SEPTUAGINT, SCROLLS
AND COGNATE WRITINGS

SOCIETY OF BIBLICAL LITERATURE
SEPTUAGINT AND COGNATE STUDIES SERIES

Series Editor
Leonard J. Greenspoon

Editorial Advisory Committee

N. Fernández Marcos, Madrid
M. Mulder, Leiden
I. Soisalon - Soininen, Helsinki
E. Tov, Jerusalem

Number 33

SEPTUAGINT, SCROLLS
AND COGNATE WRITINGS

edited by
George J. Brooke
Barnabas Lindars, S.S.F.

SEPTUAGINT, SCROLLS AND COGNATE WRITINGS

Papers Presented to the
International Symposium on the Septuagint
and Its Relations to the Dead Sea Scrolls
and Other Writings

(Manchester, 1990)

edited by
George J. Brooke
Barnabas Lindars, S.S.F.

Scholars Press
Atlanta, Georgia

SEPTUAGINT, SCROLLS AND COGNATE WRITINGS

edited by
George J. Brooke
Barnabas Lindars, S.S.F.

© 1992
Society of Biblical Literature

Library of Congress Cataloging-in-Publication Data

International Symposium on the Septuagint and its Relations to the
   Dead Sea Scrolls and Others Writings (1990 : Manchester.)
   Septuagint, scrolls and cognate writings : papers presented to the
   International Symposium on the Septuagint and its Relations to the
   Dead Seal Scrolls and Other Writings, Manchester, 1990 / edited by
   George J. Brooke, Barnabas Lindars.
   p. cm. — (Septuagint and cognate studies series ; no. 33)
   Includes index.
   1. Bible. O.T. Greek—Versions—Septuagint—Congresses. 2. Dead
Sea scrolls—Congresses. I. Brooke, George J. II. Lindars,
Barnabas. III. Title. IV. Series.
BS744.I59 1990
221.4'8—dc20   92-5253
                                                          CIP

ISBN 1-55540-707-2

Printed in the United States of America
on acid-free paper

TABLE OF CONTENTS

Acknowledgements — vii-viii

Introduction — 1-7
  +Barnabas Lindars, S.S.F.

A. The Septuagint and the Dead Sea Scrolls

The Contribution of the Qumran Scrolls to the Understanding of the LXX — 11-47
  E. Tov (Jerusalem)

The Septuagint Manuscripts from Qumran: a Reappraisal of Their Value — 49-80
  E. C. Ulrich (Notre Dame)

The Temple Scroll and LXX Exodus 35-40 — 81-106
  G. J. Brooke (Manchester)

On the Relationship between 11QPs[a] and the Septuagint on the Basis of the Computerized Data Base (CAQP) — 107-130
  J. Cook (Stellenbosch)

The Problem of Haplography in 1 and 2 Samuel — 131-158
  R. P. Gordon (Cambridge)

The Qumran Fragments of Joshua: Which Puzzle are They Part of and Where Do They Fit? — 159-194
  L. Greenspoon (Clemson)

The Old Greek of Isaiah in Relation to the Qumran Texts of Isaiah: Some General Comments — 195-213
  A. van der Kooij (Leiden)

Statistics and Textual Filiation: the Case of 4QSam[a]/LXX (with a Note on the Text of the Pentateuch) — 215-276
  F. Polak (Tel Aviv)

The Septuagint and the Temple Scroll: Shared "Halakhic" Variants — 277-297
  L. H. Schiffman (New York)

B. The Septuagint and Cognate Writings

To Revise or Not to Revise: Attitudes to Jewish Biblical
    Translation   301-338
    S. P. Brock (Oxford)

The Translation of the Septuagint in Light of Earlier
    Tradition and Subsequent Influences   339-379
    R. Hanhart (Göttingen)

Septuagintal Translation Techniques - A Solution to
    the Problem of the Tabernacle Account   381-402
    A. Aejmelaeus (Göttingen)

281 BCE: the Year of the Translation of the Pentateuch
    into Greek under Ptolemy II   403-503
    N. L. Collins (Leeds)

The Translation Technique of the Greek Minor Versions:
    Translations or Revisions?   505-556
    L. L. Grabbe (Hull)

The Treatment in the LXX of the Theme of Seeing God   557-568
    +A. T. Hanson

Εδρα and the Philistine Plague   569-597
    J. Lust (Leuven)

Is the Alternate Tradition of the Division of the Kingdom
    (3 Kgdms 12:24a-z) Non-Deuteronomistic?   599-621
    Z. Talshir (Jerusalem)

Index of Ancient and Classical Sources   623-649
    Biblical References   649
    LXX   638
    New Testament   641
    Pseudepigrapha   641
    Dead Sea Scrolls   642
    Philo   644
    Josephus   645
    Targums   645
    Mishnaic and Related Literature   645
    Papyri   646
    Classical and Patristic Literature   646

Index of Modern Authors   651-657

ACKNOWLEDGEMENTS

The International Symposium on the Septuagint and Its Relations to the Dead Sea Scrolls and Other Writings (Manchester, 30th July-August 2nd 1990) was made possible through grants from the University of Manchester's Joint Committee on University Development, the University of Manchester's Research Support Fund, and the University's Department of Biblical Criticism and Exegesis. We are grateful to many colleagues in the University for support and encouragement before, during and after the Symposium. All the participants in the Symposium appreciated the hospitality of Hulme Hall in Manchester.

More than fifty scholars from around the world attended the Symposium. We were very pleased to welcome them to Manchester. In addition to the formal conference proceedings, participants in the Symposium had the opportunity to visit the John Rylands University Library and to see there an exhibition of items specially selected by Judith Shiel and Alexander Samely, for whose help we are most grateful.

We record with regret that, since the Symposium, two of its participants, Professor Anthony Hanson and Dr Kurt Treu, have died. Professor Hanson's contribution to the Symposium is part of this volume. We are grateful for the advice on matters of translation which we were given by Dr Treu.

This volume is arranged in two sections, one covering papers on the Septuagint and the scrolls, the other papers on the Septuagint and other cognate writings. At the head of each section are two papers delivered by key specialists; other papers in each section are arranged in alphabetical order. Though there is a large measure of consistency throughout the volume, each author has been allowed to present material distinctively. As a result, each paper has particular qualities: for example, E. C. Ulrich presents his Greek evidence unaccented as in its forthcoming publication in the DJD Series, J. Cook uses the technical presentation of the CATTS system, N. Collins provides an additional system of abbreviations, L. Grabbe has produced his own paper with lengthy technical appendixes, and so on.

Many people have helped in the production of this volume of Symposium Proceedings. We are grateful to Claude Cox, editor of SBLSCS, for preliminary and continuing advice. We are grateful to Monika Faranda Bellofiglio and others for help with translating Professor Hanhart's contribution. We are grateful to Ann Sharrock of the University of Manchester Computing Centre for technical advice and help. Above all we are grateful to Dr David Stec for the many hours of work he has undertaken in standardising the computer format of this volume. As editorial assistant he has shown both amazing attention to detail and immense determination to find solutions for the best presentation of difficult and demanding textual matters. We are very much in his debt.

George J. Brooke
Barnabas Lindars, S.S.F.

As the final touches were being made to this volume, I learnt of the sudden death of Professor Lindars.

George J. Brooke

INTRODUCTION

BARNABAS LINDARS, S.S.F.

The papers collected in this volume were delivered at a symposium on The Septuagint and its Relations to the Dead Sea Scrolls and Other Writings, sponsored by the Department of Biblical Criticism and Exegesis of the Faculty of Theology of the University of Manchester, 30th July-August 2nd 1990. The Symposium was fortunate to have the enthusiastic support of Dr Sebastian Brock (Oxford), Professor Robert Hanhart (Göttingen), Professor Emanuel Tov (Jerusalem) and Professor Eugene Ulrich (Notre Dame), who gave the main papers. As the contents of this book show, other well known Septuagint specialists came from Europe, North America, Israel and South Africa as well as a number of British Universities.

The study of the Septuagint was prominent in Britain a century ago, when there was a great deal of interest in the late second temple period (200 BCE - 100 CE) and many writings of those centuries were in the process of publication, some for the first time. The great Cambridge edition of the

Septuagint (Brooke and MacLean) was begun at this time, but ran out of steam after the First World War, and the study of the Septuagint for its own sake languished generally. However, the discovery of the Dead Sea Scrolls from 1947 has led to an explosion of interest in the intertestamental period. In particular the presence of a number of Greek fragments of the biblical books at Qumran and the discovery of the important scroll of the Greek text of the Minor Prophets at Naḥal Ḥever (8HevXIIgr) has brought Septuagintal study back into prominence. The Göttinger Septuaginta-Unternehmen has proceeded with the publication of the Göttingen edition of the Septuagint with renewed vigour, and this will eventually replace the volumes published in the Cambridge edition. The foundation of the International Organization for Septuagint and Cognate Studies in 1968 has provided the means to foster Septuagintal study worldwide by conferences and publications. Hence the past twenty years have seen the greatest activity in this field of study since the beginning of the century. It must be said, however, that Britain has not recovered its former distinction in the field. One of the aims of the Manchester Symposium was to give a new impetus to British Septuagintal scholarship.

The papers collected in this volume crystallize some aspects of the present state of Septuagint studies and indicate the likely direction of future work. Four points in particular may be mentioned. In the first place, it is now universally agreed that the Greek version began with a single translation of each book of the

Hebrew scriptures (starting with the books of the
Pentateuch) rather than with several independent
translations, so that in many cases different
readings can be related to a process of correction
or alteration to bring the text into closer
alignment with the Hebrew text over a long period.
The work of D. Barthélemy on the Minor Prophets
scroll illustrated this conclusion in a decisive
way by his discovery of the so-called Kaige
recension which it represents, and which can also
be traced in the textual phenomena of the
Septuagint manuscripts. But how far is it correct
to speak of this text as a "recension?" And
should the version of Aquila, which constitutes
the *ne plus ultra* in conformity with the proto-
Massoretic text, be regarded as a recension or a
translation? Some speak of a recension as just a
set of variants which together form a distinctive
text-type, but the Symposium was agreed this is an
improper use of the word in connection with the
Septuagint. It should be confined to cases where
the variants belong to a deliberate revision of
the text, whether to bring it closer to the
current Hebrew text, as in the *Kaige* recension, or
to improve the quality of the Greek of the
translation, as in the case of Symmachus. On the
other hand, the work of Aquila is a much more
fundamental revision, and is best regarded as a
fresh translation, even though it often uses
traditional renderings. Moreover there is
evidence that, in some books at least, Aquila was
not familiar with the *Kaige* recension. Thus in
dealing with the transmission of the Greek text it
is necessary to maintain the distinction between

textual families, or groups (such as the proto-Massoretic Hebrew manuscripts from Qumran), the Hebrew recensions (such as the proto-Samaritan text), and the Greek recensions (such as *Kaige* and Symmachus), which each have their own importance for the history of the Septuagint and its relation to the underlying Hebrew.

Secondly, the presence of Greek biblical fragments at Qumran shows that, however much the Dead Sea Community preferred to use Hebrew as its normal written language medium, there were members who were familiar with Greek, just as the more numerous texts in Aramaic point to some use of Aramaic in the community. The Minor Prophets scroll from Nahal Hever gives further evidence that the Greek scriptures were used in Palestine, and indeed one might express surprise that so few Greek biblical manuscripts were found in the Qumran caves. All this supports the growing consensus that the Jews of Palestine belonged to the larger culture region in which Greek style and language predominated, at least in the educated classes. It can be assumed that the Septuagint was used in the synagogues of the Hellenists in Jerusalem (Acts 6:9). The use of Hebrew, Greek and Aramaic only partially reflects regional differences, and the interaction between regions is often not sufficiently taken into account. More real distinctions, which have yet to be assessed in detail, are the level of education, social position, and urbanization, all of which cut across territorial divisions.

Thirdly, the Septuagint is essentially a translation and not a targumizing paraphrase.

INTRODUCTION

There is a sense in which every translation is a commentary, or contains what might be called linguistic exegesis, because it represents the translator's understanding of the text, and this is inevitably coloured by the presuppositions of the time. But this is not the same thing as deliberate modification of the text for the sake of interpretation (which might be designated as content exegesis). The aim of the translators of the Septuagint was to give a faithful rendering of the Hebrew. It is thus valuable for interpretation because it shows how words and concepts were understood at the time. Though the Septuagint translation tends to be literal by modern standards, it is not slavishly literal, and the relation to the *Vorlage* is often best described as dynamic equivalence. It is also instructive to see how the translators dealt with difficulties in the text. In addition, it is evident that the Hebrew *Vorlage* often differed from the standardized Hebrew text of MT. This makes the Septuagint an important source for the restoration of corrupt passages in MT. However, this can be a hazardous business, because, although retroversion of the Greek into Hebrew can often be regarded as certain, there are times when careful attention to the translator's style and translation habits is required to avoid false deductions. Thus the B text of Judges has a number of Hebrew-sounding expressions which have no basis in the Hebrew of Judges as such, but represent a semitizing tendency at a certain stage in the revision of the text.

Fourthly, although the translators used good

Greek according to the contemporary standards of
the Koine Greek of the eastern Mediterranean
lands, the Septuagint has its own peculiarities of
vocabulary, phrase and syntax which have often
been taken to prove the production of a special
biblical Greek for the purpose of the translation.
This idea is rightly abandoned today, as it
conflicts with the evidence that the oldest strata
of the Greek text are closest to the Koine as
known from the secular papyri and least affected
by semitisms. However, the differing skills of
the translators need to be kept in mind. Some
books, notably Exodus, show the capacity to
transfer the meaning from one language medium to
the other without conflict with the normal style
of the receptor language and without the
production of a special Jewish vocabulary. In
other cases the translators did not have this
ability, and produced a literal translation which
was heavily laden with features of the original,
especially in the use of certain prepositions and
parataxis. It was tolerable Greek if not good
Greek, but it was not the result of a deliberate
attempt to create a biblical style. On the other
hand the success of the translation made it
influential in the production of further Jewish
literature in Greek, so that later books often
imitate the style of the Septuagint (e.g., Luke
1-2).

Even these few broad generalizations are
sufficient to show that those who wish to use the
Septuagint as a tool in biblical studies need to
do so with caution on the basis of good
information and study in depth. This must now

include a proper appreciation of the information that can be gleaned from the Dead Sea Scrolls. Those who undertake such study will find that the Septuagint presents fascinating and challenging issues, which make it an absorbing field of study in its own right. This is apparent from the papers in this volume. The aim of the Symposium will have been achieved, if these papers stimulate further research.

SECTION A

THE SEPTUAGINT AND THE DEAD SEA SCROLLS

THE CONTRIBUTION OF THE QUMRAN SCROLLS TO THE UNDERSTANDING OF THE LXX[1]

EMANUEL TOV

For many areas of textual criticism the discovery of the Qumran scrolls has heralded a new era. Among other things, this pertains to the LXX, and in this paper we shall be concerned especially with that version. The major areas within LXX studies on which the new discoveries have made an impact, are, in my view: (1) the credibility of the reconstruction of the elements in the *Vorlage* of the LXX; (2) the recognition of a close relation between the LXX and specific Qumran scrolls.

We limit our remarks to the Qumran scrolls, disregarding the other texts from the Judaean Desert. The main reason for this limitation is that very few unique agreements have been found between the LXX on the one hand and the Hebrew texts from Masada, Murabba'at and Nahal Hever on the other. In general terms these texts reflect the MT.

The questions raised in this paper are not new. As early as 1959 they were touched upon by H. M. Orlinsky.[2] Likewise, they have been treated in a small monograph by R. W. Klein, *Textual Criticism of the Old Testament*. This monograph[3] has a cover bearing the subtitle "From the Septuagint to Qumran," while the title page bears a very similar subtitle "The Septuagint after Qumran." Thus in tune with the character of the subject matter of this book, a textual or editorial mishap of some kind has occurred. Incidentally, while the two subtitles obviously refer to different issues, the book in my view deals with neither. With some support from the foreword by G. M. Tucker, I think that the intended focus of the book is "The Septuagint *after* Qumran," that is, how the value and use of the LXX are assessed after the Qumran discoveries. We shall follow the lead of Klein in this matter, although he himself did not discuss the issue at any length.

I The support which the Qumran scrolls give to the credibility of the procedure of retroversion

We will first turn to the contribution of the Qumran scrolls to the reconstruction of the *Vorlage* of the LXX. It is probably no exaggeration to say that the Qumran scrolls have provided the first massive support for the correctness of an approach that has been part and parcel of scholarship for more than three centuries, namely, the reconstructing of details in the *Vorlage* of the LXX by way of retroversion. Before the days of Qumran no such external support was available

for this procedure. After all, before 1947 there
was little if any external evidence in support of
the assumption that a given deviation from the MT
in the LXX should be reconstructed into Hebrew
rather than explained away as the translator's
exegesis. The great masters in this area of
reconstruction, from Cappellus to Houbigant, and
from Wellhausen to Driver, operated with such
tools as grammars, lexica and concordances to the
Greek and Hebrew Bibles, but actually their major
source of inspiration was their intuition. Guided
by this intuition, the above-mentioned scholars,
as well as others, suggested many a retroversion
for details in the LXX which deviated from MT. In
search of support for these intuitive retroversions one cannot turn to the other ancient
translations, since these are equally suspect of
reflecting content exegesis as the LXX. Nor can
one turn to the ancient Hebrew sources such as the
biblical quotations in the Talmud, for these
Hebrew sources more or less reflect the MT.
Biblical quotations in the Apocrypha are equally
of limited value, as most of these have been
preserved in secondary languages. Thus there was
no outside source which could support retroversions from the LXX, even though such support was
often very much needed. However, here and there
an exception was visible. Thus the medieval
Hebrew text of Ben Sira, known since the end of
the last century, is of help in the reconstruction
of the parent text of the Greek translation of Ben
Sira. Two further exceptions which pertain to the
Samaritan Pentateuch (SP) on the one hand and the
Hebrew context in the MT on the other should also

be mentioned. The SP, known in the West from 1616 onwards, frequently agrees with the LXX against the MT, in pluses, minuses and differences. One is often tempted to reconstruct the *Vorlage* of the LXX to a form which is identical with the SP, and in such cases the latter thus serves as a support for the former. This type of support is important, although the nature of the agreements between the LXX and the SP has yet to be examined more thoroughly, an undertaking which at present is being prepared by a student of mine, Kim King-Re, in his doctoral dissertation. Some examples of special agreements between the LXX and the SP follow (most of them in pluses):

Exod 1:22   MT כל הבן הילוד (היארה תשליכהו)
            SP כל הבן הילוד <u>לעברים</u> (היאר תשליכון)
            LXX πᾶν ἄρσεν ὃ ἐὰν τεχθῇ <u>τοῖς Ἑβραίοις</u>
            (= T°, Tʲ)

Exod 2:21   MT ויתן את צפרה בתו למשה
            SP ויתן את צפרה בתו למשה <u>לאשה</u>
            LXX καὶ ἐξέδοτο Σεπφωραν τὴν θυγατέρα
            αὐτοῦ Μωυσῇ <u>γυναῖκα</u> = S Vᴹˢˢ

Num 3:12   MT כל בכור פטר רחם מבני ישראל
            SP + פדויהם יהיו
            LXX + λύτρα αὐτῶν ἔσονται (cf. vv 46ff)

Num 14:12   MT ואעשה אתך (לגוי גדול)
            SP ואעשה אתך <u>ואת בית אביך</u>
            LXX καὶ ποιήσω σὲ καὶ <u>τὸν οἶκον τοῦ πατρός σου</u>

Num 14:18   MT ה׳ ארך אפים ורב חסד
            SP + ואמת = Exod 34:16
            LXX + καὶ ἀληθινός

In the past, however, these unique agreements between the LXX and the SP have not been invoked as a source of support for the procedure of retroverting variants from the LXX. They may have been overlooked by scholars dealing with retroversions or possibly they were not mentioned because of a cautious approach. Such caution may have been justified, as most of the pluses consist of harmonizing elements which are by definition secondary. Indeed, scepticism has often caused scholars to brush aside these unique agreements between the LXX and the SP in the 1900 instances listed by Castellus.[4] Adherence to stereotyped views of recensions and text-types of the biblical text has led some scholars to disregard these agreements by claiming that either the LXX was translated from the SP[5] or that the SP was revised according to the LXX or conversely that the LXX was revised according to the SP.[6] Whatever the reason may have been, the unique agreements between the SP and the LXX have not been used as a source adding credibility to the procedure of retroverting variants from the LXX, in my view wrongly so.

A second source of external support for the retroversions from the LXX pertains to the MT itself. Often a word in the context or in a parallel section or book provides welcome support for a retroversion. Thus the LXX of Samuel and Kings here and there reflects Hebrew variants identical with parallel elements in Chronicles and vice versa. At the same time, these parallel data are often problematical. Inner-Septuagintal influences were at work, and hence synoptic agreements between the LXX of Samuel-Kings and the MT of Chronicles could be secondary. This pertains also to agreements between the LXX of Chronicles and the MT of Samuel-Kings. For example:

2 Sam 5:9   MT   ויקרא לה עיר דוד ויבן דוד סביב
               LXX καὶ ἐκλήθη αὕτη ἡ πόλις Δαυιδ
                    καὶ ᾠκοδόμησεν τὴν πόλιν κύκλῳ
1 Chr 11:7-8   MT   על כן קראו לו עיר דויד *ויבן
                    העיר מסביב

2 Sam 5:21   MT   ויעזבו שם את עצביהם
               LXX καὶ καταλιμπάνουσιν ἐκεῖ τοὺς
                    θεοὺς αὐτῶν
1 Chr 14:12   MT   ויעזבו שם את אלהיהם

1 Chr 10:6   MT   וימת שאול ושלשה בניו
               LXX + ἐν τῇ ἡμέρᾳ ἐκείνῃ
cf. 1 Sam 31:6 וימת שאול ושלשה בניו...ביום ההוא

Similar support can be drawn from any context in MT. E.g., the Greek plus in the LXX of Judg 16:13 can easily be retranslated on the basis of words occurring in the context.[7]

At the same time, using the context as a source for reconstructions can often be misleading, for a Greek change or plus, which is phrased like other elements in the context, could actually reflect the translator's manipulation.

Leaving the issue of support for retroversions from the context, we will now turn to the main topic of this section, viz., support from Qumran for the retroversion of variants from the LXX.

THE CONTRIBUTION OF THE QUMRAN SCROLLS 17

Since this procedure is common knowledge among specialists, let us look at some lesser known examples, first from Deuteronomy. In the following example an independent analysis of the Greek data allows for various possibilities, while the Qumran data tilt the evidence in a certain direction.

One of the central formulae of Deuteronomy is "the land which you (singular/plural) come to inherit." The two verbs used for "to come" are בו"א and עב"ר, the latter one referring to the crossing of the Jordan prior to the coming into the land.

1. הארץ/האדמה אשר אתה בא (אתם באים) שמה לרשתה (4:5; 7:1; 11:10, 29; 23:21; 28:21, 63; 30:16).
2. הארץ/האדמה אשר אתה עבר (אתם עברים) שמה לרשתה (4:14; 6:1; 11:8, 11).

The latter is a shortened formula of הארץ/האדמה אשר אתה עבר (אתם עברים) את הירדן (לבוא) שמה לרשתה, found in 30:18 as well as in 4:26, 31:13 and 32:47 (in the latter three verses without לבוא).

The Greek translator of Deuteronomy distinguishes between בו"א and עב"ר, represented respectively by εἰσπορεύομαι and διαβαίνω. There are, however, four exceptions. In 4:14, 6:1 and 11:11 εἰσπορεύομαι is used for עב"ר and in 11:29 διαβαίνω is used for בו"א. In view of the different Hebrew formulae these four exceptions could reflect inner-Greek harmonizations, but since the translation of Deuteronomy is relatively consistent, it is more likely that they represent Hebrew variations between בו"א and עב"ר. This view is now supported by Qumran evidence:

6:1 עברים] 4QPhyl B,M באים; 8QPhyl בֹּאִ֗ים = LXX εἰσπορεύεσθε

Although independent harmonizing changes in the LXX, in 4QPhyl B,M and 8QPhyl are not impossible, the assumption of actual variants is more likely.

Note also the following two examples from Deuteronomy:

Deut 5:15   MT לעשות את יום השבת
　　　　　　LXX + καὶ ἁγιάζειν αὐτήν
　　　　　　4QPhyl B (text of Deuteronomy) +
　　　　　　　　ולקדשו = Exod 20:11

The added word in 4QPhyl B supports the retroversion of the LXX as ולקדשו.

Deut 6:2   MT אשר אנכי מצוך
　　　　　　LXX + σήμερον
　　　　　　SP, 4QPhyl J,M, 8QPhyl + היום

Cf. also the LXX in the following two verses:

Deut 12:11   MT כל אשר אנכי מצוה אתכם
　　　　　　　LXX + σήμερον
Deut 12:14   MT אשר אנכי מצוך
　　　　　　　LXX + σήμερον

In the above three instances the LXX translator may have added σήμερον on the basis of many similar phrases (4:40; 6:6; 7:11; 8:1, 11; 10:13; 11:8; 13:19 etc.), one of which is in the context (6:6), but the readings in the phylacteries make it more likely that the LXX actually reflects a Hebrew variant.

Unique agreements between the LXX and the Qumran scrolls, like the ones mentioned above, abound in all books of the Bible. The reason that

THE CONTRIBUTION OF THE QUMRAN SCROLLS

only a relatively small amount of such evidence is known is that only a limited number of texts have been preserved in the Judaean Desert.

Examples such as these are naturally well known; for this reason we have so far mentioned only lesser known ones. These agreements with Qumran scrolls increase our trust in the procedure of retroverting. Before 1947 retroversions from the LXX had been attempted by generations of scholars, and we are therefore pleasantly surprised to note that words reconstructed from the LXX by such scholars as Thenius, Wellhausen, and Driver[e] have now actually been found in the Hebrew Qumran scrolls, e.g. with regard to 4QSam^a:

1 Sam 1:23   MT (אך יקם) יהוה את דברו
             4QSam^a]ה יוצא מפיך
             LXX τὸ ἐξελθὸν ἐκ τοῦ στόματός σου

Thenius had reconstructed the LXX as את היוצא מפיך and this reading has now been found in 4QSam^a.

1 Sam 1:24   MT בפרימשלשה = בְּפָרִים שְׁלֹשָׁה
             LXX בפר משלש (ἐν μόσχῳ τριετίζοντι)
             = בפרמשלש
             4QSam^a [בפר בן] בקר משלש

Thenius, Wellhausen, and Driver had reconstructed the LXX as בפר משלש and a similar reading has now been found in 4QSam^a.

1 Sam 20:30 MT בֶּן נַעֲוַת הַמַּרְדּוּת
             4QSam^b בן נערת המרדה
             LXX υἱὲ κορασίων αὐτομολούντων

Driver reconstructed the LXX as בן נערה (ה)מרדות, now found in 4QSam^b.

Deut 32:8 MT (למספר) בני ישראל
4QDeut^q] בני אל; 4QDeut^j בני אלהים
LXX^{MSS} υἱῶν (LXX^{most MSS} ἀγγέλων = α´)
θεοῦ

For generations these readings of the MT and LXX have been the topic of much discussion.⁹ It is now evident that the LXX does not reflect exegesis by the translators, but a Hebrew variant such as now found in 4QDeut^{j,q}.

Another intriguing group of examples pertains to *small* additions and changes found both in a Qumran scroll and in the LXX, as illustrated from the recently released 4QNum^b (see n. 16). Until recently the text-critical value of the LXX of Numbers was not clear. E.g.,

12:6 MT ויאמר שמעו נא
LXX καὶ εἶπεν πρὸς αὐτούς ἀκούσατε τῶν λόγων μου

It is difficult to determine whether the plus πρὸς αὐτούς reflects an added אליהם or the translator's exegesis. However, the existence of this plus in 4QNum^b strengthens the former assumption. A similar reasoning applies to other cases as well.

16:5 MT ואת אשר יבחר בו הקריב אליו
LXX καὶ οὓς ἐξελέξατο ἑαυτῷ προσηγάγετο πρὸς ἑαυτόν
4QNum^b ב[חר]

19:3 MT ונחתם אתה
    LXX καὶ δώσεις αὐτήν
    4QNum^b ונחתה אתה

22:9 MT ויבא אלהים אל בלעם ויאמר
    LXX καὶ ἦλθεν ὁ θεὸς πρὸς Βαλααμ καὶ εἶπεν αὐτῷ
    4QNum^b + אליו

22:10 MT שלח אליו
    LXX ἀπέστειλεν αὐτοὺς πρός με λέγων
    4QNum^b]אלי לאמור

Although the latter group leaves room for some doubt, there are hundreds of examples which enhance the credibility of the LXX as a text-critical tool in biblical studies.[10] They show that the intuition of generations of scholars who ventured to reconstruct the readings from the LXX has been justified. The LXX should indeed be taken seriously as a tool for the textual criticism of the Hebrew Bible. In spite of known trends of exegesis in the translation, of inner-translational corruptions and of our own ability to get back to the Hebrew text underlying the translation, much of what has been done so far in the area of retroverting the *Vorlage* of the LXX is now supported by the Qumran finds. Of course, each book must be evaluated separately. 4QSam^a has strengthened our general confidence in the LXX of that book, and 4QJer^{b,d} support the retroversion of the LXX of Jeremiah as a shorter text. At the same time, not all agreements

between the LXX and the scrolls against the MT are
relevant to the discussion. As we will see in the
case of 1QIs^a, many a concurrence between that
scroll and the LXX may be coincidental and this
may also be true for some of the aforementioned
harmonizations.

II The recognition of a close relationship
between the LXX and specific Qumran scrolls

Since many of the books of the LXX agree either
occasionally or frequently with readings in
certain Qumran scrolls, scholars have expressed
opinions about a specifically close relationship
between the LXX and those scrolls. As a result,
rightly or wrongly the term "Septuagintal scroll"
has made its entrance into the scholarly literature. However, the establishing of such a close
link is beset with problems which relate not only
to the facts themselves, such as the actual
reading of the scroll and the meaning and reconstruction of the LXX, but also to more general
issues, such as the logic behind statistical
analysis and one's overall text-critical
Weltanschauung.

In more detail, the following seven issues
should be addressed beyond establishing the
reading of the scroll and the meaning of the words
in the LXX.
1. It is often difficult to know whether a
reading of the LXX which differs from the MT
should be reconstructed as a deviating Hebrew
reading or should be regarded as the translator's
exegesis. In the latter case the item should be

disregarded. Exegesis which is common to the LXX and a particular scroll is of interest, especially when occurring frequently, but it does not pertain to textual data.

2. How is the extent of the agreement between the LXX and a particular scroll to be assessed? Does one count the items of agreement separately and if so how is this counting to be done? Usually, one counts each agreement separately, including extensive textual phenomena such as a long plus, minus or difference. However, such items lose their importance in a statistical analysis when they are included with numerous items of lesser magnitude. It is therefore in order to subdivide agreements into more significant and less significant ones.

3. The analysis centres on readings in which the LXX and a particular scroll agree against the MT. Within the web of the relations between the textual witnesses there is something unusual in this way of reasoning, to which we will soon return. But there is one question which should be mentioned immediately: Should we confine our attention to exclusive agreements between the LXX and a scroll, or should we include cases in which the LXX is joined by another ancient version, such as the Peshitta or a Targum? For the sake of the argument I am inclined to include such instances. The question is not important, however, since most instances pertain to exclusive agreements between the LXX and a scroll.

4. In the past, much stress has been laid upon the counting of agreements, while disagreements have usually been disregarded. The question

arises whether such analyses actually misrepresent the situation, especially when there is an impressive number of disagreements between the two sources. I have changed my thinking on this issue since my 1980 article mentioned in n.21. While still counting disagreements, I now believe that they do not necessarily diminish the importance of the agreements, if the agreements are indeed significant. Thus, if texts *a* and *b* are closely related in such a way that they derived one from the other or from a common ancestor, either *a* and *b* or both may have developed considerably after the stage at which they were initially linked. Such subsequent development, now visible in disagreements between *a* and *b*, should not necessarily undermine the degree of affinity recognized between the two texts.

5. In determining the special relationship between the LXX and a scroll, the textual character of the pericope or the book in question has to be taken into consideration. If there is little textual variation in a given unit, as in the case of the LXX and MT of Isaiah, the relation between these two sources on the one hand and a Qumran scroll on the other is bound to be very similar. Thus all the Isaiah scrolls from cave 4, to be published by Prof. Ulrich, agree with the MT and LXX almost equally. It is therefore often irrelevant to assess their closeness to either the MT or LXX.

6. As a rule, the determining of the relation between the LXX and the scrolls does not take into consideration the originality of the readings, especially since such a question has very few

objective aspects. However, two exceptions should be made, relating to common secondary and common original readings. With regard to the former, if the LXX and a scroll agree in a presumed common secondary reading (often an error), such an agreement may point to a very close connection between the two. Such readings have been called by P. Maas "Leitfehler" or "indicative errors".[11] However, in view of the fragmentary state of preservation of the evidence it is hard to evaluate these *Leitfehler*. The assumption of a close relation is possible, but one should realize that many other texts sharing these readings may have been lost. With regard to the shared original readings, if two texts share a reading which probably is original, while the corrupted reading is found in another source, the closeness reflected by the presumably original shared reading is less significant, since it is natural for any two texts to share original readings. This has become clear in particular with regard to readings common to the LXX and 4QSam^a. Thus to my mind the aforementioned common reading of the LXX and 4QSam^a in 1 Sam 24 reflects the uncorrupted text, while the MT has been corrupted.[12] This reading, which must have been shared by many texts which are now lost, is probably less relevant to the statistics. Obviously, in only a few cases can one state with relative certainty that a given reading is either corrupt or original.

7. Finally, the coincidence of the textual transmission should be borne in mind. We should not forget that only some of the texts have been preserved, and that any conclusions on the

relation between the LXX, MT and a scroll are
provisional, since in the hypothetical stemma of
the MSS many texts may have intervened between
these three sources.

Now the data themselves. Information on the
agreements between the LXX and the published
scrolls has been collected in the critical
apparatuses of the editions of the Qumran
fragments as well as in monographs. Special
attention has been given to a few select scrolls.
The relation between 1QIs^a and the LXX has been
treated in an article by J. Ziegler.[13] Likewise,
much attention has been given to the close
affinities between the LXX and 4QSam^{a14} and
4QJer^{b,d15} respectively.

For the purpose of this research the relation
between the individual Qumran scrolls and the LXX
has been reviewed in detail. Together with Mr Kim
King-Re, I recorded all the instances in which the
main text of the LXX agrees with one or more of
the Qumran scrolls. The point of departure for
this undertaking were the remarks in the textual
apparatuses accompanying the editions of the
scrolls, but the data were also examined independently in Hebrew and Greek. Obviously any remark
on an agreement between the LXX and a Qumran
scroll is subjective. Only such agreements were
recorded as presumably go back to a common Hebrew
reading, so that common exegesis was excluded.
The data in the LXX and the scrolls were recorded
and reviewed within the framework of the greater
database of the CATSS project, which had the
additional advantage of enabling us to study
various sets of data simultaneously, among other

THE CONTRIBUTION OF THE QUMRAN SCROLLS   27

things retroversions into Hebrew from the LXX made earlier without any connection to the Qumran scrolls and the text of the SP in its agreements with the LXX. In order to avoid misunderstandings, I should add that all the work is manual and reflects human thinking. The computer serves mainly as a tool for storing and retrieving the data on agreements and disagreements between the LXX and the scrolls.

For the purpose of this research all the published Qumran scrolls have been reviewed, as well as many unpublished ones. At this stage most of the Qumran biblical texts are known in some form or other, especially with the recent completion of five Harvard dissertations providing most of the texts of Genesis, Deuteronomy and the Minor Prophets from Cave 4 as well as the lengthy text of 4QNum^b.[16] To these I added texts of Leviticus, Joshua and Jeremiah to be published by myself, and the texts of Isaiah and those written in the palaeo-Hebrew script to be published by Prof. Ulrich. I am grateful to Prof. Ulrich for allowing me to examine his future editions of these texts. I have not yet studied the large group of Psalms texts and a smaller group of Exodus texts to be published by Prof. Ulrich. To the best of my knowledge, none of these texts is particularly close to the LXX. The biblical texts contained in the Phylacteries, mezuzot and pesharim, as well as those in 4QTest and 4QFlor have also been reviewed.

Having reviewed the evidence, I note that only a few of the Qumran scrolls are close to the LXX, to a greater or lesser degree. In my view this closeness cannot be assessed objectively. After all that has been said, our main criterion remains simple statistics based on the number of agreements, which should be subdivided into more significant and less significant. The evaluation of these statistics remains subjective. It is hard to determine the lower limit of such agreements which would establish a close relationship. The most ideal case for establishing such a relation between the LXX and a scroll is when the scroll agrees with the LXX in readings that are characteristic of the LXX, tendentious or large-scale, or all of these together.

Let us now turn to the individual texts, to be discussed in a *descending* order of closeness to the LXX. At the end of this list we will also mention a few texts that are not at all close to the LXX, but these have been referred to in this regard in recent publications.

1. Two of the three fragments that have been previously labelled 4QJer^b, and which we now name 4QJer^b and 4QJer^d,[17] display a very close relation with the Hebrew *Vorlage* of the LXX. In fact, no other Qumran text is as close to the LXX as these two fragments. Characteristic of the LXX are the short name formulae, as opposed to longer ones in the MT, and these are also found in 4QJer^d. E.g., ירחנן in 4QJer^d (ןנחר[י] , ןנח[רי]) and the LXX in 43:4, 5 as opposed to ירחנן בן קרח in the MT; נבוזרדן in 4QJer^d and the LXX in 43:6 as opposed to נבוזראדן רב טבחים in MT. Equally characteristic of the LXX are the long minuses and differences in sequence, both of which are also present in 4QJer^b which contains chapters 9-10 of

THE CONTRIBUTION OF THE QUMRAN SCROLLS   29

Jeremiah. Both of these phenomena are amply
described in the literature mentioned in n.15.
There are some minor differences between the
Jeremiah scrolls and the LXX which make it clear
that the LXX was not translated from the exact
copy found in Qumran, but from a very similar one.
Since the agreements pertain to details which are
characteristic of the LXX, it is to be assumed
that the complete scrolls of 4QJer^{b,d} would also
have agreed with the LXX in the chapters which
have not been preserved.

2. Of 4QDeut^q only a small fragment has been
preserved, and this fragment, published by P. W.
Skehan,[18] reflects several important agreements
with the LXX. Of these, note especially the
reading בני אל[(32:8) which agrees with the LXX
and differs from MT בני ישראל (see above p. 20).
It also agrees with 4Q with regard to the reading
בניו in 32:43 against עבדיו in the MT. The most
important agreement concerns four stichs of the
LXX, three of which are shared with 4QDeut^q, and
none of which agrees with the MT. Several
scholars have stressed the close relation between
the LXX and the scroll, although different views
have been expressed on the exact relation between
the MT, 4QDeut^q and the LXX.[19] Admittedly,
4QDeut^q contains only a small fragment, and the
relation between the complete text of this book
and the LXX remains a matter of speculation.
Since 4QDeut^q ends with chapter 32 of Deuteronomy
(and not with chapter 34), the complete scroll
probably contained an anthology. Our conclusion
regarding the textual character of 4QDeut^q thus

probably pertains not to that scroll, but to the text from which it was copied.

3. One of the texts, whose closeness to the LXX has been stressed time and time again is 4QSam^a. The literature on the close relation between 4QSam^a and the LXX, the main text and Lucianic tradition is quite extensive (for some references see n.14). Of special importance in this regard is the article by Cross whose title specifically speaks of "A New Qumran Fragment Related to the Original Hebrew Underlying the Septuagint" (*BASOR* 132 [1953] 15-26). Undoubtably there is an impressive number of agreements between the LXX and 4Q, although in the absence of an official publication it is not easy to calculate the extent of this agreement. The text of the first two columns is given in the above-mentioned article by Cross, while many scattered readings are listed in a monograph by Ulrich (see n.14) and in McCarter's commentary.[20] The statistics for these agreements have been listed as follows in an article by myself:[21]

Col. I (1 Sam 1:22-2:25) $4Q = LXX^B \neq MT$ 22

                                                 (possibly: 28)

                                 $4Q = MT \neq LXX^B$ 4

                                 $4Q \neq LXX^B \neq MT$ 5

                                 $4Q \neq LXX^B = MT$ 9

The relation between the sources for this column is best expressed as follows (the data for LXX^B must be distinguished from those for LXX^L):

$4Q = LXX^B$ 22 (possibly: 28) $4Q \neq LXX^B$ 18

$4Q = LXX^L$ 17(23) $4Q \neq LXX^L$ 20

$4Q = MT$ 4 $4Q \neq MT$ 41

For the second column of the scroll the

following statistics are listed in my article:
Co. II (2 Sam 3:23-5:14) $4Q = LXX^B \neq MT$ 13
$4Q = MT \neq LXX^B$ 7
$4Q \neq LXX^B \neq MT$ 4
$4Q \neq LXX^B = MT$ 6

The relation between the sources for this column is best expressed as follow:

$4Q = LXX^B$ 13 $4Q \neq LXX^B$ 22
$4Q = LXX^L$ 13 $4Q \neq LXX^L$ 15
$4Q = MT$ 10 $4Q \neq MT$ 25

These data are impressive, and they are even more impressive in the figures given by F. Polak, who refers to all known readings of the scroll.[22] His statistics are significant, especially since they are subdivided into different grammatical and syntactical categories.

However, from this impressive number of agreements one has to deduct those readings which are common to the LXX and the scroll, and which presumably reflect the original text, against a corrupted form in the MT. Long before the discovery of the scrolls, such scholars as Thenius, Wellhausen and Driver had recognized the often faulty character of the MT. In our view, the fact that the joint reading of the LXX and 4Q often contains an original reading does not prove a particularly close relation between these two sources. Many other texts may have contained that reading, while the MT, being the exception, contained an error. Since many texts have been lost, comparison between the now preserved LXX, MT and 4QSam^a presents data which can be wrongly evaluated because of the optical illusion presented by the evidence. Obviously it is a very subjective and difficult matter to earmark a certain variant as original, and the reading of MT as an error, but there are quite a few instances of such in the text under consideration, which single out 4QSam^a as a very special text. Thus, the large minus of the MT in 1 Sam 1:24 is usually recognized as a homoioteleuton as compared with 4Q and the LXX. The aforementioned reading in 1 Sam 1:23 (p. 19) is likewise considered to be a mistake in the MT. In 1 Sam 2:22 the LXX and 4Q also contain the original short text while the expanded text of the MT (v.22b) has been recognized by most scholars as a theological gloss. A certain number of the common readings of the LXX and 4Q have thus to be deducted from the list as less relevant.

One also notes a large number of significant differences between the LXX and 4Q as well as exclusive readings in both of them. However, in accordance with our previous remarks, in the putative stemma of the MSS there is room for such readings if they occurred after the point at which the two sources separated from each other. In my 1980 article (see n.21) I stressed these differences between the various sources more than I do at this stage.

I now realize that the LXX and 4Q contain a few readings which P. Maas would call "indicative," viz., leading common errors. This pertains to the extensive double reading in 1 Sam 2:23-24 and to the erroneous mention of Mephibosheth's name in 2 Sam 4:1, 2, 12 as opposed to Ishbosheth in MT in v.12 and the absence of a name in vv.1, 2. These significant common errors suffice to establish a

THE CONTRIBUTION OF THE QUMRAN SCROLLS 33

close connection between the LXX and the scroll, but this connection is not as close as in the case of the two texts mentioned above. Beyond the aforementioned original readings and common errors, the agreements between the LXX and 4QSam^a include single details which are not characteristic in any way. The relative location in the putative stemma of 4QSam^a and the *Vorlage* of the LXX cannot be further determined.

Five of the newly published scrolls show an impressive degree of agreement with the LXX, which in two instances are shared with the SP and are therefore less relevant to the exclusive relation between the LXX and the scrolls:

4. 4QDeut^c, included in S. White's Harvard dissertation (see n.16), contains, according to my calculations, 12 exclusive agreements with the LXX as well as 19 instances of disagreement. According to White,[23] this scroll "stands in the textual tradition of G." The agreements, however, are in small details, and the only argument in favour of the assumption of a close connection with the LXX is the statistical picture. On the basis of our previous remarks, these statistics alone do not prove a close connection.

Actually, in the sections covered by this scroll, there are no major differences in content between the LXX and the MT, so that it is all the more difficult to establish a close relation between any scroll and the LXX. This remark also pertains to the following texts, for which a close relation to the LXX has been recognized by many scholars.

5. 4QDeut^h, included in J. Duncan's Harvard

dissertation (see n.16), contains, according to my calculations, 9 exclusive agreements with the LXX as well as 9 instances of disagreement. According to Duncan, this text "is an important witness to a text type like that of G, at a relatively early stage."[24] Of particular interest are the various agreements between the LXX and 4QDeut[h] in Moses's blessing in Deut 33:8-11, which incidentally, are shared with the quotation in 4Q175 (4QTest) against MT.[25]

MT	וללוי אמר .. .. תמיך ואוריך לאיש חסידך אשר
4Q175	וללוי אמר הבו ללוי תמיך ואורך לאיש חסידך אשר
4QDt[h]	הבו ללו̇ נ̇י
LXX	הבו ללוי

MT	נסיתו במסה תריבהו על מי מריבה האמר לאביו ולאמר
4Q175	נסיתו במסה והרבהו על מי מריבה ⁷אמר לאביו
4QDt[h]	
LXX	לאביו ולאמר

MT	לא ראיהיו ואת אחיו לא הכיר
4Q175	לוא ראיתיכה ולאמר ליד ᵛתיכהו ואת אחיו לוא הכיר
4QDt[h]	ראיתיך
LXX	לא ראיתיך

MT	ואת בנו לא ידע כי שמרו אמרתך ובריתך ינצרו
4Q175	ואת בנו לוא ידע כי שמר אמרתכה ובריתך ינצר
4QDt[h]	בנו לא̇ ע̇ כי שמר אמרתך בריתך
LXX	שמר בריתך ינצר

MT	יורו משפטיך ליעקב ותורתך לישראל ישימו
4Q175	ויאירו משפטיך ליעקוב תורתכה לישראל ישימו
4QDt[h]	יור? מש̇פ̇ יך ל ישראל ישם
LXX	ישימו

MT	קטורה באפך וכליל על מזבחך ברך יהוה חילו
4Q175	קטורה באפך וכליל על מזבחך ברך .... חילו
4QDt^h	קטׄורה באפך וכלל על מזבחֹ ברך יהוה חילו
LXX	כליל

MT	ופעל ידיו תרצה מחץ מתנים קמיו ומשנאיו מן יקומון
4Q175	ופעל ידו תרצה מחץ מתנים קמו ומשנאו בל יקומון
4QDt^h	ופעלהׄ ׄ תרצה מחץׄ מׄ נׄיׄ ל יקומ]
LXX	משנאיו? בל יקומון
	(μὴ ἀναστήτωσαν)

This text is instructive in many ways. The Deuteronomy manuscript is very close to 4Q175[26] and the latter may well have quoted the former.[27] At the same time, it shares a few details with the LXX, the most important of which is the addition of הבו ללוי in v.8. However, the two disagree in other details, and if the words הבו ללוי have been erroneously omitted from the original text, now preserved only in the LXX, 4QDeut^h and 4Q175, the agreement between the two is not of great stemmatic importance.

6. The material preserved for 4QDeut^j is not very extensive, and its textual affiliation is not clear. This text is included in J. Duncan's Harvard dissertation (see n.16). It shares more readings with the LXX than with the other two sources, but the numbers are small. According to my statistics it agrees 4 times with the LXX against the MT, while disagreeing 6 times with that source. Nevertheless, Duncan describes this text as standing in the tradition of the LXX.[28]

7. 4QLev^d*, which is to be published by myself,

and which consists of several small fragments of
Leviticus 14-17, contains two agreements with the
LXX in long pluses and three in small details. It
disagrees with the LXX in two minor details.
Although the text is not extensive, its affiliation is clearly primarily with the LXX, and
secondly with the SP and only thirdly with the MT.

The first major addition pertains to a plus in
the scroll which reflects a plus of the SP in Lev
17:4: לעשות אתו עלה או שלמים ליהוה לרצונכם לריח
ניחח וישחטהו בחוץ ואל פתח אהל מועד לא הביאו. A
similar addition is found in the LXX, and
therefore the connection between the scroll and
the LXX is less exclusive than in the other
instances. It is significant to note that this
plus is probably secondary.[29]

8. 4QNum[b], extensively described in Jastram's
Harvard dissertation of May 1990 (see n.16),
contains a very impressive list of agreements with
the LXX. There is no common denominator for these
common readings, but a great deal of them are in
the nature of small harmonizing pluses based on
the immediate or remote context. Several of these
extra-Masoretic agreements between the LXX and the
scroll are shared with the SP, and actually, the
scroll displays a much greater similarity with the
latter version. Among other things, it shares
with the SP the major harmonizing pluses, based on
Deuteronomy (Num 20:13; 21:11, 12, 20; 27:23),
while the other harmonizing pluses of the SP must
be reconstructed for the scroll on the basis of
its column length.

9. Milik's contention[30] that 5QDeut (chapters 7
and 8) has been revised four times according to a

Hebrew text close to the *Vorlage* of the LXX would have been of special interest had the evidence been more conclusive. Indeed, two of the corrections agree with the text of the LXX against the MT (the addition of ראיתה ואשר in 7:15 and that of בם in 8:12). The third correction (8:19) is based on a reading which at best is dubious, and in my view incorrect, while the fourth instance appears to me to be irrelevant (9:2). At the same time, one notes eight instances of disagreement between the LXX and 5QDeut and two agreements in minutiae. The sum of this evidence does not favour the conclusion that this text has been corrected towards a Hebrew source close to the LXX. It should be remarked in general that no Qumran MS has as yet been found in which a systematic correction of any kind is visible, not even towards the MT.[31]

10. 4QSam^c is equally close to the MT and the Lucianic text of 2 Samuel 14-15, which in that section probably reflects the Old Greek translation.[32] It is less close to the main tradition of the LXX which in these chapters contains the *kaige*-Theodotion revision. At the same time, lack of evidence warns us not to draw any special conclusion concerning a specially close relation between the LXX and the Lucianic or Old Greek text of Samuel.

11. Even though the name of the large Isaiah scroll has been invoked in connection with the same issue under investigation at a quite early stage in research,[33] the data adduced by Ziegler (see n.13) show that there was much exaggeration in these early observations. There is actually no

evidence for the assumption of a close connection between that scroll and the LXX. There are agreements between the two, but most of them are in minutiae, and as Ziegler realized, they may be coincidental. That is, the small contextual changes such as in number, pronouns, particles, and verbal forms, which the two sources sometimes have in common could have developed independently. In other words, in many instances, a secondary change evidenced in the scroll has also been made without the basis of a Hebrew source by the translator. (For A. van der Kooij's views, see pp. 207-25 in this volume.)

12. 2QDeut^c has been described as follows by Baillet: "Le texte se rapproche de la LXX et de la Vulgate."[34] However, this fragment, of which a mere twelve words have been preserved, in whole or in part, shows no close relation whatsoever to either the LXX or the Vulgate.[35]

III

Soon after the discovery of the first Qumran scrolls scholars mentioned the possibility of the existence of a close relation between them and the LXX, though this issue has actually not been examined thoroughly. As is natural, the remarks made so far on this issue reflect the convictions of scholars concerning the status of the LXX and especially concerning the relation between the textual witnesses. It was natural then, as it still is today, for many scholars to describe the history of the textual witnesses of the Bible in terms of three recensions, families, or revisions, at the centre of which stand the MT, LXX and SP.

THE CONTRIBUTION OF THE QUMRAN SCROLLS   39

With this view as a given, it was also natural
that scholars tried to ascribe the newly-found
texts to one of the above-mentioned groups/
recensions, since no entity beyond this tripartite
division had yet been envisaged. Thus most of the
Qumran texts were ascribed to the so-called
recension of the MT, some to that of the SP and
again others to the recension of the LXX, also
named the "Egyptian family." At this moment we
need not critically assess this view, which I have
tried to refute on previous occasions.[36] Suffice
it to say that, in my view, the aforementioned
textual entities are not recensions, but rather
texts, and that more than three such texts are
known. But with this scholarly consensus on the
status of the textual witnesses as background
information, it is easy to understand how and why
certain scrolls were ascribed to the recension of
the LXX, and how they were soon described as
"Septuagintal." After all, each newly found text
had to belong, so to speak, to one of the known
recensions. If the text could not be ascribed to
the recension of the MT, according to the scholarly consensus it almost *had* to be ascribed to that
of the SP or that of the LXX. There was not room
for the assumption of a different status for the
scroll, or for different views. In the light of
this it is therefore understandable why at first
scholars thought that 1QIs^a was close to the LXX -
after all, its text is not particularly close to
the MT, and there seemed to be only one alternative, viz., to assume a close relation with the
LXX. Milik's contention that 5QDeut was revised
according to the LXX reflects a similarly limited

textual outlook, and the same pertains to Baillet's aforementioned remarks on 2QDeut^c. The same view underlies Milik's description of 5QKings: "Le peu de texte conservé n'est pas significatif du point de vue recensionel: le TM et la LXX y sont à peu près identiques."[37] Even the recently published texts display a similar outlook.

The issue at stake is one of statistics and textual outlook. In our view, a list of agreements between the scroll and the LXX does not make that text close to the LXX or "Septuagintal," so to speak, even if the list is impressive, and even if that list is greater than the agreements with the other witnesses. The LXX is just a text and not a recension. A large number of agreements with the LXX only shows that the two texts are closer to each other in the supposed stemma of the biblical texts than to the other known texts. Even if we personally do not succumb to stemmatic considerations for the biblical texts, there is nothing wrong in doing so. A large number of agreements between the LXX and a scroll could mean that the two texts were close to each other in the supposed stemma, or closer to each other than to the other known texts. However, with the enormous gaps in our knowledge we will never be able to assess the real relation between the texts.

Many of our calculations on the closeness between the LXX and a scroll are based on the accumulation of many readings, sometimes important, but usually minute. The tacit assumption behind this thinking is, as mentioned, that there were merely two or three recensions and that simple statistics can show us how close the Qumran text was to one of the three or two recensions of the biblical text. However, these texts were not in the nature of recensions, but texts, and their number was at one time much larger than two or three. Moreover, probably only a very small number of these texts is known to us. As a result, any speculation on the basis of these very fragmentary data may be utterly misleading if based on mere statistics.

Besides, the case of the LXX differs from that of the other witnesses, often wrongly named "the main witnesses" of the biblical text, viz., the MT and the SP. The MT is known to us as a textual family consisting of many individual witnesses reflecting one single text. The SP does reflect a textual-editorial recension or revision, and all texts which are exclusively close to that textual tradition indeed derived from a common background. However, the Hebrew text behind the LXX was, as far as we know, nothing but a single text, which, because of the historical circumstances of its use by the translators in Egypt and its forming the basis for the New Testament became important. Since the LXX merely represents a single text and not a family as is the case with the MT, nor a recension as is the case with the SP, our task is limited to determining the relative closeness of newly found Hebrew texts to the Hebrew text underlying the LXX. Because of the lack of relevant information on most of the one-time extant Hebrew texts, this task of comparing texts with the LXX is almost impossible, and indeed in the majority of cases no conclusive evidence is available. Statistical evidence does not suffice; it has to be combined with an analysis of the content. Thus the statistical evidence together with content analysis leads to the assumption of a very close connection between the LXX and 4QJer^{b,d}, and a somewhat less close connection in the case of 4QDeut^q and 4QSam^a.

Other texts (4QDeut^{c,h,j}, 4QSam^c) are only relevant because of the statistical situation, which, in our view may be misleading. The evidence for 4QLev^{d*} is not clear, as it may have been equally close to the SP and the LXX. For the sake of completeness 5QDeut, 2QDeut and 1QIs^a have been mentioned as well, but actually the evidence for these texts is negative. There is much evidence for a close connection between the LXX and 4QNum^b, but since that text actually is closer to the SP, the evidence is not very relevant in the present context.

Since only a few Qumran texts are close to the LXX, no overall theory should be launched, and certainly all terms like "Septuagintal scroll" should be avoided. That term, often used by scholars, is a misnomer, based on the wrong assumption that the Septuagint reflects an archetypal recension of the biblical text.

In conclusion, in Qumran, Palestine, we have found only a very small number of texts that were closely related to the *Vorlage* of the LXX. The Hebrew scrolls from which the LXX was translated mainly in Egypt, have *not* been found in Qumran, and neither should one look for them in Palestine. Since many, if not most of the biblical texts of the third and second centuries BCE were unique, there is but one place where they should be sought, namely in Egypt itself, even though ultimately they were imported from Palestine.

NOTES

1. This article was written during the author's stay at the Institute for Advanced Studies of the Hebrew University in 1989-1990. The author is grateful to the staff of the Institute for the gracious help provided during that year.

2. "Qumran and the Present State of the Old Testament Text Studies: The Septuagint Text," *JBL* 78 (1959) 26-33.

3. Philadelphia: Fortress Press, 1974.

4. These figures are based upon the data in the sixth volume of the London Polyglot (1657), part IV, 19-34, and they have been collected again by Z. Metal, *The Samaritan Version of the Pentateuch in Jewish Sources* (Tel-Aviv: Don, 1979; Hebr.).

5. Thus L. de Dieu, Seldenus, Hottingerus, and Hassencampius; for a detailed description of their views and bibliographical references, see F. H. W. Gesenius, *De Pentateuchi Samaritani origine, indole et auctoritate, Commentatio philologico-critica* (Halle: Libraria Rengeriana, 1815).

6. Thus Gesenius and Usserius; see Gesenius, *De Pentateuchi*, 13.

7. See the present author's *The Text-Critical Use of the Septuagint in Biblical Research* (Jerusalem Biblical Studies 3; Jerusalem: Simor, 1981) 107-110.

8. O. Thenius, *Die Bücher Samuels* (Leipzig: Weidmann, 1842); J. Wellhausen, *Der Text der Bücher Samuelis* (Göttingen: Vandenhoeck & Ruprecht, 1871); S.R. Driver, *Notes on the Hebrew Text and the Topography of the Books of Samuel* (2nd ed., Oxford: Clarendon, 1913).

9. For a recent discussion, see M. Fishbane, *Biblical Interpretation in Ancient Israel* (Oxford: Clarendon, 1985) 69.

10. This point has been stressed by various scholars. Among others, see the article by Orlinsky mentioned in n.2; pp.11-26 (especially p.13) of the aforementioned book by R. W. Klein and D. Barthélemy, "L'enchevêtrement de l'histoire textuelle et de l'histoire littéraire dans les relations entre la Septante et le Texte Massorétique," *De Septuaginta, Studies in Honour of John William Wevers on his sixty-fifth birthday* (ed A. Pietersma and C. Cox; Mississauga, Ont: Benben, 1984) 21-40, esp. 32-33.

11. P. Maas, *Textual Criticism*, translated by B. Flower (Oxford: Clarendon, 1958) 42 = *Textkritik*, in *Einleitung in die Altertumswissenschaft* I, VII (ed. A. Gercke and E. Norden; 3rd ed; Leipzig: Teubner, 1957).

12. The common source of MT on the one hand and LXX (= 4QSam^a) on the other hand was almost identical: בפרמשלש. According to the context, it is reasonable to assume that this word cluster originally referred to a פר (bull) in the singular (in the next verse the bull is referred to in the singular ["they slew the bull"]), i.e., "a three year old bull," and that when the spaces between the words and the *matres lectionis* were added, the common source of the LXX and 4QSam^a retained this understanding, while the MT was corrupted.

13. J. Ziegler, "Die Vorlage der Isaias-Septuaginta (LXX) und die erste Isaias-Rolle von Qumran (1QIsa^a)," *JBL* 78 (1959) 34-59.

14. See especially F. M. Cross, "A New Qumran Fragment" (see below), and for a more recent and detailed analysis, E. C. Ulrich, *The Qumran Text of Samuel and Josephus*, (HSM 19; Missoula, Mont: Scholars Press, 1978).

15. See J. G. Janzen, *Studies in the Text of Jeremiah*, (HSM 6; Cambridge, Mass: Scholars Press, 1973); E. Tov, "The Literary History of the Book of Jeremiah in the Light of Its Textual History," *Empirical Models for Biblical Criticism* (ed. J. Tigay; Philadelphia: University of Pennsylvania, 1985) 211-37; Y. J. Min, *The Minuses and Pluses of the LXX Translation of Jeremiah as Compared with the Massoretic Text: Their Classification and Possible Origins*, unpubl. diss. Hebrew University

(Jerusalem, 1977); E. Tov, "Some Aspects of the Textual and Literary History of the Book of Jeremiah," *Le livre de Jérémie* (ed. P.M. Bogaert; BETL 54; Leuven: University Press, Uitgeverij Peeters, 1981) 145-76.

16. R. E. Fuller, *The Minor Prophets Manuscripts from Qumran, Cave IV*, 1988; J. R. Davila, *Unpublished Pentateuch Manuscripts from Cave IV, Qumran: 4QGen-Ex^a, 4QGen$^{b-h,j-k}$*, 1988; S. A. White, *A Critical Edition of Seven Manuscripts of Deuteronomy: 4QDt^a, 4QDt^c, 4QDt^d, 4QDt^f, 4QDt^g, 4QDt^i, and 4QDt^n*, 1988; J. Duncan, *A Critical Edition of Deuteronomy Manuscripts from Qumran Cave IV 4QDt^b, 4QDt^e, 4QDt^h, 4QDt^j, 4QDt^k, 4QDt^l*, 1989; N. R. Jastram, *The Book of Numbers from Qumrân Cave IV (4QNum^b)*, 1990.

17. See the present author in "The Jeremiah Scrolls from Qumran," *The Texts of Qumran and the History of the Community* (ed. F. García Martínez) = *RevQ* 14 (1989-90) 189-206.

18. P.W. Skehan, "A Fragment of the "Song of Moses" (Deut. 32) from Qumran," *BASOR* 136 (1954) 12-15.

19. The most recent and detailed statement is that of P. M. Bogaert, "Les trois rédactions conservées et la forme originale de l'envoi du cantique de Moïse (Dt 32,43)," *Das Deuteronomium, Entstehung, Gesalt und Botschaft* (ed. N. Lohfink; BETL 68; Leuven: University Press, Uitgeverij Peeters, 1985) 329-40. For earlier discussions, see especially P. W. Skehan, "A Fragment" (n.18); E. A. Artom, "Sul testo di Deuteronomio XXXII, 37-43," *Rivista degli studi orientali* 32 (1957) 285-91; R. Meyer, "Die Bedeutung von Deuteronomium 32,8f.43 (4Q) fur die Auslegung des Moseslieds," *Verbannung und Heimkehr. W. Rudolph zum 70 Geburtstage* (ed. A. Kuschke; Tübingen: Mohr, 1961) 197-209.

20. P. K. McCarter, *I-II Samuel* (AB 8,9; Garden City, NY: Doubleday, 1980,1984).

21. "Determining the Relationship between the Qumran Scrolls and the LXX: Some Methodological Issues," *The Hebrew and Greek Texts of Samuel, 1980 Proceedings IOSCS, Vienna* (ed. E. Tov; Jerusalem: Academon, 1980) 45-67.

22. See pp. 216-55 in this volume.

23. White, *Critical Edition* (see n.16) 123. See also p. 121: "4QDt^c appears to be a manuscript

located in the textual tradition of G. In cases of shared error, it agrees with G most often against either M and/or S, although there is some overlap."

24. Duncan, *Critical Edition*, 77.

25. 4Q175: 14-20 is copied from *DJD* V (Oxford: Clarendon, 1968) 58. 4QDeut^h is copied according to the transcription of Duncan, *Critical Edition*, fragment 9. The text of the SP follows the edition of A. and R. Sadaqa, *Jewish and Samaritan Version of the Pentateuch* (Tel-Aviv: Rubin Mass, 1961-1965).

26. The texts are almost identical in the preserved section. Note that 4Q175 contains two corrections which emend the text common to its base text and that of the Deuteronomy manuscript: ישימו, וכליל.

27. The quotation from the same text in 4QFlor (174), fragments 6-7 is not extensive enough to determine its textual filiation.

28. Duncan, *Critical Edition*, 112: "In summary, 4QDt^j may be characterized as a "full" or "expansionistic" type of text, which stands in the tradition of G of Deuteronomy."

29. The text expands v.4 according to v.3, and therefore does not add substantial details to the implication of the law. See earlier commentators: B. Baentsch, (*HKAT*; Göttingen: Vandenhoeck & Ruprecht, 1909) 389; K. Elliger, *Leviticus*, (HAT 4; Tübingen: Mohr, 1966) 219.

30. *DJD* III (Oxford: Clarendon, 1962) 169-171.

31. See E. Tov, "The Textual Base of the Corrections in the Biblical Texts Found in Qumran," *Forty Years of Research in the Dead Sea Scrolls* (in press).

32. See my own analysis quoted in n.21, especially 58-61. Ulrich, on the other hand, particularly stresses the links with the Lucianic tradition: "4QSam^c: A Fragmentary Manuscript of 2 Samuel 14-15 from the scribe of the Serek Hay-yahad (1QS)," *BASOR* 235 (1979) 1-25.

33. Upon the publication of this scroll, scholars were quick to remark on its agreements with the LXX. For details see the discussion by H. M.

Orlinsky in the article quoted in n.2 and see also his own analysis.

34. *DJD* III (Oxford: Clarendon, 1962) 61.

35. If anything, this text, written in the Qumran orthography, agrees more with the MT against the LXX than vice versa.

36. For the latest formulation of my views see *Bqwrt nwsh hmqr'* (Jerusalem: Mossad Bialik, 1989) ch 3 and my article "Groups of Texts Found at Qumran" (in press).

37. *DJD* III (Oxford: Clarendon, 1962) 172.

THE SEPTUAGINT MANUSCRIPTS FROM QUMRAN: A REAPPRAISAL OF THEIR VALUE

EUGENE ULRICH[*]

There were eight Septuagint or Septuagint-related manuscripts found at Qumran and, though none were found at Masada or Murabbaʿat, a ninth was found at Nahal Hever (Wadi Habra):

4Q119	4QLXXLev^a	[Rahlfs 801]
4Q120	pap4QLXXLev^b	[Rahlfs 802]
4Q121	4QLXXNum	[Rahlfs 803]
4Q122	4QLXXDeut	[Rahlfs 819]
4Q126	4QUnid gr	
4Q127	pap4QparaExod gr	
7Q1	pap7QExod	[Rahlfs 805]
7Q2	pap7QEpJer	[Rahlfs 804]
	8HevXIIgr	[Rahlfs 943]

All these Greek manuscripts have been published or submitted for publication in *Discoveries in the Judaean Desert*.[1] Patrick Skehan had prepared editions of 4QLXXLev^a, pap4QLXXLev^b, and 4QLXXNum and published editions of the first and last prior to his death on September 9, 1980. I published 4QLXXDeut along with a list of all the variants of the LXX manuscripts from Qumran in 1984. The larger fragments of the unidentified papyrus with the Exodus motif (4Q127) have recently been published in the Festschrift honoring our colleague and symbolic ἄρχων in the world of the Septuagint, Robert Hanhart. Maurice Baillet published the tiny fragments from Cave 7 in 1982. And Emanuel Tov's publication of the Greek Minor Prophets scroll appeared earlier this year (1990).

John Wevers, with whom both Skehan and I communicated and shared our work on the Cave 4 LXX Mss as it developed, included that evidence in his Göttingen editions of *Leviticus* and *Numeri*,[2] and in 1982 he published an article which examined the variants in 4QLXXNum.[3] I am unaware that anyone, with the single exception of Wevers, has analysed the list of variants from the Qumran Greek Mss published in 1984 and used its evidence for refining our knowledge of the history of the LXX. I described the purpose of that article as "simply the attempt at objective presentation of the data, not the analysis of their significance..." and confessed that I would "undoubtedly fail to resist proposing such an analysis in a future study."[4]

In this article I now propose to analyse some of those variants. First, the variants of 4QLXXLev^a will be studied methodically. Secondly, as a result of that study some reflections will be

required concerning the Hebrew text(s) which lay
behind the Old Greek translation (OG) and other
Greek witnesses. Thirdly, some of the variants of
4QLXXNum will be studied. And finally,
conclusions will be offered re-evaluating the
significance of the variants of these two мss.

At least one caveat should preface this
analysis. Throughout the article texts will be
compared and terms used such as "the scroll," "the
Massoretic Text," and "the LXX." In order not to
become engulfed in a constant quagmire of qualifications, it will be necessary to focus on a
particular Qumran text, on the MT, and on the
edition of the LXX edited by John Wevers ($\mathfrak{G}^{ed}$).
But it must constantly be borne in mind that all
texts are quite stratified — they contain many
original readings, a certain number of unique
errors, a certain number of errors inherited from
parent texts, usually some intentional expansions
or clarifications, and often some revisions
(whether fresh or inherited) for a variety of
purposes. It is perfectly logical, therefore, to
maintain that the same text is original in one
reading and secondary in the very next reading.
It is unlikely, however, that we should accept the
hypothesis that correction of the original Greek
toward the Hebrew text which became dominant in
the Massoretic *textus receptus* is randomly
scattered. For example, it is a plausible
hypothesis that 4QLXXLev$^{\alpha}$ might represent a
revision toward the proto-MT of a text like that
transmitted in the fourth-century Codex Vaticanus

($\mathfrak{G}^B$); conversely, it is also a plausible hypothesis that the text in $\mathfrak{G}^B$ might represent a revision toward the proto-MT of a text like that in 4QLXXLev^a. But it is implausible that both 4QLXXLev^a and $\mathfrak{G}^B$ could each be revised toward the proto-MT in 40-50% of their readings. That is, although all texts are to a certain degree mixed texts and systematic revision toward the eventually dominant MT is to be expected in certain early texts, such revision is not to be expected to have permeated one text in half measure and a different text in different half measure.

I. The Variant Readings of 4QLXXLev^a

For the purposes of this article a "variant reading" will be any reading, beyond the purely orthographical, preserved on the extant Qumran fragments which differs from $\mathfrak{G}^{ed}$, $\mathfrak{G}^B$, or the MT. There are 16 such variants in 4QLXXLev^a.[5] For each variant the lemma will present the reading of 4QLXXLev^a; the readings of $\mathfrak{G}^{ed}$, the MT, the Samaritan Pentateuch (ᛉ), and other relevant versions will be distributed as their affiliation dictates. Comments will follow on aspects of the translation and variants, especially the question whether an alternative Hebrew text might lie behind the OG or might have influenced the Greek variants. Then the following pair of contrasting possibilities will be explored and articulated: (a) if the reading in $\mathfrak{G}^{ed}$ represents the original Old Greek translation (OG), then how is the reading in 4QLXXLev^a to be explained? (b) if the

THE SEPTUAGINT MANUSCRIPTS FROM QUMRAN   53

reading in 4QLXXLev^a is the OG, then how is the
reading in 𝕲^{ed} to be explained? A decision
between the possibilities will be postponed until
all the variants have been reviewed and the
reflections in Part II have been considered.

Lev 26:4 [τον υετον τ]ηι γηι υμων ℨ^J(מיטריא
דארעכון)] τον υετον υμιν 𝕲^{ed} = גשמיכם MTᴍ (cf.
Ezek 34:26)

𝕲^{ed} is a correct, but not completely literal,
translation of the Hebrew as represented in MTᴍ,
whereas 4QLXXLev^a can be seen as a free
translation of the sense of the same Hebrew.
Occurrences, however, such as מטר־ארצך = τον υετον
τη γη σου in the similar list of covenant
blessings in Deut 28:12, demonstrate that
4QLXXLev^a could also be reflecting more literally
a different Hebrew *Vorlage*. Targum Pseudo-
Jonathan could also be a reflection of the same
Hebrew that lay behind 4QLXXLev^a, or it could be a
similar but independent expansion.

   (a) If 𝕲^{ed} is original, then it should be seen
as a translation of a text like MTᴍ, and 4QLXXLev^a
is either a legitimate, free translation of the
same Hebrew or a literal reflection of a slightly
different Hebrew *Vorlage*. (b) If 4QLXXLev^a is
original, then 𝕲^{ed} is probably the result of a
revision toward MT.

Lev 26:4 τον ξυλινον καρο[ ] (καρπον?)] τα ξυλα
(ξυλινα G-426) των πεδιων αποδωσει τον καρπον
αυτων 𝕲^{ed} = ו(ע)ץ השדה יתן פריו MTᴍ

𝔊^ed is again a correct, almost literal, translation of MTм, whereas 4QLXXLev^a is a free translation of the sense, though it would apparently have read "the land will give its produce and its arboreal fruit" in contrast to "the land will give its produce, and the trees of the fields will give their fruit." With regard to the Hebrew *Vorlage*, the similar phrase του καρπου του ξυλινου = מפרי העץ in the next chapter (Lev 27:30) shows that 4QLXXLev^a may perhaps depend upon a slightly different Hebrew text.

(a) If 𝔊^ed is original, then it would be a literal translation of a text like MTм, and the scroll would be either a free translation of the same Hebrew or possibly a literal reflection of a different Hebrew *Vorlage*. (b) If the scroll is original, then it is either a legitimate, free translation of the same Hebrew as MTм or possibly a literal reflection of a different Hebrew *Vorlage*, and 𝔊^ed is probably the result of a revision toward the MT.

Lev 26:5 αμητος A B* 121 мss Philo Aeth] αλοητος 𝔊^ed = דיש MTм

דיש as a noun (= αλοητος, "threshing") is a *hapax legomenon* in the MT, occurring only here. The verbal root (דוש = αλοαν) occurs 5 times, including twice in Judges (8:7 and 8:16). In the latter two instances the meaning is metaphorical, and 𝔊^A translates metaphorically with καταξαινειν "crush to pieces," a correct but more free rendering instead of the more literal αλοαν.

THE SEPTUAGINT MANUSCRIPTS FROM QUMRAN 55

Illustrating the problems that we are dealing with throughout, the MT in Judg 8:16 presumably errs with a divergent Hebrew reading, וידע for וידש ('ayin for šin).[6] Note also מהאב, an error in the MT for מתעב at Amos 6:8, discussed under Lev 26:11 below.

αμητος is most often used for קציר ("harvest"). It is possible that קציר occurred in the Hebrew *Vorlage* (or was mistaken for בציר two words later), though there is no proof. But in principle, there is no more reason to suspect that the substitution of "harvest" for "threshing" or vice-versa should occur at the Greek stage than at the Hebrew stage. If the word (whether דיש or קציר) was clear in the Hebrew text being translated, the translator certainly knew both the meaning of the Hebrew word and the proper Greek word for it, and could have produced a precise translation. If there were no palaeographic error (ΑΛΟΗΤΟΣ > ΑΛΛΗΤΟΣ), then the substitution was made on the basis of sense or common usage. Note similar variation in Amos 9:13, some of which might be due to cross-influence.

Either (1) αλοητος is the OG, correctly translating the Hebrew preserved in MT𝔐, but then the variant αμητος is difficult to explain except as a revision toward an undocumented Hebrew variant; or (2) αμητος is the OG, attested by the earliest witnesses, and αλοητος is a revision toward MT𝔐.

(a) If 𝔊*ed* is original, then it is simply the accurate translation of a Hebrew text like MT𝔐,

and the scroll is either a palaeographic error, or
a smoothing of the text (from the less frequent to
the more frequent expression), or even a
correction toward a Hebrew text with קציר in
place of דיש. (b) If the scroll is original, then
𝔊*ᵈ would be a revision toward the MT.

Lev 26:5,6 [κ]αι πολεμος——[υμων 3°] ad fin 6 O
Mss La¹⁰⁰(πολεμος] gladius La¹⁰⁰) Arab Co Syh =
MTₘ(και πολεμος] וחרב MTₘ)] ad fin 5 𝔊*ᵈ; ad fin
5 et 6 A Bᵐᵍ F M´Mss

This clause fits better at the end of v 6, but
it fits adequately at the end of either verse
while arguments can also be adduced against its
position at the end of either verse. The best way
to explain the variant positions in 𝔊 is to see
the problem at the Hebrew stage. On the one hand,
the clause may have been a secondary insertion
into the early Hebrew; the "few chasing many"
motif is found without the "war" motif in Deut
32:20, Josh 23:10, and Isa 30:17. On the other
hand, the clause may have been original but
omitted through parablepsis (בארצכם^בארצכם if at
the end of v 5; ורדפ-^וחרב if at the end of v 6)
and reinserted in the margin of a Hebrew text;
then Hebrew Mss could have inserted it in either
of the two places. The point of interest here is
that the OG would have translated it at whichever
point it occurred in the OG *Vorlage* and subsequent
Greek Mss would have placed it wherever their
respective Hebrew texts (if any) had it.⁷

(a) If 𝔊*ᵈ is original, I would suggest that its order is due to its being translated from a Hebrew *Vorlage* which had that order; then the scroll would be seen as a correction toward a Hebrew text whose order was that attested by the MT. (b) If the scroll is original, then it should be seen as an accurate translation of a Hebrew text like the MT, and 𝔊*ᵈ would be either an unintentional displacement or a correction toward an early variant Hebrew which similarly could be an unintentional displacement.

Lev 26:6   [o]εκφοβων / υμας F Mss Arm Syh(υμας sub ÷) = 𝔖ᵖ] tr 𝔊*ᵈ(sub ÷ G); > υμας Bo = מחריד MT𝔐𝔖°

On one level this is an insignificant reading, for it seems unrelated to the Hebrew. In none of the 12 occurrences of ואין מחריד throughout the MT is there a direct object expressed in Hebrew, and usually the Greek does not include one. But the OG here appears to have added the direct object for sense (cf. also 𝔊Jer 26[MT46]:27), and the alternate tradition appears to have transposed for reasons of style. On another level, however, this reading serves to illustrate another type of variant which must be kept in mind —— purely inner-Greek variants. This means that extra caution must be used, for at times variants may be purely inner-Greek yet independently happen to agree with the MT or some ancient Ms and thus be assigned to false causes.

Lev 26:8   πεντε υμων Syh(π. εξ υ.)] εξ υμων
πεντε $\mathfrak{G}^{ed}$; מכם חמשה MT𝔐

Both are correct translations of the MT𝔐, but the reading of the scroll appears more natural, whereas that of $\mathfrak{G}^{ed}$ is a more closely literal reflection of the MT. Is a variant Hebrew *Vorlage* for the scroll's reading likely? It is possible, but there is no reason to suppose so.

(a) If $\mathfrak{G}^{ed}$ is original, then the scroll is to be seen as a stylistic revision. (b) If the scroll is original, then $\mathfrak{G}^{ed}$ is probably a revision toward the MT.

Lev 26:9   [και εσται μο]υ η διαθηκη εν υμιν[ ]]
και στησω την διαθηκην μου μεθ υμων (διαθ. υμιν *b*;
...*pactum meum in uobis* Arm^{te}) $\mathfrak{G}^{ed}$ Aeth Arm Bo =
והקימתי את בריתי אתכם MT𝔐

The nominative in the scroll requires that η διαθηκη be the subject of its verb. The scroll's reading probably reflects a Hebrew not far from והי(ת)ה בריתי בתוככם (cf. Ezek 37:26) or ובריתי אתכם —— note והרביתי אתכם (!) just before והקימתי in the MT.

(a) If $\mathfrak{G}^{ed}$ is original, then it is to be seen as a literal translation of a text like the MT, and the scroll is either a revision toward an alternate, undocumented Hebrew, a revision for style or theological nuance, or an error. (b) If the scroll is original, then $\mathfrak{G}^{ed}$ quite probably must be seen as a revision toward the MT.

THE SEPTUAGINT MANUSCRIPTS FROM QUMRAN   59

Lev 26:10   [εξοισετ]ε μετα των νεων] εκ προσωπου
νεων εξοισετε 𝔊*ed* = מפני חדש תוציא MT𝔐

4QLXXLev^a could be freely translating a Hebrew
text identical with the MT, a slightly different
text, or even a text such as תוציאו עם חדש,
whereas 𝔊*ed* is a virtually literal reflection of
the MT.

(a) If 𝔊*ed* is original, then the scroll could
be seen as an early revision toward a Hebrew text
such as that just suggested (less likely) or as a
revision for style. (b) If the scroll is
original, then 𝔊*ed* quite probably must be seen as
a revision toward the MT.

Lev 26:11   βδελυξομαι 126(βδελλυξωμαι) Arab]
βδελυξεται η ψυχη μου 𝔊*ed* = תגעל נפשי MT𝔐

Both readings occur in both Hebrew and Greek
—— βδελυσσομαι = מתאב (read מתעב, Amos 6:8) and
εβδελυξατο η ψυχη αυτων = תתעב נפשם (Ps
107[𝔊106]:18) —— so it is difficult to decide
whether the difference is here due to *Vorlage*,
style, or theological influence.

If 𝔊*ed* is original, then it is a literal
reflection of a text like the MT or possibly a
free translation of a text with אגעל, and the
scroll could be seen as an early revision toward a
Hebrew text with אגעל or as a revision for style.
(b) If the scroll is original, then it is probably
a translation from a Hebrew text such as אגעל or
possibly a free translation of a text like the MT,
and 𝔊*ed* probably must be seen as a revision toward
the MT or as a euphemistic revision.

Lev 26:12 και εσομ[αι   ]] και εμπεριπατησω εν
υμιν και εσομαι υμων θεος ⌕•d = והתהלכתי בתוככם
והייתי לכם לאלהים MT𝔐; και εμπ. εν υμιν ad fin tr
131

The scroll did not have και εμπεριπατησω εν
υμιν at the beginning of this verse. It has space
for about four short words to follow, but there is
no way to determine whether the two clauses were
transposed (with 131) or some other covenantal
formula followed. In either case it is possible
that it followed a different Hebrew *Vorlage*.

(a) If ⌕•d is original, then it is to be seen
as a close translation of a text like the MT, and
the scroll presents an error (parablepsis or
transposition), a revision toward an undocumented
variant Hebrew text, or a theologically or
stylistically altered text. (b) If the scroll is
original, then it is a translation of an
undocumented variant Hebrew text or an error
(parablepsis or transposition), and ⌕•d quite
probably must be seen as a revision toward the MT.

Lev 26:12 μοι εθν[ος]] μου (μοι Mss) λαος (εις
λαον b Armt•) ⌕•d La Arm Bo 2 Cor 6:16; לי לעם MT𝔐

The preponderant usage of both the LXX and the
later recensions is λαος for עם when referring to
Israel, and εθνος for גוי and for עם when
referring to peoples other than Israel. The LXX
does use εθνος, however, to refer to Israel, at
least once in Leviticus (19:16) where the Hebrew
probably had עם, as well as in the promises to the

ancestral bearers of the covenant (cf. Gen 18:18; 46:3). These latter translate גוי, it is true, but the point is that the LXX has established the occasional use of εθνος to refer to Israel, even to reflect עם. In contrast, it is very difficult to imagine εθνος being substituted —— intentionally or in error —— for an original λαος. Moreover, Wevers does endorse εθνος as the OG at Lev 19:16 for עם referring to Israel. Thus it would appear that εθνος was the OG translation here at 26:12, with λαος as the routine revisional substitution.

(a) If $\mathfrak{G}^{\bullet d}$ is original, then the scroll can only be seen as an uncanny error or unusual substitution. (b) If the scroll is original, then $\mathfrak{G}^{\bullet d}$ is a secondary, routine lexical revision toward the MT.

Lev 26:13   τον ζυγον το[υ δεσμου] MSS La[100]] τον δεσμον του ζυγου $\mathfrak{G}^{\bullet d}$ Aeth Arm Bo; מטה עליכם (כם)על מטה MT4Q(-עול מטות)

There are too many possibilities for these readings to allow a firm conclusion regarding the original translation and its subsequent fate. There are both literal and figurative meanings of both nouns in addition to both literal and figurative meanings as understood by later editors and later copyists at the transmission stage, plus the possibility of interference from Ezek 34:27. Thus, the reading is best left as questionable and able to be decided in either direction.

Lev 26:14 μου 2° MSS La[100] Aeth Bo] + ταυτα 𝔊*d
Arm = הָאֵלֶּה MT𝑚

The scroll reads well without ταυτα, and there
is no reason to suspect it was intentionally or
accidentally omitted, whereas the word seems
superfluous in 𝔊*d and is best interpreted as a
revision toward the MT.

Lev 26:15 αλ[λα] 1° 𝔊*d La Aeth Arm Bo] וְאִם MT𝑚;
אִם MT[MSS] 𝑚[MSS] 𝔖𝔙

The OG, this time with all Greek MSS in agreement, had αλλα as a good and free translation of
the meaning of (ו)אם in its context.

Lev 26:15 [προστα]/γμασι μου] κριμασιν μου
𝔊*d La Aeth Arm Bo; מִשְׁפָּטַי MT𝑚

The OG three times uses προσταγμα for משפט in
Leviticus (see 18:26; 19:37, and later in this
chapter, 26:46), but it also uses κριμα five times
for משפט in Leviticus (including vv 15 and 43 in
this chapter, but note κριμα for חק in v 46). For
θ´ and α´, however, κριμα became the recensional
lexeme for משפט, whereas προσταγμα became the
recensional lexeme for חק or פקוד. Thus, if one
of the variants should be recensional, it would be
κριμασιν.

(α) If 𝔊*d is original, then the scroll simply
presents the substitution of a synonym,
intentional or not. (b) If the scroll is
original, then 𝔊*d could also be simply a synonym,
or it could be a secondary, routine recensional
lexical revision toward the MT.

THE SEPTUAGINT MANUSCRIPTS FROM QUMRAN   63

Lev 26:15   α[λλα ωστε?]] ωστε (2°) ♯•d = ‹להפרכם›
MTм; και ωστε 392 Aeth; και 44 75 Arm

This final reading is too uncertain to bear the weight of any solid argument or conclusion.

II. The Hebrew *Vorlage* behind the Greek Translation

Having studied the variant readings preserved by 4QLXXLev^a and suggested two possible vantage points from which to understand their interrelationship, it is tempting to draw a conclusion concerning which approach commends itself as more cogent. But first some explicit reflection on the character of the Hebrew text lying behind the Greek variants may help provide a more informed conclusion.

It is gratifying to note that a sophisticated, up-to-date understanding of the Hebrew *Vorlage* for the Septuagint has reached wide international scope. The parade example is Emanuel Tov's justly celebrated monograph, *The Text-Critical Use of the Septuagint in Biblical Research*,[8] but numerous others come to mind, only a few of which can be mentioned here. Anneli Aejmelaeus, in an article which offers both judicious breadth and specialized focus on the text of Exodus, concludes:

> All in all, the scholar who wishes to attribute deliberate changes, harmonizations, completion of details and new accents to the translator is under the obligation to prove [that] thesis with weighty arguments and also to show why the divergences cannot have originated with the *Vorlage*. That the

translator *may* have manipulated his original does not mean that he necessarily did so. All that is known of the translation techniques employed in the Septuagint points firmly enough in the opposite direction.[9]

Julio Trebolle, in a series of books and articles concentrating on Samuel-Kings, has demonstrated repeatedly that a Hebrew text divergent from the Massoretic *textus receptus* both explains the translation of the OG and at times provides a superior Hebrew text.[10] Sharon Pace Jeansonne has provided analogous demonstrations for the book of Daniel, showing that the claim of "Theological *Tendenz*" on the part of the Greek translator cannot be maintained.[11]

In 1980 Zaki Aly and Ludwig Koenen published an edition of P.Fouad 266, and in the introduction Koenen says:

> the appearance of the new rolls was hailed by R. Hanhart [in *OLZ* 73 (1978) 39-46, esp.40] as the beginning of a new era of studies in the text of the *Septuagint*. P.Fouad 266, indeed, shows that already in the middle of the first century B.C. the text of the Greek *Genesis* and *Deuteronomy* was basically steady, though the results of continuous attempts to bring the Greek text into closer accord with the Hebrew are clearly recognizable. Therefore, agreements between the new papyri and the Masoretic text against the majority of the best manuscripts of the later tradition do not necessarily establish what may be regarded as the original text of the Septuagint, but may very well result from later assimilations. Textual criticism of the same type as is known from the Christian era and is particularly connected with the name of Origen had already begun in the first century B.C., if not even earlier. This should be of no surprise. As soon as an authoritative Greek translation existed, attempts must have started to improve it and

to eliminate discrepancies between the Greek and the Hebrew.[12]

It is from this perspective —— that Greek texts must be evaluated in the light of the possibility that they represent a faithful translation of an ancient Hebrew text at variance with the Massoretic *textus receptus* —— that I propose a reassessment of the value of the variants of the LXX mss from Qumran.

I have a high respect for John Wevers' work, both because he has produced eleven volumes on the Greek text of the Pentateuch,[13] and because as a personal friend I know what a learned and indefatigable worker he is. But on this one point it seems that a review of the evidence is in order, since (1) 4QLXXLev^a is a pre-Christian witness three or four centuries earlier than our other Greek witnesses to Leviticus, (2) none of its variants are "errors" but are intelligible alternate readings, yet (3) none of its readings are selected as representing the OG.

Wevers, of course, is aware of the possibility of an alternate Hebrew parent text as the basis of the Old Greek of Leviticus:

> A Masoretic text of the entire Hebrew canon is available, and though it is not the exact form of the text which the translators rendered into Greek, it is an invaluable guide to it. The editor usually knows the parent text which was being translated and this serves as a reliable guide for eliminating various scribal errors from the Greek text tradition.[14]

Thus the question becomes whether and when an alternate Hebrew is considered the source of specific variants. As an example let us consider three instances concerning which preposition among attested variants is to be selected in the OG. In the *Text History of the Greek Leviticus*, Wevers says, "Prepositions occasionally create problems, though the critical text can often be determined by reading the Hebrew text."[15] First, in discussing Lev 24:8 (παρα vs. ενωπιον), he says, "The lectio difficilior which renders the MT literally is here to be preferred."[16] In this instance I do not disagree with the choice of παρα but rather pause at the reason adduced; παρα may render the MT (מאת) literally, but does that mean that παρα is necessarily the OG rather than a secondary revision of the OG back toward the proto-MT? More importantly, when using the criterion "determined by reading the Hebrew text," is *the* Hebrew text presumed to be the MT?

For a second instance, at Lev 1:15 (προς 1° vs. επι),[17] again I do not disagree but rather stress that in such cases, just as it is necessary to check the meaning involved, so too is it equally necessary to consider whether an inadvertent אל vs. על variant in the *Vorlage* lies at the root of the Greek variant. The אל vs. על confusion of laryngeals is frequent in the text transmitted in the MT,[18] as it is in the ancient manuscripts from Qumran.[19]

For the third instance I do disagree. At Deut 31:5 the MT has the frequent promise, ונתנם יהוה לפניכם ("The Lord will give [your enemies] into your power"). There are three Greek variants:

ενωπιον υμων, υμιν, and εις τας χειρας υμων, and Wevers selects και παρεδωκεν αυτους κυριος ενωπιον υμων as the OG translation. In his *Text History of the Greek Deuteronomy*, after discussing another locus where the decision on the originality of υμιν was difficult, Wevers says, "Much simpler to decide is the case of υμιν in 31:5 where for Deut ενωπιον υμων, [Vaticanus and other witnesses] read υμιν. The verb modified is παρεδωκεν. The difficult παρεδωκεν...ενωπιον υμων which is a literal equivalent to the MT was smoothed out by the change. The same kind of simplification took place in [the hexaplaric and other witnesses] where εις τας χειρας υμων was substituted for ενωπιον υμων."[20] Thus, ενωπιον υμων is viewed as original, and υμιν and εις τας χειρας υμων as the results of smoothing and simplification.

Here there is evidence for the alternate choice. Hellenophiles who usually wear a slight wince when reading some of the Greek found in the LXX, do not wince noticeably more at παρεδωκεν... ενωπιον υμων than at numerous other parts of the translation. It is hard to escape the suspicion that Wevers presumes that the לפניכם found in the MT was the reading that the OG translator saw in the Hebrew copy being translated. The same sentence, however, occurs elsewhere in Deuteronomy, and at one occurrence (Deut 7:23) where the MT has לפניך and 4QpaleoDeut[r] also has לפניך, another Deuteronomy scroll has בידך. These may be viewed as synonymous variants. When one seeks the OG translation, one finds only εις τας

χειρας σου (without relevant variant) in the ᴍs
tradition. I would maintain that probability
rests on בידך as the Hebrew word in the text (or
at least in the mind) of the OG translator at that
point, and that the OG translator translated
faithfully. We do not need the Qumran evidence,
however, for the ⅏ had already taught us this
lesson: in Deut 2:36 where the MT has (...נתן)
לפנינו, the OG has εις τας χειρας ημων (without
relevant variant), and the ⅏ has בידנו —— quite
probably the word encountered in the Hebrew text
used by the OG translator.

Such examples are frequent and widespread, a
small sampling of which follows:

Exod 1:5	4QExod^b	חמש ושבעים נפש
	MT	שבעים נפש
	𝔊	ψυχαι...πεντε και εβδομηκοντα
		75/70 people
Lev 3:1	4QLev^b	קרבנו ליהוה
(cf. 2:12, 14)	MT	קרבנו
	𝔊	το δωρον αυτου τω κυριω
		his offering (+to the Lord)
2 Sam 10:6	4QSam^a	[ורא]ישטוב (=error)
Jos., *Ant.* 7:121	MT	ואיש טוב
	𝔊	και Ειστωβ (Ιστοβον Josephus)
		the men of Tob

THE SEPTUAGINT MANUSCRIPTS FROM QUMRAN 69

2 Sam 7:23	4QSam^a	ואהלים (=error)
[*om* 1 Chr 17:21]	MT	ואלהיו
	𝕲	και σκηνωματα
		tents/its gods
Isa 23:1-2	4QIsa^a	^{2}למודמו
	MT	למו : ^{2}דמו
	𝕲	^{2}τινι ομοιοι γεγονασιν
		(=^{2}למי דמו)
		^{2}Who are they like...?
		/ to them. ^{2}Be still!
Dan 8:3	4QDan^b	[איל א]חד גדול
	MT θ´	איל אחד
	𝕲	κριον ενα μεγαν
		a (+great) ram
Dan 8:4	4QDan^a	W,E,N,S
	MT θ´	W,N,S
	𝕲	E,N,W,S (E,W,N,S, 967)
		West,East,North,South

The conclusion to be drawn is that there was a wide variety of Hebrew texts available and in use when the OG translation of the various books was made and for several centuries during the early transmission of the OG. One must treat the elasticity of the Hebrew text with caution, to be sure, but one also must not underrate the variation in the Hebrew text abundantly demonstrated by the Qumran MSS and the versions. To underrate it will cause distortion in the understanding of the LXX and the forces behind its translation and transmission.

III. The Variant Readings of 4QLXXNum

With those general reflections on the Hebrew *Vorlage* of the LXX, we can now turn to 4QLXXNum. There are 17 variants in 4QLXXNum, 13 of which are unique, only 4 finding support in other Greek MSS.[21] Again, only one — where 𝕲ᴮ has an obvious error and 4QLXXNum has strong support from the MS tradition — is accepted in the Göttingen critical edition as an attestation of the OG. Some of the variants in 4QLXXNum are of minor significance, some remain ambiguous. The value of 4QLXXNum as a witness to the OG will hinge primarily on four variants (viewing the fourfold occurrence of αρτηρ- vs. αναφορ- as a single variant).

Num 3:40   αριθμησον] επισκεψαι 𝕲*ᵉᵈ; פקד MTᴍ

Five factors point with varying degrees of strength to αριθμησον as the OG.

(1) Lagarde had discovered the general, but not universal, rule of thumb that if two variants occur in the MS tradition, both correct and acceptable, one in literal agreement with the MT and the other more free, then the freer rendering is (other things being equal) to be selected as the OG and the literal rendering is to be seen as secondary revision toward the MT (see points 3 and 4 below).

(2) No evidence surfaces to question Αριθμοι as the original Greek title of the book, and the title surely derives from occurrences of the word in the text.[22]

(3) επισκεπτεσθαι became the standard recensional equivalent for פקד, while αριθμειν was used for מנה. Thus, where פקד occurs in the Hebrew with επισκεπτεσθαι/αριθμειν in the Greek witnesses, if recensional revision is at work, αριθμειν is probably the OG and επισκεπτεσθαι the recensional revision.[23]

(4) Consider the way translators and revisers work. If the translator sees פקד in the Hebrew of Numbers and is translating fresh, both επισκεπτεσθαι (as a literal translation) and αριθμειν (as a freer, contextual translation, suggested by the title and content of the book plus occurrences as early as 1:2b) are options, as are other possible words. If a reviser sees פקד in the proto-MT and is revising the OG back toward that Hebrew text, one might (as θ´ and α´ certainly would) change αριθμειν to επισκεπτεσθαι; there would be no reason to change επισκεπτεσθαι to αριθμειν on the basis of the Hebrew. If one is copying the Greek text from another Greek text without reference to the Hebrew, one might change επισκεπτεσθαι to αριθμειν for contextual meaning. Thus, αριθμειν is due either to the original translation stage or to the later Greek transmission stage, but it is not due to the recensional stage.

(5) Finally, 2 Sam 24:1-9 narrating David's census has both αριθμειν and επισκεπτεσθαι. Insofar as this passage falls in a section usually considered recensional, the most logical explanation would be that the occurrences of both

αριθμειν and επισκεπτεσθαι together represent the OG unrevised in that passage, and that this in turn argues in favor of αριθμειν in 4QLXXNum as the OG revised in $\mathfrak{G}^B$.

Num 4:6   [α]ρτηρας] αναφορεις $\mathfrak{G}^{ed}$; + αυτης O f
          Arab Syh; + ab ea Bo; בדיו MTω
Num 4:8   αρτηρας] αναφορεις $\mathfrak{G}^{ed}$; בדיו MTω
Num 4:11 αρτη[ρας]] αναφορεις $\mathfrak{G}^{ed}$; בדיו MTω
Num 4:12 αρτηρος] αναφορεις $\mathfrak{G}^{ed}$; המוט MTω

It will be clearest to quote Wevers' exposition:

> Characteristic of the [4QLXXNum] revision is the substitution of αρτηρας for (τοὺς) ἀναφορεῖς. The word occurs four times in this fragmentary text, three times for בדים (4:6,8,11) and once for מוט (4:12)....
>
> In each case the reference in MT is to the staves by which the ark was to be carried. Apparently the reviser felt that ἀναφορεύς was an agent noun, i.e. a "carrier" rather than the means of carrying; in fact, in v.12 the [$\mathfrak{G}^{ed}$] text could easily be interpreted as referring to the bearers instead of the carrying staves.... I suspect that the use of αρτηρ to designate staves for carrying the ark instead of ἀναφορεύς is meant to avoid possible confusion in meaning for ἀναφορεύς as an agent rather than an instrument for carrying.
>
> ...[In] the case of αρτηρ, ...this variant seems to be rooted in the desire to clarify the Greek text. It is not the kind of variant which is more Hebraic than [the OG] as would be expected from the so-called καίγε recension; rather it is a variant clarifying a Hebraic kind of Greek by a more idiomatic text.[24]

To my mind the opposite conclusion seems more persuasive, though neither Wevers nor I can offer much more to support our views on this pair of

variants. I would simply note three points.
(1) Although sporadic revision certainly occurred in the interests of clearer Greek in specific cases, Symmachus is our only ancient example of systematic recension for clearer Greek, and even he retains a large measure of Hebrew recensional material. (2) More importantly, αναφορευς is clearly used as a recensional substitute: Aquila uses it but never αρτηρ for בד. (3) The argument Wevers gives (Greek idiomatic clarity) is usually an argument used to demonstrate the OG translation in contrast to more wooden recensional revision.

Num 4:7   υ[α]κινθι/[νον] = תכלת MT𝔐]
ολοπορφυρον 𝔊*od

υακινθος means "dark blue" and usually translates תכלת. ολοπορφυρος means "dark red/purple" and usually translates ארגמן. The adjective here refers to the cloth (ιματιον) spread over the table of the bread of the presence. Although in the previous two variants there was no reason to suspect an alternate Hebrew text, here it is a question of the Hebrew *Vorlage*. The Hebrew text from which the OG was translated could have had either תכלת or ארגמן. But, since the Greek always translates the other colors throughout this passage mechanically and faithfully, I would maintain that the OG translator correctly translated whichever Hebrew word (he thought) lay before him. The alternate Greek text would have to be a mistake or an early

revision toward an alternate Hebrew text. It is
impossible to decide with the evidence available.

Num 4:14   τα σπ[ονδεια] = הַמִּזְרָקֹת MT𝔐(קרה- 𝔐)] τον
καλυπτηρα 𝔊ᵉᵈ

τα σπονδεια means "cups"; τον καλυπτηρα is
simply an error. The issue is whether the error
was made by the OG translator and was later
corrected in 4QLXXNum toward the correct Hebrew,
or whether the correct OG is faithfully
represented by 4QLXXNum and became distorted (as
in 𝔊ᵉᵈ) later in the transmission stage. It
appears impossible to decide between these
possibilities on the strength of the evidence
available.

Conclusions

Part II argued that it is essential to consider
the possibilities for the Hebrew original which
the OG was attempting to translate. Often it is,
but often it is not, identical with the Massoretic
textus receptus. Having studied the variants of
4QLXXLev^a and several of the more important ones
in 4QLXXNum, it is now appropriate to reappraise
their value as witnesses to the OG.

4QLXXLev^a displays 15 variants from the text of
𝔊ᵉᵈ (plus a sixteenth where it and 𝔊ᵉᵈ both
represent the OG in a variant from MT𝔐) —— 15
variants in 28 less-than-half-extant lines of
manuscript! But none of these variants are
errors. All are sensible readings, constituting
an alternate text or translation. Is Kahle

correct that prior to the LXX translation there were divergent Greek targumim? No. These variants are embedded in a text that shows 75% agreement with $\mathfrak{G}^{ed}$. Thus 4QLXXLev^a and $\mathfrak{G}^{ed}$ are two representatives of the same translation, one or both of which has developed a total of 15 changes. Some or all could be isolated changes in either text. One or other text (but presumably not both) could display a pattern of revision, most commonly sought as recensional revision of the OG back to the emergingly dominant proto-MT.

On closer inspection, we note that of the 15 variants, 7 are unique and 3 others are attested by only one or two MSS. All the readings in 4QLXXLev^a can be seen as adequate, free ways of translating the MT or possibly as more literal translations of a slightly variant Hebrew text.

Despite the fact that this MS comes from the late second or the first century BCE —— three or four centuries earlier than our next earliest witnesses —— not one of its readings is accepted for the Göttingen critical text. Rather, for every variant the reading that agrees with the MT is chosen. My assumption is that Wevers' selection is partly based on the weight of the MS tradition (not a bad argument!). But I think all would agree that in many points our MS tradition does not take us all the way back to the OG translation. I am not certain, but I propose that 4QLXXLev^a penetrates further behind our oldest witnesses, especially with εθνος (Lev 26:12) and plausibly with τον ξυλινον καρπον (Lev 26:4), the πολεμος clause in its correct place (Lev 26:6^{fin}), and βδελυξομαι (Lev 26:11).

If we seek a comprehensive pattern for the majority of readings in 4QLXXLev^a vis-à-vis the Göttingen edition —— either seeing the text in the Göttingen edition as an accurate translation (the OG) of the proto-MT and 4QLXXLev^a as secondary (simplification, smoothing, error, etc.), or seeing the Qumran text as an acceptable free translation (the OG) of the proto-MT or a more literal translation of a slightly variant *Vorlage* and the text in the Göttingen edition as a revision toward the proto-MT —— I think the latter has stronger probability on its side. In short, predominantly throughout Part I the (b)-pattern seems more consistent.

4QLXXNum displays four crucial variants from the text of 𝔊^{ed}. The analysis of the first two indicated my preference for interpreting the Qumran text as the OG and the readings in 𝔊^{ed} as recensional (partly because επισκεπτεσθαι and αναφορευς are documentably recensional substitutes). The evidence available for the remaining two variants is admittedly insufficient. But the reading of 𝔊^{ed} is clearly an error in the fourth and apparently an error in the third, while the much older witness presents correct readings in both. The cumulative evidence suggests that 4QLXXNum, just as 4QLXXLev^a above, presents the superior witness to the Old Greek translation.

NOTES

*Author's note: It is a pleasure to thank the
Revd Prof. Barnabas Lindars, SSF, and Dr George
Brooke for their invitation to present this paper
at the University of Manchester, and to thank the
University of Notre Dame and the National Endow-
ment for the Humanities for their support of the
long-term work which this paper represents.
  The editions of the LXX мss have been accepted
by Oxford University Press. As a service to
scholars, variants and other information from the
editions are presented here. Although the present
article may appear before the more complex *DJD*
volume does, the rights remain with Oxford
University Press.

1. The publications of the Greek scrolls are as
follows:
  4QLXXLev^a: P. W. Skehan, "The Qumran Manuscripts and Textual Criticism," *Volume du congrès,
Strasbourg 1956* (VTSup 4; Leiden: Brill, 1957)
148-60, esp. 157-60;
  4QLXXNum: P. W. Skehan, "4QLXXNum: A
Pre-Christian Re-working of the Septuagint," *HTR*
70 (1977) 39-50; partial publication: "The Qumran
Manuscripts and Textual Criticism," esp. 155-7;
  4QLXXDeut plus the variants from all the LXX
Exodus-Deuteronomy scrolls: E. Ulrich, "The Greek
Manuscripts of the Pentateuch from Qumrân,
Including Newly-Identified Fragments of
Deuteronomy (4QLXXDeut)," *De Septuaginta: Studies
in Honour of John William Wevers on His
Sixty-Fifth Birthday* (ed. A. Pietersma and C. Cox;
Mississauga, Ont.: Benben, 1984) 71-82;
    pap4QparaExod gr: E. Ulrich, "A Greek
Paraphrase of Exodus on Papyrus from Qumran
Cave 4," *Studien zur Septuaginta — Robert
Hanhart zu Ehren* (ed. D. Fraenkel, U. Quast, and
J. W. Wevers; Göttingen: Vandenhoeck & Ruprecht,
1990) 287-94;
    pap7QExod and pap7QEpJer: Baillet in M.
Baillet, J. T. Milik, and R. de Vaux, *Les 'petites
grottes' de Qumrân* (DJD 3; Oxford: Clarendon,
1962) 142-3 and Pl. 30;
  8HevXIIgr: Emanuel Tov with the collaboration
of R. A. Kraft, *The Greek Minor Prophets Scroll*

from *Nahal Hever (8HevXIIgr)* (DJD 8; Oxford: Clarendon, 1990); preliminary publication: D. Barthélemy, *Les devanciers d'Aquila* (VTSup 10; Leiden: Brill, 1963) 163-78.

2. J. W. Wevers, ed., *Leviticus* (Septuaginta: Vetus Testamentum Graecum II.2; Göttingen: Vandenhoeck & Ruprecht, 1986); *Numeri* (Septuaginta: Vetus Testamentum Graecum III.1; Göttingen: Vandenhoeck & Ruprecht, 1982).

3. J. W. Wevers, "An Early Revision of the Septuagint of Numbers," *Eretz-Israel* 16: *H. M. Orlinsky Volume* (Jerusalem: Israel Exploration Society, 1982) 235*-9*.

4. Ulrich, "The Greek Manuscripts," 82.

5. Only 15 variants are listed in "The Greek Manuscripts," 78-9. The additional variant (see και εσομ[αι] in Lev 26:12 below) occurs on a tiny fragment identified subsequently to that 1984 article.

6. For an alternate, well-argued explanation based on the root ידע II "be submissive," see Barnabas Lindars, "Some Septuagint Readings in Judges," *JTS* [n.s.] 22 (1971) 1-14; and earlier, D. Winton Thomas, "The root ידע in Hebrew," *JTS* 35 (1934) 298-306.

7. For the issue of the placement of this clause at the end of v 6 or v 5, the detailed question whether πολεμος is a free rendering of חרב or possibly a more literal rendering of קרב (see Job 38:23; Ps 68[67]:31[30]; 78[77]:9; Dan o´ θ´ 7:21; Qoh 9:18) need not be settled here.

8. E. Tov, *The Text-Critical Use of the Septuagint in Biblical Research* (Jerusalem Biblical Studies 3; Jerusalem: Simor, 1981).

9. Anneli Aejmelaeus, "What Can We Know about the Hebrew *Vorlage* of the Septuagint?" *ZAW* 99 (1987) 58-89, esp. 71.

10. See most recently, Julio Trebolle Barrera, *Centena in libros Samuelis et Regum: Variantes textuales y composición literaria en los libros de Samuel y Reyes* (Madrid: Consejo Superior de Investigaciones Científicas, 1989); see also "Redaction, Recension, and Midrash in the Books of Kings," *BIOSCS* 15 (1982) 12-35; and "From the 'Old

Latin' through the 'Old Greek' to the 'Old Hebrew' (2 Kings 10:23-35)," *Textus* 11 (1984) 17-36.

11. Sharon Pace Jeansonne, *The Old Greek Translation of Daniel 7-12* (CBQMS 19; Washington: Catholic Biblical Association, 1988); see also S. Pace, "The Stratigraphy of the Text of Daniel and the Question of Theological *Tendenz* in the Old Greek," *BIOSCS* 17 (1984) 15-35.

12. Zaki Aly with Ludwig Koenen, *Three Rolls of the Early Septuagint: Genesis and Deuteronomy* (Papyrologische Texte und Abhandlungen 27; Bonn: R. Habelt, 1980) 1-2.

13. In addition to the five critical editions of the Greek Genesis-Deuteronomy and the five companion text-history volumes, see his recent *Notes on the Greek Text of Exodus* (SCS 30; Atlanta: Scholars Press, 1990).

14. J. W. Wevers, "II. Die Methode," *Das Göttinger Septuaginta-Unternehmen* (Göttingen: Vandenhoeck & Ruprecht, 1977) 18.

15. J. W. Wevers, *Text History of the Greek Leviticus* (MSU 19; Göttingen: Vandenhoeck & Ruprecht, 1986) 76.

16. *Text History of the Greek of Leviticus*, 77.

17. Ibid.

18. Note also, e.g., the מהאב error in the MT (for מתעב) in Amos 6:8 discussed under Lev 26:11 above.

19. At 2 Sam 14:30 the MT and 4QSam^c each make this same error in different words within a single line: see E. Ulrich, "4QSam^c: A Fragmentary Manuscript of 2 Samuel 14-15 from the Scribe of the *Serek Hay-yahad* (1QS)," *BASOR* 235 (1979) 1-25, esp. pp. 3, 7, 14 (2 Sam 14:30; 15:3 [II.12,24]).

20. J. W. Wevers, *Text History of the Greek Deuteronomy* (MSU 13; Göttingen: Vandenhoeck & Ruprecht, 1978) 127.

21. See "The Greek Manuscripts," 80-1.

22. H. B. Swete (*An Introduction to the Old Testament in Greek* [rev. ed. by R. R. Ottley; New York: Ktav, 1968] 214-5) considers the Greek titles "probably of Alexandrian origin and pre-

Christian in use" and notes that some of them are used in Philo and the NT.

23. This is not, of course, a decisive argument, for a principle of the recensionists was to choose one of the several OG precedents and standardise it as the recensional equivalent. But it is nonetheless an argument.

24. J. W. Wevers, "An Early Revision," 236*-8*. In the last paragraph Wevers is talking about the επισκεπτεσθαι/αριθμειν variant and says: "As in the case of αρτηρ, so this variant [επισκεπτεσθαι/αριθμειν]...." But he is making the same point about the two variants.

THE TEMPLE SCROLL AND LXX EXODUS 35-40

GEORGE J. BROOKE

I. Introduction

The purpose of this short paper is to investigate those passages of the Temple Scroll (11QT^a) which correspond in some measure with Exod 35-40[1] to discover whether the Hebrew text of Exodus reflected in some parts of 11QT^a can be described as offering an example of what may have been akin to a Hebrew *Vorlage* for the translator of the LXX of these chapters. If so, then a small contribution will have been made to the debate concerning whether or not the differences between the LXX and the MT tradition for Exod 35-40 are all the responsibility of the Greek translators and traditors.[2]

It is not the intention here to argue that the text of Exodus used and adapted by the Temple Scroll belongs to any one particular text-type. E. Tov has already demonstrated that it is not possible to determine that 11QT^a as a whole has a special affinity with either the MT, the LXX or the SP; he concludes that "the scroll contains a textual tradition which agrees now and then with one or other of these early texts."[3] This study bears out Tov's conclusion, though with two qualifications. On the one hand, Tov's analysis of textual affiliation is concerned rightly with precise words and phrases whose biblical source can be exactly identified, but this study is more concerned with the exegetical tendency of texts and textual traditions. On the other hand, it could be that for 11QT^a more attention should be paid to its source analysis,[4] for Tov's conclusion may be correct for the scroll as a whole but particular sections of 11QT^a may nevertheless reflect one of the early texts fairly consistently.

The early columns of 11QT^a are concerned with the construction and furnishing of the temple building and the altar (11QT^a 3-13:7) and several scholars have followed Y. Yadin in identifying allusions to the tabernacle of Exod 35-40 in this part of the scroll.[5] Unfortunately it is these same columns of 11QT^a which are the least well preserved. This paper is thus based on a double handicap: not only are the columns where the use of Exod 35-40 might be most readily discerned very badly damaged, but also allusions to Exod 35-40 have to be discerned through the adaptation of its subject matter from the tabernacle to the temple, adaptation which includes the reformulation of the biblical sources, the combination of biblical texts from different contexts, abbreviation and harmonization. Furthermore, when using tabernacle traditions, sometimes the compiler focussed on the plan of Exod 25-31, sometimes on its supposed execution described in Exod 35-40, the section under consideration in this paper; sometimes the descriptions of the same item in these two sources agree word for word, thus making it very difficult to determine which biblical text is acting as the base text for the composition in 11QT^a.

Apart from 11QT^a, for Exod 35-40 two manuscripts of Exodus from Qumran so far partly published have yielded intriguing but insufficient information to provide for an investigation of this sort.[6] A virtually totally illegible photograph of 4QExod^f (Exod 40:8-27) was published in the catalogue *Scrolls from the Wilderness of the Dead Sea.*[7] F.M. Cross has dated the manuscript to the mid-3rd century BCE. He has claimed that in his initial decipherment of the text few variants (from the MT) are to be found. "In verse 17, the traditional text reads: 'And on the first day of the month, the tabernacle was erected.' In this manuscript, after the phrase 'in the second year,' the phrase 'since they went out of Egypt' is added, an addition also found in the Septuagint and Samaritan versions of Exodus."[8]

Columns 42-45 of 4QpaleoExod^m have yielded a little more: parts of Exod 35:1, 22; 36:21-24; 37:9-16. The principal variants have been published by J.E. Sanderson.[9] She justifiably concludes that "the complicated questions involved in the tabernacle account have not been illuminated by the discovery of the scroll, because it is scarcely extant in the second half of that account, and whenever it is extant in the first or second parts, it agrees consistently with Sam/MT against G."[10]

As neither 4QExod^f nor 4QpaleoExod^m seem to be able to offer any direct help towards understanding the peculiarities of LXX Exod 35-40, the apparent evidence of 11QT^a becomes all the more important. This is especially so since there is an emerging consensus that 11QT^a is made up of several different sources,[11] and even if the composition of 11QT^a is to be dated in the second or first century BCE,[12] some of its sources may well belong in the third century BCE or possibly earlier. Thus it could be that the treatment of the Hebrew textual traditions of Exod 35-40 which may be apparent in 11QT^a 3-10 are approximately contemporary with what is usually supposed to be the similar interpretative activity of the Greek translator.

Before describing some of the possible minor agreements between 11QT^a 3-10 and LXX Exod 35-40, it is important to mention that 11QT^a may also reflect parts of MT Exod 35-40 which are not represented in LXX Exod 35-40. The most obvious case of this may concern the incense altar which is nowhere explicitly mentioned in LXX Exod 35-39, but which features in 11QT^a 3:10, almost certainly alluding to Exod 35:15.[13] There are other less clear instances of the same phenomenon. For example, although it is difficult to know whether the allusion is to the plan (Exod 26:29: בתים לבריחם) or its execution (Exod 37:27: לבתים מדולחים בתים לכלי המזבח), 11QT^a 33:13 (לבדים) could contain an allusion to MT Exod 37:27, a verse which does not have a counterpart in LXX Exod 36-39. Or again, in 11QT^a 36:3 the terminology for the inner angles ([ ] מן הֽמֽקֽצוע [ )

seems to reflect Exod 36:28 (לְמִקְצֹעֹת), another verse of the MT without a counterpart in the LXX.[14]

Thus it is not possible to say that the compiler of 11QT^a knew only of a Hebrew text that was akin to the *Vorlage* of LXX Exod 35-40, but nor is it possible to say with certainty that he was working solely with a text-type like that now represented in the MT. Though the evidence which has survived is very fragmentary, the number of parallels and minor agreements in textual or exegetical matters between 11QT^a and LXX Exod 35-40 over against the MT (and usually SP) is sufficient to merit the following listing from which can be drawn a few tentative conclusions.

II. 11QT^a 3-10 and LXX Exod 35-40: Possible Minor Agreements

1. 11QT^a 3:8-12. The discussion of the festivals (Exod 34:18-35:3) is omitted from 11QT^a 2; 11QT^a 3 seems to begin directly with the subject of the construction of the temple and, in echoing Exod 35:4ff., uses tabernacle traditions. Yadin correctly identified Exod 35:5-16 as the principal biblical source at the start of 11QT^a 3.[15]

11QT^a 3:8-12 contains a very fragmentary text: line 8 mentions that all the vessels of the sanctuary are to be of pure gold, line 9 mentions the mercy seat, also of pure gold, line 10 seems to mention the incense altar and the table, line 11 the plates, line 12 the bowls of pure gold and the censers. The list does not correspond in order or in form with either tradition of the tabernacle (Exod 25; 35) in either Hebrew or

Greek. It is a summary section, most of the items being mentioned in more detail later on. Of note, however, is the phrase זהב טהור, "pure gold," for which Yadin pointed to Exod 37 where the phrase is repeated several times.[16] In moving from Exod 35:5-16 to 37:6-16 it can be seen that what takes five lines in 11QT^a takes many more verses in the MT than a fully restored 11QT^a could contain. In MT Exod 37:6 the mercy seat of pure gold is mentioned, the table comes in 37:10, its vessels in 37:16. Since the MT of Exod 37 contains nothing that might match the introductory phrase concerning all the vessels of 11QT^a 3:8, effectively what takes ten verses in the MT, is reduced to or represented in four lines in 11QT^a. Furthermore, whereas the seemingly longer MT text does not mention the incense altar until Exod 37:25, the shorter text of 11QT^a finds room to mention it immediately together with the mercy seat.

Two matters in the Greek text may be relevant at this point. To begin with Exod 37:6-16 is represented in LXX Exod 38:5-12 in a much shorter form: in particular the Greek, like 11QT^a 3:8-12, has nothing that corresponds with the detailed measurements of MT Exod 37:6 and 10, nor anything that describes the frame of the table (MT Exod 37:12, 14). Secondly, like the MT the Greek has no reference in this section to the incense altar, but whereas the MT has the incense altar in 37:25-28, the Greek makes no clear mention of it in LXX Exod 35-39. Its probable presence in 11QT^a 3:10 provides yet another example of how the description of this particular piece of furniture seems to be handled especially fluidly in the tradition.[17]

2. 11QT^a 3:13. Yadin proposed that the end of this line should be restored according to the textual tradition represented by Exod 35:14 in the LXX and SP. He reads the end of the line as והמנורה וכ]ול כליה reflecting the LXX's καὶ τὴν λυχνίαν τοῦ φωτὸς καὶ πάντα τὰ σκεύη αὐτῆς and the SP's את מנורת המאור ואת כל כליה against the MT's ואת מנרת המאור ואת כליה.[18] Nothing much need be made of this proposed agreement between 11QT^a and the LXX, since the lack of כל in the MT is easily explained as omission through homoioarchton, but it shows that mistakes or a sense of strangeness do not belong all on the side of the LXX.

3. 11QT^a 3:14-16. Just as both 11QT^a 3:8-12 and LXX Exod 38:5-12 seem to represent shorter forms of the Hebrew tradition than that now preserved in the MT for MT Exod 37:6-16, so something similar may be seen in the next few lines of 11QT^a 3:14-16. At the start of a new paragraph 11QT^a describes the altar of the burnt offering and its grating (11QT^a 3:14-15). The text then becomes very fragmentary. For the second extant phrase of line 16 ([פ לראות פ]) Yadin commented that it is most likely that these words refer not to the altar but to another vessel mentioned in Exod 38. Because of the consistent understanding in Jewish tradition that the laver was made of mirrors (מראות), Yadin proposed that 11QT^a 3:16b-17 concerned the laver.[19]

Whilst all these suggestions are conjectural,

if along the right lines, then in these few lines of 11QT^a we would be able to observe, once again with reference to LXX Exod 38, a shorter Hebrew text similar to that which may lie behind the composition of the earlier lines of 11QT^a 3:8-12. In the MT the altar of burnt offering is introduced at Exod 38:1, the laver at 38:8. In 11QT^a 3:14-16 only two lines of the text may separate the two items. Intriguingly, in LXX Exod 38 the items are also described and discussed in a shorter form than that of the MT. The description of the altar of burnt offering, its utensils, and grating comes in LXX Exod 38:22-24;[20] the description of the laver appears in LXX Exod 38:26. The intervening LXX 38:25 mentions the oil and closely parallels MT Exod 37:29 which follows on directly from the altar of incense in the MT. 11QT^a 3:10 has already spoken of the incense altar in a different order from both MT and LXX, but its mention there may account for why there is probably no mention of anything parallel with LXX Exod 38:25 at this point in 11QT^a. Although it cannot be maintained that 11QT^a 3:14-16 represents a Hebrew text akin to the *Vorlage* of the LXX, both 11QT^a and the LXX contain shorter traditions than that represented in the MT.

4. 11QT^a 3:17. This line is very fragmentary. Yadin transcribed it as: .[נחו̇]שה   [. ף̇ ימס[. He suggested that נחושה may still refer to the laver, the subject of 11QT^a 3:16; in addition he reckoned that ימס[was the start of a verb in the third person plural, suggesting a restoration of כסף ימסו. If so, "after a description of bronze

and golden vessels, the author began to describe the silver ones and their accessories as in Ex. xxxviii:10f."[21] This comparison might be of little significance except that it is precisely this phrase in Exod 38:10-12 (ורי העמדים וחשקיהם כסף) which is consistently not represented in LXX Exod 37:8-10, though it is represented in LXX Exod 37:15 and 17 (MT Exod 38:17, 19).[22] Is it possible that, through its apparent use in a different context in 11QT^a, the lack of the phrase in the LXX Exod 37:8-19 represents the existence of a Hebrew *Vorlage* different from the MT rather than being simply understood as the abbreviating activity of the Greek translator? We may never know.

5. 11QT^a 7:12-13. In 11QT^a 7 lines 9-12 contain an instruction concerning the mercy seat and the cherubim which seems to be based on Exod 25:17-22, especially v. 22, and on Exod 35:12. Immediately in 11QT^a 7:13 in a new paragraph the subject matter changes to the veil. Whereas Exod 25:23-40 continues not with the veil but the table, the lampstand and the altar of incense, Exod 35:12 mentions the veil in association with the mercy seat. Because of that Yadin suitably identified Exod 35:12 as the controlling biblical influence in the ordering of 11QT^a 7:12-13.[23] In 11QT^a 7:13 the instruction is to make the veil of gold. This is so distinctive that it may have distracted Yadin and others from noticing a further comparison with LXX Exod 35:12.[24]

LXX Exod 35:12 follows its rendering of what is equivalent to MT Exod 35:12 with καὶ τὰ ἱστία τῆς αὐλῆς καὶ τοὺς στύλους αὐτῆς καὶ τοὺς λίθους τῆς σμαράγδου καὶ τὸ θυμίαμα καὶ τὸ ἔλαιον τοῦ χρίσματος. The first two phrases match Exod 35:17a, the last two objects, "the incense and the oil of anointing," correspond with part of MT Exod 35:15, but "the emerald stones" have no counterpart in the Hebrew. D. Gooding remarks forcefully: "There can be no reasonable doubt that the Greek list has suffered dislocation; and when it is seen that the court hangings are not only out of place but come exactly where the incense altar should be, one cannot help thinking that some accident or else some inept editing is responsible for the omission of this altar from the list, and the insertion of the court hangings in their present position."[25]

Now it is clear that LXX Exod 35:12 follows the mercy seat and the veil with the hangings of the court, whereas 11QT^a 7:13-14 follows the cherubim and the ark with a detailed description of the golden veil. Both texts seem to take liberties with the supposed Hebrew tradition at the same point, and both differences concern fabrics. The text of 11QT^a 7 is too fragmentary to read after 7:14, so any further comparison of the immediate contexts is not possible. However, the seemingly anomalous mention of the emerald stones in LXX Exod 35:12a would appear to point directly to the ephod. In LXX Exod 35:27 the Hebrew שהם is specified as emerald, as it is also in LXX Exod 36:13 (MT 39:6), both passages being concerned with the shoulder pieces of the ephod. Thus LXX Exod 35:12a combines the veil, the ephod and the curtains in one short, though somewhat awkwardly

THE TEMPLE SCROLL AND LXX EXODUS 35-40   91

expressed summary. These same items also seem to be the subject of a combined reordering in LXX Exod 36-37, an apparently deliberate arrangement to place all the specially coloured woven items together, an arrangement which is here anticipated in the introductory summary of LXX Exod 35:12.

All this rearrangement may be the work of the translator of the Greek, but surely the processes at work in 11QT^α need to be kept in mind too. On the one hand, 11QT^α 7:13 and LXX Exod 35:12a diverge from a supposed Hebrew *Vorlage* at the same point; on the other hand, the combination of the woven cloth items together is anticipated in LXX Exod 35:12a and found in both 11QT^α 10 (see below for details) and LXX Exod 36-37. 11QT^α 7 and 10 cannot provide evidence for the Hebrew *Vorlage* of the Greek translation, but 11QT^α attests an adjustment and adaptation of the Hebrew text which is not without echoes in the Greek.[26] It is therefore possible that not everything in the peculiar arrangement of the Greek of Exod 35:40 is the responsibility solely of the Greek translators and traditors.

6. 11QT^α 8:7. 11QT^α 8:5-6 seem to be based on Exod 25:23-24, but it is difficult to determine how those verses have been represented in 11QT^α 8:7. The text is very fragmentary (] ...מֹ לֹ[ ), so any suggestion is highly problematic, but Yadin noted as follows: "The letters are cramped, and it is difficult to determine how the text continued. Since the scroll uses Lev. xxiv in l. 8, this line appears to have contained a shorter text than in Ex. xxv, perhaps one more like Ex. xxxvii:27f.,

but even shorter. The *tet* possibly suggests
טבעות, which are essential throughout the
discussion, but because of the different versions
of MT and the LXX variation, a definite suggestion
is again difficult."²⁷ MT Exod 37:27, part of the
description of the incense altar, as has been
noted above, is absent from LXX Exod 35-39, but
Yadin's indication that here there may be a
shorter text may be significant for how we
understand the apparent lack of the incense altar
material from LXX Exod 35-39, or at least its
misrepresentation.

7. 11QT^a 9:3-4. The discussion in numbers 1 and
3 has tentatively suggested some similarity
between 11QT^a 3:8-16 and LXX Exod 38:6-12, 22-26.
Some confirmation that a Hebrew textual tradition
like that represented in 11QT^a was known to the
translator of the LXX comes from 11QT^a 9:3.
Though in 11QT^a 9:2 the surviving letters
(יה וּפְרְחִי [) can be restored in the light of MT
Exod 25:31 and 37:18, in 11QT^a 9:3 a different
source is needed. In this section of the
description of the lampstand only two words remain
at the end of 11QT^a 9:3 (משני צדיה). Yadin noted
that this combination of words is not to be found
in the MT in either Exod 25 or 37, the likely
sources. However, a similar text is reflected in
LXX Exod 38:14 (ἐξ ἀμφοτέρων τῶν μερῶν αὐτῆς), on
the basis of which he makes a restoration of
11QT^a.²⁸

For 11QT^a 9:4 where a similarly small amount of
text is preserved, Yadin noted that the text of
Exod 25:32-33, where the subject matter is

discussed, cannot be followed in its entirety.[29] Rather, it might be that a shorter text, like that represented in LXX Exod 38:13-17, might have existed as a Hebrew source both for 11QT^a 9:4 and the LXX. We cannot really be any more precise because there are several problems with the LXX text in itself, but awareness of the processes at work in the handling of the tradition in 11QT^a shows that those problems should not all necessarily be approached from the standpoint that the Greek translator(s) and traditors are solely responsible for the variations.[30]

8. 11QT^a 9:11-12. Whereas the discussion of most of the examples in this paper is based on slender evidence, the treatment of this example is based on an argument from silence! 11QT^a 9:11 ends with ככרים which Yadin suggested should be read as a dual form indicating "two talents."[31] The subject under discussion in 11QT^a 9 is the lampstand and Exod 25:31-40 seems to be the principal biblical source behind the description. The ambiguity of Exod 25:39 has given rise to an extensive debate concerning whether the lampstand, and all its lamps and connected utensils were made from one talent of gold, or whether the lampstand alone was made from one talent, another talent being used for everything else. The problem was apparently resolved in one way in LXX Exod 25:39 (πάντα τὰ σκεύη ταῦτα τάλαντον χρυσίου καθαροῦ) which states that all the vessels or utensils were made from a talent of pure gold, thus implying that yet another talent was needed for the lampstand itself. The LXX, therefore, seems to interpret

Exod 25:38-39 as meaning that two talents of pure gold were needed for the lampstand and all its utensils; this seems to agree with 11QT^a 9:11. For the purposes of this study the whole matter is an argument from silence because whereas MT Exod 37:24 subsequently seems to clarify the issue by declaring, "He made it and all its utensils of a talent of pure gold" (עשה אתה ככר זהב טהור ואת כל כליה), the LXX has nothing corresponding with this Hebrew verse. Perhaps the LXX omits any mention of the amount of pure gold because for Exod 25 the decision has already been made to interpret the Hebrew to mean that two talents of gold were required. To this extent 11QT^a and LXX seem to agree in their exegetical handling of the tradition, if not in their wording of the text.

9. 11QT^a 10. 11QT^a 10 contains 18 very fragmentary lines, some of which (2, 6, 7, 15, 16, 18) contain no extant letters at all. The last preserved part of column 9 contains the description of the lampstand, column 11 begins the commands concerning the altar for the burnt offering and the commands for the festival sacrifices. What remains in column 10 suggests that the subject is probably the screen at the vestibule entrance or at one of the gates to the inner court, or, possibly, both. Yadin proposed that possible sources for the column are Exod 26:36-37 and 36:37-38 which describe the screen of the entrance to the tent of the meeting, and Exod 27:16-17 and 38:18-19 which describe the screen of the gate of the tabernacle court.[32]

E. Qimron has restored the column as follows:[33]

1. [רב]
3. [ח
4. [ורת עמוד
5. [לזכרון
8. [שער יהיו
9. [חמה מעל השער
10. [מרום דֹף הולך תולע
11. [רמל]מ[עלה מזה עמודים
12. [ים ארגמן אדום וראשי
13. ה ש]ני[ש ל]   [לה
14. א]רגמן ותולע [[על
17.   ] באמה

When we inquire more precisely what biblical sources may have influenced the composition of the passage, it immediately becomes clear that no single text is being rigidly followed. For lines 8-17 the key extant words are שער (1. 8), שער (1. 9), תולע (1. 10), עמודים (1. 11), ארגמן אדום (1. 12), א]רגמן ותולע (1. 14), and אמה (1. 17). In Exod 38:18, seemingly the closest parallel to this section, the words that occur in the same order as in 11QT^a 10:8-17 are ארגמן, ותולע, שער, and אמה. Exod 38:19 opens with ועמדיהם.[34]

The mention of the pillar(s) in both 11QT^a 10:4 and 11 suggests that more than Exod 38 alone is referred to here, since Exod 38:18-19 only refers to pillars once. Exod 36:37-38 share several phrases with Exod 38:18-19, as Yadin has observed in relation to this section of 11QT^a.[35] Furthermore the mention of the pillars in 11QT^a 10:4 probably needs to be taken with לזכרון of 10:5, a possibility which has lead J. Milgrom to suppose that Exod 38:25-28, on the use of the half-shekel which features in Exod 30:16, may be the source for that section of the column.[36]

In other places the handling of biblical source material by the editor(s) of 11QT^a shows that it is not simply a matter of copying out texts, with some minor amendments. Rather, the author of 11QT^a tends to isolate a base text to which he adds relevant material from a secondary text and possibly from other supplementary texts.[37] The texts are often linked through catchword association. Thus it could be that, rather than seeking to isolate merely the passages which have been used as sources, some attempt might be made at how those sources have been woven together with a base text, a secondary text and other supplementary texts. 11QT^a 10 is too fragmentary to allow this in detail, but from such a perspective something of the differences in the order of key words between 11QT^a and Exodus can be explained.

It seems correct with Yadin to reckon that both Exod 36:37-38 and 38:18-19 are being used in this section of 11QT^a, but some account must be given for the presence of לזכרון in 11QT^a 10:5. To what does it refer? Nowhere in biblical sources is זכרון associated with a veil or curtain, particularly not in Exod 26-28 or 36-38. However, זכרון occurs five times in the sections of Exodus under discussion here. In Exod 28:12 it occurs twice: "And you shall set the two stones upon the shoulder-pieces of the ephod, as stones of remembrance (זכרן) for the sons of Israel; and Aaron shall bear their names before the Lord upon his two shoulders for remembrance (זכרן)." The fulfilment of this instruction is described in

Exod 39:7: the stones on the shoulder pieces of
the ephod are "stones of remembrance (זכרון) for
the sons of Israel, as the Lord commanded."
According to Exod 28:6 the ephod is made of blue
and purple and scarlet stuff (תכלת וארגמן תולעת
שני). לזכרון also occurs in Exod 28:29: "So Aaron
shall bear the names of the sons of Israel in the
breastpiece of judgment upon his heart, when he
goes into the holy place to bring them to
continual remembrance before the Lord." Lastly,
as mentioned above, Milgrom has pointed to Exod
30:16 in which half-shekel atonement money is
appointed for the service of the tent of meeting,
"that it may bring the people of Israel to
remembrance before the Lord," and according to
Exod 38:25-28 the silver derived from the
half-shekel offering was used to overlay "the
bases of the veil" (Exod 38:27).[38]

With all this information, it would appear that
there are two possible and not necessarily
mutually exclusive ways of interpreting לזכרון in
11QT^a 10:5. On the one hand, as Milgrom has
proposed, through its association with the use of
the half-shekel for the service of the tent of
meeting, it might reflect a concern with the
overlay of the bases of the pillars used somehow
to hold the veil; this would help towards
explaining the use of עמוד in line 4. Yadin
commented that while Milgrom's suggestion was
plausible, "too little remains of the text either
to accept his views or reject them."[39] On the
other hand, its more widely attested association
with the ephod's adornment might suggest that in
11QT^a 10 we are faced with a section that links

all the items together which are made from blue, purple, and scarlet material: the ephod and its adornments (Exod 28:12, 29; 39:7), the screen of the entrance to the tent of meeting (Exod 26:36-37; 36:37-38), and the screen of the gate of the tabernacle court (Exod 27:16-17; 38:18-19). The difficulty in seeing the ephod and its adornment as a part of the temple furnishings might be overcome from two angles. Firstly, by noting that when the consecration of priests is mentioned in 11QT^a 15:3-17:5 the items of priestly vestment are assumed, not described, thus possibly implying that they have been mentioned earlier in the text. Secondly, by acknowledging that the high priest's clothes clearly symbolize the sons of Israel, as is explicitly stated in Exod 28:11, and that such symbolism suitably anticipates the description of the association of the temple gates with the sons of Israel in 11QT^a 39:11-13.[40] In the context of this discussion it is striking that 11QT^a 39:11-13 follows immediately after a section on the half-shekel as a remembrance (לזכרון; 11QT^a 39:8-10).[41]

Yadin correctly stated that there is insufficient textual evidence in 11QT^a 10 for a definite conclusion to be reached,[42] but it is important also to consider the implications of either suggestion in relation to the Greek text of Exod 35-40. It is well known that the principal section of those chapters where there is a very different order of items in the text is LXX Exod 36-38. The order of items for Exod 36-37 in the LXX can be summarized as follows:

LXX	MT	Subject
Exod 36:1-8a	36:1-8a	Offerings stopped
Exod 36:8b-38	39:1b-31	Priestly vestments
Exod 37:1-2	36:8b-9	The 10 curtains
Exod 37:3-6	36:35-38	Veil and screen
Exod 37:7-21	38:9-23	The court hangings

The LXX has all the woven or embroidered items described in order, from the Holy of Holies (high priest's robes) outwards. The link is not only that the goods are all cloth, but also their colour. The key phrase, "of blue, purple, and scarlet" (ἐξ ὑακίνθου καὶ πορφύρας καὶ κοκκίνου), or some variation of it, occurs in LXX Exod 36:9, 10, 12, 15, 29, 30, 32, 37 (all for priestly vestments); 37:3 (for the veil), 5 (for the screen for the door of the tent), 16 (for the screen for the gate of the court).[43] It is also important to note that the Greek does not correspond *verbatim* with the MT, but shows a marked tendency to represent a shorter text, especially where the text represented by the MT has seemingly unnecessary repetitions.[44]

Overall it might just be possible that 11QT^a 10 represents some part of Exod 26 as the base text. Exod 26:1 introduces the curtains immediately after the description of the lamp (11QT^a 9). However, in association with the curtains, all the woven cloth items are introduced, possibly the high priest's vestments (Exod 39:7), the veil (Exod 36:35-36), the screen (Exod 36:37-38), and the remaining curtains, notably the screen for the gate of the court, this last item being described in terms of Exod 38:18-19, the fulfilment parallel to Exod 27:16-17.

If 11QT^a 10 is constructed in this way, it would be a way which is characteristic of other parts of this section of 11QT^a. This possibility is the strongest indication that we have evidence from the second temple period, close to the time of the translation of the Pentateuch into Greek, of a Hebrew text which juxtaposes the contents of Exod 36-39 in a way not dissimilar to that of the arrangement of the same passages in LXX Exod 36-37. 11QT^a 10 is not the Hebrew *Vorlage* for LXX Exod 36-37, but it hints that there may have been a Hebrew text arranged similarly from which the Greek translator could have worked. At least the arrangement in LXX Exod 36-37 reflects the practice of the interpretation of the text as it was transmitted; that practice is now known to us in 11QT^a in a Hebrew form datable to within two or three centuries of the redactional completion of the book of Exodus itself.

III. Conclusion

Any conclusion must clearly be extremely tentative, but in the light of the sections of the Temple Scroll discussed here it is possible that the text of the Temple Scroll may provide evidence for the existence of source material in Hebrew which may go part of the way towards explaining some of the differences between the LXX and the text represented by the MT for Exod 35-40. Whilst the interpretative skills of the Greek translator of Exod 35-40 should not be denied, nevertheless some of the LXX text's principal characteristics, discernible especially in the order and brevity of its *Vorlage*, are now vaguely recognizable in part of the Temple Scroll, particularly 11QT^a 3 and 10. Moreover it is striking that quite possibly this transmission of a particular Hebrew text of Exodus, exegetically adjusted, in the Temple Scroll is approximately contemporaneous with the translation of a not dissimilar Hebrew *Vorlage* into Greek.[45]

NOTES

1. All biblical references are to the Hebrew text as in *BHS* unless otherwise stated. The siglum 11QT^a refers to the principal copy of the Temple Scroll on which all the information in this paper is based.

2. Y. Yadin began the process by trying to discern whether the LXX text type lay behind particular sections of 11QT^a: *The Temple Scroll* (Jerusalem: The Israel Exploration Society, The Institute of Archaeology of the Hebrew University of Jerusalem and the Shrine of the Book, 1983). All references in this paper are to this English edition of Yadin's work, since it includes several corrections and additions. The complexity of the problem discussed in this paper is witnessed to by the fact that there are some anomalies in Yadin's index to the LXX Exod (*The Temple Scroll*, II, 476): the reference to Exod 37 at II, 35 is a reference to MT Exod, not the LXX as listed in the index; likewise Exod 37:27f., at II, 31 is a reference to MT Exod not to the LXX (which lacks any mention of the incense altar in 35-39); again, Exod 38:8 at II, 9 refers to MT Exod, the parallel for which in the LXX is LXX Exod 38:26. Likewise LXX Exod 38:14 is incorrectly listed in the index to the MT Exod: *The Temple Scroll*, II, 468.

3. "The 'Temple Scroll' and Old Testament Textual Criticism," *Eretz Israel* 16 (1982) 255*. Tov's work focusses mainly on Deut. For Exod he lists (p. 104) the evidence of the versions only for Exod 34:13 (MT: ואת אשריו); the LXX, SP, Syr, Tg. Onq. and Tg. Ps.-J. all agree with 11QT^a in having a 3rd plural pronominal suffix. Overall he notes (p. 109) the following: 11QT^a = LXX = SP ≠ MT: 22x; 11QT^a = LXX ≠ SP ≠ MT: 26x; 11QT^a = SP ≠ LXX: 2x; 11QT^a = SP = MT 6x; 11QT^a ≠ SP: 11x.

4. As worked out initially by A. M. Wilson and L. Wills, "Literary sources of the *Temple Scroll*," *HTR* 75 (1982) 275-88.

5. Yadin, *The Temple Scroll*, I, 46. Followed by J. Maier, *The Temple Scroll: An Introduction, Translation and Commentary* (JSOTSup 34; Sheffield: JSOT Press, 1985) 58; M. Delcor, "Is the Temple Scroll a Source of the Herodian Temple?" *Temple Scroll Studies* (ed. G. J. Brooke; JSPSup 7; Sheffield: JSOT Press, 1989) 69-70; H. Stegemann, "The Literary Composition of the Temple Scroll and its status at Qumran," *Temple Scroll Studies*, 133.

6. The most recent list of the relevant Exodus manuscripts from Qumran with their contents is F. García Martínez, "Lista de MSS procedentes de Qumrán," *Henoch* 11 (1989) 166-68. In addition E. Ulrich has listed the Exodus manuscripts with their correct designated sigla in "The Biblical Scrolls from Cave 4: An Overview and Progress Report on their Publication," *RevQ* 14 (1989-90) 207-28.

7. *Scrolls from the Wilderness of the Dead Sea* (London: Trustees of the British Museum, 1965), 14, plate 3. Some details of the orthography of 4QExod^d based on Cross's transcriptions are to be found in D. N. Freedman, "The Massoretic Text and the Qumran Scrolls: A study in Orthography," *Textus* 2 (1962) 92-102.

8. *Scrolls from the Wilderness of the Dead Sea*, 23. For the purposes of this study it is worth recalling Cross's description of 4QExod^a (now properly designated 4QExod^b: see E. Ulrich, "The Biblical Scrolls from Cave 4," 215, n.19), even though that MS contains nothing from Exod 35-40: "One Exodus manuscript (4QEx^a) belongs systematically to the Egyptian textual tradition reflected in the Septuagint; though at points it seems to offer a more consistent form of that

tradition than the Septuagint itself:" *The Ancient Library of Qumran and Modern Biblical Studies* (Garden City, N.Y.: Doubleday. 1958), 137; plate opposite p. 101.

9. The complete list of variants she has published include only four for Exod 35-40: (1) in having Exod 36:21-24 4QpaleoExod^m agrees with MT and SP against LXX; (2) in Exod 36:23, lacking in LXX, 4QpaleoExod^m reads נגב תימ[נה] with MT against SP's נגבה תימנה; (3) 4QpaleoExod^m seems to have Exod 37:9-16 in the form represented by the MT and SP; (4) at Exod 37:13 4QpaleoExod^m has the unique reading of על ארבע against MT's and SP's לארבע: *An Exodus Scroll from Qumran: 4QpaleoExod^m and the Samaritan Tradition* (HSS 30; Atlanta: Scholars Press, 1986) 342-3.

10. *An Exodus Scroll from Qumran*, 310.

11. Wilson and Wills, "Literary sources of the Temple Scroll," have been followed, e.g., by H. Stegemann, "The Literary Composition of the Temple Scroll and its Status at Qumran," *Temple Scroll Studies*, 132-43.

12. The date of the compilation and redaction of 11QT^a must be distinguished from the actual date of the manuscript; the latter is generally dated to the end of the 1st century BCE or beginning of the 1st century CE; so, e.g., H. Stegemann, "The Literary Composition of the Temple Scroll and its Status at Qumran," *Temple Scroll Studies*, 124.

13. D. W. Gooding argues that it is not a case of plain, straightforward 'absence' of the golden altar, but a confusion of the golden altar with the bronze altar, a confusion discernible in LXX Exod 39:14-21 (MT Exod 39:33-41): *The Account of the Tabernacle: Translation and Textual Problems of the Greek Exodus* (TextsS 6; Cambridge: University Press, 1959) 66-69. Whatever the case, the same confusion does not seem to exist in 11QT^a, so the matter can be counted as an instance of disagreement between LXX Exod 35-39 and 11QT^a.

14. For 11QT^a 34:13 see Yadin, *The Temple Scroll*, I, 47; II, 143; for 11QT^a 36:3 see Yadin, *The Temple Scroll*, II, 152-53.

15. *The Temple Scroll*, I, 46; II, 4.

16. *The Temple Scroll*, II, 6. זהב שהור occurs in Exod 37:2, 6, 11, 16, 17, 22, 23, 24, 26.

17. See D. W. Gooding, *The Account of the Tabernacle*, 66-69, for discussion of the incense altar and LXX Exod 35-40.

18. *The Temple Scroll*, II, 8.

19. *The Temple Scroll*, II, 9. See Gooding, *The Account of the Tabernacle*, 69-72 for detailed discussion of the laver in LXX Exod 35-40.

20. LXX Exod 38 lacks any reference to the incense altar. Yadin noted (*The Temple Scroll*, II, 8) that the author of 11QT^a 3:15 has tried to clarify difficult biblical passages which may have been his sources and that retroverted translations for the same passages in the LXX show that the LXX was engaged in a similar task of clarification. Gooding (*The Account of the Tabernacle*, 52-53) has argued that LXX 38:22 does not really represent either its parallel command in Exod 27 nor the story in Num 16:36-40. MT Exod 38:1-2 (LXX Exod 38:22) is discussed in detail by K. G. O'Connell, *The Theodotionic Revision of the Book of Exodus* (HSM 3; Cambridge, Mass.: Harvard University Press, 1972) 47-55. O'Connell concludes that Theodotion's version is an accurate translation of the present MT, a revision towards it.

21. *The Temple Scroll*, II, 9.

22. The laver is lacking from the Greek until LXX Exod 38:26.

23. *The Temple Scroll*, II, 27.

24. Yadin described only the problems surrounding the traditions concerning the veil and its composition (*The Temple Scroll*, I, 181; II, 27-28). Likewise Maier (*The Temple Scroll*, 68) describes only the golden aspects of the veil.

25. *The Account of the Tabernacle*, 68.

26. On 11QT^a 7:13 Yadin eventually concluded that the scroll preserves a tradition prescribing a golden veil "or - even more likely - a golden veil *in addition* to the ordinary one" (*The Temple Scroll*, II, 28).

27. *The Temple Scroll*, II, 31.

28. *The Temple Scroll*, II, 34-5.

29. *The Temple Scroll*, II, 35.

30. See D. W. Gooding, *The Account of the Taber-*

nacle, 55-6, for an account of what he sees as an abbreviating process in LXX Exod 38:13-17.

31. *The Temple Scroll*, II, 37-8; alongside the MT Yadin took note of the various evidence of the LXX, the targums, b. *Menah* 88b, Rashi, Maimonides (*Code: Laws Concerning the Temple* 3:6), and Nachmanides.

32. Yadin, *The Temple Scroll*, II, 40; he also noted Exod 40:33 and the interesting comment of Josephus (*War* 5:212-14): "Before these hung a veil of equal length, of Babylonian tapestry, with embroidery of blue and fine linen, of scarlet also and purple, wrought with marvellous skill. Nor was this mixture of materials without its mystic meaning: it typified the universe. For the scarlet seemed emblematical of fire, the fine linen of the earth, the blue of the air, and the purple of the sea; the comparison in two cases being suggested by their colour, and in that of the fine linen and purple by their origin, as one is produced by the earth, and the other by the sea. On this tapestry was portrayed a panorama of the heavens, the signs of the Zodiac excepted" (trans. H. St. J. Thackeray, LCL 3, 265).

33. "לשרננו" ,"לנוסחה של מגילת המקדש" 42 (1977-78) 138; the reading for 11QT^a 10:10 comes from Qimron's article, "New readings in the Temple Scroll," *IEJ* 28 (1978) 162.

34. עמוד occurs in 11QT^a 10:4 as well as 10:11 which would be the instance that would match Exod 38:19 the best.

35. *The Temple Scroll*, II, 40; Yadin considered that אמה in 11QT^a 10:17 was possibly a reference to the measurements of the screen in Exod 38:18 (*The Temple Scroll*, II, 43).

36. "Further Studies in the Temple Scroll," *JQR* 71 (1980) 3-5.

37. See, e.g., my discussion of the biblical sources for the Day of Atonement in 11QT^a 25:10-27:10 in "The Temple Scroll: A Law unto Itself?" *Law and Religion* (ed. B. Lindars; Cambridge: James Clarke, 1988) 41; also the detailed study by D. D. Swanson, *The Temple Scroll and the Bible: The Methodology of 11QT*, unpublished Ph.D. dissertation, Manchester, 1980.

38. "Further Studies in the Temple Scroll," *JQR* 71 (1980) 3-5; Milgrom notes the way 4Q159:6-7 seems

to parallel 11QT^a inasmuch as the half-shekel was to be paid only once by each male.

39. *The Temple Scroll*, I, 411.

40. 11QT^a 39:11-13 (בקדם מזרח) reflects Exod 38:13 (LXX Exod 37:11) where a similar phrase is used of the sides of the tabernacle court (לפאת קדמה מזרחה): Yadin, *The Temple Scroll*, II, 167.

41. A similarly worded passage on the gates occurs in 11QT^a 44. That the half-shekel is mentioned in 11QT^a 39:8-10 may make it less likely that it was also mentioned in 11QT^a 10:5.

42. *The Temple Scroll*, I, 411.

43. The phrase is also found in the introduction to the section in LXX Exod 35:6, 7, 23, 25 as in 11QT^a 3:2.

44. As at LXX Exod 37:8-10 (MT Exod 38:10-12) where the phrase ווי העמדים וחשקיהם כסף is lacking three times, but is translated by Theodotion; see, O'Connell, *Theodotionic Revision*, 298.

45. For similar conclusions with regard to the exegetical concerns of 11QT^a see the contribution of L. H. Schiffman in this volume; for a similar viewpoint with regard to the Hebrew *Vorlage* of Exod 35-40 see the contribution of A. Aejmelaeus, also in this volume.

ON THE RELATIONSHIP BETWEEN 11QPSa AND THE SEPTUAGINT ON THE BASIS OF THE COMPUTERIZED DATA BASE (CAQP)[1]

JOHANN COOK

1. INTRODUCTION

One of the major problems facing the textual critic is the enormous amount of data which inevitably has to be coped with.[2] Fortunately relatively recent developments concerning computer applications have provided new possibilities for the handling of these masses of data and are at the same time acting as a novel stimulus for that data's interpretation. This incentive is felt in various fields of research. Co-operation in the field of computerized research has certainly benefited from this development.[3] One example of this co-operation is the computerized data base for the Qumran biblical scrolls, which has the Computer-assisted Tools for Septuagint Studies (CATSS) data base as basis.[4] Using an already existing data bank saves time and in addition leads amongst other things to the standardization of transcription signs.[5]

The Computer-assisted Qumran Project (CAQP) was developed in order to research a multitude of matters concerning the Dead Sea scrolls.[6] Because of the outstanding theoretical base of the parallel-alignment concept and the adaptability of the CATSS data base, it was decided to use this existing and, it must also be said, comprehensive data bank as an indispensable basis for creating a useful computerized tool with which these various matters can be studied. This was carried out in the following manner. The second of the two main columns of the CATSS data base, i.e. the Greek column, was removed programmatically and was replaced by eight columns, each describing a specific aspect of a difference between the Massoretic Text (MT) and a given scroll.[7]

The textual basis for this exegetical tool was the *Biblia Hebraica Stuttgartensia* (*BHS*) for the MT and for the scrolls, where available, it was the material from the Discoveries in the Judaean Desert (DJD) volumes. However, the largest amount of published material, at least of the major texts was included in the data base from other extant sources.

In order to create a useful and flexible data base some of the abbreviations of CATSS were used. However, because of the structural difference between the Qumran data and the Greek data, it was necessary to develop a unique system that suits the biblical scrolls. Moreover, it was decided to encode and describe every difference that is encountered in a specific scroll or fragment.

Consequently a specific sign is used for every possible deviation in the Qumran data in comparison with the MT.

The standard monograph by E. Y. Kutscher, *The Language and Linguistic Background of the Isaiah Scroll (1QIsa^a)*,[8] together with E. Qimron's work, *The Hebrew of the Dead Sea Scrolls*,[9] were used as basis for devising the sigla applied to describe the characteristics of the Qumran readings. For other abbreviations the reference work by J. A. Fitzmyer, *The Dead Sea Scrolls, Major Publications and Tools for Study*,[10] was utilized.

The following sample of the Layout is used in the description of the scrolls:

1). MT, followed by one or two square brackets or minus/plus signs. The large a-Psalm scroll from cave eleven is used as reference (] 11a when MT and Qumran agree, when not]]11a is used). The number 11 refers to the eleventh cave and "a" to the a-scroll).

2). The Qumran text, as in the source (in this instance indicated by 11QPSa).

3). Notes on the matres lectionis, subdivided into various groups:

3).1 Aleph
)1 aleph added in final position - e.g. KY)
3).2 Waw
W1 waw as ML for o (stressed long vowel)-YQ+WL
3).3 He
H1 he for aleph
3).4 Yod
Y1 yod as ML long vowel - DWYD / HSYR

4). Orthography referring to phenomena that either are (+) or are not (-) found in the text.

4).1 Spelling
4).1.1 Defective (minus) etc.
- W

4).1.2 Plene (plus)
01 - KWL
5). Scribal notes
c3 (correction by superscript)
6). Textual status
The relationship between a specific scroll and other texts (e.g. LXX, Peshitta, Sam Pent, etc.) is defined in this column.
7). Textual notes
as - assimilation of consonants
8). Syntactical notes.
In this column only the syntactical differences between Qumran and MT are described.

    These descriptions can be researched by extracting the needed information from the data base as done below. In this case the versatile program, dBase IV plus, was used. Although the data base contains large amounts of data, practically all the published material, for the purpose of this article, I included only data from 11QPSa. The purpose of this paper is primarily to demonstrate the multi-purposeness of the Qumran data base. In this current paper I therefore concentrate on one of these other above-mentioned aspects, namely the question of the relationship between the scrolls and the ancient versions of the Old Testament (OT). Since the data base is not as yet known to all Septuagint and Qumran scholars, as an introduction I also treat some of the other aspects briefly. Consequently I do not intend providing final answers as to the above-mentioned relationship or for that matter to related issues such as questions pertaining to canonical issues.[11]

This endeavour should also be seen as a follow-up of a contribution I made before a group of Qumran scholars at the Institute for Advanced Studies in Jerusalem in January 1990. I am indebted to those scholars for their constructive remarks and reaction.[12] There I endeavoured to demonstrate some of the applications of this data base, concentrating on orthographical characteristics.[13] The point I attempted to make at that meeting is the commonplace that it is futile to base analyses on unrepresentative evidence. I am of the opinion that the computerized data base for the Qumran biblical scrolls will put us in a position to obtain representative material that could act as the basis for novel interpretations. This certainly applies to orthographical issues, although it is also applicable to numerous other aspects of the biblical text, *inter alia*, the question as to the exact content of the relationship between the scrolls and other writings.

2. THEORETICAL REFLECTION

As a necessary theoretical orientation let me begin by treating some specific methodological issues and, as an additional motivation, demonstrating what can actually be done by means of this flexible tool.

2.1 MT as basis for comparison

It is necessary at this stage to treat, albeit cursorily, the issue of the choice of the MT as the basis for comparison, as this has methodological implications. This was done only because the MT is probably the best representative complete Hebrew text available, although it does have its own peculiarities and problems.[14] Methodological problems are undoubtedly involved in this choice. The fact that many of the texts or fragments are unpointed represents only one of these problems. However, this deliberate choice does not mean that the assumption is made that the *Vorlagen* of the scrolls or fragments were identical to those of the MT. Many of the differences between the MT and a specific scroll or fragment should actually be ascribed to *Vorlagen* differences. It has to be stressed that the MT is used solely as a convenient basis for comparison.

2.2 Scribal character of 11QPSa

Determining the scribal character of a writing is a prerequisite for the evaluation of the scroll; to mention only one aspect: the creative attitude of the scribe/tradent towards his source. In the larger Isaiah scroll one finds a multitude of roots that seem to be the result of misunderstanding or different interpretations on the part of the scribe. In the description of this scroll a category "substitution of roots (sr)" was consequently included in the data base, which occurs in many cases. The same situation does not obtain in 11QPSa, which contains relatively few such descriptions.

As far as scribal notes are concerned the following abbreviations are used in the data base, having been extracted for research purposes:
ma (marginal notes/words)
cl (correction by crossing out with line)

11QPSa AND THE SEPTUAGINT

c2 (correction by dots)
c3 (correction by superscript)
\ (reconstruction by editor).

A selection of these notes concerning 11QPSa is printed below for demonstration purposes: C3 indicates scribal corrections by means of superscript.

```
11QPSa   p 119   42 W/)(NH       ]]11a W/{)}(NH              C3
11QPSa   p 119  140 W/(BD/K      ]]11a W/(B{D)/KH      28   C3
11QPSa   p 119  154 RYBH         ]]11a RYB{H}                C3
11QPSa   p 119  155 Y$W(H        ]]11a {Y$W(H}               C3
11QPSa   p 121    2 M/(M         ]]11a M/{(}M                C3
11QPSa   p 122    3 H/BNWYH      ]]11a H/BNW{Y}H             C3
11QPSa   p 123    1 N&)TY        ]]11a @N{&}[)T]Y            C3
11QPSa   p 124    7 W/)NXNW      ]]11a {[W/)NX]*N[W]}        C3
11QPSa   p 130    2 $M(H         ]]11a [..]*(H {*?}          C3
11QPSa   p 137    1 Y$BNW        ]]11a Y$B{N}W               C3
11QPSa   p 139   17 R)$/YHM      ]]11a R{)}$/YHM             C3
11QPSa   p 141   10 )(BWR        ]]11a )(B{W}R               C3
11QPSa   p 143    3 DK)          ]]11a DK{)}                 C3
11QPSa   p 143    5 B/KL         ]]11a B/{K}WL     W3 01    C3
11QPSa   p 143    6 (YPH         ]]11a ({Y}PH                C3
11QPSa   p 144    1 H/MLMD       ]]11a H/MLD{M}              C3
11QPSa   p 145    2 --+          ]]11a {W/BRWK}              C3
11QPSa   p 145    3 W/MHLL       ]]11a W/{M}HWLL   W5       C3
11QPSa   p 145    6 W/GDWLT/YK   ]]11a W/GDWL{W}T/YKH28C3
11QPSa   p 145   15 NWTN         ]]11a N{W}TN                C3
11QPSa   p 145   15 )T           ]]11a {)T}                  C3
```

From the above list it would seem that far less scribal activity took place in the Psalm scroll than for example in the large Isaiah scroll. Of course the difference in size of these scrolls must be accounted for in order for viable comparisons to be drawn. This could mean that the scribe was actually more conscientious towards his *Vorlage* than was the case with the 1QIsa scribe. This is an important observation, as in many cases there seem to be only minute differences between the scroll reading and other texts, which could easily be the result of scribal activity.

Although this is evidently a generalization the point to make is that it is indeed possible to determine the exact content of scribal and other activities, such as the orthographical systems followed by a specific scribe(s).

2.3 Orthography[15]

The following tables give an indication of the orthographical characteristics found in some of the published scrolls, once again with special reference to the above-mentioned Psalm scroll:

2.3.1 Distribution of orthographical characteristics

2.3.1.1 Added "aleph"

a) KY =) 1 [KY)]

11QPs	t (83) d (67) m (16)
11QpLev	t (25) d (17) m (8)
1QIsa	t (323) p (185) Is 1-18; 35-66 d (126)
	Is 19-33 m (12)
1QIsb	t (107) d (58) m (49)
4QDana	t (1)
4QDanb	t (1)
4QDanc	t (9) d (2) m (7)
4QSama	t (10) d (3) m (7)
4QSamb	t (17) d (3) m (14)
4QSamc	t (10) m (10)
Sam Pent	d

2.3.1.2 Combination "waw"/"he" as a depiction of final mater lectionis for the o-vowel

a) KH = W2   04 (KWH)

11QPs	t (3) d (3)
11QpLev	t (25) d (17)
1QIsa	t (52) p (38) Is 34-66 d (13) Is 1-31
	m (1)
1QIsb	t (15) d (7) m (8)
4QDana	m (1)
4QDanb	m (1)
4QIsa	m (1)

```
4QpIsa      p (1)
4QpIsc      t (4) p (2) m (2)
4QSama      m (1)
4QSamb      m (1)
4QSamc      p () t ()
Sam Pent    d
```

2.3.1.3 "He" added to the end of words/lexemes

a) HY) = 17 (HY)H)

```
11QpLev     t (2) m (2)
1QIsa       t (9) p (4) d (5)
1QIsb       t (4) d (2) m (2)
4QDana      t (2) m (2)
4QDanc      d (1)
4QSama
4QSamb      m (1)
4QSamc      p (1)
Sam Pent    d
```

b) HW) = 16 (HW)H)

```
11QPs       t (4) d (1) m (3)
11QpLev     t (19) d (3) m (16)
1QIsa       t (97) p (31) Is 34-66 d (61) Is 1-33
                                           m (4)
1QIsb       t (14) d (5) m (9)
4QpIsc      p (1) m (1)
4QDana      t (9) d (2) m (7)
4QDanb      t (8) m (8)
4QDanc
4QSama      t (2) m (2)
4QSamb      t (3) m (3)
4QSamc      m (1)
Sam Pent    d
```

2.3.1.4 Addition of "He" to specific suffixes.

a) L/K

```
11QPs       t (7) p (6)
11QpLev
1QIsa       t (51) m (3)
1QIsa       masc t (25) p (18) Is 34-66 d (7)
1QIsa       fem t (23) p (6) d (17) Is 34-66
1QISb       t (20) d (14)
4QIsa       m (3)
4QpIsc      m (1) p (1)
4QDana      m (4) d (1)
4QDanb
4QDanc      m (2)
4QSama      t (3) p (2) m (1)
```

4QSamb   m (2)
4QSamc   p (2)
Sam Pent   d

b) 2nd person plural /YK

11QPs   t (109) p (89) d (5) m (15)
11QpLev   t (5) d (5)
1QIsa   t (221)
              p [65] (1) Is 1-33; (39) Is 34-45 and
                                            (25) Is 47-66
              d [146] (55) Is 1-36; 1 Is 36-45 and
                                            (90) Is 45-66
              m (10)
1QIsb   t (98) d (54) m (44)
4QDana   t (3) d (1) m (2)
4QDanb   t (4) p (1) m (3)
4QDanc   t (5) d (1) m (4)
4QSama   d (1)
4QSamb   d (1) m (1)
4QSamc   t (7) p (1) m (6)
Sam Pent   d

c) Suffix 3rd plural /M

11QPs   t (42) p (3) d (17) m (22)
11QpLev   t (20) d (9) m (12)
1QIsa   t (190) p (30) d (145) m (15)
1QIsb   t (73) d (41) m (32)
4QDana   m (1)
4QDanb
4QDanc   d (1) m (1)
4QSama   m (1)
4QSamb   d (1)
4QSamc
Sam Pent   d

d) Suffix 2nd person plural /KM

11QPs   t (45) d (19) p (3)
11QpLev   d (8)
1QIsa   t (155) p [102] (17) Is 1-33; (85) Is
                                                34-66
              d [49] (38) Is 1-33; (11) IS 34-66
                                             m (4)
1QIsb   t (51) d (35) m (16)
4QPIsc   t (2) p (2)
4QDana
4QDanb
4QDanc
4QSama
4QSamb
4QSamc

| 8QGef1 | d (3) |
| Sam Pent | d |

As can be seen from these printed tables in certain scrolls specific orthographical forms predominate.[16] 11QPSa contains "plene" forms as well as defective ones. With this broad orientation as general background some aspects of the complicated relationship between the scrolls and the versions can now be treated.

3. RELATIONSHIP BETWEEN 11QPSa AND THE VERSIONS (ESPECIALLY LXX)

Studies of this nature in the past exhibit certain shortcomings, *inter alia*, the question of unrepresentativeness. In most cases researchers tended to concentrate on one aspect of this relationship, namely the differences between various writings. The most conspicuous characteristic in this regard, however, is that variants were forced into specific theoretical frameworks. The threefold system of the MT, LXX and SP types of readings, as far as the Pentateuch is concerned, is probably the best known.[17] To avoid this minefield one must not only concentrate on differences but also observe, as has already been said, the total situation. With the help of the data base the exact content of the agreements as well as the differences between the biblical scrolls and relevant writings can consequently be determined. It is also possible to determine those readings that are unique as far as the scrolls (in this case 11QPSa) are concerned.

3.1 Agreements

In order to determine the exact content of this

category a file was extracted from the data base of all the instances where the indicator 11QPSa]11a occurs in the data base. Out of a total number of 2942 there were 1237 cases of this sign. Of course the fragmentary nature of the data is a problematic factor. Lacunae are indicated by the siglum]]11a [...]. In addition specific sigla are used in order to depict uncertain readings [the at sign (@) indicates a highly probable reading and the asterisk (*) an uncertain reading]. There are 243 instances of this category. All these sigla together amount to 829, which means that in 586 instances the text of the scroll is totally fragmentary. Converted into a percentage this means that out of a total of 2356 words 11QPSa agrees with MT in 1237 instances, that is 53% of the time. There is clearly a great measure of agreement between these writings.

3.2 Differences

The differences between the scroll and MT measured on a macro scale are determined by extracting from the data base all the instances indicated by the sign]]11a, followed by the difference and its description. Out of a total of 3844 there are 1015 instances of the appropriate sign. This means that in approximately 26% of the total data base of the Psalm scroll there are differences between 11QPSa and MT. When the lacunae are discarded (586) the percentage rises somewhat to 34%. The number of differences is thus substantially lower than the similarities, although still significant enough to merit drawing legitimate conclusions.

The nature of these various differences must be taken into account. By far the largest number of differences are the result of orthographical differences. As far as the rest of the differences is concerned I have selected a number of representative examples from the data base for discussion purposes. These can be classified into the following categories:

3.2.1 Possible *Vorlage* differences

a) 11QPSa p 101 1 W/M$P+   ]]11a   [..]@$P+[19]

The Qumran text reads $P+ with an at sign (@) to indicate that the reading is highly probable. The LXX has KRISIN - "Judgement," which could perhaps indicate another Hebrew *Vorlage*. $P+ according to KB has as part of its semantic field the nuance "acts of judgement." H&R demonstrates that it was used as an equivalent for either M$P+ or $P+. The majority of occurrences is, however, M$P+. Peshitta reads W/DYN), which could be a rendering of any one of the above-mentioned Hebrew words. Whether M$P+ or $P+ was in fact the *Vorlage* of this reading is consequently uncertain.

b) 11QPSa p 102 1 Y(+P   ]]11a   Y(+W[.]

It is unclear whether the Qumran reading represents a root other than MT. According to KB Y(+W, from the root (+H means "to enwrap, to cover." MT has the root (+P, "to faint away," and LXX AKHDIASH - "to be deeply afflicted." The fragmentary nature of the readings impedes a clear-cut answer, as it is of course possible that the added waw simply represents a plene reading and that the "Pe" actually deteriorated.

c) 11QPSa p 119 49 DBR   ]]11a   DBR/YKH

Th´ O´ (TWN LOGWN SOU) and LXX (TON LOGON SOU) agree with 11QPSa as opposed to MT. A´ (RHMATOS), on the other hand, corresponds with MT and not with 11QPSa. S´ (LOGWN EMWN), on the contrary, has a totally different, unique reading. Pesh (MLT/K) corresponds with 11QPSa against MT. It would seem as if these readings represent different *Vorlage(n)*.

d) 11QPSa p 119 71 (NYTY   ]]11a   (NYT/NY.

Certain Septuagintal readings of the OG, Th´, O´ (ETAPEINWSAS ME) agree with Qumran as opposed to MT. The Pesh [)TMKKT] on the other hand reads like MT. Although contextual analyses need to be made of each translation unit, it does seem possible that here we find different *Vorlagen*, with 11QPSa and LXX agreeing.

e) 11QPSa p 119 110 W/M/PQWD/YK   ]]11a PQWD/YKH -WC/-pre 28[19]

LXX agrees with MT. It is, however, interesting to note that in the immediate context of this verse 11QPSa does not have added "waw"'s. This applies to the following examples:

11QPSa p 119 105 W/)WR   ]]11a   )WR   -WC
11QPSa p 119 108 W/M$P+/YK]]11a   M/M$P+/YKH
                                       -WC/ pre+M 28
11QPSa p 119 109 W/TWRT/K   ]]11a   TWRT/KH -WC 28
11QPSa p 119 110 W/M/PQWD/YK]]11a   PQWD/YKH
                                       -WC/-pre M 28
11QPSa p 119 113 W/TWRT/K   ]]11a   TWRT/KH -WC 28

It must consequently be possible that these differences are the result of the scribe, especially when it is taken into account that the LXX does agree with MT in all these instances.

f) 11QPSa p 119 119 H$BT   ]]11a   X$BTY.

Whether this difference represents a graphic error or a deviating *Vorlage* is unclear, especially because the root X$B, "to regard," exists. MT, on the other hand, reads H$BT from the root $BT, "to mop up, to put to an end." LXX has the reading ELOGISAMHN, "to reckon," which agrees with Qumran (also as far as the person is concerned) and not with MT. This could be an indication of a common *Vorlage*.

g) 11QPSa p 119 130 Y)YR]]11a W/H)R +WC 81

LXX has FWTIEI ("will enlighten") without the consecutive KAI which represents an agreement with MT as opposed to 11QPSa. The Pesh on the other hand reads W/)NHR, "and will enlighten" (Aph. from NHR), which agrees with Qumran and not with MT.

Before any conclusions can, however, be drawn these readings must be thorougly researched. The grammatical categories at stake need to be analysed, for in biblical Hebrew the "waw" consecutive plus the perfect has the same semantic value as the imperfect. It is a question whether this also holds true for the Peshiṭta. Evidently each writing must be studied individually. There are three examples of the category 81 (indication of a perfect in a scroll instead of an imperfect) and only in the instance under discussion is an added "waw" in play (cf. below). As a matter of fact in practically all instances (at least those that are not fragmentary) imperfects are rendered by means of imperfects in 11QPSa. With the help of relational data bases all these issues can be studied simultaneously.[20]

```
11QPSa p 109 31  Y(MD     ]]11a    (MD  81    LXX, Pesh, V
11QPSa p 119 130 Y)YR     ]]11a    W/H)R +WC 81 Pesh
11QPSa p 148 5   YHLLW    ]]11a    HLLW       81
```
h) 11QPSa p 119 131 Y)BTY   ]]11a   T)BTY

LXX - EPEPOQOUN - "I longed after" Pesh W/SKYT - "I waited for." Both words Y)B and T)B are interchangeable and mean basically the same, i.e. "to long for."

3.2.2 Plusses/minuses

a) 11QPSa p 102 24 --+   ]]11a   KY (LXX 102 23)

The plus in the scroll occurs nowhere else and could be the result either of a deviating *Vorlage* or an endeavour by the scribe to interpret.

b) 11QPSa p 102 29 --+   ]]11a   L/@DWR

LXX, Pesh and V have the equivalent of this addition.

c) 11QPSa p 119 68--+   ]]11a   )DWNY

Pesh and LXX agree with 11QPSa and not with MT.

d) 11QPSa p 119 107 --+   ]]11a   K/)MRT/KH

LXX (TON LOGON SOU) and Pesh (MLT/K) have similar readings.

e) 11QPSa p 119 108 N)   --+

LXX reads DH which can be correlated with N). Some Hebrew mss and Pesh agree with 11QPSa.

f) 11QPSa p 119 128 KL   ]]11a   ---

Some Hebrew mss, LXX and Pesh agree with MT, indicating a possible corresponding Hebrew *Vorlage*.

g) 11QPSa p 119 131 KY   ]]11a   ---

Hebrew mss and Pesh agree with 11QPSa.

3.2.3 Differences of number

a) 11QPSa p 102 26 W/M(&H   ]]11a   W/M(&Y

In Ps 102:26 the LXX, Targum, some Hebrew mss

and 11QPSa agree contrary to MT. They read plural instead of singular.

b) 11QPSa p 119 16 DBR/K]]11a DBR/YKH
Specific Hebrew mss, the LXX and Pesh have plural readings.

c) 11QPSa p 119 17 DBR/K]]11a DBR/YKH
Specific massoretic mss, LXX and Pesh agree with 11QPSa.

d) 11QPSa p 119 18 M/TWRT/K]]11a M/TWRWT/YKH
Specific Hebrew mss agree with 11QPSa.

e) 11QPSa p 119 82 KLW]]11a KLTH
The LXX (ECELIPON) agrees with MT as opposed to Qumran.

f) 11QPSa p 119 105 DBR/K]]11a DBR/YKH
Specific Hebrew mss and the Targum have plural readings.

g) 11QPSa p 119 105 L/NTYBT/Y]]11a L/NTYBWT/Y
V and LXX agree with 11QPSa as opposed to MT. Pesh, on the other hand, agrees with 11QPSa.

h) 11QPSa p 119 114 L/DBR/K]]11a L/DBR/YKH
One Hebrew ms and some Greek mss agree with 11QPSa. LXX and Pesh agree with MT as opposed to 11QPSa.

i) 11QPSa p 119 142 CDQ]]11a [C]DQWT
LXX and Pesh agree with MT as opposed to 11QPSa.

j) 11QPSa p 119 152 M/(DT/YK]]11a M/(DT/KH
LXX (EK TWN MARTURIWN) agrees with MT as opposed to 11QPSa, whereas Pesh (SHDWT/K) agrees with 11QPSa and not with MT.

3.2.4 Added or omitted "waw's"

a) 11QPSa p 102 27 KLBW$]]11a W/KLBW@$
The added "waw" has a corresponding addition in

LXX, S´ and V.

b) 11QPSa p 119 17)XYH   ]]11a   W/)XYH

Some Massoretic mss and Qumran readings contain the added "waw."

3.2.5 Graphic changes/scribal errors?

a) 11QPSa p 119 17 GML   ]]11a   GMWR

The root GMWR ("to bring to an end, for the benefit of") differs from MT GML ("to do good") and LXX (ANTAPODOS "to render a recompense"). It is possible that this difference represents a graphic change.

b) 11QPSa p 119 20 GRSH   ]]11a   GR$H

MT (GRSH, "to be crushed") seems to have a different nuance to 11QPSa (GR$H, "to drive out"), although a graphic error or difference could be possible. The LXX reading (EPEPOQHSEN, "to be longing for") is probably an exegetical reading, which could have influenced the Pesh (CB), "to wish".

c) 11QPSa p 119 37 B/DRK/K   ]]11a   K/DBRK/KH

Various mss and Tg agree with 11QPSa. This pericope is filled with terms such as "righteousness," etc., which could have led to a deliberate scribal change in 11QPSa. On the other hand the consonants B and K are easily interchanged.

d) 11QPSa p 119 70 $($(TY   ]]11a   *$*([$]W(Y

A Hebrew ms, A´, S´ and 11QPSa have a noun from the root $((- "to take delight". MT, on the contrary, has a verb of this root $((. LXX - EMELEQSA is a participle "to meditate." Pesh (N+RT) also reads a verb "to keep" with MT as opposed to 11QPSa.

e) 11QPSa p 119 107 XY/NY   ]]11a   XWN/NY as below
f) 11QPSa p 119 108 M/M$P+/YK   ]]11a   W/M$P+/YKH

LXX (TA KRIMATA SOU) with MT as opposed to 11QPSa. Pesh (W/MN DYN/YK) with Qumran as opposed to MT.

g) 11QPSa p 119 116 M/&BR/Y   ]]11a   M/M&BR/Y

LXX (APO THS PROSDOKIAS MOU) agrees with MT as opposed to 11QPSa. Pesh (MN SBRY), on the other hand, agrees with MT as opposed to 11QPSa.

h) 11QPSa p 119 156 XY/NY   ]]11a   XWN/NY

The MT reading (XY/NY) "revive me" is a Pi'el imperative of the root XYH. 11QPSa - XWN/NY - could be understood as a participle of XNN (plene) with a suffix 1.sg. However, it is probably an imperative sg. of XNN ("be gracious unto me"). LXX (ZHSON) and Pesh ()XNY) agree with MT as opposed to 11QPSa.

3.2.6 Orthographical differences

As stated earlier most of the differences between MT and 11QPSa can be ascribed to this category. I quote some examples only.

a) 11QPSa p 119 59 (DT/YK   ]]11a   (DWWT/YKH

LXX reads EIS TA MARTYRIA and agrees with 11QPSa as opposed to MT. Pesh (L/$BYL/YK) also agrees with 11QPSa.

b) 11QPSa p 119 61 (WD/NY   ]]11a   (WDW/NY   mss
c) 11QPSa p 119 85 $YXWT   ]]11a $XT   ms
d) 11QPSa p 119 92 B/(NY/Y   ]]11a   B/(WWN/Y

One Hebrew ms, as well as LXX (EN TH TAPEINWSEI MOU, "in my affliction") and Pesh (B/MWKK/Y) agree with MT as opposed to 11QPSa.

3.2.7 Transpositions

One example only is quoted.
11QPSa p 119 107 K/DBR/K ---

This might be the result of a transposition. 11QPSa reads K/)MRT/KH before the verb XWN/NY, whereas MT has the verb XYN/Y first.

3.3 Unique readings

Of this category there are ample examples. I once again include only a few examples.

a) 11QPSa p 102 18 TPLT   ]]11a   TWL(T

The apparently unique reading in Ps 102:18 TWL(T for TPLT means according to KB "worm, maggot." Do we have here a different *Vorlage* or is it the result of a graphic error? The reference does correspond with the idea of the "lowness" of man as phrased especially in Ps 103 and could indeed represent a unique reading.

b) 11QPSa p 119 37 XY/NY   ]]11a   XWN/NY uni[21]

Compare the discussions of verses 107 and 156 above.

c) 11QPSa p 119 41 XSD/K   ]]11a   XSD   suf -K
d) 11QPSa p 119 43 L/M$P+/K   ]]11a   L/DBRN/KH uni

Many Hebrew mss, LXX, Pesh and the Targum differ from MT only as far as the number is concerned.

e) 11QPSa p 119 44 L/(WLM --- uni
f) 11QPSa p 119 45 B/RXBH   ]]11a   B/RXWB/YH uni
g) 11QPSa p 119 83 HYYTY   ]]11a   (&YT/NY uni
h) 11QPSa p 119 83 XQ/YK   ]]11a   XSD/KH

LXX (TA DIKAIWMATA SOU, "your laws") and Pesh (W/PWQDN/YK, "and your laws") agree with MT as opposed to 11QPSa.

i) 11QPSa p 119 87 B/)RC   ]]11a   M/)RC

11QPSa AND THE SEPTUAGINT   127

One could argue here for a graphic confusion of
the prepositions MN and B. The LXX (EN TH GH) and
Pesh (B/)R() agree with MT as opposed to 11QPSa.
j) 11QPSa p 119 106 L/$MR   ]]11a   L/(&WT uni
k) 11QPSa p 119 106 M$P+/Y   ]]11a   M$P+ uni
l) 11QPSa p 119 109 W/TWRT/K]]11a   TWRT/KH uni
m) 11QPSa p 119 110--+   ]]11a   )NY uni
n) 11QPSa p 119 111 KY   --- uni
   LXX - OTI and Pesh - M+L agree with MT as
opposed to 11QPSa.
o) 11QPSa p 119 117 B/XQ/YK]]11a   XWQ/YKH uni
p) 11QPSa p 119 129 PL)WT   ]]11a   PLGY NPT
   LXX reads QAUMASTA - "wonderful" corresponding
with MT, but disagreeing with 11QPSa. The Pesh
reads RWRBN - "magnificently," which also agrees
with MT as opposed to Qumran. Apparently this
reading was adapted by the scribe/translator in
the light of verse 136 (PLGY MYM).
q) 11QPSa p 119 153 KY   ]]11a   --- uni

4. CONCLUSIONS

I have endeavoured to demonstrate that, in
addition to the orthographical patterns that can
be determined by means of the data base, it is
also possible to determine the content of the
relationship between the Qumran scrolls and some
of the related writings, especially the LXX.
Taking the broader perspective into account one
can conclude that this relationship is rather
complicated. In order to obtain an objective
picture one should of course compare LXX with MT
independently. In many instances the LXX actually
agreed with MT as opposed to 11QPSa. Concentrating
on the relationship in 11QPSa it became clear that

there is a great measure of agreement between
these writings. I have also demonstrated that the
differences between these writings are relatively
few. There are also, albeit only a few, unique
readings to be found in 11QPSa.

I am fully aware of the relative value of these
conclusions. Before one can actually draw final
conclusions even as to the precise extent of the
relationship under discussion, one needs to
research all available material on the Psalms.
This still needs to be done. There are,
fortunately, much more data available for research
purposes than treated here. I do hope that I have
succeeded in making researchers aware of the
possible applications of the data base, especially
taking into account the unlimited possibilities
opened by the hyper text and relational data base
structures.

NOTES

1. I decided upon the abbreviation CAQP (Computer-assisted Qumran Project) for this project. This applies to more than just the biblical scrolls; recently it was decided to include non-biblical material in the data base as well. In addition a comprehensive bibliographical data base on Qumran literature is available at the Department of Semitic Languages and Cultures of the University of Stellenbosch. Throughout the study the literal distinguishing mark of each manuscript is presented on the line, not supralinearly as is generally the practice: thus 11QPSa = 11QPs^a.

2. See J. Cook, "New Horizons in Textual Criticism," *Text and Context: Old Testament and Semitic Studies for F. C. Fensham* (ed. W. Claassen; JSOTSup 48; Sheffield: JSOT Press, 1988) 53.

3. There are surely some examples where scholars were apt not to cooperate (see J. Cook, "Interpreting the Peshitta," *JNSL* 15 [1989]), although generally there exists good cooperation between computerized research projects. The "Bible et Informatique" congresses have played a constructive role in this regard: see E. Tov, "Achievements and Trends in Computer-assisted Biblical Studies," *Colloque "Bible et informatique: méthodes, outils, résultats", Jerusalem, 9-13 Juin 1988* (Paris-Genève: Champions-Slatkine) 33-60.

4. The data base is a joint international endeavour by the author, Prof. J. A. Sanders of the Ancient Biblical Manuscript Center at Claremont, California, and Prof. E. Tov of Jerusalem.

5. It was decided, for instance, to follow the CATSS transcriptions. For the purposes of this paper this transcription is also printed in the quotation and discussion of pertinent readings.

6. I should like to thank the SA Human Sciences Research Council and the University of Stellenbosch for financial support of the data base.

7. See J. Cook, "The Qumran (Biblical Scrolls) Data Base," *JNSL* 14 (1988) 32-38.

8. STDJ 6; Leiden: Brill, 1974.

9. HSS 29; Atlanta: Scholars Press, 1986.

10. SBLSBS 8; Missoula: Scholars Press, 1977.

11. As raised, e.g., by J. A. Sanders, "More Psalms of David," *The Old Testament Pseudepigrapha* (ed. J. H. Charlesworth; London: Darton, Longman and Todd, 1985) 2.609-24; and by G. J. Brooke, "Psalms 105 and 106 at Qumran," *RevQ* 14 (1989) 267-92.

12. I also thank Prof. Sanders for the constructive comments he has made in the past concerning this research.

13. "Orthographical Peculiarities in the Dead Sea Biblical Scrolls," *RevQ* 14 (1989) 292-305.

14. See F. E. Deist, *Witnesses to the Old Testament* (Pretoria: NG Kerkboekhandel, 1989) 10-11.

15. The following abbreviations are applicable to specific descriptions in the data base: A´=Aquila; d=defective; H&R=Hatch and Redpath; i=indecisive; KB=Koehler and Baumgartner; m=miscellaneous; ML=matres lectionis; MT=Massoretic text; No=textual notes; Nu=number; O´=Origen; OG=Old Greek; p=plene; Pesh=Peshitta; pre=preposition; ref=textual reference; S´=Symmachus; Sc=scribal notes; t=total; Tg(g)=Targum(im); Th´=Theodotion; ms(s)=Massoretic manuscripts; V=Vulgate; Vs=versions.

16. 1QIsa contains interesting patterns: see J. Cook, "Orthographical Peculiarities in the Dead Sea Biblical Scrolls," 292-305.

17. See the comments of E. Tov. "A Modern Textual Outlook Based on the Qumran Scrolls," *HUCA* 53 (1982) 15-16.

18. In order to demonstrate the structure of the data base, I quote the precise extractable phrase which is to be discussed in each individual case.

19. This is the way the differences are described in the data base. -WC indicated that 11QPSa lacks a "waw;" the same applies to -pre. The number 28 is an indication of the plene vowel letter "he" in the 2nd person suffix.

20. This concept has been put into practice in the Qumran project by B. A. Nieuwoudt: "Beyond CATSS: Using Relational Databases for Text-Critical Research," *Literary and Linguistic Computing* 4/4 (1989) 254-59.

21. This is the abbreviation for a unique reading.

THE PROBLEM OF HAPLOGRAPHY IN 1 AND 2 SAMUEL

ROBERT P. GORDON

While it has become the custom to link the recognition of the biblical literary technique of "resumptive repetition" with H. M. Wiener who touched on the subject in a study published in 1929,[1] *Wiederaufnahme*, the underlying equivalent in German, was, as M. Anbar has recently pointed out, a term already in use among nineteenth-century scholars such as A. Dillmann, C. Steuernagel and J. Wellhausen.[2] Still, we shall leave the defining to Wiener:

> Where an editor desired to incorporate something, he frequently inserted it, and then resumed the original narrative, repeating the last phrase before the break with more or less accuracy.[3]

So far as can be judged, the first serious discussion of this literary phenomenon comes in an article by C. Kuhl published in 1952.[4] Kuhl had reviewed Wiener's book back in 1929[5] and had even fleetingly invoked "resumptive repetition" on the penultimate page of his own 1930 monograph on

Daniel 3.[6] Whereas Wiener had been occupied with the historical books, Kuhl in his *ZAW* article sought evidence of *Wiederaufnahme* mainly in the prophets, though he also noted possibilities for the source criticism of the Pentateuch.

Ten years after Kuhl's article I. L. Seeligmann included *Wiederaufnahme* among several compositional techniques discussed in his essay on Hebrew narrative and biblical historiography.[7] The word "compositional" is used advisedly here, since Seeligmann observed that what Kuhl had regarded as an editorial technique should be seen as, in the first instance, an aspect of narrative composition. The same point was made by S. Talmon who dealt with the subject, at greater or lesser length, in several studies published in the 1970s. In his article on Ezra in *IDBSup* he noted several instances of what he called "repetitive resumption" in that book,[8] and in a joint article with M. Fishbane on the structuring of the book of Ezekiel the technique is again observed - and not surprisingly in view of the fact that Kuhl had already found Ezekiel a generous contributor in this area.[9] Talmon's most detailed discussion comes, however, in his article on synchroneity and simultaneity published in 1978.[10] He points out that medieval commentators like Rashi and Nachmanides occasionally explain features in biblical narrative in terms of "resumptive repetition," even if they do not expound a worked out theory of the phenomenon. Since the early 1970s appeal to "resumptive repetition" or *Wiederaufnahme* in commentaries and other studies, including the "narrative art" genre, has become

HAPLOGRAPHY IN 1 AND 2 SAMUEL   133

more common.

The application of the *Wiederaufnahme* principle in the LXX area is already in evidence in Kuhl's 1930 monograph mentioned above. Kuhl sought to trace the stages of development in the greatly expanded Greek version of Daniel 3 partly on this basis; however, just because he is dealing with Greek additions, the question is not yet one of adjudication between rival Hebrew and Greek readings. For this development we have to refer, in the first instance, to the work of J. Trebolle Barrera on Kings[11] and to the final report of the Hebrew Old Testament Text Project (HOTTP) of the United Bible Societies, published in 1982.[12] In the interests of manageability comment will, at this point, be confined to the latter. In their discussion of the notorious "and the boy was a boy" (1 Sam 1:24) the committee concluded that the Greek *Vorlage* had taken advantage of the obscurity of והנער נער to insert between the two words a not conspicuously original addition aimed at tidying up one or two halakhic problems relating to Hannah's vow.[13] The committee, perhaps wisely in this case, make no reference to *Wiederaufnahme*, but then they also fail to do so in their discussion of 1 Sam 10:1 where, "not without hesitation," they decided that, instead of the MT having suffered omission by haplography as is often suggested, the LXX *Vorlage* had incorporated additional material which ends with the same word as had occasioned (and immediately precedes) the addition.[14] This is getting closer to *Wiederaufnahme*, though still without the use of the term.

The HOTTP committee have therefore described in

one or two cases a *Wiederaufnahme* type of situation in the LXX, but without explicit reference to the existence of such a technique elsewhere. This omission is remedied with style, and from a basically similar ideological standpoint, by Stephen Pisano in his substantial Fribourg dissertation on additions and omissions in Samuel published in 1984.[15] The whole of Pisano's investigation is conducted in terms of what he calls "haplogenic" and "non-haplogenic" readings.

> When an editorial addition has been inserted into the text in this way, so that the first and last word or phrase are identical, and when the absence of the addition in the other texts would lead one to think that this absence might be explained by haplography, such a text may be designated "haplogenic" (p. 12).

Pisano's study is divided into two main parts, the first dealing with ordinary (or "non-haplogenic") pluses in the LXX and MT and including a section on pluses and minuses in 4QSam$^\alpha$ in relation to the MT (pp. 17-156), and the second concerned with haplogenic pluses in the LXX and MT (pp. 157-282). The final section in Part I (pp. 119-56) discusses double translations in the LXX and acts as a bridge to Part II inasmuch as it is in the conclusion to the section that the evidence for the haplogenic technique of insertion first comes into view (pp. 154-56). Here Pisano offers some general comments on the examples of double translation that he has just been discussing, and especially on the way in which the alternative translations have been inserted in the text. He quotes from a paper on LXX Samuel published by F. H. Woods in 1885 in which Woods comments on occurrences of apparent haplogenic omission in MT Samuel.[16] Woods's observation deserves repeating because of the very relevant, commonsense, point that he has to share with us.

> It frequently happens, however, that what at first sight looks like omissions from this cause (*sc.* homeoteleuton) in the Hebrew prove, on closer examination, to be merely alternative renderings of the LXX, because, from the nature of the case, these alternatives generally begin or end with the same words as the clauses to which they correspond (p. 27).

It is clear from the context that Woods is merely commenting on what might, for present purposes, be called "casual haplogeny," it being *in the nature of the case* that there should be an impression of haplogeny since, as Woods notes, "these alternatives generally begin or end with the same words as the clauses to which they correspond." The *intentional* creation of haplogenic effect is a quite separate issue, but Pisano claims to have found already in his list of double translations two instances of deliberate "pseudo-homeoteleuton," at 2 Sam 2:22 and 18:18. In the first case he regards the sentence καὶ πῶς ... πρὸς 'Ιωάβ (1°) as the later, MT-type, reading and the second sentence καὶ ποῦ ... ἀδελφόν σου as Old Greek (OG) (p. 127). It could be, of course, that the MT-type reading omitted τὸν ἀδελφόν σου not from haplogenic considerations but simply because it was an unproblematical part of the text that was being corrected.[17] Moreover, the inclusion of the words τὸν ἀδελφόν σου in the revised reading would, in Pisano's terms, have contributed at least as much to the haplogenic effect as would their exclusion, the situation then being the same as in some other places where haplogeny is invoked (e.g. 2 Sam 13:27, 34). The position at 2 Sam 18:18, as Pisano explains it, is that the second translation (probably *kaige*) was inserted in B after στήλην (1°) and itself ended with the same word (p. 143). The resultant text does have a haplogenic appearance, though again it might be argued that retranslation was limited to that part of the sentence where the actual difficulty was believed to lie.

To form a balanced view of what is happening in regard to double translations in LXX Samuel we would do well to consider that it is for only two "significant pluses" out of thirteen discussed by Pisano that haplogenic insertion is being suggested. And, as we have seen, the eligibility of 2 Sam 2:22 is very much open to doubt. We may fairly question, therefore, whether this exceeds the incidence of "casual" haplogeny that might be expected in the circumstances. Moreover, there is even one passage where the reverse process may be seen at work, if we follow Pisano's explanation. At 2 Sam 20:22 ("And the woman went to all the people, and she spoke to all the city in accordance with her wisdom" [LXX^{Ant}]) the additional "and she spoke to all the city" is treated as "an expansion based on the context" with "city" replacing "people" to avoid repetition (p. 151). If this is the case, haplogeny, as well as repetition, has been avoided.

We come now to the second main part of Pisano's

work, in which he discusses haplogenic pluses in the LXX and MT. As regards the LXX, he concludes that, of nineteen cases examined, at least fifteen represent haplogenic expansion on the part of this version (pp. 238-39). In only one instance (2 Sam 15:20b) is homeoteleutic failure in the MT regarded as certain. By contrast, none of the ten theoretically possible cases of haplogenic addition in the MT is actually regarded as such (pp. 281-82). The LXX is accused of haplography on six occasions and is suspected of deliberate omissions on three other occasions. It will be seen, then, that the old charge against the MT of being haplography-prone is now shifted decisively in the direction of the LXX.[18]

1. *Shorter Pluses*

We deal first with four very short pluses which Pisano has characterized as haplogenic. The inclusion of three of them, at least, is surprising in view of Pisano's stated intention (p. 13) of excluding all one- and two-word, and many three-word, pluses from his discussion. As throughout the remainder of this paper, the main issue is not that of haplography in the MT versus haplogeny in the LXX, but whether, even if the superiority of the MT is conceded for the sake of argument in each case, the LXX text can be described as haplogenic and, if so, whether the haplogenic effect is contrived or merely coincidental.

i. At 1 Sam 3:15 Pisano (pp. 164-66) favours treating the LXX plus "and he arose in the morning" as secondary, with "in the morning" functioning as the resumptive element. But do we have to imagine that an editor who wished to say that Samuel "lay until the morning *and awoke early* and opened the doors ..." felt obliged to repeat בקר / πρωί simply because of his desire to insert his additional verb? Moreover, if we were to assume a Hebrew *Vorlage* containing the verb שכם, its frequent association with the prepositional בבקר ("in the morning") would have to be taken into account.

ii. Haplogenic insertion is also suggested by Pisano (pp. 172-74) for LXX 1 Sam 12:8 where the expanded text reads: "When Jacob *and his sons* came to Egypt *and Egypt humbled them*, then our fathers cried out to the Lord." Again it is argued that, for the addition of a single word – ויענום in the assumed LXX *Vorlage* – מצרים was inserted to create a haplogenic effect. However, the fact that without the repetition of מצרים the inserted verb would, strictly speaking, lack a subject has not been given due weight. Haplogenic intent seems less likely still when we consider the addition of ובניו ("and his sons") in the LXX *Vorlage* earlier in the verse, since the question of haplogeny does not arise there and, as Pisano notes, the two additions appear to stand or fall together.

iii. Although there is a theoretical possibility of haplography in the MT at 1 Sam 13:5 the shorter reading is usually preferred. Pisano (p. 175) thinks that the Greek addition "and they went up *against Israel*" is haplogenic because it follows "And the foreigners assembled for war *against Israel*," but this is another instance of the device being invoked for the sake of the addition of a verb and - though this would only apply if there was a Hebrew original - its accompanying preposition. Close repetition of the kind which the LXX text creates is, moreover, stylistically defensible in both Greek and Hebrew and could in this case be used to emphasize the enormity of the problem which faced the Israelites. Furthermore, while the originality of the plus may well be questioned, Pisano's explanation that it falls into the category of "completing the unsaid" seems not to take account of the occurrence of ויעלו later in the verse.

iv. A fourth instance of the short addition comes in 1 Sam 23:6 where the longer (LXX^B) reading is: "And it came to pass that when Abiathar son of Abimelech fled to David, [and] he came down with David to Keilah, having an ephod in his hand." This rendering construes the sentence differently from Pisano, for whom καὶ αὐτὸς μετὰ Δαυειδ is an insertion to explain that Abiathar was still with David (pp. 207-8). Support for Pisano's interpretation could be found in the Antiochene text which is in essential agreement with LXX^B except for the four additional words, but if LXX^B represents an earlier stage in the Greek tradition, then the relatively smooth reading of LXX^{Ant} will not be of much help. We should note, moreover, that both the MT and LXX^{Ant} by having Abiathar flee to David at Keilah, set up a surface tension with the account of Abiathar's flight in the previous chapter, for 22:20-23 belongs to the pre-Keilah phase of David's outlawry. It may well be, then, that the whole clause καὶ αὐτὸς ... κατέβη is intended to deal with that issue: Abiathar *came down with* David to Keilah.[19] If so, the syntactical isolation of καὶ αὐτὸς μετὰ Δαυειδ ceases and the case for haplogeny diminishes. Stylistically the repetition of the name David in such a clause is unexceptionable and might even be judged superior to the pronominal alternative, "and he came down with him..." Thus Pisano's explanation of the LXX plus as "the result of the desire to explain Abiathar's presence in Keilah, or, more specifically, to emphasize the fact that he was still there with David" (p. 208) goes adrift at the point where it attempts to be more precise.

2. *Longer Pluses*

Pisano considers fifteen passages involving longer pluses on the part of the LXX and, as we have noted, concludes that in only one case, 2 Sam 15:20b, is the Greek unreservedly to be preferred to the MT because of haplographic failure in the latter (pp. 236-38). He also regards the Greek additions at 2 Sam 13:21, 27 as very probably original (p. 238), and in this he may well be correct, though in both verses, as he notes, there could have been supplementation from references elsewhere, viz. 1 Kgs 1:6 and 1 Sam 25:36 respectively. At 2 Sam 13:21 there is the possibility of loss by homeoarcton in the MT, but even if the Greek plus is judged to be secondary it is important from the standpoint of the present study to note that the passage which might, in those circumstances, have influenced the verse begins with ולא, the potentially haplogenic element in 2 Sam 13:21-22. The presence of ולא

might then have nothing to do with symmetrical interpolation. Again, even if we suppose the Greek to have suffered secondary expansion in verse 27, the addition of a sentence saying that "Absalom gave a party like the party of a king" (cf. 1 Sam 25:36), following upon a sentence ending with "the king," does not necessarily indicate haplogenic intent.

In his detailed discussion of 1 Sam 29:10 (pp. 208-17) Pisano shows a slight preference for the MT but without much conviction, as is evident from his later summing up (pp. 238-39). As regards the haplographic argument he observes: "No accident of haplography can account for MT's shorter text whereas the repeated imperative could have given a creative scribe the pretext he needed to insert additional material, where the resulting text would *seem* to have occasioned a haplography in MT" (p. 217). Pisano is inclined to treat the two main clauses in the MT of this verse as double readings, but even this does not relieve the sentence just quoted of an inbuilt contradiction. There is no more evidence of haplogeny in the LXX than there is of haplography in the MT - where even McCarter maintains his usual form only by positing three stages of textual corruption within the MT.[20]

If Pisano were correct in his admittedly tentative explanation of LXX 1 Sam 29:10 this would constitute an interesting departure from the general pattern of haplogenic insertion in Samuel inasmuch as here *both* occurrences of the catch-word (or its approximation) are present in the MT. A clearer instance of the same is envisaged by Pisano (pp. 157-63) for 1 Sam 1:24 where the two occurrences of נער (Gk παιδάριον) are separated by a lengthy plus in the Greek and 4QSam^a. A number of scholars have rightly pointed out that straightforward haplography would not account for the loss from the MT of the addition represented by LXX and 4QSam^a, which is partly why some prefer to stay with the MT despite its doubtful appearance. Pisano (p. 163) thinks that an editor "has taken advantage of the repeated נער" in order to make an insertion, but the same ultimate effect could as easily, and at least as convincingly, be attributed to an editor's conviction that the text had suffered a (non-mechanical) omission between the occurrences of נער. In other words, the insertion was made in order to break up the puzzling statement that "the boy was a boy," and the claimed haplogenic effect is coincidental.

We are left, then, with ten of the pluses which, according to Pisano, can be shown "with varying degrees of certitude" (p. 239) to be haplogenic in character. These will be discussed in what follows, under four sub-headings.

i. *Problem cases*

Four of the passages examined by Pisano do not, in this writer's view, offer even *prima facie* evidence of haplogeny.

1 Samuel 3:21. In his discussion of the several omissions/additions in the MT and LXX of 3:20-4:1 Pisano notes that no simple textual error can account for the absence of the sentence καὶ 'Ηλεὶ ... Κυρίου from the MT of verse 21 (p. 30), and that might also be expected to be the end of the matter as far as haplogeny is concerned. However, at a later stage in the book 3:21 is included among the references which are thought to have haplogenic additions in LXX (p. 238, n. 259). This is puzzling until it is observed in the footnote on p. 240 that haplogeny is only involved if a reconstruction proposed by O. Thenius and P.K. McCarter is followed. And yet in the original discussion of the verse Thenius' rearrangement of the verse-order had been rejected as "unsatisfying" (p. 30). This explanation, understandably resisted by Pisano, involves positing a composite text in which MT 4:1a, absent in the LXX, is followed by the above-mentioned Greek addition plus the variant Greek version of 4:1b, thus creating circumstances in which haplography could - and did, according to Thenius and McCarter - afflict the MT.

1 Samuel 10:1. Most accept as original the Greek addition which expands Samuel's speech to Saul on the occasion of the latter's anointing as king. Barthélemy and his colleagues recognize that הלוא כי is defensible on the basis of 2 Sam 13:28, and that there is a sufficient basis for omission by homeoarcton in כי משחך, but they come down on the side of the MT: "Le comité, non sans hésitation, a reconnu en ce 'plus' une insertion de tissu conjonctif avec reprise du mot ayant servi de prétexte à cette insertion."[21] Pisano admits the possibility of accidental omission in the MT but claims that "in a true haplography, כי should have fallen out as well" (p. 168). However, since he also accepts the legitimacy of the expression הלוא כי, he must be open to the possibility of homeoarcton involving כי משחך. Pisano (p. 169) suggests that an addition has been made in the LXX "at" the words משחך יהוה, which sees him in essential agreement with Barthélemy's committee in their final verdict, but unless LXX οὐχὶ represents MT הלוא כי, rather than simply הלוא as seems more likely,[22] Pisano's suggestion of haplogenic insertion at משחך יהוה is itself open to the charge of failing to take account of כי. This conjunction is represented straightforwardly by ὅτι in the LXX plus.

1 Samuel 10:21. Pisano (p. 172) notes that straightforward haplography would not explain the MT's apparent omission of the words "and they brought near the clan of Matri man by man," however his own suggestion of haplogenic insertion overlooks the existence of εἰς ἄνδρας (=לגברים) in the Greek. The presence of this phrase complicates the argument for haplographic omission from the MT[23] and just as surely stands in the way of a theory of haplogenic insertion. What repetition there is in the plus is but the serial repetition characteristic of lot-casting procedures and accounts of them (cf. Josh 7:16-18).[24]

1 Samuel 15:12-13. "It was, therefore, around Saul's name that the plus was inserted into the text, the result being that we have, in OG, a text whose structure appears to be 'haplogenic.'" So Pisano (p. 206) summarizes the situation in LXX[B] at 1 Sam 15:12-13. It is not at all apparent, however, in what way the LXX[B] text could be seen as haplogenic in any meaningful sense of the term, and it turns out that the real occurrence of haplogeny is in LXX^Ant which, by its misconstruing of OG, created a doublet on MT "and Samuel came to Saul" (v. 13), so "completing the haplogenic form of the text and establishing a text which led Thenius and others to make a correction where, in fact, the 'homeoteleuton' was the product of Ant's misunderstanding of OG's insertion" (pp. 206-7).[25] But a mistaken expansion of the OG phrase πρὸς Σαούλ into "and Samuel came (ἦλθεν) to Saul," so that it now parallels the original OG "and Samuel came (παρεγένετο) to Saul," which comes immediately after the plus, hardly constitutes an example of haplogenic insertion as a deliberate editorial ploy such as usually interests Pisano.

ii. *Translational haplogeny*

It is surely significant as regards Pisano's theory of haplogenic insertion in biblical texts that he does not limit the phenomenon to the Hebrew scribal tradition. In at least two cases, 1 Sam 14:42 and 30:24, the haplogenic effect is attributed to the Greek translator(s) (pp. 203, 218-19). The first of these pluses is not highly regarded by critics and could be seen as one of Pisano's better examples of haplogenic insertion inasmuch as there is almost exact correspondence between "Cast between me and Jonathan my son" and the LXX addition, "and they cast between him and Jonathan his son," yet, for obvious reason, this plus will also require mention in the subsection that follows. The short plus ὅτι οὐχ ἧττον ὑμῶν εἰσιν at 1 Sam 30:24 is, in Pisano's judgment, an addition made by the Greek translator of the verse. It also is given short shrift by most critics, many of them failing to take it under their notice at all. The haplogenic factor in this case consists of the similarity between ὅτι and διότι, which immediately follows the short plus. If it had been a question of a Hebrew original *both* Greek conjunctions could have been taken to represent כי and an occurrence of haplography, real or apparent, would perhaps be arguable, even if the basis were as slim as a monosyllabic conjunction. When, however, the theory rests on no more than the resemblance between ὅτι and διότι *and* their "imaginary retroversion" (p. 219) into Hebrew we may wonder whether haplogeny comes into the picture at all.

iii. *Reported action/speech*

Three references come in for consideration under this heading: 1 Sam 14:42; 2 Sam 13:34; 14:30. The first has already been mentioned in the preceding subsection ("Translational haplogeny") and its attractiveness from the standpoint of Pisano's thesis has been acknowledged. Nevertheless, the plus consists in part of reporting that what Saul had commanded was carried out, from which it could be argued that the repetition is "in the nature of things." The Greek plus at 2 Sam 13:34 has been well received by text critics, though it is sometimes charged with having merely supplied what was felt to be lacking in the Hebrew, viz. a report by the watchman of what he had seen.[26] Even if it is secondary, however, the fact that it is report will still favour the verbatim recounting of what has been witnessed.

At 2 Sam 14:30 Pisano, for whom LXX^{Ant} (minus τὴν μερίδα Ἰωάβ) represents OG, regards the Greek

plus as secondary (pp. 232-36). The insertion is
thought to have been made "at" ויצהר and to end at
καὶ λέγουσιν "thus creating a text in OG which
appeared to be 'haplogenic' in form because of the
repetition of ἐνεπύρισαν" (p. 235). This view of
OG is facilitated by the decision that τὴν μερίδα
Ἰωάβ is secondary, since otherwise the Greek
reads very like an uninterrupted rendering of the
MT, with the plus beginning at καὶ παραγίνονται.
We must note, nonetheless, that, however
attractive the case for treating αὐτὰς as the
(sole) original object of ἐνεπύρισαν (1°), the
reconstructed Hebrew text of 4QSam^c cited by
Pisano has the Hebrew equivalent of τὴν μερίδα.
Moreover, there is the small consideration that,
according to Pisano's explanation, it is the *plus*
that represents ויצהר accurately in καὶ
ἐνεπύρισαν, whereas the supposed actual equivalent
of ויצהר coming immediately after the plus is
ἐνεπύρισαν, which must retrovert as הציתו/הצתו.
In the end it may be as simple, and as desirable,
to begin the plus at καὶ παραγίνονται, and in that
case such repetition as there is could be put down
to the report character of the addition.

iv. *Other pluses*

The remaining pluses are at 1 Sam 13:15; 14:41,
and in both instances a *prima facie* case for
haplogenic insertion in the longer text could be
made out. At 13:15 the omission from the MT of a
large plus ("[from Gilgal] ... from Gilgal") *per*
homeoteleuton is widely accepted. Even Barthélemy
and his colleagues are favourably disposed, noting
against Keil and Stoebe that the difficulty in the
expression εἰς ἀπάντησιν ὀπίσω is not an argument

against the originality of the plus, but just an indication that it is not the creation of the Greek translator.[27] Still, if haplography were not responsible for the difference between the Hebrew and the Greek the question of haplogeny might legitimately arise, as Pisano (pp. 175-83) suggests.

In its Greek form, 14:41 elaborates upon the lot-casting procedure in a way that many text critics find irresistible. Pisano very fairly declines to come down on the side of either the MT or LXX, though he suspects that the presence of another sizeable plus in the Greek of verse 42 points to editorial supplementation rather than to coincident haplography (pp. 183-99). At the least, we may observe with A. Toeg[28] - though Pisano (pp. 198-99) contests this point - that the LXX is almost certainly superior to the MT in having "Lord God of Israel" as address to God, in accordance with normal usage. MT "And Saul said to the Lord God of Israel, 'Give tāmîm,'" is anticlimactic and unconvincing. We should also note that, since all hinges on the repetition of the word "Israel," as regards haplogenic effect, there is repetition of the full phrase "Lord God of Israel" midway through the Greek plus.

3. *The Minuses*

In his comparatively short section entitled "'Haplogenic' pluses in MT" (pp. 243-82) Pisano finds fault with the MT in only one out of ten references discussed, viz. 2 Sam 6:3-4 where accidental dittography of six words is judged to have taken place. In six other places the LXX is thought to have suffered omission by haplography, while in three others *deliberate* omission of words is suspected. Two of these three are of interest here because Pisano thinks that the excision was purposely made at a point where a word or phrase was repeated, with the result that there is the *appearance* of omission by haplography in the Greek. At 1 Sam 2:31-32 LXX[B] and 4QSam[a] have nothing corresponding to MT את־ישראל ... מהיות, and Pisano (p. 248) believes that an editor took advantage of the similarity between מהיות זקן בביתך and ולא יהיה זקן בביתך to remove the sentence in which judgment was passed on Eli personally. In this instance it is not so easy to explain the shorter text on the basis of haplography, which means that deliberate omission is a possibility. But whether the omission of מהיות ... את־ישראל should be attributed to design or to necessity is a fair question, for once the sentence dooming Eli was marked for excision, one or other of the references to aged members among his descendants probably also had to go, otherwise the same thing would be repeated in two adjacent clauses.

The omission of the reference to the five golden mice in the LXX at 1 Sam 6:4 may have come about because of the difficulty in squaring this datum with 6:18 where the number of the mice is said to be according to the number of towns belonging to the Philistine lords.[29] But if this is so, the impression of homeoteleutic omission, because of the formal similarity of the phrase immediately preceding, is probably coincidental.

Pisano was not the only one who, in the early

1980s, was suggesting homeoteleutic *omission* as an editorial technique affecting the transmission and citation of the books of Samuel. It is interesting in this connection to note the observations of another scholar who, independently of Pisano, heads in the same direction. The year after the publication of Pisano's volume, G.J. Brooke published his study of 4QFlorilegium in which he discusses, at one point, a quotation of 2 Sam 7:11-14 which appears to have suffered three omissions by homeoteleuton within its brief compass.[30] But homeoteleuton on this scale strikes Brooke as too much of a coincidence:

> We are thus pushed to the conclusion that the text of 2 Sam 7 has received some deliberate editing at this juncture; and this is tantamount to saying that omission through homeoteleuton may be correctly considered as a correct exegetical principle used here by the author deliberately! (p. 111)
> What was formerly in scholarship described as a scribal error is now to be seen as the correct use of a valid exegetical technique. (p. 112)

It has to be said that the homeoteleutic element involved in the first two omissions consists of the second person masculine singular suffix כה-,[31] nevertheless it is noteworthy that Brooke is thinking in terms of deliberate homeoteleutic omission such as Pisano envisages in the final section of his book (pp. 281-82).

So is there "haplogeny" within the Hebrew and Greek textual traditions of Samuel? Several complicating factors make a final judgment difficult. In most cases there is the possibility of accidental haplography as an alternative explanation, and the evidence is frequently such as to make the decision between haplography and haplogeny extremely difficult. In some cases it is doubtful whether the basic criterion for haplogeny has been met, and always we have to reckon with the possibility that the haplogenic effect is "casual" or "coincidental."

Haplogeny not only at the Hebrew level but also in a couple of places at the Greek-translational level is envisaged by Pisano.[32] Is this a weakness of his case? Or have text-critics been twice wrong in this respect? And is there evidence of haplogenic insertion/omission as an authorial or editorial technique in ancient Greek literature? In a postscript to Kuhl's *ZAW* article on *Wiederaufnahme* J. Hempel[33] notes a study by E. Hirsch of the literary style of the Fourth Gospel in which Hirsch discusses a number of insertions which might now qualify for description as "haplogenic."[34] In his short discussion of *Wiederaufnahme* in Ezekiel B. Lang[35] adverts to the scribal tendency to include marginal additions in classical Greek texts, often with the lemma, or *Stichwort*, and often enough in the wrong place - hence the formulation of "Brinkmann's Law" in connection with the reconstruction of texts in their original form.[36] But the direct comparability of this to Septuagintal haplogeny is difficult to see, unless the whole issue is turned into one of marginal readings and their incorporation in the text. It is also apropos here to observe that in Samuel the Vaticanus and Antiochene texts do not always agree in respect of an alleged case of haplogeny (e.g. 1 Sam 14:41; 15:12-13; 30:24).[37]

Presumably this says something about the awareness of, or the importance attached to, "haplogeny" within the LXX tradition.

It is clear that, on a standard view of the MT vis-à-vis LXX in Samuel, we are talking about, perhaps, a few dozen instances of haplography in the Hebrew; if so, the transmission of the Hebrew text of Samuel has been attended by uncommon troubles. But do manuscripts suffer the fate of being haplography-prone to the extent often assumed for MT Samuel? Plainly, where the relationship of the MT and LXX is concerned, any attempt to answer this question statistically is bound to involve an unacceptable number of value judgments. On the other hand, some statistics, for what they are worth, can be produced for another ancient version of an Old Testament book. Thanks to the remarkably detailed introduction accompanying the Leiden edition of the Peshitta of 1-2 Kings it is possible to compile statistics in relation to mechanical omissions in the Syriac version of these books.[38] Two manuscripts stand out as being more haplographic in tendency than the others, viz. 9a1 (and dependants), which has twenty-seven omissions by haplography in the forty-seven chapters of Kings, and Ms 17a10 which has fifty-six such omissions. It is noticeable, on the other hand, that omissions of twenty words approximately, as would compare with some of the alleged haplographies in MT Samuel, are rare indeed in any of the manuscripts collated for the Peshitta of Kings. Furthermore, no manuscript has lengthy omissions in adjacent verses in the manner of 1 Sam 14:41-42.

HAPLOGRAPHY IN 1 AND 2 SAMUEL 153

The evidence of the foregoing study would suggest that there may be a slight amount of evidence for Pisano's thesis. As it happens, one of the stronger examples that could have served his purpose - 2 Sam 15:19-20 - is discussed without reference to haplogeny in the first part of his book (pp. 136-37). Here the addition is in the *kaige* (LXX^B) text, and its potentially haplogenic significance becomes all the clearer when it is compared with OG (LXX^{Ant}). To be sure, the situation overall becomes more complicated once we begin to consider the contribution of Trebolle Barrera, nevertheless some initial comment on how his findings relate to those of Pisano will be appropriate.

Trebolle Barrera's first major foray into Samuel - excepting an earlier article on an aspect of the account of Absalom's rebellion - comes in his 1989 volume in which forty-seven of the hundred passages from Samuel-Kings briefly reviewed come from 1 and 2 Samuel.[39] Only three of the fifteen references which feature in Pisano's list of probable cases of haplogenic addition in the LXX are discussed by Trebolle Barrera, but they will suffice to show the great differences between these two scholars despite their shared interest in *Wiederaufnahme* as a (compositional and) editorial technique within the biblical textual tradition. The passages in question are 1 Sam 1:24; 3:15 and 29:10. It should be noted that although Trebolle Barrera refers to Pisano's monograph a dozen times, this is mainly in the form of footnote references to relevant page numbers in Pisano. In no sense could he be said to interact with Pisano.

The situation at 1 Sam 1:24 is nothing if not complex, and here Trebolle Barrera (pp. 46-48) pays particular attention to the repetitions that are a feature of this verse, and of the one that follows, when the evidence of the MT, 4QSam^a and LXX is combined. Even so, his judgment as regards the "tautologous" והנער נער of the MT is that something comparable to what is in 4QSam^a and LXX has been lost at this point. Creative interpolation in a short, primitive text of the MT-type is not envisaged.

At 1 Sam 3:15 the LXX has, in Trebolle Barrera's opinion (p. 48), double readings based on the graphically similar verbs שכב and שכם: "And Samuel lay until the morning" and "And Samuel awoke early in the morning." Pisano, as we saw earlier, regards the LXX plus as a filling out of the elliptical reading of the MT, "And Samuel lay until the morning and opened the doors ...," so again these two scholars see things differently. Either could be right, but Pisano may call on the support of the Qumran fragment *4Q160* ("The Vision of Samuel") where, in what is obviously a free rendering of our verse, the verb ויקם ("and he rose") is supplied, no doubt to ease the slightly awkward transition presented by the MT.[40]

A further difference between Pisano and Trebolle Barrera is apparent at 1 Sam 29:10 where the latter (pp. 83-85), for all that he regards the Greek plus as secondary to the narrative, appears to think that it was once present in the MT and was lost by haplography. This being so, the second imperative in the MT ("and you shall rise early in the morning") is seen not as a synonymous/repetitive reading (so Pisano) but as a resumptive repetition coming after the interpolated material which still survives in the LXX. Trebolle Barrera, moreover, regards the references to the appointed place, by which is meant Ziklag, in LXX verse 10 *and* in MT/LXX verse 4 earlier in the chapter as secondary elements intended to bind ch. 29 in with chs 27 and 30 as also relating, in part, to David's "Ziklag phase."

To all this there can be but one conclusion, namely that much checking of worked examples and governing methods will be necessary before the true worth of *Wiederaufnahme* as a basis for text-critical judgments concerning the Hebrew and Greek Bible traditions can be determined.

NOTES

1. *The Composition of Judges II 11 to 1 Kings II 46* (Leipzig: J.C. Hinrichs, 1929) 2.

2. M. Anbar, "La 'Reprise,'" *VT* 38 (1988) 385.

3. *The Composition*, 2.

4. "Die ‹Wiederaufnahme› - ein literarkritisches Prinzip?" *ZAW* NF 23 (1952) 1-11.

5. See *TLZ* 54 (1929) cols. 345-47.

6. *Die drei Männer im Feuer. Daniel Kapitel 3 und seine Zusätze* (BZAW 55; Giessen: A. Töpelmann, 1930) 163.

7. "Hebräische Erzählung und biblische Geschichtsschreibung," *TZ* 18 (1962) 314-24.

8. art. "Ezra," *IDBSup* 322.

9. S. Talmon and M. Fishbane, "The Structuring of Biblical Books. Studies in the Book of Ezekiel," *ASTI* 10 (1975-76) 129-53 (144-46).

10. "The Presentation of Synchroneity and Simultaneity in Biblical Narrative," *Scripta Hierosolymitana* 27 (1978) 9-26, esp. 12-17; cf. A. Berlin, *Poetics and Interpretation of Biblical Narrative* (Sheffield: Almond, 1983) 126-28; B.O. Long, "Framing Repetitions in Biblical Historiography," *JBL* 106 (1987) 385-99.

11. J. Trebolle Barrera, "Testamento y muerte de David. Estudio de historia de la Recensión y Redacción de I Rey., II," *RB* 87 (1980) 87-103 (87-98); "Redaction, Recension, and Midrash in the Books of Kings," *BIOSCS* 15 (1982) 12-35; "Recensión y redacción de 2 Re 17,7-23 (TM LXX^B/ LXX^L VL)," *Simposio Biblico Español (Salamanca, 1982)* (ed N. Fernández Marcos, J. Trebolle Barrera, J. Fernández Vallina; Madrid: Universidad Complutense, 1984); *Jehú y Joás. Texto y composición literaria de 2 Reyes 9-11* (Institución San Jerónimo 17; Valencia: Institución San Jerónimo 1984); *Centena in Libros Samuelis et Regum: Variantes Textuales y composición literaria en los libros de Samuel y Reyes* (Textos y Estudios "Cardenal Cisneros" de la Biblia Políglota Matritense 47; Madrid: CSIC, 1989); "Textual Variants in $4QJudg^a$ and the Textual and Editorial History of the Book of Judges," *RevQ* 14 (1989-90) 229-45.

12. *Critique textuelle de l'Ancien Testament. 1. Josué ... Esther* (ed. D. Barthélemy; OBO 50/1; Fribourg/Göttingen: Éditions Universitaires/ Vandenhoeck & Ruprecht, 1982).

13. *Critique*, 143.

14. *Critique*, 163.

15. *Additions or Omissions in the Books of Samuel. The Significant Pluses and Minuses in the Massoretic, LXX and Qumran Texts* (OBO 57; Freiburg/Göttingen: Universitätsverlag/Vandenhoeck & Ruprecht, 1984).

16. F.H. Woods, "The Light Thrown by the Septuagint Version on the Books of Samuel," *Studia Biblica. Essays in Biblical Archaeology and Criticism* (ed. S.R. Driver, W. Sanday, J.

Wordsworth; Oxford: Clarendon, 1885) 21-38.

17. Pisano's statement (p. 155) that "the repetition of πρὸς Ἰωάβ in cod B surrounds the second translation" is at odds with his view that "the Greek was corrected according to MT only as far as אל־יואב" (p. 127).

18. Cf. the writer's comment in his short review of Pisano in *VT* 37 (1987) 384.

19. Cf. P.K. McCarter, *1 Samuel* (AB 8; Garden City: Doubleday, 1980) 369.

20. *1 Samuel*, 426.

21. *Critique*, 163.

22. Cf. McCarter, *1 Samuel*, 171.

23. Cf. McCarter's retroversion, *1 Samuel*, 190.

24. On this verse see further *Critique*, 165.

25. Cf. Pisano, *Additions*, 241.

26. Cf. Pisano, *Additions*, 231.

27. *Critique*, 179.

28. "A Textual Note on 1 Samuel XIV 41," *VT* 19 (1969) 493-98 (497).

29. Cf. Pisano, *Additions*, 249-57 (256-57).

30. G.J. Brooke, *Exegesis at Qumran. 4QFlorilegium in its Jewish Context* (JSOTSup 29; Sheffield: JSOT Press, 1985) 111-16.

31. There are seven forms ending in ־כה within vv. 11b-12.

32. See above, sect. 2.ii.

33. *ZAW* NF 23 (1952) 11.

34. "Stilkritik und Literaranalyse im vierten Evangelium," *ZNW* 43 (1950-1) 128-43 (133).

35. "A Neglected Method in Ezekiel Research," *VT* 29 (1979) 42-44.

36. A. Brinkmann, "Ein Schreibgebrauch und seine Bedeutung für die Textkritik," *Rheinisches Museum für Philologie* NF 57 (1902) 481-97; cf. H. Herter, "Zur Lebensgeschichte des Apollonios von Rhodos," *ibid.*, NF 91 (1942) 316-17; M. Gronewald, "Platonkonjekturen nach der 'Brinkmannschen Regel,'" *ibid.*, NF 119 (1976) 11-13.

37. N. Fernández Marcos notes that he has not

found "the use of apparent homoioteleuta to insert secondary additions to the narrative" among Antiochene expansionist techniques: "Literary and Editorial Features of the Antiochian Text in Kings," *VI Congress of the International Organization for Septuagint and Cognate Studies, Jerusalem 1986* (ed. C.E. Cox; SBLSCS 23; Atlanta: Scholars Press, 1987) 294.

38. *The Old Testament in Syriac According to the Peshiṭta Version*, II,4: *Kings* (prepared by H. Gottlieb and E. Hammershaimb; Leiden: E.J. Brill, 1976) LXXVII-LXXXI.

39. See note 11 above.

40. See DJD V (Oxford: Clarendon, 1968) 9.

THE QUMRAN FRAGMENTS OF JOSHUA: WHICH PUZZLE ARE THEY PART OF AND WHERE DO THEY FIT?

LEONARD GREENSPOON

The fragments of the book of Joshua found at Qumran have not yet been published. In spite (or, one might more cynically suggest, because) of this fact, these relatively sparse remains have been cited as supportive or at least collaborative evidence for several diverse, even contradictory, opinions on the question of textual affiliation.

In the first and still best known statement on this matter Frank Cross declared: "The *historical books* are represented by two MSS of *Joshua*, both of which follow the tradition of the *Vorlage* of the Greek text."[1] In this form,[2] Cross's evaluation entered into the mainstream of scholarship, as can be seen from J. Alberto Soggin's popular commentary on Joshua: "The text of LXX^B can be found in Hebrew in two manuscripts from Qumran."[3] Cross's judgment can also be detected in the unfortunately garbled account reported in Martin Woudstra's Joshua commentary: "Among the discoveries at Qumran are two manuscripts of the

Vaticanus."[4] From such murky channels we can return to the clear-flowing waters of the mainstream by noting that as recently as 1988 Carol Newsom cited Cross's opinion as authoritative.[5]

In fact, Cross is incorrect in his stress on the DSS-LXX link for the book of Joshua. In making this statement, I do not intend to enter into a discussion or criticism of Cross's view of textual affiliation as opposed to that of Emanuel Tov, Shemaryahu Talmon, or others. Rather, I mean that, based on the largely quantitative approach favored by Cross,[6] the Joshua fragments are far closer to the Masoretic Tradition than they are to that which underlies the Old Greek (OG) translation. As a graduate student of Frank Cross in the mid-70s I was given access to this material. I reported my findings at a southeastern regional meeting of the Society of Biblical Literature in 1978, and they subsequently entered into the "public domain" through their inclusion by Robert Boling in the introduction to his Anchor Bible commentary on Joshua which was published in 1982.[7] On the basis of material provided by me, Boling writes (p. 110): "Greenspoon's study of the fragments leads him to the conclusion that the 4Q Joshua manuscripts are in the same tradition of the full, expansionistic text as Joshua in the MT, the type which Cross labels Palestinian. This clearly suggests relationships very different from those seen, for example, in Samuel fragments from Qumran which display a Hebrew text much more closely related to the *Vorlage* of the Old Greek translation."

Although Boling does not report any individual readings from the Scrolls, he does use one of my reconstructions, based in part on the Qumran text, in the eclectic version he translates at 7:13.[8] I must admit to a heady feeling upon being identified - along with the likes of Moses, to say nothing of J and E - as an "author" of the Hebrew Bible!

In his masterful summary and analysis of Scrolls research through the mid-1980s, Tov notes that 4QJosh^{a,b} are among numerous Scrolls not written in Qumran orthography, and he concludes that 4QJosh^a (at least), along with other Qumran material, belongs in the category of "sources *additional* to those known before."[9] Such a designation is supportive of his overall view of textual history.[10] Tov does not cite any specific readings from 4QJosh in this article or in his earlier discussions of Joshua.[11]

Thus it is that these fragments have been judged as closely linked to the LXX, to the MT, and as forming an essentially independent witness. The first-listed option is, in my opinion, no longer viable. Although Cross has not formally, or at least publicly, abandoned it, in private correspondence he has indicated a marked change in the direction of his thinking on this issue.[12] Nonetheless, we cannot altogether exclude the possibility that some qualitatively important (that is, generally speaking, secondary) readings are indeed shared by the LXX and 4QJoshua.[13]

Before proceeding to the Joshua fragments themselves, I wish to say something about my own approach to such material. I tend to avoid

theoretical constructs, at least in the initial
stages of inquiry, preferring to listen as the
"material speaks for itself." I attempt to figure
out, in concrete terms, what ancient scribes or
translators did, what this tells us about their
apparent goals, and how and why they proceeded in
one direction (or several related directions)
rather than in others.[14] Where possible, I draw
parallels from the modern world. Thus, in a
recent article, I sought to illuminate the otherwise unknown (and unknowable?) motivations of the
ancient reviser Theodotion on the basis of a
comparison with the 20th century translator/
reviser Max L. Margolis.[15] In like manner, I want
to uncover or recover as fully as possible the
modus operandi of the scribe(s) responsible for
the manuscript(s) of Joshua that I am studying.[16]

In so doing, I make it a practice to avoid
value judgments, even those of the type still
common in textual criticism today. For example,
the New Testament critic Elden Epp adjures us to
distinguish carefully between garden variety
readings and *significant* readings. In Epp's
opinion only the latter merit the lofty designation "variant."[17] In practice, such precision may
be not only desirable, but even necessary, when
dealing with a massive amount of material. For
briefer remains, on the other hand, the more
comprehensive the approach, the better. Given the
fragmentary nature of most Qumran scrolls, no
purpose is served by the initial elimination of
any group of readings from further scrutiny.

It is also regular text critical practice to
delineate readings in terms of their alleged

"superiority" or "inferiority." The problem with these designations is that, left un- or badly defined, such terms are susceptible to any number of possible meanings. Generally, they represent modern value judgments based on closeness to or distance from a hypothetical "original." Considerations of this sort were probably far from the mind of any ancient scribe.

I prefer to focus my attention on the individual scribe in the belief that he chose (if indeed he had a choice) to incorporate into his text what he considered to be the best available reading for every passage, given the conditions and contexts in which he worked. It may well be that such wording is neither "original" nor even "suitable" in our opinion, but such judgments should not be allowed to color our thinking when trying to understand an ancient figure whose perceptions of suitability may have been quite different from our own. Even today, many well-educated, sane people prefer to "walk through the valley of death" rather than tread upon some more correct, but less familiar terrain (as most modern translations would have us do). A neutral stance should not, however, blind us to the fact that some scribes (or translators, for that matter) are more competent than others and that all scribes (or, again, translators) are more or less careful at given moments in the tedious process of preparing or producing a text.

Having considered these preliminary matters, I return to the book of Joshua at Qumran. In the mid 1950s Frank Cross made an initial determination that the extant fragments of Joshua originally formed part of two separate manuscripts: the fragments from 4QJosh^a cover chapters 6, 7, 8, perhaps also 9 (if the scribe of this manuscript placed the Ebal-Gerizim incident in its OG position [see below]), and 10. The 4QJosh^b fragments consist of material from chapters 2, 3, 4, and 17.

When I first worked on these fragments and my eyes (and mind) were sharper than at present, it seemed to me that both scrolls could be dated paleographically to c. 100 BCE.[18] In discussing the nature of their text, Cross had spoken of both as sharing a common textual affiliation.[19] My analysis also led me to consider all of the extant Joshua material in common. Consequently, in the present paper, I move freely between fragments of both scrolls.[20]

In my own analysis of these fragments, I am struck by two phenomena, one of which is pervasive, the other sporadic but nonetheless significant. First, this (or, these) scribe(s) had no knowledge of the distinctive features of the LXX tradition for the book of Joshua. To put it another way, there are no qualitatively important readings definitely shared by the LXX and 4QJoshua. As noted by Tov,[21] agreement is more significant when it involves secondary rather than original readings.[22]

The MT of Joshua is rather full and expansionistic, of the type Cross was wont to designate Palestinian.[23] Tov reckons that the OG of Joshua is shorter than the MT by only about 5%.[24] However, in several key chapters (e.g., 6 and 8), the percentage is notably higher and elsewhere it *seems* to be so even if it is not. Fullness and expansion are also the predominant characteristics of the 4QJoshua fragments. It is, therefore, tempting simply to locate the Qumran material in the same tradition as the MT. This would explain their many shared secondary expansions and also, in my opinion, independent additions on the part of the Qumran scribe.[25]

At this point, it is necessary to bring in the other phenomenon referred to above: equally worthy of note, if not equal in number, are 4QJoshua readings that retain the original, un-expanded text either in common with the LXX or, of even greater interest, uniquely preserved at Qumran. These readings point to our scribe's access to a source or resource outside the tradition that we associate with the MT of Joshua. These are among the questions and issues I address as we proceed. Although I include several transcriptions along with this paper, I do not attempt to reproduce or discuss every reading.[26]

At Josh 2:11-12 only five words are visible on the leather of 4QJosh[b]: קמה עוד רוח באיש (in the middle of v 11) and השבעו (at the beginning of v 12). For these words, there are no variations between the MT and the OG. In the gap off the leather, I reconstruct an haplography of 15 or 16 characters, to obtain a line approximately 41 characters in length.[27] Since accidental omissions are common and particularly so when, as here, homoioteleuton is the likely culprit ([מפניכם] כי יהוה אלהיכם), the length of the material dropped may be of no significance. However, I have noticed several other similar instances,[28] suggesting the possibility that the Qumran scribe was working at least part of the time from an exemplar that contained relatively short lines, fewer than 20 characters in length.[29]

The fragments covering 3:15-17 offer more substantial evidence for the textual affiliations of 4QJosh (at least of 4QJosh[b]). The unadorned "ark" (הארון) of the first line I have transcribed (see the first transcription in the Appendix at the end of this paper) is identical to the MT and original in this context. A secondary expansion reflective of ברית יהוה developed in the Greek tradition. As Tov correctly emphasizes, common retentions of original readings do not have the same qualitative significance as shared expansions or other secondary elements.[30] Repeated instances of such retentions, however, do have a quantitative, and (I would argue) ultimately a qualitative, force.

This fragment also contains the only intralinear placement that I have detected in the Joshua fragments at Qumran. The scribe wrote כימי קציר alone, which is, I think, the original reading here (uniquely preserved in 4QJosh).[31] Expansion in the MT took the direction of כל ימי (קציר; the OG has (ὡσεὶ ἡμέραι θερισμοῦ) πυρῶν = חטים. That word appears between the lines in 4QJoshua and also in the text of one of the psalms of Joshua (4Q379).[32] We cannot be certain that this addition in 4QJosh represents an intentional correction. If this word was introduced onto the leather by someone other than the original scribe,[33] then it is likely that it was not known to that scribe on the basis of whatever resources he had available to him.³⁴ So, we may suggest, at this point (at least), he was unfamiliar with a reading that came to be part of the LXX tradition, but he was familiar with, and uniquely passed on, the original wording of this phrase.³⁵

Only a few letters are preserved on the leather for the first verses of chapter 4. Even combined, their testimony is elusive. With respect to one word, מזה at v 3, 4Q and OG unite in omitting this secondary reading found in the MT. For the rest, it is clear that the text of 4Q is not as lengthy as the MT and may approximate the likely *Vorlage* of the OG. One phrase not found in the LXX, but present in the MT, was almost certainly absent as well from 4Q: ממצב רגלי הכהנים. This omission contains about 16 characters and again suggests an exemplar in which relatively short lines were occasionally overlooked by the 4Q scribe. At best, the evidence is here inconclusive.³⁶

At least 6 verses of Chapter 6 are represented by a half dozen or so fragments that have been fitted together to present a fairly clear picture of 4Q-MT affinities (see transcription number 2). As is well known, this chapter is not easy in any version and even more difficult when traditions are compared. Nonetheless, it is clear that the MT does present a text at least occasionally expanded beyond the original and beyond the *Vorlage* of the OG.³⁷ At verses 6, 7, 8 and 9 (and probably also in v 10, where there is ample room for the additional MT wording ולא יצא מפיכם דבר) 4Q shares some of this expansion with the MT. In verses 5 (without כל before העם [on the leather] or עירה [conj]) and 9 (after ברית [so also 3:15

above]), 4Q along with MT lacks distinctive OG expansions. 4QJosh also exhibits two unique readings in chapter 6 (v 5: רעלה; v 7: [ויאמר] יהושע). It is equally attractive to posit the scribe's knowledge of a text within the MT tradition at these points also.

The evidence for chapter 7 is more complex. However, without forcing this evidence to suit my own purposes, I am convinced that we are drawn to a similar conclusion with respect to textual affiliation. The very first legible phrase (see transcription number 3), at 7:12, is a unique Qumran reading: ולא פנים. In context, this expansion is both appropriate and a rather clever word play, given the fact that the פנה-root appears three times earlier in the same verse (twice as preposition, once as verb). I suggest that the scribe himself is the "source" of this addition, partly because its length is considerably shorter than that hypothesized for his exemplar. More to the point, a scribe accustomed to an expansionist text might well, sooner or later, try his own hand at it. Of course, it is not clear that a given scribe would be conscious of the fullness of a text he was copying (what, for example, would be his basis for comparison?), but it is possible that his exemplar was constructed in such a way that its expansionistic character was apparent to the scribe.[38]

At 7:13 there are as many distinctive 4Q-LXX agreements (plural suffixes on בקרבכם and אויביכם, vs. singular in MT) as there are shared 4Q-MT readings (singular תוכל, vs. plural in LXX and the probable addition of the word ישראל). As I

reconstruct the textual history of this verse,³⁰
the plural forms are original. The subsequent
introduction of the word "Israel" triggered a
shift from plural to singular forms in verbs and
suffixes alike. This shift was carried out, to
varying degrees, in 4Q and in MT. Seen in this
light, the two agreements with the LXX are less
significant (being original) than the secondary
readings (one probable and one definite) shared
with MT.

At 7:14 4Q has suffered another haplography at
the first occurrence of a repetitive phrase
containing אשר ילכדנה יהוה and a form of the verb
קרב. No significant difference divides MT from
the presumed *Vorlage* of the LXX at this point, but
it may be worthy of note that the missing clause
could fit on two lines of about 15/16 characters
each.

Later in v 14, 4Q again splits its allegiance
between the LXX (תקריבו) and the MT (יקרב). In my
opinion, both are retentions of an original
variation in verb forms. Finally, at 7:15, we
observe the graphic (and aural) similarity between
the unique 4Q reading בהם and the equally
secondary MT בחרם; the LXX is pristine and
original at this point.

A half dozen fragments contain portions of vv
3-19 of chapter 8 (see transcriptions numbers 4
and 5), another episode exhibiting extensive
differences between LXX and MT - with the latter
frequently fuller and expansive. For the text
covering vv 3-5, the pattern already discerned
continues: two possible agreements between 4Q and
MT with respect to single-word additions (ראו and

מאד [both in v 4]) and one probable agreement with respect to a short, original text in the face of a fuller LXX: 4Q, MT: כי יצאו לקראתני; LXX adds the explicit ישבי העי.⁴⁰ The situation in v 4 also recalls 7:15: LXX exhibits a short text, while the brief additions in MT (לעיר) and 4Q (אל העיר) strongly suggest mutual interdependence at some stage.

Readings gleaned from the next three verses offer further support, but it is not clearcut. For vv 7 and 8, the reconstructed 4Q text approximates to the fuller MT. But two *caveats* are in order: (1) 4Q and MT are not, in their present forms, identical, although an hypothesized haplography in 4Q at v 8 (תציתו את העיר) would line them up quite closely. (2) It is not easy to determine the OG here, that is, to sort out original wording from inner-Greek developments.⁴¹

For 8:7-9, then, the meaningful reconstruction is difficult, but within the realm of possibility, even probability.⁴² What are we to say for what follows? Four lines of the scroll are constrained to contain five verses of material (MT 8:10-14), with very few letters extant on the leather. There is no reasonable reconstruction that allows us to suggest that this scribe squeezed a text as long as that represented in the MT into a space thus constricted.

On the back of the photograph of the two fragments that contain these verses, Cross wrote: "8:10-18, cf. short LXX text." Do these fragments, unlike others we have looked at, reflect the "short LXX text" of Joshua? The first reading visible on the leather is promising in this regard: זקנים, with the LXX, against MT (זקני ישראל) for v 10. Equally enticing is the sole reading on the fourth line: לקראהם (MT: לקראת ישראל) at the end of v 14. However, the shorter 4Q-LXX is in both cases original. Three words appear on the second line: עלו אתו וישרבו. The first two seem to be a reversal of order in a reading common to the MT and OG at v 11. The next word is not found here in either the MT or the probable *Vorlage* of the OG; it may be a variant of the verb (ויגשו) that they both apparently share. If this is so, a very short line, of only 34 characters, connects זקנים of v 10 with these words in v 11.

The opposite dilemma - too many words for too little space - confronts us in the next line, which ends with the word כראות, found at the beginning of v 14 in both the MT and the OG. We readily concede that the concept of "too many words" is dependent on the MT of these verses, for it is certainly possible to fit an LXX-type text into the space. But we are not sure what cause or combination of causes led to the less full LXX at this point.[43]

In point of fact, we are unable to reconstruct anything with confidence here.[44] For the rest of v 14, it does seem that 4Q contains the longer wording of the MT, or else it is impossible to know how to fill the gap from כראות at the beginning of v 14 to לקראהם at the end.[45]

The last line of these fragments contains the words בידך אל העי, written in a different hand, most likely by a different scribe. This may represent a note originally attached to v 18 and

serving as a correction of העיר (so LXX) to עיר
(=MT) there. Such an interpretation reverses the
pattern of "correction" found at 3:15 and is at
variance with the pattern operative elsewhere as
well. However, we cannot be sure how this phrase
initially functioned, nor can we overlook the
frequency with which the variant forms have been
independently generated when עיר and עי appear in
the same context.[46]

It is difficult to determine the original
wording of 8:18 and thus to assess the
significance of a possible 4Q-LXX agreement at
that point. At 8:35, on the other hand, 4Q-LXX
agreement is certain: they both add את יהושע
after צוה משה. Moreover, this is just the sort of
secondary reading that is particularly important
for determining textual affiliation (and that
links 4Q and MT elsewhere in these fragments).
Without ignoring this piece of "negative"
evidence, I think it is only fair to point out how
easily this addition could arise independently,
especially in the book of Joshua. It is this
latter factor of (probable?) independent
development that characterizes the definite 4Q-LXX
agreement at 8:35 [9:2] and the possible common
text at 8:18.[47] Independent generation is not, in
my opinion, a viable explanation for most of the
4Q-MT secondary agreements we note elsewhere in
the scrolls. Therein lies the difference.[48]

This section of the scroll also offers several
more routine 4Q-MT agreements: the presence of
[בספר] התורה at the end of 8:34 (where OG [9:2]
has ἐν τῷ νόμῳ Μωυσῆ [presumably = בתורת משה] [cf.
MT 8:31 and OG 9:2]), the absence of האנשים in MT

and (probably) 4Q at v 35,⁴⁹ and the 4Q-MT agreement (בקרבם) at what is the close of v 35 in the MT (cf. OG: τῷ Ισραηλ = בקרב ישראל [so Margolis, Book of Joshua, 150]).

These shared readings, as interesting as they are, seem pedestrian in comparison with the two unique additions - one of a few words, and one of a few lines - that 4Q contains here. The first occurs in v 35 where MT has נגד כל קהל ישראל, and OG εἰς τὰ ὦτα πάσης ἐκκλησίας υἱῶν Ισραηλ. I suggest the reconstruction of something like נגד כל]קהל אשר עברו[את הירד]ין[, which connects this episode with the crossing of the Jordan River in chapters 3-5. I have not been able to identify the source of the longer addition at the close of this section.⁵⁰

In speaking of these verses primarily as 8:34-35, I have, perhaps subconsciously, situated them in their MT position. As is well known, the episode at Ebal and Gerizim is narrated later, after the first two verses of chapter 9, in the LXX.⁵¹ So far as I can tell, on the basis of this fragment, it is not possible to determine where the scribe located these verses.

Finally, we turn to chapter 10 (see transcriptions numbers 6 and 7). Again, approximately a half dozen fragments have been joined to cover a number of verses: here vv 3-11. In the first group of verses (3-5) there are at least three potentially significant agreements between 4Q and MT: אדני צדק, where the OG has אדני בזק;⁵² השלימה in the singular (which is original), where the OG in the plural reveals the influence of the same form from v 1; and, of more importance, both

ויאספו and ויעלו at the beginning of v 5, where the OG reflects only the second item of this doublet. The lack of בני before ישראל at v 4, unique to 4Q, may be original, but (as is often the case with the phrase) this cannot be determined with certainty.

The next three fragments (not transcribed here) cover 10:8-10. Three or perhaps four times in these verses 4Q and MT agree against the OG (two singular suffixes [OG plural], one instance of word order, once without בני in the common phrase לפני [בני] ישראל [where the LXX has this word][53]).

The last word of 10:10 and then 10:11 are found next in sequence. There are several places where readings held in common by 4Q and MT might present contrasts with the OG. But certainly the most interesting reading here is in 10:11 (see transcription number 7), where 4Q's unmodified אבנים uniquely preserves the original wording. OG's "hail" is easily supplied from the context, and the MT's description of the stones as "large" is in keeping with the nature of the divine: He wouldn't bother throwing down a bunch of pebbles, would He?

In his unpublished work on 4QJosh[b], Tov also provides an analysis of fragments covering a number of verses in chapter 17. It is his judgment that 4Q-MT agreements, against the OG, are especially prominent in these fragments.

In the preceding paragraphs, I have sought to present a fair and full appraisal of how I evaluate the remains of the book of Joshua found at Qumran. There are five points to note.
(1) This material shows a wide acquaintance with

distinctive readings preserved in the MT, usually in the direction of full texts judged to be secondary expansions. (2) The scribe(s) responsible for these scrolls were not reluctant to incorporate material of their own creation, material I judge to be "in the spirit" of the MT. (3) In at least two cases and perhaps another one or two, 4QJoshua material uniquely preserves the original text, and in several other places the fragments transmit original readings not preserved in the MT. (4) Where original readings are not unique to 4Q, they are shared with the LXX; however, in the absence of any (many?) 4Q-LXX agreements in the more significant area of secondary readings, it is not necessary to posit any acquaintance on the part of these scribes with the distinctive features of the LXX tradition. (5) In addition, I suggested in a tentative fashion that the exemplar of both of these manuscripts was written in relatively short lines, 15-16 characters in length.

In what direction do these data point? No simple answer suggests itself. In order to do full justice to the complexity of the issues involved, it would be necessary to enter into an extended discussion of the literary history of the book of Joshua, something that Emanuel Tov, A. Graeme Auld, Alexander Rofé, and others have assayed with considerably more elegance than I could.[54]

At this point, perhaps, a few general comments may suffice. There is no question that the MT of Joshua is longer, fuller, more extensively elaborated than the LXX of the same book.[55] Is this difference in length due primarily to the Old Greek translator's Hebrew *Vorlage* or to his manipulation, generally in the direction of curtailment, of a Hebrew text essentially equivalent to the MT? As is fairly well known, the latter judgment was that of Max L. Margolis.[56] On this point, however, he was wrong. Already in 1914 Samuel Holmes had argued that the Old Greek translator prepared a generally faithful, if not literal, rendering of the Hebrew text that lay before him.[57] For the modern period, Harry M. Orlinsky first pointed out the flaws in Margolis' understanding of how the Old Greek translator operated.[58] The correctness of the position taken by Holmes and Orlinsky has been subsequently confirmed by Tov, Auld, and myself, among others.[59]

There is, in short, no question that the isolation and determination of Old Greek readings in Joshua brings us, to some degree, into contact with its Hebrew *Vorlage*. The precise proximity of this contact is a matter of some disagreement. It is Tov's judgment that "this translation contains many examples of very free exegesis in both small and large details, but at the same time it reflects faithfully many details of its *Vorlage*, *inter alia* many significant Hebrew variants."[60] I tend to limit the scope of what Tov terms "free exegesis" and find myself in general agreement with Tov's later characterization of the Old Greek translation as "relatively free to relatively literal."[61] I also feel that there is considerable validity to Fernandez Marcos' overall judgment that, in many blocks of material, the OG accurately reflects its Hebrew *Vorlage* at the level of "major deviations," less so in the matter of individual words and phrases.⁶²

Be that as it may, there can be no doubt (1) that a Greek tradition for the book of Joshua is recoverable, (2) that this tradition was less full than the developed MT, but that (3) it also contained a number of distinctive features, including material additional vis-à-vis the MT.⁶³ As mentioned several times above, I do not detect any sure signs of this tradition in secure or probable 4Q readings.

It should be added, at the risk of redundancy, that the determination of original versus secondary readings cannot be made on anything other than an individual basis. Even after we have recovered the shorter OG of a passage and are convinced that it accurately, though not necessarily literally, reflects its *Vorlage*, we have not completed, but only begun, the comparative, sometimes intuitive, process of sorting out secondary development from original text. In this paper, I have alluded more than once to my own judgment on specific instances, but (in the nature of the text critical enterprise) I am far from convinced that I am correct each time.

We have portrayed the scribes responsible for 4QJoshua as working largely within an MT "context." That this kind of text - shall we call it proto-MT? - was in existence around 100 BCE is hardly surprising. We are, of course, free to jettison Cross' designation of this type of text as Palestinian, for we cannot be certain that the scribes of these manuscripts worked in Palestine at Qumran or anywhere else.[64] But is it not likely that they did?

For me at least, it is tempting to envision two groups of near-contemporaries having access to proto-MT Hebrew manuscripts: a pair of scribes, on the one hand; one or two more translators/revisers, on the other. For the latter, I have in mind the unknown individual(s) responsible for the *kaige*-Theodotionic version of Joshua, preserved in Origen's sixth column and elsewhere. The Hebrew text to which this individual's (Old) Greek text was revised is remarkably similar to the developed MT. This (these) individual(s) may have worked only a few decades later or maybe even at the same time as the scribes responsible for the Joshua scrolls found at Qumran. I suspect that *kaige*-Theodotion is (also) to be located in Palestine.[65]

But differences soon intrude. To an extent, they entail certain natural, even necessary, contrasts between scribe and translator.[66] However, it is another sort of contrast that I wish to make at this point: I believe I can reconstruct what the translator was doing, how he did it, and perhaps even why; for the "Qumran" scribe, I have nothing beyond very tentative suggestions to offer. With respect to *kaige*-Th it is, I think, fairly straightforward. He had before him a form of the Old Greek of Joshua, which he proceeded to revise to a proto-MT form of Hebrew.[67] In the process, he retained as much as possible of the Greek that lay before him, even when he was compelled to correct that text. The mindset of such a reviser is conservative, even reverential, with respect to his base text, but at

the same time he cannot avoid dealing with its
obvious inadequacies vis-à-vis the foreign language text to which he is revising. Considerations
of community and audience vie for his attention
with these concerns for text. A difficult
balancing act, no doubt, in antiquity as well as
in the modern world. Theodotion I judge to have
been remarkably successful in this entire
enterprise.[68]

For the scribe(s) whose work ended up at
Qumran, even if it did not originate there, the
reconstruction of activities is anything but
straightforward.[69] But we should not be deterred
from attempting to understand the scribal process.
as outlined above, I consider it likely that this
scribe made use of an evolving (that is,
expanding) form of the tradition eventually
designated MT. From the sources or resources at
his command he may well have derived a sense that
expansion was not simply possible, but even
desirable. How would one arrive at such a
judgment? After all, the MT of Joshua would not
strike even a careful reader as particularly full
or expansionistic, unless that reader had some
basis, biblical or extra-biblical, for comparison.

One possibility is that the manuscript used by
the scribe (let us hypothesize he used only one
written source or manuscript) was one into which
numerous marginal and intralinear notations had
been introduced. Essentially, then, his "copy"
would have consisted of a relatively primitive,
original text of Joshua, which had been
extensively "marked up" either by our scribe
and/or by others.[70] In this way, we could explain

the presence of both original readings and of so many secondary expansions in the Qumran manuscripts. The material thus introduced reflected a fairly advanced stage in the development of the MT, and additionally it stimulated our scribe to undertake expansions of and on his own.

Analogies for this type activity can be amply documented, as Max L. Margolis demonstrated in a speech of his that I annotated and published under the title, "Ars Scribendi: Max Margolis' Paper 'Preparing Scribe's Copy in the Age of Manuscripts.'"[71] In this address Margolis shows that the editor responsible for the Joshua portion of the Complutensian Polyglot handed the typesetter a thoroughly worked-over manuscript (B-McL: *b*). Only this explanation accounts for the otherwise bewildering assortment of readings displayed in the great Polyglot.[72] In the same paper Margolis cited another parade example of this phenomenon: editors of the Sixtine edition of the Greek Old Testament, which was based on Vaticanus, gave their typesetters a marked-up copy of the already published Aldine print. Some distinctive Aldine readings remained uncorrected, however, and these crept into the Sixtine edition.[73]

Margolis also referred, although without much comment, to another type of analogy, which is perhaps even closer to what I envision. In his analysis of the Greek manuscripts of Joshua, he was led to go beyond the *trifaria varietas* of Jerome and to propose a fourth, Constantinopolitan, family. Its dependence on Origen's

Hexapla is, in Margolis' view, obvious, but equally obvious is its access to a source that retained proper names in their earlier, perhaps original form. Thus, although secondary readings predominate, an earlier stratum does shine through.[74]

I do not know if I have correctly discerned the nature and substance of what "crept" into or "shines" forth from the 4QJoshua fragments. Nor do I know how this scribe's work was received when it was presented to its original or subsequent audiences. As an object of study and analysis, it may be judged - in antiquity as in the modern world - by one set of standards. Another series of criteria, only partially recoverable for us, was used by the community for whom this version of the words and deeds of Joshua became Sacred Writ. And, I cannot help thinking, there were some in that community who would be pleased that a portion, albeit a small portion, of *their* text survived. I share their pleasure.

Additional Note:

Emanuel Tov has offered us not only an alternative to Cross' Theory of Local Texts, but also at least a partial description and evaluation of the context in which Cross formulated his hypothesis.[75] As narrated by Tov, Cross was too quick to organized the manuscript evidence from Qumran according to the well-known tripartite and bipartite divisions of previous generations. But why did he act in this manner? And what about others in similar circumstances? Is it simply the comfort one derives from following traditional categorizations, or an intellectual laziness that allows earlier scholars to do our thinking?[76] I do not think that such negative evaluations do justice to scholars or scholarship in general. Without commenting on any specific example, I would like to introduce a somewhat different perspective that could be brought to bear in evaluating many individual cases.

In a recent issue of *The New York Review of Books*, R. C. Lewontin reviewed a book by Harvard biologist Stephen Jay Gould.[77] Gould's work deals with fossil discoveries at Canada's Burgess Shale. According to Gould, its initial discoverer willingly "shoehorned" the fossils into the then standard classification of animals. That was near the turn of the century. Only seventy years later did a group of individuals come along and recognize that many of these fossils reflected life forms radically different from what had previously been known.[78]

What causes one individual or groups to take a conservative view of fossil (or manuscript) discoveries, while another adopts an outlook that is nothing short of revolutionary? For author Gould, the key lies in the socio-economic class to which the investigator belongs or with which he identifies. Reviewer Lewontin counters that these distinctions more likely "arise from the fact that professional scholarship is a way of building a life, and that successful careers are constructed" along one of "two patterns for a high status life." One, represented by the original discoverer, is "to become part of the political hierarchy of the field," immersed in the bureaucratic and

organizational side. The other, exemplified by
Gould's heroic young Turks, entails rebelling
"against the orthodoxy of their predecessors and
saying something new." Such revision, common not
only in evolutionary biology, does not depend on
ideological conflict, but rather on more general
scholarly, even temperamental bases. Who is to
say where the greater value lies? And why should
we be forced to do so?

Appendix

More significant readings are underlined, but no
attempt is made to distinguish sure from merely
probable text.

Transcription 1. Josh 3:15-16 (4QJosh^b)

נשאי הארון נטבלו ב[קצה המים והירדן מלא על כל גדותיו]

חטים

בימי קציר ויעמדו המים הירדים מ[למעלה ...   [

Transcription 2. Josh 6:5-10 (4QJosh^a)

גדולה ונפלה חמ[ות העיר תחתיה] ועלה הע[ם אי]ש [נ]גדו
[ויקרא

יהושע בן נון אל ה[כהנים ויאמר אלהם] שאו א[ת ארון
הברית]

ושבעה כהנים ישא[ו שבעה שופרות יוב]לים לפני [ארון
יהוה ויאמר]

יהושע אל העם [עברו וסבו את העיר והחלוץ יעבר לפ]ני
[ארו]ן [יהוה]

[ויהי כא]מר [יהושע אל העם ושבעה הכהנים נשאים שב]עה
שופ[רות

[היובלים] ל [פני יהוה עברו ותקעו בשופרו]ת וארון [ב]רית יהוה הולך

[אחריהם והחלוץ הולך לפני הכהנים תקעו [הש]נ[פ]רות והמ [אס]ף הולך

[אחרי הארון הלוך ותקוע בשופרות ואת העם צוה יה]ושע לא [מר לא

[תריעו ולא תשמיעו את קולכם ולא יצא מפיכם דבר] עד י[ום אמרי

Transcription 3. Josh 7:12-15 (4QJosh^a)

[יפנו לפני איביהם] ולא פנים כי היו לחרם ולא אוסיף להיות

[עמכם אם] לא תשמידו החרם מקרבכם קום קדש את העם ואמרת

[התקדשו] למחר   כי כה אמר יהוה אלהי ישראל חרם בקרבכם

[ישראל לא] תוכל לקום לפני אויביכם עד הסירכם החרם מקרבכם

[ונקרבתם] בבקר לשבט [יכם ו]היה השבט אשר ילכדנו יהוה תקריבו

ל[בתים והבית אשר ילכדנו יהו]ה יקרב לגברים והיה הנלכד בהם

ישרף [באש אתו ואת כל אשר לו כי] עבר את ברית יהוה כי עשה

Transcription 4. Josh 8:3-5 (4QJosh^a)

יהושע וכל עם המלחמה [לעלות העי ויבחר יהושע שלשים אלף איש

גבורי החיל וישלחם [לילה ויצו אתם לאמר ראו אתם ארבים]

THE QUMRAN FRAGMENTS OF JOSHUA

אל העיר מאח [רי העיר אל תרחיקו מן העיר מאד (?) והייתם
כלכם נכנים [

ואני וכל [העם אשר אתי נקרב אל העיר והיה כי יצאו
לקראתנו כאשר [

ברא [שנה... [

Transcription 5. Josh 8:7-9 (4QJosh^a)

[א]ת הע[יר ונתנה יהוה]

[אלהיכם בידכם והיה כתפשכם את העי]ר באש [כדבר יהוה
תעשו ראו [

[צויתי אתכם וישלחם יהושע ויל]כו א[ל ... [

Transcription 6. Josh 10:3-5 (4QJosh^a)

[אדני]

צדק מלך [ירושלם אל הוהם מל]ך [חברו]ן [ואל פראם מלך
ירמות ואל יפיע [

מלך לביש ואל ד[ביר] מ[ל]ך עגלון לאמר עלו אלי
וע[זרני ונכה את גבעון [

[כ]י השלימה את [יהו]שע ואת ישראל ויאספו ויעל[ו ... [

Transcription 7. Josh 10:11 (4QJosh^a)

ויהוה השליך עליהם אבנים מן השמ[ים עד עזקה וימתו רבים
אשר מתו [

באבני הברד מאשר הרגו [בני ישראל ... [

NOTES

1. P. Benoit et al, "Editing the Manuscript Fragments from Qumran," BA 19 (1956) 84. This article is an English translation of "Le Travail d'édition des fragments manuscrits de Qumran," RB 63 (1956) 49-67. Since Cross presumably presented his initial findings in English, it seems appropriate to report them in that language.

2. For a later formulation, see, e.g., F. M. Cross, The Ancient Library of Qumran (rev. ed.; Garden City, NY: Doubleday, 1961) 151 n. 84: "The Joshua manuscripts at Qumran are systematically 'Septuagintal' in character."

3. J. A. Soggin, Joshua (OTL; Philadelphia: Westminster, 1972) 19.

4. M. Woudstra, Joshua (NICOT; Grand Rapids, MI: Eerdmans, 1981) 40. Woudstra's (mis)placement of Greek manuscripts at Qumran is apparently based on a mis- or hasty reading of Soggin. On this see L. Greenspoon, "The Use and Abuse of the Term 'LXX' and Related Terminology in Recent Scholarship," BIOSCS 20 (1987) 21.

5. C. Newsom, "The 'Psalms of Joshua' from Cave 4," JJS 39 (1988) 58 n. 6.

6. On this point, see several articles by E. Tov, including "The Textual Affiliations of 4QSam^a," JSOT 14 (1979) 37-53, esp. 50-51; "Determining the Relationship between the Qumran Scrolls and the LXX: Some Methodological Issues," The Hebrew and Greek Texts of Samuel (1980 Proceedings IOSCS, Vienna) (ed. E. Tov; Jerusalem: Academon, 1980) 45-67; "A Modern Textual Outlook Based on the Qumran Scrolls," HUCA 53 (1982) 11-27, esp. 20-21. See also K. A. Mathews, "The Leviticus Scroll (11Qpaleo Lev) and the Text of the Hebrew Bible," CBQ 48 (1986) 171-207, esp. 194-95.

7. R. Boling, Joshua (AB 7; Garden City, NY: Doubleday, 1982).

8. Boling, 219. For details see below.

9. Tov, "Hebrew Biblical Manuscripts from the Judaean Desert: Their Contribution to Textual Criticism," JJS 39 (1988) 15 n. 39, 32. Earlier ("The Growth of the Book of Joshua in the Light of the Evidence of the LXX Translation," Scripta

Hierosolymitana 31 [1986] 322) he had cited the longer ending of ch. 8 (as he does here [p. 6 n. 5]) in support of this contention: "The ending of chapter 8 in that scroll [4QJosh^a] differs from all other known sources, so that its textual independence *vis-à-vis* the other sources should be recognized." I draw a different conclusion from the evidence of chapter 8 (see below).

10. For what has now become the classic formulation of Tov's view, see his "Modern Textual Outlook."

11. E. Tov, "Midrash-Type Exegesis in the LXX of Joshua," *RB* (1978) 50-61, and "Growth of Joshua," 321-39.

12. See also Tov ("Growth of Joshua," 322): "When I read this scroll [4QJosh^a] I thought at first that its contents were relevant to the LXX. This is not the case."

13. In this paper I use both the term "LXX" and the expression "OG," but not interchangeably (see my "Use and Abuse"). The earliest (recoverable form of the) Greek translation of Joshua is designated the OG. In general, it is the Hebrew *Vorlage* of this Old Greek that is of most interest. It is possible, moreover, that the scribe responsible for the Qumran scrolls of Joshua (also) came into contact with readings that reflect the distinctive secondary developments in the Greek textual traditions. On such occasions, I make use of the broader term LXX.

14. Very few researchers have explicitly addressed such questions. Among those who have, I have especially profited from reading J. E. Sanderson, *An Exodus Scroll from Qumran: 4QpaleoExod^M and the Samaritan Tradition* (HSS 30; Atlanta, GA: Scholars Press, 1986). See, in particular, ch. VI (pp. 261-306): "Editorial and Scribal Processes in the Late Second Temple Period as Exhibited in the Text of Exodus." See also Tov ("Hebrew Biblical Manuscripts," 20-27) and E. C. Ulrich ("Horizons of Old Testament Textual Research at the Thirtieth Anniversary of Qumran Cave 4," *CBQ* 46 [1984] 616-19) for discussion and further bibliographical references.

15. L. Greenspoon, "Biblical Translators in Antiquity and in the Modern World: A Comparative Study," *HUCA* 60 (1989) 91-113. There are, to be sure, several dangers inherent in such

comparisons, i.e., reading modern categories and concerns back into the past. However, I am committed to "the general notion that 'translators will be translators,' even when they are separated by a time period as extended as 2,000 years. Today's translators are confronted by many of the same problems as their ancient counterparts, and their solutions to these problems do not differ as much as we might suppose" ("Biblical Translators," 94 n. 8). This holds equally true, I submit, for revisers and scribes.

16. See below on the number of manuscripts and possibly also the number of scribes involved.

17. E. J. Epp, "Toward the Clarification of the Term 'Textual Variant,'" *Studies in New Testament Language and Text: Essays in Honour of George D. Kilpatrick on the Occasion of his sixty-fifth Birthday* (ed. J. K. Elliott; Leiden: Brill, 1976) 153-73.

18. See my remarks in Boling, 110.

19. See n. 1 above.

20. In forthcoming *DJD* volumes Ulrich is responsible for 4QJosh^a, Tov for 4QJosh^b. Both have shared their findings with me, and for that I am most grateful.

21. For specific references, see n. 6 above.

22. I base this characterization only on what I can read on the leather and on what I can reconstruct with a high degree of probability.

23. For recent statements of Cross' overall views, see F. M. Cross, "The Evolution of a theory of Local Texts," *Qumran and the History of the Biblical Text* (ed. F. M. Cross and S. Talmon; Cambridge: Harvard University Press, 1975) 306-20; and "Problems of Method in the Textual Criticism of the Hebrew Bible," *The Critical Study of Sacred Texts* (ed. W. Doniger O'Flaherty; Berkeley: Graduate Theological Union, 1979) 31-54.

24. Tov ("Growth of Joshua," 326): "In Joshua, on the other hand, the LXX lacks not more than 4-5%, a proportion similar to that in Ezekiel."

25. For the latter, Tov seems to suggest that such "non-MT" expansions preclude the designation of our scrolls as "MT." See, e.g., the material quoted in n. 9 above. In my opinion, this conclusion does not necessarily follow from the

evidence. On this, see further below. Earlier in the same article ("Growth of Joshua," 321f), Tov writes more generally: "There is one further source which also differs considerably from MT... I refer to a Hebrew scroll from Cave 4 in Qumran, 4QJos^a, fragmentary in nature, but rather extensive and often different from MT."

26. No one today can ignore the legitimate concerns of his fellow scholars to have access as quickly as possible to as much Qumran material as possible. My decision not to publish photographs is, I hope, balanced by my willingness to share the photographs with interested scholars upon their request.

27. Tov (private communication), allowing for considerably longer lines at this point, reconstructs in accordance with the full MT.

28. See below, e.g., at 4:3 and 7:14; cf. 7:12.

29. On the length of lines in "anterior" copies, see, e.g., M. L. Margolis, "Textual Criticism of the Greek Old Testament," *Proceedings of the American Philosophical Society* 67 (1928) 190-91; and more recently, V. A. Dearing, "A New Explanation for the Discontinuities in the Text of Isaiah 1-10," *The Critical Study of Sacred Texts* (ed. W. Doniger O'Flaherty; Berkeley: Graduate Theological Union, 1979) 77-93.

30. See references in n. 6 above.

31. Tov (private communication) reads the preposition ב rather than כ at beginning.

32. Newsom, "Psalms of Joshua," 67. The direction of dependence or indeed whether there is any dependence cannot be determined with certainty.

33. Tov (private communication) favors this view, as do I.

34. We are prone to speak of the addition of חמשים as a "correction" toward the LXX. However, there is no way of knowing what motivated someone to add this word. If this is an example of the work of a "corrector," he seems to have been a singularly lazy or disinterested individual.

35. The wording of this "suggestion" is purposely vague and minimalist.

36. Some observers may suspect that here I am veering away from a likely 4Q-LXX connection in order to protect my hypothesis. In my defense I can respond that this connection is at best only possible or suggestive.

37. On this see the relevant discussions in S. Holmes, *Joshua: The Hebrew and Greek Texts* (Cambridge: University Press, 1914); M. L. Margolis, *The Book of Joshua in Greek* (Paris: Paul Geuthner, 1931); Boling, *Joshua*; Tov, "Growth of Joshua;" and other sources.

38. More on this below.

39. A reconstruction that Boling (p. 219) accepted. See also above.

40. But none of these appears on the leather.

41. On this see also the sources listed above in n. 37.

42. In any event, these verses cannot be said to offer anything other than supporting evidence for an argument with securer bases in other passages.

43. For further details see the sources listed above in n. 37.

44. The task of reconstruction, never an easy one, is even more difficult here because of the curious, unique reading exhibited by 4Q on the leather earlier in v 11.

45. Having largely discounted the significance of a possible 4Q-LXX connection just above, I am in no position to insist on the importance of a probable 4Q-MT agreement here. But, I suppose, there is some force in even inconsistent insistence.

46. On this latter point see M. L. Margolis, "Ai or the City? Joshua 8.12, 16," *JQR* 7 (1917) 491-97.

47. I have purposely used the broader term "LXX" to indicate some uncertainty, at least in my mind, about the wording of the OG in these cases.

48. I am sensitive to the criticism that I have simply "explained away," rather than fairly examined, evidence contrary to my hypothesis. Nonetheless, it seems more profitable, if less prudent, to argue our case as forcefully as possible.

49. On the original text here see the sources listed above in n. 37.

50. Although, in my opinion, the Qumran scribe himself "composed" the longer and probably also the shorter addition here, I suspect that some discerning scholar will be able to link the substance of this unknown additional material with a known development within the midrashic tradition. That identification will have to await the fuller publication of this scroll. There may, in addition, be some connection between these additions and the Psalms of Joshua, especially 4Q379 (see Newsom, "Psalms of Joshua," 65-68).

51. On this section as a late addition, see E. Tov, "Some Sequence Differences between the MT and the LXX and Their Ramifications for the Literary Criticism of the Bible," *Journal of Northwest Semitic Languages* 13 (1987) 152-54.

52. Cf. Judg 1:4-7. On the question of originality see Boling (*Joshua*, 278), who also wrote the commentary on Judges for the Anchor Bible.

53. But we cannot be certain about the OG.

54. For Tov, see "Midrash-Type Exegesis," "Some Sequence Differences," and "Growth of Joshua" (all cited earlier). For Auld, see A. G. Auld, *Studies in Joshua: Text and Literary Relations* (Unpub. diss.; University of Edinburgh, 1976); "Cities of Refuge in Israelite Tradition," *JSOT* 10 (1978) 26-40; "Textual and Literary Studies in the Book of Joshua," *ZAW* 90 (1978) 412-17; "The Levitical Cities: Texts and History," *ZAW* 91 (1979) 194-206. For Rofé, see A. Rofé, "The end of the Book of Joshua in the Septuagint," *Henoch* 4 (1982) 17-35 (a Hebrew version appeared earlier in *Shnaton* 2 [1977] 217- 27); and "Historico-Literary Criticism Illustrated by Joshua 20," *I. L. Seeligmann Volume* (ed. A. Rofé and Y. Zakovitch: Jerusalem, 1983) 137-50. The above listing is not intended to be exhaustive.

55. See above. Note also the preponderance of asterisks in Origen's hexaplaric edition of this book.

56. Typical of Margolis' judgment is the following statement ("Textual Criticism," 196): "On the whole he [the Old Greek translator]

handled his Hebrew freely, repeatedly curtailing the text."

57. For Holmes see above n. 37.

58. H. M. Orlinsky, "The Hebrew *Vorlage* of the Septuagint of the Book of Joshua," *Congress Volume 1968* (VTSup 17; Leiden: Brill, 1969) 187-95.

59. For Tov and Auld see above n. 54. See also L. Greenspoon, "Theodotion, Aquila, Symmachus, and the Old Greek of Joshua," *Eretz-Israel* 16 (1982) 82-91; and *Textual Studies in the Book of Joshua* (HSM 28: Chico, CA: Scholars Press, 1983).

60. Tov, "Midrash-Type Exegesis," 51.

61. Tov, "Growth of Joshua," 327f n. 18. "At the same time," Tov continues, "the freedom of the translator is often predictable, so the reconstruction of the Hebrew base is often easier than shown by mere statistics."

62. N. Fernandez Marcos, "The Use of the Septuagint in the Criticism of the Hebrew Bible," *Sefarad* 47 (1987), esp. 70-71.

63. For a detailed examination, see Tov, "Growth of Joshua."

64. Recall that Tov, ("Hebrew Biblical Manuscripts," 15 n. 39) placed 4QJoshua^{a,b} in the category of "Biblical texts *not written* in the Qumran orthography."

65. For the material in this paragraph, see my "Biblical Translators." On the last point, see esp. p. 112.

66. See, for example, H. M. Orlinsky, "The Septuagint as Holy Writ and the Philosophy of the Translators," *HUCA* 46 (1975) 89-114. The thrust of his argument should, in my opinion, be accepted as operative in evaluating the work of any translator, unless compelling counterarguments can be adduced.

67. A further distinction, between translation and revision, is also necessary: "As distinct from a translation, which entails the fresh rendering of a text from one language into another, a revision is most dependent on an existing text in the same language. It is a matter of degree: no translator, however original, is totally unaware of earlier renderings, nor is even the most slavish reviser without knowledge of the foreign language

text that stands behind the earlier translation with which he works. Or, to put it another way, it's a matter of starting point: the translator begins with the foreign language text; the reviser, with a text in his own language." See my "A book 'Without Blemish': The Jewish Publication Society's Bible Translation of 1917," *JQR* 79 (1988) 17.

68. As I wrote at the end of *Textual Studies* (pp. 380-81): "Theodotion, in our opinion, embodies those concerns that a reviser or translator ought to display. First of all, he was faithful to and respectful of the text he was revising. Secondly, he was knowledgeable of and careful with the text to which he was correcting. And, perhaps most important, he took into account the needs of his intended audience and produced a text in which the flavor of neither the Hebrew (as with Sym.) nor the Greek (as with Aq.) was lost." The jury is likely to be more mixed in assessing the success of Margolis and the translation committee he headed.

69. As is also true with any such reconstruction (Tov, "Modern Textual Outlook," 26-27 n. 70).

70. The terms in quotation marks are familiar to any editor. Their appropriateness in this context is explained below.

71. *JQR* 71 (1981) 133-50. See also "Ars Scribendi; Pars Reperta," *JQR* 72 (1982) 43-44.

72. For further details see also L. Greenspoon, "Max L. Margolis on the Complutensian Text of Joshua," *BIOSCS* 12 (1979) 43-56.

73. See further M. L. Margolis, "The Aldina as a Source of the Sixtina," *JBL* 38 (1919) 51-52.

74. M. L. Margolis, "Specimen of a New Edition of the Greek Joshua," *Jewish Studies in Memory of Israel Abrahams* (New York: Jewish Institute of Religion, 1927) 309-11; reprinted in *Studies in the Septuagint: Origins, Recensions, and Interpretations* (ed. S. Jellicoe; New York: KTAV, 1974). For further details on Margolis' *C* recension, see his "'Man by Man,' Joshua 7, 17," *JQR* 3 (1913) 327; and "Hexapla and Hexaplaric," *AJSL* 32 (1916) 137-38.

75. See Tov, "Modern Textual Outlook."

76. I hasten to add that these explanations are not Tov's, nor are they attributable to anyone in particular. They simply reflect one sort of inference that could reasonably be drawn from any such situation.

77. R. C. Lewontin, "Fallen Angels: *Wonderful Life: The Burgess Shale and the Nature of History*, by Stephen J. Gould," *The New York Review of Books* (June 14, 1990) 3-7.

78. Analogies with the manuscript discoveries at Qumran readily suggest themselves.

THE OLD GREEK OF ISAIAH IN RELATION
TO THE QUMRAN TEXTS OF ISAIAH:
SOME GENERAL COMMENTS

ARIE VAN DER KOOIJ

I

Since the discoveries in the caves at Qumran in the late forties and in the early fifties, the Old Greek of Isaiah (hereafter: LXX Isa) is no longer the only witness to the early history of the text of Isaiah. Among the large number of (fragments of) biblical texts the following Isaiah-texts have been found:
- 1QIsa^a, a complete scroll, the only one among the biblical texts from Qumran; dating from the late second century BCE.
- 1QIsa^b, preserved in a fragmentary state, with major parts from Isa 41 onwards; dating from the late first century BCE.
- 4QIsa^{a-r}, fragments of about 17 scrolls;[1] dating from the period 150 BCE - 70 CE.
- 5QIsa (5Q3), a tiny fragment, dating from the first century CE.[2]

For 1QIsa^a and 1QIsa^b official editions are available,[3] but up to the present the edition of the 4Q fragments has not yet appeared.[4] Yet we know something about these fragments because P. W. Skehan has published a list of the contents of all the 4QIsa MSS,[5] and F. J. Morrow, a student of his, has catalogued and analyzed all the variants of these MSS in his dissertation, entitled *The Text of Isaiah at Qumran*.[6]

As is well known the above mentioned QIsa-texts are not the only texts with regard to the book of Isaiah found at Qumran. We also have parts of *pesharim* on several passages from Isaiah.[7] The large number of biblical Isaiah texts, together with these *pesharim* and, furthermore, the many instances of citations from and allusions to passages from Isaiah,[8] make it fully clear that this book was a favorite one at Qumran. For our subject, LXX Isa in relation to the QIsa-texts, we limit ourselves to the biblical texts from Qumran.

Both LXX Isa and the QIsa-texts go back to the period of c. 150 BCE until 70 CE. These texts are important witnesses to that early period of the history of the text of the Hebrew Bible, the period before c. 100 CE, i.e. before the proto-masoretic text dominates the scene. The period before 100, or maybe even before the first century CE, is characterised by the well known and much discussed variety and fluidity of biblical texts and text traditions. This applies also to our Isa-texts from that period: they too display a variety, as may be clear from the following characterizations.

LXX Isa and 1QIsa^a both reflect a free approach

towards their *Vorlage*, as appears from deviations and variant readings of a linguistic nature, as well as from contextual changes such as harmonizations. Both texts are also characterized by interpretative renderings or readings.

1QIsa^b, on the other hand, is a text of quite a different type, reflecting a conservative attitude towards its *Vorlage*. Though paleographically younger than 1QIsa^a, as far as its orthography is concerned 1QIsa^b is much older. As a copy it belongs to the accurate type,[9] and being very close to MT it can therefore be regarded as a pre-masoretic text.[10]

The fragments of 4Q are to be seen as a third group:[11] as a whole they offer a large number of variants, but these variants are, in general, rather insignificant. The 4QIsa-texts hold a position somewhere between 1QIsa^a and 1QIsa^b, being closer to the (proto)-masoretic text than to 1QIsa^a. According to Morrow the variants of 4QIsa are due to 5 tendencies: (a) breakdown of Hebrew grammar and usage; (b) breakdown of Hebrew pronunciation; (c) substitution of more normal or current diction, including the interpretation of difficult or unusual words in terms of what is known; (d) a harmonizing tendency with regard to person; (e) influence of similar biblical passages on each other.[12]

So one can discern three kinds of Isa-texts.[13] As far as the QIsa-texts are concerned, a three-fold variety is attested in one and the same region, namely Judea. This means that these data cannot be accounted for by the theory of local text-types.[14]

Though LXX Isa as well as QIsa are indeed to be considered as early witnesses, as stated above, one should not forget two important differences between them: in contrast to QIsa the Old Greek, as a translation, is not a text written in the language of the Hebrew Bible itself, and the Old Greek is not attested by any manuscript dating from the time when the original translation was presumably made. Because of these two aspects LXX Isa is in fact only an indirect witness to the early history of the text of Isaiah.

On the other hand, however, LXX Isa has the advantage of being a complete text. Though this is, quite exceptionally, also the case with 1QIsa^a, all other QIsa-texts, as well as all remaining biblical texts from Qumran, have been preserved in only a fragmentary state.

After these introductory remarks we will now deal with our subject matter, LXX Isa in relation to QIsa, from two points of view:
1. LXX Isa together with QIsa against MT.
2. LXX Isa compared with QIsa.

II

Because all these materials are witnesses to the earliest attested period of the text of Isaiah it is of course most important to look for "pre-masoretic" readings which are older than (proto-)MT. As we all know the number of variants offered by our texts, be it directly or, in the case of a translation, indirectly,[15] is very large. However, for several reasons most of them are of a secondary nature. A particular element which limits the value of alternative readings is the fact that they are not supported by all available witnesses.

It will be clear that variants shared by LXX Isa together with all QIsa-texts are of particular weight, the more so when 1QIsa^b joins in. However, these cases are very rare.[16] By way of example we refer to three quite interesting cases which are found in the last verses of Isaiah 53:

53:11

יראה MT] יראה אור 1QIsa^a, 1QIsa^b, 4QIsa^d, LXX Isa (δειξαι αυτω φως)

53:12

חטא MT] חטאי 1QIsa^a, 1QIsa^b, 4QIsa^d, LXX Isa (αμαρτιας)

לפשעים MT] לפשעיהם 1QIsa^a (המה-), 1QIsa^b, 4QIsa^d, LXX Isa (δια τας αμαρτιας αυτων)

The fact that these variants are attested by all the early witnesses so far available for these verses strongly favours the assumption that they are to be seen as belonging to the pre-masoretic text of Isaiah.[17] This is the more probable since 1QIsa^b, a conservative type of text, joins the other texts.

Cases of combined evidence from LXX Isa and the QIsa-texts versus MT are very rare indeed. Though the most important MS, 1QIsa^b, is only fragmentarily preserved, because of the nature of this MS one can safely assume that the rare cases of combined evidence point to a pre-masoretic text of Isaiah which is very close to (proto-)MT.

III

We will discuss now our second point, LXX Isa compared with the QIsa-texts. As we have seen, the QIsa-texts fall into three groups: 1QIsa^a, 1QIsa^b, and 4QIsa. What can be said about the relationship between LXX Isa and 1QIsa^a, 1QIsa^b, and 4QIsa respectively?

As far as the matter of recension is concerned, it has become clear that there is no particular connection between LXX Isa and any one of the three groups of QIsa-texts.[19] This holds not only for 1QIsa^{b19} and 4QIsa,[20] but also for the most interesting text, 1QIsa^a. It should be stressed that not only do LXX Isa and 1QIsa^a deviate in many instances from MT but both are also mutually divergent in a large number of cases, whereas the number of common readings versus MT is relatively very small. In his valuable discussion of these agreements, J. Ziegler offers some suggestions with regard to the common readings: some were present in the *Vorlage* of LXX Isa, be it in the text, or in the margin, and others, in particular the lexical variants, were part of a scholarly tradition.[21] As always, the difficulty is to know whether a variant reading is going back to a *Vorlage*, or is due to the method of the author (scribe or translator). In light of the overall character of our texts one is more inclined to ascribe agreements on word-level to a common practice of both authors rather than to their *Vorlagen*.

So, quite different from the state of affairs with regard to the books of Samuel and Jeremiah, notable agreement between LXX Isa and even one (group of) QIsa-text(s), against MT, does not emerge from a comparison between these texts. This does not mean, however, that there is no relationship or connection at all. It is to be asked whether, on the basis of characteristics other than that of textual agreements, LXX Isa has something in common with any one of the QIsa-texts.

Apart from a few readings, it can be stated that 1QIsa^b and 4QIsa do not have any particular trait in common with LXX Isa, though it must be admitted that a comparison with 1QIsa^b, and even more with 4QIsa, is complicated by the fragmentary state of these Isa-texts. But, unlike 1QIsa^b and 4QIsa, it is 1QIsa^a which has something in common with LXX Isa. Both texts, dating from the same period, the second half of the second century BCE, differ markedly from MT, and both reflect a free approach towards their *Vorlagen*.

We will concentrate therefore, in the rest of our paper, on the question of the relationship between LXX Isa and 1QIsa^a.

In his lecture during the IOSOT-congress at Strasbourg in 1956, P. W. Skehan, dealing with the relationship between LXX Isa and 1QIsa^a, stated that 1QIsa^a "illustrates ... an exegetical process at work within the transmission of the text itself, in Hebrew."[22] He referred to Ziegler's study, *Untersuchungen zur Septuaginta des Buches Isaias*, in which it is suggested that cases of borrowings from other books into the text of Isaiah, as well as cases of harmonizations within the book itself may already have been present in the *Vorlage* of LXX Isa. Skehan applied this idea to 1QIsa^a; LXX Isa and 1QIsa^a are, he then remarked, "mutually illustrative, because the cave 1 manuscript gives us, for the first time in Hebrew, the kind of glossed and reworked manuscript that the LXX prototype must have been."[23] However, with regard to all this, determining which variants go back to the *Vorlage* and which are due to the author remains highly problematic.

Though the usual method of comparison on word-level is quite understandable for text-critical purposes, this approach is too limited with regard to LXX Isa and 1QIsa^a, since these texts reflect a free approach. This means that an analysis of variant readings has to be carried out within the scope of the nature of each of these texts itself, before a comparison with the other text is made. In my opinion, though a lot of research has been done, further research is needed on LXX Isa and 1QIsa^a, each in their own right, before an adequate comparison can be made.

It is commonly agreed that in these texts under discussion a free approach towards their *Vorlage* is visible. But what do we assume about the nature of a translation like LXX Isa when we speak of a "free approach," or of a "free translation?"

The distinction between a "literal" and "free" translation is a very old one indeed. In ancient times, scholars like Cicero and, like him, Jerome were well aware of these two types of translation: the literal one was characterised by the expression *verbum pro verbo*, and the free one by *sensus de sensu*.²⁴ Though very useful, these designations constitute but a broad distinction.

A free approach means, in fact, two things: (a) a free attitude towards the *Vorlage*, and (b) a free representation of it. A free rendering, first of all, concerns the language of the *Vorlage* in several respects (grammatical, syntactical, semantic, stylistic, and idiomatic). In case of a translation into Greek, the aim is to produce an adequate rendering in good Koine Greek.²⁵ Further, a free approach may also have to do with the *content* of the *Vorlage*. In such a case the translator apparently feels free to deviate from his *Vorlage* (also) with respect to content, for some reason or other.

As for the characteristics of a free approach in the sense of a free translation, the following aspects or tendencies apply:
- the aim of writing good Koine Greek, both with respect to syntax and to idiom;
- inconsistency, or variety, of lexical choices; different word order as well;
- grammatical and contextual changes, such as harmonizations;
- that of adding or subtracting words or phrases.²⁶

As we know from past research, these aspects, and others as well, are typical of LXX Isa.²⁷

Today, we live in the era of the computer, the great advantage of which is that quantitatively as well as percentilely literalness can be measured in a more accurate way than ever before. Furthermore and importantly, it is now more readily possible to detect patterns on a syntactical or stylistic level in Greek as part of the method of a translator. In relation to these matters we now have some interesting results from the well known CATTS project.[28]

However, in particular with regard to free translations, such as LXX Isa and LXX Job, these findings, though of a great help, have their limits. The conclusion, based on earlier research or on modern research by means of the computer, that the data justify the characterization of "free approach," leaves several questions unanswered. It is helpful and important to know that certain variants, pluses or minuses, are due to contextual changes, but the question remains open whether they are intentional or unintentional. It is also important to know that the lexical choices display a great measure of inconsistency, but the question whether they are pure guesses or deliberate choices, serving some (contextual) interpretation, remains open. Let us state it in this way: for what purpose or purposes did the author of LXX Isa, or *mutatis mutandis* the scribe of 1QIsa^a, use the "free approach"? In short, one wants to know more than simply whether the attitude of the translator towards his *Vorlage* was literal or free.

Instead of guessing whether a translator made a guess, or made his translation from intuition, or whether he harmonised rather mechanically or not, a more detailed analysis of a text such as LXX Isa is needed. As I have argued elsewhere,[29] with regard to LXX Isa I prefer the following approach: each pericope should be analysed in detail, both on a linguistic level and on the level of

contents, including a comparison with MT. Thus
one can attempt to determine whether, and to what
extent, deviations in LXX Isa from MT are serving
a particular interpretation of the actual context.
If so, they provide us with little evidence that
might go back to a different *Vorlage*.

Our choice for the pericope as the basis for
closer research has to do with the scribal and
reading practices of the ancient world. This
aspect is particularly interesting with regard to
1QIsa^a. In this scroll the pericopes are clearly
indicated by a nuanced system of text-division.[30]
As to 1QIsa^a I prefer also a more holistic, and
less atomistic approach, by which I mean that
there should be a close reading of a pericope,
including an analysis of its syntax, its form and
its contents, taking seriously its own variants,
its own division and subdivision. In terms of
antiquity, such a reading means in fact the
reconstruction of the ἀνάγνωσις, the "reading
aloud" of the text, which implies, particularly in
the case of an unvocalised text, a first
interpretation of it.

As an example I may refer to my analysis of LXX
Isa 8:11-16 and 1QIsa^a 8:11-18.[31] Both passages I
have analysed in the way just mentioned. The
conclusion was reached that each passage
constitutes a coherent text in its own right,
containing a form and content quite different from
the other, and each one is different from MT as
well. Deviations or variant-readings turned out
to be part of a particular interpretation.

Let me give some examples:
- MT Isa 8:11 has the reading ויסרני, "and YHWH

instructed me (not to go the way of this people)."
LXX offers in its place the rendering ἀπειθοῦσι
(presumably via the root סרר), "they disobey," and
together with other deviations from MT this
rendering makes perfect sense, though one quite
different from that of MT: persons with power,
leaders, do not obey the way of this people.
- In MT Isa 8:15 the verb כשל, "to stumble" is
used. In LXX this verb has been rendered here by
ἀδυνατήσουσι. This equivalent for כשל does not
occur in the rest of LXX Isa, nor in the other
books of the LXX. In our pericope, however, this
rendering makes perfect sense: the strong leaders
shall became "powerless." A nice example of a
lexical choice in view of the actual context in
Greek (vs. 11).
- In 1QIsa^a, the text of 8:11 has the reading
יסירנו, "He (YHWH) will cause us to turn away
(from walking in the way of this people)." A
close reading of our pericope, including this
variant, reveals that this reading serves a
particular interpretation of Isa 8:11ff.
- This pericope of 1QIsa^a also contains an
interesting case of text-division: within 8:12-13
(see col. VIII, l. 6) the scroll displays an
interior subdivision marked by a blank space in
the line. As a result, the words את יהוה צבאות
are not part of vs. 13, as is the case in MT, but
figure as the last words of vs. 12. Reading the
text of 1QIsa^a as it stands, an understanding of
this text different from MT emerges. Our variant
in vs. 11 and this subdivision create in the text
of 1QIsa^a "a strong emphasis on the group of the

prophet and his followers, standing as a group opposed to the people."[32]

My conclusion is that in these, and other cases as well,[33] the passages involved constitute a deliberate composition. This means that the authors are not to be regarded simply as dragoman-translators or copyists, but more likely as scribes and scholars. Or to put it in terms of antiquity; they are to be seen as "oratores," rather than "interpretes."[34]

This conclusion may help us in finding an answer to our question concerning for what purpose the authors of LXX Isa and 1QIsa^a used the free approach. But again one wants to know more. For two further questions arise, namely, (a) *why*, for what purpose, did the authors produce their text as a deliberate composition, and (b) *how* did they produce their text.

The first question is a hermeneutical one; it has to do with the status of our texts, being prophetical books dating from the hellenistic period. As has been argued first of all by I. L. Seeligmann, LXX Isa contains passages which reflect an understanding of the prophecies of Isaiah as predictions of what happened in the time of the translator.[35] This means that LXX Isa may be read and understood (i.e. decoded) as a collection of prophetical oracles like Daniel 11 or Book III of the Sibylline Oracles.

As I have argued elsewhere,[36] 1QIsa^a also contains texts which reflect such an actualization of prophecy, an understanding of prophecies typical of the Qumran community as appears from the *pesharim*. In this respect 1QIsa^a 8:11 is a most interesting case: the tenor of this verse, within the pericope to which it belongs, agrees with the use of this verse in other texts from Qumran. This text appears to be "an important text in the self-understanding of the Qumran covenanters."[37] So the most natural conclusion is that 1QIsa^a 8:11ff reflects the attempt of legitimating the Qumran community on the basis of this passage.

Our second question, concerning *how* such a text was produced, has to do with the interpretation technique of the time. How was the *Vorlage* read and interpreted, and which exegetical devices were used? It will be clear that this question is of crucial importance for the matter of the *Vorlage*.

At the end of this paper I return to the relationship between LXX Isa and 1QIsa^a, the texts on which we have concentrated our discussion. What do both texts have in common? Both texts are, in my view, "mutually illustrative," not only with regard to their free approach, but also in the way in which both authors have used this free approach. My tentative conclusion is, that they, as scribes and scholars, have made the effort to create new texts with a meaning of their own, presumably with the ultimate purpose not only to modernize the text linguistically, but also to actualize the prophecies of Isaiah.

Of course, further research has to be carried out, in order to get a better knowledge of both texts in their own right, and hence to be able to carry out a comparison between both as adequately as possible. But if we are on the right track, it would mean that both texts reflect some literary activity of scribes resulting in updated texts of Isaiah, kinds of new editions of the book. It would also mean that the significance of their relationship lies not so much in their being the earliest witnesses to the text of Isaiah, but more in particular in their being kindred pieces of Jewish literature from the hellenistic era.

NOTES

1. For further information, see now E. Ulrich, "The Biblical Scrolls from Qumran Cave 4: An Overview and a Progress Report on their Publication," *RevQ* 14 (1989-90) 225-26. See also P.W. Skehan, "Qumran, Textes bibliques," *DBSup* 9 (1978) cols. 811-12 (here 4QIsa^{a-q}).

2. See DJD III, 173. Beside these findings at Qumran, a very small fragment was found outside Qumran: Mur Isa, a fragment containing parts of Isa 1:4-14; see DJD II, 79-80.

3. For 1QIsa^a: M. Burrows, J.C. Trever and W. H. Brownlee, *The Dead Sea Scrolls of St. Mark's Monastery, Vol. I: The Isaiah Manuscript and the Habakkuk Commentary* (New Haven: ASOR, 1950); for corrections, see E.Y. Kutscher, *The Language and Linguistic Background of the Isaiah Scroll (1QIsaa)* (STDJ 6; Leiden: Brill, 1974) passim. For 1QIsa^b: E. L. Sukenik, אוצר המגילות הגנוזות (Jerusalem: Bialik, 1954); for additional fragments, see DJD I, p. 66.

4. It was announced at the Groningen congress in 1989 that this edition would be part of volume 9 of the DJD series: see E. Ulrich, *RevQ* 14 (1989-90) 227. However, at the Manchester congress Ulrich told me that meanwhile the decision has been taken not to publish the 4QIsa materials in volume 9.

5. See note 1.

6. F. J. Morrow, *The Text of Isaiah at Qumran* (Ph.D. Dissertation, The Catholic University of America, 1973; Ann Arbor, Michigan: University Microfilms, 1977).

7. See DJD III, 95-96; DJD V, 11-30.

8. As for citations, see the Index of Biblical Passages in: J. A. Fitzmyer, *The Dead Sea Scrolls. Major Publications and Tools for Study* (SBLSBS 8; Missoula: Scholars Press, 1975) 163-65. A large number of allusions to the book of Isaiah is to be found in the Hodayot. See P. Wernberg-Moeller, "The contribution of the Hodayot to biblical textual criticism," *Textus* 4 (1964) 133-75.

9. For the notion of "accuracy", see Josephus, *Contra Apionem* 1:43. See also my *Die alten Textzeugen des Jesajabuches* (OBO 35; Fribourg: Universitätsverlag; Göttingen: Vandenhoeck & Ruprecht, 1981) 113-14.

10. For an opinion different from what is generally held, see G. Garbini, "1QIsa^b et le Texte d'Isaie," *Henoch* 6 (1984) 17-21. For the terminology, "pre-masoretic", "proto-masoretic" and "masoretic", see D. Barthélemy, "Text, Hebrew, history of," IDBSup 881.

11. Being such a tiny fragment 5Q3 is left out of consideration.

12. F. J. Morrow, *Text of Isaiah*, 171.

13. See also F. J. Morrow, *Text of Isaiah*, 171.

14. We need not enter the discussion about the origin of the QIsa-texts (whether they are written by the Qumran community, or by people outside Qumran): see E. Tov, "The Orthography and Language of the Hebrew Scrolls Found at Qumran and the Origin of these Scrolls," *Textus* 13 (1986) 31-57.

15. We leave aside here the question of whether these variants are real variants or "pseudo-variants", i.e. variants in the mind of the translator. For this term, see E. Tov, *The Text-Critical Use of the Septuagint in Biblical Research* (Jerusalem Biblical Studies 3; Jerusalem: Simor, 1981) 228-30.

16. Cf. P. W. Skehan, "The Text of Isaias at Qumran," *CBQ* 17 (1955) 42.

17. Cf. D. Barthélemy, *Critique textuelle de l'Ancien Testament. 2. Isaïe, Jérémie, Lamentations* (OBO 50/2; Fribourg: Universitätsverlag; Göttingen: Vandenhoeck & Ruprecht, 1986) 406. On the other hand, J. Koenig is of the opinion that the reading אור of 1QIsa^a has been derived by the scribe of the scroll, via analogical interpretation, from Isa 9:1; see J. Koenig, *L'herméneutique analogique du Judaïsme antique d'après les témoins textuels d'Isaïe* (VTSup 33; Leiden: Brill, 1982) 274-83. For critical remarks, see my review-article in *BibOr* 43 (1986) col. 373.

18. See also the article by E. Tov in this volume.

19. 1QIsa^b is, in fact, close to (the *Vorlage* of) Kaige-Theodotion Isaiah.

20. On 4QIsa variants supported by LXX, see F. J. Morrow, *Text of Isaiah*, 182-84.

21. J. Ziegler, "Die *Vorlage* der Isaias-LXX und die erste Isaias-Rolle von Qumran 1QIsa^a," *JBL* 78 (1959), 59 = J. Ziegler, *Sylloge. Gesammelte Aufsätze zur Septuaginta* (MSU 10; Göttingen: Vandenhoeck & Ruprecht, 1971) 509: "Varianten ... von einer Gelehrtenschule mündlich tradiert und auch schriftlich in separaten Verzeichnissen fixiert ..."

22. P. W. Skehan, "The Qumran Manuscripts and Textual Criticism," *Volume du Congrès Strasbourg 1956* (VTSup 4; Leiden: Brill, 1957), 151.

23. *Ibid.*, p. 151.

24. See G. J. M. Bartelink, *Hieronymus, Liber de optimo genere interpretandi* (Epistula 57) (Mnemosyne Sup 61; Leiden: Brill, 1980).

25. See also J. Barr, *The Typology of Literalism in Ancient Biblical Translations* (MSU 15; Göttingen: Vandenhoeck & Ruprecht, 1979) 289; I. Soisalon-Soininen, "Zurück zur Hebraismenfrage," *Studien zur Septuaginta Robert Hanhart zu Ehren* (ed. D. Fraenkel, U. Quast, J. W. Wevers; MSU 20; Göttingen: Vandenhoeck & Ruprecht, 1990) 37: "Eine freie Übersetzung drückt den Inhalt der Ausgangssprache in der Zielsprache so aus, dass der Wortlaut der Übersetzung in keiner Weise von dem allgemeinen Sprachgebrauch der Zielsprache abweicht."

26. For similar aspects, see J. Barr, *Typology of Literalism*, 294-96, and E. Tov, *Text-Critical Use*, 54-62.

27. See in particular J. Ziegler, *Untersuchungen zur Septuaginta des Buches Isaias* (Alttest. Abhandl. XII,3; Münster: Aschendorffschen Verlagsbuch-handlung, 1934).

28. See e.g. E. Tov - B.G. Wright, "Computer-Assisted Study of the Criteria for Assessing the Literalness of Translation Units in the LXX," *Textus* 12 (1985) 149-87; G. Marquis, "Word Order as a Criterion for the Evaluation of Translation Technique in the LXX and the Evaluation of Word-Order Variants as Exemplified in LXX-Ezekiel," *Textus* 13 (1986) 59-84; id., "Consistency of Lexical Equivalents as a Criterion for the Evaluation of Translation Technique as Exemplified in the LXX of Ezekiel," *VI Congress of the International Organization for Septuagint and Cognate Studies, Jerusalem 1986* (ed. C. E. Cox; SBLSCS 23; Atlanta: Scholars Press, 1987) 405-24. For critical remarks with respect to method, see I. Soisalon-Soininen, "Methodologische Fragen der Erforschung der Septuaginta-Syntax," *VI Congress IOSCS*, 425-44 (= I. Soisalon-Soininen, *Studien zur Septuaginta-Syntax. Zu seinem 70. Geburtstag am 4. Juni 1987* [ed. A. Aejmelaeus und R. Sollamo; AASF B, 237; Helsinki: Suomalainen Tiedeakatemia, 1987] 40-52); id., "Zurück zur Hebraismenfrage," *Studien zur Septuaginta*, 35-51.

29. A. van der Kooij, "Accident or Method? On 'Analogical' Interpretation in the Old Greek of Isaiah and in 1QIs^a," *BibOr* 43 (1986) cols 366-76.

30. See J. M. Oesch, *Petucha und Setuma* (OBO 27; Fribourg: Universitätsverlag; Göttingen: Vandenhoeck & Ruprecht, 1979).

31. A. van der Kooij, "The Septuagint of Isaiah: Translation and Interpretation," *The Book of Isaiah, Le Livre d'Isaïe* (ed. J. Vermeylen; BETL 81; Leuven: Peeters, 1989) 127-33; id., "1QIsa^a Col. VIII,4-11 (Isa 8,11-18): A Contextual Approach of its Variants," *RevQ* 14 (1989-90) 569-81.

32. A. van der Kooij, *RevQ* 14 (1989-90) 580.

33. See J. M. Coste, "Le texte grec d'Isaïe XXV 1-5," *RB* 61 (1954) 36-66; A. van der Kooij, "The

Old Greek of Isaiah 19:16-25: Translation and Interpretation," *VI Congress IOSCS*, 127-66.

34. For this distinction in relation to the ancient versions, see S. P. Brock, "Translating the Old Testament," *It is Written: Scripture Citing Scripture. Essays in Honour of Barnabas Lindars* (ed. D. A. Carson and H. G. M. Williamson; Cambridge: University Press, 1988) 87-98.

35. I. L. Seeligmann, *The Septuagint Version of Isaiah* (MVEOL 9; Leiden: Brill, 1948). See also: J. C. M. das Neves, *A Teologia da Traduaçao Grega dos Setenta no Livro de Isaías (Cap. 24 de Isaías)* (Lisboa: Universidade Católica Portugesa, 1973); A. van der Kooij, *Die alten Textzeugen*; J. Koenig, *L'herméneutique analogique*.

36. A. van der Kooij, *Die alten Textzeugen*, 81-97.

37. G. J. Brooke, *Exegesis at Qumran. 4QFlorilegium in its Jewish Context* (JSOTSup 29; Sheffield: JSOT Press, 1985) 319.

STATISTICS AND TEXTUAL FILIATION:
THE CASE OF 4QSAM^a/LXX
(WITH A NOTE ON THE TEXT OF THE PENTATEUCH)

Frank H. Polak

This paper aims to propose a method to determine the relationship between the MT and the ancient witnesses to the text of the Hebrew Bible. Our first step is classifying the variants into categories. In order to establish affinities the data in these categories are analyzed statistically. On the basis of these findings one may establish descent by the standard methods of textual criticism. That is to say, our approach is similar to the stemmatic method, but it will be based on statistics.

By the statistical method we can prove the following theses:

a. 4QSam^a and the parent text of the Old Greek of the Book of Samuel descend from one common exemplar (ב), which differs from the ancestor of MT and represents a revision of the ancient text.

b. 4QpaleoExod^m and the Samaritan Pentateuch (SP)

of the Book of Exodus represent one and the same
revision ש (including also 4Q158 11-12) made on
the basis of Proto-MT (מ), but they do not descend
from the same manuscript. These texts are related
to MT, which is, however, closer to Proto-MT. The
LXX is not related to מ.
c. 11QpaleoLev, MT and SP of the Book of Leviticus
are all independently related to Proto-MT (מ); the
Old Greek is not related to this text.
d. Both in Exodus and in Leviticus the Old Greek,
SP and the scrolls have been influenced by a
revision of the ancient text (R).
Of course, similar theses have already been
expressed in the past, but they have also been
challenged. The statistical method enables us to
turn scholarly intuitions into conclusive
evidence.

I

The relationship between 4QSam^a and the LXX
poses a dilemma. On the one hand, the scroll
contains numerous readings that differ from the
MT, but match the OG according to LXX^B or the
(proto-)Lucianic version. On the other hand, the
scroll also contains many variants that are not
attested by the Greek; therefore we cannot bluntly
state that 4QSam^a is identical with or directly
related to the parent text of the LXX. Cross has
tried to solve this problem by assuming that both
the LXX (the Egyptian text in his system) and the
Qumran scroll (the Palestinian recension) represent a scribal reworking that has bypassed the MT
(of Babylonian descent).[1] In this point he is

followed by Ulrich, in his discussion of the
relation between the scroll and the text used by
Josephus.[2] On the other hand, Tov has argued that
the disagreements between the scroll and the LXX
are more numerous and more important than indicated by Cross and Ulrich; he has also pointed out
that in some sections, independent variants are
more frequent than in other parts.[3] Thus he
considers the scroll an independent witness, not
to be characterized as "Septuagintal." Tov's call
for more precision in the statistical treatment of
the material provided the starting-point for our
investigation.[4] First I wish to set out some of
the principles of the statistical approach; next I
address the question why this method should be
used.

Before turning to the figures, we must determine what to count. Arithmetically the interchange
וישחט/וישחטו (1 Sam 1:25) has the same value as a
long addition, but in fact its status is quite
different. The first variant is no more than a
common interchange of singular and plural, whereas
a long addition pertains to the structure of the
text, might represent exegesis, and on all
accounts has far more implications. It would be a
serious error to count both variants together in
one class.[5] Therefore, analysis of the figures
must be preceded by an objective classification:
1. Obvious mechanical variants,
2. Substitution / interchange of words within the
same syntactic slot,
3. Longer / shorter syntactic slots (expansion or
condensation),

4. Presence / absence of entire syntactic slots (addition or omission),
5. Presence / absence of entire clauses or sentences (addition or omission),
6. Complicated redactional processes,
7. Changes in word order.

These categories are not quantitive. The point is not that the phrase היוצא מפיך is longer than דברו (1 Sam 1:23), but that it occupies the same slot in the sentence. By the same token, the expansion of ויחזק to ויחזק שאול in 1 Sam 15:27 is quite different from the addition of בן נר in אבנר בן נר. In the former case the longer reading introduces an explicit subject into the sentence, whereas in the latter instance, a given slot has been expanded; without this expansion, sentence structure and meaning still remain the same. Categorization has the additional advantage of enabling us to differentiate between various processes. For example, two manuscripts may represent one and the same revision, without descending from one common ancestor; this would be evident from the data, for we would find significant differences in the categories of redactional processes and large plusses, but not in the class of substitution.

For our inquiry each one of the categories has been divided into subgroups. The first subgroup includes all cases of agreement between the scroll and the LXX (as against MT): a. 4Q = LXX / against MT. On the other hand, disagreement between the Old Greek and the scroll covers three subgroups: b. 4Q = MT / against LXX; c. LXX = MT / against 4Q; d. all witnesses at variance.

STATISTICS AND TEXTUAL FILIATION 219

The last subgroup, e. indeterminable, is not taken into account.

In order to examine the relationship between the witnesses to the text, we assume at the outset that there are no significant relations between the texts. This is our "zero-hypothesis" (H_o); the aim of our statistics is to refute it ("reject H_o"). If H_o is correct, laws of chance lead us to expect every one of the sub-groups (a) - (c) to contain the same number of variants, that is *circa* 30 % of the total score. In order to illustrate this assumption, we suppose a lottery with a hundred prizes to divide (X=100), and 2,000 participants, who are equally distributed over 4 clubs with 500 members each, or .25 of the *population* [probability=p(x)]. There is no reason to presume that the allotment of the prizes should not be the same for each club: in the long run each club should win .25 of the total of prizes, namely 25. This is the "*expectation*" [p(x).X]. "Expectation" is thus an objective theoretical quantity, following from the figures alone. Of course, in reality there may be *deviations* from the theoretical expectation. In that case, we have to ask whether this deviation can be explained by the figures alone (there may always be "flukes"), or whether we must assume that the result has been conditioned by outside constraints. For example, the results of a lottery might be influenced by a hidden magnet under the roulette-table. If certain mathematical functions (e.g. Chi-square) show that the figures alone suffice to explain the deviation, it is "insignificant;" if the deviation is too large to allow for such explanation, the distribution of the data is considered "significant." Let us apply these concepts to the text of the Book of Samuel. If we consider the agreement between (most of) the witnesses the "main stream of tradition," we may regard disagreement (variance) as a deviation from the main stream. The critic notes all cases in which at least one of the witnesses contains a variant, and thus reaches a total number of variants (X). Since all witnesses have the same extent, the probable occurrence of variants is equal for each of them.[6] In the Book of Samuel the probability of deviation MT = the probability of deviation LXX = the probability of deviation 4Q = 1/3 of the total number of variants. For X=75, one would expect every witness to contain 25 variants.

Moreover, in some cases all readings must be different from each other. From a statistical point of view, this is the overlapping of two disagreements (q,r), expressed by the product of their probabilities [p(q).p(r)].[7] Let me illustrate this principle by means of the following example: out of a group of 100 neighbours, 10 (p=.10) like football and 10 (p=.10) play chess. How many football fans may be expected to play chess? This question concerns the overlapping of these two subgroups, and the answer is given by the product of both frequencies: 0.1 . 0.1 . (X) = .01 (X) = 1. In the Book of Samuel the probability of all readings being different = 1/3.1/3 =1/9. Altogether we have 10 units: p(a) - (c) =3/9 each; p(d)=1/9. That gives .30 for (a) - (c), and 0.10 for (d). So, if every one of the sub-groups (a) - (c) contains circa 30 % of the readings, whereas the fourth subset contains about 10 % of the total score, this is in keeping with the theoretical expectation. Therefore, H_o cannot be rejected. On the other hand, H_o must be rejected in the following cases:

a. The sub-groups (a) - (c) contain significantly more (or less) than 30 %. Whatever our personal preferences, in this case we can only conclude that there is a certain relationship between the witnesses.

b. If rubrics (a) - (c) are more or less equal and rubric (d) small or non-extant (significantly smaller than 10 out of a total of 100), we conclude that all texts have influenced each other and all are interdependent. (If we have less than a total of 100 readings this conclusion is not warranted.)

c. Sub-group (d) contains significantly more examples than expected (at least 11 variants out of a total of 50), whereas rubrics (a) - (c) are of equal size. In such a case, all three witnesses are independent.

The statistical method has considerable advantages to offer. Classical textual criticism, as developed in 19th century classical philology, requires the critic to establish the filiation of texts on the basis of two criteria: common corruptions and common characteristic variants. If two texts have striking corruptions in common, it is assumed that they descend from one exemplar that contained these corruptions. If the critic cannot detect enough common corruptions, he checks significant common readings; failing this, he tries his luck with a large number of less significant readings.[8] In any case, the factors common to the manuscripts should always be more than mere chance.[9]

This method has come under heavy attack for a variety of reasons, and in biblical studies it is not very useful:
1. It is not always clear which reading is original, and which one is secondary. The decision which variant constitutes a corruption, is always a matter of personal preference. Hence this type of analysis necessarily involves subjective judgment.[10] Moreover, one cannot always determine whether a secondary reading in fact arose by corruption, or whether it represents exegesis or revision for ideological or linguistic reasons. If some textual witnesses contain common features relating to exegesis and linguistic revision, this does not imply that they are related to one and the same manuscript. Agreement of this kind might very well be caused by the influence of exegetical tradition and may even be coincidental. For example, in the pericope of the Blessing of the Sabbath SP reads ויכל אלהים ביום הששי מלאכתו אשר עשה, whereas the MT has ביום השביעי (Gen 2:2). The fact that the LXX also speaks of the sixth day does not mean that its *Vorlage* and the Samaritan descend from one common exemplar: both these witnesses may well represent an exegetical tradition that aims to avoid a reference to divine activity on the seventh day.
2. It is even more difficult to draw the line between significant and meaningless variants. Following Maas, one might state that a significant variant is one which cannot have been invented by

the medieval scribe.[11] This criterion, however, can only rarely be applied to the biblical text: we are not dealing with medieval copyists, but with scribes in a period in which the literary tradition of biblical Hebrew has still not been forgotten. These scribes and translators are the predecessors and contemporaries of the poets and writers who composed the books of *Ben Sira* and *Jubilees*, and the *Hodayoth Scroll*. Viewed from another angle, a reading may be called significant if it cannot have arisen by sheer accident. This definition, too, is vague. For instance, Mathews considers the variance ואהלים/ואלהיו (2 Sam 7:23 according to LXX, 4QSam^a) to be significant.[12] Another scholar might, however, regard this as a matter of exegesis, or even as a common metathesis. Another criterion for "significance" is idea content. A variant that relates to content is significant, but an interchange like כאשר/מכל אשר (1 Sam 2:16) is not. The problem is, however, that for textual analysis interchanges that are "significant" in this sense, are necessarily suspect, since they may always involve exegesis. The example of ואהלים/ואלהיו is a case in point.

3. The classical approach is based on the assumption that the manuscripts in question are not "contaminated," i.e., that in copying his exemplar the scribe has not been influenced by additional manuscripts or oral tradition. Of course, if the manuscripts in question have been subject to influence from other traditions, common readings do not prove common descent or filiation: the variant may issue from alternative traditions.[13]

For biblical studies this point is decisive: the frequency of the "double readings" shows that in this area contamination prevails everywhere. Exegetic tradition is a contaminating factor par excellence. In short, the classical approach does not offer any solutions for the problems posed by the transmission of the text of the Hebrew Bible. On the other hand, we must acknowledge that only this approach can provide the foundations on which to base textual criticism. Hence we must not abandon the stemmatic method, but overcome the difficulties involved.

In my opinion, these problems may be solved by statistics. For statistical analysis it does not matter whether a given variant is "significant," "secondary," "corrupt" or "insignificant." What counts, is number. Agreements (common variants) are significant, if their number is "significantly" larger than expected. If that is the case the textual critic must reject the hypothesis that these texts are independent; he may then proceed to examine the connections between them by his own criteria. This approach can also be applied to contaminated manuscripts: if two manuscripts have a large number of "contaminations" in common, this is a very meaningful feature of the transmission.

The statistical method does not require that there be no exceptions to the rule. If there are twenty cases of agreement of 4QSam=LXX (against MT), and ten cases of disagreement (three cases of 4QSam=MT and seven cases of LXX=MT, with an expectation of nine), the statistician still detects a significant connection between the

scroll and the LXX. The exceptions are a matter
of chance. Hence, the result of our analysis will
be less rigid than a stemma properly speaking. In
fact, it should rather be regarded as a stream-
diagram, indicating different undercurrents within
one river-bed. Thus, statistical analysis meets
all our demands for certainty, without committing
us to the subjective presuppositions of the
classical approach. I do not pretend that
statistics are totally and unequivocally
objective. On the contrary, interpretation of
statistical data is a matter of common sense and
critical judgment. One may draw the wrong
conclusion. But on the whole this approach is far
more objective and well-founded than common text-
critical arguments.

In the next section I have listed and
categorized those passages of 1 Sam 1-2 Sam 10
for which the $4QSam^{a}$ readings have been published
with the complete context of the fragment in which
they have been found; only in this case can one be
certain of being acquainted with all agreements
and disagreements;[14] additional variants (mainly
from Ulrich's discussion of the scroll) have been
presented as "additional examples;" they have been
marked with an asterisk, and will not figure in
the statistical analysis. Data on 2 Sam 11-24 are
to be presented in separate tables; instead of LXX
I shall mainly (but not always) quote the Lucianic
recension, in particular where LXX^{B} represents
Kaige. I have not adduced readings based on
reconstructions of lacunae; a reconstruction of
this kind may be attempted in view of our final
results, but should not appear in a discussion of

the basic data. This statistical method is not concerned with the question which reading is primary and which one secondary. In classical textual criticism, however, this is a central problem, and therefore we shall indicate those cases in which we may take it for granted that MT is primary (@M), that Q is primary (@Q) or that LXX is primary (@G); cases in which both LXX and Q have the primary text have been indicated by @@. Our judgment was quite subjective, and has been based on the recognition of supposedly "obvious" lexical difficulties (ld), "obvious" exegesis proving that the other reading is secondary (ex), as well as considerations pertaining to grammatical structure (str) and context (ctxt); synonymous readings have been indicated by =. Details that are important for the understanding of the reading but do not constitute variants in themselves, have been adduced within curly brackets.

II

1. Obvious mechanical variants

In this category I have listed those readings for which LXX and/or 4QSam^a "undoubtedly" offer the primary text. In this case common variants LXX=4Q may derive independently from the ancient text.

a. LXX = Q / against MT

@@ld   1   1;24 בפרים שלשה MT] Q,LXX
                   [בפר (בן) בקר] (Q+ משלש)
@@gr   2   2:21 כי פקד MT] LXX,Q ויפקד
@@str 3   2 Sam 6:3-4 חדשה-בגבעה MT
                 (dittography)] LXX,Q> = 1 Chr 13:7

STATISTICS AND TEXTUAL FILIATION

        disagreement LXX / Q
    b. Q=MT / against LXX -0
    c. LXX=MT / against Q -0
    d. all witnesses at variance

@Q	1	5:9	גתה Q] MT {הסבר} אתר =Luc.; LXX >
2 Sam			
@Q	2	6:5	[עז ר]בשירים Q] MT עצי ברושים =1 Chr 13:8; LXX doublet
=	3	6:6	נדון Q (נידן?)] MT נכון; LXX νωδαβ; 1 Chr 13:9 כידן

                2 Sam 11-24
     a. Q = LXX / against MT

@@	1*	13:39	דוד המלך MT,LXX] Luc.LXX^{MN}, [רו]ח המלך Q
@@	2*	18:9	וַיִּתַּן MT] LXX,Q ויתל (passive)
@@	3*	24:17	[רא]נכי הרעה Q] MT ואנכי העריתי הָרֵעֹתִי = LXXMSS (majority, including AMNB^{ab},Luc. = Copt.,Eth.); 1 Chr 21:17 והרע הרעתי ; Tg. Neb.= MT but also has כענא ביד רעיא

This category is too small to be taken into account.

2.Interchange of words

The second category is far more important for our purposes, since it includes small-scale phenomena, which can only be transferred from one manuscript to the other by copying.

     a. Q = LXX / against MT
a) function words/grammatical interchange

=	1	1:25	וישחט=Q] MT וישחטו=LXX (Luc. plural)
@@str	2	2:4	חתה MT] LXX,Q חתים
@Mstr	3	2:10	יְחַתּוּ MT] LXX,Q יחת (causative)
=	4	2:20	וברך ... ויאמר MT] LXX,Q ... לאמר
=	5	2:21	עם MT] LXX,Q לפני
	6	2:32	בביתך MT] LXX,Q בביתי
=	7	5:10	הָסֻבָּה MT] LXX,Q [הסבות]ם
2 Sam			
=	8	3:29	ואל MT] LXX,Q ועל

	9	3:33	עַל LXX,Q] אֶל MT
=	10	3:34	בנחש[תי]ם LXX,Q] לנחשתים MT
=	11	6:3	עַל LXX,Q] אֶל MT
=	12	6:9	לאמור LXX,Q] {וַיִּרָא} וַיֹּאמֶר MT = 1 Chr 13:12

Additional examples:

=	1*	2:36	לאמר LXX,Q] וַאמָר MT
	2*	3:4	שמו[ו]אל Q] אֶל שמואל MT; LXX σαμουηλ σαμουηλ
=	3*	8:18	הֵהֵם LXX,Q] הַהוּא MT
=	4*	9:18	אֶת שמואל LXX,Q] אֶל שמואל MT
=	5*	14:47	ובמלכי צובה LXX,Q] ובמלך צובה MT
=	6*	31:3	עַל LXX,Q] אֶל MT

2 Sam

|=| 7* | 2:5 | עַל LXX,Q] עִם MT |
|=| 8* | 3:1 | הולך וד[ג]ל LXX,Q] הלכים ודלים MT הולך וגדול |

b) lexemic interchange

@@ex	13	1:23	היוצא מפיך LXX,Q;] אֶת דבריו MT
=	14	2:20	ישלם LXX,Q] יָשֵׁם MT
=	15	2:22	לכל LXX,Q] לבני MT
@Mldex	16	2:29	תביט LXX,Q] תבעטו MT (cp. v. 32; רהבשׁת; laryngual)
@Mex	17	2:29	להבריאכם MT] Q להבריך; LXX ἐνευλογεῖσθαι (etym. √ ברך)
@Q	18	5:9	הֵסַבּוּ אתו Q] סבו גחה MT; LXX: τὸ μετελθεῖν αὐτήν
=	19	10:26	יהו[ר]ה LXX,Q] אלהים MT
	20	10:27-11:1	ויהי כמו Q] ויהי כמחריש MT = LXX חדש

2 Sam

=	21	3:23	אֶל דוד LXX,Q] אֶל המלך MT
@M	22	3:34	כנב[ו]ל Q] כנפול MT; LXX ὡς ναβαλ
@M	23	4:12	מפיבשת LXX,Q] אִישׁבֶשֶׁת MT
	24	5:9	ריבנה עיר LXX,Q] וִיבן דוד MT (1 Chr 11:8 ויבן העיר)
=	25	6:5	בני LXX,Q] בית MT

Additional examples:

@Mld	10*	6:3	ו[נ]כפר LXX,Q] ונרדע MT
=	11*	9:18	העיר LXX,Q] הַשַּׁעַר MT
=	12*	9:19	(ר/ו) הוא LXX,Q] הָרֹאֶה MT
=	13*	10:25	[ומ]ר למק LXX,Q] לביתו MT (cf. 6:2)
=	14*	11:8	שבעים אלף LXX,Q] שלשים אלף MT
=	15*	15:29	ישרב LXX,Q] ישקר MT
@Mex	16*	17:4	ארבע LXX,Q] שש MT

STATISTICS AND TEXTUAL FILIATION 229

=	17*	25:3	והאיש [MT רהוא] LXX,Q
	18*	27:10	על מ[י] MT אל] LXX,Q
=	19*	30:29	הקיני MT] LXX,Q הקנזי (י/ז), metathesis)

2 Sam
| | 20* | 3:3 | כלאב MT דליה] LXX,Q (<דליהו?;) 1 Chr 3:1 דניאל) |
| @Mex | 21* | 7:23 | ואלהיו MT] Q ואהלים; LXX καὶ σκηνώματα (1 Chr 17:21 >) |

Disagreement Q / LXX
b. Q = MT / against LXX

=	1	2:23 כדברים האל[ה] MT=Q] LXX κατὰ τὸ ῥῆμα τοῦτο
@M	2	5:10 עקרו[ן] MT=Q] LXX εἰς ἀσκαλῶνα (cf. LXX 17:52)
=	3	2 Sam 6:6 אל MT =Q, Luc. πρός] LXX ἐπί

c. LXX = MT / against Q

=	1	2:18 חגור MT =LXX περιεζωσμένον] חוגר Q
=	2	2:29 מראשית MT=LXX ἀπαρχῆς] מראש Q
=	3	2:29 מנחת MT = LXX θυσίας] מנחות Q
=	4	5:8 יטב MT =LXX μετελθέτω] י[סבו] Q

2 Sam
=	5	3:29 כל בית אביו MT = LXX] Q [ו]ל כ בית יואב
	6	3:28-29 מדמי ... יחלו MT=LXX] Luc, ודם [אבנר] בן נר י[חול Q
@Q	7	6:2 מבעלי {יהודה} MT=LXX] Q מבעלה (1 Chr 13:6 בעלתה)
@Mld	8	6:13 שור ומריא MT =LXX] Q שב[עה] פרים [ושבע]ה אילים = 1 Chr 15:26

Additional examples:
=	1*	1:11 יעבור MT=LXX] Q יעלה
=	2*	14:32 אל MT=LXX εἰς] Q על; =Luc. ἐπί
=	3*	26:11 החנית MT=LXX] Q חניתו

d. all at variance

	1	2:20 שאל MT] LXX ἔχρησας; ה[שאיל]ה Q
	2	2:9 רגלי MT] Q ודרך; LXX: colon deest
	3	5:11 מהומת מות MT] Q [מ]המת יהו[ה] or הומת [מ]; LXX σύγχυσις

2 Sam
| | 4 | 3:34 הֻגָּשׁ MT] Q הגש; LXX^BA προσήγαγεν (MNrell., Luc. -γες) |

5   4:4   היה MT] Q ויהי; LXX οὗτος

e. indeterminable

1:22 [י]פְנֵי אֶת MT,Q] LXX τῷ προσώπῳ (=?
אל פני, לפני)
1d   9:24 [ה]עליה/ורהעליה MT] Q <; LXX
Ulrich / [ה]עלינה] McCarter
27:10 וראל...ועל MT] Q ועל...וראל; LXX
κατά...κατά
= 2 Sam 5:8 שנאו k שׂנְאֵי q MT] LXX καὶ τοὺς
μισοῦντας ~ q ; Q שנאה

2 Sam 11-24

a. Q = LXX-Luc. / against MT

a) function words/grammatical interchange

=   1   24:16 היה MT] LXX^{LucMNrell},Q עמד
(1 Chr 21:15 עמד)

Additional examples:

=   1* 12:17 עליו MT=LXX] Luc.,Q אליו
=   2* 13:24 עם עבדך MT=LXX] Luc.,Q אל עבדו
=   3* 18:3 ישימו MT=LXX] Luc.,Q י[ש]י[מ]ו
=   4* 20:10 אל החמש MT=LXX^{AN}] Q על החמש (=Luc.)
=   5* 20:10 רדפו MT] LXX^{AN},Luc,Q ירדף
=   6* 21:6 יתן (ינתן)k q MT; k=Luc]
LXX^{AMNrell},Q [ונ]תנו להם; LXX^{B} δότω
(~ q)
@Mld 7* 23:1 הֻקַם {עַל} MT] Q {אל} הקים = LXX,
Luc.

b) lexemic interchange

8* 11:4 וַתָּשָׁב MT =LXX] Luc. καὶ ἀπῆλθεν;
Q [וא]ותב
@Mex 9* 13:3 יונדב MT=LXX] Luc.,Q [י]הרנתן
=   10* 18:9 ואבשלום MT=LXX] Luc., Q והוא
=   11* 18:11 עשרה MT=LXX] Luc.,LXX^{MN},
Q [חמ]ש[י]ם
@Mld 12* 23:1 {הֻקַם} עַל MT] Q אל {הקים} = LXX
κύριος, Luc. ὁ θεός
13* 23:3 משל..משל MT~LXX] Q מושל...מושל
= Luc. ἄρξον...ἄρχε

=   14* 24:15 ה' MT=LXX] Luc.,Q אלוהים
{* 22:51 ישעורה MT =LXXplur.,Ps] Q ישועה=Luc.
{* 22:33 מערוזי MT~LXX] Luc.,Q מאזרני=Ps המאזרני
{* 22:46 ממסגרותם MT=LXX] Luc.,Q ממסגרוהם

STATISTICS AND TEXTUAL FILIATION   231

{* 22:49 הצילני MT = LXX,Ps] Luc.,Q הצרני

Disagreement Q / LXX
b. Q = MT / against LXX

=   1* 11:4 ותבוא אליו MT = Q] LXX καὶ
              εἰσῆλθεν πρὸς αὐτήν
=   2* 18:6 [ה]שדה MT=Q,Luc.] LXX εἰς τὸν
              δρυμόν (=ביער)
{* 22:36 ישעך MT=Q] LXX σωτηρίας μου

c. MT = LXX / against Q

=   1* 12:14 את איבי ה' MT =LXX,Luc., OL;]
        את דבר ה' Q (= Copt.)
{* 22:48 הנתן MT =LXX,Luc.] Q נהן/[...]

How significant are these figures? In statistics this issue is settled by means of mathematical functions, such as Chi-square (X^2). This function is based on the difference between "expectation" and "actual score," in relation to the expectation itself: it is the sum ($\underline{\Sigma}$) of the squares of the differences between expectation and actual score ($[E(x)-x]^2$), divided each time by $E(x)$: $\Sigma[E(x)-x]^2/E(x)$.[16] The outcome of this function is significant, if and only if it is beyond a certain limit (α), which may assume several values: α = .05 , .025, .01, .005, .001. What is the meaning of limits? One must keep in mind that a function such as X^2 defines a graph; the limit (α) denotes an upper percentage of a certain part of the surface of the graph: α = .05 means that α is the limit beyond which there lies .05 (5 %) of the surface of the graph. For our data (with three undefined factors = degrees of freedom) the upper percentage .05 is reached with 7.81473. Any figure below this number lies to the left of the limit; any number > 7.81473 lies to the right. Since this is an extremely small part of the graph (<5 %), chances that the outcome still depends on the figures only, are slight. The higher the outcome, the smaller the remaining part of the surface and the slighter the chances that the result depends on the figures only. For $\alpha=.05$ these chances are 5 in a hundred, that is out of a hundred results five would be coincidental. For $\alpha=.025$, the odds are 25 in a thousand (five in two hundred); for $\alpha=.001$ the odds are one in a thousand.

Let us now proceed with the analysis of the data for category 2.

Statistical analysis (2)

	score	frequency	expectation	x^2
Q = LXX / against MT	25	.610	12.3	13.113
Q = MT / against LXX	3	.073		7.0317
LXX = MT / against Q	8	.195		1.5033
all at variance	5	.122	4.1	0.1976
Total	41	1		21.8456

Extremely significant for $\alpha=0.001$ (>16.266; v=3)

This result is extremely significant. The chances that it is coincidental (that is: H_o is correct), are far less than one in a thousand. Hence we must conclude that the scroll and the Septuagint version of Samuel belong to one and the same branch, as against MT.

A similar result has been obtained for 2 Sam 11-24:

	score	frequency	expectation	x^2
Q = LXX / against MT	16	0.833	5.7	18.6123
Q = MT / against LXX	2	0.111		2.4018
LXX = MT / against Q	1	0.056		3.8754
all at variance	0	0	1.9	1.9
Total	19	1		26.7895

Once again extremely significant for $\alpha=0.001$ (>16.266; v=3).

STATISTICS AND TEXTUAL FILIATION

3. Slots longer / shorter
a. Q = LXX / against MT

a) MT shorter

@Mex	1	1:24	באיפה אחת קמח MT] LXX: καὶ ἄρτοις καὶ οιφι σεμιδάλεως ; Q [...] לחם[17]
=	2	2:2	אין[1] כ]יא אין[MT] Q,LXX
@@str	3	2:25	יחטא MT] LXX,Q [יחטא]חטא[19]
@Mstr	4	2:25	אל יהוה Q [MT אלהים = LXX πρὸς κύριον

2 Sam

=	5	3:28-29	מדמי...יחלו MT=LXX] Luc, Q ודם [אבנר בן נר י]חול
=	6	4:12	בן] נר + LXX,Q [MT אבנר

b) MT longer

=	7	2:16	מכול אשר[19] MT] LXX,Q
=	8	2:21	ותהר ותלד MT] LXX,Q ותלד עוד (cf. LXX 2 Sam 12:24; Gen 4:25)
=	9	2:22	כל MT] LXX,Q <(את אשר, cf.22b MT)
=	10	5:10	אלהי צבאות MT] LXX,Q צבאות
=	11	10:26	החיל {וילכו} MT] LXX,Q בני החיל
=	12	2 Sam 5:6	כי אם MT] LXX,Q כי

Additional examples:

=	1*	1:13	והנה היא MT] LXX,Q והיא (casus pendens)
@Mstr	2*	2:30	אמר אמרתי MT] LXX,Q אמרתי
	3*	3:4	אל שמואל MT] Q [שמו]ראל; LXX σαμουηλ σαμουηλ
@Mex	4*	6:1	ולקסמים MT] LXX,Q + [למעונ]ני[ם (cf. Deut 18:10,14)
@Mex	5*	6:3	ארון MT] LXX,Q + ברית ה'
	6*	6:4	וחמשה עכברי זהב MT] LXX,Q >
@@ld	7*	10:4	שתי לחם MT] LXX δύο ἀπαρχὰς ἄρτων; Q [...ה]נופות

2 Sam

=	8*	2:15	לבנימין MT] LXX,Q לבני בנימין
@@ctxt	9*	8:4	אלף[1] MT] LXX,Q + ר]כב]

Disagreement Q / LXX
b. Q = MT / against LXX

a) MT shorter

=	1	2:16	האיש MT,Q] LXX = האיש הזבח (cf. 2:15)

2 Sam

=	2	3:1	ודוד MT = Q] LXX = ובית דוד

| = | 3 | 3:27 אחיר MT= Q אחיהו] LXX = אחי יואב
(Luc. = MT) |
| = | 4 | 3:28 עד עולם MT = Q =LXX^B] LXX^{MLuc}. = מעתה ועד עולם |

b) MT longer

| = | 5 | 5:8 ארון אלהי ישראל MT=Q] LXX > ישראל |

Additional examples:

=	1*	1:12 ועלי MT = Q] LXX = עלי הכהן
=	2*	10:14 דוד שאול MT = Q] LXX ὁ οἰκεῖος αὐτοῦ
=	3*	26:12 מקיץ כי MT = Q] LXX > כי

c. LXX = MT / against Q

a) MT shorter

=	1	1:24 בפרים MT, בפר LXX] Q + בקר [בן]
=	2	2:16 ויאמר {אליו} האיש MT] LXX καὶ ἔλεγεν ὁ ἀνήρ; Q ור[מ]ר האיש וענה
=	3	5:10 ארון האלהים MT=LXX] Q ארון אלהי ישראל

2 Sam

=	4	3:34 כל העם MT=LXX] Q > העם
=	5	3:25 אבנר בן נר MT = LXX] Q > בנר[א]
=	6	3:34 אסרות MT=LXX] Q+ בזקים
=	7	6:13 שר ומריא MT = LXX,Luc.] Q [שבעה] פרים ושבע[ה אילים] = 1 Chr 15:26

b) MT longer

| = | 8 | 2:21 הנער MT=LXX] Q< |
| = | 9 | 2:25 אביהם MT =LXX] Q > |

Additional examples:

| = | 1* | 8:6 לעבדים MT = LXX] Q עבדים |

d. all at variance

| = | 1 | 2:14 בכיור או בדוד או בקלחת או בפרור MT (4 nouns)] LXX εἰς τὸν λέβητα τὸν μέγαν ἢ εἰς τὸ χαλκίον ἢ εἰς τὴν κύθραν (3 nouns); Q: בסיר או בפרור (2 nouns)[20] |
| = | 2 | 2:15 ראם לא ולקחתי MT] LXX: καὶ οὐ μὴ λάβω; Q ולקחתי (possibly < ולא ולקחתי LXX= לקחתי) |

2 Sam

| = | 3 | 4:10 לאמר הנה MT] Q [כי לאמ]ר; LXX ὅτι; Luc λέγων ὅτι |
| = | 4 | 5:11 חרשי אבן קיר MT] Luc,Q קיר חרשי קיר (=VL ≃ 1 Chr 14:1); LXX^{BMN} > קיר |

STATISTICS AND TEXTUAL FILIATION 235

=   5   6:7   לִ]פְנֵי Q [MT עִם אֲרוֹן הָאֱלֹהִים
                     הָאֱ[לֹ]הִ[ים] = 1 Chr 13:10; LXX doublet

Additional examples:

        1* 6:20 הָאֱלֹהִים הַקָּדוֹשׁ ה' MT] LXX >$_{NLuc,MSS}$,^{21}
                     ה' הָאֱלֹהִים ;Q > הָאֱלֹהִים (=LXX^{NLuc,MSS})

2 Sam 11-24
a. Q = LXX / against MT

=   1* 19:8 כִּי אִם אֵינְךָ MT] LXX,Q כִּי אִם אֵינְךָ
=   2* 19:10 הַמֶּלֶךְ MT] LXX,Q + דָּוִד
@@   3* 15:31 וְדָוִד MT] LXX,Q [ד]ויד[לוד]ר
{* 22:39 וְאֹכְלֵם וַאֲמַחֲצֵם MT dupl.] LXX, Luc., Q
[אֲמַחֲ]צֵם=Ps18
{* 22:43 אֶרְקָעֵם אַדְּקֵם MT dupl.] Q אֶרְקָעֵם = Luc,
LXX^{Pe}; LXX^{Sam} אַדְּקֵם

Disagreement Q / LXX
b. Q = MT / against LXX

=   1* 15:2 עַל יַד MT =Q] Luc. ἐπί; LXX ἀνὰ χεῖρα

c. MT = LXX / against Q:

=   1* 13:32 בְּנֵי MT =LXX,Luc.] Q pr. כֹל
=   2* 15:2 דֶּרֶךְ הַשַּׁעַר MT=LXX,Luc.] Q הַדֶּרֶךְ
=   3* 18:10 אִישׁ אֶחָד MT =LXX] Q אִישׁ
{* 22:37 תַּחְתֵּנִי MT=LXX] Q>

Statistical analysis (3)

	score	frequency	expectation
Q = LXX / against MT	12	.4	9.3
LXX = MT / against Q	9	.2667	
Q = MT / against LXX	5	.1667	
all at variance	5	.1667	3.1
Total	31	1	x^2 = 3.946

This distribution is insignificant. This rubric contains quite a few cases of agreement LXX=MT, whereas the scroll offers many particular variants, including two shorter readings.

4. Presence/absence of slots

a. Q = LXX / against MT

a) MT shorter

=   1   1:24 ותעלהו עמה] LXX καὶ ἀνέβη μετ' αὐτοῦ εἰς σηλωμ ≃ Q ותעל אותו שילה (cf. בית הֵ֗ שלו in the penultimate clause)

@@ctxt 2   5:8 ישראל MT] Q + [גתה] = LXX εἰς γεθθα

@@ctxt 3   5:8 ישראלᵃ MT] LXX,Q + [גתה]

@@ctxt 4   2:20 והלכו MT] LXX,Q וילך האיש

=   5   2:32 יהיה MT] LXX,Q + לך (note : בביתי pro MT בביתך)

2 Sam

@Mctxt 6   3:7 ויאמר MT] LXX,Q + [בן מפיבשת] שאול

@Mctxt 7   4:2 היו MT] LXX,Q + למפיבשת

=   8   6:6 וישלח עזא MT] LXX,Q + [את] ידו = 1 Chr 13:9

b) MT longer

=   9   2:17 נאצו האנשים MT] LXX,Q > האנשים

@@str 10   5:10 לאמר MT] LXX,Q + למה (haplography)

2 Sam

=   11   3:3 אשה נבל הכרמלי MT] LXX,Q [ה]כרמלית

=   12   3:36 טרבᶠⁱⁿ MT] LXX,Q >

Additional examples

@@ctxt 1*   2:27 במצרים MT] LXX,Q + עבדים

=   2*   2:27 אליו MT] LXX,Q >

=   3*   2:28 לפני MT] LXX,Q >

=   4*   10:25 איש ... שמואל {וישלח} MT] LXX,Q {וישלח} שמואל ... וילכו איש

=   5*   15:27 ויחזק MT] LXX,Q + שאול

=   6*   15:31 וישתחו שאול MT] LXX,Q > שאול

=   7*   24:15 מִי MT] LXX,Q + אהה

=   8*   24:19 לִיᶠⁱⁿ MT] LXX,Q >

2 Sam

=   9*   3:7 ושמה MT] LXX,Q >

@Mctxt 10*   4:1 וישמע MT] LXX,Q + [בשת]מפי

=   11*   7:23 לכם MT] LXX,Q > (=1 Chr 17:21)

=   12*   10:5 לדוד MT] LXX,Q + האנשים [על] = 1 Chr 19:5

Disagreement Q / LXX

b. Q = MT / against LXX

2 Sam

        1   3:32 העםᶠⁱⁿ MT=Q] LXX + ἐπὶ αβεννηρ

STATISTICS AND TEXTUAL FILIATION

  2   4:12 בחברון MT = Q,LXX^{MN}Luc] LXX^{BA} >
  3 10: 6 עמון MT=LXX,Luc.] Q + אלף ככר
               כסף = 1 Chr 19:6

Additional examples:

      1* 24:18 ויאמר MT = Q] LXX + σαουλ

c. LXX = MT / against Q

  1   2:23 שמע MT=LXX] Q + [...]דברי
  2 2 Sam 6:2 יהודה MT = LXX] Q קריו]ת אל
               ליהודה [אשר] יערים 1= Chr 13:6

Additional examples:

=   1* 9:7 לנערו MT=LXX] Q>

d. All at variance

  1   2:16 אליו MT] LXX >; Q אל נער הכוהן
  2   2:16 קַטֵּר יַקְטִירוּן MT, // 2:15] LXX
          θυμιαθήτω (=יקטר passive); Q יקטר הכוהן
          (>infin.=LXX; + subject)
  3 2 Sam 5:1 ויאמרו לאמר MT] Luc לאמר>;
          ויאמרו>=LXX^{MN}, 1 Chr 11:1; LXX^{BAyck}
          ויאמרו לו

Additional examples:

      1* 11:9 מחר תהיה לכם ישועה MT ≃ LXX αὔριον
          ὑμῖν (+ἔσται Luc.) ἡ σωτηρία] Q [...]
          מיהוה התש]ועה[
      2* 28: 1 {במחנה} וְאַנְשֶׁיךָ MT = LXX] Q +
          [למ]לחמה יזרעאל

e. indeterminable

1 Sam 2:2 ואין צור כאלהינו MT = Q] for צור LXX
has δίκαιος; possibly ≃ MT (transl. techn.);
possibly = צד(י)ק; in connection with the latter
possibility, we should pay attention to the fact
that Q has a long gap which might be reconstructed
as ואין צדיק כאלהינו (Cross; see below).

2 Sam 11-24

a. Q = LXX,Luc. / against MT

  1* 12:16 וישכב MT] LXX^{MNrell},Luc,Q + בשק
  2* 13:37 גשור MT] LXX,Q + [בא]רץ

3* 24:18 ויאמר לו MT =LXX,~ Chr 21:18]
Luc, Q > לו

Disagreement LXX / Q
b. Q = MT / against LXX,Luc.
1* 12:16 ושכב MT ~ וישכב Q] >LXX$^{Baya}_2$
2* 12:16 וילן MT = LXX] >Luc,Q
4* 18:3 העם [ויאמר] MT=Q,Luc.] LXX καὶ εἶπαν

c. LXX=MT / against Q
1* 11:3 החתי MT=LXX] Q + יואב כלי [ונ]ושא
1* 11:4 מטמאתה MT =LXX,Luc.,L] Q >
3* 12:15 ויאנש MT=LXX,Luc.] Q >
(haplography, cf. ויבקש, v. 16)

d. all at variance - 0

Statistical analysis (4)

	score	frequency	expect	x^2
Q = LXX / against MT	12	.6	6	6
Q = MT / against LXX	3	.15		1.5
LXX = MT / against Q	2	.1		2.667
all at variance	3	.15	2	.5
Total	20	1		10.667

Significant for α=0.025 (>9.3484; v=3).

Chances that this constellation is coincidental are less than 25 in a thousand. Although this result is far less obvious than the outcome for category 2, the connection between the scroll and the LXX is quite convincing.

5. Presence / absence of clauses / sentences
a. Q = LXX / against MT
a) MT shorter
1   1:24:והנער MT] LXX + μετ' αὐτῶν (v.25) καὶ προσήγαγον ἐνώπιον κυρίου καὶ ἔσφαξεν ὁ πατὴρ αὐτοῦ τὴν θυσίαν, ἣν ἐποίει ἐξ ἡμερῶν εἰς ἡμέρας τῷ κυρίῳ, καὶ προσήγαγεν τὸ παιδάριον καὶ ἔσφαξεν τὸν μόσχον καὶ προσήγαγεν αννα ἡ μήτηρ τοῦ παιδάριου κτλ (repetitive; possible

STATISTICS AND TEXTUAL FILIATION 239

			epanalepsis); Q + 'ה לפני ויבאו עמם[
	2	2:9 LXX,Q [MT כי לא לנוד]ר נדן נתן	אשר כ]הזב[ח את אבי]ך רישחט ²²ימימה לה'. וישחט את הפר ותבא את [... וי ברך שנ]י צדיק[
	3	2:10 κύριος LXX [דוש]ק + Q [k MT מריבו	ἅγιος
	4	2:24 שמע LXX,Q + כיא כן תעשרן אל[	לו[א טוב]ו[ת השמועות] אשר אני שרמע
2 Sam			
	5	8:7 ירושלים ויביאם MT [LXX,Q + גם	(LXX: καὶ ἔλαβεν αὐτά) [ל]אחר שושק מלך מצרים] [ב]על[יתו אל יר]ו[שלים] בימי רחבעם בן שלו[מה] [ארתם] [לקח

b) MT longer

	6	2:22 מועד-ואת MT] LXX,Q >	
	7	2:31-32 ישראל-מהירות MT] LXX,Q >²⁴	

Disagreement Q / LXX

b. Q = MT / against LXX

1	1:24 גמלהו כאשר Q,MT] LXX >	
2	2:9 חסידו-ידמר רגלי MT ~ Q ודרך	
	LXX > ח[]סידו ישמר[...]	
1*	8:18 ההוא MT ~ Q] הם LXX + ὅτι ὑμεῖς ἐξελέξασθε ἑαυτοῖς βασιλέα	fin
2*	15:29 להנחם MT=Q,Luc] LXX^NMSS αυτος (some MSS >) απειλησει και ουκ εμμενει	

c. LXX = MT / against Q

@Mex	1	1:22 עולם עד MT=LXX] Q + והו[תיה]ונת חייו ימי כול עולם עד נזיר (end clause parallels עולם עד...וישב)
@Mex	2	2:16 Q transposes (or repeats) 2:13 (והמזלג)-2:14a (excl. 'וגר יעשה ככה) before 2:17 (with many stylistic adjustments that will not be discussed now). Also Q adds: ...]מח ד[ב]ל רוב שר[ק הימין
@Mex	3	2:22 מאד MT=LXX] Q +[...] שנה תשעים בן
	4	6:9 'ה יהודה ארון MT=LXX] Q + [ויבוא] = Luc.
@Qex	5	11:1 init MT=LXX] Q pr

ורנ]חש מלך בני עמון הוא לחץ את בני גד ואת בני
ראובן בחזקה ונקר להם כו[ר]ל [ע]ין ימין ונתן אי[ן מה
ופחד] על [י]שראל ולוא נשאר איש בבני ישראל אשר
בעו[בר] [הירדן אש]ר ל[וא נ]קר לו נח[ש מלך] בני עמון

כּוֹל עין ימין רק שבעת אלפים איש [נסר מפני] בני עמרן
ויבאו אל [י]בש גלעד
ויהי כמו חדש ויעל נחש העמרני ויחן
(inter lineas) [גלעד] על יביש
6 11:9-10 LXX=MT] Q inserts line :
[...]; [...]לכם פתחו ה[...]
continuation next line: [ו]יאמר[ו] אנש[י]

d. all at variance

1 2 Sam 6:7 MT על השל[ח ידו]] LXX >; Q [על אשר
שלח ידו] אל [ה]ארון = 1 Chr 13:10.

e. indeterminable

1 1:22 MT עד יִגָּמֵל הנער] LXX ἕως τοῦ
ἀναβῆναι τὸ παιδάριον, ἐὰν ἀπογαλακτίσω
αὐτό (4Q has עד אשר יגמל; does ἐὰν
reflect a similar reading?)

2 Sam 11-24

a. Q = LXX / against MT

@@ 1* 13:21 MT ויחר לו מאד] LXX,Q + ולוא עצב]
את רוח אמנ[ון בנו כי אה]בו כי בכור[ו הוא]
2* 13:27 MT בני המלך] LXX,Q + [ויעש אבשלום
משתה כמשתה ה[מ]ל[ך]
{* 2 Sam 22:37 MT=LXX] Q: ולא מעדו קרסלי
interlineary addition (doubl.), and additionally
(on line) + [...] ול[א עמדו קמי עלי] = Luc.
b. Q = MT / against LXX: - 0

c. MT = LXX / against Q

1 24:16 Q + [דויד את] MT=LXX היבסי וישא
עיניו ... בי[ן] הארץ ובין [הש[מ]י]ם
וחר[ב]ו שלופה בידו [נטויה על ירושלים] ...
והזקנים על פנ[יהם מחכ]סים ב[ש]קים
2* 24:20 MT = LXX (including עברים עליו
Luc.)] Q + [מתכסים] בשקים וארנא דש חטים

Statistical analysis (5)

	score	frequency	expectation
Q = LXX / against MT	7	0.4375	4.8
Q = MT / against LXX	2	0.125	
LXX = MT / against Q	6	0.375	
all at variance	1	0.0625	1.6
Total	16	1	x^2 = 3.1667

This result is insignificant.
In this category the connection with the OG is
even less obvious than in rubric 3; on the other

STATISTICS AND TEXTUAL FILIATION 241

hand, the text of the scroll is slightly more independent. These tendencies are still more obvious in the categories of 6-7 (redactional phenomena and changes in word order). In rubric 6 we count one agreement LXX=MT against 4Q, and one case of disagreement between all witnesses; rubric 7 contains 1 case of agreement Q=LXX, 1 agreement Q=MT, and 3 agreements MT=LXX; of course these results are not susceptible to statistical analysis.

6. Complicated redactional phenomena

1:28 'וישתחו שם לה [MT] LXX 2:11 καὶ κατέλιπεν (many MSS -πον) αὐτὸν ἐκεῖ ἐνώπιον κυρίου; Q [ר]והשתחה שם ?הו[ר]והתנ/[?הו]והעזב]; order of words: MT=Q, against LXX.

2 Sam 10: 6

MT=LXX

את ארם בית רחוב
- - - ואת ארם צובא עשרים אלף רגלי
ואת מלך מעכה אלף איש ואיש טוב
שנים עשר אלף איש
- - - -

Q

- - - -
[ומן ארם מ]עכה [...ומצנב]ה רכב ופרשים
[...]ם אלף רכב [ואת מלך מעכה רא]ישטוב
- - - -
[ובני] עמון נאספר מן ה[ערים]
(ובני עמון נאספו מעריהם 1 Chr 19:6-7 ~)

7. Changes in word order

a. Q = LXX / against MT

1* 24:20 תחת היום הזה/אשר עשיתם MT] LXX,Q
[תחת אשר עשית]ה לי היום [הז]ה

2 Sam

2* 2:7 עליהם/למלך MT] LXX,Q ~
1 5:13 עוד/לדוד MT] LXX,Q (1 Chr 14:3 דויד עוד)

Disagreement Q / LXX

b. Q = MT / against LXX

1   10:26   Q ˜ MT וילכו עמו /החיל אשר...בלבם
            וילכו בני החיל / אשר... ˜ :LXX] (בלבבם)
            בלבבם עם שאול

1* 15:30   Q= MT נגד זקני ישראל ונגד עמי]
            נגד זקני עמי ונגד ישראל = LXX

c. LXX = MT / against Q

2 Sam

1   3:34   ?אן]סורות Q [MT=LXX ידך לא אֲסֻרוֹת
            ידיך לא[

2   3:34   MT =order LXX] הֻגָּשׁוּ /לא לנחשתים
            בנחש[תי]ם לא הגש Q

3   5:8a   הפסחים...והעורים = LXX^{BA}, Luc.]
            ו]א[ת הע]ורים ואת הן]פסחים[Q
            העורים והפסחים = LXX^{MN,MSS} cf. MT v. 6
            (=LXX^{BAMN}; Luc. ˜); cf. v. 8b: MT עור
            ופסח =Q,LXX

e. indeterminable

1 Sam 2:2

```
                    MT                        Q
[ואין צדיק כאלהינו]       - - -
[ואין בלח]ך        כי אין בלתך
ואין צור כאלהינו     ואין צור כאלהינו
```

LXX
καί οὐκ ἔστιν δίκαιος ὡς ὁ θεὸς ἡμῶν
οὐκ ἔστιν ἅγιος πλὴν σοῦ
    - - -

The view that the phrase καί οὐκ ἔστιν δίκαιος ὡς ὁ θεὸς ἡμῶν corresponds to MT ואין צור כאלהינו implies a change in word-order. In this case Q might be considered to contain a doublet, which also involves changes in the order of the phrases (Cross; see above).

2 Sam 11-24

a. Q = LXX / against MT

1* 11:5   אנוכי הרה LXX,Q] MT הרה אנכי
2* 15:2   ויקרא אבשלום אליו MT] LXX,Luc.,
           ויקרא לו אבשל]ום[Q

3*   19:12 ודבר כל ישראל בא אל המלך אל ביתו²
      MT] LXX,Q והמלך^{init}-אל ביתו¹
[לה]שיב [את המלך] [אל ביתו ודבר כול ישראל
בא אל המלך והמלך דויד שלח] אל צדוק הכו[הן]
(NB: צדוק הכוהן against MT,LXX)

III

Next we compare the agreements for categories
2-5; for the sake of comparison the data have been
given per 100.

Comparative Frequency

	2	4	3	5
Q = LXX / against MT	.61	.6	.4	.4375
Q = MT / against LXX	.073	.15	.1667	.125
MT = LXX / against Q	.195	.1	.2667	.375
All at variance	.122	.15	.1667	.0625
Significance α=	.001	.025	insignificant	

Categories 2 and 4 contain a significant number of
agreements between the scroll and the OG (> 60 %;
as against 30-40 % disagreements); on the other
hand, in categories 3 and 5 one notes the high
number of deviations that are characteristic of
the scroll, as borne out by the percentage of
singular readings:

Singular readings per 100

	2	4	3	5
MT	.732	.75	.548	.5
Q	.317	.3	.451	.375
LXX	.195	.25	.326	.125

4QSam^a is much more individualistic than the LXX.
In comparison with the table of the agreements we
see that the more freedom the scroll is allowed,
the less it is related to the OG. Its connections
with the MT are rather weak, although in rubric 3
the agreement Q=MT is remarkable. On the other
hand, there is a relatively strong affinity
between MT and the LXX, especially in rubric 5.

Agreements per 100

	2	4	3	5
Q=LXX	.694	.706	.462	.4667
LXX=MT	.222	.176	.192	.4
Q=MT	.083	.118	.346	.1333
Significance α=	.001	.025	insignificant	

These data warrant two conclusions.

1. The extremely high agreement between Q and the OG in categories 2 and 4 indicates that the scroll and the LXX version of Samuel belong to one and the same branch, as against MT. In other words, they are related to one hyparchetype.

As these rubrics include many insignificant variants in the sub-group 4Q=LXX, these two witnesses appear to represent one common manuscript tradition; otherwise it would be extremely difficult to account for the similarity. No doubt a scribe may decide to write מכל אשר for כאשר (1 Sam 2:16), or למקומו for לביתו (10:25). It is, however, highly unlikely that two different scribes would introduce the same "insignificant" revision time and again. Hence we can only assume that 4QSam^a and LXX ultimately descend from one and the same manuscript (or alternatively: textual tradition).

2. Rubrics 2-5 (categories 3 and 5 in particular) also contain many divergences between LXX and the Scroll. Hence we need a more precise definition of the relation between these witnesses.

As this issue cannot be settled by means of statistics, we have to apply the traditional methods of textual criticism. This way we shall also deal with the issue of the relationship between the scroll and the Hebrew parent text of

Chronicles. These considerations will provide some clues concerning the date of this textual tradition.

IV

In many cases MT obviously has the primary text as against the secondary variant of 4QSam[a] and LXX. First we must mention those passages in which the scroll and the OG agree in referring to Mephiboshet, whereas the original text undoubtedly meant Ishboshet:[25]

2 Sam 3:7 ויאמר MT] LXX,Q + [מפיבשת בן] שאול
   4:1 וישמע MT] LXX,Q + [מפי]בֶשֶׁת]
   4:2 היו MT] LXX,Q + למפיבשת
   4:12 אישבשת MT] LXX,Q מפיבשת

Since it is quite impossible to explain these readings as the product of some common, recurring corruption, they must represent a particular exegesis. This surmise is borne out by the following examples of exegetical variants:

2. Interchange

2:29 להבריאכם MT] Q להבריך, LXX ἐνευλογεῖσθαι
  (=etym. ✓ ברך)
2:29 תבעטו MT] LXX,Q תביט (cf. v. 32 והבטת;
  problem of laryngeal)
2:10 יחתו MT] LXX,Q יחת (causative)
2 Sam
3:34 כנפול MT] Q [כנב]ול; LXX ὡς ναβαλ
6:13 שור ומריא MT =LXX] Q [שב]עה[פרים ושבעו]ה
  [אילים =1 Chr 15:26
6:3 וינדע MT] LXX,Q ו[נ]כפר
7:23 ואלהיו MT] Q ואהלים, LXX καὶ σκηνώματα
  (1 Chr 17:21 >)
11:4 ותבוא אליו MT = Q] LXX καὶ εἰσῆλθεν πρὸς
  αὐτήν
23:1 הקם על MT] Q הקים אל;cf. LXX (κύριος), Luc.
  (ὁ θεός)

3. Longer/shorter slots

1:24 באיפה אחת קמח MT] LXX καὶ ἄρτοις καὶ οιφι σεμιδάλεως; Q [...] לחם (the variant σεμιδάλεως reflects interpretation; cf. Lev 2:1,4; 7:12)
6:1 ולקסמים MT] LXX,Q + [למעונ]נים (cf. Deut 18:10,14)
6:2 ארון MT] LXX,Q + ברית ה'

4. Presence/absence of slots

15:27 ויחזק ,MT] LXX,Q + שאול
2 Sam 3:3 אשת נבל הכרמלי MT] LXX,Q [ה]כרמלית

5. Presence/absence of clauses/sentences

1:24 והנער MT] LXX + μετ' αὐτῶν (v. 25) καὶ προσήγαγον ἐνώπιον κυρίου καὶ ἔσφαξεν ὁ πατὴρ αὐτοῦ τὴν θυσίαν, ἥν ἐποίει ἐξ ἡμερῶν εἰς ἡμέρας τῷ κυρίῳ, καὶ προσήγαγεν τὸ παιδάριον καὶ ἔσφαξεν τὸν μόσχον καὶ προσήγαγεν αννα ἡ μήτηρ τοῦ παιδαρίου κτλ' (repetitive; possible epanalepsis); Q + [עמם ויבאו לפני ה' וישחט אביו את[הזב]ח כ[אשר [יעשה מימים ימימה לה' וישחט את הפר ותבא את [...
Since according to LXX=Q the ox is slaughtered twice, and Samuel is presented more than once to the sanctuary, the longer text must be regarded as secondary.
2:9 נתן נד]ר לנוד]ר ויברך שנ]י MT] LXX,Q כי לא צדיק] (actualisation)
2:24 שמע MT] LXX,Q + [א לו]ר כיא כן תעשון אל טרב]ות השמערות] אשר אני שׁרמע
2:31-32 מהיות-ישראל MT] LXX,Q >
2 Sam 8:7 ויביאם ירושלים MT] LXX,Q + אורחם [] גם לקח] (אורחם) (LXX: καὶ ἔλαβεν αὐτά) אחר שרשק מלך מצרים] [ב]עלותו אל יר]ושלים] בימי רחבעם בן שלו]מה]

These variants represent revision and exegesis. Thus it appears that 4QSam[a] and the parent text of LXX derive from one common manuscript ב, which offers a revision. This revision does not make itself felt in MT, which testifies to the unrevised text (א).[26] Hence we may justify the position of both Cross-Ulrich and of Barthélemy:[27]

STATISTICS AND TEXTUAL FILIATION

the scroll and the OG belong to one branch, which
is characterized by exegesis, revision and
"literary initiative." On the other hand, this
text also contains many readings that appear to be
original: it is an independent witness to the text
of Samuel.

Still, sections 2-5 also include a large number
of divergencies between LXX and Q. Hence it
appears that both texts have continued to develop
the basic revision each in its own way. This
justifies Tov's caution, that the Scroll is not to
be identified with the parent text of LXX.[28] But
these reservations should not prevent us from
recognizing the connection between these two
texts. Rather, we should conclude that the parent
text of LXX is closer to the original text of ב
than is the Scroll, which represents a further
development of this branch. This conclusion is
confirmed by an expansion of Q that is not
attested in the LXX:

1:22
MT (=LXX)   ונראה את פני ה' וישב שם עד עולם
Q   [ונראה] את פנ[י] ה' וישב לפני [ה']...עד עולם
            ונת[היהר נזיר עד עולם כול ימי חייו

The characteristic expansion of Q is a further
development of the text of the Old Greek, which
represents Samuel as a temple oblate: (1:11)

       LXX   MT
καὶ δώσω αὐτὸν   ונתתיו
ἐνώπιόν σου   לה'
δοτὸν   = נתון   ‎- - -
ἕως ἡμέρας θανάτου αὐτοῦ = עד יום מותו   כל ימי חייו

The equation δοτὸν = נתון is based on LXX Num 3:9:
δόμα δεδομένοι = נתונם נתונם (a similar rendering

occurs in Num 8:16; 18:6). Hence it is quite probable that the parent text of the LXX had נתוּן in 1 Sam 1:11.[29] In fact, it is plausible that the midrash of the Chronicler, who mentions Samuel as one of the Levites (1 Chr 6:12-13, 18-19) was also based on this reading: according to Num 3:9, 8:16 and 18:6 the Levites have been dedicated to the service of the Temple as נתונים. Obviously the text of 4QSam^a represents a similar exegetical endeavour to give a contemporary expression to Samuel's place in the cult. This is a powerful example for the scroll's independent development beyond the ancient prototype.

Additionally, we have to consider the following examples:

1:24 בפרים שלשה MT [Q בקר משלש [בן בפר; LXX בפר משלש
2:16 אליו MT [LXX >; Q: אל נער הכוהן
(specification of the addressee)

Possibly the LXX has, in its turn, been influenced by the unrevised text (א).[30] This surmise would account for a constellation such as 2 Sam 6:13 שב[עה] פרים ושבע[ה אילים] Q [LXX=MT שור ומריא = 1 Chr 15:26.

V

This passage presents one of the agreements between the scroll and Chronicles. This type of agreement bears implications for dating the text of ב, for it might suggest that this revision already existed at the time that the Book of Chronicles was composed. We must, however, also consider the possibility that this agreement really is an independent residue of a more ancient

STATISTICS AND TEXTUAL FILIATION

text form. This assumption applies to all primary readings and synonymous variants:

2 Sam 6:2   מבעלה Q [LXX = MT מבעלי {יהודה}
            (בעלתה 1 Chr 13:6)
    6:2   אל קרי[ו]ת יערים [אשר] Q [LXX = MT יהודה
            = 1 Chr 13:5 ליהודה
    6:5   עצי ברושים MT] Q בשירים[ו עז] 1= Chr 13:8;
            LXX doubl.
    6:9   לאמור = 1 Chr 13:12 [LXX,Q] MT {וַיִּרָא} וֵיאמר
    5:9   ויבנה עיר LXX,Q [MT ויבן דוד (1 Chr 11:8
            (ויבן העיר)
    6:6   וישלח עזא [את] LXX,Q [MT וישלח עזא...וַיֹּאחֶז
            וישלח עזא את ידו לֶאֱחֹז 1 Chr 13:9, ידו ויאחז
    6:7   ל[ו]פני הא[ו]ל[ור]ה[י]ם Q] MT עם ארון האלהים
            = 1 Chr 13:10; LXX doubl.
   10:5   לדוד MT] LXX,Q + האנשים [על] = 1 Chr 19:5

As these readings may well derive from the original text of the Book of Samuel, they cannot be used to prove that the Book of Chronicles and ב represent one common hyparchetype.

On the other hand, some data suggest that the Chronicler was already acquainted with a revised text. The Ark tale relates that God smote Uzza for his "error" since he had touched the Ark: 2 Sam 6:7 על השל MT] LXX >. The Chronicler explains: "because he had put forth his hand to the Ark" (1 Chr 13:10 על אשר שלח ידו אל הארון); the scroll, which has a long gap and אל [ה]ארון, must have offered a similar reading.

In 2 Sam 8:7, Q has a long addition concerning the subsequent fate of the golden shields David had dedicated to the Temple:
גם []אותם [ל]קח + LXX,Q [MT ויביאם ירושלים
[מצרים מלך שרשק אחר] :LXX) καὶ ἔλαβεν αὐτά)
[ב]עלוחו אל יר[ו]שלים[ ]בימי רחבעם בן שלו[מה]
Since this chapter deals with David's conquests, the reference to the subsequent history of the

Temple does not belong to the original text.[31] It is part of a later revision that aimed at unification of the various allusions to the history of the Temple and its treasures. Hence the reference to Shishak's campaign (cf. 1 Kgs 14:25-26). This expansion has a sequel in the LXX. After the reference to the copper taken from Hadadezer (8:8), the translator continues: ἐν αὐτῷ ἐποίησεν Σαλωμων τὴν θάλασσην τὴν χαλκῆν καὶ τοὺς στύλους κτλ´ This text has not been preserved in the fragments of the scroll, but it is quite similar to the addition of 1 Chr 18:8 בה עשה שלמה את ים הנחשת ואת העמודים ואת כלי הנחשת. Thus, the Chronicler was acquainted with the expanded version of this pericope. True, in this context he does not mention Shishak's expedition (contrast 2 Chr 12:9); but this fact does not jeopardize our argument: the Chronicler may have omitted it in order to avoid its juxtaposition to David's grandiose conquests. Thus, we are dealing with a typically Chronistic revision of the text of ב. This recension appears to have been the Chronicler's *Vorlage*.[32]

Decisive variants, however, are rare. Moreover, there might be a counter-example: 2 Sam 7:23 ואלהיו MT] Q ואהלים = LXX καὶ σκηνώματα (1 Chr 17:21 >) If the Chronicler really were dependent on ב, one would expect him to read ואהלים. On the other hand, if he read ואלהיו, the omission would not be surprising. Still, he might have been acquainted with both variants; in that case the omission might be explained as a conscious decision to suspend judgment.

Another difficulty is that the Chronicler does

not substitute מפיבשת for אישבשת. On the
contrary, he mentions אשבעל (1 Chr 8:33; 9:39),
whereas 2 Samuel has אישבשת. Moreover, he is
still acquainted with the name מריבעל (9:40; 8:34:
מריב בעל), obviously the original reading of which
מפיבשת is the exegetical recast (2 Samuel has
ירבשת where the Book of Judges has ירבעל). This
might suggest that he used a unique ancient source
for his genealogies. On the other hand, the
parent text of Chron might represent a stage of ב
that precedes the <u>Vorlage</u> of LXX.

This tentative suggestion is compatible with
two alternative hypotheses:
a. ב is an ancient revision, which was subject to
a process of ongoing reworking in LXX and Q; this
reworking, however, is no more than a continuation
of the ancient revision and does not present new
tendencies. If the ancient state of this revision
was already at the disposal of the Chronicler, it
must have been in existence circa 400 BCE.
b. Possibly ב was based on an ancient recension
(ג). Such variants as the scroll's reading at 2
Sam 6:13 may also belong to this stratum. The
decision whether this revision is pre-exilic or
not is a matter of redaction history. In any case,
both ב and the Chronicler may have used this text,
but א has not.

A second revisionist tendency is censorship.
This has not affected the Scroll, but is rather
plausible in MT and LXX of the Book of Samuel.
1. 2 Sam 24:16 היבסי MT =LXX] Q + את דויד[וישא
שלופה ו[חרב] ו[הש[מ]י]ם בין הארץ בין ... עיניו
פנ]יהם על והזקנים ... ירושלים על נטויה] בידו
ב[שקים מתב]סים

1 Chr 21:16

וישא דויד את עיניו וירא את מלאך ה' עמד בין הארץ
ובין השמים וחרבו שלופה בידו נטויה על ירושלים ויפל
דויד והזקנים מכסים בשקים על פניהם

In this pericope the numinous tension is
overwhelming. Nowhere is the presence of the
destroying Angel so threatening. There is a stark
contrast between the Angel on high, with his sword
drawn and stretched out against Jerusalem on the
one hand, and David and the elders, prostrated on
the ground and wearing sack-cloth (high / low;
drawn / covered). This text is far more forceful
than similar pericopes in the Hebrew Bible (Jos
5:13-14; Num 22:23,31); in post-biblical
literature one finds nothing comparable. The
clause וחרבו שלופה בידו is matched by the Akkadian
phrase tamḫat qašta ina idīša, šalpat namsaru
zaqtu ša epēš tāḫazī, which describes Istar's
posture in the dream revelation to the šabrū of
Assurbanipal ("holding the bow in her hands, drawn
the sharp sword for waging battle," Streck,
Assurbanipal 116-7, Cyl. B, V: 54-55). Therefore,
the most plausible explanation for our textual
constellation is that in MT and LXX an original
pericope has been omitted in order to attenuate
the numinous tension.[33]

2. 1 Sam 11: 1 init MT=LXX] Q pr

[ונ]חש מלך בני עמון הוא לחץ את בני גד ואת בני ראובן
בחזקה ונקר להם כ[ו]ל ע[י]ן ימין ונתן אי[ן מ]ה ופחד]
על [י]שראל ולוא נשאר איש בבני ישראל אשר בע[בר]
[הירדן אש]ר ל[וא נ]קר לו נח[ש מלך] בני עמון כול עין
ימין רק שבעת אלפים איש [נסו מפני] בני עמון ויבאו
אל [י]ב[ש] גלעד

(inter lineas)

ויהי כמו חדש ויעל נחש העמוני ויחן על יביש [גלעד]

The originality of the shorter text of MT=LXX has been defended as against the longer text of 4Q, since the latter could be considered a secondary, midrashic expansion, aiming to explain how the Ammonites, who live to the east of the Gilead, could attack a town near the Jordan. The remarkable motif of the blinding of the right eye has been viewed as a midrashic reverberation of the Jabesh episode (MT v. 1).[34] Redoubling, however, is a well-known literary trope (note the Joseph narrative, *Enūma Eliš* and the Sumerian account of Gudea's dreams), and certainly not especially midrashic. The conquest is necessary from a literary point of view: the fact that almost all the Gilead has been conquered by a brutal enemy constitutes a national calamity which reaches its climax in the attack on Jabesh. At this stage divine salvation enters through the actions of Saul, who is thus worthy of being king over all Israel. In this version of the narrative Saul's victory carries far more weight than the mere rescue of Jabesh, since the initial threat is far greater. In the shorter text the pericope of Nahash's conquest of Gilead has been removed because of the terrible disgrace implied by the defeat. Thus the longer text appears to be the original one.

3. In the LXX the short text of 1 Sam 17-18 also appears to represent censorship. The shorter version avoids three embarassing details: the fact that for forty days Goliath's challenge had not been met (in the LXX David acts immediately,

v. 11, 32); David's humiliation at his brother's hand (v. 28); and the fact that Abner and Saul did not know who he was, despite 16:14-23.[35]

Hence א should not be identified with Proto-MT. This hypothetical text represents a continuation and revision of א.

Our findings may be summarized in the following stream-diagram:
1. According to hypothesis (a) Chron. represents an ancient state of ב.

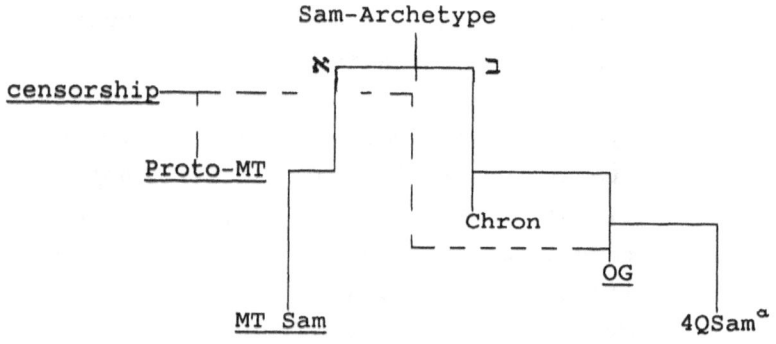

Censorship has been indicated by underlining.
2. According to hypothesis (b) Chron. and ב derive both from ג:

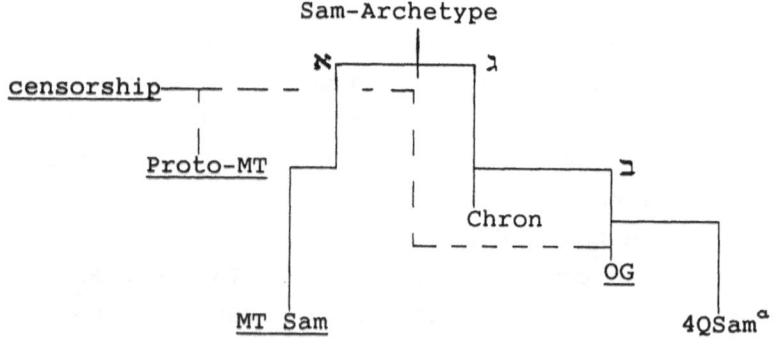

Thus, statistical analysis, based on objective classification, enables us to enrich and to deepen our insight into the relations between the texts.

VI

This method may also be applied to the question of the relation between MT, the Qumran texts, the Samaritan Pentateuch and the LXX. At this preliminary stage we propose the pilot examination of two cases: the texts related to 4QpaleoExod^m and to 11QpaleoLev. Sanderson has concluded that MT, SP and 4QpaleoExod^m belong to the same textual tradition, but that LXX is an older offshoot of the main branch.[36] This conclusion is borne out by statistical analysis.[37] The category of small-scale expansion is particularly important:

3. Longer/shorter slots

	score	frequency	expectation	x^2
LXX deviant	18	.4615	8	12.5
MT deviant	8	.205		0
SP deviant	2	.051		4.5
Q deviant	4	.103		2
Q=LXX/SP=MT	2	.051	2.333	0.0475
Q=SP/LXX=MT	5	.128		3.0488
Q=MT/SP=LXX	0			2.333
Total	39			24.4293

Extremely significant for $\alpha=.001$ (>22.458; $v=6$)

5. Presence/absence of clause/sentence

	score	frequency	expectation	x^2
LXX deviant	7	.368	2.5	8.1
MT deviant	1	.052		.9
SP deviant	0			2.5
Q deviant	2	.11		0.1
Q=LXX/SP=MT	0		3	3
Q=SP/LXX=MT	9	.4736		12
Q=MT/SP=LXX	0			3
Total	19			29.6

Although the outcome is unreliable because of the low expectation (< 5), it is quite suggestive (>22.458; beyond α=.001 for v=6). These figures indicate that SP, MT and the Exodus scroll belong all to one and the same branch of the tradition (מ = Proto-MT). Both SP and 4QpaleoExod^m have undergone secondary revision. It is, however, less easy to determine whether beyond revision there is a specific textual connection between these witnesses. In some cases the reading SP=4QExod seems to be secondary as against MT:
Exod
22:3   שנים MT] SP,4QExod שנים אחד (=4Q158 11,6; so frequently in SP; cf. Dan 3:19 חד שבעה)
22:6   וגנב MT] SP, 4QExod ו]נגנב (Niph'al for original MT Pu'al)
7:10   ויבא...אל פרעה MT] SP,4QExod לפני...ויבא פרעה (=LXX ἐναντίον), cf. parall. וישלך לפני פרעה ולפני עבדיו in continuation.
8:14   ותהי הכנם MT] 4QExod ויהי הכנים; SP ותהי הכנים
32:11   יחרה MT] SP,4QExod יחר (unexpected apocopat.)
17:16   עד דור ודו]ר SP מדר ודור MT] 4QExod לדר דר (cf SP 3:16 לדוך ודור for MT לדר דר; Prov 24:27 ketib לדר דר; qere לדר ודר)

Unique readings of SP

7:4   בשפטי]ם MT=4QExod] SP במשפטים (easier lexeme)
28:4   וכתנת MT=4QExod] SP כיתנת
10:11   לא כן MT=4QExod,LXX] SP לכן
21:29   השר]ו יפק]ל MT=4QExod,LXX] SP הבהמה תסקל

These variants prove that 4QExod and SP form one family (ש), which branched off from Proto-MT. Moreover, SP is a later offshoot of ש. Still, the scroll does not preserve the original form of ש either, as shown by some secondary variants:
23:31   רשתי MT=SP] 4QExod רש]מתי(vid)
32:11   ו]בזרוע חזקה MT] 4QExod ה חזק]ה וביד חזקה (conflate); SP ובזרוע נטוים =LXX

STATISTICS AND TEXTUAL FILIATION   257

10:21 וְיָמֵשׁ חֹשֶׁךְ MT=SP,LXX] 4QExod > (lexic.
diffic.; apparently redundant)

Thus 4QpaleoExod^m too is no more than an offshoot
of 𝔖, though it is closer to the original state of
this recension than is SP.

It appears that the particular revision common
to 4QpaleoExod^m and SP (𝔖) was concerned mainly
with the addition of sentences and paragraphs on
the one hand, and the expansion of given syntactic
slots on the other hand. In other respects,
however, the Scroll and SP are not particularly
close; they do not descend from one and the same
manuscript. On the contrary, in those cases, in
which the revision did not affect the proto-MT
reading (𝔐), 4QpaleoExod^m mainly equals MT.
LXX forms another branch (𝔊), splitting off before
the node of 𝔖 (SP-4QExod). Thus we arrive at the
following stream-diagram:

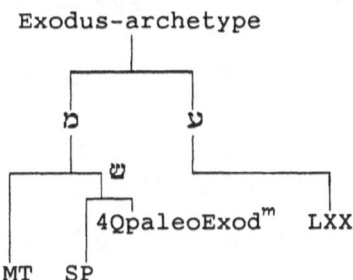

VII

In the Book of Leviticus the situation is
slightly different. Both Tov and Mathews have
reached the conclusion that MT, 11QpaleoLev, SP
and the LXX are all independent of each other.[39]
The data suggest, however, that 11QLev is

dependent on the same traditon as MT. It is a
maverick development of Proto-MT, unconnected with
SP and LXX.

Statistical Analysis of 11QLev
1 Mechanical Variants

1   14:17   תנוך MT=SP,LXX] Q ועאתנוך? (Puech 171-
172 prefers to read ראתנוך, apparently a conflation with ראש)

2 Interchange

a. Q = LXX = SP / against MT

1   21:8   מְקַדְּשְׁכֶם MT] מקדשם Q,SP=LXX
@M2 22:25   מָשְׁחָתָם MT] SP, Q משח[תים = LXX

b. Q = MT = SP / against LXX

@M3   15:2   ואמרתם] LXX ἐρεῖς
= 4 17:3   מבית ישראל] LXX τῶν υἱῶν Ισραηλ
= 5 17:4   האיש ההוא] LXX ἡ ψυχὴ ἐκείνη
@M6 18:28   הגוי MT=SP=Q] LXX τοῖς ἔθνεσιν
= 7 21:8   וקדשתו MT=SP=Q] LXX καὶ ἁγιάσει αὐτόν*
             (cf.MT 16:19; 21:15,22)³⁹
= 8 22:22 הקריבו MT=SP=Q] תקרבו] LXX προσάξουσιν*
             (cf. MT 22:18; similar interchange: LXX
             22:20)
= 9 21:8   אלהיך MT=SP=Q] LXX κυρίου τοῦ (B>) θεοῦ
             ὑμῶν* (cf. MT 22:25)

c. LXX = MT = Q / against SP

=10 27:12   אֹתָה MT,LXX,Q] אתר SP

d. LXX = SP = MT / against Q

=11 11:27   על כפיו MT=SP,LXX] Q [גחר]נו על גחר[נו (Puech
             170)
=12 24:14   הוצא MT=SP,LXX] הציאו Q (Puech 178)

e. MT = Q / SP = LXX

=13 20:2   האמר] תדבר=SP LXX
=14 26:20   הארץ] השדה SP = LXX + ὑμῶν

f. MT = LXX / SP = Q

=15 20:2   מבני] מבית SP=Q

LXX indeterminable

a. Q = SP / against MT

@M 1 18:27   האל MT] SP האלה=Q
@M 2 20:3   ולחלל] SP וחלל=Q
@M 3 25:31   יָחָשֵׁב MT] SP, Q יחשבו (LXX also has

STATISTICS AND TEXTUAL FILIATION

plural, no evidence)
@M 4 25:34 הִוא] Q,SP הוּא
QM 5 26:22 וְהִשְׁלַחְתִּי] Q, SP ושלחתי
@M 6 27:13 יִגְאָלֶנָּה] Q,SP יגאלנו

b. Q = MT / against SP

=   7 10:6 אֵל...וּאֵל [מר]ולאיתן ולאלעזר MT,Q] SP אל...ואל;
       LXX προς...και ελεαζαρ και ιθαμαρ
=   8 18:30 בָּהֶם] SP בהן
@M 9 24:9 וא[כל]הוּ MT=Q] SP ואכלוה
@M 10 24:9 הוּא] SP היא
= 11 25:35 יָמוּךְ MT=Q] SP ימך
@M 12 25:35 והחזקת] SP וחזקת

c. SP = MT / against Q

= 13 24:12 ויניחהו SP,MT] Q ויניחר אחר

d. All at variance

= 14 26:24 אַף אֲנִי MT] SP גם אני; Q אני (LXX καγώ
       indeterminable)
      21:6 קֹדֶשׁ MT] Q ...[דש]... (Puech 175);
       קדשים SP (cf. opening verse; LXX has plural,
       no evidence for Vorlage)

3 Longer / shorter slots

a. SP = Q = LXX / against MT

=   1 13:42 בקרחת MT] Q,SP,LXX בקרחתו

b. Q = MT = SP / against LXX

=   2 17:5 והביאום] LXX και οίσουσιν* (cf.
       14:42; 16:12)
=   3 17:3 וישראל] LXX + ἢ τῶν προσηλύτων τῶν
       προσκειμένων ἐν ὑμῖν = או הגר הגר
       בתוככם (this phrase is extant in LXX^BA, but
       is omitted by many MSS; Wevers relegates it
       to the apparatus; see Puech 174)
=   4 21:7 כי] LXX>
    5 25:29 ממכרו] LXX>*
    6 25:31 גאלה] LXX λυτρωταὶ διὰ παντός * (cf.
       MT 25:32)
@M 7 27:12 כערכך הכהן MT=SP,Q] LXX και καθότι ἂν
       τιμήσεται ὁ ἱερεύς (=27:14)
    8 27:13 חמישתו MT=SP, Q חמישיתו] LXX τὸ
       ἐπίπεμπτον* (cf. MT 27:15, 19; the Greek has
       the suffix in 22:14, but not in 5:16;
       27:27, 31)
    9 27:19 גאל יגאל] LXX >גאל*

c. LXX = MT = Q / against SP

= 10   17:4   להקריבו] SP [LXX=Q=MT להקריב
@M11   22:21 וכל מום כל] SP [LXX,Q,MT מום

d. LXX = MT = SP / against Q

@M12   10:7   ופתח אהל Q] LXX,SP=MT ומפתח אהל מועד
                מועד
= 13   14:18 כפר Q] LXX,SP=MT כף הכהן, cf. v. 17
                (Puech 171)
@M14   17:2   >Q] LXX,SP=MT ואל בניו
                (homoioarchton)
= 15   22:21 או בבקר Q] LXX,SP=MT בבקר
@M16   22:25 בהם Q] בם
@M17   25:32 עולם תהיה ללוים LXX,SP=MT] Q <תהיה
@M18   25:30 (לא ketib)] ἐξόυσα τῆ=SP,LXX אשר לו
                לו Q
= 19   25:31 וביובל] Q ביובל

e. SP = MT / Q = LXX

= 20   18:30 כי אני Q] SP=MT ἴδε LXX^B=אני
{*=   19:2   אל[ע]דת Q] SP=MT אל כל עדת = LXX τῇ
              συναγωγῇ (problem of space)}
@M21   26:24 [בְּ]קְרִי Q קרי בחמת=LXX

f. Q = MT / SP = LXX

= 22   13:3   וראהו MT=Q] SP,OG וראה
= 23   22:24 ומעוך] SP מעוך=LXX
= 24   27:17 אם] SP ראם=LXX

LXX indeterminable

a. MT = SP / against Q

= 1   21:8   Q כי לחם] MT,SP כי את לחם
= 2   24:10 Q האיש] איש
= 3   26:19 Q< אה] MT,SP את שמיכם
= 4   27:19 את חמשית Q] MT=SP חמשית

b. MT = Q / against SP

= 5   23:27 כפרים] SP [MT,Q ה[כְּ]פָרִים (LXX also
              > article)
= 6   24:10 הישראלי] SP ישראלי ישראלי
SP=Q / against MT : 0
All at variance : 0
Indeterminable: 11:27 [כֹּ]; [..] Q הולך] MT וְכָל הֹלֵךְ
                SP, LXX וכל ההלך

4 Presence / absence of slots

a. Q = MT = SP / against LXX

@G 1   15:3   זאת תהיה] LXX καὶ οὗτος = וזאת

STATISTICS AND TEXTUAL FILIATION

= 2 21:8 לך] LXX>*
= 3 23:28 ירם כפרים הוא] LXX + ὑμῖν* (cf. MT 23:32)

b. MT = Q / SP = LXX

@M 3 25:35 רחי] SP + אחיך = LXX

c. Q = SP / against MT / against LXX

= 4 14:16 והזה מן MT] SP=Q והזה מן השמן שבע באצבעו שבע; LXX καὶ ῥανεῖ ἑπτάκις τῷ δακτύλῳ (+ αὐτοῦ MSS)

LXX indeterminable
All at variance

= 5 26:24 אף אני ;SP גם אני, LXX κἀγώ)] Q>

5. Presence / absence of clause/sentence

a. LXX = MT = SP / against Q

= 1 4:25 ושפ]ך... Q , [MT=SP,LXX ואת כל דמו ישפך
= 2 4:26 המזבחה כחלב זבח השלמים וכפר עליו הכהן MT=SP,LXX] Q ...[ה וכפר]; Puech (169) adduces additional fragments and suggests the reading ליהו]ה וכפר על[יו הכה]ן ונ[סלח לו (cf. v. 31)
= 3 18:27] Q + [א...]תם תירשו את אדמתם (derivative from 20:23-24)

b. MT = SP = Q / against LXX

4 21:7 ²לא יקחו] LXX >*
5 23:24 מקרא קדש] LXX + ἔσται ὑμῖν * (cf. MT v. 27,21,36)

d. MT = Q / LXX = SP

= 6 17:4 אהל מועד] SP + לא הביאו לעשות אתו עולה או שלמים לה' לרצונכם לריח ניחוח וישחטהו בחוץ ואל פתח אהל מועד= LXX

e. LXX = Q / against SP / against MT

@M 5 15:3 מזובו] SP + טמא הוא, כל ימי זוב בשרו = LXX + Q... ז ימי כל בו ; והחתים בשרו מזובו αὕτη ἡ ἀκαθαρσία αὐτοῦ ἐν αὐτῷ ... (continuation= SP)

7. Changes in word-order.

a. Q = MT = SP / against LXX

@M 1 19:3 אמו / ואביו] LXX πατέρα αὐτοῦ καὶ μητέρα αὐτοῦ

LXX indeterminable
a. SP = MT / against Q
= 2 22:22 ויבלח/ילפת] Q ⁻

Leviticus - Survey

	2-inter	3 exp	4 add	5 cls	7 order	total	p
MT deviant	2	1	0	0	0	3	.06
LXX deviant	7	8	3	2	1	21	.42
SP deviant	1	2	0	0	0	3	.06
Q deviant	2	8	0	3	0	13	.26
MT=Q/SP=LXX	2	3	1	1	0	7	.14
MT=SP/LXX=Q	0	2	0	0	0	2	.04
MT=LXX/SP=Q	1	0	0	0	0	1	.02
total	15	24	4	6	1	50	
p	.3	.48	.08	.12	.02		

Frequency per 100

	2-inter	3 exp	4 add	5 cls	7 order
MT deviant	.133	.042	0	0	0
LXX deviant	.467	.333	.75	.333	1
SP deviant	.067	.083	0	0	0
Q deviant	.133	.333	0	.5	0
MT=Q/SP=LXX	.133	.125	.25	.167	0
MT=SP/LXX=Q	0	.083	0	0	0
MT=LXX/SP=Q	.067	0	0	0	0

x^2 for categories 2-4

	2-inter	3 exp	4 add	total	exp	x^2
MT deviant	2	1	0	3	8.5	3.5589
LXX deviant	7	8	3	18		10.6176
SP deviant	1	2	0	3		3.5588
Q deviant	2	8	0	10		0.265
MT=Q/SP=LXX	2	3	1	6	3	3.00
MT=SP/LXX=Q	0	2	0	2		0.3333
MT=LXX/SP=Q	1	0	0	1		1.3333
altogether	15	24	4	43		22.6669

Highly significant for $\alpha=0.005$ (>18.5476; v=6)

Once again the LXX stands out as an independent witness. On the other hand, there is a significant connection between MT, SP and 11QLev, all three apparently deriving from Proto-MT. In the rubric of interchange and substitution (2) the Scroll is closest to MT; its deviations are most numerous in the categories of expansion (3) and clause addition (5). Still, the deviation of 11QLev is only slightly larger than expected (a score of 10 as against an expectation of 8.5). Thus 11QpaleoLev is no more than a secondary development of Proto-MT.

In order to examine these affinities more closely, we must analyse the agreements between the witnesses pair by pair.

Pair by pair agreement

2   Interchange

	Tot	MT	p	Q	p	SP	p	LXX	p
SP	14	9	.6429	10	.7143			6	.4286
Q	13	10	.7692			10	.7692	3	.2308
MT	13			10	.7692	9	.6923	4	.3077
LXX	8	4	.50	3	.375	6	.75		

Significance of pairs:
(1) Q=MT - (2) SP=Q - (3) SP=MT - (4) SP=LXX - (5) MT=LXX - (6) Q=LXX

3 expansion

	Tot	MT	p	Q	p	SP	p	LXX	p
SP	22	18	.818	9	.409			13	.5455
Q	16	13	.8125			9	.5625	5	.3125
MT	23			13	.5652	18	.7826	10	.4348
LXX	16	10	.625	5	.3125	12	.75		

Significance of pairs:
(1) SP=MT - (2) Q=MT - (3) SP=LXX - (4) MT=LXX - (5) SP=Q - (6) Q=LXX

In the rubric of substitution/interchange of words, the most important connection is that between the scroll and MT, with the agreements SP=MT and Q=SP as runners-up. On the other hand, in the category of syntactic expansion the most obvious connection is between SP and MT, followed by Q=MT and SP=LXX. Nevertheless, on the whole the agreements between MT and the scroll are the most important, with the connection SP=MT coming in second. Within the branch of Proto-MT, MT is closer to 11QLev than to SP.

There is no significant relationship between the scroll and the SP. True, there is a singular agreement Q=SP, whereas MT and LXX testify to two different variants, but this constellation does not contradict the general picture: 14:16 והזה מן שבע SP=Q] MT והזה מן השמן באצבעו שבע; LXX καὶ ῥανεῖ ἑπτάκις τῷ δακτύλῳ (+ αὐτοῦ MSS). This agreement seems to be related to a special revision (R), on which we shall comment later. This revision is also the source for the exceptional case of SP, Q and MT all carrying different readings (Q=LXX as far as transmitted): 15:3 טמא הוא, כל ימי זוב בשרו והחתים SP + מזורבו [...] Q + בשרו מזורבו בו כל ימי ז = LXX αὕτη ἡ ἀκαθαρσία αὐτοῦ ἐν αὐτῷ ... (continuation=SP). On the other hand, there are some interesting agreements between SP and LXX, especially in the area of secondary readings:

2. Interchange

@M 22:25 מָשְׁחָתָם] SP, Q [משח]תים] = LXX/ not specific
=   21:8 מְקַדִּשְׁכֶם MT] מקדשם Q,SP=LXX
=   13:3 וראהו MT=Q] וראה SP, LXX
=   13:42 בקרחתו MT] בקרחת Q,SP,LXX

STATISTICS AND TEXTUAL FILIATION

= 22:24 מעורך=LXX [מעורך SP] ורמעורך
= 27:17 ראם=LXX [אם SP] וראם
= 20:2 הדבר=LXX [האמר SP] הדבר
= 26:20 השדה= LXX + ὑμῶν [הארץ SP] השדה

3. longer/shorter

= 25:35 אחיך=LXX [נחי SP + אחיך
@M 15:3 טמא הוא כל ימי זוב בשרו מזובו [SP + ורהחתים בשרו מזובו ;Q + ...[ז מי יכל בו =LXX αὕτη ἡ ἀκαθαρσία αὐτοῦ ἐν αὐτῷ ... (continuation=SP)
= 6 17:4 לא הביאו לעשות אתו עולה [SP + אהל מועד או שלמים לה' לרצונכם לריח ניחוח וישחטהו בחוץ =LXX ואל פתח אהל מועד

What is the status of those readings? In answering this question, one must first of all notice that the agreement SP=LXX is far from massive. No one would compare this constellation with the convergence 4QSam^a and LXX in the Book of Samuel. Basically there are two possibilities.

1. Some of these readings are original, such as: Exod 18:6 הנה חתנך בא אליך where MT has אני חתנך בא אליך.[40] A very significant representative of this category is the SP reading *a'itinna* (=LXX, Tg. Onq.) for MT אֲחַטֶּנָּה (Gen 31:39; some manuscripts actually read אחיטנה). Loewenstamm has shown that this reading still reflects the ancient and original text, explained by the Akkadian *ḫiātu*= "to make good," "to indemnify."[41] Of course, an original reading like this cannot be considered evidence for a specific genetic relation between LXX and SP in Genesis.

2. Other variants appear to derive from common exegesis. Here I wish to quote three meaningful long readings:

a. Exod 22:4   MT

כי יבער איש שדה או כרם
ושלח את בעירה ובער בשדה אחר

מיטב שדהו ומיטב כרמו ישלם

SP = LXX, 4QpaleoExod^m

וכי יבער איש שדה או כרם
ושלח את בעירו ובער בשדה אחר
שלם ישלם (ἀποτείσει LXX) משדהו כתבואתה
ואם כל השדה יבעה (כיבער= ḤΣΑΖΑ=?ָהַשָׂדֶה יְבַעֶה) (LXX καταβοσκήσῃ)
מיטב שדהו ומיטב כרמו ישלם

4QpaleoExod has:...] כל [..; all the plus is
extant in 4Q158 11, 6-9. The provision
that שלם ישלם משדהו כתבואתה is apparently
no more than a restriction of the main
stipulation מיטב שדהו ומיטב כרמו ישלם.

b. Lev 15:3   MT

וזאת תהיה טמאתו בזובו
רר בשרו את זובו
או החתים בשרו מזובו

טמאתו הוא

SP ≃ LXX

וזאת תהיה (ὁ νόμος ὁ τούτου καὶ) טמאתו בזובו
רר בשרו את זובו
או החתים (והחתם LXX) בשרו מזובו
טמא הוא SP ;LXX=[טמאתר היא] בו Q
= LXX αὕτη ἡ ἀκαθαρσία αὐτοῦ ἐν αὐτῷ
כל ימי זוב בשרו והחתים (והחתם LXX) בשרו מזובו SP
Q [...ז כל ימי;
טמאתו היא

STATISTICS AND TEXTUAL FILIATION   267

The plus of LXX and SP is a mere repetition of the previous clause.

c. Lev 17:4

MT = Q

ואל פתח אהל מועד לא הביאו

להקריב קרבן לה' לפני משכן ה'
דם יחשב לאיש ההוא

SP = LXX

ואל פתח אהל מועד לא הביאו
לעשות אתו עולה או שלמים לה' לרצונכם
לריח ניחוח וישחטהו בחוץ
ואל פתח אהל מועד לא הביאו
להקריב קרבן לה' לפני משכן ה'
דם יחשב לאיש ההוא

In this verse the plus of SP=LXX is a superfluous specification. In these three passages both SP and the LXX present the same longer text; in Exod 22:4; Lev 15:3 this variant has the support of 4QpaleoExod^m and 11QpaleoLev respectively. But in Lev 17:4 the scroll has the shorter text (=MT). Hence one might suggest that these variants are original, or that they descend from an ancient hyparchetype P, the presumed ancestor of the parent text of the OG and SP.[42] That would, however, be a grave error. If long additions are not supported by less conspicuous phenomena, such as substitution and small-scale expansion, they may well derive from exegetical influences. In our case this explanation is quite plausible. All these additions have a similar structure: the longer version presents an additional case and/or a doublet, and then proceeds to state the legal case as presented in the short version (MT). That is to say, in all cases we are dealing with an exegetical addition, rounded off by a resumptive repetition. LXX, SP and the scrolls derived these additions independently from the same ancient revision, indicated by R. R's influence on 11QpaleoLev was only partial. Hence we obtain the following stemma:

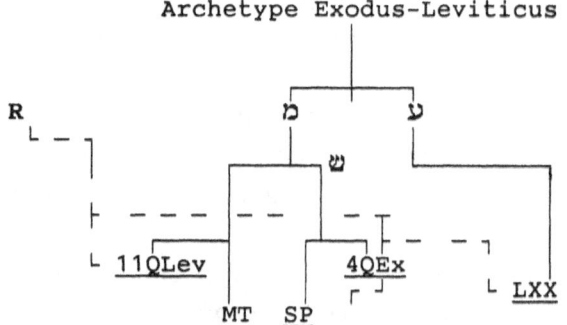

Underlining indicates the influence of R.

Statistical analysis, based on objective classification, puts the analysis of the relation between manuscripts and translations on reliable foundations. Hence this method may provide us with a better insight into the lines of textual transmission proper, and may also throw more light on ideological and linguistic revisions. It is an excellent starting point for the study of the history of the text.

NOTES

1. F. M. Cross, "The Evolution of a Theory of Local Texts," *Qumran and the History of the Biblical Text* (ed. F. M. Cross and S. Talmon; Cambridge Mass./London: Harvard University, 1975) 306-320, esp. n. 11 on p. 316-7.

2. Ulrich, *The Qumran Text of Samuel and Josephus* (HSM 19; Missoula Mont.: Scholars, 1978) 149.

3. Tov, "Determining the Relationship between the Qumran Scrolls and the LXX: Some Methodological Issues," *The Hebrew and Greek Texts of Samuel: 1980 Proceedings IOSCS - Vienna* (ed. E. Tov; Jerusalem: Academon, 1980) 45-67.

4. Tov, "A Modern Textual Outlook Based on the Qumran Scrolls," *HUCA* 53 (1982) 11-27, esp. p. 21. But see now his contribution to this volume.

5. The importance of "insignificant" variants has been stressed by: B. M. Metzger, "The Caesarean Text of the Gospels," *JBL* 64 (1945) 457-489, esp. p. 488-89. The quantitative approach of Colwell and the statistical method of Griffiths are in certain respects similar to my suggestions, but differ from them in (a) the breadth of the textual spectrum, and (b) their tendency to disregard the traditional methods of textual judgment. Tov (in this volume) accepts the statistical method, but suggests that its validity be restricted to "secondary readings," since primary readings descend directly from the Urtext. True, Tov is aware of the difficulty in distinguishing between primary and secondary readings, but he seems to underestimate its subjectivity. 1 Sam 1:24 is a case in point: should this reading be disregarded, since it has been considered primary, or should it be regarded as secondary? Moreover, suppose two manuscripts A and B have only a large number of primary readings in common, as against another group of manuscripts (c). The classical approach does not permit us to construct any connection between MSS A and B, whereas according to the statistical method we may conclude that they form a branch; subsequent philological inquiry would

show that this branch derives directly from the Urtext.

6. Since we deal only with these passages for which readings are extant in the fragments of 4QSam^a, one might say that the scroll prescribes the extent of the sample. Still, the extent is the same for all witnesses.

7. On the concept of overlapping ("joint events") see W. L. Hays, *Statistics for the Social Sciences* (London/New York: Holt, Rinehart & Winston; 2d. ed., 1974) 142-3, 150-1

8. V. A. Dearing, *A Manual of Textual Analysis* (Berkeley/Los Angeles: California University, 1959) vii; see also: D. W. Gooding, "An Appeal for a Stricter Terminology in the Textual Criticism of the Old Testament," *JSS* 21 (1976) 15-25.

9. P. Maas, *Textual Criticism* (transl. from German by B. Flowers;, London: Oxford University, 1958) 4-5; M. L. West, *Textual Criticism and Editorial Technique* (Stuttgart: Teubner, 1973) 32.

10. An additional difficulty is that we are dealing with texts in different languages. A comparison of manuscripts in one and the same language can always rely on an analysis of common errors, idiosyncrasies, - such as the reading בלבם MT / בלבבם 4QSam^a (1 Sam 10:26) -, and orthography; it is easy to point to obvious mechanical errors. In a discussion of a Hebrew text and a Greek translation, the issue is far more complicated: it is not easy to detect graphic errors, since we must always keep in mind the translator; objective data on orthography etc. are not available.

11. More precisely: a separative error (indicating that two texts do not belong to one and the same branch of the tradition) should not be one which might have been corrected by the medieval scribe. A conjunctive error (indicating that two manuscripts do belong to one and the same branch) should not be such that two scribes might have committed it independently (e. g. omission by homoeoteleuton); see Maas, *Criticism* 3, 42-52; M. H. Goshen-Gottstein, "Hebrew Biblical Manuscripts - Their History and Their Place in the HUBP Edition," in: Cross-Talmon, *History* 42-89, esp. p. 78-83 (=*Biblica* 48 [1976] 279-84). For the general definition see: L. D. Reynolds and N. G. Wilson, *Scribes and Scholars - A Guide to the*

Transmission of Greek and Latin Literature
(London: Oxford University; 2d ed., 1974) 190.

12. K. A. Mathews, "The Leviticus Scroll
(11QpaleoLev) and the Text of the Hebrew Bible,"
CBQ 48 (1986) 171-207, esp. p. 195-6. For the
exegetical problem of this verse see S. R. Driver,
*Notes on the Hebrew Text and the Topography of the
Books of Samuel*, (London: Oxford University; 2d
ed., 1913) 278; A. Geiger, *Urschrift und
Uebersetzungen der Bibel* (Breslau: Hainauer, 1857)
289-291; note the exegetical interchange implied
by the midrashic *Tiqqun Sopherim* לאהליו / לאלהיו
(1 Kgs 12:16). The phrase ותרגנו באהליכם (Deut
1:27) inspires R. Shim'on ben Tarphon to explain:
תרתם וגיניתם באהלו של מקום (b. Shebu 47b); this
comment might allude to a reading באלהיכם, which
would suit the complaint "בשנאת ה' אתנו" רגו' in
the continuation of this verse.

13. Maas, *Criticism*, 9; J. Willis, *Latin Textual
Criticism* (Urbana-Chicago: Illinois University,
1972) 19-29. In New Testament textual criticism
the problem of contamination is extremely grave,
as shown by: E. C. Colwell, *Studies in Methodology
in Textual Criticism of the New Testament* (NTTS
IX; Leiden: Brill, 1969) 69-72. On the frequency
of conflation in the Hebrew Bible ("double
readings") see: S. Talmon, "Double Readings in the
Massoretic Text," *Textus* 1 (1960) 144-85; id.,
"The Textual Study of the Bible - A New Outlook,"
in Cross-Talmon, *History*, 321-400. The argument
that conflation ("horizontal copying") is far more
frequent in classical manuscripts than generally
assumed, has been proposed by: R. D. Dawe, *The
Collation and Investigation of Manuscripts of
Aeschylus* (Cambridge: Cambridge University, 1963)
23-93, 151-64.

14. For 1 Sam 1:22-2:6; 2:12(?)-25 I refer to: F.
M. Cross, "A New Qumran Biblical Fragment related
to the original Hebrew underlying the Septuagint,"
BASOR 132 (1953) 15-28. The data on 1 Sam 2:8-10,
31-32; 5:8-10; 10:25-26; 2 Sam 6:2-9,13-17; 8:7-8;
10:6-7; 24:16 have been culled from Ulrich,
Qumran. For 2 Sam 3:23-5:13 I refer to the
systematic enumeration in Tov, "Relationship,"
55-7. For 1 Sam 10:27-11:1 see: F. M. Cross, "The
Ammonite Oppression of the Tribes of Gad and
Reuben: Missing Verses from 1 Samuel 11 Found in
4QSamuel[a]," *History, Historiography and Interpretation* (ed. H. Tadmor and M. Weinfeld; Jerusalem:

Magnes, 1983) 149, 153; note the corrected
transcription in: E. Tov (ed.), *Samuel*, 107.

15. LXX οὗ ἔχρησας = אשר השאלה might reflect an
original השאלה (3rd prs. fem.), interpreted as 2d.
pers. Q [ה]השאיל might then be taken as a
reformulation of השאלה; MT שאל לה' might represent
an exegetical correction. On the other hand, the
MT reading might also be original, since it may
represent the narrator's voice, which takes over
after Eli's blessing. The LXX form ἔχρησας
appears to be related to the problem of Elkana's
status in this narrative. I hope to deal with
this issue at another opportunity; see: J.
Wellhausen, *Der Text der Bücher Samuelis*
(Göttingen: VandenHoeck & Ruprecht, 1871) 41-42;
and also S. D. Walters, "Hannah and Anna: The
Greek and Hebrew Text of I Samuel 1," *JBL* 71
(1988) 385-412.

16. S. Siegel, *Nonparametric Statistics for the
Behavioral Sciences* (New York/Tokyo: McGraw-Hill,
1956).

17. The variant σεμιδάλεως (=סלח) for MT קמח
represents adaptation to the pentateuchal
halakhah, cf. Lev 7:12; 2:1, 4; Num 6:14, 15 and
see: F. Foresti, "Osservazioni su alcune varianti
di 4QSam^A rispetto al TM," *RivB* 29 (1981) 45-56,
esp. p. 55; see also: A. Rofé, "The Nomistic
Correctures in Biblical Manuscripts and its
Occurrence in 4QSam^α," *RevQ* 14 (1989) 247-254.

18. The tautological infinitive may occur in the
protasis; in legal contexts: Exod 21:5; 22:3, 11,
12, 16, 22, 25; Lev 13:7, 22, 27, 35; 14:48;
15:24; 19:7; 20:4; Num 30:13, 16; 35:26; in
homiletic discourse: Exod 23:22; Deut 8:19; 11:13,
22; 15:5; 28:1; Josh 23:12; 1 Sam 12:25; 1 Kgs
9:6; Jer 17:24; 22:4; Lam 5:22 (only case in
poetry!); in narrative and dialogue: Judg 14:12; 1
Sam 1:11; 20:6, 7, 9, 21; 2 Sam 18:3; 1 Kgs 20:39;
22:28; Jer 38:17; 42:10. Since this construction
is problematic in late biblical Hebrew, there is a
strong presumption in favour of the 4Q=LXX
reading.

19. For the reading of 4Q=LXX cf. אשר תארה ב/ככל:
Deut 14:26; 2 Sam 3:21; 1 Kgs 11:37).

20. Probably LXX represents הסיר הגדול (= λέβης
Exod 16:3; 1 Kgs 7:45; 2 Kgs. 4:38-41; = סף 2 Sam
17:28; כיור 1 Kgs 7:40; χυτρόπαυλος = כיר/כיור).

It is impossible to determine whether he had בדוד,
פארור or בקלחת. דוד and קלחת are both difficult
words. χύτρα = פארור (Num 11:8; Judg 6:19; Joel 2:6;
Nah 2:10) or= קלחת (Mic 3:3); χαλκεῖον = סיר (Job
41:22; 2 Chr 35:13: בסירות ובדודים ובצלחות = ἐν
τοῖς χαλκείοις καὶ ἐν τοῖς λέβησιν); דוד =
κάρταλλος (2 Kgs 10:7).

21. Ulrich (*Qumran*, 64) finds here "a proto-
Lucianic revision towards 4Q which nearly
thoroughly penetrated the tradition." Rahlfs
considered the B reading the result of an
inner-Greek haplography (κυρίου ˆ ἁγίου).

22. This amalgam is an instructive accumulation of
doublets. LXX καὶ προσήγαγεν is repetitive and
might indicate epanalepsis. It is rather unlikely
that MT would have arisen out of parepiblepsis
because of homoeoteleuton. This proposal could
only be justified by the weak similarity ויבאר ˆ
והבא). See also: Foresti, "Varianti," 55.

23. Ulrich (*Qumran*, 45) adds אחר in his
reconstruction of Q and the parent text of the
LXX, cf. Vetus Latina *postea*.

24. In 2:31-32 MT includes the clause והבטת צר
מעון בכל אשר ייטיב את ישראל which is non-extant in
LXX=4Q (Ulrich, *Qumran*, 58-59.). In the given
context this phrase might well be secondary; it
looks, however, like an adaptation of the
difficult verse 29: למה תבעטו ... אשר צויתי מעון,
for which LXX has καὶ ἵνα τί ἐπέβλεψας ... ἀναιδεῖ
ὀφθαλμῷ = צר מעון ... למה תביט. LXX has the
adaptation only; see Wellhausen, *Text*, 49. 4QSam[a]
has תביט.

25. See the survey of Ulrich, *Qumran*, 41-43.

26. F. M. Cross, "Evolution," 316-7, n. 11;
Ulrich, *Qumran*, 149.

27. D. Barthélemy, "La Qualité du Texte
Masorétique de Samuel," in: Tov (ed.), *Samuel*,
1-44.

28. Tov, "Relationship," 53-57.

29. Ulrich, (*Qumran*, 39-40) supposes that the
parent text of LXX read נזיר. For another opinion
see: K. Budde, *Die Bücher Samuel* (KHAT 8;
Tübingen/Leipzig: Siebeck & Mohr, 1902) 8, against
Wellhausen, *Text*, 38. On the status of the Temple
oblate in the Ancient Near East see: E. A.

Speiser, "Unrecognized Dedication," *IEJ* 13 (1963) 69-73; M. Elat, "History and Historiography in the Story of Samuel," *Shnaton* 3 (1978) 8-28, esp. p. 8-10., viii-ix (Hebr., Engl. summary). According to the opinion of Foresti, "Varianti," 52 the LXX text derives from Num 18:6 (so also Rofé, "Correctures," 251). But he does not take into account the data from the Ancient Near East.

30. Ulrich (*Qumran*, 197) speaks of influence by the Kaige revision, which amounts to the same, since Kaige is a revision of OG in accordance with Proto-MT. See also 2 Sam 6:2.

31. Wellhausen (*Text*, 175) considers the "plus" of the LXX a later addition. In a Temple Chronicle such an addition would be quite plausible; for the view that the original sources of the book of Kings included a Chronicle of this kind see: ב. מייזלר, "היסטוריוגרפיה ישראלית קדומה", הכינוס העולמי למדעי היהדות, י"ם תשי"ב, 357-361; esp. p. 60.

32. This result also disposes of the possible argument that the text of Chronicles has undergone partial revision towards ב.

33. *Pace* S. Pisano, *Additions or Omissions in the Books of Samuel: The Significant Pluses and Minuses in the Massoretic, LXX and Qumran Texts* (OBO 57; Freiburg- Göttingen: Universitätsverlag Freiburg - Vandenhoeck & Ruprecht, 1984) 112-4; A. Rofé, *The Belief in Angels in the Bible and in Early Israel* (2 vols,; Jerusalem: Makor, 1979), 1. 184-190, 194-7; 2.xix-xx (Hebr,; Engl. summary).

34. A. Rofé, "The Acts of Nahash according to 4QSam$^{\alpha}$," *IEJ* 32 (1982) 129-33.

35. See: J. Lust, "The Story of David and Goliath in Hebrew and Greek," *The Story of David and Goliath - Textual and Literary Criticism* (ed. D. Barthélemy, D. W. Gooding, J. Lust, E. Tov; OBO 73; Freiburg-Göttingen: Universitätsverlag Freiburg - Vandenhoeck & Ruprecht, 1986) 5-18, 87-91, 121-8; E. Tov, "The Nature of the Differences between MT and the LXX in 1 Sam. 17-18," ibid., 19-46, 92-4, 129-37; on the other hand see: D. W. Gooding, "An Appraoch to the Literary and Textual Problems in the David-Goliath Story," ibid., 55-87, 99-106, 114-120, 145-154; F. Polak, "Literary Study and "Higher Criticism" According to the Tale of David's

Beginning," *Proceedings of the Ninth World Congress of Jewish Studies, A: The Period of the Bible* (Jerusalem: World Union Jewish Studies, 1986) 27-32.

36. J. E. Sanderson, *An Exodus Scroll from Qumran: 4QpaleoExod^m and the Samaritan Tradition* (HSS 30; Atlanta: Scholars, 1986) 256-9, 308-11. For a similar view see: H. M. Wiener, "The Pentateuchal Text: A Reply to Dr. Skinner," *Bibliotheca Sacra* 71 (1914) 218-268, esp. pp. 222-235, 244-248.

37. For four witnesses it is hardly sound to set an *a priori* probability. Hence I have distinguished between the probability of the deviation of one of the four witnesses (=.25 x the total number of one deviation), and the probability of paired readings a=b/c=d (=.333 x the total number of paired variances). For the small number of variants in our corpus the expectation of three or four different variants is totally negligible.

38. E. Tov, "The Textual Character of 11QpaleoLev," *Shnaton* 3 (1978) 238-44 (Hebr.; Eng. summary); see also E. Tov, "Outlook" 17-21 ; K. A. Mathews, "Scroll." For some important corrections and additions, on the base of infrared photographs, see: E. Puech, "Notes en marge de 11QPaléoLévitique. Le Fragment L, des fragments inédits et une jarre de la grotte 11," *RB* 96 (1989) 161-183.

39. Mathews, "Scroll," 187-194 lists a large number of LXX readings that in his opinion should not be taken into account, since they may reflect translation technique and exegesis. In many cases this procedure is obviously justified, but he has also disregarded some variants that must be considered genuine. I have marked these passages with an asterisk. In general, one should carefully consider the "Septuagintal" variants of a text such as 4QDeutPhylN (4Q151; *DJD* VI, [Oxford 1977] 72-74).

40. SP, LXX and 4QDeutPhylN all share the same plus on Deut 32:15: ויאכל יעקב וישבע; this clause is matched by similar phrases in Deut 8:12-14 (פן תאכל ושבעת...ורם לבבך ושכחת את ה' אלהיך), Hos 13:6 (כמרעיתם וישבעו, שבעו וירם לבם, על כן שכחוני) and Neh 9:25-26 (ויאכלו וישבעו וישמינו ויתעדנו בטובך הגדול וימרו וימרדו בך). The last passage has וישבע and וישמינו in sequence, just like the non-MT reading of Deut 32:15. All these passages

deal with the same motive: sin as a result of satiety (κόρος). See also Deut 31:20.

41. S. E. Loewenstamm, "אנכי אחמטנה," ZAW 90 (1978) 410; Z. Ben-Ḥayyim, *The Literary and Oral Tradition of Hebrew and Aramaic Amongst the Samaritans, IV: the Words of the Pentateuch* (Jerusalem: Academy Hebrew Language, 1977) 382. It is to be noted that Tg. Onq. also understand אחמטנה as reimbursal. The Samaritan Targum has אמרקנה; normally the Pi'el of חטא is rendered by סלח (cognate to Akkadian *sulluhu*).

42. This possibility has been suggested by J. D. Purvis, *The Samaritan Pentateuch and the Origin of the Samaritan Sect* (HSM 2; Cambridge/Mass.: Harvard University, 1968) 80-82. Purvis (p. 84) admits that the agreement SP=MT is far more massive, but assumes that this results from a revision of SP towards Proto-MT. In view of the character of the agreements this explanation is rather implausible. And how are we to explain that this revision obliterated most agreements with the LXX, but left many unique readings untouched and preserved some "striking" secondary variants? This constellation can only be explained on the assumption that these variants were already extant in Proto-MT; this hypothesis contradicts the presupposition that the agreements SP=LXX derive from the hyparchetype *P*.

THE SEPTUAGINT AND THE TEMPLE SCROLL:
SHARED "HALAKHIC" VARIANTS*

LAWRENCE H. SCHIFFMAN

Introduction

It has long been known that the Septuagint (LXX) contains numerous translations which evidence interpretations otherwise known from Rabbinic sources, both halakhic and aggadic.[1] One of the great challenges facing scholars of textual criticism in regard to the LXX has been to distinguish actual textual variants from interpretations,[2] and to some extent the Rabbinic parallels have helped to caution against the facile assumption that all variations constitute true textual variants, by which we mean those which result from the history of transmission of the text.

The discovery of the Dead Sea Scrolls stimulated numerous important contributions to our understanding of the Hebrew texts which lie behind the ancient versions, and of the nature of the biblical texts from which these versions were translated. At the same time, the biblical exegesis of the scrolls has yet to yield up its important contribution to this same issue.

One prime example of a resource for this kind of study is the *Temple Scroll* (11QT).[3] This scroll, one of the largest in the Qumran corpus, presents us with a rewritten and reredacted Torah. The author/redactor of this document, writing in the early Hasmonean period, had available to him a variety of sources regarding the building of the Temple, purity laws, the laws of the king, and other topics.[4] These he skillfully wove together into an imitation Torah, adding his own interpretations and views, and completing his Torah by composing the Deuteronomic Paraphrase with which the scroll ends. Among these sources were certainly some of Sadducean origin, as is now clear from comparison of laws and interpretations in the *Temple Scroll* with those of 4Q *Miqsat Ma'aseh Ha-Torah* (MMT), on the one hand, and from comparison of 4QMMT with tannaitic sources, on the other hand.[5]

The *Temple Scroll* contains numerous biblical passages which have been either copied or adapted and expanded. It is clear that the author/redactor and his sources had before them *Vorlagen* of the canonical Torah, in its present shape, which demonstrated genuine textual variation when compared with the Masoretic Text (MT). To this textual base, the author(s) added their own interpretations and adaptations. One of the challenges to scholarship is to distinguish these layers. In other words, we must attempt to determine from examination of the scroll which variants with MT (used here as a standard) are the result of textual transmission (genuine textual variants) and which are tendentious, intentional changes by the author or some previous source or *Vorlage*.[6]

We have elsewhere investigated at length the section at the end of the *Temple Scroll*, the Deuteronomic Paraphrase, which in our view is the composition of the author/redactor of the complete scroll.[7] This section, which is the closest of all the sections of the scroll to the text of the Pentateuch, presents us with an excellent opportunity to inquire into the nature of the biblical text which stood before the author. One of the interesting phenomena we have found, the subject of the present paper, is that there are a number of cases in which the scroll presents a text which varies from that of MT, and agrees with the LXX, in which the variation clearly has halakhic significance.[8]

These shared variants, which we term "halakhic" variants, are cases where the readings in the scroll and the LXX either represent a different legal ruling than that of MT, or seek to clarify a legal question left undetermined in MT. In effect then, there are two types of halakhic variants. One we may term prescriptive, and the second exegetical. By halakhic, we mean relating to issues of Jewish law. We recognize fully that this may be an anachronistic or even somewhat inaccurate term, since it derives from the Rabbinic corpus. Nonetheless, we lack a better designation for the unique combination of ritual, civil, and ethical law which characterizes Judaism in all its ancient manifestations.

This study will examine the halakhic variants which occur in the Deuteronomic Paraphrase of the *Temple Scroll* which are shared with the LXX. We should emphasize that these examples must be seen in the proper context. Numerous examples of halakhic variants between 11QT and MT exist which are not shared by the LXX. Yet this study is limited to those which are. These examples will be discussed in order of their occurrence in the book of Deuteronomy, which is not the order in which they appear in the scroll. Finally, conclusions about the nature of these variants and their value for our understanding of both the scroll and the LXX will be drawn.

Variants

(1) Deut 12:22

11QT 53:07-53:8 is an adaptation of Deut 12:20-28 and deals with non-sacral slaughter. Lines 4-5 read:

> You shall eat (it)[9] in your gates, both the pure and the impure[10] among you (בכה) together.[11]

Comparison with MT (v. 22) indicates that 11QT has the addition בכה, "among you," not found in MT. This plus solves a halakhic problem in the text. MT is ambiguous and can be interpreted to mean that one may eat both impure and pure (i.e. non-kosher and kosher) animals outside of the Temple area, just as one eats of the gazelle and hart. The addition of בכה is intended to resolve this ambiguity. That the author of the scroll was indeed concerned with this matter can be seen from

another modification he introduced, the change in
the word order of verses 22-23. He placed the
mention of the gazelle and the hart at the end of
the sentence, so as to remove the mistaken
impression that the pure and impure are to be
compared with these animals. In this respect he
also was harmonizing this text with Deut 12:15.

The LXX to Deut 12:22 reads, ὁ ἀκάθαρτος ἐν
σοὶ καὶ ὁ καθαρὸς, "the impure among you and the
pure." This same variant is found in the Samaritan
which has: הטמא בך והטהור.[12] This variant seems,
like the reading in the *Temple Scroll*, to be
intended to make the point that the text is not
discussing impure or pure animals, but rather
those Israelites who are ritually pure or impure.

This is an example of the exegetical variety of
halakhic variant as it attempts to make certain
that the text of Deuteronomy will not be
misunderstood in an important halakhic context.
While the scroll has gone much further in its
attempt to eliminate this ambiguity, as evidenced
by its rewriting of the surrounding passage in a
different order, it is clear that the LXX
represents an attempt to clarify the same matter.

(2) Deut 13:7

11QT 54:19-55:1 is a virtual quotation (as
restored) of the law of the enticer to idolatry in
Deut 13:7-12. The text begins (lines 19-21):

> And if your brother, the son of your father
> or the son of your mother, or your son or
> your daughter, or the wife of your bosom, or
> your neighbor who is like you, shall entice

you secretly saying, "Let us go and worship other gods"....[13]

In quoting Deut 13:7 the text of the scroll includes the phrase בן אביך או, "son of your father or," which is lacking in MT.[14] It is clear from the most cursory examination of the list of relatives included here that the son of your father, i.e. your brother or half brother, belongs in this list. The purpose of the list is to indicate that the requirement of having no mercy on such an enticer extends even to one's closest relatives.[15]

The same variant is found in the LXX which adds ἐκ πατρός σου ἢ, "from your father or," after "your brother." Indeed, the Samaritan also has בן אביך או בן אמך.[16] In view of the requirement of this reading for the sense of the verse, its prevalence in Second Temple times, and its presence in 4QDeut^c,[17] it is certain that we are dealing here with a genuine reading which was found in a *Vorlage* available to the author.

In this case, we are dealing with a halakhic variant of prescriptive nature, since this variation effects the specific details of the law. In other cases, one is not allowed to testify against close relatives. Here, however, the Torah specifically makes an exception. Accusations and testimony of enticing to idolatry may be made even by these relatives who normally do not testify against each other.

In this example we cannot be certain if MT is primary and the other versions all added the father to correct the text, or if the text originally included the son of the father and MT represents a defective text. In any case, the author of the scroll had a text before him which included this additional phrase and he simply quoted from it.

(3) Deut 13:14 and 16

11QT 55:2-14 parallels closely Deut 13:13-19, the commandment regarding a city which has been led astray to idolatry, עיר הנדחת in Rabbinic parlance.[18] Here we read in lines 2-7:

> If you hear regarding on[e of your cities which] I give you [in which] to dwe[ll], the following:[19] "Some worth[less] peo[p]le among you have gone out and have led astray all the [in]habitants of their city, saying,[20] `Let us go and worship gods' which you have not known," then you must ask, inquire and investigate carefully.[21] If the accusation turns out to be true (and) correct, (that) this abomination has been performed among (the people of) Israel, you must kill all the inhabitants of that city by the sword, destroying[22] it and all (the people) that are in it. And all its domesticated animals[23] you must kill by the sword.[24]

This passage contains two instances of the presence of כול, "all," where it is not found in MT. 11QT adds כול indicating that all the inhabitants must worship idols for this law to apply (line 3), and again that all the inhabitants be killed (line 6). These are clearly halakhic modifications.

In the case of the requirement that all the

inhabitants be lead astray to idolatrous worship for this law to apply, the ruling of the scroll contrasts with that of the tannaim who require only that the majority of the inhabitants worship idolatrously (*m. Sanh.* 4:1). The scroll may have been influenced here by Gen 18:24-25 in which Abraham asks God how he can take the lives of the righteous along with the sinners.[25] Ezek 18:1-20 which likewise expects that only those who violate the law will suffer divine punishment may also have been a factor here. In any case, according to the *Temple Scroll*, collective responsibility was not possible. Only those who actually worshiped idols could be included in the idolatrous city. The possibility that we are dealing here with a polemic against the Hasmonean practice of destroying pagan cities must also be considered.

That all the inhabitants of the idolatrous city are to be killed, also emphasized by the scroll, contrasts with the view of some tannaim that the children of the idolatrous city are to be spared (*t. Sanh.* 14:3).[26]

Both these additions of כול correspond with the reading of the LXX which has πάντας in both these passages.[27] These are indeed halakhic variants, intended to indicate these specific rulings. But the parallel with LXX shows that these changes may have taken place in the *Vorlage* of the author, and may not be original to the *Temple Scroll*. Regardless, the additions of כול in the scroll or its *Vorlage* and the LXX were intended to polemicize against specific views which we know from later tannaitic sources.

(4) Deut 15:22

11QT 52:7-12 is almost a quotation of Deut 15:19-23. Dealing with the blemished firstborn animal, lines 10-11 prescribe:

> In your gates you shall eat it, the impure and the pure among you (בכה) together, like the gazelle and the hart.[28]

In quoting the text of verse 22, the scroll has בכה, "among you," which is not found in MT. The purpose of this variant, like that discussed above in Deut 12:22, is to eliminate the ambiguity of the verse, which could have been misunderstood to mean that kosher and non-kosher animals could be eaten. The addition clarifies that it is the pure and impure Israelites who may eat of the blemished firstborn which is slaughtered in a non-sacral context. Here again, this exegetical halakhic variant is shared by the LXX[29] which has: ὁ ἀκάθαρτος ἐν σοὶ καὶ ὁ καθαρός, "the impure among you and the pure."

(5) Deut 17:3

11QT 55:15-56:04 is copied almost verbatim from Deut 17:2-7. In lines 17-18 the specific offense of the idolatrous individual is outlined:

> and he (or she) goes and serves other gods and bows down to them, either to the sun (או לשמש), or to the moon, or to any of the host of heaven....[30]

In this passage, the scroll has או, "or," where the conjunctive -ו, usually "and," and sometimes "or," appears in MT. What is at stake here is a very minor point of interpretation with legal ramifications. Verse 3 as it appears in MT is ambiguous. The text of MT can be misconstrued to require that to be guilty of idolatrous worship one must worship both idols ("other gods") and astral bodies. In order to dispel this possibility of misinterpretation, the scroll, or his *Vorlage*, substituted אֹו for the ambiguous conjunctive -וְ.

The situation in the LXX to this passage is somewhat complex.[31] LXX in most manuscripts preserves absolutely no conjunction, so that it is as if a colon is placed after "other gods" such that the sun, moon, and other astral bodies are the "other gods" in question. Such an interpretation would severely limit the applicability of this law to astral worship alone, and seems to fly in the face of its simple meaning and the history of its interpretation. More likely is the reading of other LXX MSS which have ἤ, "or," and which agree with the reading of the *Temple Scroll*.[32] This second LXX text represents the same interpretive process we have seen in the scroll.

In this case, some LXX manuscripts and the scroll share a halakhic variant of the exegetical variety which seems to be a secondary change designed to remove ambiguity. We cannot tell if both these sources derived this reading from their *Vorlagen* which were in agreement, or if they independently arrived at this interpretation.

Indeed, from the point of view of the LXX, one cannot even really consider the translation of a -וְ conjunctive (assuming this to be the reading of the *Vorlage*) to be a variant, only a correct interpretive translation. Yet in any case, the

THE SEPTUAGINT AND THE TEMPLE SCROLL

scroll and some manuscripts of the LXX share the same halakhic variant or exegesis.

(6) Deut 17:9

11QT 56:05-11 is an adaptation and expansion of Deut 17:8-13.[33] This passage deals with the requirement to heed the decisions of the authorities. Lines 07-1 command:

[And you shall come to the priests (and?)[34] the Levites, o]r (או)[35] to the [j]u[dges[36] who will be (in office) in those days].[37]

The scroll has the conjunction או where MT to Deut 17:9 has -ו, usually "and." The text as it appears in MT can be taken to require that the cases described in verse 8 must be tried before "the Levitical priests and the judge."[38] Such a procedure would require a verdict of lay and priestly judges. The reading או, "or," provides the option of trying the case either in a priestly venue or in a lay court. According to the editor's reconstruction, the scroll would allow either a court of priests and Levites, or a group of judges. A parallel in 11QT 61:7-9 would support the notion that the reading of the scroll included the Levites as a separate group, not simply as a description of the priests. Indeed, the Qumran sectarian texts expect that priests, Levites and Israelites would all be part of the court.[39]

Certain manuscripts of the LXX to Deut 17:9 also have ἤ, "or," in agreement with the *Temple Scroll*. Indeed, this is the reading of several manuscripts of the MT, the SP and the Lucianic and Theodotionic renderings.[40] This reading, like that of the the scroll, would clearly indicate that the meaning of ו- in this passage is "or."

In this case, in both the scroll and the Greek readings in question, we are dealing with a halakhic variant the purpose of which is exegetical. We cannot be certain if this variant was independently introduced by the author of the scroll or if he found it in the text of Deuteronomy in front of him. Alternatively, he may have been familiar with this exegesis which is found elsewhere, and adapted the biblical text accordingly.[41]

(7) Deut 18:5

11QT 60:1-15 specifies the Levitical and priestly emoluments as understood by the author. Lines 10-11 are almost a quotation of Deut 18:5:

> For I have chosen them (the priests) from among all your tribes to stand before Me, and to serve and to pronounce the benediction in My name, him (Aaron) and all his sons forever.[42]

The author of the scroll has reformulated this verse in the first person, so that God addresses the people of Israel directly. This is one of the characteristic features of the style of the scroll and testifies to the author's theology of direct divine revelation without the intermediacy of Moses. Yet the key variant with MT is the presence in the scroll of "and to pronounce the benediction" (ולברך), not found in MT. On the one hand, this variant results from harmonization with Deut 10:8, "to serve Him and to pronounce the benediction in His name," (לשרתו ולברך בשמו), and

21:5, "to serve Him and to pronounce the benediction in the name of the Lord" (לשרתו ולברך בשם ה')[43] which appears in 11QT 53:3.[44] At the same time, the reading of 11QT is designed to emphasize the obligation of the priests (and only the Aaronide priests) to pronounce the priestly blessing found in Num 6:22-27. This benediction was recited daily in the Second Temple[45] and the author of the scroll expected this pattern to continue in his ideal sanctuary.

The very same harmonization is found in the LXX to Deut 18:5 which reads, καὶ εὐλογεῖν ἐπὶ τῷ ὀνόματι αὐτοῦ, "and to pronounce the benediction in his name." The very same reading appears in the SP.

In this case we again see a halakhic variant of the prescriptive type. The text as found in 11QT, LXX and the SP, the result of harmonization, seeks to emphasize the obligation of the priests to recite the priestly blessing. We cannot claim that this interpretation is original to the scroll. It may already have been in the author's *Vorlage*.

(8) Deut 21:6

11QT 63:05-8 corresponds to the expiation ceremony to be conducted in case a body is found, as described in Deut 21:1-9. Lines 4-5 provide:

> Then all the elders of that city which was nearest to the body shall wash their hands upon the head of (על ראש) the heifer whose neck was broken in the stream.[46]

The parallel in MT does not have the word ראש, "head," and instead commands in verse 6 that the elders "wash their hands upon the heifer."⁴⁷ The text in the scroll is clearly intended to clarify a halakhic requirement, namely that the washing of the hands be done in such a manner as the water drip down over the head of the heifer the neck of which has already been broken.⁴⁸ The water from the lustrations is expected to flow back into the stream and in some way to purify the earth of the transgression of the murder of the innocent man whose body was found.

A similar requirement is found in tannaitic law. *M. Sota* 9:6 and *Sifre Devarim* 209⁴⁹ state that the washing is to be performed over the place where the animal's neck was broken, i.e. over the back of the neck. Apparently, the very same ruling was adopted by the scroll.

The reading of the LXX, ἐπὶ τὴν κεφαλὴν τῆς δαμάλεως, "over the head of the heifer," also indicates the very same ruling. In this case the LXX and the scroll represent the same prescriptive halakhic addition to the biblical text. What we still do not know is whether for the author of the scroll this addition was found in his *Vorlage*. In any case, this is a shared prescriptive halakhic variant.

(9) Deut 21:12

11QT 63:10-64:03 details the laws of the woman taken captive in war, and follows Deut 21:10-14 with modifications.⁵⁰ Lines 12-13 provide:
> Then you shall bring her into your house, and you shall shave her head and pare her nails, and remove her captive's garb.⁵¹

This version of Deut 21:12 differs from MT in an

important aspect. Whereas, according to MT, the captive woman herself is supposed to perform the three actions described in the verse,[52] according to the version of the *Temple Scroll* these actions are to be done by the prospective husband.

The text of 11QT differs in regard to a second detail. The first and third actions to be performed are clear, the shaving of the head and the removal of the captive's garb. Yet what of the second? The ambiguous use of the verb עשה led to controversy in tannaitic times regarding whether the text meant to cut the nails or to grow the nails.[53] The text of the scroll, requiring that the prospective husband undertake these actions, makes clear its view that the "doing" of the nails refers to paring them. This action can be undertaken by the man; obviously "growing" cannot.

Both rulings of the *Temple Scroll* are found in the LXX which accordingly translates, καὶ περιονυχιεῖς αὐτήν, "and you shall cut her nails." The LXX, like the scroll, requires that the actions be performed by the husband and that the nails be cut, not grown.

In this case we have a variant between 11QT and MT which has ramifications in regard to two halakhic issues. The scroll and the LXX have the identical text. It is hard to believe that this common variant would have come into existence independently in both places. Rather, it seems that both these sources had such a text in their *Vorlage*. This text may itself be tendentious, but there is no way to be certain.

Conclusion

In the Deuteronomic Paraphrase at the end of the Temple Scroll there are a variety of shared halakhic variants, some exegetical and some prescriptive, which are found in both the scroll and the LXX. In these cases, we cannot assume that the scroll has originated the particular reading, especially in passages which deal with halakhic matters known to have been debated in Second Temple times. In general, the examples we have examined are cases in which we must conclude that either the author/redactor of the scroll found these variants in his *Vorlage* or that he knew of the exegesis represented in the LXX and incorporated this interpretation into his scroll. In either case, it seems that the rulings of the shared halakhic variants cannot be considered to be original to the *Temple Scroll*.

It is important to keep these shared variants in perspective. They amount to a small minority of the many differences between the text of 11QT and MT. Many of the other variants, however, which are of similar nature to those we have studied here, must be assumed to emerge from the text base of the Bible available to the scroll or its source. Others, however, no doubt originate with the scroll, as is clear from detailed study.

From the point of view of Septuagint studies, our comparisons illustrate the fact that whereas many variations between LXX and MT result from variants in the *Vorlage* of the LXX, this is not the only possibility. Often exegesis has been introduced into LXX readings such that they do not constitute real variants with MT. This is clearly the case with many of the variants between 11QT and MT as well.

From the perspective of the history of Judaism we must emphasize the intimate links between the scribal process of passing on texts, and the exegetical process of interpreting them. Interpretations are often evident in ancient biblical manuscripts and translations, and some of these were introduced secondarily in the process of transmission. In the *Temple Scroll* we have perhaps the most extreme example, because of the purposeful rewriting of the Torah.

Let us finally emphasize that the *Temple Scroll* cannot be looked at as an anthology of variant biblical texts. It includes many genuine textual variants, but these are only a few of the many variations with MT which have been created as a result of the intentional exegetical, halakhic and literary activity of the author/redactor and his sources, all of which reshaped the biblical material for their own purposes. Yet in some cases the author/redactor had before him biblical texts which already included such interpretations, of which those shared with the LXX are a small part.

NOTES

* This study was written during my tenure as a Fellow in the Institute for Advanced Studies of the Hebrew University of Jerusalem, Israel. I wish to thank the staff of the Institute for their gracious assistance.

1. Z. Frankel, *Ueber den Einfluss der palästinischen Exegese auf die alexandrinische Hermeneutik* (Leipzig: Joh. Ambr. Barth, 1851).

2. On interpretation in the LXX see E. Tov, "The Septuagint," *Mikra, Text, Translation, Reading and Interpretation of the Hebrew Bible in Ancient Judaism and Early Christianity* (ed. M. J. Mulder; CRINT 2:1; Assen/Maastricht: Van Gorcum, Philadelphia: Fortress, 1988) 176-8.

3. Y. Yadin, *The Temple Scroll* (3 vols; Jerusalem: Israel Exploration Society, 1983).

4. A. Wilson, L. Wills, "Literary Sources for the Temple Scroll," *HTR* 75 (1982) 275-88.

5. See L. H. Schiffman, "The Temple Scroll and the Systems of Jewish Law of the Second Temple Period," *Temple Scroll Studies* (ed. G. J. Brooke; JSPSup 7; Sheffield: JSOT Press, 1989) 239-55; "The New Halakhic Letter (4QMMT) and the Origins of the Dead Sea Sect," *BA* 53 (1990) 64-73; "*Miqsat Ma'aseh Ha-Torah* and the *Temple Scroll*," *RevQ* 14 (1990) 435-57.

6. See E. Tov, "'Megillat Ha-Miqdash' U-Viqoret Nusah Ha-Miqra'," *Eretz-Israel* 16 (1981/2) 100-11.

7. L. H. Schiffman, "The Deuteronomic Paraphrase of the *Temple Scroll*," to appear in *RevQ* (1991).

8. The text of the LXX used here follows J. W. Wevers, ed., *Septuaginta Vetus Testamentum Graecum Auctoritate Academiae Scientiarum Gottingensis editum*, vol. III, 2, *Deuteronomium* (Göttingen: Vandenhoeck & Ruprecht, 1977) and A. E. Brooke, N. McLean, eds., *The Old Testament in Greek*, Vol. I, Part III, *Numbers and Deuteronomy* (Cambridge: University Press, 1911).

9. Meat slaughtered in a non-sacral context.

10. The scroll switches the order of reference as Deuteronomy has "the impure and the pure." Such variations are not uncommon in the scroll and result either from genuine textual variants in the scroll's *Vorlage*, or from sloppiness on the part of the author or a copiest.

11. All translations in this paper are mine. On

this passage, cf. Yadin, *The Temple Scroll*, 2.238.
See also below, on Deut 15:22.

12. Tov, "'Megillat Ha-Miqdash'," 106.

13. Cf. the commentary of Yadin, *The Temple Scroll*, 2.245 and L. H. Schiffman, "Laws concerning Idolatry in the *Temple Scroll*," to appear in the H. Neil Richardson Memorial Volume. (ed. L. M. Hopfe; Winona Lake: Eisenbrauns).

14. The reading of 11QT is confirmed here by MS. b. See A. S. van der Woude, "Ein bisher unveroffentlichtes Fragment der Tempelrolle," *RevQ* 13 (1988) 89-92. For a full discussion of this fragment, see the Appendix in Schiffman, "Laws concerning Idolatry."

15. The absence of the brother through the father in MT was felt by the tannaim in *Sifre Devarim* 87 (ed. L. Finkelstein; New York: Jewish Theological Seminary of America, 1969, p. 151). Accordingly, they understood אחיך as referring to him, separating this word from בן אמך which follows.

16. Tov, "'Megillat Ha-Miqdash'," 106.

17. Fragments 21 and 22 in S. White, *A Critical Edition of Seven Manuscripts of Deuteronomy: 4QDt^a, 4QDt^c, 4QDt^d, 4QDt^f, 4QDt^g, 4QDt^i, and 4QDt^n* (Cambridge, Mass.: Harvard University Doctoral Dissertation, 1988) 62-63.

18. On this passage, cf. Yadin, *The Temple Scroll*, 2.247-9 and Schiffman, "Laws concerning Idolatry."

19. This is the meaning of לאמר in this context.

20. 1QDeut^a preserves Deut 13:13-14 in fragmentary form (D. Barthélemy, J. T. Milik, *Qumran Cave I*, [DJD 1; Oxford: Clarendon Press, 1962] 55). No variants with MT except those occasioned by Qumran orthography can be found there.

21. השיב here modifies all three verbs, not only the first as in Yadin's translation (*The Temple Scroll* 2.247, 401).

22. Taking החרם as an infinitive absolute used in the gerundive sense, rather than as an imperative.

23. I.e. permissible, edible animals.

24. 4QDeut^c Fragment 24 (White, 66-67) preserves the words את בהמתה. As noted by White, the phrase is missing in some Greek manuscripts as a result of homoioarchton. Based on this reading, A. Rofé,

Mavo' Le-Sefer Devarim (Jerusalem: Akademon, 1988) 64 n. 14, would omit the entire phrase (up to the end of the verse) from the text of Deuteronomy.

25. Yadin, *The Temple Scroll*, 2.247.

26. In line 8 the scroll even adds כול again to say that all animals must be destroyed. The notion that all the animals are to be killed disagrees with the tannaitic view that certain animals designated as offerings are to be saved (*t. Sanh.* 14:5 and *Sifre Devarim* 94 [ed. Finkelstein, p. 156]). The Tosefta records disagreement as to which kinds of offerings are to be exempted, whereas the *Sifre* excludes all offerings.

27. Tov ("'Megillat Ha-Miqdash'," 106) refers only to the addition in line 3 where he notes that the SP is in agreement with MT.

28. See Yadin, *The Temple Scroll*, 2.234.

29. In this case, however, the SP agrees with MT (Tov, "'Megillat Ha-Miqdash'," 106).

30. See Yadin, *The Temple Scroll*, 2.249 and Schiffman, "Laws concerning Idolatry."

31. The SP is in agreement with MT (Tov, "'Megillat Ha-Miqdash'," 106).

32. Tov, "'Megillat Ha-Miqdash'," 106.

33. In light of the many variations with MT found in the preserved portions of this text, it is unlikely that Yadin's proposed text of 05-07 (*The Temple Scroll*, 2.250) should be considered anything more than, in his words, a "suggested reconstruction."

34. The conjunction does not appear in MT to Deut 17:9 which has הכהנים הלוים, "the Levitical priests." Nonetheless, Yadin (*The Temple Scroll*, 2.250) reconstructs with the conjunction in light of והלויים in 11QT 61:8 (*The Temple Scroll*, 2.278) which has no equivalent in MT.

35. The bottom of the *waw* is preserved so that no reading other than this is possible (cf. Yadin, *The Temple Scroll*, 2.251).

36. Yadin restores the plural based on its appearance in the parallel in 11QT 61:9 which is derived from Deut 19:17 where the plural appears. It is also possible to restore the singular in our

passage as does Tov ("'Megillat Ha-Miqdash'," 107) who indicates that the SP also has the singular.

37. See Yadin, *The Temple Scroll*, 2.251.

38. Cf. *Sifre Devarim* 153 (ed. Finkelstein, p. 206).

39. See L. H. Schiffman, *Sectarian Law in the Dead Sea Scrolls, Courts, Testimony and the Penal Code* (BJS 33; Chico; California: Scholars Press, 1983) 26-28.

40. Yadin, *The Temple Scroll*, 2.251.

41. Note that the scroll made no such change in 11QT 61:8-9.

42. See Yadin, *The Temple Scroll*, 2.273-74.

43. Tov, "'Megillat Ha-Miqdash'," 107.

44. With modification to direct divine discourse in the first person.

45. *M. Tamid* 5:1, 7:2; *m. Sota* 7:6.

46. See Yadin, *The Temple Scroll*, 2.284.

47. This is also the reading of the SP (Tov, "'Megillat Ha-Miqdash'," 108). This phrase is not preserved in 4QDeut^f Fragments 17-19 (White, 188; see n. 17).

48. J. Maier, *The Temple Scroll, An Introduction, Translation & Commentary* (JSOTSup 34; Sheffield: JSOT Press, 1985) 132.

49. Ed. Finkelstein, p. 243.

50. On this law see Yadin, *The Temple Scroll*, 1.364-7; my forthcoming article, "Laws pertaining to Women in the *Temple Scroll*," to appear in *The Dead Sea Scrolls, Forty Years of Research* (ed. D. Dimant and U. Rappaport; Jerusalem: Magnes Press); and M. R. Lehmann, "The Beautiful War Bride (יפת תאר) and other *Halakhoth* in the *Temple Scroll*," *Temple Scroll Studies* (ed. G. J. Brooke; (JSPSup 7; Sheffield: JSOT Press, 1989) 265-71.

51. See Yadin, *The Temple Scroll*, 2.286.

52. The SP here is in agreement with MT (Tov, "'Megillat Ha-Miqdash'," 108).

53. *Sifre Devarim* 212 (ed. Finkelstein, pp. 245-46); *b. Yebam.* 48a; cf. Targumim.

SECTION B

THE SEPTUAGINT AND COGNATE WRITINGS

TO REVISE OR NOT TO REVISE: ATTITUDES TO JEWISH BIBLICAL TRANSLATION

SEBASTIAN BROCK

The Qumran finds of fragments of Hebrew biblical manuscripts have undoubtedly revolutionized our understanding of the transmission of the text of the Hebrew Bible. A similar revolution in our understanding of the early history of the Septuagint can be said to have occurred as a result of the discovery of the Twelve Prophets Scroll in Greek from Nahal Hever, and the brilliant interpretation of their significance by Fr Dominique Barthélemy. In this paper I shall not be concerned directly with the relevance of these Greek fragments for Septuagint studies per se, or with their contribution to textual criticism; my perspective will instead be a much broader one, for I shall try to sketch the outlines of the picture that is emerging, largely as a result of these finds, of the polarisation of attitudes to biblical translation that was taking place during the last two centuries before the turn of the Common Era.

Barthélemy's initial article, announcing the find of the Greek XII Prophets fragments, appeared in 1953, most aptly entitled "Redécouverte d'un chaînon manquant de l'histoire de la Septante."[1] The significance of Barthélemy's announcement for LXX studies was quickly recognized by Peter Katz (P. Walters), to whose inspiration and guidance I owe my own initiation into LXX studies; Katz contributed two articles, "Frühe hebräisierende Rezensionen der Septuaginta und die Hexapla,"[2] and "Justin's Old Testament quotations and the Greek Dodekapropheton Scroll,"[3] a paper given at the first Oxford Patristic Conference in autumn 1955. Barthélemy's full study, accompanying his preliminary publication of the fragments, came in 1963 with his book *Les devanciers d'Aquila*,[4] in which he brought out the implications of these fragments for a proper understanding of the early history of the Septuagint as a whole (I use the term in its traditional wider sense, not restricted, as it properly should be, to the Greek Pentateuch). When Barthélemy wrote, the exact provenance of the XII Prophets fragments was still unknown to him; the discovery of some further fragments from the scroll in excavations in Nahal Hever in 1961, however, resolved this enigma; these were published by Lifshitz in 1962,[5] and so today the official designation of the fragments is 8HevXIIgr (with the Göttingen Septuaginta Unternehmen's siglum 943). The publication of the complete materials in the series Discoveries in the Judaean Desert, accompanied by a full set of photographs, appeared in early 1990;[6] this exemplary edition, prepared by Emanuel Tov, now provides the firm basis for all future work on the manuscript, which dates, according to the most expert advice obtainable, probably from the late first century BCE.

As is by now well known, the Greek XII Prophets fragments contain a text of the Old Greek translation of the XII Prophets which has been revised fairly systematically in order to conform it to the Hebrew text; this revision in turn served as a basis for Aquila's further revision, carried out in the first half of the second century CE. Furthermore, as Barthélemy, and subsequently others, have shown, traces of the same, or similar work of "correction" can be identified in the manuscript tradition of many other parts of the Septuagint.[7] The details of all this, and the problem of nomenclature - *kai ge* recension, proto-Theodotion, etc. - , are not our concern here; rather, what is of prime importance is the fact that we now have direct evidence from the first century BCE that in some circles a need had been felt to revise the Old Greek translation and bring it closer into line with the Hebrew original. (I leave open the question of whether or not the revisers consciously sought out an authoritative form of the Hebrew text, and were aware of the plurality of Hebrew text forms in currency, though this seems very likely).

If we move on half a century or so in time we encounter a totally different attitude to the Septuagint, an attitude that is implicitly hostile to the idea that the Septuagint needed revising and "correcting." I refer of course to Philo's famous account of Septuagint origins in Book II of his *Life of Moses*.[9] A number of details are worth noting. Philo stresses that the translators' aim was to preserve the "original form and shape" (τὴν ἐξ ἀρχῆς ἰδέαν καὶ τὸν τύπον) of the divine laws, not "taking away, adding, or altering anything" (μήτ' ἀφελεῖν τι μήτε προσθεῖναι ἢ μεταθεῖναι) [34]; accordingly they began with prayer to God, asking "that they might not fail in their purpose," and to this God assents (ἐπινεύει) [36]. Then, as they worked "they became as it were possessed (ἐνθουσιῶντες) and, under inspiration (προεφήτευον), wrote, not each several scribe something different, but the same word for word, as though dictated to each by an invisible prompter" [37]. He then goes on to say that witness to the excellence of their translation is provided by those who know both languages: such people regard the original and the translation "with awe and reverence as sisters, or rather as one and the same, both in matter and in words, and speak of the authors not as translators but as prophets and priests of the mysteries (οὐχ ἑρμηνέας ἐκείνους ἀλλ' ἱεροφάντας καὶ προφήτας), whose sincerity and singleness of thought have enabled them to go hand in hand with the purest of spirits, the spirit of Moses" [40].

Philo's aim in this passage is to place the translation on a par with the original: the Greek is not a "daughter version", but a "sister", an equal with, indeed "one and the same", with the original; that this should be so is thanks to the fact that the translators had worked under divine inspiration, communing at the same time with the spirit of Moses. Philo of course has a hidden agenda here: he is polemicizing against those who sought to revise and correct the Septuagint, and by claiming that the Septuagint is itself inspired he is undercutting the position of the would-be revisers: their work is totally unnecessary. (Because the problem of the differences between the Hebrew and Greek would not go away, subsequent Christian apologists for the Septuagint simply updated Philo's presentation: since the translators were themselves prophets, any differences between the translation and the original were to be explained as deliberate "updatings" of divine revelation for the benefit of the Gentile world).[9]

In Philo and in the Greek XII Prophets fragments, then, we have clear evidence of two completely different, and conflicting, attitudes to biblical translation current around the turn of the common era: the basic point at issue was "do the original Greek translations require revising or not?" This was not, however, a matter that had only recently come to the surface, for we can trace the debate back to the late second century BCE. From that period we again have two key documents at hand, the preface that Ben Sira's grandson provided for his translation of his grandfather's work, and the treatise addressed to Philokrates, purporting to be by Aristeas, an official at the court of Ptolemy II, but which modern scholarship assigns to the end of the second century BCE. Both are familiar documents, but the hidden agenda behind the latter has only

become clear once the implications of the Greek
XII Prophets fragments had been brought out.
Expressing feelings which any translator of a
literary text can share, Ben Sira's grandson asks
the readers of his translation "to make allowances
whenever you think that, in spite of all the
devoted work that has been put into the translation, some of the expressions I have used are
inadequate. For what is said in the Hebrew does
not have the same force when translated into
another language. Not only the present book, but
even the law itself, as well as the prophets, and
the other writings, are not a little different
when spoken in the original."[10] Here the
translator is simply drawing attention to the fact
of differences between the Greek translations of
the Hebrew biblical books and their originals; he
does not actually go on to make the inference that
the Greek translations accordingly are in need of
revision. That some contemporaries had made this
inference, and were revising the original translations is rendered very likely if we look at the
polemic which underlies the account of the origins
of the Greek Pentateuch in Aristeas' so-called
"Letter to Philokrates." Correctly understood,[11]
the account is aimed at undermining the position
of would-be revisers of the original translation.
The following points in particular deserve
noticing:
- it is admitted at the outset that copies of the
Hebrew Pentateuch available at Alexandria were not
very accurate [30];
- fully aware of this deficiency in the Hebrew
manuscripts available locally, an embassy is sent

to Jerusalem, the source of religious authority, and it is none other than the High Priest himself who provides a copy of the Hebrew Pentateuch; and to emphasize that this was no ordinary copy but one with the highest credentials, it is stated that it was even written in golden letters [32ff, 176];

- not only does the High Priest provide the Hebrew text from which the translation is to be made, but he also provides the translators themselves; these translators, it goes without saying, were men of the highest ability, but, more important still, they represented the whole of Israel, six men being selected from each of the twelve tribes [46-7, 121];

- the translation which they go on to make proves to be so accurate that any subsequent revision (διασκευή) is totally unnecessary; furthermore, anyone who dares to make any changes is laid under a curse [310-11].

This final point, concerning revision, is a very telling one: there would have been absolutely no reason to mention such a thing if no one at that time had yet thought of revising the original translation. Once we realize that, in his account of Septuagint origins, the author of Aristeas is polemicizing against those who wished to revise the original translation, then we can recognize the force of the other points as well which he is making: in each case he is answering objections to the original version made by the revisers. We can reconstruct the main features of the argument as follows:

Revisers: the original translation was made in Egypt from poor Hebrew originals that happened to be available locally. Aristeas: it was indeed made in Egypt, but the poor quality of the local Hebrew manuscripts was recognized, and so care was taken to get a copy that had the highest religious authorization possible. Furthermore, although it was made in Egypt, it was not a provincial affair, for the translators were from Palestine and were representatives of the whole of Israel.

The revisers of course will also have made what was undoubtedly their strongest point, that the translation was not always as accurate as it might be. In response to this undeniable fact Aristeas, like many others in similar positions, simply takes refuge in counter assertion and the use of threat: no revision is necessary, and anyone who attempts to undertake any is under a curse.

It is significant that, living a century and a half or so after Ps.Aristeas, when revision of the Greek Bible was evidently quite widespread in some Jewish circles, Philo sees the need to resort to even higher religious authority than the High Priest in Jerusalem: for him the translators were inspired by God himself and worked in harmony with the spirit of Moses.

Josephus, retelling the story of Septuagint origins as found in Aristeas, makes an interesting change at the end of the account of the work of translation.[12] No mention is made of the curse laid upon would-be revisers; instead, according to Josephus' presentation, when the finished translation was read out, everyone present, including, Josephus specifies, the chief officers of the

Jewish community, "requested that, since the translation had been so successfully completed, it should remain as it was and not be altered. Accordingly, when all had approved this idea, they ordered that, if anyone saw any further addition made to the text of the Law or anything omitted from it, he should examine it and make it known and correct it; in this they acted wisely, that what had once been judged good might remain for ever." The sentence "if anyone saw any further addition made to the text of the Law....he should....correct it" is actually ambiguous: who is correcting whom? Taken out of its immediate context the words could imply "if anyone notices additions or omissions to the Law made by the translators, they should publicize this and make the appropriate correction." The previous words, however, to the effect that the translation was not to be altered, must mean that the additions and omissions were being made to the original Greek translation by revisers, and that where these "corrections" had been noticed they were themselves to be "corrected" away. Possibly the ambiguity of the passage is deliberate, since there is clear evidence that Josephus here and there made use of a "revised" text of the Septuagint.[13]

So far, then, my aim has been to highlight the co-existence, within Judaism of the late Hellenistic and early Roman period, of two totally different attitudes to biblical translation, one seeing the need for revision, the other denying this need. Our modern sympathies may be with the revisers, but as I shall try to show later on,

Philo's position also has something to be said for
it, when seen in the light of modern problematics
in biblical translation. First, however, we
should return to the LXX as a translation, but
this time looking at it, not from the point of
view of the various Jewish communities which used
it, but from the wider perspective of translation
practice in general in the ancient world.[14]

Although we do not have formulations concerning
the norms of translation practice until the time
of Cicero and Horace, it is sufficiently clear
that these norms were already in practice a couple
of centuries earlier. Essentially, two different
modes of translation procedure existed side by
side, one employed for literary translation, the
other for translations of legal, governmental,
commercial and other "practical" texts. Translators of literary texts rendered their originals
in a very free fashion, so that we would often
call the end result a re-creation rather than a
translation; practitioners of this style of
translation such as Cicero had nothing but scorn
for the other style which was literal in
character, proceeding *verbum e verbo*. Cicero
speaks of himself as translating *ut orator*,
disassociating himself from *interpretes indiserti*
"clumsy hack-translators," the sort of person to
whom Horace too deprecatingly refers as *fidus
interpres* "the slavish hack-translator."

The Pentateuch, being both a literary and a
legal text, did not fit such a schema, and
furthermore, being the first large-scale
translation of an oriental religious text into
Greek,[15] no precedent was available to the

original translators, who no doubt worked on an entirely *ad hoc* basis. Only subsequently, when accumulated experience in translating from Hebrew into Greek had provided the opportunity for some reflection on the practice of "biblical translation," (only then) did there come into being some consensus over what was the proper procedure for such translation. From the work of the Jewish revisers of the Greek Bible we can see that, at least for them, the ideal for the Biblical translator was to work *verbum e verbo*. In due course this principle of biblical translation came to be expressly made by Jerome, in his letter to Pammachium; ardent admirer of Cicero that he was, Jerome openly and emphatically states that when he is translating from Greek into Latin he works *sensus de sensu*, that is, following the norms laid down by Cicero for literary translation; but, he goes on, there is one exception, the Sacred Scriptures "where even the order of words is a mystery:" accordingly in this case, and in this case alone, it is right to proceed *verbum e verbo*, that is, to adopt the literalist style of Cicero's and Horace's despised *interpres*. Since the literal style of biblical translation became the norm in the Christian world until the Renaissance for all translation, we can readily see how Horace's derogatory epithet *fidus*, used of the *interpres*, came to be understood in a quite different and positive sense, so that every translator of late antiquity and the middle ages held the *fidus interpres* as his ideal.

In an illuminating preface to the Latin translation of the writings of Dionysius the

Areopagite the translator comments "if someone should consider the translation opaque and obscure, he should realise that I am just the translator (*interpres*) of this work and not its *expositor*."[16] The *expositor* is the interpretative translator, of whom Cicero would have approved, whereas the *interpres* is the literal translator, the object of Cicero and Horace's contempt, who had, nevertheless, come into his own having gained prestige as the ideal biblical translator. These two terms can usefully serve us as we examine some of the main characteristics of the two conflicting ideals of translation.

Although there is a continuum between the extremely free style of translation advocated by Cicero and the very literal,[17] there is nonetheless an identifiable dividing point which distinguishes, albeit sometimes more in theory than in practice, the *expositor* from the *interpres*. The *expositor* (who conforms more to the modern idea of a translator) is essentially reader-oriented, whereas the *interpres* is essentially oriented towards his source text. Put in tabular form we have the following set of basic oppositions:

expositor	*interpres*
– translation oriented towards reader;	– translation oriented towards source text;
– translator has a self-confident attitude to his role;	– translator has a self-deprecating attitude to his role;

- translator will seek
  to resolve any difficulties in the original and
  will shun nonsense
  renderings;
- unit of translation
  is large (i.e. phrase,
  sentence or even
  paragraph);
- concern is primarily
  with the *signifié*,
  what is signified by
  the word employed;
- dynamic renderings
  will be preferred (e.g.
  use of cultural
  equivalents, change
  of grammatical
  categories).

- translator will
  simply pass on any
  difficulties in the
  original, even if
  the rendering makes
  nonsense;
- unit of translation
  is small (i.e. word,
  or even bound
  morpheme);
- concern is primarily
  with the *signifiant*,
  the actual word
  employed;
- formal renderings
  will be preferred,
  including exact
  representation of
  grammatical cate-
  gories;
- a concern for
  stereotyping (i.e.
  regular use of
  lexical
  equivalents), etymo-
  logizing renderings
  etc, free use of
  syntactic and
  semantic calques.

Under each heading there is, of course, considerable scope for variation, and so, for example, one
interpres, or literal translator, may exhibit a
quite different set of concerns from another.

Since much of this paper is at a fairly high level of abstraction, we might do well at this point to anchor ourselves in reality by looking briefly at some actual examples.

I take first a brief sample, Nah 2:6, taken more or less at random from the better preserved portions of 8HevXIIgr, in order to illustrate the sorts of interest that lie behind this revision. For convenience of reference the Greek texts are divided into eight units, corresponding to the eight words in MT.

Nahum 2:6

MT   יזכר אדיריו יכשלו בהלכותם (K=; כהם-) Q) ימהרו
        חומתה והכן הסכך:

LXX   (1) καὶ μνησθήσονται
8HevXIIgr   (1) om   "   -σεται
LXX   (2) οἱ μεγιστᾶνες αὐτῶν
8HevXIIgr   (2) om δυναστῶν αὐτοῦ
LXX   (2a) καὶ φεύξονται ἡμέρας
8HevXIIgr   (2a) om   om   om
LXX   (3) καὶ ἀσθενήσουσιν
8HevXIIgr   (3) om   "
LXX   (4) ἐν τῇ   πορείᾳ   αυτῶν
8HevXIIgr   (4) "   ταῖς πορεία[ι]ς   "
LXX   (5) καὶ σπεύσουσιν
8HevXIIgr   (5) "   ταχυνοῦσιν
LXX   (6) ἐπὶ τὰ τείχη (+ αὐτῆς BS Eth)
8HevXIIgr   (6) "   "   "   -
LXX   (7) καί ἑτοιμάσουσι
8HevXIIgr   (7) "   -ασε[ι]
LXX   (8) τὰς προφυλακὰς αὐτῶν
8HevXIIgr   (8) [τ]ὸ ἐπικάλυμμα om   + space

The following points deserve singling out, taking the units in turn.

TO REVISE OR NOT TO REVISE 315

(1) - (2): LXX, in order to have the same subject throughout the verse, has made οἱ μεγιστᾶνες subject; the reviser, however, is more interested in effecting a formal equivalence of grammatical categories, and so LXX μησθήσονται (passive sense) is altered to μνησθήσεται (active sense), to provide a formal equivalence with יזכר, and the former subject of the verb now becomes dependent upon it. In (1) the reviser again shows his concern for formal equivalence by removing καί (one of several features in the revision which are preserved in the Achmimic translation of the LXX). In (2) three further alterations are made: the exact equivalence of the Hebrew suffix is provided, the article is removed, and a lexical alteration is made in order to achieve greater consistency: at Nah 3:10 LXX uses μεγιστᾶνες for נכבדיה (evidently kept by the reviser), and so the reviser alters to δυναστῶν which LXX already uses for אדיריך at 3:18.

(2a): the phrase, absent from MT and the reviser's *Vorlage*, is excised (in the Syrohexapla it is obelized, but with the note "but not with an obelus in the Hexapla;" the phrase is omitted in the manuscript group C).

(3): the reviser naturally, in the light of (2a), omits καί.

(4): LXX represents the *Qere*, whereas the reviser's Hebrew text will have had the *Ketib* (the correction has left its influence in the LXX manuscript tradition, being found in Alexandrinus and a few other witnesses).

(5): the reviser fails to remove καί, but makes a lexical alteration probably in order to achieve the stereotyped equivalence of מהר - ταχύνω, characteristic of the early revisers and, subsequently, of Aquila.

(6): the reviser fails to represent the suffix (for which there is some LXX manuscript evidence, presumably of hexaplaric origin).

(7) - (8): the corrections made here are similar in character to those made in (1) - (2).

After (8) the rest of the line in 8HevXIIgr is left empty. One of the interesting features of this revision is the evident desire on the part of the reviser even to reproduce features of the format of the original;[19] thus he observes verse division, as well as the distinction between *petuḥah* (open) and *setumah* (closed) sections.[20] Although there is usually considerable agreement between the scroll and the Masoretic sections, it so happens that this particular *petuḥah* does not feature in the Leningrad codex.

For my next examples I take particular translation features, starting with the handling of יהוה צבאות. Since the phrase does not occur in the Pentateuch the subsequent LXX translators had no ready made option to take over; it is not surprising, consequently, that in the later books of the LXX we find the various translations divided up in their practice between three different choices:

(1) The transliteration Σαβαωθ occurs in Joshua, I Kingdoms, Isaiah and I Esdras.
(2) The dynamic rendition Παντοκράτωρ[21] is found in a wide range of books, including Jeremiah, XII Prophets and Ben Sira.
(3) The more formal rendering τῶν δυνάμεων

(which, however, goes against Hebrew grammatical usage) is to be found most notably in Psalms.

Subsequent handling of the phrase, both within the LXX textual tradition and outside it, is complex, and here I just draw attention to three main features:

- Diaspora Judaism not surprisingly has a preference for *Pantokrator*. This is shown, for example, by its use in Ps.Aristeas in the late second century BCE and by Philo a century and a half later; Philo indeed tacitly substitutes Παντοκράτωρ for Σαβαωθ in his quotations from LXX Isaiah.[22]

- The author of the revision in 8HevXIIgr regularly alters Παντοκράτωρ to τῶν δυνάμεων, following the precedent set by the translators of LXX Psalms.[23]

- Although Theodotion and Symmachus stay with this preference for τῶν δυνάμεων Aquila takes a further step and provides the more literal τῶν στρατιῶν.[24]

The main feature of interest here from our present perspective is the fact that the reviser behind the XII Prophets fragments does not here innovate himself, but draws on translation usage already developed by a translator of one of the later books of the LXX.

The equation of the Torah and Light found in *b.Meg.*16b (אורה זו תורה) had a two-fold basis: Prov 6:23 ותורה אור, and the association of the verb הורה "teach" with אור "light" reflected in the rendering of that verb by φωτίζω "illumine." This is a feature adopted by the reviser behind

8HevXIIgr;[25] whether or not this was his own
innovation is, however, unclear,[26] but in any case
his practice was simply taken over by Aquila.
Given Philo's great interest in light imagery, one
wonders, in passing, whether it was his hostility
to the idea of revising the LXX, or just ignorance
of this usage, that lies behind his failure to
take advantage of a rendering that would have been
so conducive to his way of thinking.[27] More to
the point, however, are two passages in Ps.Philo's
Liber Antiquitatum Biblicarum where *illuminare* is
used with *legem* as object[28] in contexts which
strongly suggest that the original Hebrew had הורה
and the Greek translation φωτίζω. There is in
fact a number of indications that the Greek
translator of *Liber Antiquitatum Biblicarum* must
have been working in the general tradition of the
Hebraising revision evidenced in 8HevXIIgr,
although active perhaps a century or so later.[29]
The relevance of this point will become clear in
my last example.

Gen 6:2, describing the descent of the בני
האלהים to cohabit with the daughters of men, is a
passage of some consequence in the history of
exegesis, where much hinges on the identity of the
בני האלהים. The general pattern of early
interpretation has been well set out by
Alexander[30] and others. As far as the Jewish
Greek tradition is concerned we have four
different renderings:

- the LXX textual tradition is itself divided
between οἱ υἱοὶ τοῦ θεοῦ and οἱ ἄγγελοι τοῦ θεοῦ
(the former is also ascribed to Theodotion).

- Aquila οἱ υἱοὶ τῶν θεῶν.
- Symmachus οἱ υἱοὶ τῶν δυναστευόντων (compare both Palestinian and Babylonian Targum traditions).

If we are to believe the editions of Rahlfs (both 1926 and 1935) and Wevers, the original LXX rendered the phrase literally, οἱ υἱοὶ τοῦ θεοῦ. Katz,[31] however, was in my opinion entirely correct to prefer the rendering οἱ ἄγγελοι as original here; this would place the translator in the same tradition as two other texts from the early Hellenistic period, Enoch 6:2 and Jub.4:15.

If the dynamic rendering, οἱ ἄγγελοι, is restored to the status of being the original LXX, the οἱ υἱοὶ, a formal equivalent, will belong to a subsequent revision which has found its way into much of the LXX manuscript tradition. That the Theodotion who also attests it is not the second-century Theodotion, but an earlier reviser is suggested by the fact that we have evidence for the same rendering of בני האלהים in Gen 6:2 by *filii dei* in Ps.Philo (*Bib. Ant.* 3:1).

Aquila's choice of a yet more formal rendering, οἱ υἱοὶ τῶν θεῶν provides a good example of the way in which the literalist translator, or *interpres*, makes no attempt to resolve theological difficulties in his source text. Symmachus,[32] on the other hand, belongs to a period when the phenomenon of the Targum, as we know it, had come into existence, that is, a version where (as we shall see)[33] the translator now felt free to combine the role of *interpres* with that of *expositor*, being at liberty to do this since his version now functioned just as a subordinate appendage to the Hebrew text. Symmachus, even though his translation was probably intended to function independently of the Hebrew, simply took advantage of this newly gained "freedom" acquired by the Targumists.

I return to more general considerations. Given the prestige of the Hebrew original, to which both Ps.Aristeas and the revisers bear witness, it is not surprising that the *interpres*, with his reverential attitude towards his source text, should have become the model for the biblical translator at an early date. Nevertheless, while the original translators of the Greek Pentateuch would hardly have seen themselves in such a role, people like Ps.Aristeas and (especially) Philo in later generations were quite happy to accept them, not as *interpretes*, but as *expositores*, interpretative translators, - on the understanding, of course, that the interpretative element was not of human, but of divine, origin.

Whereas Ps.Aristeas had located the source for the authentication of the Greek translation of the Pentateuch in the Jerusalem High Priesthood, and Philo in God himself, the revisers held the Hebrew original to be the sole source of authority; associated with this was a growing feeling that the Hebrew language was the unique source of revelation. Although it was only with the destruction of the Second Temple and the loss of the land that a new ideology fully emerged, making the Hebrew language the locus of revelation both for the written and for the oral Torah,[34] the roots of this can be traced back much earlier, to passages in Jubilees[35] and elsewhere. Expression was given to this in the growth of traditions that Hebrew was the original language, was the language of heaven (with the practical consequence that if petitionary prayers were to be heard, they had to be in Hebrew, since the angels did not understand Aramaic),[36] and that this was the language of the Sanctuary duly used by the Patriarchs when they spoke to God in the Targumim.[37]

Such an attitude to the unique role of Hebrew as the language of divine revelation effectively ruled out the possibility that a biblical translation could legitimately enjoy any authority at all independently of the Hebrew original. Since, however, for practical purposes Aramaic translations were nonetheless needed in areas most closely subject to Rabbinic authority, a compromise was reached by attaching the translation to the original, and ensuring that it was always read as an appendage to the original, indicating clearly its subordinate nature. This had the practical advantage that, since the translation was no longer in danger of being seen as substituting for or replacing the original, it could be treated more as an exposition of the original, instead of as an authoritative translation. Thus in the Targumim, whether Palestinian or Babylonian, the consciously interpretative element is high, seeing that the Targum translator was consequently free to regard his task as that of the *expositor*, and no longer just that of the *interpres*.[38]

The idea that a particular language or languages had an exclusive claim to religious authority was, it seems, not confined to Rabbinic Judaism in the early centuries of the common era. The Neoplatonist Iamblichus of Chalkis (in Syria), whose life spanned the end of the third century and early decades of the fourth, has a passage in the Seventh Book of his *De Mysteriis* which is of considerable relevance for us, since it provides us, *mutatis mutandis*, with an insight into something of the rationale behind this claim that only the original language of a religious text carried true authority. Because of its interest I shall quote a fairly extensive passage, using the early nineteenth-century translation of that remarkable Platonist, Thomas Taylor.[39]

> For because the Gods have shown that the whole dialect of sacred nations, such as those of the Egyptians and Assyrians, is adapted to sacred concerns; on this account we ought to think it necessary that our conference with the Gods should be in a language allied to them. Because, likewise, such a mode of speech is *the first and most ancient* [my italics]. And especially because those who first learned the names of the Gods, having mingled them with their own proper tongue, delivered them to us, that we might always preserve unmovable the sacred law of tradition, in a language peculiar and adapted to them. For if anything pertains to the Gods, it is evident that the eternal and immutable must be allied to them.
> VII.5 You object, however, "that he who hears words looks to their signification [τὰ σημαινόμενα], so that it is sufficient the

concept remains the same, whatever the words
may be that are used." But this thing is not
such as you suspect it to be. For if names
subsisted through compact [κατὰ συνθήκην, i.e.
convention],[40] it would be of no consequence
whether some were used instead of others. But
if they are suspended from the nature of
things, those names which are more adapted to
it will also be more dear to the Gods. From
this, therefore, it is evident that the
language of sacred nations is very reasonably
preferred to that of other men. To which may
be added, that names do not entirely preserve
the meaning when translated into another
language; but there are certain idioms in each
nation which cannot be signified by language
to another nation. And in the next place,
though it should be possible to translate
them, yet they no longer preserve the same
power when translated.[41] Barbarous names,
likewise, have much emphasis, great
conciseness, and participate of less
ambiguity, variety and multitude.

Iamblichus goes on to complain that the Greeks are
always changing things, whereas the "Barbarians
[non-Greeks] are stable in their manners, and
firmly continue to employ the same words. Hence
they are dear to the Gods, and proffer words which
are grateful to them, but which it is not lawful
for any man by any means to change [διαμείβειν]."

Particularly interesting in this passage is the
opposition between *signifiant* and *signifié*: the
interlocutor, as a typical representative of Greek
culture, interposes the objection that, provided

you pay attention to the *signifié* [τὰ σημαινόμενα], nothing too serious will be lost in translation. Iamblichus, however, counters this by in effect saying that the *signifié* is in fact inherent in the *signifiant*. The interlocutor's sympathies will thus be with the translator who works *ut expositor*, whereas those of Iamblichus himself will in principle be with the *interpres*, though he is in fact taking the further step taken in Rabbinic circles, denying the possibility that a translation of a religious text can carry authority by itself.

It so happens that we have another voice from the pagan world which displays an approach analogous to that which Philo took with respect to the Septuagint. In a papyrus fragment of the second century CE[42] an unknown writer tells how, after a delay, he had taken up the translation of an Egyptian religious text having been specifically instructed by the god to do so. In other words, no doubt all too aware of the difficulties involved, he anticipates any potential criticism by claiming divine authorization from the start - very much as, in the sixteenth century, Luther took the precaution of making analogous claims for his translation of the Bible.[43]

At this point it may be helpful to recapitulate briefly. In the course of the half millennium or so that followed the initial translations into Greek of the books of the Pentateuch we are able today, thanks to the finds in the Judaean Desert, to discern the general contours of Jewish reflection on the novel phenomenon of biblical translation. For convenience we can distinguish between five main stages, where the third and fourth in fact represent two contemporary, rather than successive, developments:

(1) The earliest translators, lacking any real precedent, work in an *ad hoc* fashion, producing somewhat uneven renderings that veer between the rather free and the literal. At this stage there is no clear awareness of the sharp dichotomy in translation practice, probably already current in the gentile world, between the literary translator (or *expositor*) and the non-literary (or *interpres*).

(2) Subsequent translators, while often drawing on the Greek Pentateuch for their choice of vocabulary, usually aim at (and achieve) a more even rendering - and a more literal one, for by now the biblical translator consciously sees himself in the role of *interpres*, rather than that of *expositor*.

(3) By the end of the second century BCE at the latest, the need was seen in some circles (probably Palestinian) to "correct" the earlier versions, bringing them closer into line with the Hebrew. At first this work of correction will probably have been sporadic and unsystematic; later, however, and certainly by the late first century BCE, the process of correction had become much more systematic, both in the techniques developed, and in the extent to which these techniques were applied, evidently covering whole groups of books. What we have surviving, both in the form of early fragments, and relics incorporated into the later manuscripts of the LXX, are very incomplete witnesses to a number of

different attempts at "correction," of which that represented by the XII Prophets fragments from Nahal Hever was probably both the most systematic and the most extensive. The culmination of this process of "correction" is of course Aquila's *ekdosis* in the second century CE. The earlier "correctors" often drew on the usage and experience of the translators of the later books of the LXX (our stage 2), and notably the Psalter, while the subsequent "correctors" built upon the work of their predecessors.

(4) Contemporary with the developments outlined in stage 3 will be the reaction of diaspora Judaism, which had no interest in revision of the original translations. To counter the arguments of the "revisers," at first we have the original Greek Pentateuch provided with a highly respectable pedigree and the assertion that the original translators had duly followed the (later) ideal of literal translation (Ps. Aristeas); subsequently, when this latter point could no longer carry any real conviction, the translation was boldly put on a par with the original, on the grounds that it too was divinely inspired (Philo).

(5) Probably not until after the destruction of the Second Temple, the course undertaken by literalist revisers, with their great concern for the *signifiant*, was carried to its logical conclusion: no translation at all, however literal, could do justice to the original language of revelation: that language now took on a sacral character which obviated the possibility of any translation carrying authority independent of the Hebrew original. Where translations were needed

for practical purposes, their subordinate character was made plain to everyone by the fact that they were read out in synagogue, a verse (or a group of verses) at a time, after the Hebrew: this subordinate position had at the same time a great advantage, for it meant that the translation could now also function as commentary: in other words, the translator could legitimately combine the role of *expositor* with that of *interpres*, in contrast to the Septuagint "revisers" who will have seen themselves solely as *interpretes*. This explains why the Targumim, in contrast to the other ancient versions, are highly interpretative in character (even in the case of the seemingly very literal Onkelos and Jonathan). The sacralization of the Hebrew original, with the concomitant denial of the possibility of independent authoritative translations, of course neatly countered Philo's position, which was presumably that of much of the Diaspora: but by the mid second century this no longer mattered in Egypt since the Egyptian Diaspora seems to have suffered virtually total eclipse after the revolts of the early second century CE; furthermore, there was positive advantage, in that the emergent Christian Church, being essentially based in the Diaspora, had early on adopted the Septuagint as its authoritative Scripture. One wonders what the situation was in the evidently flourishing Jewish diaspora communities of Asia Minor: unfortunately our sources are completely silent on this matter.[44]

It was against this general background of varying, and increasingly polarized, attitudes to biblical translation, that Christianity emerged. Given the early dominance of Greek as the literary language of Christianity and the general ignorance of, and lack of interest in, Hebrew, it is no surprise that the early church took over Philo's position on the Septuagint, regarding it as enjoying equal status, as "sister," with the original Hebrew. (Subsequently the LXX was even seen in some Christian circles as being superior to contemporary Hebrew Bibles, on the grounds that the latter had been corrupted by wilful alteration subsequent to the date of the translation). Nonetheless, it was not the case that the work of the revisers was entirely without its influence on early Christian writers; thus Paul on occasion, when it suits his purposes, cites the Septuagint in its revised form, as in 1 Cor 15:54 where he quotes Isa 25:8 in a form which agrees with the "corrected" translation εἰς νῖκος for לנצח (LXX εἰς τέλος).[45] Similarly the author of the Letter to the Hebrews speaks of Isaac as μονογενής, rather than ἀγαπητός (as in LXX), evidently reflecting a revised form of the Septuagint text of Gen 22:1 which was also known to Josephus (*Ant.* 1:22). And in the mid second century Justin, a native of Palestine, sometimes quotes the XII Prophets in a revised form which is very close to that represented by the Greek fragments from Nahal Hever. But it was in the early third century, with Origen's revision of the Septuagint text, bringing it into conformity with the Hebrew, that the Jewish revisers had their closest Christian follower as far as the Septuagint was concerned. As it happened, however, the influence of the

Jewish revisers' attitude to biblical translation was much more effectively, albeit indirectly, felt outside the field of the Septuagint, for whenever the Greek New Testament came to be translated into other languages, the ideal procedure for such translation always came in due course to be seen as that of the *interpres*, and not that of the *expositor*. Thus we can observe the same pattern of development that we found in the Jewish Septuagint: through lack of experience and precedence the initial translations were uneven and so later generations felt the need to bring them into line with the original, adopting the *verbum e verbo* procedure of the *interpres*. These revisions in some cases were carried out using highly sophisticated techniques of mirror translation, rivalling the work of Aquila and his predecessors. As it happens this pattern of development can nowhere be better observed than in the history of the Syriac biblical versions where the process of refinement in the techniques of literal translation continues over two or more centuries:[46] first the Peshitta revision of the Old Syriac Gospels, a somewhat inconsequential piece of work completed in the early fifth century; then the much more systematic work of Polycarp, completed in 507/8 at the behest of Philoxenos of Mabbug; and finally the tour de force of mirror translation - in reality, yet a further revision - undertaken by Thomas of Harkel in Alexandria c. 615 at the same time that Paul of Tella was producing the translation of Origen's revised Septuagint text which we know today as the Syrohexapla.

The fashion for a highly literal style of source-oriented translation reached its height in the Syriac Churches in the seventh century, and a similar phenomenon can be observed in contemporary Latin and Armenian translations. The seventh century was of course the moment when another new monotheist religion emerged. It is a remarkable fact that from the very start Islam took the step that had previously been taken in Rabbinic Judaism of sacralizing the language of revelation, thus ruling out translation of the Qoran as a legitimate option. Whereas in Judaism the emphasis put on the *signifiant* at the expense (as we might say) of the *signifié* had first led to the very literal translations of Aquila and his predecessors, and then, as a logical consequence, to the denial of any authority at all to an independent translation, in Christianity the same preoccupation with the *signifiant* that we witness in Christianity's various cultural traditions in the seventh century was never followed by that further logical step of confining the true *signifié* of the *signifiant* to the source language – for the simple reason that Greek as a source language became effectively cut off, both politically and religiously, at just that time from the languages into which the mirror translations were being made. It is almost as if Islam had stepped in and taken up the option followed by Judaism some six centuries earlier, but which Christianity had been prevented by circumstances from even considering.

Let me conclude by drawing attention to a few of the relationships between these ancient

attitudes to biblical translation and our own -
and to some of the ironies implicit in these
relationships.

As academics, our sympathies will naturally be
with the general aims of the revisers and their
search for accuracy. We are not so likely,
however, to want to adopt their methods of literal
translation (though of course they do have some
followers today), nor are we likely to take the
step taken in Rabbinic Judaism, of ruling out the
legitimacy of independent translations of the
Hebrew Bible - though it could be said that, by
moving away from a single recognized version to a
multiplicity of modern versions, constantly
rivalling and replacing one another, we are
implying much the same thing. It is, after all,
what we in effect do with the great classics of
literature, where, furthermore, the schoolboy crib
serves as a ladder to reach the original text:
unlike the Targumim, however, these cribs are not
consciously interpretative, seeing that we now
have the separate commentary to serve that
purpose.

Now it is of course ironic that, while the
sympathy of modern scholarship is likely to lie
with the position of those within Judaism who
sought to revise the Septuagint, rather than with
those who accorded it an inspired origin, the
general practice of modern biblical translation
resolutely stands in the tradition of the
expositor, and it is only a few, like Rosenzweig
or Chouraqui, who choose to follow in the tradition of the *interpres*. It is intriguing, however,
that in a recent discussion of the question of

what stage in the history of the Hebrew text should be taken as the basis for modern translations,[47] Barthélemy has come up with a suggestion that would in fact lend legitimacy to the stand on the Septuagint taken by Diaspora Judaism. Barthélemy suggests that in dealing with the Hebrew Bible it would be helpful to make a distinction between two kinds of authenticity, which he terms literary and scriptural authenticity, the former representing the original form of the text, the latter representing a form of the text whose use in a religious community over a period of time has accorded to it some form of authority. Since, in the case of the Hebrew Bible, literary authenticity is an unattainable ideal, the modern translator has to follow the other option, but here he has to make a choice, for, whereas only one form of text can in theory ever lay claim to literary authenticity, many forms of text can be said to possess scriptural authenticity. Barthélemy himself proposes, sensibly enough, the proto-Masoretic text as a suitable candidate in the case of Christian translations from the Hebrew Bible, but he points out in passing that, using the criterion of scriptural, rather than literary, authenticity means that the ancient versions, sometimes themselves in different forms, could equally legitimately be seen as having scriptural authenticity - which is exactly what Philo was saying in his own terms of the Septuagint. And I think it would be generally accepted that, if a translation is to be successful, the translator needs to have a true feeling for the text he is translating - and this too is precisely what Philo was saying when he spoke of the Septuagint translators as "communing with the spirit of Moses."

Plus ça change plus c'est la même chose: the issues and controversies raised over biblical translation within Judaism of the Hellenistic and Roman period are clearly still alive in the late twentieth century, even though the terms of argument have changed.

Abbreviations:
ANRW   Aufstieg und Niedergang der römischen Welt
PAAJR Proceedings of the American Academy for Jewish Research
RB   Revue biblique
TU   Texte und Untersuchungen

NOTES

1. *RB* 60 (1953) 18-29. The fragments turned up in August 1952.

2. *ZAW* 69 (1957) 77-84.

3. *Studia Patristica* 1 = *TU*, no 63 (Berlin: Akademie-Verlag, 1957), 343-53.

4. (VTSup. 10; Leiden: E. J. Brill, 1963). A sequel to J. Smit Sibinga's *The Old Testament of Justin Martyr*, I, *The Pentateuch* (Leiden: E. J. Brill, 1963) is very much a desideratum.

5. B. Lifshitz, "The Greek documents from the Cave of Horror," *IEJ* 12 (1962) 201-7.

6. E. Tov, *The Greek Minor Prophets Scroll from Nahal Hever (8ḤevXIIgr)* (DJD 8; Oxford: Clarendon Press, 1990).

7. A handy survey by K. G. O'Connell can be found in *IDBSup*, 377-81.

8. Philo, *Life of Moses* 2:25-44, quoted from the translation by F. H. Colson in vol. 6 of the LCL edition.

9. For this aspect see especially H. Karpp, "'Prophet' oder 'Dolmetscher'. Die Geltung der LXX in der Alten Kirche," *Festschrift für G. Dehn* (Neukirchen: Kreis Moers, 1957) 103-17 (esp. 107ff), and P. Benoit, "L'inspiration des Septante d'après les Pères," *L'Homme devant Dieu. Mélanges offerts au Père Henri de Lubac* (Paris: Aubier, 1963) I.169-87.

10. REB (the NEB's translation is not satisfactory here). For the translator's intended meaning see J. Barr, *The Typology of Literalism in Ancient Biblical Translations* (Nachrichten der Akademie der Wissenschaften in Göttingen, phil.-hist. Kl. Nr 11; Göttingen: Vandenhoeck & Ruprecht, 1979) 317-8.

11. For the interpretation followed here see A. F. J. Klijn, "The Letter of Aristeas and the Greek Translation of the Pentateuch in Egypt," *NTS* 11 (1965) 154-8, S. P. Brock, "The Phenomenon of the Septuagint," *OTS* 17 (1972) 11-36 (esp. 23ff), D. Barthélemy, "Pourquoi la Torah a-t-elle été traduite en grec?" *On Language, Culture and Religion. In Honour of Eugene A. Nida,* (Approaches to Semiotics 56; The Hague: Mouton, 1974) 23-41 = D. Barthélemy, *Études d'histoire du texte de l'Ancien Testament* (OBO 21; Fribourg/Göttingen: Éditions Universitaires/Vandenhoeck & Ruprecht, 1978) 322-40 (esp. 32-4/331-3), H. M. Orlinsky, "The Septuagint as Holy Writ and the philosophy of the translators," *HUCA* 46 (1975) 89-114.

12. The texts are conveniently juxtaposed in A. Pelletier, *Flavius Josèphe adapteur de la Lettre d'Aristée* (Études et Commentaires 45; Paris: Librairie C. Klincksieck, 1962) 307-27. (Pelletier discusses *Ant.* 12:108-9 on pp.188-9). I cite the translation by R. Marcus in vol. 7 of the LCL edition.

13. For a good example see my "A doublet and its ramifications (I Sam. 23,1 LXX)," *Bib* 56 (1975) 550-53. The use of ἔκτισεν instead of LXX ἐποίησεν (Gen 1:1) in *Ant* 1:27 may well be another case: see A. Paul, "Le récit de la creation dans les 'Antiquités juives' de Flavius Josèphe," *Hellenica et Judaica. Hommage à V. Nikiprowetsky* (Leuven/Paris: Editions Peeters, 1986) 129-37. For Samuel E. C. Ulrich finds that Josephus used "a slightly revised form of O[ld] G[reek]": see his *The Qumran Text of Samuel and Josephus* (HSM 19; Missoula: Scholars Press, 1978) 259.

14. For the following see my more detailed discussion, with references, in "Aspects of translation technique in Antiquity," *GRBS* 20 (1979) 69-87, reprinted in my *Syriac Perspectives on Late Antiquity* (London: Variorum Reprints, 1984) ch.3.

15. On this point see my "The phenomenon of the Septuagint."

16. For this introduction see W. Schwarz, "The meaning of *fidus interpres* in medieval translation," *JTS* 45 (1944) 73-8.

17. This point is well made by Barr, *The Typology of Literalism*.

18. For the tension between *signifiant* and *signifié* see the interesting discussion in L. G. Kelly, *The True Interpreter* (Oxford: Blackwell, 1979) 162ff.

19. One might suggest that the presence in the scroll of the tetragrammaton in the palaeo-Hebrew script was intended to reflect the same use of the palaeo-Hebrew script for the divine name in the Hebrew Vorlage from which the reviser was working.

20. For this aspect see Tov, *The Greek Minor Prophets Scroll*, 9-12, with the literature cited there.

21. For the Greek background to the term (not found outside the LXX before the late Hellenistic period) see O. Montevecchi, "Pantokrator," *Studi in Onore di A. Calderini e R. Paribeni* (Milan: Ceschina, 1957) 2:401-32.

22. The popularity of Pantokrator is evident from the materials collected by R. Marcus, "Divine names and attributes in Hellenistic Jewish literature," *PAAJR* 2 (1930/1) 39-67.

23. For this aspect see O. O. Munnich, "Contribution à l'étude de la première revision de la Septante," *ANRW* II.20.1 (Berlin/New York: W. de Gruyter, 1987) 190-220.

24. Aquila's rendering has surprisingly left its mark in *The Life of Adam and Eve* 38:3. τῶν may be secondary.

25. 8HevXIIgr has φω[τιει] at Hab 2:19 and Justin attests the same revision at Mic 4:2. On this feature see M. Smith, "Another criterion for the kai ge recension," *Bib* 48 (1967) 443-5, and compare the variant יאירו for MT יורו at Deut 33:10 in 4QTestim, on which see G. Vermes in *VT* 8 (1958) 436-8.

26. This depends on one's understanding of the textual history of the LXX 4 Kms, where φωτίζω is attested at 12:3; 17:27, 28 in *L* as well as in the mainstream LXX (the latter is a part of Barthélemy's "Palestinian recension"): has *L* also come under the influence of the revision here? If so, *docuit*, preserved in Eth. only at 17:28, will be the sole relic of the original LXX reading. In Judg 13:8 συμβιβασάτω will be the original reading, and φωτισάτω the revision; so, rightly, W. R. Bodine, *The Greek Text of Judges, Recensional Developments* (HSM 23; Chico: Scholars Press, 1980) 19-20.

27. For φωτίζω in Philo, see F. N. Klein, *Die Lichtterminologie bei Philon von Alexandrien und in den hermetischen Schriften* (Leiden: E. J. Brill, 1962) 50-61. Since Justin, who definitely does know this revisional practice (see note 23) is the first writer to use φωτισμός with its special Christian baptismal sense, it is tempting to suggest that there might be some link here; Y. Ysebaert, *Greek Baptismal Terminology. Its Origins and Early Development* (Graecitas Christianorum Primeva 1; Nijmegen: Dekker & Van de Vegt, 1962) 164-78, is, however, cautious on this point. The logical extension of φωτίζω for הורה would be φώτισμα/-μός for תורה, but this step appears never to have been taken (it is worth observing that, while *T.Levi* 14:4 speaks of τὸ φῶς τοῦ νόμου, *Ap.Const.* II.5.7. has τὸν φωτισμὸν τοῦ νόμου).

28. 12:2 *legem illuminabit*; 23:10 *sed dedi eis legem meam et illuminavi eos ut facientes hec vivant* (God is speaking).

29. The following are some notable renderings which are in the tradition of Aquila and his predecessors: the frequent use of *Fortis* and (especially) *Fortissimus*, corresponding to Aquila's ἰσχυρος for אל (cf also *2 Apoc. Bar.* 13:2); *Bib. Ant.* 3:8 *odor requietionis* (Gen 8:21, LXX ὀσμὴν εὐωδίας), where the second element reflects an etymologizing ἀναπαύσεως (Hebrew ניחוח), attested for Aquila; *Bib. Ant.* 3:9 *figura cordis* (Gen 8:21 יצר לב; LXX ἡ διάνοια) where *figura* reflects πλάσμα of Aquila at Deut 31:21 etc. (at Hab 2:18, where LXX already uses πλάσμα, the reviser behind 8HevXIIgr naturally leaves the text unchanged).

30. P. S. Alexander, "The Targumim and the early exegesis of the 'Sons of God' in Gen 6," *JJS* 23 (1972) 60-71.

31. P. Katz, *Philo's Bible* (Cambridge: Cambridge University Press, 1950) 20-21, and P. Walters (Formerly Katz), *The Text of the Septuagint* (Cambridge: Cambridge University Press, 1973) 255. M. Harl, *La Bible d'Alexandrie. I. La Genèse* (Paris: Éditions du Cerf. 1986) 125, likewise sees "angels" as the original reading.

32. For Symmachus as a Jewish, rather than a Judaeo-Christian, translator, see A. E. Salvesen, *The Translation of Symmachus in the Pentateuch and its Place in Exegetical Tradition* (Journal of Semitic Studies Monograph Series; Manchester, 1991).

33. See below (with note 38).

34. See A. Paul, "La Bible Grecque d'Aquila," *ANRW* II.20.1 (Berlin/New York: W. de Gruyter, 1987) 221-45 (esp. 230ff).

35. *Jub.* 12:26.

36. *b. Shabb.* 12b.

37. See, for example, Gen 2:19, 11:1, 22:1 etc. in *Tg. Neofiti.*

38. See further my "Translating the Old Testament," (ed. D. A. Carson and H. G. M. Williamson; *It is written: Scripture Citing Scripture. Essays in Honour of Barnabas Lindars* Cambridge: Cambridge University Press, 1988) 87-98.

39. Thomas Taylor (tr.), *Iamblichus on the Mysteries* (3rd ed. London: Stuart and Watkins, 1968) 293-5, 298.

40. Iamblichus alludes to the long-standing argument over whether names were given θέσει or φύσει.

41. Compare the translator's preface to Ben Sira.

42. P.Oxyrh. XI. 1381. Among the many discussions of these and other relevant texts, see especially C. Préaux, "De la Grèce classique à l'Égypte hellénistique: traduire ou ne pas traduire," *Chronique d'Egypte* 42 (1967) 369-83; see also D. N. Wigtil, "The independent value of ancient religious translations," *ANRW* II.16.3 (Berlin/New York: W. de Gruyter, 1986) 2052-66.

43. On this see W. Schwarz, *Principles and Problems of Biblical Translation. Some Reformation Controversies and their Background* (Cambridge: Cambridge University Press, 1955) ch.6.

44. The opening of Melito of Sardis's Paschal Homily may be of relevance here, as reflecting local synagogue usage: ἡ μὲν γραφὴ τῆς ἑβραικῆς ἐξόδου ἀνέγνωσται, "The Scripture of the Hebrew Exodus has been read," i.e. the lection from Exodus in Hebrew; for this sense see G. Zuntz, "On the opening sentence of Melito's Paschal Homily," *HTR* 36 (1943) 299-315.

45. See especially D. A. Koch, *Die Schrift als Zeuge des Evangeliums* (BHT 69; Tübingen: J. C. B. Mohr (Paul Siebeck), 1986) 61-3; Koch has a section "Vorpaulinische Septuagintarezensionen in den Zitaten des Paulus" on pp. 55-81.

46. See further my "Towards a history of Syriac translation technique" *IIIe Symposium Syriacum* (R. Lavenant, ed. Orientalia Christiana Analecta 221; Rome: Pontificio Instituto Orientale, 1983) 1-14.

47. D. Barthélemy, *Critique textuelle de l'Ancient Testament*, I (OBO 50/1; Friburg/ Göttingen: Editions Universitaires/Vandenhoeck & Ruprecht, 1982) 65*-114* (esp. 103*ff.).

THE TRANSLATION OF THE SEPTUAGINT
IN LIGHT OF EARLIER TRADITION
AND SUBSEQUENT INFLUENCES

ROBERT HANHART

"The Septuagint and its relations to the Dead Sea Scrolls and other writings": the theme of this symposium has once again drawn attention to the problem which has always stood at the centre of Septuagint research and on which new light has been thrown by the recent finds of Hebrew and Greek texts. Those texts are very close in time to the event which summarily we would designate as "the Greek translation of the 'Holy Scriptures' of the OT" and as "the formation of the Alexandrian Canon of the Septuagint."

I propose to formulate the problem as three questions. 1. Given that the formation and transmission of our witnesses are to be set in the period of the process of the formation of the LXX itself, which also was variously shaped, to what extent can the extant witnesses give us information about the Hebrew *Vorlage* of the OT writings, the *Vorlage* as it was received by the

LXX translators? 2. To what extent are they documents testifying to the most ancient text-form of the translation itself? 3. To what extent are they witnesses of its earliest recension, i.e., interpretation?

I will not deal extensively with the first question, concerning the form of the text of the Hebrew originals which the translators had as *Vorlagen* and which can be documented and reconstructed today, because the editing of the Dead Sea scroll texts, which are of utmost importance for this problem, has not yet been finished, but more especially because this subject area has been dealt with in an exhaustive and competent manner by other contributors to the Symposium. Rather, I will concentrate on the question of the most ancient form of the LXX itself, its position in the context of Jewish and non-Jewish Greek tradition and its significance as the object of the earliest Jewish and non-Jewish interpretation.

Our theme, "The Translation of the LXX in Light of Earlier Tradition and Subsequent Influences," is thus narrowed down to the following questions. To what extent and in what ways can the original form of the texts of the translation be illuminated from the Greek tradition available to the translators? Secondly, because later parts of a translation may be best explained in the light of texts already translated, to what extent can a relationship of mutual dependence be perceived within the history of the formation of individual translations? And, thirdly, how did the translations themselves in their fixed canonical form become the object of interpretation, thus bringing about a new literary genre, the commentary?

I

This basic limitation to the consideration of Greek tradition cannot, however, free us from some preliminary discussion of the first link between translation and earlier tradition, namely, the relationship between the Hebrew original and the Greek version based upon it. On the basis of insights which derive from the discovery of Hebrew biblical texts contemporary with the period of the translation of the books of the LXX, I perceive this relationship with regard to translation technique, from book to book, in the following ways. 1. As a matter of first principle the Greek translation must be considered as a faithful rendering of the original as far as content and form is concerned, a rendering exact even in grammatical and syntactical details like those involving parataxis, the article and pronouns. 2. Within this principle, in the course of the history of translation, there is some initial freedom as far as formal possibilities are concerned. In other words, there is a possibility of "free translation", which J. Barr in his work, "The Typology of Literalism in Ancient Biblical Translations,"[1] has described as an alternative possibility to "literal translation". In this the essence of the original is rendered more adequately by a formulation that deviates from the formal rules of the original language, yet corresponds with the linguistic character of the language into which the translation is made, than it is by the formal slavish rendering of "literal translation." 3. The faithful rendering of the original remained such a basic requirement throughout the entire period of the work of translation that already in the earliest period - not just in subsequent history - it became the basis of recensional activity, that is, the principle behind every new checking of translations against the original.

With regard to the original form of the Hebrew this means - and thus far I agree with the text-historical views of F. M. Cross[2] - that nowadays, where it deviates from the MT, the text of the LXX must be taken seriously, in the manner of the text-critical presuppositions of O. Thenius, J. Wellhausen and in a certain sense also of P. A. de Lagarde, as witness to an underlying Hebrew text-form which we are able to reconstruct. With regard to the original form of the Greek translation, this means that deviations from the MT must be noticed but should only in the rarest cases be taken as the peculiar expression of the translator by means of which he wants to interpret - let alone reinterpret - his *Vorlage*. The LXX - and this is true for all the books translated - is **interpretation** only insofar as a decision is made between various possibilities of understanding which are already inherent in the formulation of the Hebrew *Vorlage* and thus given to the translator. Furthermore, the LXX is the **actualisation** of the contemporary history of the translator only when the choice of the Greek equivalent is capable of doing justice both to the factuality and history of the original Hebrew witness and also to

EARLIER TRADITION AND SUBSEQUENT INFLUENCES   343

the contemporary history of the translator. The
LXX is essentially *conservation*.

1. In Dan 11:29 the Hebrew expression ולא תהיה
כראשנה וכאחרנה can mean either "this time it will
not be like the last time" or "this time it will
not be like the last time and the one before
that." The author of the more recent translation
of Daniel rendered the Hebrew expression with the
formulation καὶ οὐκ ἔσται ὡς ἡ πρώτη καὶ ὡς ἡ
ἐσχάτη and so decided in favour of the latter
possibility. The translation is formally
completely faithful, but corresponding with the
facts of history and by relating it to the three
Egyptian campaigns of Antiochus Epiphanes, the
translator has given an interpretation where the
Hebrew original and the more ancient translation
of Daniel (καὶ οὐκ ἔσται ὡς ἡ πρώτη καὶ ἡ ἐσχάτη)
left open both possibilities.[3]

2. When the translator of Deuteronomy, both in
the law for the king of Israel (17:14-15) and also
in the curse against him in case of disobedience
(28:36), rendered the term for the highest
authority amongst the people, "king" (מלך), with
the equivalent "ruler" (ἄρχων), then he actualized
both law and curse for the Hellenistic cultic
community of his own period. He did that by
choosing his vocabulary, in accordance with the
text, both to preserve and to remind; the word is
adequate both for the pre-exilic monarchical
representative and also for the post-exilic high
priestly one.[4]

3. According to the pioneering and still
fundamental insights of I. L. Seeligmann, when the
translator of the book of Isaiah saw the Assyrian

and Babylonian oppressor of the original prophetic oracle resurrected in the Seleucid persecutor, then it is precisely his literal translation (the original and the translation being so very nearly the same) which makes the translator's contemporary history transparently visible in the Greek form of the history of the prophet's time. On the other hand, there are actualisations which seemingly deviate from the original, like the announcement of the death of the oppressor in Isaiah 14 corresponding to the death of Antiochus Epiphanes "in the mountains" (ἐν τοῖς ὄρεσιν; 2 Macc 9:28; Isa 14:19). According to the modern text-historical evidence already mentioned, such actualisations, which anyway are exceptions which confirm the rule, must be attributed to a corresponding tendency within the Hebrew tradition, as it was available to the translator, rather than to any actualizing intention of the translator.[5]

II

This identification of the nature of the initial and original relationship of "the Septuagint to its earlier tradition", i.e., the determining of the relationship of the Greek translation to its Hebrew original, must form the basis for answering our first question about the Greek tradition in which the translators are rooted, tradition which could be reflected in the kind of translation, choice of words and formulation.

This understanding of the formation of the LXX translations and of their relationship to the Hebrew original which is their prototype should never be abandoned. Although in the course of transmission there were textual changes, these were kept within narrow limits, because like the Hebrew original the translation attained canonical status at an early stage. From all this it necessarily follows in the first place that the non-Israelite Greek tradition as known to the translators must have been altered beyond recognition; there is no evidence for earlier stages in the transmission of Greek tradition within the Israelite sphere because of the stringent laws of translation.

From this same dependence of the translation on its prototype, which did not allow the translator to introduce meaning which was not given by the original itself, it necessarily follows secondly that the Greek equivalent chosen by the translator - James Barr's thesis in *The Semantics of Biblical Language* has its origins here - should be semantically explained only on the basis of the relation between the translation and the original text. Explanations based on abstract etymologies distinct from a particular context or based on some other context in which the same expression occurs and which may have been known to the translator should be discounted.

From this same understanding it follows thirdly - and this is the point, as far as I can see, at which the consequences of Barr's thesis need careful qualification - that the choice of the Greek equivalent, if influenced by Greek tradition known to the translators, might have been made with the deliberate intention either of eliminating from the translation's Greek vocabulary those expressions which were loaded too greatly with religious, cultural and political ideas of Greek tradition, or of creating new expressions for the particular ideas of Israelite faith and thought.

1. As a first example of this we can consider how the Greek translations represent the Hebrew original for altar (מזבח); in the Hebrew original the same term is used for the altar of Yahweh and for pagan altars. For pagan altars the term βωμός is used, a term rooted in ancient Greek tradition as far back as Homer. However, with only a few explicable exceptions, for the altar of Israel's God the construction θυσιαστήριον is used, a noun which still remains unattested in non-biblical literature. These two equivalents for מזבח reflect a consistent translation technique which distinguishes between Israelite and non-Israelite altars within the same sentence. Thus, concerning the question of whether the altar built by the Eastern tribes at the Jordan was an altar of Yahweh, whereas the Hebrew reads ביהוה אל תמרדו ... בבנתכם לכם מזבח מבלעדי מזבח יהוה אלהינו (Josh 22:19), the Greek translation is μὴ ἀπόστητε ἀπὸ κυρίου διὰ τὸ οἰκοδομῆσαι ὑμᾶς βωμὸν ἔξω τοῦ θυσιαστηρίου κυρίου τοῦ θεοῦ ἡμῶν. As confirmation that here we have evidence of the intention within the translation to reject as well as positively to choose a certain Greek equivalent because of its use and meaning in earlier Greek tradition, the same distinction occurs again in the latest period of translation, in 1 Macc 1:59, as an interpretation of the Danielic שקוץ משומם: θυσιάζοντες ἐπὶ τὸν βωμόν, ὃς ἦν ἐπὶ τοῦ θυσιαστηρίου.[6] Even those passages in which

θυσιαστήριον is used to translate מזבח, where it refers to an altar for pagan worship, cannot be used as evidence against this assertion. All these cases are in the Deuteronomistic history: the altar building of Gideon (Judg 6:25, 28, 30-32), of Jeroboam at Bethel (3 Kgdms 12:32-33; 13), of Ahab (3 Kgdms 16:32), the cultic reforms of Elijah (4 Kgdms 18), and of Josiah (4 Kgdms 23).[7] In each case it is a question of the contrast of true and false worship; formally the same expression is needed to designate the two opposing cultic places. Here we are dealing with true or false worship at one and the same "altar of Yahweh."

2. A second example concerns OT statements relating to unexpected events which according to more ancient Greek thought would correspond with the idea of fate. Nowhere in the LXX are OT statements of this sort rendered with genuine expressions for this theologoumenon, τύχη, είμαρμένη, μοῖρα, nor with the term συμφορά which only occurs in those parts of the canonical Apocrypha which were originally written in Greek. On the one hand, the Greek translators chose clearly neutral terms for "event" or "accident," such as σύμπτωμα for מקרה as a designation for the disaster which "does not come from Yahweh" (1 Kgdms 6:9), or συνάντημα for the same expression in the theology of Qohelet: מקרה אחד יקרה את כלם = συνάντημα ἓν συναντήσεται τοῖς πᾶσιν αὐτοῖς (2:14).[8] On the other hand, apart from the popular etymology of the name גד as ἐν τύχῃ in Gen 30:11, the term τύχη appears in the whole LXX[9] only in Third Isaiah (65:11) as the personified

designation for the foreign deities גד and מני, next to δαιμόνιον which is equally used only for idolatry: הערכים לגד שלחן והממלאים למני ממסך = ἑτοιμάζοντες τῷ δαιμονίῳ τράπεζαν καὶ πληροῦντες τῇ τύχῃ κέρασμα. These lexicographic discoveries can hardly be explained in any way other than as a conscious delimitation against earlier Greek tradition which, if taken over without reflection, would have risked a syncretistic understanding in the translation.

3. A third example involves the alternative Greek equivalents for "God of heaven," the Hebrew אלהי השמים, the Aramaic אלה שמיא. In the LXX in literal translation this appears as ὁ θεὸς τοῦ οὐρανοῦ, in free translation as ὁ ὕψιστος, but the usage of the latter is restricted to texts in which the translation of ὁ θεὸς τοῦ οὐρανοῦ could have resulted in a similar syncretistic danger through an identification of God with Ζεὺς οὐράνιος, i.e., Ὀλύμπιος (2 Macc 6:2), such as texts dealing with the Seleucid persecution and its effects.[10] This is so in the more ancient translation of the Book of Daniel and in the more ancient tradition of Ezra-Nehemiah (1 Esdr),[11] so that, according to the findings of J. A. Montgomery, the Greek translation corresponded exactly with the intention of the Hebrew-Aramaic usage of the OT in delimiting Israel's God against the Canaanite Baal of heaven.[12] In this way, it was only through the act of translation that the limitation of the Israelite use of this name was realized in the Persian to Hellenistic period, just as in the earlier Hebrew-Aramaic original of the pre-Persian period. As a result, there is

EARLIER TRADITION AND SUBSEQUENT INFLUENCES   349

here not only some further indication of how translation-equivalents were oriented towards the intention of the original, but also an argument, though one not proven, for the suggestion that through the choice of the equivalent an existing Greek expression could be formed anew in the light of the contemporary history of the translators, whether apologetically or polemically.[13]

The theological intention within Israel with respect to these two equivalents becomes transparent within the translation-tradition of the LXX itself when the two possibilities of the Greek rendering of אלהי השמים are realized at the point at which this theologoumenon gained greatest actuality in the history of Israel, i.e., in the reference by Cyrus to the God of Israel which in the Greek form of Cyrus' edict in the more ancient translation of 1 Esdras seems like a protest against any identification of Persian religious politics with the syncretistic one of the Seleucid in the person of Ζεὺς οὐράνιος: ἐμὲ ἀνέδειξεν βασιλέα τῆς οἰκουμένης ὁ κύριος τοῦ 'Ισραηλ, κύριος ὁ ὕψιστος (1 Esdr 2:3). The literal and more recent translation of 2 Esdras should be attributed to a time in which this danger no longer existed to the same extent: πάσας τὰς βασιλείας τῆς γῆς ἔδωκέν μοι κύριος ὁ θεὸς τοῦ οὐρανου (1:2).

However, the strongest evidence for the assertion that the form and content of the Greek translation is, in the final analysis, based solely on the statements of the Hebrew original and not on existing tradition possibly known to the translators, lies in the recognition that nowhere in the entire LXX can a translation be identified which can be shown to be literarily dependent upon such a non-biblical tradition. This is the case even where such a contact between the two cultures might suggest itself because of common content, as in the traditions of the OT on the history of the ancient Near East and the similar concerns of the history work of Herodotus, or as in the Priestly and Yahwistic accounts of creation and the similar Platonic ideas of creation, or as in the postulates of OT law, prophecy and wisdom that are similar to Platonic, Stoic or Sceptic teachings in their ethical demand.

The LXX translators never had the freedom to take over non-Israelite tradition in its written form into the context of their translations. Whereas most obviously in the Hebrew tradition the wisdom instruction of Amenemope is translated into the context of the book of Proverbs (22:17-23:12),[14] the sole freedom given to the LXX translators is that of rendering a canonized original into a form which was intended also to be canonized. The freedom given to them was not that of alteration; rather, theirs was the responsibility of preservation. This responsibility demanded a direct bond with the prototype, the original text, even where the adoption of earlier non-Israelite Greek tradition suggested itself because of the similarity of didactic or historical subject matter. Nobody would want to deny that there is anthropologically conditioned common ground in the thought of various religions and cultures, but where an identity of statement is nevertheless recognizable, it may be explained from the medium of earlier Greek tradition only when the formulation of the Greek translation does not at the same time correspond with the keeping of these laws of translation-technique.

But even if this condition is fulfilled, to postulate direct dependence on non-Israelite Greek tradition cannot necessarily be granted.

1. A first example of this is the rendering of the Hebrew term for "create" (ברא) at Gen 2:4a by forms of γίνεσθαι, "to become:" אלה תולדות השמים והארץ בהבראם = αὕτη ἡ βίβλος γενέσεως οὐρανοῦ καὶ γῆς ὅτε ἐγένετο. This is unique in the whole of the OT; something equivalent is to be found elsewhere only in Exod 34:10 where ברא does not designate God's creation, but his miraculous activity, and in Isa 48:7 where it designates his creation of new salvation in contrast with the original creation.[15] But it would be an error to conclude from this evidence that at the very seam between the Priestly and Yahwistic accounts of creation the translator wanted to explain their difference through his choice of words, as if it was based on the speech of Timaeus about the creation of the world (27c1-47e2). The translator is not trying to say that there is a Platonic distinction between that which is (τὸ ὂν ἀεί) in the Priestly account and that which is to become (τὸ γιγνόμενον ἀεί) in the Yahwistic one.

2. A second example can be found in the central message of the OT prophetic understanding of the law in Mic 6:8: הגיד לך אדם מה טוב ומה יהוה דורש ממך כי אם עשות משפט ואהבת חסד והצנע לכת עם אלהיך. This is rendered in the LXX as: εἰ ἀνηγγέλη σοι,

ἄνθρωπε, τί καλόν, ἢ τί κύριος ἐκζητεῖ παρὰ σοῦ, ἀλλ' ἢ τοῦ ποιεῖν κρίμα καὶ ἀγαπᾶν ἔλεος καὶ ἕτοιμον εἶναι τοῦ πορεύεσθαι μετὰ κυρίου θεοῦ σου; This deviates a little from the Hebrew original and shows some common ground with the inner relation of God, humanity and law which the Athenian defines in the *Laws* of Plato. The "readiness to walk with God" of the LXX (ἕτοιμον εἶναι τοῦ πορεύεσθαι μετὰ κυρίου θεοῦ σου) corresponds with the Platonic idea of the just or reasonable man (ἔμφρων) as one who is solely concerned with belonging to those who follow God (ὡς τῶν συνακολουθησόντων ἐσόμενον τῷ θεῷ δεῖ διανοηθῆναι πάντα ἄνδρα [*Laws* 716b]). The definition of good or just action in the LXX (καλόν for טוב), doing right and practising mercy (ποιεῖν κρίμα καὶ ἀγαπᾶν ἔλεος), corresponds with the Platonic definition of actions pleasing to God, following God rightly (δίκη) and purposefully walking humbly and lawfully (ἧς ὁ μὲν εὐδαιμονήσειν μέλλων ἐχόμενος συνέπεται ταπεινὸς καὶ κεκοσμημένος [*Laws* 716a]). The LXX and Plato seem to have in common that which apparently deviates from the Hebrew original, namely, the fact that in both traditions the relation of being to God, the "walking with him," i.e., "following him," is depicted separately from the manner of this existence, which in the one is the doing of the law, justice and mercy, and in the other is the practice of right and humility. However, this agreement should not be traced back to a tradition independent of the Hebrew original but should rather be explained on the basis of the translator's attempt to achieve an adequate

rendering of the original text's message.
ἕτοιμον εἶναι is the translation which causes the seeming correspondence with Plato, but the term it renders, הצנע, has a range of meaning in the Hebrew original. One meaning is "being humble, being broken before him" (Vulgate: sollicitum ambulare cum deo tuo; Luther, 1545: Demütig sein fur deinem Gott). The only OT reference which provides secure etymological evidence for this is Prov 11:2 where צנוע (also understood by the LXX as ταπεινός) is contrasted with the one who has become proud (זדון, ὕβρις); this evidence should not be proudly dismissed! The other meaning is that of the LXX: ἕτοιμον εἶναι. Thus this adjustment of meaning in the LXX is simply due to the meaning of the original being disputed, at the time of the translators as well as today, a dispute which can be traced through the etymologies of the same root in Nabatean and Arabic, "acting," "accomplishing," and Ethiopic, "being firm."

3. A third example involves the OT **concept of history** and its message in the period when even the author of the Hebrew-Aramaic original may be supposed very probably to have had knowledge of the non-Israelite Greek tradition of history. This concerns the teaching of the concept of the kingdom in apocalyptic history; the depiction of Hellenistic times from Alexander the Great to the Seleucid religious persecutions is apocalyptically hidden in the Book of Daniel. The formulations of both Greek Daniel translations in some passages seem to be closer to the historical witnesses of the Graeco-Roman historians from Polybius to

Diodorus Siculus and Livy, witnesses which certainly depend upon more ancient but lost historical tradition, than to the formulation of the Hebrew-Aramaic *Vorlage*. However, in none of these passages can literary dependence on that existing tradition be demonstrated.

At this point, where OT and Greek tradition touch each other with respect to the details of historical events and circumstances, the almost total lack of any proven literary contact is an even stronger argument against dependence on any existing written Greek tradition than in the other parts of the OT where the common ground consists merely in anthropological presuppositions about the idea of creation or about ethical action. The two possible exceptions which I will now discuss allow for the possibility of some literary contact between the earlier non-Israelite tradition of Greek historiography and the translation of the LXX, but the evidence of these exceptions tends to confirm the rule.

a. In the first place the Danielic concept of history concerning the kingdoms is likely to be completely literarily independent from any earlier traditions concerning the myth of world ages symbolized by metals, as is represented in Hesiod at the end of the 8th century BCE, and from traditions concerning the historiographical principle of sequential kingdoms attested since Ktesias in the early 4th century BCE. Independence from such traditions in the two Greek translations of Daniel can be explained on the grounds that in the Daniel apocalypse the two concepts of the growing decay of the ages,

EARLIER TRADITION AND SUBSEQUENT INFLUENCES 355

depicted in the four metals, and of the sequential kingdoms are unified in such a way as necessarily to require formulation completely independent from known literary examples. In particular the idea of growing decay, the basic thought in the poetry of Hesiod, could only have been integrated with difficulty into the Danielic conception. This lack of dependence is all the more worthy of attention because the choice of the Greek equivalent in the more ancient translation of Daniel is a unique agreement with Greek tradition outside the OT which is obviously a literary phenomenon close to the conception of the teaching about the kingdoms.

This unique agreement concerns the killing of the fourth beast, symbolizing the fourth kingdom, Macedonia, in Dan 7:11. This slaying is presented in the Aramaic *Vorlage* with the general term קטל:
חזה הוית עד די קטילת חיותא והובד גשמה ויהיבת ליקרת אשא. In the more ancient translation of Daniel this is rendered by a word which is a unique translation equivalent and which is rarely attested elsewhere, ἀποτυμπανίζειν: καὶ ἀπετυμπανίσθη τὸ θηρίον, καὶ ἀπώλετο τὸ σῶμα αὐτοῦ καὶ ἐδόθη εἰς καῦσιν πυρός. This term is used for a certain type of death penalty, perhaps crucifixion,[16] with which the violent death of Labhasi-Marduk, the penultimate Babylonian king, is depicted in the *Babyloniaca* of Berossus which was written under Antiochus I in the early 3rd century BCE: ἐπιβουλευθεὶς δὲ διὰ τὸ πολλὰ ἐμφαίνειν κακοήθη ὑπὸ τῶν φίλων ἀπετυμπανίσθη (Josephus, *Ag.Ap.* 1:148). In view of the unique occurrence of the term as a translation,[17] it

should be interpreted as an attempt by the translator of the more ancient Daniel translation to make clear, in a way which was not yet apparent in the Aramaic original, the concept of the increasing decay of the world kingdoms through violent events from the downfall of the Babylonian empire to that of Macedon.[18]

b. The second possible exception concerns the apocalyptically hidden depiction of the history of the kingdoms of the Ptolemaic-Seleucid Diadochoi in the great audition of Daniel 11. It would appear that the unique style of apocalyptic writing both in the Hebrew original and in the two Greek translations would display literary independence from any earlier non-Israelite tradition. The translation reflects a famous event in the third Egyptian campaign of Antiochus Epiphanes (Dan 11:29),[19] the confrontation before Alexandria between the Seleucids and the Romans in the person of the messenger Popilius Laenas. He demanded obedience to the Senatus consultum, requiring that the enemy should leave Egypt, before he left the circle which he had drawn around himself with his stick. Even though they depart little from their Hebrew *Vorlage*, Dan 11:30 (ובאו בו ציים כתים ונכאה) is rendered in both Greek translations in such a way that knowledge of these well recorded events seems to be reflected from a different tradition, historical rather than apocalyptic. Even if this conjecture may seem too daring with respect to the more recent θ translation (καὶ εἰσελεύσονται ἐν αὐτῷ οἱ ἐκπορευόμενοι Κίτιοι) because it can be explained technically as a straightforward translation, at

EARLIER TRADITION AND SUBSEQUENT INFLUENCES 357

least with regard to the Seleucids being
disheartened (ונכאה) when faced by Roman power the
unique equivalent (καὶ ταπεινωθήσεται) seems to
have been chosen in complete accord with the
historical facts according to which the Seleucid
king withdrew his troops to Syria, according to
Polybius,[20] in a "downcast and despondent" mood
(βαρυνόμενος καὶ στένων), and, according to
Diodorus Siculus,[21] he submits to the will of the
Roman, being "despondent and helpless"
(καταπεπληγμένος ... πρὸς ἀμηχανίαν ἐλθών). In
the more ancient o´ translation, which reveals its
awareness of the event by the interpretative
rendering of "ships of the Kittim" (ציים כתים) as
"Romans" (Ῥωμαῖοι), the description of the event
must be seen in proximity to existing tradition
from outside the OT because it is especially the
very parts of the translation which deviate from
the MT which are most clearly in contact with it.
According to o´ it is the Romans who "drive away"
and who "become angry against him:" ἐξώσουσιν
αὐτὸν καὶ ἐμβριμήσονται αὐτῷ. The deviating
Hebrew *Vorlage* can be reconstructed only
speculatively: perhaps הריחוהו for ונכאה, and
וזעמו as a doublet of the following וזעם.
However, the statement in o´ which replaces the
report about the Seleucid becoming disheartened
corresponds precisely with the characterisation of
the Roman messenger Popilius as we know it from
Greek and Roman historical traditions: according
to Pliny his move against Antiochus Epiphanes was
"a furious and arrogant deed" (πρᾶγμα βαρὺ μὲν
δοκοῦν εἶναι καὶ τελέως ὑπερήφανον),[22] and
according to Livy he had a rough nature and

insulting harshness (asperitas animi),[23] an expression which according to the *Lexicon* of Cyril, the most ancient biblical lexicography, serves as a synonym to clarify ἐμβριμᾶσθαι: ἐμβριμώμενος, μετὰ αὐστηρότητος ἐπιτάττων.[24]

III

The theme "The Translation of the LXX in Light of Earlier Tradition" actually points to a problem inherent within the formation of the individual works of translation which in their entirety form the Alexandrian canon. It is a problem which involves the two aspects of existing tradition and the development of a tradition of subsequent influences. This is not a matter of how the translators explained the Hebrew original from intellectually analogous statements in non-Israelite Greek tradition, that corresponds with the inner intention of all LXX translators. Rather, it is a question of how the translators explained the Hebrew original from analogous formulations in the OT witnesses themselves; it is thus a question concerning the possibility of illuminating such analogous statements by translating in a way that was not explicitly represented in the statement of the original.

We are dealing here with a phenomenon which has its origin in the original of the Hebrew-Aramaic tradition itself. It is evident at least in the processing of the earlier prophetic tradition in later apocalyptic as has been seen by I. L. Seeligmann who has described the "presuppositions of the midrash-exegesis" of the Isaianic witnesses in the Book of Daniel.[25] But this phenomenon really gains significance only through the act of translation into a foreign language which in a certain sense must always involve interpretation. A meaning is produced that has not existed before in the history of the formation and transmission of the original text.

The act of translation leads necessarily to the question about analogous formulations in the context of the original as a whole as received by the translator. The identity of the Greek rendering of the Hebrew *Vorlage* in statements which are identical in content but different in form is the only clear evidence of some literary dependence, evidence that we are dealing with one and the same translator or that the translator of one statement knew the translation of another and used it as an authority. In spite of all the unknown factors which relativize any discussion of the evidence, the identity of these kinds of formulations also provides the strongest evidence which can act as a criterion for a chronological ordering of the individual works of translation.

This problem cannot be solved purely through the use of word statistics for assessing translational techniques. In fact the whole issue concerning the adoption of an existing tradition of translation on the basis of which there is the possibility of illuminating the intention of the original has so far been clearly solved only in one instance: with the translation of the Torah. The Letter of Aristeas confirms that the Torah was the basis of the translation of all the remaining writings of the Palestinian canon. Thus the theologoumenon that the Torah is the origin of the canon and basis of the נביאים ראשנים, אחרנים and of the כתובים is actualised and confirmed in the translation of the LXX itself. However, the chronology of the formation of the individual writings in the original text itself, as postulated today more or less convincingly through the application of historical-critical criteria, is no longer reflected in the LXX translation.

1. The promise of eschatological blessing in Amos 9:13 (ונגש חורש בקצר) is represented in the LXX by the Greek translation of the similar promise in the Holiness Code in Lev 26:5 (והשיג לכם דיש את בציר): καὶ καταλήμψεται ὑμῖν ὁ ἀλοητὸς τὸν τρύγητον.[26] This not only shows the basis of the tradition of translation in a technical sense, but also has brought about an interpretative relationship between the two statements as far as their content is concerned. Such a relationship does not exist in the original Hebrew. The substitution of the persons (ploughman and reaper) by their action and its timing (threshing and wine harvest) is an interpretation in the LXX of Amos from the perspective of the promise of the Holiness Code. That the season of growth will be a sign of blessing could also have been intended in Amos itself. However, the taking over of the actions from the promise of the Holiness Code (threshing and wine harvest in place of ploughing and reaping the grain)[27] demands an understanding of the translation in which, provided that the rules in the Holiness Code are obeyed, the temporal promise of earthly blessing is identified with the eschatological one of the new earth in Amos. But this identification does not contradict

EARLIER TRADITION AND SUBSEQUENT INFLUENCES   361

the eschatological orientation of the promise in Amos in its LXX form as can be demonstrated from the second part of the *parallelismus membrorum*. Assimilation to the corresponding statement in the Holiness Code, which in synthetic parallelism promises earthly blessing (ובציר ישיג את זרע), would have been equally possible, but the translator of LXX Amos puts emphasis on the eschatological character of the promise in the second part of the statement of Amos (ודרך ענבים במשך הזרע) through a free translation and with almost antithetical intention: καὶ περκάσει[28] ἡ σταφυλὴ ἐν τῷ σπόρῳ. As a metaphor of eschatological fertility that can only mean, "Already with the sowing - in the seed and with its appearance - the fruit matures."

2. I have already noted that in Dan 11:30 in both Greek translations[29] it is probable that the translators had knowledge of the historical fact of the appearance of the Romans in Egypt as portrayed in the wrath of the Roman commander and the humiliation of the Seleucid. In the more recent θ translation of the same event the relationship between Dan 11:30 and the mysterious prophecy of Balaam which lies behind the apocalyptic statement is made explicit by a translation equivalent that deviates from the MT but is common to both texts. The MT of Num 24:24 is רצים מיד כתים וענו אשור וענו עבר. In both Numbers and Daniel צים, "ships,"[30] is rendered with a form of the verb יצא (ויוצאים?): ἐξελεύσεται ἐκ χειρὸς Κιτιαίων (Num 24:24), εἰσελεύονται ἐν αὐτῷ οἱ ἐκπορευόμενοι Κίτιοι (Dan 11:30). This not only proves that the more recent translation

of Daniel is dependent upon the translation of the
Torah, but it also provides an interpretation of
the statement in Daniel in light of the existing
translation of the prophecy of Balaam; this
interpretation was not provided in the Hebrew
original. The "going out," ἐκπορεύεσθαι, does
not reflect part of the battle as in the Hebrew
original, but the inner intention of the prophecy
itself: it is the Kittim, who in Daniel are the
apocalyptic symbolic expression for the Romans as
the more ancient Greek translation discloses
(Ῥωμαῖοι), from whom the announced event
proceeds. In the Danielic teaching about the
kingdoms this "going out" is the first sign of the
disintegration of the last kingdom, Macedonia,
symbolized by the most terrible animal. Implied
in this are the rise and fall of subsequent
earthly kingdoms, but from the perspective of the
final end their ups and downs are portrayed
subordinately within the last period of fallen
creation.[31]

It may not, therefore, be an over-
interpretation to understand the eschatological
vision of the Greek Daniel tradition in the light
of the Greek form of the oracle of Balaam as that
tradition knew it. The Greek oracle of Balaam
still remains the earliest interpretation for the
proper understanding of the Hebrew original of the
Balaam pericope which has probably been partly
destroyed. The Greek Balaam oracle is a vision
according to which, in face of earthly suffering
still to come, even the chosen people of Yahweh in
their earthly form must be destroyed: "Alas, who
shall live when God accomplishes these things

EARLIER TRADITION AND SUBSEQUENT INFLUENCES   363

(ὅταν θῇ ταῦτα ὁ θεός; cf. משרמו אל)? From the
Kittim it will proceed (καὶ ἐξελεύσεται ἐκ χειρὸς
Κιτιαίων; cf. ורצים מיד כתים); they shall destroy
Assyria, they shall destroy the Hebrews, they
shall all perish together (καὶ κακώσουσιν Ἀσσούρ,
καὶ κακώσουσιν Ἑβραίους, καὶ αὐτοὶ ὁμοθυμαδὸν
ἀπολοῦνται; cf. רעני אשור ועני עבר וגם הוא עדי
אבד)."

Corresponding with this explanation is the
recognition that the interpretative intention of
the Greek translation of Daniel, resting on the
basis of existing LXX tradition, can develop and
become even more intensified beyond the Torah. In
relation to the Hebrew tradition it has been noted
by I. L. Seeligmann that the Danielic apocalypse
relates to the prophecy of Isaiah as midrash.[32]
Likewise the Greek translation of Daniel relies on
LXX Isaiah in such a way that the anti-godly
power, personified in Daniel by Antiochus
Epiphanes, is identified through analogous
statements, which do not feature in the Hebrew
Vorlage, with the personification of the anti-
godly Assyrian oppressor at the time of Isaiah.
This is done in such a way that this paragon is
lifted out of the immediate historical context
and elevated into a symbol of the eschatological
adversary, which in NT terms is the "Antichrist."

3. The use made of Isa 10:14 provides another
example. Isa 10:14 reads: τὴν οἰκουμένην ὅλην
καταλήμψομαι τῇ χειρὶ ὡς νοσσιὰν καὶ ὡς
καταλελειμμένα ᾠὰ ἀρῶ ("I have grasped the whole
earth with my hand as a nest and as forsaken eggs
I have gathered it"). In the more recent θ
translation of Dan 8:25 there is a place where the

Hebrew original can only be constructed with difficulty: the expression באפס יד ישבר ("by no human hand, he shall be broken") appears as ὡς ᾠὰ χειρὶ συντρίψει ("as eggs he will destroy them by hand"). On this basis אפס appears to presuppose a metathesis from the original אסף of Isa 10:14, the niphal ישבר appears as the hiphil ישביר, and ביצים was inserted from Isaiah (by the translator?). By using the existing Greek translation of Isaiah the interpretative intention of the translator of Daniel is evident: he seeks to describe the last work of the destroyer as his anti-godly rule over the whole world.

IV

The problem of "the translation of the LXX in light of subsequent influences" includes three areas lying as it were in three concentric circles around a centre which is the Greek translation of the Palestinian canon. The first circle embraces Greek literature, which either as translation or as originally written in Greek, is associated with the translated Palestinian canon and together with it constitutes the Alexandrian canon. To this can be added a second circle of Greek tradition in which the Alexandrian canon, to various extents, is considered to be Holy Scripture and the object of interpretation. Its basis is the Jewish-Hellenistic literature up to Philo and Josephus; from a purely intellectual perspective this circle also includes the early Christian and Gnostic witnesses. To the third circle belongs the "secular" Greek non-Jewish and non-Christian

EARLIER TRADITION AND SUBSEQUENT INFLUENCES   365

literature in which the witness of the Alexandrian canon is dealt with as the object of praise or polemic.

Over against the internal literary dependence within the Greek translation of the Palestinian canon itself which I have already described, in all three cases here the dependence upon existing tradition is of a different kind. It is not that the earlier tradition of translation serves as the basis for interpretative translations of analogous statements as regards content; rather, the canonical significance of the Greek translation of the Palestinian canon in Hellenistic Judaism provides the basis for the possible formulation of interpretative statements to which theological legitimacy is due only because of their connection to the authority of the translated Palestinian canon.

The prologue to the Greek translation of the wisdom of Jesus Sirach in the second century BCE testifies to the distinction that was made between canonical and apocryphal and shows that within the Alexandrian canon an understanding of what is "apocryphal," i.e., that which does not belong to the Palestinian canon as translated into Greek, is legitimized and authorized only in connection and in light of that canon. From this and only from this is it explicable that in these apocryphal writings, associated with the translated Palestinian canon, was it possible not only to transmit reminiscences of, appeals to and actual quotations from the canonical witnesses, but in some places, even though only in the margin and again as the exception that proves the rule, there are also cases of the adoption of material from non-Israelite Greek traditions in a form hardly changed and which would have been unthinkable in the translation of the canonical witnesses. The integration of these statements into the Alexandrian canon as a whole and the context they thus acquired convey to these statements their only legitimate meaning in the eyes of the originators of canonisation.

Already the references of apocryphal witnesses that recall the Greek tradition of the law, prophets and writings are to be understood in some places not as pure repetition, resumption and thus authorized quotation, but as a form of reference to the earlier word according to which it can be interpreted in the light of non-Israelite Greek tradition and in delimitation against it.

1. In one of these apocryphal writings, originally written in Greek, we encounter the earliest formulation which explicitly states the theologoumenon of *creatio ex nihilo*. 2 Macc 7:28 contains the phrase οὐκ ἐξ ὄντων ("not from what is"). This is to be explained from the point of view of the witness as well as from that of the founder of the Alexandrian canon in such a way that with this statement the more ancient creation accounts of the OT in their Hebrew and Greek forms are interpreted in the sense of "creation out of nothing" and are thus delimited against any other idea of how the world came into being. In the translation of the priestly creation account in the LXX the paratactic syntax of the first two sentences leaves open the two possibilities of understanding given by the Hebrew *Vorlage*, that

EARLIER TRADITION AND SUBSEQUENT INFLUENCES   367

is, the creator's first work in the creation of the heaven and earth can be seen as either *creatio ex nihilo* or in terms of the pre-existence of the invisible and unformed earth as the power of chaos. But this ambiguity is interpreted in 2 Macc 7:28 as the creation of heaven and earth out of nothing, just as in the creation account in Job 26:7. In the MT Job 26:7 reads: נטה צפון על תהו תלה ארץ על בלי מה. The Greek is only transmitted in Origen's Hexapla but doubtless rested on a more ancient pre-Theodotion tradition: X ἐκτείνων βορέαν ἐπ'οὐδέν X κρεμάζων γῆν ἐπὶ οὐδενός. The meaning of οὐδέν, "nothing," is open; it can be understood as either a definition of that which was pre-existent for the creator or as designating creation as the first act.

Delimitation against the idea of creation as a forming out of pre-existent material may also be recognized in the choice of the Greek equivalent for the terms תהו ובהו and בלי מה from Genesis through Job to 2 Maccabees: ἀόρατος καὶ ἀκατασκεύαστος → οὐδέν → οὐκ ἐξ ὄντων. ἀόρατος is the Platonic expression for the world of ideas that exists and lies behind "becoming" (*Sophist* 246a-c; *Theaetatus* 155e). Likewise at a still later time the translation of the priestly creation account seems to be a mockery of pre-Socratic philosophy by the Jewish translators of the second century CE: ἡ δὲ γῆ ἦν κένωμα καὶ οὐθέν (Aquila), θὲν καὶ οὐθέν (Theodotion). These translators imply that whatever had been philosophized about existence and non-existence, from Parmenides to Democritus, is found within the scope of that which the OT God of creation created in the beginning.

2. Some cases which are not dealing with delimitation against non-Israelite Greek tradition are debates with it. Primarily these concern ideas that are common to Israelite and non-Israelite realms intellectually or anthropologically. The basic intention of the Israelite tradition lies in its concern to interpret the common idea in form and content according to its first genuinely Israelite written attestation.

Perhaps this is shown most clearly by the treatment within Israelite Hebrew and Greek tradition of the theologoumenon of God's self-sufficiency, a motif which is common also in non-Israelite sources. It is formulated in Israelite sources differently from its treatment in the Hellenic-Greek cultural area; in this case the much abused antithesis between Hebrew and Greek thought is justified. In the OT this motif is formulated in terms of the wants and the activity of Israel's God. In 1 Kgs 8:27 (cf. 2 Sam 7:5-7) God is depicted as initially refusing to live in a house built by man; then, in Ps 50:12-13 he rejects presumptuous human worship, especially self-complacent sacrifice; finally, in Isa 46:7a he mocks the way that idols need human help. By contrast this motif appears in the Greek-hellenistic tradition from Xenophanes through Plato, from the Stoa down to Plutarch as a general aphorism, a perception of the nature of the godhead achieved through the *via negationis*:[33] ἀπροσδεὴς μὲν γὰρ ὁ θεὸς ἁπλῶς. (Plutarch, *Aristides-Cato maior*, Cato 31). It is this kind

EARLIER TRADITION AND SUBSEQUENT INFLUENCES 369

of assertion which is implied, even where it shows great similarity to the OT mockery of idols, as in the poetic form of Euripides' polemic against the anthropomorphic worship of idols, put into the mouth of Heracles:

ἐγὼ δὲ τοὺς θεοὺς οὔτε λέκτρ'ἃ μὴ θέμις
στέργειν νομίζω, δεσμά τ'ἐξάπτειν χεροῖν
οὔτ'ἠξίωσα πώποτ'οὔτε πείσομαι,
οὐδ'ἄλλον ἄλλου δεσπότην πεφυκέναι
<u>δεῖται γὰρ ὁ θεός, εἴπερ ἔστ'ὀρθῶς θεός,</u>
<u>οὐδενός·</u> ἀοιδῶν οἵδε δύστηνοι λόγοι
(Heracles 1341-46)
I deem not that the Gods for spousals crave
Unhallowed: tales of Gods' hands manacled
Ever I scorned, nor ever will believe,
Nor that one God is born another's lord.
<u>For God hath need, if indeed he be,</u>
<u>Of naught</u>: these be the minstrels' sorry
tales.[34]

That is a philosophical aphorism put in a dramatic form and thus put into action.

This theologoumenon, therefore, appears in non-Israelite Greek tradition as a *terminus technicus* for the perception of the monotheistic deity's nature gained through the *via negativa*. It is also expressed but in line with OT tradition in a Greek form in the apocryphal parts of the Alexandrian canon in 2 and 3 Maccabees: σὺ κύριε, τῶν ὅλων ἀπροσδεὴς ὑπάρχων (You Lord, who need nothing at all; 2 Macc 14:35); σοι τῷ τῶν ἀπάντων ἀπροσδεεῖ καὶ παραδοξάσας ἐν ἐπιφανείᾳ μεγαλοπρεπεῖ (You have no need of anything and when glorified by your magnificent manifestation...; 3 Macc 2:9). It has not been sufficiently noticed by those, such as E. Norden and M. Dibelius,[35] who first pointed out the contact between biblical Greek and secular Greek traditions, that these statements should not be interpreted as the sudden intrusion of Greek-hellenistic religious ideas into the biblical tradition, but rather as a reminder and interpretation of OT statements by means of intellectually related non-Israelite categories which in their new context gain a genuinely OT significance. This is so because the immediate reference of these statements is the OT *locus classicus* of the sufficiency of Yahweh, his not needing an earthly sanctuary as described in Solomon's prayer of dedication for the temple (3 Kgdms 8:27).

With regard to the Jewish-hellenistic taking over of Greek philosophical tradition we are dealing with a phenomenon similar to the adoption of mythical tradition; in that case H. Jonas distinguished between the "means of depiction and existence,"[36] and a similar distinction was made by H. Conzelmann as follows: "we must distinguish more sharply than is customary between mythical material and reflective mythology as a current form of theology."[37] In the case under consideration here it is the recollection of the God of Israel who is present in history. In 3 Kgdms 8:26, in Solomon's prayer for the dedication of the temple, this is expressed in terms of the promise of the perpetual Davidic dynasty: πιστωθήτω δὴ τὸ ῥῆμά σου τῷ Δαυὶδ τῷ πατρί μου. It is taken up in 2 Macc 14:34 in the invocation of God who always defends his people: ἐπεκαλοῦντο

EARLIER TRADITION AND SUBSEQUENT INFLUENCES 371

τὸν διὰ παντὸς ὑπέρμαχον τοῦ ἔθνους ἡμῶν. And again it is taken up in 3 Macc 2:7 before the impending danger of the Ptolemaic desecration of the temple when Simon invokes the God who drowned Pharaoh and his army in the sea: ἐπεδιώξαντα αὐτὸν σὺν ἅρμασιν καὶ ὄχλων πλήθει ἐπέκλυσας βάθει θαλάσσης.

All these instances are recollections of the God of Israel who is the creator of heaven and earth and as such stands sovereign above creation. The Greek rendering of the Hebrew of 1 Kgs 8:27 in Solomon's prayer of dedication is ὁ οὐρανὸς καὶ ὁ οὐρανὸς τοῦ οὐρανοῦ <u>οὐκ ἀρκέσουσίν σοι</u>. The last phrase, "are not enough for you," a unique LXX equivalent and something of a *via negativa* within Israelite tradition, is meant to express merely the superiority of the creator over all creation, not any need beyond his creation. However, as such, it prepares for the *direct* relating of the Greek *terminus technicus* and the Israelite creation statement in a sense which is not given by the Hebrew *Vorlage*, namely the perception that Israel's God is by his very nature not in need of the universe he created. This is made explicit in 2 Macc 14:35, τῶν ὅλων ἀπροσδεὴς ὑπάρχων, and similarly in 3 Macc 2:9 where ὁ τῶν ἁπάντων ἀπροσδεής is the creator of the universe and the one who has chosen Jerusalem: κτίσας τὴν ἀπέραντον καὶ ἀμέτρητον γῆν ἐξελέξω τὴν πόλιν ταύτην.

Finally, the fact that the God of Israel, being self-sufficient, has nevertheless chosen an earthly sanctuary for his name reveals his grace - a concept completely alien to Greek thought. The apprehensive question in the Solomonic prayer of 3

Kgdms 8:27, "If heaven and the highest heaven are not sufficient for you, how can this house be which I have built?", seems to find its interpretation and its answer in the original Greek tradition of the Alexandrian canon, firstly in 2 Macc 14:35 in terms of divine pleasure, ηὐδόκησας ναὸν τῆς σῆς σκηνώσεως ἐν ἡμῖν γενέσθαι, and secondly in 3 Macc 2:9 in terms of holiness: ἡγίασας τὸν τόπον τοῦτον εἰς ὄνομά σοι.[38]

3. In the apocryphal literature of the Alexandrian canon some ideas are taken from Greek tradition but do not have intellectual or anthropological analogies in Israelite thought and are transmitted neither in deliberate opposition to Greek thought nor in debate with it. As with the adoption of ancient Egyptian proverb material in the wisdom tradition of Israel,[39] the meaning of these ideas is clearly given by the genuinely Israelite context of their usage.

In the "king's mirror" of Wis 9:15 human nature confronted by divine wisdom is depicted in terms of the dualism of the soul and the body which weighs it down:

φθαρτὸν γὰρ σῶμα βαρύνει ψυχήν,
καὶ βρίθει τὸ γεῶδες σκῆνος νοῦν πολυφρόντιδα.

For a perishable body weighs down the soul,
And this earthly tent burdens the mind so full of thought.

In an almost unguarded way this reflects the Platonic teaching that describes the soul as weighed down by the visible world of embodiment and thus as hindered from becoming part of the invisible world of pure ideas. Indeed, because of

EARLIER TRADITION AND SUBSEQUENT INFLUENCES   373

the use of the same words, Wis 9:15 may even be designated as a quotation from the *Phaedo*: ἐμβριθὲς δέ γε, ὦ φίλε, τοῦτο οἴεσθαι χρὴ εἶναι καὶ βαρὺ καὶ γεῶδες καὶ ὁρατόν· ὃ δὴ καὶ ἔχουσα ἡ τοιαύτη ψυχὴ βαρύνεταί τε καὶ ἕλκεται πάλιν εἰς τὸν ὁρατὸν τόπον φόβῳ ἀιδοῦς τε καὶ Ἅιδου (81c), "And, my friend, we must believe that this (i.e., the corporeal [σύμφυτον, σωματοειδές]) is burdensome (ἐμβριθές) and heavy (βαρύ) and earthly (γεῶδες) and visible (ὁρατόν). And such a soul is weighed down (βαρύνεται) by this and is dragged back into the visible world, through fear of the invisible (ἀιδές) and of the other world."[40] But because this teaching is integrated consistently into the context of genuinely OT anthropology the Platonic anthropology appears merely as a subordinate element, one among many possibilities for paraphrasing the nature of fallen creation when confronted by the creator God who alone saves. The OT anthropology in the context is confirmed in Wis 9:1-2 through the use of "the word" (ὁ λόγος) and the divine "wisdom" (σοφία). These terms are used, as in the sense of Prov 8, for describing the creative activity of Israel's God and they thus take the place of the Platonic invisible world of truth (Wis 9:1-12). It is only through the gift of divine wisdom and the holy Spirit that human action can be wise: βουλὴν δέ σου τίς ἔγνω, εἰ μὴ σὺ ἔδωκας σοφίαν καὶ ἔπεμψας τὸ ἅγιόν σου πνεῦμα ἀπὸ ὑψίστων; (Wis 9:17)

It is not possible to discuss further the second circle of biblical literature in which the Alexandrian canon is variously "Holy Scripture" and the object of interpretation nor the third

circle of non-biblical Greek tradition which knows
the Alexandrian canon or parts of it as an
existing tradition with which it stands in
dialogue. Suffice it to say by way of providing
some perspective that to understand the nature of
the second circle there must be a basic
distinction between the literature which, though
preserving the forms of statements of the
Alexandrian canon, takes up in large degree
non-Israelite Greek tradition in form and content
(i.e., the wisdom, historical and prophetic/
apocalyptic pseudepigrapha), and the literature
which as actual commentary presupposes the
traditional material of the Alexandrian canon as
"Holy Scripture"; within Judaism these are the
writings of Philo and Josephus. By contrast the
third circle, i.e. the circle of the non-biblical
secular Greek tradition engaged in a debate with
the writings of the Alexandrian canon, does not
become conspicuous before the period when the last
representatives of ancient philosophy, Celsus and
Porphyry, question the truth of the Jewish-
Christian witnesses. An exception which again
proves the rule is the Genesis quotation found in
Περὶ ὕψους, a work which it is difficult to locate
in time and place but which almost certainly
belongs to an earlier period.

And this, in reverse, is exactly the situation
in which the translators of the OT found
themselves when faced with the earlier
non-Israelite Greek tradition: the serpent has
bitten itself in the tail!

NOTES

1. *Nachrichten der Akademie der Wissenschaften in Göttingen* (I. Phil-hist. Kl. 11 = Mitteilungen des Septuaginta-Unternehmens 15; Göttingen: Vandenhoeck & Ruprecht, 1979) 275-325

2. Best expressed summarily in *The Ancient Library and Modern Biblical Studies* (Garden City, N.Y.: Doubleday, 1958) 120-45 = *Die antike Bibliothek von Qumran* (Neukirchen: Neukirchener Verlag, 1967) 154-79.

3. Cf. R. Hanhart, "Die Übersetzungstechnik der Septuaginta als Interpretation (Daniel 11,29 und die Ägyptenzuge des Antiochus Epiphanes," *Mélanges Dominique Barthélemy* (ed. P. Casetti, O. Keel, and A. Schenker; OBO 38; Fribourg: Editions universitaires/Göttingen: Vandenhoeck & Ruprecht, 1981) 135-57.

4. Cf. R. Hanhart, "Die Bedeutung der Septuaginta für die Definition des 'hellenistischen Judentums'," *Congress Volume: Jerusalem 1986* (ed. J. A. Emerton; VTSup 40; Leiden: E. J. Brill, 1988) 67-80.

5. Cf. I. L. Seeligmann, *The Septuagint Version of Isaiah* (Mitteilungen ex Oriente Lux 9; Leiden: E. J. Brill, 1948) 83-84; R. Hanhart, "Die Septuaginta als Interpretation und Aktualisierung (Jesaja 9,1[8,23]-7[6])," *Isac Leo Seeligmann Volume* III (ed. A. Rofé and Y. Zakovitch; Jerusalem: E. Rubinstein, 1983) 331-46.

6. For further examples for pagan altars of the equivalence מזבח-βωμός see Exod 34:13; Deut 7:5, 12:3; Num 23:1, 2, 4, 14, 29, 30; 2 Par 31:1; Isa 17:8, 27:9; Jer 11:13. Exceptions to the use of βωμός for the altar of Yahweh are Num 3:10 (without a *Vorlage* in the MT), Sir 50:12 (Heb: המערבות), 14 (Heb: מזבח; cf. המערבות in 14b), 2 Macc 2:19; note also that Josh 22:34 is not an exception since the problem of whether the altar there is an altar of Yahweh presupposes the distinction clearly (cf. Josh 22:29). For the whole subject see S. Daniel, *Recherches sur le Vocabulaire du Culte dans la Septante* (Etudes et Commentaires 61; Paris: Klincksieck, 1965) 15-54 (cf. my review in *OLZ* 65 [1970] 358-62); E. Tov,

"Die griechischen Bibelübersetzungen," *ANRW* II, 20:1 (1987) 121-89; here p. 146.

7. Cf. 4 Kgdms 16:10 (Ahaz), 18:22 (the Rabshakeh), 21:1-3 (Manasseh). The corresponding translations in the prophetic books are also to be explained in this sense: Hos 4:19, 8:11 (Ephraim), 10:1, 2, 8 (altars of Israel); Amos 2:8, 3:14 (Bethel); Ezek 6:4-13, 8:5 (with the exception of Judg 2:2?).

8. Cf. Qoh 2:15, 3:19, 9:2-3.

9. This is true also for the apocryphal parts of the Alexandrian canon; the text of 2 Macc 7:37 attested in codices A' (τύχην for the original ψυχήν; recorded by Hatch and Redpath without versional attestation) is of course secondary.

10. Cf. R. Hanhart, "Fragen um die Entstehung der LXX," *VT* 12 (1962) 139-63; here pp. 159-60.

11. Cf. for the moment, R. Hanhart, *Text und Textgeschichte des 1. Esrabuches* (Mitteilungen des Septuaginta-Unternehmens 12; Göttingen: Vandenhoeck & Ruprecht, 1974) 11-18.

12. J. A. Montgomery, *The Book of Daniel* (ICC; Edinburgh: T. & T. Clark, 1927) 158.

13. The clarification of the history of the term ὕψιστος must start from here. Still important is W. Bauer, *Griechisch-deutsches Wörterbuch zu den Schriften des Neuen Testaments und der übrigen urchristlichen Literatur* (5th ed; Berlin: A. Töpelmann, 1958); the 6th edition (ed. K. and B. Aland; 1988) offers nothing new in this respect.

14. Cf. O. Eissfeldt, *Einleitung in das Alte Testament* (3rd ed.; Tübingen: J. C. B. Mohr, 1964) 641-43 = *The Old Testament: An Introduction* (Eng. tr. P. R. Ackroyd; Oxford: B. Blackwell, 1965) 474-75.

15. Exod 34:10: אעשה נפלאת אשר לא נבראו בכל הארץ, ποιήσω ἔνδοξα ἃ οὐ γέγονεν ἐν πάσῃ τῇ γῇ; Isa 48:7: עתה נבראו ולא מאז, νῦν γίνεται οὐ πάλαι. In Ps 148:5b הוא צוה ונבראו is rendered by the double translation αὐτὸς εἶπεν καὶ ἐγενήθησαν, αὐτὸς ἐνετείλατο καὶ ἐκτίσθησαν which corresponds literally with Ps 32(33):9 הוא אמר ויהי הוא צוה ויעמד) and displays the synonymity of κτίζεσθαι and γίνεσθαι in the usage of the LXX.

16. Since Demosthenes, Lysias, Aristotle (LSJ 225

and Sup 21); in the LXX at 3 Macc 3:27 it is torture with the τύμπανον; cf. 2 Macc 6:19, 28.

17. The more recent θ translation renders it with the general term ἀναιρεῖν peculiar to this book but elsewhere used for various terms expressing killing: ἀνηρέθη τὸ θηρίον καὶ ἀπώλετο, καὶ τὸ σῶμα αὐτοῦ ἐδόθη εἰς καῦσιν πυρός.

18. J. J. Scaliger's identification of Labhasi-Marduk on the basis of this tradition of Berossus with the Danielic Belshazzar of Dan 5, and of the last Babylonian ruler Nabonidus with the Danielic Darius the Mede has indeed been historically refuted with respect to Belshazzar by the Nabonidus texts from Ur which present him as the son of Nabonidus; but as a legendary identification, as is suggested for Daniel between Nebuchadnezzar and Nabonidus, especially concerning the legend of the dream and madness of Nebuchadnezzar in Dan 4, by the Qumran text of the dream of Nabonidus (cf. R. Hanhart, *Zur Zeitrechnung des I. u. II. Makkabäerbuches* [BZAW 88; Berlin: A. Töpelmann, 1964] 88, n. 55), it would constitute a still more explicit interpretation of the growing decline of the Babylonian-Macedonian kingdom: "Canonum Isagogicorum," *Thesaurus temporum Eusebii Pamphili* (Amsterdam: apud J. Janssonium, 1658) III.296-97; cf. *Opus de emendatione temporum* (Geneva: Typis Roverianis, 1629) 579-80.

19. Cf. pp. 343, 361-63.

20. Polybius, *Historiae* 29.27.8

21. Diodorus Siculus, *Bibliotheca Historica* 31.2.2

22. *Historiae* 29.27.4; so also Diodorus Siculus, *Bibliotheca Historica* 31.2.1, adopted from Polybius.

23. *Historiae* 45.12: "a hard, brusque man" (Th. Mommsen, *Römische Geschichte*, 3.10, dtv 6054 [1976] 304).

24. Cf. J. F. Schleusner, *Lexicon in LXX*, London: J. Duncan, 1829, 1.753; adopted from J. Chr. Biel, *Lexicon in LXX* (ex b. autoris manuscripto edidit ac praefatus est E. H. Mutzenbecher; Hagae Comitum: J. A. Bouvink, 1779) 1.517; cf. Mutzenbecher's "*Praefatio*," pp. xviii-xix; according to *Suidae Lexicon* (ed. A. Adler; Stuttgart: B. G. Teubner, 1967) 2.255 (#963), cf. 2.276 (#1212-13) Σ = Συναγωγή.

25. I. L. Seeligmann, "Voraussetzungen der Midraschexegese," *Congress Volume: Copenhagen* (VTSup 1; Leiden: E. J. Brill, 1953) 150-81.

26. The allocation is probably encouraged by the metathesis of הׁשיג, which from the Pentateuch onwards is a frequent equivalent for καταλαμβάνειν, with נגשׂ (for which there is an equivalence only in Amos 9:13) in the *Vorlage* of the translator of Amos.

27. On the problem of understanding cf. above all W. Rudolph, *Amos* (KAT XIII/2, 1971) 283-84.

28. For דרך in the sense of progression, ripening, see Schleusner, ad loc.

29. See pp. 356-57.

30. Known with this significance in LXX Isa 33:21 (πλοῖον), but not in Ezek 30:9 where the term is missing from the original translation and is transcribed by Aquila, Theodotion and the Hexaplaric and Lucianic recension, each in a different way.

31. Cf. R. Hanhart, "Kriterien geschichtlicher Wahrheit in der Makkabäerzeit," *Drei Studien zum Judentum* (Theologische Existenz heute 140; München: Chr. Kaiser, 1967) 7-22; here pp. 11-12.

32. Cf. nn. 5 and 25; I. L. Seeligman, "Voraussetzungen der Midraschexegese," 171; *The Septuagint Version of Isaiah*, 82.

33. Cf. E. Norden, *Agnostos Theos* (Leipzig: B. G. Teubner, 1913) 13-14; M. Dibelius, *Paulus auf dem Areopag* (Heidelberg: Carl Winter, 1939) = *Aufsätze zur Apostelgeschichte* (FRLANT 60; 2nd ed.; Göttingen: Vandenhoeck & Ruprecht, 1953) 29-70, here 42-45, with classical evidence, p. 43, n. 2; cf. also H. Conzelmann, *Die Apostelgeschichte* (HNT 7; Tübingen: J. C. B. Mohr, 1963) 98-99.

34. Eng. tr. A. S. Way, *Euripides* (LCL; London: Heinemann; New York: Macmillan, 1912) 3.239; German Tr. available in U. von Wilamowitz-Moellendorff, *Griechische Tragödien* (9th ed.; Berlin: Weidmannsche Buchhandlung, 1922) 1.363.

35. In their interpretation of Paul's Areopagus speech (see n. 33), where the breaking of the Greek philosopheme through OT faith in God is given in the denial of the temple as the place

where God lives (Acts 17:24-25), even though veiled.

36. *Gnosis und spätantiker Geist* (FRLANT 51; 2nd ed.; Göttingen: Vandenhoeck & Ruprecht, 1954) 1.48-49: "Den inhaltlich angebbaren Ausgangselementen, welche es auch seien, kann die gnostische Idee nur ihre Darstellungsmittel, nicht ihr Dasein zu verdanken haben."

37. "The Mother of Wisdom," *The Future of Our Religious Past: Essays in Honour of Rudolph Bultmann* (ed. J. M. Robinson; London: SCM, 1971) 232 = "Die Mutter der Weisheit," *Zeit und Geschichte: Dankesgabe an Rudolf Bultmann zum 80. Geburtstag* (ed. E. Dinkler; Tübingen: J. C. B. Mohr, 1964) 227 = *Theologie als Schriftauslegung: Aufsätze zum Neuen Testament* (Beiträge zur evangelische Theologie 65; München: Kaiser, 1974) 169.

38. It is only a further step in the same direction when in Jewish hellenistic tradition beyond the Alexandrian canon, in Josephus' interpretative paraphrase of the Solomonic prayer of dedication, the nature of God is defined as ἀπροσδεής, but with a view to considering the very possibility of creaturely service, whether it be the construction of the temple or sacrifice: ἀπροσδεὲς γὰρ τὸ θεῖον ἁπάντων καὶ κρεῖττον τοιαύτης ἀμοιβῆς (*Ant.* 8.111).

39. Cf. p. 350.

40. Eng. tr. H. N. Fowler, *Plato* (LCL; London: Heinemann; Cambridge: Harvard University, 1914) 1.283.

SEPTUAGINTAL TRANSLATION TECHNIQUES -
A SOLUTION TO THE PROBLEM OF THE TABERNACLE
ACCOUNT

ANNELI AEJMELAEUS

The new era in biblical criticism, opened by the discoveries in the Dead Sea area, has brought about new attitudes towards textual criticism of the OT and, in particular, the use of the LXX in it. When readings previously known only through the LXX were actually found in Hebrew manuscripts or fragments of them, this meant an increase of confidence in the work of the LXX translators. It is no longer possible for a scholar to assume off-hand that a divergence between the MT and the LXX was caused by the translator - either his carelessness or free rewriting - without serious consideration of the possibility of a different Hebrew *Vorlage*. This new attitude - and no particular textual discovery - is my point of departure in this paper.

This basic attitude of confidence in the LXX translators also has another root. It is supported by the study of translation techniques.

The more one learns about the work of the LXX translators, the clearer it becomes that they ought to be looked upon, not as editors or revisers, but primarily as translators who - each of them in their own way - aimed at a faithful rendering of their Holy Scripture.[1]

One of the greatest textual problems in the Greek Pentateuch is the end of Exodus, the section dealing with the tabernacle. Chs 25-31 and 35-40 give tiresome and detailed accounts of the tabernacle and the various items in it, its curtains and pillars, the ark, the table, the lampstand, the copper altar and the golden altar, the priests' vestments and the court hangings and so on. The first section (Chs 25-31) contains instructions for the building and the production of the whole. The second section (Chs 35-40) goes through all the details again in the form of a report of how everything was realized. As is well known, the problem lies in the second section: in the LXX it is somewhat shorter than in the MT and reveals quite a different order of items.

In the first section, where the LXX and the MT agree, the account begins with the ark, the table, and the lampstand, i.e., the furniture of the tabernacle (ch 25), then continues with the tabernacle itself, its curtains and wooden frames, the veil and the door-screen with their pillars (Ch 26), then come the altar of burnt offering and the court (Ch 27). The vestments of the priests (Ch 28) and their ordination (Ch 29) form the first ending of the instructions, and the items that follow, the altar of incense, the copper laver, and the recipes for anointing oil and incense, obviously represent a later stratum in the instructions.

As for the second section, neither the MT nor the LXX follows the order of the first section. The MT begins with the tabernacle (Ch 36), goes on with the furniture, connecting items mentioned in the beginning of the first section to those in the later addition (Chs 37-38), then comes the court (Ch 38) and finally the priests' vestments (Ch 39).

In the LXX, the second section is opened by the priests' vestments, but after that the order is partly the same as in the MT: first the tabernacle, then the furniture. Only the court has a different location, between the tabernacle and the furniture. But there are also minuses in the LXX. The making of the tabernacle is reported very briefly, without the mention of the goats' hair tent or the wooden frames, their bases and bars, etc. (MT 36:10-34). The most prominent item neglected in the LXX is the altar of incense (MT 37:25-28); its making is not reported at all. However, it is not absent altogether: it appears twice in the lists of Ch 40.

The most difficult part in the LXX text is Ch 38. The report of the realization of the ark, the table and the lampstand is much shorter than in the MT, lacking measurements and other details. The account of the metalwork (LXX 38:18-26), on the other hand, is without exact equivalent in the MT. It collects together pillars, bases, capitals, hooks, and pegs, contradicting what has been said about them before, and connects these with the report of the making of the copper altar

and the copper laver. Each verse in the account
of the metalwork begins with the pronoun οὗτος,
obviously referring to Bezalel, but laying
exceptional stress on the subject. Moreover, this
οὗτος-section contains midrash-type explanations
of the origin of the copper used for both the
altar (v 22) and the laver (v 26), the former
having been made of the censers of the followers
of Korah (cf. Num 16:36-40) and the latter of the
mirrors of the women doing service at the door of
the tabernacle. The second explanation is also
found in the MT (38:8). Neither of these
explanations is suitable in this context in which
Israel is still supposed to be at Mount Sinai.

In short, the two different versions of the
second section and the first section each give the
items in different orders. A certain logic,
however, might be discovered in each of them. In
the first section, it is natural to begin the
instructions with the most sacred objects inside
the tabernacle. The disorder towards the end of
the first section was again caused by later
additions. In the second section, on the other
hand, the MT reports the construction of the
tabernacle before its furniture, which is logical
in the sense that the tabernacle had to be built
before the furniture could be placed in it. The
order of the furniture is from inside outwards,
except for the laver which is always reported
after the altar of the burnt offering, although
its place was between the tabernacle and the
altar. The priests' vestments could be regarded
as not being part of the tabernacle, although
necessary for the service in it, and this would

explain their location at the end of the account.

But the LXX, with all its defects, also has a certain logic. The order of the items is according to the materials used. The priests' vestments, the tabernacle, the veil, the door-screen, and the court hangings all involve woven materials. Supporting pillars and some other hard objects, to be sure, are mentioned among the soft ones, but the many details of the framework of the tabernacle are all absent. At the end of this part of the account Oholiab is said to be the designer of all the fabrics, though the consistent use of verb forms in the plural implies that he was thought to have had several co-workers. The second part presents the works of Bezalel, the ark, the golden table (just as in LXX 25:23, not only overlaid with gold), the lamp-stand, and all the various metalworks, including the copper altar and the copper laver. This part of the account in the LXX uses verb forms in the singular and ends with the inventory of the amounts of metals used. Neither of the two types of texts could be said to reveal total disorder. The differences do not seem to be accidental.

Now, the question is: what is the relationship between the Hebrew and Greek versions of the second section? I do not think it would be correct to start with the question: how did the Greek text come into existence? Many have started with this question and ended up with the answer that all the differences are caused by the translator or translators. Since this kind of editing and abridging would be most unusual in the Greek Pentateuch and not easily ascribed to the translators, various theories have been developed to explain it. It has been fairly common to assume that the second section or part of it was not present in the Hebrew text used by the translator. The original translation of Exodus would thus have been shorter and would not have contained the problematic passages. That the second section or part of it was not by the same translator as the first section was thought to be proved by differences in the Greek terminology used for the various details of the tabernacle. And once this unknown, later, second translator-editor had been brought on stage, all the worst things could be blamed on him.

The latest extensive study on our problem, D. W. Gooding's, *The Account of the Tabernacle*,[2] goes through the evidence in great detail and corrects many errors of the past. The most important result of this study concerns the variations in the translation of technical terms. According to Gooding, this variation is not indicative of different translators but is rather a characteristic feature of the translators of the Greek Pentateuch. This means that at least most of the second section comes from the same translator as the first section and the rest of Exodus. But from the translator's freedom in variation of terminology, Gooding further concludes that also the minuses in the second section can be attributed to the carelessness of this translator and to his impatience with the repetition of technical details. As for the order of the Greek text, Gooding regards it as the result of rearrangement by a later editor. This editor he also holds responsible for the contradictions of Ch 38.

Needless to say, I cannot agree with Gooding's final solution, which in my opinion is based on a false idea of what can be expected from the LXX translators. I also find it difficult to assume such large scale editorial activity on the Greek text early enough not to be witnessed by the extant manuscripts and contradictory to the known recensional activity that had the MT - or a text very close to it - as its criterion as well as to the attitudes expressed in the *Ep. Arist.* What we need now is a new reading of the Greek text with more understanding and fewer assumptions. This is my first point.

And now the second: theories concerning the translating and editing of the Greek text have been so attractive that almost no serious attention has been paid to the possibility of a different Hebrew *Vorlage*. According to Gooding, "it seems unnecessary ... when so many of the Greek's peculiarities can definitely be traced to the Greek translator and editor."[3] Nevertheless, what scholars of the Hebrew text tell us about the different strata of the source P and strata later than P in the tabernacle account is not irrelevant to our problem and ought not to be disregarded. In the first section, the existence of later additions is obvious, and the second section itself is considered to be altogether later than the first section. Part of the second section, which uses the phrase "as the Lord commanded Moses," is generally regarded as earlier than the rest of the second section. Thus, we must regard

the whole account of the tabernacle as the outcome
of gradual growth, textual and editorial growth
that may have carried on for some time.[4]

For this reason, it is necessary to ask: how
did both the Hebrew and the Greek texts come into
existence and what is their relationship to one
another? To find a better solution to our problem
one must assume less about the Greek text and
translator and more about the Hebrew. In short,
the *Vorlage* of the LXX must be taken more
seriously into consideration. My discussion of
the problem begins with a report of my reading of
the Greek text and ends with a suggestion for a
theory concerning the relationship between the
Hebrew and the Greek texts.

Translation technique. The LXX translators
must always be discussed as individuals, book by
book, including the translator of Exodus. In the
various translation-technical studies which
describe the translators' way of handling
typically Hebrew syntactical phenomena, Exodus has
proved to be one of the most freely translated
books in the LXX and one of those in which the
requirements of Greek idiom have been best taken
into account. This translator was capable of
using free renderings that are perfectly
appropriate in their context, but he also used
literal renderings. He was capable of changing
grammatical construction in order better to meet
the requirements of Greek, but he did not always
do so. He was free enough to change the word-
order of the original, but, actually, most of the
time he followed the original word-order. He
could add and omit words and grammatical items,

but he obviously did not do so out of indifference or carelessness. Even in the free renderings he mostly proves to be faithful to the original. He may be characterized as a competent translator, one of the best, but still not perfect. He made his mistakes too.[5]

Does this characterization fit the second section of the tabernacle account as well? It is very difficult to compare this section with the rest of Exodus or with any other text, because its contents and form are so uniquely monotonous, almost the mere listing of technical details. It is hard to find phenomena that appear throughout Exodus frequently enough to make a full comparison possible. For this reason, I shall confine myself to presenting a few scattered examples of free translation from these chapters, examples that go with the description above.

One of the indicators of free translation and consideration for the Greek idiom is the use of the Greek participial constructions the *part. coni.* and the *gen. abs.* The former is found in the rendering of a coordinate clause in (1) Exod 35:10 καὶ πᾶς σοφὸς τῇ καρδίᾳ ἐν ὑμῖν ἐλθὼν ἐργαζέσθω - וכל חכם לב בכם יבאו ויעשו (SP יבוא ועשה). (Another example is found at 40:20).[6] The *gen. abs.* appears as the rendering of the Hebrew ב + *inf. cstr.*, along with another good rendering of the same idiom, a subordinate clause, in (2) Exod 38:27 εἰσπορευομένων αὐτῶν εἰς τὴν σκηνὴν τοῦ μαρτυρίου ἢ ὅταν προσπορεύωνται πρὸς τὸ θυσιαστήριον λειτουργεῖν, ἐνίπτοντο ἐξ αὐτοῦ - 40:32 בבאם אל אהל מועד ובקרבתם אל המזבח ירחצו.

(Another case of a subordinate clause as the rendering of ב + *inf. cstr.* is 40:36).⁷

A change of construction from coordination to subordination, another feature of free rendering, can be observed in (3) Exod 36:28 ἵνα μὴ χαλᾶται τὸ λογεῖον ἀπὸ τῆς ἐπωμίδος - 39:21 ולא יזח החשן מעל האפד.⁸

In the rendering of relative clauses there is a change to a nominal expression in (4) Exod 36:2 πάντας τοὺς ἑκουσίως βουλομένους - כל אשר נשאר לבו, and a good example of correct handling of a preposition in (5) Exod 35:24 καὶ παρ' οἷς εὑρέθη - וכל אשר נמצא אתו.⁹

The Greek verb ἔχειν is not very common in the LXX, because it has no equivalent in Hebrew. Two examples - out of seven in Exodus - are, nevertheless, found in our text: (6) Exod 36:2 πάντας τοὺς ἔχοντας τὴν σοφίαν - כל איש חכם לב (N.B. the omission of איש); and (7) Exod 36:30 ᾧ ἂν ἔχον κύκλῳ τὸ περιστόμιον ἀδιάλυτον - 39:23 שפה לפיו סביב לא יקרע.¹⁰

The last example also contains the free rendering ἀδιάλυτον corresponding to a Hebrew clause.¹¹ Further examples of free formulations that we would include under the title of dynamic equivalence in modern translation are found in (8a) Exod 35:5 πᾶς ὁ καταδεχόμενος τῇ καρδίᾳ - כל נדיב לבו, (8b) Exod 35:22 πᾶς ᾧ ἔδοξεν τῇ διανοίᾳ - כל נדיב לב, (9) Exod 35:31 καὶ ἐνέπλησεν αὐτὸν πνεῦμα θεῖον σοφίας καὶ συνέσεως καὶ ἐπιστήμης πάντων - וימלא אתו רוח אלהים בחכמה בתבונה ובדעת ובכל מלאכה, (10) Exod 36:10 καὶ ἐτμήθη τὰ πέταλα τοῦ χρυσίου τρίχες ὥστε συνυφᾶναι σὺν τῇ ὑακίνθῳ - 39:3 וירקעו את פחי הזהב וקצץ פתילם לעשות בתוך

SEPTUAGINTAL TRANSLATION TECHNIQUES   391

התכלת,[12] and (11) Exod 37:21 'Ελιάβ ... ὃς ἠρχιτεκτόνησεν τὰ ὑφαντὰ καὶ τὰ ῥαφιδευτὰ καὶ ποικιλτικὰ ὑφᾶναι ... - 38:23 --- אהליאב --- חרש וחשב ורקם.

Free renderings like these should not be taken as examples of the carelessness of the translator - no more here than in the case of a modern translator - but rather as evidence of his striving towards natural Greek expressions, expressions that are accurate and appropriate in their context but formally diverge from the original. This very same striving towards idiomatic Greek is characteristic of the whole book of the Greek Exodus, and furthermore, the kinds of free renderings exemplified above are typical of this translator.

As for the rendering of technical terms, about which much has been written, the variation of equivalents actually seldom disturbs the reader. In spite of the variation, the meaning of the whole is preserved in most cases. Sometimes it looks as if the translator tried to find a better equivalent each time a certain word appeared again. Among the weaving terminology and names of the wooden parts of the tabernacle there are many rare words and *hapax legomena*, which show that the translator tried to find the correct words. He seems to have preferred more specific terms rather than general ones. Obviously he had difficulties in picturing for himself what the objects described in these passages actually looked like - just as we have - and it must be admitted that he also made mistakes, e.g., trying to fit in the capitals (κεφαλίδες) either for אדנים or for ווים.

But true to his habits, he did not compare parallel passages or go back to correct and make them even.

Indications of a different Vorlage. In a close reading of the chapters in question one cannot avoid getting the impression that several small details of the Greek text indicate a different *Vorlage*, e.g., (1) Exod 35:3 + ἐγὼ κύριος (cf. 31:13 where the parallel passage contains ὅτι ἐγὼ κύριος ὁ ἁγιάζων ὑμᾶς - כי אני יהוה מקדשכם), (2) Exod 38:4 εὑρεῖς τοῖς διωστῆρσιν ὥστε αἴρειν - 37:5 לשאת (---) (cf. 37:14 בתים לבדים לשאת), (3) Exod 38:5 τὸ ἱλαστήριον ἐπάνωθεν τῆς κιβωτοῦ ἐκ χρυσίου - 37:6 כפרת זהב (cf. 40:20 הכפרת על הארן מלמעלה LXX and 25:21 הכפרת על הארן מלמעלה - τὸ ἱλαστήριον ἐπὶ τὴν κιβωτὸν ἄνωθεν), (4a) Exod 38:9 τὴν τράπεζαν τὴν προκειμένην - 37:10 את השלחן, (4b) Exod 39:17 τὴν τράπεζαν τῆς προθέσεως - 39:36 את השלחן (cf. Num 4:7 על שלחן הפנים - ἐπὶ τὴν τράπεζαν τὴν προκειμένην), (5) Exod 38:13 τὴν λυχνίαν, ᾗ φωτίζει - 37:17 את המנרה (cf. 35:14 את מנרת המאור - τὴν λυχνίαν τοῦ φωτός and Num 4:9 את מנרת המאור - τὴν λυχνίαν τὴν φωτίζουσαν[13]). It is hard to see why a translator would have added features like these. A further example of a different *Vorlage* could be seen in that the table is described as golden - not only overlaid with gold - both in Exod 25:23 and 38:9.[14]

In several cases the Greek text reads in small details with the SP, against the MT, e.g., (6) Exod 40:17 ἐκπορευομένων αὐτῶν ἐξ Αἰγύπτου - SP לצאתם ממצרים (>MT), (7) both the SP and the LXX lack Exod 35:14 ראה נרתיה, 38:25 בשקל הקדש (LXX 39:2), (8) Exod 38:4 ὥστε αἴρειν αὐτὴν ἐν αὐτοῖς -

37:5 MT לשאת את הארן, SP לשאת את הארן בהם,
(9) Exod 37:15 καὶ αἱ ἀγκύλαι αὐτῶν ἀργυραῖ –
38:17 MT וווי העמודים וחשוקיהם כסף, SP כסף ווויהם.
A further interesting feature, although not necessarily indicating interdependence, is that both the SP and the LXX use verb forms in the plural in the section of the priests' vestments 36:8-38LXX/39:1-31MT, whereas the MT vacillates between the singular and the plural.[15]

Thus, it seems that there were differences in the *Vorlage*, and that the translator reproduced even small details of it. Why should the minuses then be his own work? As far as I know this translator, I refuse to believe that he had a Hebrew text like the MT which he then abbreviated, not to mention his rearranging it. I cannot see why he should have taken such trouble. Why would he have left out the making of the altar of incense, precisely the object that has been added later to the whole? Why would he have been more accurate in the translation of the "as the Lord commanded"-section, precisely the part that is considered to be older than the rest of the second section? There are too many coincidences. And what is most important, it is difficult to find motives for a translator undertaking such troublesome changes to the original. I cannot see that the translator would have done anything more than translate his *Vorlage*.

But still there is something that requires explanation in the οὗτος-section Exod 38:18-26, the report of the metal work. It is not hard to imagine how this section would look in the Hebrew. What is difficult is to see how a passage with ten openings by the pronoun הוא and the perfect tense would stylistically fit into the chapters in question. This style is highly exceptional, but perhaps still not absolutely impossible in Hebrew. The closest parallels I can find are 2 Kgs 14:7, 22, 25; 15:35; 18:4, 8, which tell about the achievements of various kings during their reign. However, if it is difficult to accept this style in Hebrew, it is at least as difficult to try to explain why anyone would have created this οὗτος-style in Greek. Another difficulty in this section is the series of contradictions with information given in other chapters, which Gooding stresses. Be it in Hebrew or in Greek, the only possible explanation for this section is that someone filled it in, because he thought that the account was lacking something, viz. parts of the frame-work of the tabernacle and the making of the copper altar and the copper laver. Whether in Hebrew or in Greek, this hand was a rather late one and not one that could be praised for his skill. I would prefer to regard these verses as an addition in the Hebrew *Vorlage*.

The relationship of the two texts to one another. Now, supposing that the translator of the Greek Exodus translated his *Vorlage* rather faithfully, we have two different Hebrew versions of the second section of the tabernacle account to compare with one another. The next question is: which one can more easily be explained relative to the other? Since they have so much in common, they must have a common origin. One of them abbreviates or the other adds and fills in. One of them moves items in one direction or the other

one in the opposite direction. We should perhaps
not speak of an original text and a secondary text
in this connection, but rather of a more primitive
edition and a developed edition. Which is which?
This must be decided by answering the question:
what has been the motive behind the development?

If we compare the two versions of the second
section with the first section, the section of
instructions, the one that differs more from the
instructions is the one represented by the LXX,
whereas the MT repeats most of the details of the
first section. In my judgment, the MT is the more
developed text, and its development was motivated
by the idea that the realization of the tabernacle
in all its detail should correspond to the
instructions. This is a motive powerful enough
for all the changes made, filling in measurements
and details and changing the order of items. It
would be more difficult to motivate changes in the
opposite direction, towards greater divergence
between the sections.

Furthermore, regarding the version found in the
LXX as more primitive helps us to understand why
it is such as it is. Actually, it would have been
natural for the report of the building of the
tabernacle to proceed in quite a different order
from that in the instructions, in an order according to the workers and the materials. And the
report could have been much briefer than the
instructions, more like a summary. Indeed, it
would have been enough to say that they did "as
the Lord commanded Moses."

As a matter of fact, such a summary can be
found in Ch 39. Altogether there are five

summaries that list the parts of the tabernacle and its furniture (Exod 31:7-11; 35:11-19; 39:13-23LXX/39:33-43MT; 40:1-16; 40:18-33), and in all five there are differences between the MT and the LXX. The summary in Ch 39 is most interesting, because in it M. Noth discovered features that connect it with the original P, particularly in the concluding remark: "According to all that the Lord had commanded Moses, so the people of Israel had done all the work. And Moses saw all the work, and behold, they had done it; as the Lord commanded, so they had done it. And Moses blessed them" (vv 42-43).[16] In the LXX this summary appears in a more primitive form than in the MT: it lacks the altar of incense and the copper laver. This kind of a summary would have been possible in the phase when the first section only contained Chs 25-28.

According to Noth, the absence of an incense altar from the source P was due to conscious opposition to foreign cults.[17] In the MT the second section as well as all the summaries presuppose Chs 30-31 and the existence of the incense altar in the first section. Thus, no part of the second section in the MT could have formed the second section in P.[18] The second section of the LXX, on the other hand, does not report construction of the incense altar, and two of the summaries, those in Chs 39 and 35, lack both the incense altar and the copper laver, whereas the two lists in Ch 40 lack the copper laver, but mention the golden incense altar. The various summaries in the LXX seem to represent different stages in the development of the text, but in the

MT, the very uniformity of the summaries is a sign of deliberate editing of the text.

Another interesting feature of the text of Ch 39 represented by the LXX is that it does not mention the wooden frames of the tabernacle. It would not be surprising, if this were also a primitive feature. With the wooden frames inside and the various coverings over the tabernacle, the fine woven curtains decorated with cherubim would have been invisible for the most part. The normal way to put up a tent would have been with the aid of pillars, cords and pegs, and these are all present in the summary of Ch 39.[19]

It is difficult to say exactly which details would have belonged to the first edition of the second section, but it seems probable that there was a short, early form of it, to go with the shorter form of the first section, still lacking Chs 30-31. Perhaps it contained a report of the collecting of materials and the calling of workers (Ch 35) and then a summary of the work like that in Ch 39. Since the report of the making of the priests' vestments is part of the "as the Lord commanded"-section and very similar in the MT and the LXX, it may have been one of the first constituents of the second section. But then more and more details of the first section were repeated in the second section, features were added to the first section and these again gradually repeated at several points of the second section.[20] The text of the *Vorlage* of the LXX actually represented a halfway phase in the development. It was incomplete and inconsistent and had perhaps also suffered in the hands of scribes. Through editorial additions, harmonizations and rearrangements the development was brought to an end in the MT, but in a way that had changed the nature of the second section from a report of the work done to a repetition of the instructions in the past tense.[21]

The LXX thus represents an earlier phase in the development of the text. But which text could be called the original text? The situation is complicated by the fact that the differences were not caused by textual development or corruption. It is a matter of definition, whether one wishes to call the final result of editing the original text or rather to attach this label to that which is chronologically earlier. As a matter of fact, none of the texts in the OT are original in the sense that they have not been edited. So, it is possible to regard the MT as the original finished product.

To conclude, in cases of divergence between the MT and the LXX, we usually ask whether they have resulted from the free translation or a different Hebrew *Vorlage*. We seldom come to think that these two do not exclude one another. Since they are not alternatives, it is possible to have both free translation and a different *Vorlage* in the same text. And this is the case in the tabernacle account.

NOTES

1. See the present writer's "Translation Technique and the Intention of the Translator," *VII Congress of IOSCS*, Leuven 1989, to be published in SCS (Scholars Press) 1991.

2. D. W. Gooding, *The Account of the Tabernacle Translation and Textual Problems of the Greek Exodus* (TextsS New Series 6; Cambridge: Cambridge University Press, 1959). For a review of earlier research, see Gooding's pp. 3-7, and *La Bible d'Alexandrie: L'Exode,* Traduction du texte grec de la Septante, Introduction et Notes par A. le Boulluec & P. Sandevoir (Paris: Cerf, 1989) 61-67.

3. Gooding, *Account*, 99 n. 1. For criticism of this attitude, see the present writer's "What Can We Know about the Hebrew *Vorlage* of the Septuagint?" *ZAW* 99 (1987) 68-69.

4. See e.g., B. Baentsch, *Exodus-Leviticus* (HKAT 1/2; Göttingen: Vandenhoeck & Ruprecht, 1900) 286-87; N. Noth, *Das zweite Buch Mose, Exodus* (ATD 5; 8th ed.; Göttingen: Vandenhoeck & Ruprecht, 1988) 187-188, 192-197, 220-221; R. Smend, *Die Entstehung des Alten Testaments* (Theologische Wissenschaft 1; 2nd ed.; Stuttgart-Berlin-Köln-Mainz: Kohlhammer, 1981) 46, 48, 51-52. - I am grateful to Prof. Arie van der Kooij for drawing my attention to the work of his predecessor a hundred years ago, *viz.* Abraham Kuenen, *An Historico-Critical Inquiry into the Origin and Composition of the Hexateuch* (translated from the Dutch, with the Assistance of the Author, by P. H. Wicksteed, London: Macmillan, 1886). Kuenen already saw in the divergencies of the Septugintal version reason to "suspect that the final redaction of these chapters was hardly completed - if indeed completed - when that translation was made, i.e., about 250 B.C." (p. 73). He rejected the theory of two successive translators which was put forward by his contemporary J. Popper (*Der biblische Bericht über die Stiftshütte* [Leipzig: Hunger, 1862]), because "we have no right to place the original Greek translator between the composition of *Ex.* xxxix., xl. (+*Lev.* viii.) and the compilation of

xxxvi.-xxxviii." (p. 80), an opinion still worth noting.

5. For a characterization of this translator and examples of his technique, see the present writer's article in *ZAW* 99 (1987) 71-77. A similar picture of this translator is given by J. E. Sanderson, *An Exodus Scroll from Qumran* (HSM 30; Atlanta: Scholars Press, 1986) 247-55.

6. Cf. the present writer's *Parataxis in the Septuagint* (AASF [=Annales Academiae Scientiarum Fennicae] B Diss 31; Helsinki: Suomalainen Tiedeakatemia, 1982) 88-109.

7. Cf. I. Soisalon-Soininen, *Die Infinitive in der Septuaginta* (AASF B 132; Helsinki: Suomalainen Tiedeakatemia, 1965) 80-93, 188-90.

8. Cf. the present writer's *Parataxis*, 68-72, 179.

9. Cf. Soisalon-Soininen, "The Rendering of the Hebrew Relative Clause in the Greek Pentateuch," *Studien zur Septuaginta-Syntax* (ed., A. Aejmelaeus & R. Sollamo; AASF B 237; Helsinki: Suomalainen Tiedeakatemia, 1987) 55-61.

10. Cf. Soisalon-Soininen, "Der Gebrauch des Verbs ἔχειν in der Septuaginta," *Studien zur Septuaginta-Syntax*, 181-88.

11. Cf. Exod 25:15 ἀκίνητοι - לא יסרו ממנו.

12. Cf. Soisalon-Soininen, *Die Infinitive*, 54; the use of ὥστε with a final infinitive, instead of τοῦ, seems to be a characteristic of Exod.

13. 4QLXXNum reads here τη]ς φαυσεως, the *b*-group του φωτος. Whichever is the original text in Num 4:9 - Prof Eugene Ulrich in his paper attaches great importance to 4QLXXNum - the plus in Exod 38:13 fits well among the renderings of מָאוֹר.

14. Cf. J. W. Wevers, *Notes on the Greek Text of Exodus* (SCS 30; Atlanta: Scholars Press, 1990), which I was able to consult only after finishing this paper. Wevers does not regard the above examples as indications of a different *Vorlage* (for Exod 25:23 p. 402; 35:3 p. 575; 38:4, 5, p. 621; 38:9 p. 622).

15. For the relation between the LXX and the SP, see Sanderson, *An Exodus Scroll*, 256-57.

16. Noth, *Exodus*, 225-26.

17. Noth, *Exodus*, 192-93.

18. See also Baentsch, *Exodus-Leviticus*, 286-87.

19. Noth is suspicious about the wooden frames of the tabernacle, but finds the text homogeneous; see *Exodus*, 172.

20. Some features (e.g., the mention of the workers in Ch 31) may even have been added to the first section in anticipation of the second.

21. Kuenen, *An Historico-Critical Inquiry*, 73, already saw the development in a very similar way.

THE TABERNACLE ACCOUNT
Sec.I Exod 25-31 MT = LXX

Ch 25   ark and mercy-seat
        table (LXX: golden)
        lampstand.
Ch 26   tabernacle of ten curtains
        tent over the tabernacle
        wooden frames for the tabernacle
        veil and its 4 pillars
        door-screen and its 5 pillars
Ch 27   altar (for burnt offering)
        court with its hangings and pillars
        olive oil for lamp
Ch 28   priests' vestments
Ch 29   ordination of priests
Ch 30   altar of incense
        atonement money
        copper laver
        anointing oil
        incense
Ch 31   calling of Bezalel and Oholiab

Sec.II Exod 36-40 MT   Sec.II Exod 36-40 LXX

Ch 36   Bezalel and Oholiab start   Ch 36   Bezalel and Oholiab start
                                                       priests' vestments
        tabernacle of 10 curtains   Ch 37   tabernacle of 10 curtains
        tent over tabernacle
        wooden frames for the tabernacle
        veil and its 4 pillars   veil and its 4 pillars
        door-screen and its 5 pillars   door-screen and its 5 pillars
                                                       court with its hangings and
                                                       pillars
Ch 37   ark and mercy-seat   Ch 38   ark and mercy-seat
        table overlaid with gold   golden table
        lampstand   lampstand
        altar of incense
        anointing oil and incense
                                                       report of metalwork including:
                                                       copper altar
Ch 38   altar of of burnt offering   anointing oil and incense
                                                       copper laver
        copper laver
        court with its hangings and
        pillars
        inventory of metals used   Ch 39   inventory of metals used
Ch 39   priests' vestments
        list of finished work   list of finished work
Ch 40   list of items to be erected   Ch 40   list of items to be erected
        list of items having been   list of items having been
        erected   erected

281 BCE:
THE YEAR OF THE TRANSLATION OF THE
PENTATEUCH INTO GREEK UNDER PTOLEMY II

NINA COLLINS

Most scholars today consider that the Pentateuch was translated into Greek some time before the middle of the third century BCE.[1] Using previously neglected testimony from the Church Fathers, this discussion will suggest the precise year.

Firstly, in order to identify the likely period of the event, the literary accounts will be briefly surveyed. This will enable an evaluation of the various dates given by sources which place the translation in a definite year. Those that fall around the period implied by the literary accounts will be more closely examined, especially in relation to the start of the reign of Ptolemy II. An explanation of their differences will show that all refer back to a single year, when the Greeks commemorated the translation of the Law. From this will follow the date remembered by the Jews. Two further problems relating to the translation will then be discussed. This will reveal the use of two kinds of sources for early accounts of the translation of the Law.

THE LITERARY EVIDENCE - WHICH KING WAS INVOLVED?

The most famous of the many literary accounts concerning a translation of the Pentateuch into Greek is preserved in the document entitled the *Letter of Aristeas*.[2] Although some of the historical details in this work have been questioned, and several probable errors observed,[3] most scholars accept its broad outline of events.[4] These include a report of the liberation of Jewish slaves who were originally brought to Egypt by Ptolemy I, also called Lagus, the father of the King. Aristeas thus sets the translation in the reign of Ptolemy II, the son and successor of Ptolemy I, whom he further identifies as Ptolemy,[6] the son of Lagus,[7] the husband of Arsinoë, his sister-wife.[8]

Aristeas himself hints that other Greek versions of the Pentateuch were made before the version he describes.[9] However, only later accounts of the translation are extant. These give the same basic story as Aristeas, and it is with these that the present discussion is concerned. Many of them also attest the link with Ptolemy II, often called Philadelphus.[10] One only, the account of the philosopher Aristobulus, is probably independent of Aristeas.[11] Others, such as Josephus,[12] and the literary account of

281 BCE: THE YEAR OF THE TRANSLATION

Eusebius,[13] may be almost totally derived from Aristeas. Yet others, for example, Philo[14] and Justin Martyr,[15] may have used him in part. All in all, although independence from Aristeas is difficult to prove and the identity of the king is often unclear, a possible total of up to thirty-four sources state or imply that the Law was translated under Ptolemy II.[16]

A lesser number of authorities, four probably reliable and others less so, claim that the translation was made under the father of Philadelphus, Ptolemy I, also called Soter.[17] These can not be wholly dependent on Aristeas, because the latter refers only to Ptolemy II. Some authors note also that Demetrius of Phalerum was involved in the work.[18] According to Diogenes Laertius, Demetrius was sheltered by Ptolemy I, but was "imprisoned in the country" after this King had died.[19] Thus, if the translation was made while Soter was alive, the presence of Demetrius is not in dispute. But if Diogenes is correct, Demetrius was not active after Soter's death, when Philadelphus was King. Yet, though the majority of sources claim that the translation was made under Ptolemy II, no scholar has rejected Demetrius' role.

More confusion is caused by the philosopher Aristobulus, who states that the translation was made when Soter was alive, although Philadelphus was King.[20] Similarly, Clement of Alexandria implies that either Soter or Philadelphus was King at the time.[21] Both authors mention the role of Demetrius, but neither can be wholly dependent on Aristeas. There are even two sources which place the translation outside the reigns of Soter or his son.[22]

Can any of this evidence be reconciled?

If we consider the weight of the testimony as a whole, the answer is yes. Since most of the witnesses involve Soter or his son, and two even involve both, it appears that in some way (not yet known), both Kings were connected with the translation of the Law. Only one period reasonably fits this description, namely, the time around the succession, when Philadelphus replaced Soter, his father, on the throne. With this working hypothesis, it would appear that the statements of most witnesses can probably be reconciled.[23]

Let us now turn to the sources which place the translation in a definite year. These are listed below in two groups: [1] Those dating the event early in the reign of Philadelphus, which began around 285 BCE;[24] [2] The remaining sources, which give a range of dates, outside or late in Philadelphus' reign. This King died in 246 BCE.

[1] SOURCES DATING THE TRANSLATION EARLY IN PHILADELPHUS' REIGN

1. Eusebius, Latin *Chronicle*: "in the reign of Philadelphus, 2nd year of the 124th Olympiad" (July 283 to July 282 BCE)[25]

2. Epiphanius, *Weights and Measures* (Syriac): "in the 7th year of Philadelphus, more or less"[26]

3. Cyril of Alexandria, *Contra Iulianum* I 16: "the 124th Olympiad" (July 284 to July 279 BCE)[27]

4. Zacharias of Mitylene, *The Syriac Chronicle*: "280 years and more before the birth of our Lord", citing Eusebius' *Chronicle*[28]

281 BCE: THE YEAR OF THE TRANSLATION

5. Bar Hebraeus, *The Chronography*: "in the 6th year of Philadelphus"[29]

6. Eusebius, *Syriac & Armenian Chronicle*: "year 1737 of Abraham" (autumn 279 to autumn 278 BCE)[30]

7. Michael the Syrian, *Chronicle*: "5th year of Philadelphus, the 125th Olympiad"[31]

[2] REMAINING SOURCES, WHOSE DATE IS OUTSIDE OR LATE IN PHILADELPHUS' REIGN

(A) AFTER HIS REIGN:

1. John Chrysostom: "100 years or more before the birth of Christ"[32]

2. Pseudo-Athanasius: "230 years before the birth of Christ"[33]

(B) BEFORE HIS REIGN:

1. Nicetas of Heraclea: "301 years before the birth of Christ"[34]

2. Pseudo-Theodoretus: "301 years before the coming of Christ"[35]

(C) LATE IN HIS REIGN:

1. Georgius Syncellus: "the 132nd Olympiad" (July 252 to July 248 BCE)[36]

The literary evidence reviewed briefly above suggests that the date of the translation falls around the time when Philadelphus replaced his father as King. It can be seen that the dates in Group [1] above fall sufficiently close to this time to account - in theory - for the conflicting attributions of the literary works, although none of them fall in the reign of Ptolemy I. Moreover, whereas the seven sources in Group [1] give a date for the translation early in the reign of Ptolemy II, the five others in Group [2] give a wide range of dates - two after the reign of Philadelphus, two before his reign and one well into his reign. Thus, since in general, the more united testimony of the majority of witnesses is slightly to be preferred, but chiefly from the weight of evidence of the literary accounts (although it may ultimately be shown that few are based on a primary source), the following discussion will focus on the testimony of the seven authorities in Group [1].

THE CHRONOLOGICAL SYSTEMS OF THE SOURCES

The sources quoted above use four basic methods to indicate their dates - Olympiads, years of Abraham, years before Christ and regnal years of a king. In Ptolemaic times, regnal years were recorded in Macedonian or Egyptian years. It is obvious that these dates can be understood only if the simple principles behind their calculation are known. These are set out below.

1. Olympiads and Olympiad Years[37]

Olympiad years followed the Attic year, each year beginning and ending at the first new moon after the summer solstice. For the early years of Ptolemy II, the year began at the beginning of July.[38]

With this system, the time between the accession of a king and the beginning of an Olympiad year was suppressed (that is, not counted), and Olympiad Year 1 of a new king was reckoned from the first full Olympiad year which followed his accession. In practice therefore, the Olympiad year when the ruler died was added to

281 BCE: THE YEAR OF THE TRANSLATION   409

the reign of the dead king, even though he may have lived for only part of this year.

One Olympiad consisted of four Olympiad years. The first Olympiad began at the first Olympic festival in 776 BCE.[39] The precise year of an event is expressed with reference to the 1st, 2nd, 3rd or 4th year of a numbered Olympiad. The number of each year within each Olympiad should not be confused with the Olympiad regnal years of a king, especially with the first four years of his reign, since there are four years in each Olympiad. The Olympiad years of a king begin at the accession of each king, and are thus independent of the *continuous* passage of Olympiad dates. For example, in Diagram 5 (below), the 2nd Olympiad year of the reign of Ptolemy II is reckoned from the start of the co-regency in December 285, and this falls in the 2nd year of the 124th Olympiad. In Diagram 6, the 2nd Olympiad year of the reign of Philadelphus is reckoned from the *end* of the co-regency and falls in the 4th year of the 124th Olympiad.

2. Egyptian Regnal Years[40]

Regnal years were reckoned from Thoth 1 to Thoth 1, the first day of the Egyptian new year. The partial year between the accession of a king and the following Thoth 1 was counted as one whole year, as if it were reckoned from Thoth 1 that preceded the accession of the king. The partial year between the death of a king and the following Thoth 1 was suppressed (not counted). For the years 285-280 BCE, Thoth 1 fell on the 1st or 2nd of November, that is, near the end of a Julian year.[41]

3. Macedonian Regnal Years[42]

The regnal year of a king began on the date of accession and each regnal year began and ended with the anniversary of that event. The period between the beginning of a regnal year and the death of a king (assuming he did not die on the anniversary of his rule) was counted as one regnal year. As a result, the total number of Macedonian regnal years gradually exceeded the number of concurrent Olympiad and Egyptian (and Julian) years.

4. Years of Abraham[43]

The first year of Abraham started with the birth of Abraham in the Hebrew autumn month of Tishri, and each year began and ended at the annual anniversary of his birth. The year of Abraham 1240 corresponds with the first year of the first Olympiad 776/5 BCE. When years of Abraham are used to count regnal years, the count of regnal years begins with the first full year of Abraham after the accession of the king, as for Olympiad regnal years.[44]

5. The Years before Christ

This system used simple Olympiad years, which were counted backwards from the birth of Christ. (The similar system in use today was introduced by Petavius in 1627 CE). The exact Julian year of a date thus depends on the year assumed for the birth of Christ.[45]

281 BCE: THE YEAR OF THE TRANSLATION

The span of the different chronological years is compared below:

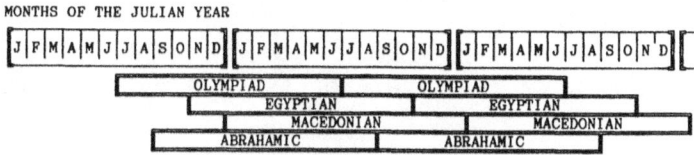

DIAGRAM 1: THE RELATIONSHIP BETWEEN OLYMPIAD, EGYPTIAN, MACEDONIAN & ABRAHAMIC YEARS IN THE EARLY REIGN OF PTOLEMY II

There are two points to consider when reckoning the length of the reign of a king, according to his regnal years: (1) What was the date that marked the limits of a whole regnal year? This was measured from one date in the year to the same date in the following year. (2) How did the system deal with partial years of a reign? Were these counted or suppressed (not counted)? A partial year could occur [a] at the beginning of a reign, between the accession of a king and the start of a new regnal year and [b] at the death of a king, between his death and the start of a new regnal year.

The description of specific chronological years above shows that the Egyptian system counted the partial year at the beginning of a reign as a whole regnal year and suppressed the partial year at the end. The Olympiad system suppressed the partial year at the beginning of a reign and counted the partial year at the end as a whole regnal year. The Macedonian system did not have a partial year at the beginning of a reign because the regnal year began (and ended) on the date of accession. The last partial year of a king was the period between the start of his last regnal year (the annual anniversary of the date of his accession) and his death, which was counted as a whole regnal year.

THE REGNAL YEARS OF PHILADELPHUS UP TO HIS 13TH YEAR

One task remains before examining the dates. Since at least two are clearly related to the start of Philadelphus' reign (the dates of Epiphanius and Bar Hebraeus), it is important to know how, and from when, the King counted the length of his reign. This is particularly urgent in relation to the start of the reign of Philadelphus because for the last part of his father's reign, Soter ruled in conjunction with his son.[46] This period has been called a co-regency. It began at the end of December in 285 BCE, and ended over two years later by the 12th March in 282 BCE, when Soter died.[47] It is important to know if the years of this period were numbered with the reign of Soter or with his son.

Contemporary papyri and ancient historians who state the years of his rule show that while Soter was alive, the period of the co-regency was added to Soter's reign.[48] This was accepted at first by Ptolemy II, so that for 13 years after Soter had died, Philadelphus counted the years of his reign from the annual anniversary of Soter's death.[49] Thus, for at least 15 years after the event (that is, from the start of the co-regency, plus the two or so years of the co-regency plus the next 13 years), even Philadelphus did not consider that during the co-regency he was himself King. It appears therefore that between December 285 and March 282, the future King was still subordinate to his father, so that *at the time that it occurred*, the period was not a co-regency in the true sense of the term.

But, as indicated above, a change occurred sometime just before his 13th year when Philadelphus back-dated his reign to the start of the co-regency, thus lengthening his reign with the co-regency years.[50] The back-dating of his reign was probably announced on the annual anniversary of the start of the co-regency. Thereby the Macedonian years of the reign of Philadelphus increased by 3, and the Egyptian years increased by 2.[51]

As a result, sources which come after this change consistently assume that the rule of Philadelphus began from the beginning of the co-regency and not (as is actually the case), from its end. Thus, without exception, ancient historians who state the length of the reign of Philadelphus all claim that the King ruled for 38 Olympiad (or, 39 Macedonian) years. None gives the more accurate 36 Olympiad years. These writers all lived after the King's chronologically significant 13th year, when he back-dated his reign.[52]

However, just as any tyrant who re-writes history after the event (knowing full well the true facts as they stand), Philadelphus could not alter events *as they had occurred*. It is critical therefore that the records of dates before Philadelphus' 13th year are carefully scrutinized, to see if they relate to the start of the co-regency, or to its end.

This observation is fundamental to the argument below. The majority of literary sources give the impression that the translation was made soon after the death of Soter, in the time of the changeover of the Kings, that is, well *before* the original 13th year of Soter's son. This can be seen from the dates in Group [1] above - none of them fall *after* the time of the change. As a result, although the original record of the event was undoubtedly made in relation to the end of the co-regency, it is probable that writers who lived well *after* the 13th year of Philadelphus interpreted the date from the *beginning* of this time.

It is thus necessary to establish the length of the co-regency, as it was measured by Philadelphus, so that the degree of error of these ancient sources is known. This can be done by establishing the dates of events during the regnal years of the King for the first few years after the start of the co-regency. These include the annual anniversaries of his rule which would have been celebrated if the reign of Philadelphus had started at the beginning of the co-regency. These are listed below, with their corresponding Julian months. Further accuracy is not needed, as it is necessary to establish only the relevant chronology of events, and not their absolute dates:

281 BCE: THE YEAR OF THE TRANSLATION

TABLE I - SIGNIFICANT DATES AT THE START OF THE CO-REGENCY[53]

DATES BCE	SIGNIFICANCE OF DATE
I Thoth, 2 Nov 285	First day of Egyptian New Year
24 Dystros, end of Dec 285	Start of co-regency
1 July 284	Start of 1st Olympiad year of 124th Olympiad
1 Thoth, 2 Nov 284	First day of Egyptian New Year
24 Dystros, Jan 283	End of 1st Macedonian year of co-regency
1 July 283	Start of 2nd Olympiad year of 124th Olympiad
1 Thoth, 2 Nov 283	First day of the Egyptian Year before Soter's death
24 Dystros, Jan 282	End of 2nd Macedonian year of co-regency
By 29 Artemisios, mid March 282	Death of Soter
1 July 282	Start of 3rd Olympiad year of 124th Olympiad
24 Dystros, Jan 281	End of 3rd Macedonian year of the co-regency
29 Artemisios, April 281	1st anniversary of Soter's death
24 Dystros, Feb 280	End of 4th Macedonian year of the co-regency
29 Artemisios, April 280	2nd anniversary of Soter's death

These dates and events are arranged horizontally below:

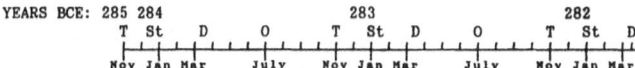

DIAGRAM 2: THE RELATIVE CHRONOLOGY OF EVENTS AND DATES
IN THE CO-REGENCY

Key to the symbols:

T - *Th*oth I, the date of the Egyptian new year, which fell in November,

St - the *St*art and anniversary of the co-regency, which fell around the beginning of the Julian year;

D - the *D*eath of Soter and anniversary of this event, in March/April;

O - the end of the old and start of the new *O*lympiad year on July 1.

Diagram 2 enables us to calculate the length of the co-regency in Macedonian, Egyptian and Olympiad years:

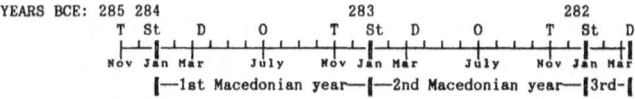

DIAGRAM 3: THE LENGTH OF THE CO-REGENCY IN MACEDONIAN YEARS[54]

Each full Macedonian year starts and ends on the annual anniversary of the co-regency on Dystros 24. It may be noted that unlike the Julian year, the length of successive Macedonian years varied according to their intercalation. Thus, Dystros 24 does not correspond to the same date in successive Julian years.

The 1st Macedonian year of the co-regency extends from the start of the co-regency at the end of December 285 BCE to Jan 283 BCE; the 2nd year, from Jan 283 BCE to Jan 282 BCE. The 3rd Macedonian year is a partial year, from Jan 282 (Dystros 24) till the death of Soter in March 282, and is counted as one whole Macedonian year. The exact date in March is not important, so long as Soter's death took place *before* the next annual anniversary of the co-regency, Dystros 24, which fell in January of 281.

The co-regency thus lasted for 3 Macedonian years.[55]

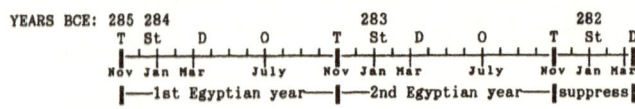

DIAGRAM 4: THE LENGTH OF THE CO-REGENCY IN EGYPTIAN YEARS

The 1st Egyptian year began in November, before the start of the co-regency at the end of December 285 BCE, and ended at the following Thoth 1, November 284 BCE. The 2nd Egyptian year extended from this latter date till Thoth 1, in November 283 BCE. Soter died in March 282, which is before the next Thoth 1, so this last period (a partial year, from Thoth 1 in November 283 BCE till his death) was suppressed (not counted).

The co-regency thus lasted for 2 Egyptian years.[56]

As far as the length of the co-regency in Olympiad years is concerned, the 1st Olympiad year began in the summer after the start of the co-regency, from July 284 to July 283; the 2nd Olympiad year was a partial year, from July 283 to the death of Soter in March 282, but was counted as one whole Olympiad year. This means that co-regency lasted for 2 Olympiad years.[57]

Let us now examine those sources which give a date for the translation early in the years of Ptolemy II, starting with the earliest - the date recorded by Jerome in the Latin *Chronicle* of Eusebius, assuming that Jerome accurately transmits his source.

THE DATE IN JEROME'S LATIN *CHRONICLE* OF EUSEBIUS

The *Chronicle* states that the translation was made when Philadelphus was King, in "the second year of the 124th Olympiad," that is, sometime between July 283 and July 282 BCE.

As discussed above, there are two ways in which this date could be understood - either from the end of the co-regency or from the start. An examination of his evidence shows that Eusebius himself understood the date from the beginning of this time when he states that Ptolemy II ruled for 38 years.[58] This itself is conclusive - the number can be derived only if the years of the co-regency are counted with his reign.[59] A further indication is that Eusebius misplaces the death of Soter by placing this event two years earlier than it occurred so that it falls immediately before the beginning of the reign of Philadelphus. Had he known of the co-regency, the reigns of Soter and Philadelphus would have overlapped.

The *Chronicle* therefore ignores the co-regency, although Eusebius had read Porphyry[60] who records the event.[61] Porphyry also seems unaware of the chronological significance of this time, although his remark that the reign of Soter should be reduced by its length hints of some concern. But this is no surprise - Porphyry and Eusebius lived well over five centuries after Philadelphus had decided that the start of the co-regency marked the start of his rule.[62]

The date of Eusebius must therefore be corrected by reckoning this time in relation to the *end* of the co-regency, rather than from its *start* Thus, instead of counting the years from the start of the co-regency in December in 285 BCE, the count must begin from the death of Soter in March 282.

Firstly, therefore, we must consider the chronology of Eusebius in relation to the beginning of the co-regency rather than its end, in the way that this date was received by Eusebius in Olympiad years. As it now stands, the period covered by Eusebius' date extends from July 283 to July 282. This was originally recorded either in Macedonian or, possibly, Egyptian chronology, but not in Olympiad chronology, as the latter was

281 BCE: THE YEAR OF THE TRANSLATION

invented after the time of Philadelphus.[63] The relationship between (a) the Olympiad year of the translation given by Eusebius and (b) the corresponding Macedonian and Egyptian years in the reign of Philadelphus, reckoned from the beginning of the co-regency, is shown in the shaded areas of the diagram below:

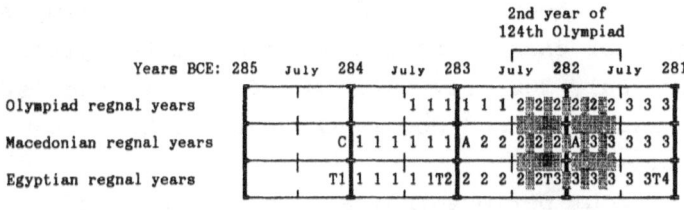

DIAGRAM 5: THE RELATIONSHIP BETWEEN PHILADELPHUS' (A) OLYMPIAD, MACEDONIAN
& EGYPTIAN REGNAL YEARS & (B) THE 2ND YEAR OF THE 124TH OLYMPIAD

The years above are arranged according to Julian years, starting in January and ending in December, Using the dates from Table 1 above in *approximate* positions,

- C refers to the start of the Co-regency at the end of December 285;
- A refers to the yearly Anniversary of the co-regency.
- T indicates Thoth 1, the date of the Egyptian new year.

The shaded area in the diagram above shows that the 2nd Olympiad year of the 124th Olympiad (the date of the translation, according to Eusebius) overlaps the regnal years of Philadelphus in four separate periods.

    (1) The 2nd Macedonian year, from July to A,
    (2) The 3rd Macedonian regnal year, from A to July
    (3) The 2nd Egyptian regnal year, from July to Thoth

(4) The 3rd Egyptian year from Thoth to July.

This shows that when the date of the translation was converted into Olympiad chronology by the source of Eusebius, the latter must have known the month of the event in relation to the start of the Olympiad year - otherwise, it would be impossible to place the date in an exact Olympiad year. For example if the event had taken place before July 282, it would have fallen in the 1st Olympiad year, and not in the 2nd, as Eusebius notes.

The four periods indicated by the date of Eusebius must now be transferred to the *end* of the co-regency, *in the way that the event was recorded before the 13th regnal year of Philadelphus*. This will reveal the relationship between these periods and (a) the years BCE, (b) the month of the death of Soter, and (c) their Olympiad date.

This is shown in the diagram below which differs in the following details from that above: (1) the years under review begin at the end of the co-regency, i.e. from 282 to 280 BCE; (2) D refers to the *D*eath of Soter; (3) d indicates the anniversary of the *d*eath of Soter. The latter marks the moment of change in Philadelphus' Macedonian regnal years, before he back-dated the years of his reign. The four periods of direct interest now fall in the 4th year of the 124th Olympiad:

281 BCE: THE YEAR OF THE TRANSLATION

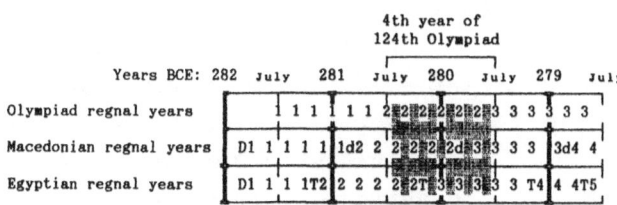

DIAGRAM 6: THE 4 REGNAL PERIODS OVERLAPPING THE 2ND YEAR OF THE 124TH OLYMPIAD, WHEN RECKONED FROM MARCH 282, THE END OF THE CO-REGENCY

The shaded area in the diagram above indicates the four significant periods in the 2nd and 3rd Macedonian and Egyptian years of Philadelphus reckoned from the *end* of the co-regency. These lie:

(1) Between July 281 and March 280, the king's 2nd Macedonian year;

(2) Between April 280 and July 280, the king's 3rd Macedonian year;

(3) Between July 281 and Thoth (November) 281, the king's 2nd Egyptian year;

(4) Between Thoth (November) 281 and July 280, the king's 3rd Egyptian year.

It is not possible at this stage to decide in which of these periods the translation was made. This will emerge from a discussion of the date of Epiphanius, the younger contemporary of Eusebius.

THE DATE OF THE TRANSLATION RECORDED BY EPIPHANIUS

Epiphanius states that the translation was completed "in his (i.e., Philadelphus') seventh year, more or less."[64] What is the significance of the phrase "more or less"?

While discussing the ministry of Jesus, the apologist Justin Martyr (*c*.100-*c*.165 CE) states that Jesus "waited for 30 years, more or less, until John appeared."[65] In the context of the life of Jesus, evidence from other sources suggests that the words "more or less" indicate that Jesus had not yet completed 30 full calendar years. This means that when John appeared, Jesus was less than 30 years old, that is, he was 29 years old plus part of a year.[66] The phrase *more or less* used in conjunction with a number thus refers to the previous integer. On this basis, a baby at birth would be "one, more or less" until his first birthday, when he would be "two, more or less." Otherwise, as far as whole years are concerned, he remains at naught till the first anniversary of his birth.[67] The statement of Epiphanius that the King was in his 7th year "more or less" thus suggests that Philadelphus had not yet completed 7 years of his reign, that is, he was still in year 6 of his reign. Convincing confirmation from antiquity that this is indeed correct comes from the great scholar Bar Hebraeus, who frequently states that he is based on Epiphanius and records that the translation took place in the 6th year of Ptolemy II.[68] Even without the explicit acknowledgement of Hebraeus to Epiphanius, it is difficult to see from where else his date was derived; no other source gives this regnal year.

We must now decide whether or not the date of Epiphanius should be counted from the start of the co-regency or from the end. There are two indications that he counted from the start.

Firstly, Epiphanius (like Eusebius) lived over five centuries after the fiction was established that the reign of Philadelphus began at the start

281 BCE: THE YEAR OF THE TRANSLATION

of the co-regency - no ancient historian contests this fact. It is likely therefore that Epiphanius followed the opinion of Eusebius, his illustrious older contemporary.

Secondly, Epiphanius (like Eusebius) states that Philadelphus reigned for 38 years.[69] This shows conclusively that he counted the reign of Philadelphus from the start of the co-regency, because the number includes the co-regency years.

The date as it now stands in Epiphanius must thus be adjusted to read from the end of the co-regency, as it was originally recorded at the time of the event. This will reduce the regnal year of the date of Epiphanius by the length of time of the co-regency years. The numerical value of this period depends on the method used by Philadelphus to approximate the time of the co-regency to a *whole* number of regnal years, which then could be added to the years of his reign.

The need to decide on a *whole* number of years arises from the simple fact that each annual anniversary (just as, for example, each annual birthday) must mark a *whole* number of years. Should the annual anniversary of the years of a reign add a fraction of a year, apart from the fact that this would not make sense, it would be obvious that the reign had not begun when its incumbent claimed. The method used by Philadelphus to calculate the length of the co-regency has been described above, following Diagrams 3 and 4. These show that this period was reckoned as 2 Egyptian years or as 3 Macedonian years. The increase in Philadelphus' Egyptian regnal years was thus made by the addition of "2" to his Egyptian years, or "3" to his Macedonian years. Contemporary records show clear evidence of such numerical jumps in Philadelphus' Egyptian and Macedonian regnal years.[70]

THE DATES OF EPIPHANIUS AND EUSEBIUS COMPARED & HARMONIZED

A. A Double Date for the Translation of the Law

Eusebius and Epiphanius were contemporaries - Epiphanius was born around 315 CE, when Eusebius was about 55, and was about 25 years old when Eusebius died. Epiphanius moreover cites Eusebius by name[71] and uses information from the *Chronicle* and other books of Eusebius in his own work.[72] However, each transmits a different date for the translation of the Law. This strongly suggests that by the late 3rd century CE, there existed two parallel traditions for this date. It is possible therefore that the dates of Eusebius and Epiphanius represent a double date - the chronologer's gold - and the disparity between them is more apparent than real. If so, a convincing reason must be offered to account for their difference. In fact, this has already been found: if the date of Eusebius is reckoned from the *end* of the co-regency, whereas the date of Epiphanius is taken from the *start*, their values must approach. Thus, if the dates of Eusebius and Epiphanius are adjusted to begin from the same time, it is possible that both may agree.

B. The Back-dating of Years and Events Before 270 BCE

As described above, probably by 270 BCE, in the 13th year of his rule, Philadelphus back-dated his reign counting his years from the end of the co-regency in 282 BCE. From this time, therefore, his Macedonian Year 1 began in December 285. This was the start of the co-regency and the new start of his reign. But what of the *original* Year 1, that began in March 282? In order to avoid the confusion that would occur if different years were given the same number, or different numbers used for the same regnal year, it was necessary *retrospectively* to re-number the regnal years of Philadelphus before his original 13th year, starting from the beginning of the co-regency, in order to conform with the back-dating of his reign. Events were thus kept "in proper sequence and with proper interval."[73] In this way, Philadelphus could claim as his own the prestige for the years of the co-regency and the glory for its events, such as the *megale doxa* promised by Aristeas for the translation of the Law.[74]

After this re-numbering of regnal years, any event which fell within a certain year would be automatically re-dated with the re-numbering of that year. The re-dating of years and events may have arisen unofficially, as a simple convenience in referring to the past. Alternatively, this procedure may have been an official policy of Philadelphus. If so, it was restricted to records under the aegis of the King, or to those to which he had access and of which he knew. The contemporary inscriptions made by the priests of the

Bucheum before the King's 16th regnal year are
examples of records which were out of his
control.[75] Consequently, these were not redated
and thus still reveal the true start of his reign
by counting his years from the *end* of the
co-regency.[76] The date of the translation used by
the source of Eusebius may well be a further
example of a date recorded in its original form.

C. The True Significance of Epiphanius' Date

It is likely, therefore, that when Philadelphus
back-dated the years of his reign, the date of
Epiphanius, "the 6th year of Philadelphus," was
adjusted (i.e., re-dated) from its original lower
value, in order to conform with the new numbering
of the back-dated years. Thus, if the date of
Epiphanius is expressed in Macedonian years, just
as the King added "3" to make up his Macedonian
years (see Diagram 3), this date *originally* noted
that the translation was made in the 3rd Macedonian year of the King (6 minus "3"). Similarly, if
the date of Epiphanius was expressed in Egyptian
years, just as Philadelphus adjusted his Egyptian
years by adding "2," then, the original date of
the translation fell in the King's 4th Egyptian
year (6 minus "2," see Diagram 4).

According to Epiphanius, therefore, the
translation was completed either in the 3rd
Macedonian year or the 4th Egyptian year of
Philadelphus. Of these values, only the 3rd
Macedonian year coincides with one of the four
periods suggested by the date of Eusebius (see
Diagram 6 above). Thus, assuming that the dates
of Eusebius and Epiphanius represent two parallel

281 BCE: THE YEAR OF THE TRANSLATION

transmissions of the original date, the translation of the Law took place in 280 BCE, in the 3rd Macedonian year of Philadelphus, counting from the end of the co-regency. Moreover, it appears that the date of Epiphanius was made in Macedonian (rather than Egyptian) years.

Using the same values to make up the Egyptian or Macedonian years of Philadelphus, a similar but opposite procedure can be followed with Eusebius' date. If this was derived from an original record of events (that is, if the date is reckoned from the *end* of the co-regency), then, "2" must be *added* to the possible Egyptian years, and "3" to the possible Macedonian years. For the numbers of Philadelphus' Egyptian and Macedonian years according to Eusebius, see Diagrams 5 and 6.

In this way, according to Eusebius, the translation took place either in Egyptian years 4 or 5 (2 plus "2," or, 3 plus "2"), or in Macedonian years 5 or 6 (2 plus "3," or, 3 plus "3"). The latter - indicating Philadelphus' 6th Macedonian year - is the only regnal year that agrees with the date of Epiphanius. This indicates that, according to the combined information of Eusebius and Epiphanius, the translation was made in the original (i.e., before the back-dated) 3rd Macedonian year of Philadelphus, which fell in 280/279 BCE.

The combined testimony of Eusebius and Epiphanius enables further precision. The 2nd Olympiad year of Philadelphus' true reign overlaps the 3rd Macedonian year of the King in the year 280, in the period between (a) the anniversary of the death of Soter in April 280 BCE and (b) the beginning of July in 280 BCE (see Table 1 and Diagram 6). The translation was thus made between April and June in 280 BCE.[77]

THE SOURCES OF THE DATES OF EUSEBIUS & EPIPHANIUS

The discussion above suggests the date of the translation transmitted by Epiphanius is derived from a date originally recorded for the event, which was subsequently re-dated, in accordance with the re-dating of Philadelphus' regnal years. Otherwise, it must be assumed that Epiphanius himself adjusted the date. But this is not likely as the change probably occurred around the time that the King back-dated the years of his reign in 270 BCE, six centuries or so before Epiphanius lived. Thus, if the translation was commemorated in 280 BCE, the date of Epiphanius assumed its present value at least 10 years after the event it records.

On the other hand, if Eusebius (or his source) had used the date of Epiphanius, thus claiming that the translation was completed in the 6th year of Philadelphus, then, counting the Macedonian years of the King from the beginning of the co-regency, the event falls in the 125th Olympiad, between January 279 and January 278. This overlaps part of (a) the second half of the first Olympiad year, and (b) the first half of the second Olympiad year. If the month of the event were known, and lies between April and July (as indicated in the harmonization of the dates of Eusebius and Epiphanius above) the date could be placed in the second half of the first year of the 125th Olympiad (between January and July in 279

281 BCE: THE YEAR OF THE TRANSLATION   429

BCE), see Diagram 7 below. However, as Eusebius does not transmit this date, it is clear that he could not have used the same source as Epiphanius.

```
                              July
285    ....................|..................C-M¹
284    M¹-M¹-M¹-M¹-M¹-M¹-M¹ |O¹-M¹-O¹-M¹-O¹-M¹-O¹
283    M¹-A-O¹-M²-O¹-M²-O¹- |M²-O²-M²-O²-M²-O²-M²
282    O²-A-M³-O²-M³-O²-M³- |O³-M³-O³-M³-O³-M³-O³
281    M³-A-O³-M⁴-O³-M⁴-O³- |M⁴-O⁴-M⁴-O⁴-M⁴-O⁴-M⁴
280    M⁴-A-M⁵-O⁴-M⁵-O⁴-M⁵ [St]-O¹-M⁵-O¹-M⁵-O¹-M⁵
279    M⁵-A-O¹-M⁶-O¹-M⁶-O¹- |M⁶-O²-M⁶-O²-M⁶-O²-M⁶
278    M⁶-A-O²-M⁷-O²-M⁷-O²- |M⁷-O³-M⁷-O³-M⁷-O³-M⁷
```
DIAGRAM 7: HOW EUSEBIUS WOULD HAVE INTERPRETED THE DATE OF EPIPHANIUS

Key to symbols:
[St] marks the St̲art of the 125th Olympiad
O^1, O^2 etc., M^1, M^2 etc., indicates successive years of O̲lympiad or M̲acedonian years, from the start of the co-regency. The Olympiad years are numbered according to their position in a specific Olympiad. Thus, the series M^6-O^1-M^6-O^1-M^6-O^1-M^6 etc. indicates the overlap of the 6th M̲acedonian year and the 1st O̲lympiad year of the 125th Olympiad.
C marks the start of the C̲o-regency
A marks the A̲nniversary of the start of the C̲o-regency
The 6th Macedonian year of Philadelphus is underlined

From where was the date of Eusebius derived? As Eusebius himself used Olympiad dates, it is possible that his date originates from an earlier Olympiad chronicle complied by Eratosthenes, who appears to have invented Olympiad chronology.[78] Eratosthenes arrived in Alexandria after 246 BCE (after the death of Philadelphus), when he was about 30 years old, at the invitation of Euergetes to tutor his son.[79] It is reasonable to assume that while in Alexandria, he had access to official Ptolemaic records and thereby saw an original record of the date the translation. This stated that the work was commemorated in the third Macedonian regnal year of the King, sometime between the Macedonian months corresponding with April (the anniversary of Soter's death in the month of Artemisios) and the summer solstice around July 1. Eratosthenes then converted this date into Olympiad years, and, believing that the rule of Philadelphus began from the beginning of the co-regency, started the count of regnal years from the beginning of this time. There is little doubt that the back-dated length of the reign of Philadelphus was well established by the time the King died.[80] This would account for Eratosthenes' mistake when he converted the date of the translation into Olympiad chronology. Furthermore, as the number of each Olympiad year changes after the summer solstice (in practice, after the 1st July), just as the number of the Julian year changes on January 1st, a record of the month of the event enabled him to place the translation in an exact year. If the original record of the date of the event had not included the exact month, it is possible that Eratosthenes (and subsequently, Eusebius), would have been obliged to date the translation less accurately, perhaps in the broader period of the four years of the 124th Olympiad.

The basic difference between the dates of Epiphanius and Eusebius thus lies in the fact that, whereas Epiphanius is transmitting a year which was re-dated from its contemporary date (in order to conform with the re-numbered years after the back-dating of the King's reign), the date of Eusebius is a direct reflection of the true date of the event as it was originally recorded. The date used by Eusebius thus represents an original record of an event which occurred before the true 13th year of the King in 270 BCE. Unlike the date

281 BCE: THE YEAR OF THE TRANSLATION

of Epiphanius, the date of Eusebius was not re-dated when the King back-dated his reign.

This means that the date of Eusebius refers to an event that actually took place. Otherwise, there is no significance in the contemporary record of events. It can hardly be imagined that the Ptolemaic regime would note the date of a contemporary event which had not occurred. Neither is it likely that a Hellenistic chronographer anticipated an essential need of the future Christian Church by inventing the date of the translation of the Law (although, subsequently, the Church provided the framework in which this date was preserved). In short, a true understanding of the dates of Eusebius and Epiphanius confirms the historical fact, evident from the very existence of the Greek Pentateuch and the language in which it is composed, that a translation of the Law was made and commemorated in the first half of the 3rd century BCE, in the reign of Ptolemy II. This is independently confirmed by the many literary accounts of the translation, which also add further details of the event. The dates of Eusebius and Epiphanius thus endorse the basic historicity of Aristeas and the literary accounts.

It is clear, therefore, that Eusebius and Epiphanius each used two separate sources for their work, one literary and the other chronographic. Since both sources place the translation in the reign of Philadelphus, they must both refer to the same event. Thus, whereas the date of Eusebius is derived from a contemporary record, transmitted via a Hellenistic chronicle, his literary account comes from Aristeas, and a small literary synopsis accompanies the entry in the *Chronicle*. Aristeas may also be the source of the details of the translation furnished by Epiphanius, but the latter's date for the event is derived from a separate chronological source based on an original record of the event which was re-dated after the 13th year of Philadelphus in 270 BCE.

SUMMARY

This investigation on the date of the translation of the Law rests on the reliability of the dates transmitted by of Eusebius and Epiphanius. It is clear that these authors lived many years after the event they record. However, the fact that although transmitted in different chronologies (thus representing independent traditions), both refer to the same period of time (the 3rd Macedonian year of Ptolemy II) is a strong indication that both witness the truth. It appears therefore, that by the end of the third century CE, there existed two parallel dates for the translation of the Law, each correct according to the chronology it used. These are the earliest records of the date that have survived. One, recorded by Eusebius, was based on Olympiad chronology and thus places the translation in an Olympiad year. The other, noted by Epiphanius, relates to Philadelphus' Macedonian regnal years, and places the translation in a Macedonian year.

Moreover, the fact that they are recorded in different chronologies can be exploited to enable a more accurate date for the translation to be deduced than if each existed on its own. This is because the precise date to which each refers is shown in the overlap of the relevant years. Thus, the period in which the translation was made emerges when the dates of Eusebius and Epiphanius are evaluated together. In this way, the date which marks the translation of the Law is narrowed down from one particular Olympiad or Macedonian year, to the smaller period when the relevant Macedonian and Olympiad years overlap. This occurs between April and the beginning of July in 280 BCE. An understanding of the dates of Eusebius and Epiphanius in relation to the start of the reign of Philadelphus thus reveals that, according to the tradition of the Greeks, the translation was completed between April and the start of July in 280 BCE.

According to Olympiad chronology, this date falls in the 4th year of the 124th Olympiad. Calculated from the beginning of the co-regency according to Macedonian chronology, it falls in Philadelphus' 5th Macedonian year. However, although Epiphanius transmits this latter date, he refers to the 6th (not, the 5th) Macedonian year. The discrepancy of 1 is due to the mechanical, rather than *true* re-dating of the 3rd Macedonian year of Philadelphus to the 6th Macedonian year (the value transmitted by Epiphanius), which occurred when Philadelphus back-dated his reign, in order to award himself a whole number of years. As a result, a value of "3" was simply added to the original date, instead of a true calculation of the date in relation to the start of the co-regency. Epiphanius thus transmits the earliest record of the adjusted date.

On the other hand, the date of Eusebius is a direct reflection of the date that was originally recorded for the event. Since it has not been adjusted in the same way as the date of Epiphanius, the date of Eusebius must have been recorded before the 13th year of Philadelphus in 270 BCE. This means that, if the translation was commemorated in 280 BCE (as the argument above suggests), the date of Eusebius was recorded no longer than ten years *after* the event. As there would be little point in waiting for up to 10 years to note the date of a contemporary event, this suggests that the date was originally recorded at the time of the event, that is, in the 3rd Macedonian year of the King (although, sadly, this notice is now lost).

If indeed the dates of Eusebius and Epiphanius can be traced back to an original record of the event, the event that they record must have occurred. The dates of Eusebius and Epiphanius thus independently and accurately confirm the literary accounts of Aristeas (and others) that a translation of the Pentateuch was made when Philadelphus was King.

The methodology used here for deducing the date of the translation will again be used later in this discussion to answer two further questions: (1) Why do the sources differ in their identification of the King when the translation was made? (2) When did Demetrius of Phalerum leave the court of Philadelphus? The fact that the same

281 BCE: THE YEAR OF THE TRANSLATION

principles can be applied to suggest sensible solutions for these problems will help to confirm the validity of the arguments used above.

But first, the later Greek versions of the date of the translation from Group [1][91] will be examined. This will show that all are derived either from Eusebius, or from Epiphanius, or from them both.

1. THE DATE DERIVED FROM EPIPHANIUS:
BAR HEBRAEUS

The 13th century scholar Bar Hebraeus states that the translation of the Law took place in the 6th year of Ptolemy II.[92] In a different section of the same work, which also records details of this event, he cites Epiphanius by name.[93] The latter, it will be remembered, wrote that the translation took place "in the seventh year, more or less" of Ptolemy II, which refers to Philadelphus' 6th year.[94] It is clear that Bar Hebraeus has interpreted the date of Epiphanius, which he transmits.

2. THE DATE DERIVED FROM EUSEBIUS:
CYRIL OF ALEXANDRIA & ZACHARIAS OF MYTILENE

Cyril of Alexandria records that the Law was translated in the 124th Olympiad, the same Olympiad chronicled by Eusebius, July 284 to July 280 BCE.[95] The dates of Cyril are probably derived from his contemporary Eusebius.[96] But unlike Eusebius, it is strange that Cyril does not give a specific Olympiad year. It is possible therefore that he also took account of the date transmitted by his other contemporary Epiphanius, which, taken as it stands, *appears* to fall in the year 279/8, the second half of the first Olympiad year and the first half of the second Olympiad year in the 125th Olympiad (see Diagram 7). His possible margin of error was thereby reduced if Cyril referred only to a specific Olympiad, without further detail.

The source of Zacharias for the date of the translation is not in doubt. His dependence on Eusebius is clearly proclaimed with the words that the translation took place "as the Chronicle of Eusebius of Caesarea declares, 280 years *and more* before the birth of Christ." According to the Latin version of the *Chronicle*, Christ was born in the 3rd year of the 194th Olympiad. As there are 4 years in each Olympiad, the date of the translation given by Eusebius is separated from the birth of Christ by 281 years. The date of Zacharias is thus merely approximated to the nearest ten. This is indicated by the phrase "and more" in the quotation above. Similar approximations are made by this writer in other contexts, e.g., "*about* the space of 130 years after [Ptolemy II], Ptolemy Philometer ... exerted himself ... to write down ... the limits of the lands under their sway."[87] Zacharias thus claims that the Law was translated over 280 years before the birth of Christ.

It remains only to decide if Zacharias was dependent on the Latin *Chronicle* of Eusebius or the Armenian version. The latter gives a difference of 278 years between the translation in the 1,737th Abrahamic year and the birth of Christ in the 2,015th Abrahamic year. The claim of

281 BCE: THE YEAR OF THE TRANSLATION

Zacharias that the translation was made "280 years or more," is thus proof that he was based on the Latin *Chronicle* of Jerome, rather than an archetype of the Armenian text.

3. THE DATE DERIVED FROM BOTH EUSEBIUS & EPIPHANIUS: THE *ARMENIAN CHRONICLE* OF EUSEBIUS

This text states that Philadelphus became King in year of Abraham 1733 and that the translation was made in year of Abraham 1737.

It is well known that the dates in the Armenian *Chronicle* differ from those of Jerome.[88] As far as concerns the translation of the Law, not only is there a difference in the absolute dates of the accession of Ptolemy II and the translation of the Law, but these times also differ in relation to each other - in Jerome, the translation falls in Ptolemy's 2nd Olympic year, but in the Armenian *Chronicle*, it occurs in his 5th regnal year, reckoned in years of Abraham. It is obvious that the years in each *Chronicle* do not indicate some relative passage of time. The discussion here is not concerned with the cause of specific differences between the Latin and Armenian versions,[89] but will consider the date of the translation in the Armenian *Chronicle* in relation to the date that it claims for the start of the reign of Philadelphus, in the same way that the dates for events in the reign of Philadelphus were originally recorded using Macedonian or Egyptian years.

Year 1733 of Abraham (the year of the accession of Philadelphus in the Armenian *Chronicle*) is marked A^1 in the diagram below. The fact that the Armenian *Chronicle* is based on the Latin version of Jerome (see further below) indicates that, just as implied by Jerome, the start of the reign of Philadphus must be dated from the beginning of the co-regency. This is confirmed by the claim in the *Chronicle* that Philadelphus reigned for 38 years. It is assumed here that the *Chronicle* starts the count of regnal years in the year of Abraham which started *after* the beginning of his reign began, just as the count of regnal years according to Olympiad chronology.[90]

Since the *Chronicle* states that the Law was translated in the year of Abraham 1737, the date of the translation falls between the start of the year of Abraham 1737, and the end of this year in 1738.

Let us now identify the Macedonian year of the King in which this *Chronicle* places the translation of the Law. It is known that the anniversary of the co-regency took place near the start of a Julian year (see Diagram 2). Thus, counting the 1st Macedonian regnal year from the start of the Julian year in 283 BCE,[91] the 2nd in 282, etc., it then follows that the 6th Macedonian year of Philadelphus began in 278 BCE, marked M^6 in the diagram below. This Macedonian year overlaps part of the year of Abraham 1737 in which the *Chronicle* places the translation of the Law. The Armenian *Chronicle* thus places the translation in Philadelphus' 6th Macedonian year, the same year indicated by Epiphanius. The overlap is underlined in the diagram below:

281 BCE: THE YEAR OF THE TRANSLATION   439

```
Years                                              Years of
BCE                           A                    Abraham
284      ............................  ........
283      .Ac.M¹.M¹.M¹.M¹.M¹.M¹.M¹.M¹.M¹ |A¹-M¹-A¹   1733
282      M¹aM²-A¹-M²-A¹-M²-A¹-M²-A¹-M²- |A²-M²-A²   1734
281      M²aM³-A²-M³-A²-M³-A²-M³-A²-M³- |A³-M³-A³   1735
280      M³aM⁴-A³-M⁴-A³-M⁴-A³-M⁴-A³-M⁴- |A⁴-M⁴-A⁴   1736
279      M⁴aM⁵-A⁴-M⁵-A⁴-M⁵-A⁴-M⁵-A⁴-M⁵- |A⁵-M⁵-A⁵   1737
278      M⁵aM⁶-A⁵-M⁶-A⁵-M⁶-A⁵-M⁶-A⁵-M⁶- |A⁶-M⁶-A⁶   1738
```

DIAGRAM 8: NUMBER OF YEARS BETWEEN THE ACCESSION OF PTOLEMY II &
THE TRANSLATION OF THE LAW, ACCORDING TO THE ARMENIAN CHRONICLE

Key to symbols:
The 1st full year of Abraham, A^1, of the reign of Philadelphus began in the
autumn following his Accession, Ac.
A^1, A^2 etc., M^1, M^2 etc., indicates successive years of Abraham and Macedonian
years in the rule of Philadelphus. Thus, the series A^5-M^6-A^5-M^6 etc. indicates
the overlap of the 5th year of Abraham (A^5) and the 6th Macedonian year (M^6).
| indicates the start of a year of Abraham

The horizontal line in the diagram above shows when the 5th year of Abraham overlaps the 6th Macedonian year of Philadelphus, which suggests that the Armenian *Chronicle* used the date of the translation given by Epiphanius. This was expressed in Abrahamic years, in relation to the date assumed for the start of the reign of Philadelphus.

It is thought that the Armenian *Chronicle* was derived from the work of the early fifth century monks, Panodorus and Annanius, who prepared a Greek redaction of Eusebius' *Chronicle*, about a quarter of a century after the Latin version of Jerome.[92] The Armenian version is thus ultimately based on Eusebius and Jerome, but was modified by the introduction of the chronological system of years of Abraham. It is thought that the present work may be derived from a single manuscript emanating from these monks, which was produced

about a thousand years after Eusebius.[93]
According to Syncellus, Panodorus and Annanius were contemporaries and flourished in the time of Theophilus, bishop of Alexandria in 388-416 CE. Panodorus also lived in the time of the emperor Arcadius, 383-408 CE. It was thus about the year 400 CE that Panodorus may have re-edited the *Chronicle*. It is possible, in fact, that Panodorus published his work before 408 and Annanius between 408 and 416 CE.[94] As Epiphanius lived *c*.315-*c*.403 CE, he pre-dates the monks who could thus have consulted his work.[95] They may thereby have used the date of Epiphanius to "correct" that of Jerome when they re-edited the *Chronicle* of Eusebius.

THE DATE DERIVED FROM THE *ARMENIAN CHRONICLE*:
MICHAEL THE SYRIAN

This author states that the translation was made in the 5th year of Philadelphus, in the 125th Olympiad.[96] The source of his work on early history can ultimately be traced to the *Chronicle* of Eusebius, probably through the Armenian version.[97] This is confirmed by Diagram 8 above - from the beginning of the reign of Philadelphus, the date of the translation falls in the 5th year, reckoned by Abrahamic years. The 125th Olympiad begins in July 280 BCE.

THE JEWISH DATE PRESERVED IN *MEGILLAT TAANIT*

The date preserved by the Jews can now be considered in relation to the period between April and July in 280 BCE, when the Greeks recorded the translation of the Law. This is preserved in *Megillat Taanit*, and states that the translation

281 BCE: THE YEAR OF THE TRANSLATION 441

was finished by the 8th of Tevet.[98] No year is given for the event.

The Jewish year consists of twelve lunar months. An extra month may be inserted between the months of Adar and Nisan, so that the lunar year keeps pace with the longer solar year.[99] Counting from Tishri (the first month of the year), Tevet is the fourth, Adar the sixth, and Nisan the seventh month of the year. The first day of Tevet thus precedes the 15th of Nisan by three and a half or four and a half lunar months. Thus, for all the regnal years of Philadelphus, the 8th of Tevet could *never* have fallen between Artemisios 29 (April) and the start of summer at the end of June. In fact, Tevet always falls around the months of December or January. This means that if the translation of the Law was commemorated between April and the start of summer in 280 BCE, the Jewish date refers to a separate event.

This event exists. According to Aristeas, after the translation was completed, two ceremonies were held. The first took place on the island of Pharos for the benefit of the Jews, in the presence of the translators and the entire Jewish community of Alexandria, including the priests and leaders of the people, when the whole translation was read aloud.[100] It is reasonable to assume that the date of this event was remembered by the Jews.[101]

Some time later, a second, more sumptuous ceremony was held at the court of Philadelphus.[102] This was again attended by the translators and the whole translation was read to the King who then

gave generous, individual gifts to the Jews. If
only a few of these details are correct, a
celebration of magnificence took place. It is
possible that this event was recorded in the
annals of the King, and was transmitted (with
interpretation) by later sources in Greek.

As a result, assuming the date calculated for
the celebration of the Greeks is correct, the
simple fact that the 8th of Tevet cannot coincide
with this time provides mutual confirmation for
the veracity of the record of two ceremonies
furnished by Aristeas and the date preserved by
the Jews.

It thus appears that a ceremony for the Greeks
was held between April and June in 280 BCE. This
was preceded by a ceremony for the Jews on the 8th
of Tevet. This month corresponds with the period
December to January. The 8th of Tevet, which
falls just after the first quarter of the month,
therefore probably indicates a time in December.
This estimate has been confirmed by calculation
which suggests that the 8th of Tevet in 281/80 BCE
corresponds with 28/29 December in 281.[103]
Assuming that the weather in Alexandria has
remained more or less the same for the last two
thousand years,[104] this date appears to be in
accord with Philo's description of the annual
commemoration of the translation held on the
Pharos, when some celebrants "lay on the sandy
beach in the open air" and others put up tents.[105]
The fact that some people merely lay on the beach
suggests that the celebration was held only on one
day. But if so, why the necessity for tents?
This detail makes sense if the weather in Alexan-

281 BCE: THE YEAR OF THE TRANSLATION 443

dria and, by extension, the weather on the Pharos, was rainy and/or windy in December, which is indeed the case.[106]

The description by Aristeas of the ceremony on the Pharos held by the Jews shows that it took place *after* the translation was complete.[107] The Jewish record thus marks the actual date of completion of the work.

The true (traditional) dates, the mechanically re-dated and the correctly re-dated dates in the regnal years of Philadelphus are listed in the table below. The two dates which are extant - the day and month of the Jewish date and the date of Epiphanius, later cited by Bar Hebraeus - are underlined. The remaining dates are deduced:

	JEWISH DATE	GREEK DATE
TRUE DATE BCE	<u>29th(?) December</u> 281	April-July 280
ORIGINAL MACEDONIAN DATE IN THE YEARS OF PTOLEMY II	2nd Macedonian year	3rd Macedonian year
DATE MECHANICALLY RE-DATED AFTER PTOLEMY II BACKDATED HIS REIGN	5th Macedonian year	<u>6th Macedonian year</u>
DATE CORRECTLY RE-DATED FROM START OF CO-REGENCY	4th Macedonian year	5th Macedonian year

TABLE 2: DATES CONNECTED WITH THE TRANSLATION OF THE LAW

By a happy coincidence, Olympiad chronology embraces both the original (true) Jewish and Greek dates. The former falls *after* July in 281 and the latter *before* July in 280. This being the case, according to Olympiad years, both dates occur in the 4th year of the 124th Olympiad (see Diagram 6).

As is the case for many other ancient literary remains, the exact date of the translation emerges from records which are external to the text.[109]

TWO ANCIENT *CRUCES* RELATED TO THE TRANSLATION OF THE LAW

The methodology employed in the investigation of the date of the translation will now be used to throw light on two ancient problems, briefly noted above: (1) Why some authors link the translation with Soter, a larger number with Philadelphus his son, and a few with both; (2) The timing of the withdrawal of Demetrius of Phalerum from the court of Philadelphus. This will also indicate the kind of sources available to authors prior to Eusebius, who give accounts of the translation of the Law.

(1) PTOLEMY I OR PTOLEMY II?

The brief review of the literary evidence at the beginning of this discussion showed that some ancient authors link the translation with Ptolemy I, a larger number with Ptolemy II, and a few with both. Using the principles on which the date of the translation has been deduced, it is now possible to determine the cause of these discrepancies, both the number and name.

Two errors may be involved, the first by the source of Eusebius, and the second by Eusebius himself. The first of these has already been discussed - it is possible that the source of Eusebius (Eratosthenes?) placed the original date of the translation in relation to the beginning of the co-regency, rather than to its end (see text above, after Diagram 7). The resulting incorrect

281 BCE: THE YEAR OF THE TRANSLATION   445

date, the 2nd year of the 124th Olympiad, was then used by Eusebius in the *Chronicle*. This date will now be considered in relation to each of the dates set by Eratosthenes and Eusebius for death of Soter.

The dates relevant to this discussion are set out below:

EVENT	TRUE DATE	DATE IN EUSEBIUS'CHRONICLE
Alexander died	10 June 323, 1st year of 114th Olympiad	1st year of 114th Olympiad
Soter assumes power	Between July 322 & July 321, 3rd year of 114th Olympiad	Between July 324 & July 323, 1st year of 114th Olympiad
Soter died	March 282, 2nd year of 124th Olympiad	Between July 285 & July 284, 4th year of 123rd Olympiad He ruled for 40 Olympiad years
Translation of Law	Between April & July 280, 4th year of 124th Olympiad	2nd year of 124th Olympiad
Philadelphus died	January 246, 2nd year of 133rd Olympiad	2nd year of 133rd Olympiad He ruled for 38 Olympiad years

Let us first consider the date of Soter's death set by Eusebius. An examination of the *Chronicle* suggests this was fixed in relation to dates of the deaths of Alexander and Philadelphus which Eusebius found in an Olympiad chronicle on which he based his own work. Alexander died in June 323 BCE, and this date was correctly placed (perhaps by Eratosthenes) in the 1st year of the 114th Olympiad, that is, between July 324 and July 323 BCE.[109] Philadelphus died in January 246 BCE, and this date was placed (again perhaps by Eratosthenes) in the 2nd year of the 133rd Olympiad.[110] The traditional lengths of the reign of Soter and Philadelphus available to Eusebius were respectively 40 and 38 Olympiad years.[111] Eusebius thus counted forwards for 40 Olympiad years from the death of Alexander, so that the death of Soter fell between July 285 and July 284, in the 4th year of the 123rd Olympiad. Or else, he counted backwards for 38 Olympiad years from the death of Philadelphus. Either way, Soter's death fell in the 2nd year of the 124th Olympiad. This was because the sum of the lengths of the official reigns of Soter and Philadelphus correspond by chance *exactly* with the number of years between the deaths of Alexander and Philadelphus, when these are measured in Olympiad years.

The *Chronicle* of Eusebius thus removed evidence of the co-regency. This was possible because by chance the duration of the co-regency is equal to the duration of time between the death of Alexander and Ptolemy's assumption of power in 322/1 BCE.[112] Both consist of two Olympiad years. The loss of time by the overlap of the co-regency thus compensates exactly for the extra time that must be allowed between Alexander's death and Soter's rule. Perhaps Eusebius was not aware of this delay, although it is almost certain that he knew of the co-regency.[113]

However, records indicating the correct year of the death of Soter have been preserved and others have been assumed.[114] As a result, it is known that Soter died by March 282 BCE, two Olympiad years earlier than the date set by Eusebius (the 2nd Olympiad year of the 124th Olympiad).[115] Since Philadelphus began his sole reign by counting his regnal years from the death of his father, the date of Soter's death must have been recorded *when it happened* in Soter's Macedonian

281 BCE: THE YEAR OF THE TRANSLATION

regnal years. It is likely that this was correctly converted into Olympiad chronology by the source of Eusebius. This is because the original record of this date was probably not reckoned with reference to the years of Philadelphus, and therefore did not depend for its interpretation on an intimate knowledge of the chronology of the co-regency years. There was thus no good reason for an error to arise. It must therefore be assumed that the date of Soter's death was fixed in the 2nd year of the 124th Olympiad, although there is no extant Olympiad record of this fact. This date, however, gives a period longer than 40 years between the deaths of Alexander and Soter, which suggests either that Soter ruled for more than 40 years or that he did not assume power as soon as Alexander died. For either of these reasons (perhaps the latter), it was later rejected by Eusebius.[116]

Before the time of Eusebius, therefore, two events appear to fall in the same 2nd year of the 124th Olympiad - the death of Soter and the translation of the Law.

Authors who pre-date Eusebius place the translation either in the time of Soter, or in the time of Philadelphus, or attribute the event to both kings. Authors after the time of Eusebius almost invariably refer to Ptolemy II. Let us now look in detail at each of these groups.

1. Authors pre-dating Eusebius who refer to the role of Ptolemy I

The discussion above has suggested that, according to an Olympiad chronicle which existed before the time of Eusebius, Soter's death and the translation of the Law fell in the same Olympiad year. This is significant because, according to Olympiad chronology, the last Olympiad year of a king is included with the reign of the dead king. Hence, without an indication of the relative chronology of events, any event in the last Olympiad year of a king could be attributed to this king, although it may have occurred after his death. This is unlikely to happen for events recorded in Macedonian regnal years. In this system, the date is reckoned from the start of the regnal years of a king, which end at the moment of his death. By contrast, Olympiad dates are continuous starting from the first Olympiad in 776 BCE, and are not reckoned with reference to a specific event, such as the accession or death of a king. Thus, given the basic characteristics of Olympiad chronology, the conversion from Macedonian to Olympiad dates of the date of Soter's death and the date of translation, did not help to counteract the impression that the translation was (apparently) completed in Soter's last Olympiad year, and that he was the King in power at the time.

The existence of such an Olympiad chronicle, prior to the *Chronicle* of Eusebius, thus neatly accounts for the claim of Aristobulus, Irenaeus and Clement of Alexandria, that the translation was made under Ptolemy I, although if it was completed by December 281 BCE (as argued above), Soter had been dead for over a year.[117]

When was this Olympiad chronicle prepared? Since Aristobulus is the earliest of the authors

who may have depended on such a source, it
probably existed before he lived, sometime before
the 2nd century BCE. In fact, a chronology was
probably constructed by Eratosthenes in
Alexandria, during the second half of the 3rd
century CE.[118] If further proof be needed of the
existence of such a chronicle, it can be seen in
the work of Eusebius, whose dates quoted in his
own *Chronicle* could only have come from an earlier
source.

However, it is unlikely that the authors who
link the translation with Ptolemy I actually used
a chronicle themselves. It is interesting to note
that although apparently based on a simple
chronicle of events, none of the reliable authors
who connect the translation with Soter give a date
for this event. Neither do they give the length
of the reigns of Soter or his son. This can be
contrasted with the seven sources who give a date
for the translation and who claim the involvement
of Ptolemy II, the majority of whom give the
lengths of the reigns of the Kings.[119]

This suggests that by the time of Aristobulus,
there existed a prose account of events, which was
itself based on an earlier chronicle that attested
the role of Soter in the translation. This work
was subsequently used by later authors who involve
Ptolemy I. The attraction of a chronicle in
ancient times is easily understood - compared with
the obvious bias of some Hellenistic history (for
example, the account of Manetho regarding the
Jews), a chronicle appears to be free from bias
and thus, less prone to error than a literary
account.

2. Authors pre-dating Eusebius who refer to the role of Ptolemy II

If those who attest Ptolemy I derived their claim from an early Olympiad chronicle, what was the source of those who involve Ptolemy II? It cannot be the same. We must ask, therefore, what other sources were available for authors in ancient times. Probably the most common were the earlier simple written accounts - the alternative Greek chronicles were an invention of Hellenistic times.[120] It makes sense therefore to assume that those who identify Philadelphus with the translation of the Law such as *The Letter of Aristeas*, were dependent on one or more earlier literary accounts. Alternatively, an oral tradition may have survived, as Philo and Justin both attest.[121] Compared with an early chronicle, in which the date of the translation was incorrect because of lack of knowledge of the co-regency years, it is likely that a simple literary account would have given an accurate record of events in the order they occurred. If Ptolemy II was King at the time, there would have been no reason for such sources to involve Ptolemy I. Consequently, it was probably on such sources as these that the accounts of Aristeas, Philo, Josephus, Justin, Pollux and Tertullian were based.

3. Authors pre-dating Eusebius who refer to the role of both Ptolemies

Aristobulus and Clement of Alexandria state that the translation was made under either or both Ptolemies. Common sense alone suggests that these authors are based on two sources.[122] The argument above has suggested the nature of these texts – the claim for Soter is based ultimately on the evidence of a chronicle, whereas that for Philadelphus comes from a simple prose account originating from the event.

4. Authors contemporary with and after Eusebius

Around the time of Eusebius, opinion is still divided. This can be seen in the contrasting testimony of his younger contemporaries Filaster and Cyril of Jerusalem. Filaster places the translation in Soter's reign.[123] The work of Filaster was probably dependent on Epiphanius and Irenaeus.[124] As far as concerns the King responsible for the translation, he seems to have used the testimony of Irenaeus. On the other hand, Cyril of Jerusalem (and perhaps also Pseudo-Athanasius, if his dates here are correct), implicate Ptolemy II.

The situation changes dramatically after the time of Eusebius. No reliable author after his time links the translation with Ptolemy I. On the other hand, up to 23 writers born after Eusebius link the translation with Ptolemy II.[125] The numbers of authors who identify Soter or Philadelphus with the translation, in relation to the life of Eusebius, are compared in the table below:

	PTOLEMY I	PTOLEMY II	BOTH PTOLEMIES
Authors before Eusebius	4	5	2^{126}
Contemporary with Eusebius	1	1 (or, 2)	0
Authors after Eusebius	none reliable	up to 23	0

TABLE 3: NUMBERS OF AUTHORS BEFORE, DURING AND AFTER THE TIME OF EUSEBIUS WHO ATTRIBUTE THE TRANSLATION TO PTOLEMY I, OR TO PTOLEMY II, OR TO BOTH

The unanimous testimony of those who wrote after Eusebius must be attributed directly to the alteration by Eusebius of the year of the death of Soter, and to the influential spread of the *Chronicle*, even by the time Eusebius had died.[127] This was due especially to the work of Jerome.[128] The comparatively small number of sources who attribute the translation to Ptolemy I compared to those who refer to Ptolemy II is thus due only to the vicissitudes of fate which decreed that fewer of the authors who describe the translation of the Law lived prior to Eusebius than lived after him. The differing opinions of the contemporaries of Eusebius may reflect a simple continuation of earlier traditions, or may have arisen from debate on his work which took place while Eusebius was still alive.

The sequence of events described above can be described as follows:

1. Soter died in March 282 BCE. Eratosthenes (or some other early chronologer) found a record of his death expressed in the Macedonian years of Ptolemy I and correctly placed the event in the 2nd year of the 124th Olympiad.

2. The date of the translation was originally recorded by the Greeks in the 3rd Macedonian year of Philadelphus, along with a record of the month. Eratosthenes (?) saw the original notice of the date, which he converted into Olympiad chronology. But, due to a lack of knowledge of the co-regency, the date was placed two Olympiad years earlier than it actually occurred. As a result, the date of the translation fell in the 2nd year of the 124th Olympiad.

281 BCE: THE YEAR OF THE TRANSLATION 453

3. Two significant dates now coincide - the Olympiad year of the death of Soter and the Olympiad year of the translation of the Law. Consequently, some authors, based ultimately on a chronological source with Olympiad dates, attribute the translation to this King. Others, based on a prose and/or oral account which was originally contemporary with the event itself, transmit the tradition that the work was completed under Ptolemy II. A few authors, based on both sources, claim that both Kings were involved.

4. For the date of the translation, Eusebius consulted a chronicle of events, rather than a literary account derived from such a chronicle. He accepted the date of the translation but rejected the date of Soter's death. This was reckoned by counting forward for 40 years from the death of Alexander, or counting backwards for 38 years from the death of Philadelphus. As a result, the date of Soter's death was incorrectly placed in the 4th year of the 123th Olympiad, two Olympiad years earlier than had previously been thought. Soter's death now preceded the translation by 2 Olympiad years. As a result, the date of the translation now fell in the reign of Philadelphus, and was now inevitably associated with this King. Eusebius may have been reassured, or even inspired in this chronology by the existing literary tradition which linked Philadelphus with the translation of the Law - he quotes extensively from *The Letter*, citing Aristeas by name.[129]

5. During the lifetime of Eusebius, opinion was divided. Of the two reliable sources from this

time, one attributes the translation to Soter and the other to Philadelphus.

6. After Eusebius, only doubtful sources implicate Soter. All others were influenced by Eusebius and transmit the tradition that at the time of the translation, Philadelphus was King.

To conclude - the apparent link between Soter and translation can be traced to the error originally made by Eratosthenes, the possible source of Eusebius, when he reckoned the date of the translation from the time of the start of the co-regency. This date now fell in the last Olympiad year of Ptolemy I. As a result, some sources attribute the translation of Ptolemy I. However, as this attribution is probably based on an error of chronology, it must be wrong.

Eusebius accepted the date of the translation, but rejected the date of Soter's death. The error of Eratosthenes was thus compounded when Eusebius placed the death of Soter two years earlier than the date he had received. The date of the translation now fell in the reign of Philadelphus. If it was completed by 281 BCE, the two relevant dates - the death of Soter and the translation of the Law - although now incorrect in absolute terms, were correctly placed in the order they occurred. As a result of the errors of the chronographers, all reliable sources after Eusebius claim the translation was made when Philadelphus was king.

THE RETIREMENT OF DEMETRIUS OF PHALERUM

The chronology of the co-regency also accounts

281 BCE: THE YEAR OF THE TRANSLATION

for the apparently incompatible evidence in the sources concerning the timing of the retirement of Demetrius of Phalerum from the court of Philadelphus. Diogenes Laertius, quoting Hermippus, states that Demetrius was "imprisoned in the country" after Soter died,[130] thus implying that Demetrius was not in Alexandria when Philadelphus was sole King. This suggests that Demetrius left court at the end of the co-regency, that is, he left Alexandria soon after Soter died. On the other hand, several sources attest the presence of Demetrius at the court of Philadelphus.[131] It could be argued that this is due to the fact that Demetrius was in court during the years of the co-regency when Soter was alive, although Philadelphus was King.[132] However, if the Pentateuch was translated by April 280 BCE and Aristeas (and others) correctly attest the presence of Demetrius at the final ceremony before Philadelphus,[133] Soter had already been dead for two years.

This problem can be solved with the same methodology as the problem of the date of the translation of the Law. If the evidence is to be harmonized, Demetrius was removed from court by the 13th year of Philadelphus, (i.e., before Philadelphus back-dated his reign), so that account must be taken of a later adjustment of the true dating of the event, resulting from a lack of appreciation by later authors of the chronology of the co-regency. This being the case, the fall of Demetrius happened at such a time that, when reckoned (by later sources) from the *beginning* of the co-regency, the period appears to fall in the same Olympiad year as the death of Soter, the 2nd year of the 124th Olympiad, between March and the end of July. As the last Olympiad year of a king is wholly attributed to the regnal years of this king (see above), this timing would account for the story of Diogenes that Demetrius was not employed by Philadelphus, i.e., he was "imprisoned in the country," after Soter died. The relevant period is shaded in the diagram below:

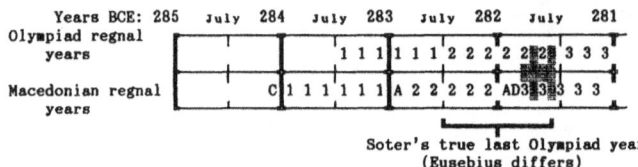

DIAGRAM 9: SHOWING THE MACEDONIAN YEAR OF PHILADELPHUS WHICH COINCIDES WITH THE OLYMPIAD YEAR OF THE DEATH OF SOTER, RECKONING FROM THE START OF THE CO-REGENCY

C refers to the start of the Co-regency, A to the annual Anniversary of the event and D to the Death of Soter in March 282.

The area shaded in the diagram above indicates a period between the death of Soter in March and the beginning of July, at the beginning of the 3rd Macedonian year of Ptolemy II. Let us now reckon this time from the *end* of the co-regency. This will indicate the corresponding years BCE. The appropriate period is again shaded in the diagram below:

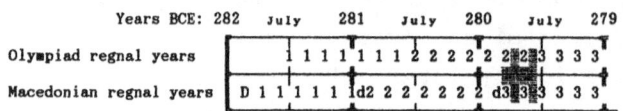

DIAGRAM 10: THE RELATIONSHIP BETWEEN THE 2ND OLYMPIAD YEAR OF PHILADELPHUS & THE PERIOD WHEN DEMETRIUS WAS DISGRACED

D refers to the Death of Soter and d to the annual anniversary of his death.

281 BCE: THE YEAR OF THE TRANSLATION

The relevant period is shown in the shaded area in the diagram above. It falls in 280 BCE, between (a) the beginning of the 3rd Macedonian year of Philadelphus, just after the April anniversary of the death of Soter (the month of the anniversary of Soter's death in 280), and (b) the 1st of July, which marks the beginning of the new Olympiad year. The departure of Demetrius thus took place in the same period of time that the Greeks commemorated the translation of the Law. If Demetrius was indeed present when the translation of the Law was read to the King,[134] the ceremony acts as a *terminus a quo*. On this basis, Demetrius left Alexandria some time between (a) the ceremony before Ptolemy in April and (b) the end of June in 280 BCE. This means he remained at court for just over two years after Soter died.

If the retirement of Demetrius took place at this time, the apparently conflicting evidence can be easily explained. After the death of Soter, Demetrius was employed by Philadelphus in Alexandria, as Aristeas and others suggest. On the other hand, it appears from information ultimately based on a false chronological report that Demetrius was removed from court after Soter died and did not work under Philadelphus, as Diogenes relates. The reasoning behind the explanation of Diogenes can be justified by historical events. Diogenes relates that Demetrius lived in Alexandria under the protection of Soter, who gave him refuge when he was expelled from Athens.[135] While in Alexandria, it appears that Demetrius advised Soter to give the succession to his elder son, the future Ptolemy Ceraunos.[136] But, by establishing a co-regency with the future Philadelphus, Soter ensured that his younger son would become the next King. Whereupon, while Soter was still alive, the dispossessed Ceraunos fled to Seleucus, King of Syria, who promised to help him gain the throne after Soter's death.[137] It thus seemed in later times that Philadelphus had good cause to remove Demetrius, a possible ally of Ceraunos, from court. Consequently, since it appeared (from a false chronological report) that all traces of Demetrius ceased in the same Olympiad year that Soter died, the idea took root that Demetrius was imprisoned by Philadelphus as soon as his father was no longer alive. The explanation of Diogenes is thus simply an ingenious and plausible fiction, contrived to harmonize the apparent chronology with the historical facts.

On the other hand, if the sources correctly attest the work of Demetrius with the translation of the Law,[138] Demetrius may have been involved in organizing the translation for Philadelphus, and then left Alexandria when this was complete. This would account for the fact that Demetrius apparently departed from court in the same period of time as the completion of this work. However, such evidence is again only circumstantial. The one connection that can be claimed between the completion of the translation and the arrest of Demetrius is that they seem to have happened in this order and in the same period of time.

To conclude: the two ancient problems discussed above - the identity of the King who presided over

281 BCE: THE YEAR OF THE TRANSLATION

the translation and the timing of the disappearance of Demetrius of Phalerum - can be discussed in the light of the existence of the co-regency and the problem for ancient chronology that this caused when it was ignored. This problem particularly concerns the dates of events in the period up to the 13th year of the reign of Philadelphus which followed the death of Soter at the *end* of the co-regency, when Philadelphus back-dated his rule. In antiquity, these years were reckoned in relation to the *beginning* of the co-regency, not its end. This fact was the basis of the investigation of the date of the translation of the Law. The use of the same methodology with positive results for two other *cruces* of antiquity is added confirmation for the validity of this approach.[130]

SOURCES OF ACCOUNTS OF THE TRANSLATION PRIOR TO EUSEBIUS

This analysis also casts light on the sources of authors prior to Eusebius, who give accounts of the translation of the Law. The discussion on Demetrius implies that Hermippus, the authority of Diogenes for the story of the imprisonment of Demetrius, was based on a source ultimately derived from a simple Olympiad chronicle, rather than on a literary account originating from the event itself. It can be assumed that the latter would have little reason to distort the relative chronology of events. On the other hand, the existence of a chronicle explains precisely how the story of Hermippus arose - ignorance of the chronology of the co-regency meant that when the

Macedonian date of the disgrace of Demetrius was converted into Olympiad chronology, this event and the death of Soter fell in the same year. A similar Olympiad chronicle prior to the time of Eusebius may also have served as the ultimate source for those authors who link the translation with Ptolemy I. Although the existence of an early Hellenistic Olympiad chronicle has long been known, the source of these authors has not been appreciated by scholars, perhaps mainly because no dates are cited in their work. It is revealed, however, by an error which could only have come from a chronicle of events. Other facts used by later authors could also have been derived from a chronicle of events, although because they are correct, they are difficult to detect.

It thus appears that in an early Olympiad chronicle prior to Eusebius, three dates were placed in the same Olympiad year. In the order they occurred, these are: (1) the date of Soter's death, (2) the date of the translation of the Law, and, (3) the date of the retirement of Demetrius. However, as both the translation of the Law and the withdrawal of Demetrius probably took place two years after Soter died, it appears that any author prior to the time of Eusebius, who associates the translation with Soter, or who omits the presence of Demetrius, used a source which was ultimately based on a chronicle of events. When both these factors are considered - (1) the identity of the King and (2) the presence or absence of Demetrius - the sources remain in the same groups indicated in the discussion above.

281 BCE: THE YEAR OF THE TRANSLATION

The one exception is Philo, who omits Demetrius, but refers to Ptolemy II.

This strongly suggests that in addition to Aristobulus and Clement, Philo's account of the translation of the Law is also based on at least two sources - (1) a literary account, originating perhaps from the event itself, which attested the role of Philadelphus and gave prominence to Demetrius (2) a chronicle, or perhaps, a prose account based on a chronicle, which caused Philo to reject completely the role of Demetrius, although this was prominent in the literary accounts.[140] In contrast with Aristobulus and Clement, who combined the facts on the Kings and the presence of Demetrius from both sources, it seems that Philo, influenced by a source based on a chronicle, reasoned logically that if Philadelphus was King, Demetrius did not take part. The omission of Demetrius in Philo is thus a rare example of true significance in an argument *ex silentio*. No other source prior to Eusebius refers to the role of Philadelphus but omits reference to Demetrius. The inclusion of Demetrius by all other authors before the time of Eusebius, who are based on a literary account, thus indicates the strength of tradition for his role.

It is interesting that although a notice of the date of the retirement of Demetrius was probably listed in an early work of chronology which Eusebius saw, the date is not given in the *Chronicle*. This may be a logical and deliberate omission by Eusebius in order to leave open the question of when Demetrius left the court. There is thus no inconsistency when Eusebius uses the report of Aristeas in his prose account of the translation of the Law, which includes a description of Demetrius' role.[141]

This discussion on the authors and their sources up to the time of Eusebius, is briefly summarized in the diagram below. This also suggests that in contrast with Josephus and Eusebius, Aristobulus did not use Aristeas:[142]

```
                    The translation was completed in the
              3rd or (re-dated) 6th Macedonian year of Ptolemy II,
         between April and 1st July, in the 4th year of the 124th Olympiad;

    ┌──CHRONOLOGICAL SOURCE──┐        ┌──PROSE SOURCE
    │                                 │
    Eratosthenes(?), after 246.BCE,   This linked the translation
    converted this date to Olympiad   with Ptolemy II, recounting facts
    years & placed it in the 2nd year as they actually took place
    of the 124th Olympiad, the same
    year as Soter's death
        │                                 │
    ──By early 2nd cent.BCE, a prose     The following authors link the
      account summarized the facts of   translation with Ptolemy II:
      the chronicle; it implicated Soter    Aristeas,──────────────
      in the translation & omitted
      the role of Demetrius
        │                                 │
      Two authors link the              Josephus, Justin,
      translation with Soter            Pollux & Tertullian
      and omit Demetrius:
      Irenaeus & Filaster
        │
        └──Aristobulus & Clement of Alexandria: attest 2 Kings
                                      & the presence of Demetrius

          ──Philo omits Demetrius, but attests Philadelphus

    ──Eusebius' Chronicle: used the Olympiad date for the
      translation, altered the date of Soter's death & omitted
      the date of the fall of Demetrius; thus, Demetrius and
      Philadelphus appear in his prose account
        │
      All reliable sources after Eusebius
      link the translation with Ptolemy II.
          None attest Ptolemy I
```

DIAGRAM 11: TO SHOW THE SOURCES OF AUTHORS UP TO THE TIME OF EUSEBIUS, IN RELATION TO THEIR TESTIMONY ON THE IDENTITY OF THE KING, & THE PRESENCE OF DEMETRIUS OF PHALERUM

HOW LONG WERE THE TRANSLATORS IN ALEXANDRIA?

The discussion on Demetrius of Phalerum has helped to confirm the claim of Aristeas that Demetrius was present at the court of Philadelphus after Soter died. Let us now examine a further detail of Aristeas in the light of the date of the translation deduced above, to see how this date relates to the timetable of the translators indicated in the text.

Aristeas claims that the translation was produced in seventy-two days (*LetAris* 307). This number coincides suspiciously with the number of translators and the number of questions answered at the seven banquets, and is clearly artificial. However, if interpreted in the way to be described, it may be related to fact. Using this interpretation in conjunction with the date of the translation deduced above, it is possible to arrive at an approximate date for the arrival of the translators in Alexandria, and thus to estimate the total length of their stay. This will cast light on one of the remarks of Ptolemy to the translators at the final ceremony before the King. In this way, a small detail of Aristeas may be confirmed.

Let us assume that the seventy-two days of Aristeas refers to the number of working days.[143] We know that the translators were religiously observant Jews because the *Letter* frequently mentions their strict concern for Jewish religious law. Seventy-two continuous days includes Sabbaths and festivals, when no writing is done. The latter is an example of "work" which is prohibited on sanctified days.[144] Thus, if the

Jewish *working* week consisted of a maximum period of five and a half days - leaving half a day for preparation for the Sabbath, and a full day for the Sabbath itself - then, seventy-two working days is equivalent to just over 13 weeks (72 divided by five and a half). Consequently, according to Aristeas, the translators "worked" just over thirteen weeks.

Let us assume that (1) the ceremony on the Pharos was held *immediately* after the completion of the translation; (2) no "work" was done over the 7 days of *Succoth*, on the day of the New Moon, or the day before a major festival, the latter to allow time for preparation; (3) *Rosh haShanah* was celebrated for one day; (4) the translators worked between *Rosh haShanah* and *Yom Kippur*; and (5) there were 30 days in Kislev, 29 days in Marheshvan, 30 days in Tishri, 29 days in Ellul. If we then allow (a) a week for the seven-day banquet that Ptolemy held for his guests[145] and (b) 3 days between the end of the banquet and the start of their task,[146] then, assuming that the translators "worked" over a period of thirteen weeks, we can count back from the 8th of Tevet and calculate the approximate date they arrived in Alexandria:

Dates	Days worked	Cumulative Total of Days Worked
Tevet, 7th to 2nd	6 days	6 days
Tevet 1st	No work (New Moon)	
Kislev 30th to 2nd	29 days	35 days
Kislev 1st	No work (New Moon)	
Marheshvan, 29th to 2nd	28 days	63 days
Marheshvan, 1st	No work (New Moon)	
Tishri 30th to 22nd	9 days	72 days
Tishri 21st to 14th	No work (Succoth + 1 day[147])	
Tishri 13th to 11th	3 days	75 days
Tishri 10th to 9th	No work (Yom Kippur + 1 day)	
Tishri 8th to 2nd	7 days	82 days
Tishri 1st to Ellul 29th	No work (Rosh haShanah + 1 day)	
Ellul 28th to 20th	9 days	91 DAYS = 13 WEEKS
Ellul 19th to 10th	to allow for the 7-day banquet plus 3 days[148]	

281 BCE: THE YEAR OF THE TRANSLATION

This suggests that the translators arrived in Alexandria around the second week in Ellul. (The date is earlier if the translators did not work during the ten days between *Rosh haShanah* and *Yom Kippur*, or if further days are disallowed for work). This gives an adequate period for a caravan or, more probably, a boat[149] to prepare and complete the journey from "Coele-Syria" to Alexandria, if the group set out after the 7th of Sivan, that is, after *Shevuoth*.

Having arrived in Alexandria, the translators were greeted immediately by the King.[150] If they had waited for the customary month, their meeting with the King may have been delayed till at least the start of Marheshvan. This is because the dates of the festivals in the month of Tishri do not allow for a consecutive sequence of seven days when Ptolemy and the translators could have dined, apart from the ten days between *Yom Kippur* and *Rosh haShanah*, whose solemnity probably precludes an encounter of this type. As a result (assuming a minimum of thirteen weeks), the activity of translation would have extended into Shevet (corresponding with January/February), and would not have been finished by the 8th of Tevet.

Thus, although Aristeas could claim that the translation was finished in seventy-two days - about two and a half months, it is more likely that the task was completed over the more credible period of about four months.[151] During the numerous periods when "work" was disallowed (during festivals and around certain times of non-festival days, such as the daily services), the translators could have conferred among themselves, orally and from memory. Aristeas implies a background activity of this kind.[152]

Two ceremonies were then held, the first before the Jews, and the second before the King. The earliest month for this latter event (according to the argument proposed above) was April. This suggests that the ceremony was held after the spring equinox (March 21st), that is after the beginning of the Passover, which falls in relation to this time.[153] The translators may thus have spent the seven days of Passover in Alexandria. If so, they remained in Egypt till at least the 22nd of Nisan (the last week of this month) and perhaps returned to Jerusalem in time for the festival of *Shevuoth*. According to the Rabbinic calendar, this falls forty-four days after the Passover week, giving the translators adequate time to travel home.

If this is the case, after the ceremony on the Pharos, the translators remained in Alexandria for the rest of Tevet and for about three more lunar months, so that by the time of the ceremony before Philadelphus, they had lived in Alexandria for at least seven and a half months - that is, from just after the start of Ellul to around the end of Nisan (from early autumn to spring).[154] In fact, if they had set out for Alexandria after *Shevuoth* and returned to Jerusalem in time for the next *Shevuoth* (as the argument above suggests), they were absent from home for almost a year.[155] It may therefore be significant that, during the final ceremony before Philadelphus, the King remarks that "it was only fair *dikaion gar* for the departure [of the translators] to take place."

281 BCE: THE YEAR OF THE TRANSLATION

Such a comment does not make sense if the translators had stayed for around thirteen weeks, but is reasonable if they were in Alexandria for about seven and a half months. Moreover, the delay between the ceremonies of the Jews and the Greeks is directly in accord with the policy of Ptolemy to encourage men of learning and culture from lands outside Egypt to reside at his court.[156]

This argument in itself does not prove the veracity of either the dates of the translation, or the details of Aristeas. Indeed, if an adequate span of time, free from festivals (apart from the Sabbath) for the journey between Jerusalem and Alexandria is taken as the starting point of the calendar of the translators, periods other than the time between *Shevuoth* and *Rosh haShanah* are also possible for their journey, although these do not fit with the length of time implied by Aristeas and the dates the completion of the translation deduced above. However, need it be assumed that the time of a journey could not include a major festival?[157] Furthermore, need we believe that the translators began their work ten days after their arrival, as Aristeas states? They may have spent a considerable time in Alexandria discussing their task, before they met with the King and started their work.

However, the fact that precise details of timing in the testimony of Aristeas can be harmonized with the dates of the completion of the translation calculated above, so that events fall neatly within the fixed framework of the Jewish calendar, is pleasing confirmation that the work could have been completed and celebrated within the times described.

ANCIENT KNOWLEDGE OF THE CO-REGENCY

The existence of the co-regency and its implications on the chronology of events in the reign of Philadelphus have been mentioned above many times. It is useful now to gather together from the literary authors the meagre evidence of this time. As might be expected, there is a gradually diminishing knowledge of these years.

Only two extant references to the co-regency exist. The first is implied by Aristobulus and the second is the direct reference of Porphyry. However, the discussion above indicates the existence of at least one further source which is now lost. It has been argued above that when Eratosthenes (the assumed source of Eusebius) converted the date of the translation into Olympiad chronology, he mistakenly placed the 3rd Macedonian year of Philadelphus (the true date of the translation) in the 2nd year of the 124th Olympiad. This means that, if the death of Soter was also placed in the 2nd year of the 124th Olympiad, Philadelphus was in his 3rd Macedonian regnal year before Soter was dead. The co-regency was thus implied by an overlap of reigns. Indeed, if the pattern of Eusebius' *Chronicle* is modelled on an earlier work, the overlap was implied by a notice recording the accession of Philadelphus, which preceded a notice of Soter's death. However, unlike the later *Chronicle* of Eusebius, it is unlikely that the early chronicle mentioned the link between the translation and Philadelphus

- otherwise, those authors which were dependent on such a source, namely, the authors who associate the translation with Ptolemy I (see above) may instead have linked the translation with Philadelphus. In an early chronicle, the tie with Philadelphus may have been thought obvious from the fact that the accession of this King began before the translation was made.[158] Moreover, unless Eratosthenes considered that the traditional 40 years of Soter's reign should be reduced by a period equal to the length of the co-regency, this scholar counted the years of the co-regency with the reigns of both Soter and his son. This was the procedure adopted by Philadelphus himself after he back-dated his reign.

The words of the 3rd century scholar Porphyry suggest that this system continued until his time.[159] However, although Porphyry was aware that the years of the co-regency were counted twice over, and, therefore, that Soter was alive during this time, he apparently considered that the procedure was incorrect, and that the traditional 40 years of the reign of Soter should be reduced by the duration of the co-regency. This implies that by the time of Porphyry, the fact that Soter was King till the end of the co-regency had been forgotten, although it was still the practice to count his regnal years till the end of this time. This trend may appear in the first extant, although oblique reference to the co-regency, which is implied by the 2nd century philosopher Aristobulus, when he states that the translation of the Law was made for both "Ptolemy Philadelphus and his father".[160] The

absence of a reference to Soter as King may
suggest that Aristobulus considered that the
translation was made when Soter was alive,
although, by this time, he had already ceded the
throne to Philadelphus. However, the lack of a
title for Soter may not be significant, so that
Aristobulus implies a time of joint rule.

Porphyry is the sole extant historical source
who clearly refers to the co-regency. Although
Eusebius had read Porphyry and thus probably knew
of this time, he dismisses it completely, giving
the traditional number of regnal years to both
Soter and Philadelphus, without having to
acknowledge that the co-regency occurred.[161] It
has been argued above that the existence of the
co-regency was also implied in an early Olympiad
chronicle, possibly in the chronicle of
Eratosthenes, in which the notice of the start of
the reign of Philadelphus preceded that of Soter's
death.[162] If this was used by Eusebius, he would
again have found evidence of the co-regency years.
However, after he had altered the date of the
death of Soter, there was no longer an overlap of
reigns and proof of the existence of the
co-regency was lost. The influence of Eusebius
was so great that no further mention of the
co-regency is found.

DATES FOR THE TRANSLATION WHICH FALL
    LATE OR OUTSIDE THE REIGN OF PTOLEMY II

A brief reference must be made to the dates
given by the sources in Group [2] above, which
fall late or outside the reign of Philadelphus.[163]
That of Chrysostom is probably the easiest to

281 BCE: THE YEAR OF THE TRANSLATION

explain.[164] His assertion that the translation was completed 100 years before the birth of Christ (although he associates it with Ptolemy II[165]) makes sense if he is referring to the Hebrew Bible as a whole. According to the prologue of Ben Sira, this was translated by 132 BCE. Chrysostom may therefore refer to the entire Hebrew Bible, rather than to the Pentateuch alone. However, this is curious in view of the fact that Chrysostom, who flourished *c.*347-407, was born just after the death of Eusebius, was a contemporary of Epiphanius and probably had access to the same sources as these men. It is thus difficult to believe that Chrysostom was ignorant of the opinion of his time which indicated that Philadelphus was involved only with the translation of the Law.

We turn now to Nicetas[166] and Pseudo-Theodoretus,[167] who claim that the translation was competed 301 years before the birth of Christ, and Pseudo-Athanasius[168] who places the event approximately 230 BCE. An examination of their dates must await further work on the text of these authors, which includes an investigation of the chronology they use. It is possible that once the latter is understood, their dates will also relate to the year 280 BCE. This is also suggested by the analysis above, which shows that all reliable sources after Eusebius associate the translation with the reign Philadelphus.

Finally, there is the date of Syncellus, who places the translation in the years July 252 to July 248 BCE,[169] a few years before the death of Philadelphus in 246. No other source places the event so late in his reign. This suggests that the date of Syncellus needs further investigation. Just as the dates of Eusebius and Epiphanius, and their dependent sources, the date of Syncellus is probably not valid as it stands.

THE HISTORY OF THE DATE OF THE TRANSLATION OF THE LAW

The history of the date of the translation recorded in the sources is summarized below in Diagram 12. Sources which are *not* extant are entered in italics, apart from the *Chronicle* of Eusebius, which is assumed to be present in the version of Jerome. Extant sources are written in simple type. No time scale is used.

This diagram shows that of all seven extant versions of the date of the translation which place this event early in the reign Philadelphus, only two are significant - the dates of Eusebius and Epiphanius. Later writers are based either on these sources, or else are derived from the evidence of both. Three main lines of transmission can thus be traced. Two are descended directly from the original date of the translation itself, via Eusebius and Epiphanius, and a third stems from the combined testimony of both. It is thus evident that Greek tradition has preserved two separate and independent records of the date that marks the translation of the Law, on which all other dates in this group depend.

A fourth line of transmission prior to Eusebius is also marked, although this does not involve the transmission of a date. This probably used the same sources as Eusebius.

281 BCE: THE YEAR OF THE TRANSLATION

1. THE DATE RECORDED BY THE JEWS

Megillat Taanit records the translation was complete on 8th of Tevet, probably at the end December 281 BCE, the original 2nd Macedonian year of Ptolemy II. No further transmission of this date took place.

2. THE DATE RECORDED BY THE GREEKS

The translation was completed between April & the start of July 280 BCE, the original 3rd Macedonian year of Ptolemy II

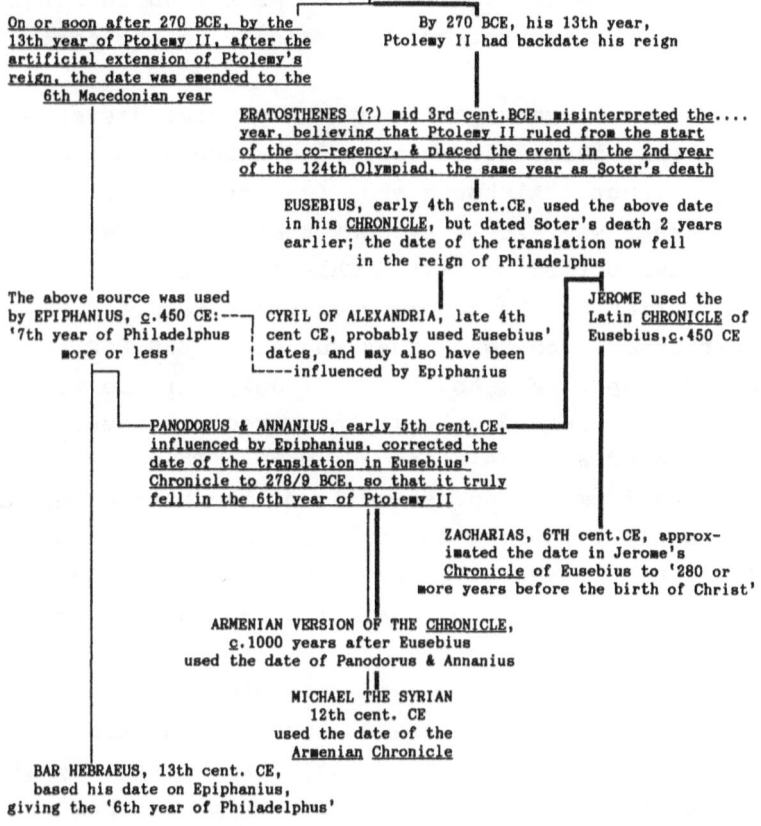

DIAGRAM 12: THE HISTORY OF THE DATE OF THE TRANSLATION OF THE LAW

Key:

Double line - transmission via Eusebius
Single line - transmission via Epiphanius
Combined single & double line - combined transmission of Eusebius & Epiphanius
Dotted line - transmission prior to Eusebius, which used the same sources as Eusebius
Interrupted line - tentative connection between Epiphanius and Cyril of Alexandria

CONCLUSION

This investigation began with a brief survey of the literary accounts of the translation of the Law, from which was surmised the likely period in which the translation was made. As a result, it was possible to list the dates preserved in Greek texts, which conformed most closely to the period implied.

Further investigation of these dates has shown that only those of Eusebius and Epiphanius are significant. Although each is expressed in a different way, it is evident that both refer to the same period of time. This is a strong indication of the accuracy of their report. Furthermore, the date they suggest - 280 BCE, between April and the start of July - falls well within the period of time that scholars have considered a translation was made. This has been deduced from an understanding of the chronology of the early reign of Ptolemy II, that is, without reference to the literary accounts of the translation, which act merely as a initial pointer for the correct time to search.

The same technique has again been used to solve two ancient problems associated with the translation of the Law: (1) the conflicting testimony of the sources concerning the King in power when the translation was made,[170] and (2) the presence of Demetrius of Phalerum at the court of Philadelphus, although he was reputedly expelled after Soter died.[171] The fact that these problems can be solved by means of the methodology earlier employed further endorses the value of its use.

281 BCE: THE YEAR OF THE TRANSLATION   475

    The discussion has also cast light on the variety of sources available to authors up to the time of Eusebius and Epiphanius, who give an account of the translation of the Law. Two types emerge: (1) a narrative source - this has long been recognized and attributed mainly to Aristeas,[172] and (2) a chronological source. This has not previously been appreciated, but is revealed in two ways. Firstly, even if literary texts do not cite dates, they include two characteristic errors that can be sensibly ascribed to an earlier chronicle of events. In relation to the translation of the Law, these errors place the translation in the reign of Ptolemy I and/or omit the role of Demetrius of Phalerum. The use of an earlier chronicle of events is also shown from the use of chronological information which can be derived from no other source. Thus, as far as Eusebius and Epiphanius are concerned, it is clear that as all earlier, literary accounts of the translation do not give a date, the two that they cite must have been derived from a chronological source. In addition, it has been argued that the dates of the translation transmitted by Eusebius and Epiphanius can each be traced back to a record contemporary with the event. The dates cited in sources after the time of Eusebius and Epiphanius are derived from either of these men, or from them both.

    There are thus two independent lines of transmission which originate from the translation of the Law under Ptolemy II - (1) a literary and/or oral source and (2) a chronological source. These confirm each other in different ways. Thus, the date of the translation deduced above has confirmed some details of the testimony of Aristeas. These include his claim that Demetrius of Phalerum worked in Alexandria after the death of Ptolemy I, and that the Jews and the Greeks held separate ceremonies to mark the completion of the translation of the Law. In addition, when the relevant facts from Aristeas are interpreted in conjunction with the dates deduced for the separate ceremonies of the Jews and the Greeks, a valid timetable for the translators can be proposed. This evidence as a whole thus suggests that in spite of much extraneous material (as far as his account of the translation is concerned) and although several of his facts are historically suspect,[173] the account of Aristeas concerning the translation of the Law is essentially true.[174]

The existence of this belief has long been apparent from the several disparate and unconnected sources prior to the time of Eusebius and Epiphanius, which all testify to this claim. It is unlikely that they are all wrong. Thus, in addition to the probably separate literary testimonies in Greek of Aristeas and Aristobulus,[175] a single date is again implied by the different chronographic records of Eusebius and Epiphanius (even if no further investigation of their significance is made), and by the very existence of the Jewish record in *Megillat Taanit*, even if the accuracy of this text is in doubt.[176] It is also implied by the several other allusions to the translation in Jewish, Aramaic texts[177] and by the oral history of the translation, noted personally, and at different times, by Philo and Justin.[178]

The present investigation provides direct evidence for the reality of this belief. Thus, it has been shown that the date of the translation given by Epiphanius is almost certainly taken directly from a contemporary record of the event; similarly, the date of Eusebius can be traced back to an Olympiad chronicle from Hellenistic times, which was itself based on a contemporary note.[179] A record of a contemporary event proves almost certainly that this event took place.

This investigation of the date of the translation into Greek is thus based on sources which are independent of Aristeas and have confirmed the essence of his basic report. As Aristeas relates, a translation of the Pentateuch was made when Philadelphus was King. The records of Eusebius and Epiphanius further establish that the Greeks noted this event in the year 280 BCE, in the period between April and the 1st of July. The Jewish record gives an alternative date. This is confirmed by the testimony of Aristeas, which reveals that the date of the Greeks followed that of the Jews. The latter probably fell near the end of December in 281 BCE. We must therefore conclude that a translation of the Pentateuch was completed under Ptolemy II, in the closing days of 281 BCE.[180]

ABBREVIATIONS

(Others according to *Journal of Biblical Literature* 95 (1976) 331-46).

A.A.M.   Alden A. Mosshammer, *The Chronicle of Eusebius and the Greek Chronographic Tradition* (Cranbury, New Jersey: Associated University Presses, 1979)

A.E.S.   Alan Edouard Samuel, *Ptolemaic Chronology* (München: C. H. Beck, 1962)

A.P.   André Pelletier, *La Letter d'Aristée à Philocrate* (Paris: Cerf, 1962)

B.G.S   Marguerite Harl, Gilles Dorival, Olivier Munnich, *La Bible Grecque des Septante* (Paris: Cerf, 1988)

C.A.H.   *The Cambridge Ancient History*^{2}, Vol VII, Part I, *The Hellenistic World*, ed. Walbank et al. (Cambridge: Cambridge University Press, 1984)

C.M.S.   J. B. Chabot, *Chronique de Michel Le Syrien, Patriarche Jacobite d'Antioche* (Bruxelles: Culture et Civilisation, 1963), Vol 1 (Reprint of Paris, 1899)

E.J.B.   Elias J. Bickerman, *Chronology of the Ancient World*^{2} (London: Thames and Hudson, 1980)

E.S.   Emil Schürer, *The History of the Jewish People in the age of Jesus Christ*, ed. Geza Vermes, Fergus Millar and Martin Goodman, Vol I (1973), Vol III.1 (Edinburgh: T. & T. Clark, 1986)

Helm   *Die Chronik des Hieronymus*, ed. Rudolf Helm (Berlin: GCS, 1956)

H.O.   Harry M. Orlinsky, "The Septuagint and its Hebrew Text," *The Cambridge History of Judaism*, Vol 2, The Hellenistic Age, ed. Davies and Finkelstein (Cambridge: Cambridge University Press, 1989), pp. 534-62.

J.E.D.   James Elmer Dean, *Epiphanius' Treatise on Weights and Measures* (Chicago, Illinois: University of Chicago, 1935)

281 BCE: THE YEAR OF THE TRANSLATION   479

J.F.   Jack Finegan, *Handbook of Biblical
          Chronology* (Princeton, New Jersey:
          Princeton University Press, 1964)

Karst   Joseph Karst, *Eusebius Werke, Die Chronik*
          (Leipzig: J. C. Hinrichs, 1911)

LetAris The Letter of Aristeas

M.H.   Moses Hadas, *Aristeas to Philocrates*
          (New York: Harper and Brothers, 1951)

P.M.F.   P. M. Fraser, *Ptolemaic Alexandria*
          (Oxford: Clarendon Press, 1972)

P.W.P.   P. W. Pestman, *Chronologie Egyptienne
          d'après les Textes Démotiques*,
          Papyrologica Lugduno-Batava, Vol XV
          (Leiden: Brill, 1967)

P.W.   Paulus Wendland, *Aristeae ad Philocratem
          Epistula* (Leipzig: Teubner, 1900). (PW
          refers to *Pauly-Wissowa*)

R.P.   R. Pfeiffer, *History of Classical
          Scholarship* (Oxford: Clarendon Press,
          1968)

S.M.S. Sidney Jellicoe, *The Septuagint and
          Modern Study* (London: Oxford University
          Press, 1968)

SSORI   Sidney Jellicoe, ed., *Studies in
          Septuagint Origins, Recensions and
          Interpretations* (New York: Ktav, 1974)

Thack.   H. St. John Thackeray, *The Letter of
          Aristeas* (New York: Society for Promoting
          Christian Knowledge, 1918)

List 1. SOURCES IMPLICATING PTOLEMY II IN THE
                    TRANSLATION OF THE LAW

Listed below are the sources in addition to Aristeas, which directly cite Ptolemy II, called Ptolemy or Philadelphus, in connection with the translation of the Law, or else imply that this king was involved, such as those which refer to Aristeas. They appear in chronological order as far as this is known. Unless otherwise noted,

they are cited according to P. Wendland (P.W.) or
A. Pelletier (A.P.):

1. Aristobulus (fl. *c*.155-145 BCE): (i) Eusebius,
HE 13.12.2, P.W., p.124; (ii) Eusebius, *HE*
7.32.16, (*Ex Anatolii de Pascha canonibus*), P.W.,
p.126.

2. Philo (*c*.30 BCE-45 CE): *De Vit.Mos.* II 25-44,
P.W., pp.90-95.

3. Josephus (b.37/8CE): (i) *Ant* 1.10, P.W., p.120;
(ii) *Ant* 12.11-18, P.W., pp.96-120, *Ant* XII 11;
(iii) *Con.Ap* 2.44-45, P.W., pp.120-21.

4. Justin (*c*.100-165 CE): (i) *Apology* 1.31, P.W.,
p.121; (ii) *Dialogue with Trypho* 71, trans.
Thomas B. Falls, *Saint Justin Martyr* (Catholic
University of America Press, Washington, 1948),
p.262; (iii) *Exhortation to the Greeks* 13, P.W.,
pp.121-23.

Justin is the earliest of the Church Fathers to
mention the translation. He refers to the King
as "Ptolemy," with no further identification.
Since the eponym "Philadelphus" was current from
the 2nd cent. BCE (see n. 10), it is possible
that Justin may be referring to Soter. However,
Justin also refers to the testimony of Aristeas
and Philo, who both indicate Ptolemy II.

5. Clement of Alexandria (*c*.150-211/16 CE): *Strom*
I.22.148, P.W., pp.124-25.

6. Iulius Pollux (2nd cent.CE): P.W., pp.136-37.
The link with Philadelphus is assumed from the
statement of Pollux that the King associated with
the translation ruled for 38 years. Ancient
historians claim that Soter ruled for 40 years,
Philadelphus for 38, see nn. 52, 111 with
text.

7. Tertullian (*c*.160-240 CE): *Apology* 18, P.W.,
pp. 126-27.

8. Eusebius (*c*.260-340 CE):
   (i) *PrEv* 8.1.5, P.W., pp. 127-28;
   (ii) *Chronicle* of Eusebius
      (a) Jerome's (Hieronymus') Latin

281 BCE: THE YEAR OF THE TRANSLATION

        Chronicle, P.W., p. 130, Helm, p. 129;
(b) Armenian *Chronicle*, P.W., p. 130,
Karst, p. 200; Karst, *Chronographia*,
p. 60, P.W., p. 129;
(c) Syriac *Chronicle* of Dionysius Tell-
Mahre (d.845 CE), P.W., pp. 131-32.

9. Epiphanius (c.315-403 CE): *On Weights and Measures*, P.W., pp. 139-48, J.E.D., §52b, §52c, §53c.

10. Athanasius (c.296-373 CE): *Synopsis Scripturae Sacrae*, P.W., p. 149.

11. St. Cyril of Jerusalem (b. before 318 - d. after 386 CE): *Catechetical Lectures* IV 34, P.W., p. 138.

12. John Chrysostom (c.347-407 CE): P.W., pp. 138-39, *Discourses against Judaizing Christians* IV I; *Homilies on Genesis* IV 4; *Homilies on St. Matthew* V 2.

13. St. Jerome (also called Hieronymus), see No.8iia above, (c.342-420 CE): P.W., pp. 162-63, *Praef. in Penti.* PLXXVIII, p. 181; *Comm. in Ezeck.* 5,12; *Comm. in. Mich.* 2,9.

14. Cyril of Alexandria, (d.444): see n. 27 with text.

15. Augustine (d. 604/5 CE): *De Civ. Dei.* XVIII 42, P.W., pp.163-64; *De Mirabilibus Sacrae Scripturae* I,9, P.W., pp. 164-65;.

16. St. Isidore (d. 450 CE): *Etymologiae* VI 3,5, P.W., p. 165.

17. Cosmas Indicopleustes (mid. 6th cent.CE): *Topogr. Christ.*, P.W., pp. 156-57.

18. Basil of Seleucia (d. c.459): P.W., p .149 (PG 85, pp. 421-22).

19. Zacharias of Mitylene, (also "Zacharias Scholasticus," d. after 536): A.P., p. 95, see n. 28 with text.

20. Ioannes Malalas (late 6th cent.CE): P.W., p. 132.

21. *Chronicon Paschale* I (compiled early 7th cent.): P.W., pp. 132-33.

22. Nicephorus (c.758-829 CE): P.W., pp. 129-30 (*P.G.* 100, p. 1009, *Chronographia Brevis*).

23. Georgius Syncellus (fl. 8th century): P.W., pp. 133-35.

24. Georgius Cedrenus (fl. 11th cent.CE): P.W., p. 135.

25. Nicetas Serrarus of Heraclea, *Catena in psalmos* (fl. 11th cent.), P.W., p. 159.

26. Leo Grammaticus: P.W., p. 136.

27. Euthymius Zigabenus (fl. early 12th cent.): *In Psalmos* P.W., p. 155.

28. Ioannes Zonaras I (fl. 12th cent.): P.W., p. 136.

29. (Pseudo-)Theodoretus: *tractatus ineditus*, P.W., pp. 150-55. See n. 35 with text.

30. Iosephi Hypomnesticum: P.W., pp. 155-56.

31. Ioannes Lydus: (i) *De Magistratibus*, P.W., p. 157; (ii) *De Mensibus*, P.W., p. 157.

32. Michel le Syrien (Patriarche Jacobite d'Antioch 1166-1199): see n. 31 with text.

33. Bar Hebraeus (1226-1286 CE): see n. 29 with text.

34. Solomon (fl. 1222 CE): *The Book of the Bee*, trans. E. A. Wallis Budge, (Oxford, 1886), Semitic Series Vol 1, Part II, p. 120.

List 2. SOURCES IMPLICATING PTOLEMY I IN THE TRANSLATION OF THE LAW

Listed below are the ancient authorities which link, or appear to link Ptolemy I with the translation of the Law. The three which most clearly refer to Soter, namely Aristobulus, Irenaeus and Clement of Alexandria, lived prior to Eusebius. Filaster was probably a younger

281 BCE: THE YEAR OF THE TRANSLATION

contemporary of Eusebius. Aristobulus and Clement implicate both Soter and his son:

PROBABLY RELIABLE SOURCES:

1. Aristobulus, in Eusebius, *HE* 7.32.16, P.W., p. 126 (*Ex Anatolii de Pascha canonibus*), quoted above, No.1.

2. Irenaeus (*c*.130-200 CE): Eusebius, *HE* 5.8.11, P.W., pp. 123-24, "Ptolemy, called Lagos, in his ambition to adorn the library which he had built in Alexandria ... besought of the inhabitants of Jerusalem that he might have their Scriptures rendered into the Greek tongue..." (A.P., p. 81, emends "Ptolemy, called Lagus" to "Ptolemy, the son of Lagus" ("Ptolémée fils de Lagos"). This is probably incorrect - see main text on "Ptolemy I or Ptolemy II?").

3. Clement of Alexandria, *Strom*.1.22.148, P.W., pp. 124-25, quoted above, No.5.

4. St. Filaster (also "Philaster"), *Diversarum Hereseon Liber CXLII*, (d. *c*.397): P.W., pp. 160-61, "haec etenim, id est LXX duorum interpretatio, sub Tolemeo rege Aegyptiorum post Alexandrum Macedonem..."

DOUBTFUL SOURCES:

5. Theodoretus (*c*.393-458 CE): *Praef. in psal.*, P.W., pp. 148-49, "Ptolemy, who ruled after Alexander..."

6. Nicetas, quoted above, No.25, who names Philadelphus, but whose date for the translation in 301 BCE implies Soter.

7. P-Theodoretus, quoted above No.29. If the proposed emendation is correct (see n. 35 with text), P-Theodoretus names Philadelphus, but his date implies Soter.

8. Zosimus Panopolitanus, see E. Nestle in James Hastings, *Dictionary of the Bible* (Edinburgh: T. & T. Clark, 1902), Vol IV, *s.v.* "Septuagint," p. 439, quoting from *de Zythorum confectione*, ed. Gruner, 1814, p. 5, "Simon the high priest of Jerusalem sent Hermes to Ptolemy Lagi, [and Hermes] translated all the Hebrew [work] for the

Greeks and Egyptians..." (Also said by Nestle to be cited by Constantine Oikonomos, *Peri ton o' hermeneuton tes Palaios Theias Graphes*, Vol II (Athens, 1845), p. 328).

VERY DOUBTFUL SOURCES:

?9. Eutychius, P.W., p. 131, *PG* 11, *Alexandrini Annales* states, "In Alexandria and Egypt, after Alexander, ruled his brother for 7 years, (or, according to a different authority, 40 years) called Philip, who was surnamed Philip Arrhidaeus. After him, Ptolemy, surnamed Alexander, whose family name was Galeb-Vzr, ruled for 27 [or, 21] years. In his 20th year, having sent to Jerusalem..."

After Philip Arrhidaeus, Ptolemy I ruled in Egypt, and not (as Eutychius states) Ptolemy Alexander, who ruled Egypt 106-88 BCE. Eutychius seems wrong with respect to the successor of Arrhidaeus, but his placement of Ptolemy Alexander following Arrhidaeus may suggest that he is confusing Ptolemy Soter with this king. If so, Eutychius appears to suggest that the translation of the Law occurred in the 20th year of Soter.

?10. *Excerpta Latina Barbari*, p. 276, P.W., pp. 130-31, attributes the translation to Ptolemy Alexander, "post Philippum, autem regnavit Alexander Ptolemaeus quem ... illi septuaginta Ebrei sapientes illam legem interpretaverunt Greco sermonei." But, Ptolemy Alexander ruled Egypt 106-88 BCE. However, as this ruler is stated to be the 3rd after the death of Alexander, this may suggest that Soter is intended - Philip Arrhidaeus and Alexander IV ruled nominally between the death of Alexander the Great and Ptolemy I.

NOTES

1. S. Jellicoe, *S.M.S.*, Chap. 1, esp. pp. 55-56; E.S., Vol III.1, p. 476; G. Dorival, B.G.S., pp. 56-58; J. A. Lee, *A Lexical Study of the*

281 BCE: THE YEAR OF THE TRANSLATION   485

Septuagint Version of the Pentateuch (SBLSCS 14; Chico, California: Scholars Press, 1983).

2. A recent comprehensive list of sources, with refs. to other collections, with excellent commentary, has been compiled by G. Dorival, B.G.S., pp. 45-50. See also E. Nestle in James Hastings, *Dictionary of the Bible* (Edinburgh: T. & T. Clark, 1902), Vol IV, *s.v.* "Septuagint," esp. pp. 438-39. A wide range of refs. is said to have been collected by Constantine Oikonomos, *Peri ton o' hermeneuton tes Palaios Theias Graphes*, 4 Vols (Athens, 1845), but I have not been able to inspect this work - Nestle cites vols. I, II and III. For bibliog. of *LetAris*, see B.G.S., pp. 43-44.

3. See, e.g., M.H., pp. 5-9, who comments on *LetAris* 180, with ref. to sea battles under Ptolemy II, esp. in relation to the life of Arsinoë II. See also historical inaccuracies listed by J. W. Wevers, "Proto-Septuagint Studies," *SSORI*, pp. 138-57, esp. p. 142. But, some historical problems listed by scholars are difficult to substantiate, see e.g., H.O., pp. 534-62, who states (pp. 543-44) that it is not likely that the completed translation was read on the Pharos, due to *problems of transportation and geography*. Orlinsky then quotes *LetAris* 301 which describes the accommodation of the translators on the Pharos. This *proves* rather than *dis*proves the possibility of a public reading at this place. Orlinsky also fails to quote the conflicting testimony of Justin Martyr: see n. 15 below. The date of the translation deduced here supports the observation of historical inaccuracies in Aristeas, e.g., his ref. to *Arsinoë* as "sister-wife" and mother of the children of Ptolemy II, *LetAris* 41 (also Eusebius, *PrEv* 8.5) may be a simple confusion with the first wife of Philadelphus, also called Arsinoë. It is interesting that Josephus may correct Aristeas in this respect, by omitting the reference to Arsinoë as a "sister," *Ant* XII. 51, referring to the first wife of Philadelphus who was the mother of his children, whereas his second marriage was childless, see C.A.H., p. 488 for a genealogical table of the Ptolemies. However, Josephus refers to the sister of Philadelphus at *Ant* XII.55. Was Josephus aware of the date of the translation of

the Law into Greek under Ptolemy II, as deduced in this discussion?

4. E.g., S.M.S, pp. 55-56; B. S. J. Isserlin, "The Names of the 72 Translators of the LXX (Aristeas, 47-50)," *JANESCU* 5 (1973), 191-97. For *contra*, see H.O., esp. pp. 541-48.

5. *LetAris* 13, 22. Aristobulus also refers to Soter as the father of Ptolemy II, Eusebius, *EH* 7 32 16

6. *LetAris* 35, 41.

7. *LetAris* 4, 12, 13, 22.

8. *LetAris* 41.

9. *LetAris* 30, see comments of G. Zuntz, "Aristeas Studies II: Aristeas on the Translation of the Torah," *JSJ* 4 (1959), 109-26, reprinted in G. Zuntz, *Opuscula Selecta*, (Manchester: Manchester University Press, 1972), pp. 126-43 and also in *SSORI*, pp. 208-25.

10. The name "Philadelphus" is thought to have come into use in the 2nd cent. BCE to distinguish Ptolemy II from other Ptolemies, see A. Yarbro Collins, "Aristobulus" *The Old Testament Pseudepigrapha*, Vol 2, ed. James H. Charlesworth (London: Darton, Longman and Todd, 1985), p. 833, n. 13. Aristeas does not use the name "Philadelphus."

11. Aristeas and Aristobulus may be independent sources for the role of Demetrius, because Aristobulus relates the main elements of Aristeas, without betraying knowledge of other elements of his work, see E.S., Vol III, pp. 474-75.

12. See e.g. the analysis of Josephus' account of the trans., *Ant* 12.12-8, by M.H., pp. 18-21. The dependence of Josephus on Aristeas is difficult to decide. For a possible change to the account of Aristeas by Josephus, see n. 3.

13. Eusebius, *PrEv* 8 2-5. The date given by Eusebius in the *Chronicle* comes from a different source which is discussed below.

14. On Philo, see M.H., pp. 21-26. For the possible sources of Philo, see SOURCES OF ACCOUNTS OF THE TRANSLATION PRIOR TO EUSEBIUS, below in the main text.

15. Justin does not mention *LetAris* by name, but states that his evidence for the involvement of

281 BCE: THE YEAR OF THE TRANSLATION

Philadelphus comes from the oral evidence of the people of the Pharos themselves, where he claims (along with Aristeas and others) that the translation was written. He also states that during his life, other sources were extant, "You may learn it from others also, and chiefly from those wise and distinguished men who have written, Philo and Josephus, but there many others besides," *Exhortations to the Greeks* 13.

16. See List 1 for sources which implicate Ptolemy II in the translation, placed at the end of this paper.

17. See List 2 for sources which implicate Soter. It is possible that Justin Martyr also implicates Soter, see List 1. Several Jewish sources give the name "Ptolemy" in connection with changes that were introduced into the translation, see Thack., pp. 89-95, and Emanuel Tov, "The Rabbinic Tradition concerning the 'Alterations' Inserted into the Greek Pentateuch & Their Relation to the Original Text of the LXX" *JSJ* 15 (1984), 65-89, esp. p. 70. They imply that some changes were made in the Greek text to avoid offending Soter's patronym, *Lagus* (=hare). This hints that Soter, rather that his son, was involved. But the date of the translation deduced here suggests that such changes were made to avoid offending Philadelphus. It may be relevant that Aristeas devotes considerable space to the discussion of unclean animals, *LetAris* 128-71. Aristeas does not use the name "Soter." The link between the translation and Soter is discussed below, "PTOLEMY I OR PTOLEMY II?"

18. The following sources implicate Demetrius directly in the translation:
  A. Before Eusebius: (1) Aristeas, *LetAris* 9,11,28 etc.;(2) Aristobulus, Eusebius, *PrEv* 13.12.2; (3) Josephus, *Ant* 12.12; *Apion* 2.44; (4) Clement of Alexandria, *Strom* I.2248; (5) Tertullian, *Apology* 18; (6) Eusebius, in his account of Aristeas, *PrEv* 8.1;
  B. Contemporary with Eusebius: (1) Epiphanius, *On Weights and Measures*, J.E.D., 52b; (2) St. Cyril of Jerusalem, *Catechetical Lectures* IV 34;
  C. After Eusebius: (1) Cosmas Indicopleustas, refers to Demetrius as "Tryphon of Phalerium;" (2) Georgius Syncellus, P.W., pp. 133-35; (3) Georgius Cedrenus, ed. Immanuel Becker (Weber,

Bonn, 1838), p. 290; (4) Leo Grammaticus, ed. I.
Becker, (Bonn: Weber, 1842), p. 50.

Other sources also link Demetrius with Ptolemy
II, in contexts other than the translation, e.g.,
the *Plautine Scholium* from Caecius; Johnnes
Tzetzes' *Prolegomena to Aristophanes* (for trans.
of these, with com. see Edward Alexander Parsons,
The Alexandrian Library (London: Cleaver-Hume
Press, 1952), pp. 108-21 and Plutarch, *Moralia*
189D cites Demetrius in connection with "Ptolemy."

19. Diogenes Laertius V 78, "Hermippus tells us
that upon the death of Casander, being in fear of
Antigonus, he fled to Ptolemy Soter. There he
spent a considerable time and advised Ptolemy,
among other things, to invest with sovereign power
his children by Eurydice. To this, Ptolemy would
not agree, but bestowed the diadem on his son [the
future Philadelphus] by Berenice, who after
[Soter's] death, thought fit to detain Demetrius
as a prisoner in the country *paraphulattesthai en
tei cho̱rai* until some decision should be taken
concerning him. There he lived in great
dejection, and somehow, in his sleep, received an
asp-bite on the hand which proved fatal." Trans.
R.D. Hicks (LCL; Cambridge, Mass.: Harvard
University Press).

On the problem of the presence of Demetrius of
Phalerum after Soter's death, see H.B.Swete, *An
Introduction to the Old Testament in Greek*
(Cambridge: Cambridge University Press, 1914), pp.
18-19; M.H., pp. 7, citing PW, s.v. "Demetrius,"
(85), 4, (1901), pp. 2817-41; R.P., pp. 95-96,
99-104; E.S., pp. 475, n. 11; P.M.F., pp. 267,
314-15, 321; B.G.S., pp. 57-58.

20. Aristobulus, (fl. c.155-145 BCE) implies that
both Philadelphus and his father were involved
with the translation, see Eusebius, *HE* 7.32.16,
(*Ex Anatolii de Pascha canonibus*), P.W., p. 126,
"... Aristobulus, who was enrolled among the 70
who translated the sacred and divine Scriptures of
the Hebrews for Ptolemy Philadelphus and his
father". See also n. 11.

Two other sources *may* imply both Ptolemy I and
II: (1) Nicetas Serrarus, of Heraclea, *Catena in
psalmos* (11th cent.), P.W., pp. 158-59, who names
Philadelphus, but whose date for the translation,
about 301 BCE, implies Soter; similarly, (2)
Pseudo-Theodoretus, P.W., pp. 150-55, see n. 35
below.

21. Clement of Alexandria (c. 150-211/16 CE), Strom I.22.148, P.W., pp. 124-25, "They say that the Scriptures, both of the Law and of the prophets, were translated from the Hebrew tongue into Greek under King Ptolemy, son of Lagus, or, as some assert, under him who was surnamed Philadelphus, Demetrius of Phalerum displaying the greatest zeal in the undertaking... "

22. John Chrysostom and Pseudo-Athanasius, see Group [2].

23. Possible reasons for the confusion regarding the identity of the king under whose aegis the translation was produced will be discussed below under "PTOLEMY I OR PTOLEMY II?"

24. The dates of the start of the reign of Philadelphus are discussed below.

25. Helm, p. 129.

26. Thack., p. 115 (English); trans. from Syriac by J.E.D., 53c.

27. P.W., p. 148; trans. Paul Burguire, *Contre Julien* (Paris: Cerf, 1985), Livre I, 16.

28. A.P., p. 95 (French); English trans. by F. J. Hamilton and E. W. Brooks, *The Syriac Chronicle known as that of Zachariah of Mitylene* (London: Methuen, 1899), p. 325.

29. A.P., pp. 95-96; English trans. by E. A. Wallis Budge, *The Chronography of Bar Hebraeus* (London: Oxford University Press, 1932), Vol I, pp. 39-40.

30. Karst, p. 200.

31. C.M.S., Livre V, VI, p. 123, also known as Michel le Grand or Michel l'Ancien, C.M.S., p. II. In the trans. of Victor Langlois, *Chronique de Michel le Grand...traduite ... sur la version arménienne du prêtre Ischôk*, (Venise: Académie de Saint-Lazare, 1868), p. 78, (A.P., p. 95, note 2), Michel le Syrien dates the translation in the 26th year of Ptolemy and claims that it took place on Cyprus, although he admits, p. 79, that others place it on the Pharos. C.M.S. places the event on the "Faros." If the 26th year is correct, Michel should be placed in Group [2].

32. *in Matth. Hom. V 2*, P.W., p. 139.

33. P.W., p. 149.

34. *Nicetae catena in psalmos*, P.W., p. 159.

35. *Pseudo-Theodoreti tractatus ineditus*, P.W., p. 153. According to the text of P.W., the event took place "before the 31st year, *pro triakostou protou etous*, before the coming of Christ." This number is suspect because no other source places the translation so close to the birth of Christ - the closest is that given by Chrysostom for which there is a good explanation - see below under "DATES FOR THE TRANSLATION WHICH FALL LATE OR OUTSIDE THE REIGN OF PTOLEMY II." The date of P-Theodoretus is thus totally anomalous. Accordingly, it is here proposed that the Greek *triakostou*, i.e., 30th, should be read *triakosiou*, i.e., 300th, that is, reading Iota for Tau. This emended number is identical to that of Nicetas, and thus may have the same historical implication i.e., it dated the translation under Ptolemy I, see n. 20 above.

36. P.W., p. 135.

37. The system is well documented, e.g., A.E.S., p. 5.

38. J.F., §114.

39. See J.F., §185. Olympiads and Olympiadic years are well documented, e.g., E.J.B., pp. 75-76; pp. 115-122 provides an easy ref. for correlating Olympiads, Olympiadic years and years BCE/CE. (The adjective used to describe one of the four years of an Olympiad is variable. A.A.M. uses "Olympiad years," see p. 35; but J.F. uses "Olympiadic years," see §187).

40. These are well documented, e.g., A.E.S., p. 4; P.W.P., p. 5.

41. See table in E.J.B., p. 118, re. 124th Olympiad. In the years 285-282 BCE Thoth 1 fell on November 2; in the years 281-278, on November 2.

42. These are well documented, e.g., A.E.S., p. 12; P.W.P., p. 5.

43. For the value of Julian years corresponding to years of Abraham, see A.A.M., p. 172; for claim that Abraham was born in Tishri (autumn) and the start of the years of Abraham, see J.F., p. 169.

44. For an example, see discussion below on the Armenian *Chronicle* of Eusebius.

281 BCE: THE YEAR OF THE TRANSLATION   491

45. For dates of the birth of Christ in early Christian texts, see J.F., p. 361.

46. According to Porphyry, "While [Soter] was yet alive, he gave the rule to his son Ptolemy, who was called Philadelphus, and he lived 2 more years under his son who had assumed power. Thus, not 40 years, but 38 are reckoned for the first Ptolemy, whom they call Soter...," Felix Jacoby, *Die Fragmente der Griechischen Historiker* (Berlin: Weidmann, 1929), Vol 2B, 260, 2 (2).

47. Dates of the reigns of Soter and Philadelphus are those of A.E.S., pp. 66, 168. For the revised date for the start of the co-regency, see Alan E. Samuel, *Greek and Roman Chronology* (München: C. H. Beck, 1972), p. 147 with n. 5. In the past, the apparent overlap of the kings has inspired the suggestion that the translation was written during the co-regency years, see e.g., J. H. A. Hart, *Ecclesiasticus* (Cambridge: Cambridge University Press, 1909), p. 262; Henry G. Meecham, *The Oldest Version of the Bible* (Holburn Publishing House, London, 1932), p. 137, quoting Bleek, *Introduction to the Old Testament* II, 400ff. This theory is not promoted here, although the existence of the co-regency is vital to the argument below.

48. A.E.S. pp. 25-26 and n. 111.

49. A.E.S., pp. 27-28, states that the back-dating occurred in the 16th year of Philadelphus, 267 BCE. Another opinion is given by Uebel, *Bibl. Orient.* 21 (1964), pp. 310-12, who presents evidence to support a change in the 13th year of Philadelphus, 270 BCE. The argument of this discussion is not affected by which of these dates is correct, because, as will be shown, the significant dates given for the translation in Group [1], i.e., the dates of Eusebius and Epiphanius, pre-date the King's 13th year. Thus, the 13th year will here be accepted as the date of the change. See Ludwig Koenen, *Eine agonistische Inschrift aus Ägypten und frühptolemäische Königsfeste* (Meisenheim: Hain, 1977), pp. 43-45, with refs.; P.M.F., Vol II, pp. 364-65.

50. See n. 49.

51. The mechanics of the addition will be detailed below in the main text.

52. The following sources which state that Philadelphus ruled for 38 years are restricted to

those which deal with the translation of the Law.
(The number after each name refers to the position
of the name in the list of sources in List 1 at
the end of this paper). (1) Julius Pollux, No.6;
(2) Eusebius' Latin *Chronicle* (see Helm, pp.
129-30), No.8iia; (3) Epiphanius, *Weights and
Measures*, J.E.D., 53c, No.9; (4) Basil of
Seleucia, P.W., p. 149, (PG 85, p. 421), No.16;
(5) Nicephorus, No.22; (6) Syncellus, ed. Bekker
(Bonn, 1847), p. 49, No.23; (7) Cedrenus, P.W., p.
135, No.24; (8) Leo Grammaticus, P.W., p. 136,
No.26; (9) 32. Michel le Syrien, No. 32, C.M.S.,
p. 232; (10) Bar Hebraeus, No.33; (10) Solomon,
Book of the Bee, No.34; (11) Armenian version of
Eusebius' *Chronicle* (the years emended from 28),
No.8iib,c.

Josephus, *Ant* XII 11, No.3i, gives the
equivalent 39 Macedonian years.

Porphyry, above n. 46, makes no reference to
the translation, but suggests that, due to the
co-regency, two years should be removed from the
regnal years of Soter, see below on "ANCIENT
KNOWLEDGE OF THE CO-REGENCY" in main text.

53. The corresponding Julian months are calculated
from A.E.S., pp. 161-67, esp. Table C, pp. 166-67.
Dates are given to the nearest Julian month, since
A.E.S. states p. 161 that the months are not
accurate before Philadelphus' 22nd year.

54. See n. 42.

55. A.E.S., p. 66, calculates the length of the
co-regency by counting full years *backwards* in the
reign of Ptolemy II, but the total effect is the
same.

56. See n. 55.

57. The length of the co-regency in Olympiad years
is not important during the reign of Philadelphus,
because the system of Olympiad years was probably
developed after his time, perhaps by Eratosthenes
in Alexandria after Philadelphus had died, see
n. 63. However, they are relevant to the evidence
of later sources - see below in main text re.
"PTOLEMY I OR PTOLEMY II?"

58. See n. 25.

59. See n. 52.

60. See n. 46. A.A.M., p. 130, notes that Eusebius

cites only two named authorities, Porphyry (in relation to Hesiod) and Apollodorus.

61. See n. 46.

62. For further discussion on the co-regency, see below under "ANCIENT KNOWLEDGE OF THE CO-REGENCY" in main text.

63. A.A.M., pp. 117-18; E.J.B., p. 87

64. "More or less" occurs in the Syriac version of Epiphanius' *Weights and Measures*, but is absent in the Greek. See J.E.D., p. 28, n. 99. The phrase appears in the trans. of Thack., p. 115.

65. Justin Martyr, *Dialogue with Trypho* 88.

66. Observed by J.F., pp. 274, 427, who cites: (1) Lk 3:23, "Jesus was about (h<u>o</u>sei) 30 when he was baptised;" (2) Irenaeus, *Against Heresies* II xxii 5, "For when [Jesus] came to be baptized, he had not yet competed his 30th year, but was beginning to be about 30 years of age;" (3) Epiphanius, *Panarion haer.* 51,16,2. ed. Karl Holl, *Die griechischen christlichen Schriftsteller der ersten drei Jahrhunderte* II (1922), p. 271, "[Jesus was] beginning to be about 30 years of age." Epiphanius puts the baptism of Jesus on Nov 8, 60 days before his 30th birthday, reckoning his birth on Jan 6, 2 BCE, see J.F., pp. 251-52.

67. The expression may in fact have originated as a way of referring to the age of a child before his first year. To overcome the problem, we refer to the age of such a child in months.

68. For Bar Hebraeus, see n. 16, No.32 in List 1. For evidence of his dependence on Epiphanius, see trans. of the history of Bar Hebraeus by E. A. Budge, *The Chronography of Gregory Abu'l Faraj* (London: Oxford University Press, 1932), p. 20, in which Epiphanius is cited in the section of this work entitled *Kings of the Hebrews*, p. 20. For a general appreciation of the debt owed to Epiphanius by Syriac writers, see J.E.D., p. viii, "...in order to trace the sources of Bar hebraeus, Karkaphensian philology and much else in Syriac literature, it proved necessary to recur time and again to Epiphanius' *Weights and Measures*." The standard of the testimony of Bar Hebraeus can be gauged from the remark by M. Sprengling & W. C. Graham, *Barhebraeus' Scholia on the Old Testament* (University of Chicago Press, Chicago, Illinois, 1931), p. vii, that he was "by far the greatest

writer in the entire history of Syriac literature."

69. See n. 52.

70. See n. 48.

71. E.g., Epiphanius, *Panarion* 29,4,1, see trans. of Frank Williams, *The Panarion of Epiphanius of Salamis, Book I (Sects 1-46)* (Leiden: E. J. Brill, 1987), p. 114.

72. J.E.D., p. 7; F. Williams (see above note) p. XII; p. 114, in *Panarion* 3,3 & 4,1 Eusebius' *HE* is used at *Panarion* 29,5,1-4, etc. see F. Williams, pp. 112-14.

73. Stated in connection with the re-numbering of the same regnal years of Philadelphus, indicated on the Mendes stele, see J Oates, A. Samuel and C. Welles, *Yale Papyri in the Beinecke Rare Book and Manuscript Library*, American Studies in Papyrology, Vol 2 (New Haven: The American Society of Papyrologists, 1967), No.28, p. 67.

74. *LetAris* 39.

75. See n. 49 for the possible difference in the years of the change noted by Samuel and Uebel.

76. For contemporary inscriptions from Bucheum, see A.E.S., p. 26.

77. Perhaps the date of the completion was marked on the actual anniversary of the reign of the King on April 6th. The anniversary of the co-regency was probably the annual birthday of the King, see A.E.S., pp. 69-70. The co-regency may have been a birthday present from Soter to his son. The splendor of the ceremony held for the translators would be appropriate for the special celebrations held by Ptolemies on their birthdays. See also P.M.F., p. 232. It is interesting that some authors of popular books have already confidently given this year, e.g., *Pears Cyclopaedia 97th Edition*, ed. Christopher Cook (London: Pelham Books, 1988), p. A3, "280 BCE;" J. O. Westwood, *The Art of Illuminated Manuscripts* (London: Bracken Books, 1988), p. 1, "about 280 BCE."

78. See n. 63.

79. R.P., p. 153. Eratosthenes lived *c*.275-194 BCE.

80. See n. 73.

281 BCE: THE YEAR OF THE TRANSLATION

81. See pp. 406-407.
82. See n. 29.
83. See n. 68.
84. See n. 66.
85. See n. 27.
86. On Cyril's use of Eusebius' *Chronicle*, see A.A.M., p. 325, n. 52.
87. See n. 28.
88. A.M.M., p. 78. For a comparison of the reliability and accuracy of the Armenian and Syriac versions of the *Chronicle*, compared with the Latin version, see A.A.M., pp. 65,74,78,81.
89. The reasons for the difference are well known, see A.A.M., pp. 73-79.
90. See n. 43.
91. See n. 43.
92. A.A.M., pp. 76-79.
93. A.A.M., p. 74.
94. A.A.M., pp. 77-79.
95. A.A.M., p. 78, p. 324, n. 48.
96. See n. 31.
97. C.B.S., pp. XXV-XXVI.
98. Appendix to *Megillath Taanith*, in *Anecdota Oxoniensia, Semitic Series*, Vol I, Part VI, Mediaeval Jewish Chronicles II (Oxford, 1895), Section II, p. 24. A variant mss. gives the 7th of Tevet.
99. E.S., Vol 1, p. 590.
100. *LetAris* 308-11.
101. *Megillath Taanith* states that when the translation was made, "darkness came upon the world for three days." This suggests that the Jewish date coincided with an eclipse of the sun. But no kind of heavenly portent appears in any of the accounts of the translation, although the latter include several miraculous events, e.g., the claim (of Aristeas and others) that the translation was completed in 72 days, Philo's claim (repeated by others) that the seventy-two translators all emerged with identical texts, so

that, (as Irenaeus and others assert), the
Scriptures were translated by the inspiration of
God. If the translation had coincided with a
notable astronomical event, surely a record of
this would have entered the literary accounts.
Moreover, no eclipse of the sun of significant
magnitude visible from Alexandria appears to have
occurred around the date 280 BCE, see J. K.
Fotheringham, "A Solution of Ancient Eclipses of
the Sun," *Monthly Notices of the Royal
Astronomical Society*, 81 (1921) 104-126, esp. p.
111. Neither can any such eclipse be recorded at
that time for Palestine or Babylon, see Theodor
Ritter von Oppolzer, *Canon of Eclipses*, trans.
Owen Gingerich (New York: Dover Publications,
1962), pp. 90-91, for the eclipses for the
astronomical year -282 (historical year 281 BCE).
A total eclipse took place over Babylon in 280
BCE. Could this have been remembered in
association with the translation?

The lack of association between the date of an
eclipse over Alexandria and the proposed year of
the translation may suggest that the reference to
the darkness of three days is a metaphorical echo
of the three days darkness that descended on
Pharaoh when he refused to allow the Jews to leave
Egypt, Exod 10:22. This plague heralded a
catastrophe of the Egyptians - the slaying of the
first born - just as the translation of the
Pentateuch heralded a catastrophe for the Jews
when their Bible was later adopted by the
Christians and used in evidence against the people
by whom it was inspired.

102. *LetAris* 312-21.

103. According to the tables in the *Calendar for
6,000 Years*, devised by A. A. Akavia, ed. David
Zakai (Jerusalem: Mossad Harav Kook, 5736-1975),
pp. 292-93, the 8th of Tevet fell on Tuesday, 28th
Dec. 281 BCE, in the Jewish year 3481. But, as
the Jewish calendar was probably not officially
fixed till the 4th cent. CE, this may not be
accurate. Using calculations based entirely on
astronomical data, Dr Robin Jakeways, of the
Department of Physics in the University of Leeds
has confirmed that the 8th of Tevet in the
historical year 281 BCE (= astronomical year -282)
corresponds with a date at the end of Dec. 281
BCE. If the original Jewish record gave the 7th of
Tevet, see n. 98, the likelihood of a date in
December rather than January is increased.

281 BCE: THE YEAR OF THE TRANSLATION

However, R. Parker and W. H. Dubberstein, *Babylonian Chronology 626 B.C.-A.D. 75* (Providence, Rhode Island: Brown Univ. Press, 1956), p. 37, calculate that the year 281 BCE was intercalated in Babylon, and indicate that the 8th of Tevet fell on the 11th Jan. But see n. 154.

104. See C.E.P. Brooks, *Climate Through the Ages* (London, Ernest Benn, 1949), esp. p. 281, "The beginning of the 'period of unchanging climate'.... stands only a few centuries before Christ;" also pp. 333-35, which dismisses appreciable changes of climate in the Mediterranean provinces of Africa, including Alexandria.

105. Philo, Moses II 42.

106. The 8th of Tevet may fall on different dates in December or possibly early January, see n. 103. During this time, the following storms (whose names may also represent feast days) and rains are recorded for Alexandria in the Coptic calender, see Mary Dungan Megalli, *On the Road in Egypt: A Motorist's Guide* (Cairo: American University in Cairo Press, 1989), p. 59: Dec 4, al Kassem, SW-NW, force 6-8, rain, 5 days; Dec 10, Ba'i al Kassem, NE-NW, force 6-7, 2 days; Dec 13, al Fayda al Sughayyara, NW, force 6-7, 2 days; Dec 21, Ba'i al Fayda al Sughayyara, SW-NW, force 6-7, 2 days; Dec 29, 'Eid al Milad, NW, force 6-8, 2 days; Jan 6, Ras al Sana, W-NW, force 6-8, rain, 2 days. It is also possible that tents were erected as protection from the sun.

107. See n. 100.

108. E.g., the production dates of the plays of the Greek tragedians.

109. The date of the death of Alexander in sources which are unlikely to have been used by Eusebius are discussed by B. Z. Wacholder, "Beginning of the Seleucid Era" in *Nourished with Peace*, ed. F. Greenspahn, E. Hilgert and B. Mack (Chico, California: Scholars Press, 1984), p. 183-211, esp. pp. 184-85, 188.

110. Helm, pp. 124-25, 132.

111. Except for Josephus and Basil of Seleucia, the sources listed in n. 52 state that Soter ruled for 40 years. Josephus gives the equivalent 41 Macedonian years and Basil gives 20 years. The latter value may be derived from the Parian

Chronicle or the *Canon* of Claudius Ptolemaeus, in which the years of Soter are reckoned from his probable true accession on Nov. 7th, 305 BCE, see A.E.S., pp. 4-5, with comment by E. G. Turner, C.A.H., p. 128 and B. Z. Wacholder, see n. 109, p. 186.

112. A.E.S., p. 30

113. See below on "ANCIENT KNOWLEDGE OF THE CO-REGENCY."

114. A.E.S., p. 30.

115. See n. 47.

116. The methods used by Eusebius for his selection of dates is briefly mentioned by A.A.M., p. 85

117. Also perhaps Justin, see comments on Justin in List 1.

118. The existence of a chronicle before the time of Eusebius has been assumed in the earlier discussion on the date of the translation of the Law, see n. 63. For a history of Greek chronography prior to Eusebius, see A.A.M., Chap. 2.

119. See n. 52

120. See n. 118.

121. Philo, *De Vit.Mos.* II 44; Justin, *Exhortation to the Greeks* 13, "We ourselves have been in Alexandria ... and have heard this story which we tell you from the inhabitants who have it handed down as a tradition of their country."

122. Thus Henry G. Meecham, *The Oldest Version of the Bible* (London: Holborn Publishing House, 1932), p. 126, "[Aristobulus] registers a double tradition."

123. Epiphanius is not relevant here. As has been shown in the main text, Epiphanius and Eusebius transmitted different traditions, i.e., used different sources for the date of the translation. Other sources may also implicate Soter, see List 2 at the end of this paper, but their texts need further investigation.

124. See Angelo di Berardino, *Patrology*, IV (Westminster, Maryland: Christian Classics, Inc., 1988), p. 131.

125. See List 1 at the end of this paper, from John Chrysostom onwards. Nicetas, Pseudo-

Theodoretus and Syncellus are probably unreliable, see nn. 34, 35 and 36.

126. If Justin Marty implicates Soter, the numbers are 5 for Ptolemy I, 4 for Ptolemy II, see List I, No.4.

127. E.J.B., p. 87-88.

128. A.A.M., p. 38. Eusebius died c.340 CE, Jerome c.342-420 CE.

129. Eusebius, *HE* 8.1.8.

130. See n. 19.

131. See n. 18 and n. 19 with text.

132. See n. 46.

133. *LetAris* 312,317. Also Josephus, *Ant*. 12.110, who may be dependent on Aristeas and Eusebius, *PrEv* 8.5, who states his dependence on Aristeas.

134. See n. 18.

135. Plutarch, *Mor* 189 d; Aelian, *VH* iii.17. For the expulsion of Demetrius from Athens, see C.A.H., pp. 55-56.

136. See n. 18 and n. 19 with text.

137. *The Cambridge Ancient History*[1] (Cambridge: Cambridge University Press, 1954), pp. 96-97.

138. See n. 18.

139. The same reasoning is used for the calculation of the date for the establishment of the Theoi Adelphoi in relation to the death of Arsinoë II, see n. 73.

140. The sources of Philo's religious thought are discussed by Burton L. Mack, "Philo Judaeus and Exegetical Traditions in Alexandria," *Aufstieg und Niedergang der Römischen Welt* II, 21.1 (1984), pp. 226-68. Philo's use of numerical sources, which may include the use of a chronicle, is well known, see e.g., Abraham Terian, "A Philonic Fragment on the Decad," in *Nourished with Peace*, see n. 109, pp. 173-82, esp. p. 180, n. 29.

141. During the life time of Eusebius, authors still refer to the role of Demetrius. Thus, he is mentioned by Epiphanius and Cyril of Jerusalem. However, after the time of Eusebius, the role of Demetrius is rarely cited - he is mentioned for certain by only three Byzantine scholars, Syncellus, Cedrenus and Grammaticus, see n. 18.

Why should this be, especially when Demetrius is included by Eusebius in his prose account of the translation? Perhaps controversy over his role continued after the time of Eusebius, which the *Chronicle* of Eusebius did not help to settle, by its omission of the date of his absence from court.

142. See nn. 11, 12 and 13.

143. It is less likely that "days" refers to calendar days of 24 hours. If this were the case, each of the 72 days of Aristeas would refer to 2 working days.

144. m.Shab 7.2.

145. *LetAris* 187-294.

146. *LetAris* 301.

147. This period will inevitably include one of the Sabbaths that have already been counted in the thirteen weeks, but this is a detail.

148. Josephus, *Ant* XII 99 has 12 days for the banquet. Does this number include the 3 days that Aristeas gives between the banquets and the start of work?

149. This method of travel by land is suggested by M.H., p. 167, n. 172. If so, the translators may have used the *Via Maris* from Rafia to El-Kantareh, see Alan H. Gardiner, *JEA* 6 (1920) 99-113. How then did the caravan cross the delta region to Alexandria? But, the extreme difficulties of travel in Sinai during summer are graphically described by Donald W. Engels, *Alexander the Great and the Logistics of the Macedonian Army* (Berkeley: University of California Press, 1978), p. 60. Moreover, Aristeas hints that the group arriving in Alexandria was heavily laden, *LetAris* 172. The translators were certainly loaded when they returned, *LetAris* 319-20 - their luggage included the complete furnishing of a dining room and 10 silver footed couches with all accessories. Engels (p. 27) notes that sea and river transport were always more efficient than land transport in antiquity. Thus, in the march from Gaza to Pelusium in October, the fleet sailed alongside Alexander's army travelling on the coast, to supply food and water, Arrian *Anabasis* 3.1.1. Perhaps the journey of the translators to Alexandria was made by boat along the coast. For sailing vessels which plied the coasts, see Lionel

281 BCE: THE YEAR OF THE TRANSLATION

Casson, *Ships and Seamanship in the Ancient World* (Princeton, New Jersey: Princeton University Press, 1971), pp. 337-38. Casson notes on p. 159 n. 7, a papyrus that refers to a coastal vessel named an *akatos*, which plied between Ascalon and Alexandria (*Sammelb*. 957.6, 2nd CE). Engels p. 59, notes that the march of Alexander between from Gaza to Pelusium (east of the Nile Delta, approximately half way to Alexandria) took 7 days. This can be compared with a voyage from Alexandria to Cyprus with unfavorable winds took only 6+ days, see Casson p. 289. It is clear that the journey from Palestine to Alexandria would be more efficiently made by sea than by land.

150. *LetAris* 175.

151. A similar telescoping of time may account in part for Nehemiah's assertion that the walls of Jerusalem were completed in 52 days, Neh 6:15, whereas Josephus gives 2 years and 4 months, *Ant* XI.v.8.

152. *LetAris* 39, 302.

153. E.S., Vol I, p. 593.

154. It is unlikely that the year 281/0 was intercalated if the 8th of Tevet in 281 BCE fell at the end of December. An extra Adar would mean that the translators spent an extra month in Alexandria.

155. The section below entitled "THE RETIREMENT OF DEMETRIUS OF PHALERUM" will suggests that the original planning for the translation took place while Soter was alive.

156. P.M.F., Chap 6, esp. pp. 308-12.

157. b. Shab 19a states that travel over the Sabbath is allowed if the journey is undertaken "for a good deed."

158. It is interesting that Eusebius in the *Chronicle* stresses the connection between Philadelphus and the translation although it is obvious from the preceding accession of the King. Was this polemic to emphasize that, according to Eusebius, Philadelphus, not Soter, was King at the time?

159. See n. 46.

160. *HE* 7.32.16. See also n. 5.

161. See n. 52 and 11 with text.

162. The discussion suggests that the following notices were found in an early chronicle which precedes Eusebius: (1) 4th year of the 123th Olympiad, the accession of Ptolemy II; (2) 2nd year of the 124th Olympiad, (a) the death of Soter, (b) the translation of the Law, (c) the fall of Demetrius.

163. See pp. 406-407.

164. See n. 32.

165. *Discourses against Judaizing Christians* I VI.

166. See n. 34.

167. See n. 35.

168. See n. 33.

169. See n. 36.

170. See Lists 1 and 2.

171. See n. 18.

172. Thus, P. W. cites all ancient accounts of the translation of the Law, including the dates, as *testimonia* of Aristeas. The only dissension from this opinion is the possibility that Aristobulus may be based on a different source, see n. 11.

173. These include historical errors, see n. 3 and material which has little direct relevance for the event of the translation. The latter includes literary embellishments, e.g., the 7 banquets, *LetAris* 187-294, the largest section of the work, taking up more that one-third of the whole; and religious propaganda, e.g., Eleazar's digression on Jewish Law, *LetAris* 128-72, see Jellicoe's brief summary of comments by scholars on the apologetic nature of Aristeas, *S.M.S.*, p. 54; also, on the religious message for the Jews in Aristeas, see Sebastian Brock, "To Revise or not to Revise: Attitudes to Jewish Biblical Translation," pp. 305-308 in this volume.

174. If the translation was completed in 281/0 BCE, further evidence of the veracity of Aristeas can be derived from an analysis of the names of the translators. The groups of names as a whole can be dated to the first quarter of the 3rd cent. BCE, see Naomi G. Cohen, "Jewish Names as Cultural Indicators in Antiquity," *JSJ* 7 (1976) 97-128.

175. See n. 11.

176. For bibliog. on *Megillat Taanith*, see E.H., Vol I, pp. 114-15.

177. See n. 17.

178. Zuntz comments that "Philo's report about an annual feast celebrated on the Pharos in commemoration of the translation seems genuine and points to an ancient tradition," see n. 9, Section VI.

179. See "THE SOURCES OF EUSEBIUS & EPIPHANIUS."

180. I would like to give thanks to the generous help of scholars with whom I have discussed, both in person and by letter, different aspects of this work, in particular, Professor A. Hastings, Mr I. Moxon, Dr H. Gottschalk, Dr R. Jakeways and Mr S. Burton, of the University of Leeds; Dr G. Brooke, and Professor B. Lindars and Dr D. M. Stec of the University of Manchester; Professor L. Schiffman, New York University; Professor E. Ulrich, University of Notre Dame; Professor G. Dorival, Université de Provence; Professor J. N. Birdsall, Birmingham; Mr L. Tweddle, The Library of the American University of Cairo; Dr C. G. Smith, the University of Oxford.

THE TRANSLATION TECHNIQUE OF THE GREEK MINOR VERSIONS: TRANSLATIONS OR REVISIONS?

LESTER L. GRABBE

Part I

According to the testimonies of the ancients, Aquila, Symmachus, and Theodotion were independent translators who rendered the Hebrew Bible into Greek. This view was reflected in handbooks up until the past few decades.[1] However, with the appearance of Barthélemy's fundamental study in 1963, the consensus has changed drastically.[2] The Greek Minor Versions are now usually presented as revisions rather than original translations, whose aim was either to bring the Greek text into line with the standardized Hebrew or to make the Greek of the LXX more idiomatic and less awkward.

---

[1] Cf. H. B. Swete, *An Introduction to the Old Testament in Greek* (revised by R. R. Ottley; Cambridge: University Press, 1914) 29-53. It was argued, however, that Theodotion revised the LXX rather than making an original translation (p. 43).

[2] D. Barthélemy, *Les devanciers d'Aquila* (VTSup 10; Leiden: Brill, 1963).

Yet in spite of this change of common opinion, the actual amount of work on the Minor Versions in the last 25 years is quite small, especially when one considers the flow of publications on the LXX itself during this same period.[3] Barthélemy's thesis has been more repeated than examined. While it is commonplace to read that the *kaige* revised the LXX and that Theodotion, Aquila, and Symmachus revised the *kaige*, little has been done systematically to confirm this hypothesis.[4] My purpose in this paper is to look more closely at Barthélemy's claim.

The Nature of the Investigation

The difficulty of such an investigation is the nature of the data for it, usually fragmentary and often unreliable quotations, and

---

[3]Most publications up to 1969 are listed in S. Brock, et al., *A Classified Index to the Septuagint* (ALGHJ 6; Leiden: Brill, 1973). From 1969 onwards, one should consult the annual *Bulletin of the International Organization for Septuagint and Cognate Studies*.

[4]For example, K. G. O'Connell (*The Theodotionic Revision of the Book of Exodus: A Contribution to the Study of the Early History of the Transmission of the Old Testament in Greek* [HSM 3; Cambridge, MA: Harvard, 1972]) has a chapter on "Aquila's Dependence on Theodotion in Exodus" (pp. 252-73). However, it consists simply in noting the agreements and disagreements between Aquila, Theodotion, and the LXX without actually demonstrating that Aquila revised Theodotion. The fact that Aquila is sometimes closer to Theodotion than to the LXX does not by itself prove dependence.

even retroversions from the Syro-Hexapla, rather than continuous texts. To overcome some of the problems, I here make use of some of the few remains of the Hexapla extant: the Mailand text of the Psalms published by Mercati.[5]

The database for this study consists of the following passages of the Psalms from the Hexapla in Mercati's edition (except for the omission of a few passages for which data are absent in some columns):

18:26-48
28:6-9
29:1-3
30:1-13
31:1-10, 20-25
32:6-11
35:1-2, 13-28
36:1-6
46:1-12
49:1-15
89:26-53

The extant fragments contain columns 2-6 of the Hexapla, indicated by letters in Mercati's edition: a: Hebrew (not preserved, the MT being used for comparison); b: Greek transliteration of Hebrew; c:

---

[5]J. Mercati, *Psalterii Hexapli reliquiae, Pars prima: Codex rescriptus Bybliothecae Ambrosianae O 39 sup. phototypice expressus et transcriptus* (Consilio et studio procuratorum Bybliothecae Vaticanae 8; Rome: Bybliotheca Vaticana, 1958); *Psalterii Hexapli reliquiae, Pars prima: Osservazione; commento critico al testo dei frammenti Esaplari* (1965).

Aquila; d: Symmachus; e: LXX (without any diacritical signs); f: Quinta, according to Mercati. This last identification is important. It means that Theodotion is not extant as such (though there do seem to be a few marginal quotations from it). However, Barthélemy has identified the Quinta of Psalms with the *kaige*.[6] Throughout this paper, the readings in col. f are referred to by the abbreviation *e'* (= Quinta). Also used are the abbreviations Aq (= Aquila) and Sym (= Symmachus).

In order to test the question of revision versus translation, three points must be kept in mind: (1) Agreements with regard to common words may not be significant since two translators could have hit on the same equivalent independently. (2) The focus of any study must be on verbs and nouns since slight difference involving articles, particles, and the like may be due to accommodation on the part of a reviser rather than an original translator. (3) Where all Minor Versions agree with the LXX consistently throughout the collection, one cannot draw conclusions since one could prove any theory by such data.[7]

Therefore, I have collated all nouns and verbs throughout the preserved fragments, except where (a) all versions give the same translation

---

[6]*Devanciers*, 47.

[7]These generally involve quite common words which are not unlikely to be translated the same by any translator, including "hand," "right hand," "eye," "heart," and the like.

throughout or (b) the data in some of the columns is not preserved. This yielded almost 400 separate examples which are recorded in Part II. Each is numbered for ease of reference through this paper. The minutiae of their assembly and recording are indicated in the introduction to Part III. Part III contains the one complete psalm in the collection as an illustration to supplement Part II.

One final comment: The results of the study are presented in statistical form. Naturally, something so complicated as the Greek versions cannot be reduced to statistics (nor is the database probably large enough to be strictly scientific, in any case). Nevertheless, the use of statistics does help to give a greater objectivity to ones analysis, as well as having value in summarizing the data. It is also not a question of whether I have not missed some words or made errors of recording--undoubtedly there are both these despite checks--but that the database is sufficiently large to render such errors of no major significance to the overall results.

Kaige Recension

The data seem to provide a reasonable confirmation of Barthélemy's thesis that the *kaige* represents a revision of the LXX. In 63 percent of the examples (245), *e'* agrees with the LXX. In the text in Part III, *e'* agrees exactly with the LXX about three-quarters of the time (76 percent). Even when the LXX is inconsistent in its renderings of the underlying Hebrew, *e'* may follow the LXX in its inexactitudes. In collating the data, it became clear that one would normally expect *e'* to agree with the LXX. This conclusion has also been supported by the analysis in Tov's recent edition of 8HevXIIgr.[8] There are certainly many differences from the LXX, but most of these can be explained as an attempt to conform more closely to the current Hebrew. (As noted above, Theodotion was not included in the database.)

Aquila's Version

Aquila agrees with *e'*, exactly or closely in 118 instances, or 30 percent. We could point to this fact and follow Barthélemy in saying that the former is a revision of the latter. However, a closer look shows that things are not so simple. We must first eliminate the examples in which LXX = *e'* = Aq since this could show a dependence of Aq on the LXX rather than *e'*.[9] (65 cases). There are

---

[8] E. Tov, et al. (ed.), *The Greek Minor Prophets Scroll from Nahal Hever (8HevXIIgr)* (DJD 8; Oxford: Clarendon: 1990).

[9] 65 instances: ## 6, 8, 10, 13-15, 19, 33, 36, 40, 42, 43, 53, 55, 57, 63, 66, 67, 78, 81, 92, 93, 96, 101-3, 105, 106, 108, 111, 117, 122-25, 132, 140, 147, 174, 188, 189, 192-94, 197, 221, 241, 242, 245, 247, 249, 260, 262, 271, 278, 285, 289, 291, 315, 345, 346, 350, 372-74.

left 33 examples of e' = Aq $\neq$ LXX.[10] To these we can add 20 examples of close agreement (e.g., Aq omits an article),[11] to give a total of 14 percent. When we look at these in detail, we find that it is not possible to draw any sort of conclusion one way or the other from about half of them.[12] Those left form the largest and most significant group, those which have more than one occurence in the Hexapla fragments. Of these, all but 5 are examples in which Aq renders consistently but e' does not. In only 5 cases do both e' and Aq render consistently in more than one occurence.[13]

Thus, where the situation can be checked most of the agreements between e' and Aquila could be accounted for as fortuitous. That is, Aquila is consistent whereas e' is not, so there would be no reason to assume borrowing. Yet even if we counted *all* of them, they still make up only 14 percent of

---

[10]##23, 35, 37, 46, 47, 51, 52, 56, 64, 94, 95, 98, 138, 179-83, 201-4, 210, 235, 239, 268, 269, 272, 284, 293, 312, 357, 380.

[11]##7, 9, 11, 27, 82, 86, 87, 133, 205-7, 250, 270, 281, 305, 316, 328, 365, 367, 375.

[12]Several are not consistently rendered by Aquila or have other problems associated with them (##23, 27, 46, 235, 239, 284, 305, 376). For an indication of the translations in other passages, I have only relied on J. Reider and N. Turner (*An Index to Aquila* [VTS 21; Leiden: Brill, 1966]) and not attempted an independent check. About 15 occur only once so that, even though they are apparently rendered consistently by Aquila elsewhere, I cannot discern how the *kaige* renders them (##11, 35, 47, 56, 64, 98, 133, 138, 250, 281, 293, 316, 328, 365, 380).

[13]## 37, 51, 52, 86, 87.

the significant words in the text, a rather small
number if Aquila ultimately depended on the *kaige*.
But could not Aquila nevertheless be a version of
kaige, despite these considerations, when one takes
into account the cases in which Aquila agrees with
the LXX and *e'* together (30 percent)? To answer
that, one must consider the following points:

First, when does a revision become so
extensive that it should be considered a new
translation? For example, there would be general
agreement that the Revised Version of 1881 was, as
its name indicates, a revision of the Authorized
Version of 1611, but what about the Revised
Standard Version? It claims to be a revision of
the Authorized Version and is certainly in that
tradition, but most of us regard it as a
translation in its own right.

Secondly, there is a more practical
consideration. The data show that Aquila attempted
a very consistent rendering, so that the same
Hebrew word (and even root in some cases) was
almost always rendered by the same Greek word.[14]
To have revised an earlier text, either the LXX or
kaige, would have required Aquila to change almost
half the words (47 percent) in the one text in Part
III. Is this a reasonable assumption? And if he
was attempting a consistent rendering, what
advantage would it be to use a version which was so

---

[14]On Aquila's technique, see K. Hyvärinen, *Die Übersetzung von Aquila* (Coniectanea Biblica, Old Testament Series 10; Uppsala: Gleerup, 1977).

often inconsistent? Would it have been easier to do this than to translate from scratch? Perhaps a definite decision is not possible, but there is little in Aquila's translation which could not be explained by assuming an original translation.

Finally, one should consider that *any* partial revision of the LXX toward the MT is likely to appear intermediate between it and the literal rendering of Aquila. That is, Aquila is a close rendering of a text very similar to the MT. Any independent revision of the LXX which remains fairly literal but also corrects the LXX to bring it more in line with the MT would *appear* to be a stage between Aquila and the LXX, even if it was not.[15]

However, even then one could allow that Aquila was refining a tradition of literal translation which had begun much earlier. As has been suggested, the *kaige* could have been a product of such a "school of literalism." We should not assume a linear progression, though, as if the most literal was chronologically later than the others. There may have been different streams of thought

---

[15] It has also been argued that Aquila never agrees with the LXX against the *kaige* (e.g., O'Connell, *Theodotionic Revision*, 252-73). This is not strictly true since even O'Connell notes an occasional agreement of Aquila with the LXX and against the *kaige* (pp. 257-58). In my study there is also some agreement with the LXX against *e'* (## 97, 370, and possibly 371). This is not much and may be due to accident or scribal error, but it must be taken account of in any assessment of the relationship between Aquila and the *kaige*.

even within a common "school" tradition, with some thinking that too literal a translation such as Aquila's was not right. That is, Aquila might represent the refinement of a technique which we already see developing in the *kaige*. But once the technique was developed, Aquila could have used it to make an independent translation of the Hebrew rather than a revision of the *kaige*.[16]

Symmachus' Version

The statistics on Symmachus do not seem to show any clear pattern:

Sym=LXX≠e'/Aq: 5% (18)[17] ⎫
Sym=e'/LXX≠ Aq: 10% (37)[18] ⎬   Sym=LXX: 14% (55)
Sym=e'≠LXX/Aq: 3% (13)[19] ⎬   Sym=e': 15% (57)
Sym=e'/Aq≠ LXX: 1% (5)[20]   ⎫
Sym=Aq≠LXX/e':   6% (23)[21] ⎬   Sym=Aq: 7% (28)

---

[16] R. A. Kraft already made a similar point in his review of Barthélemy (*Gnomon* 37 [1965] 474-83). Talking specifically of the claim that *R* represents a revision of the LXX, he notes: "It can be shown that basically independent Greek translations of basically the same Hebrew 'Vorlage' can have a great deal in common" (p. 479-80).

[17] ##23, 83, 88, 100, 149, 201-7, 220, 263, 284, 357, 375, 379.

[18] ##4, 79, 104, 112, 113, 127, 136, 139, 150-52, 163, 165, 169, 173, 177, 178, 184, 230, 232, 264-67, 283, 303, 314, 326, 332, 340, 341, 347, 349, 368, 381, 387, 388.

[19] ##45, 54, 155, 185, 186, 200, 213, 234, 244, 273, 287, 346, 369.

[20] ##37, 98, 235, 357, 365.

Sym=*e'*≠LXX: 5%
Sym=LXX≠*e'*:   5%

The statement by Barthélemy that Symmachus revised the *kaige* does not seem to bear up.²² There is no clear relationship between Symmachus and any of the other versions. On the one hand, Symmachus does sometimes agree with the LXX; on the other hand, since there seems to be no attempt to render consistently, one could see this agreement as often accidental. Nevertheless, there are instances where the LXX may lie at the basis of his translation; at least, he agrees as often with the LXX against *e'* as with *e'* against the LXX. There is also the possibility that he knew Aquila, contrary to Barthélemy, since in a number of cases he agrees with Aquila against *e'*. One might easily argue that if Symmachus is chronologically later, as the ancient sources indicate, he knew all the previous versions and happily drew from them all. This is only an impression and difficult either to substantiate or to disprove, but it does indicate his lack of dependence on any particular previous version and suggests that his should be characterized as a new translation, whatever influence there might be from his predecessors.

---

[21]##1, 3, 16-18, 30-32, 75, 121, 129, 134, 135, 208, 217, 226, 237, 251, 295, 302, 331, 353, 359.
[22]*Devanciers*, 261-62.

Conclusions

It would be foolish to make sweeping claims. I have examined only portions of one OT book. Nevertheless, this study has had the advantage of looking at complete passages rather than just isolated words or phrases of doubtful attribution. My conclusions must be judged within the limits noted. One should first observe that the whole Minor Version tradition has been influenced by the LXX. That is, even independent later translations would inevitably take a form partially determined by the LXX tradition.

The *kaige* recension identified by Barthélemy does seem to be a revision of the LXX. Most of the differences could be explained as due to the desire of the reviser to make the Greek conform more closely to a particular Hebrew text.

The question of Aquila and Symmachus is more difficult. One would be just in saying that both have been influenced in some way by the LXX tradition. Some agreements, especially in Symmachus, seem to be borrowings from the LXX and not just the translator's accidentally hitting on the same rendering. For revisions supposedly dependent on *kaige*, there is surprisingly little agreement between the former and Aquila and Symmachus. Where Aquila agrees with the *kaige*, it can usually be explained in one of two ways: (a) it is a rendering of Hebrew words for which independent translators might easily adopt the same Greek equivalent; (b) Aquila rendered the Hebrew conistently by the same Greek equivalent whereas the *kaige* only sometimes renders the same as Aquila. It seems best to designate Aquila as a new translation in its own right. Its relationship to *kaige* and perhaps even to the LXX is not a simple one, but it seems wrong to designate it only as a revision of the *kaige*.

Similarly, Symmachus is so often different from the *kaige*--as well as from the LXX and Aquila--as to make the question of a revision difficult. It seems to be an independent translation, though one could argue that the LXX, *kaige*, and Aquila all had their influence on it.

These results are necessarily provisional. I can hardly claim to have disproved Barthélemy's thesis. Indeed, one aspect of it has been supported, that the *kaige* (and by impliction Theodotion) represents a revision of the LXX. Yet it seems to me that there are major difficulties with his thesis when it comes to the two other versions. This study has suggested reasons for giving greater weight to the older idea that Aquila and Symmachus were original translators.

Part II

The following points should be noted about the collection and collation here:
1. All citations are given according to those of the Hebrew text. For LXX chapter numbers, subtract 1; verse numbers are all the same.
2. The readings of the editor are generally accepted and given without indication of abbreviation or slight differences in spelling (e.g., presence or absence of the *iota adscript*) or correction of obvious scribal error. Otherwise, the essential agreements and disagreements might not be clear. Mercati's publication must be consulted for the exact form of the text preserved. However, examples with major textual problems and those in which full data are not preserved have been omitted.
3. The words are generally organized by the theoretical Hebrew roots. Despite certain obvious problems with this, it makes clearer the translation technique used in some instances. However, a number of noun are forms recorded alphabetically rather than under a root.
4. In order to make clear the agreements and disagreements between the version, the following sigla are used:
    ..... Exact agreement with the LXX
    " Same as the word immediately above
    -- Absence of the word immediately above

אביון

(1) Psa 49:3
MT: ואביון
LXX: καὶ πένης
ε´: ....
Aq: καὶ πτωχός
Sym: καὶ πτωχός

אדמה

(2) Psa 49:12
MT: עלי אדמות
LXX: ἐπὶ τῶν γαιῶν
ε´: ....
Aq: ἐπὶ --- χθόνας
Sym: --- ταῖς γαίαις

אור

(3) Psa 18:29
MT: תאיר
LXX: φωτιεῖς
ε´: ....
Aq: φανεῖς
Sym: φανεῖς

אזר

(4) Psa 18:33
MT: המאזרני
LXX: ὁ περιζωννύων με
ε´: ....
Aq: -- περιζωννύς με
Sym: ....

אמן

(5) Psa 31:24
MT: אמונים
LXX: ὅτι ἀληθείας
ε´: ἀλήθειαν
Aq: πιστούς
Sym: πίστεις

(6) Psa 89:29
MT: נאמנת
LXX: πιστὴ
ε´: ....
Aq: ....
Sym: πιστωθήσεται

(7) Psa 89:34
MT: באמונתי
LXX: ἐν τῆι ἀληθείᾳ μου
ε´: ἐν τῆι πίστει μου
Aq: ἐν --- πίστει μου
Sym: -- τὴν πίστιν μου

(8) Psa 89:38
MT: נאמן
LXX: πιστός
ε´: ....
Aq: ....
Sym: ....

(9) Psa 89:50
MT: באמונתך
LXX: ἐν τῇ ἀληθείᾳ σου
ε´: ἐν τῇ πίστει σου
Aq: ἐν -- πίστει σου
Sym: διὰ τῆς ἀληθείας σου

אמץ

(10) Psa 31:25
MT: ויאמץ
LXX: καὶ κραταιούσθω
ε´: ....
Aq: ....
Sym: καὶ στερρούσθω

אמרה

(11) Psa 18:31
MT: אמרת
LXX: τὰ λόγια
ε´: τὸ λόγιον
Aq: -- λόγιον
Sym: -- ῥῆσις

אסף

(12) Psa 35:15
MT: ונאספו
LXX: --- συνήχθησαν
ε´: ....
Aq: καὶ συνελέγησαν
Sym: --- συνήγοντο

אף

(13) Psa 30:6
MT: באפו
LXX: ἐν τῶι θυμῶι αὐτοῦ
ε´: ....
Aq: ἐν --- θυμῶι αὐτοῦ
Sym: -- --- ὀργὴ αὐτοῦ

בוש

(14) Psa 31:2
MT: אבושה
LXX: καταισχυνθείην
ε´: ....
Aq: ....
Sym: ....

(15) Psa 35:26
MT: יבשו
LXX: αἰσχυνθείησαν
ε´: ....
Aq: ....
Sym: καταισχυνθείησαν

בטח

(16) Psa 28:7
MT: בטח
LXX: ἤλπισεν
ε´: ....
Aq: ἐπεποίθησεν
Sym: ἐπεποίθησεν

(17) Psa 31:7
MT: בטחתי
LXX: ἤλπισεν
ε´: ....
Aq: ἐπεποίθησα
Sym: ἐπεποίθησα

(18) Psa 32:10
MT: והבוטח
LXX: --- τὸν δὲ ἐλπίζοντα
ε´: ....
Aq: καὶ τὸν -- πεποιθότα
Sym: --- τὸν δὲ πεποιθότα

(19) Psa 49:7
MT: הבטחים
LXX: οἱ πεποιθότες
ε´: ....
Aq: ....
Sym: ....

בין

(20) Psa 32:9
MT: אין הבין
LXX: οἷς οὐκ ἔστι σύνεσις
ε´: ....
Aq: --- οὐκ ἔστι συνιέναι
Sym: --- --- ---- ἀνόητοι

(21) Psa 49:4
MT: תבונות
LXX: σύνεσεις
ε´: ....
Aq: φρονήσεις
Sym: σύνεσιν

בלה

(22) Psa 49:15
MT: לבלות
LXX: --- παλαιωθήσεται
ε´: --- κατατριβήσεται
Aq: εἰς κατατρίψαι
Sym: --- παλαιώσει

בלע

(23) Psa 35:25
MT: בלענוהו
LXX: κατεπίομεν αὐτόν
ε´: κατεποντίσαμεν αὐτόν
Aq: κατεποντίσαμεν αὐτόν
Sym: ....

בער

(24) Psa 49:11
MT: ובער
LXX: καὶ ἄνους
ε': ....
Aq: καὶ ἀσύνετος
Sym: καὶ ἀμαθὴς

(25) Psa 89:47
MT: תבער
LXX: ἐκκαυθήσεται
ε': ....
Aq: ἀναφθήσεται
Sym: φλεγήσεται

בצע

(26) Psa 30:10
MT: בצע
LXX: ὠφέλεια
ε': ....
Aq: πλεονέκτημα
Sym: κέρδος

בצר

(27) Psa 89:41
MT: מבצריו
LXX: ----- τὰ ὀχυρώματα αὐτοῦ
ε': ....
Aq: ----- -- ὀχύρωμα αὐτοῦ
Sym: πάντα τὰ περιφράγματα αὐτοῦ

בקר

(28) Psa 46:6
MT: בקר
LXX: --- πρωί
ε': ....
Aq: τὴν πρωίαν
Sym: --- ὄρθρον

(29) Psa 49:15
MT: לבקר
LXX: ' εἰς τὸ πρωί
ε': ....
Aq: εἰς --- πρωίαν
Sym: ἐν τῶι ὄρθρῳ

ברית

(30) Psa 89:29
MT: ובריתי
LXX: καὶ ἡ διαθήκη μου
ε': ....
Aq: καὶ -- συνθήκη μου
Sym: καὶ ἡ συνθήκη μου

(31) Psa 89:35
MT: בריתי
LXX: τὴν διαθήκην μου
ε': ....
Aq: --- συνθήκην μου
Sym: τὴν συνθήκην μου

(32) Psa 89:40
MT: ברית
LXX: τὴν διαθήκην
ε': ....
Aq: --- συνθήκην
Sym: τὴν συνθήκην

ברר

(33) Psa 18:27
MT: נבר
LXX: ἐκλεκτοῦ
ε': ....
Aq: ....
Sym: καθαρὸν

(34) Psa 18:27
MT: תתברר
LXX: ἐκλεκτὸς ἔσηι
ε': ....
Aq: ἐκλεκτωθήσῃ
Sym: καθαρεύσῃ

גאה

(35) Psa 46:4
MT: בגאותו
LXX: ἐν τῇ κραταιότητι αὐτοῦ
ε´: ἐν τῇ ὑπερηφανίᾳ αὐτοῦ
Aq: ἐν τῇ ὑπερηφανίᾳ αὐτοῦ
Sym: ἐν τῶι ἐνδοξασμῶι αὐτοῦ

גבר

(36) Psa 18:26
MT: גבר
LXX: ἀνδρὸς
ε´: ....
Aq: ....
Sym: ἄνδρα

(37) Psa 89:49
MT: מי גבר
LXX: τίς ἐστιν ὁ ἄνθρωπος
ε´: τίς ---- -- ἀνήρ
Aq: τίς ---- -- ἀνήρ
Sym: τίς ---- -- ἀνήρ

גדוד

(38) Psa 18:30
MT: גדוד
LXX: ἀπὸ πειρατηρίου
ε´: μονόζωνος
Aq: εὔζωνος
Sym: λόχου

גדל

(39) Psa 35:26
MT: המגדילים
LXX: οἱ μεγαλορημονοῦντες
ε´: ....
Aq: -- μεγαλύνοντες
Sym: οἱ καταμεγαλυνόμενοί

(40) Psa 35:27
MT: יגדל
LXX: μεγαλυνθήτω
ε´: ....
Aq: ....
Sym: μέγας

גדר

(41) Psa 89:41
MT: גדרתיו
LXX: τοὺς φραγμοὺς αὐτοῦ
ε´: ....
Aq: ---- περιφράγματα αὐτοῦ
Sym: τοὺς θριγκοὺς αὐτοῦ

גיל

(42) Psa 31:8
MT: אגילה
LXX: ἀγαλλιάσομαι
ε´: ....
Aq: ....
Sym: ἱλαρεύσομαι

(43) Psa 32:11
MT: וגילו
LXX: καὶ ἀγαλλιᾶσθε
ε´: ....
Aq: ....
Sym: καὶ εὐθυμεῖτε

גרז

(44) Psa 31:23
MT: נגרזתי
LXX: ἀπέρριμαι
ε´: ἐκβέβλημαι
Aq: ἐξέρριμαι
Sym: ἐξεκόπην

דבר

(45) Psa 18:48
MT: וידבר
LXX: καὶ ὑποτάξας
ε´: καὶ ὑποτάσσων
Aq: καὶ συνοδώσει
Sym: καὶ ὑποτάσσων

(46) Psa 35:20
MT: יְדַבֵּרוּ
LXX: ἐλάλουν
ε´: λαλήσουσι
Aq: λαλήσουσι
Sym: λαλοῦσι

(47) Psa 35:20
MT: דִּבְרֵי-
LXX: ἐλάλουν
ε´: ῥήματα
Aq: ῥήματα
Sym: λόγους

דלג

(48) Psa 18:30
MT: אֲדַלֶּג
LXX: ὑπερβήσομαι
ε´: ....
Aq: ὑπερπηδήσω
Sym: ἐπιβήσομαι

דלה

(49) Psa 30:2
MT: דִּלִּיתָנִי
LXX: ὑπέλαβές με
ε´: ἐξεῖλώ με
Aq: ἀνέσωσάς με
Sym: ἀνιμήσωμεν --

רמה

(50) Psa 49:13
MT: נִדְמוּ
LXX: καὶ ὡμοιώθη αὐτοῖς
ε´: --- ὡμοιώθη ------
Aq: --- ἐξωμοιώθησαν -----
Sym: --- σιωπηθήσονται -----

דמם

(51) Psa 30:13
MT: יִדֹּם
LXX: καταυγῶ
ε´: σιωπήσηι
Aq: σιωπήσηι
Sym: ἀποσιωπήσηι

(52) Psa 35:15
MT: דָּמּוּ
LXX: κατενύγησαν
ε´: ἐσιώπησαν
Aq: ἐσιώπησαν
Sym: ἠρέμουν

הגה

(53) Psa 49:4
MT: וְהָגוּת
LXX: καὶ ἡ μελέτη
ε´: ....
Aq: καὶ -- μελέτη
Sym: καὶ -- μηνυρίσει

הדר

(54) Psa 29:2
MT: בְּהַדְרַת-
LXX: ἐν αὐλῆι
ε´: ἐν εὐπρεπείᾳ
Aq: ἐν διαπρεπείᾳ
Sym: ἐν εὐπρεπείαι

הלך

(55) Psa 32:8
MT: תֵלֵךְ
LXX: πορεύσηι
ε´: ....
Aq: ....
Sym: ὁδεύσεις

(56) Psa 35:14
MT: הִתְהַלָּכְתִּי
LXX: οὕτως εὐηρέστουν
ε´: ----- ἐμπεριεπάτησα
Aq: ----- ἐμπεριεπάτησα
Sym: ----- ἀνεστράφην

(57) Psa 89:31
MT: יֵלֵכוּן
LXX: πορευθῶσιν
ε´: ....
Aq: ....
Sym: ὁδεύσωσιν

הלל

(58) Psa 35:18
MT: אֲהַלְלֶךָּ
LXX: αἰνέσω σε
ε´: ....
Aq: ὑμνήσω σε
Sym: ὑμνήσω σε

(59) Psa 35:28
MT: תְּהִלָּתֶךָ
LXX: τὸν ἔπαινόν σου
ε´: τὸν αἴνεσίν σου
Aq: --- ὕμνησίν σου
Sym: τὸν ὕμνον σου

(60) Psa 49:7
MT: יִתְהַלָּלוּ
LXX: καυχώμενοι
ε´: ....
Aq: ὑπνούμενοι
Sym: ἀλαζονευόμενοι

המה

(61) Psa 46:4
MT: יֶהֱמוּ
LXX: ἤχησαν
ε´: ἠχήσουσι
Aq: ὀχλάσουσιν
Sym: ἠχούντων

(62) Psa 46:7
MT: הָמוּ
LXX: ἐταράχθησαν
ε´: ἤχησαν
Aq: ὤχλασαν
Sym: συνήχθησαν

הפך

(63) Psa 30:12
MT: הָפַכְתָּ
LXX: ἔστρεψας
ε´: ....
Aq: ....
Sym: μετέβαλες

הר

(64) Psa 30:8
MT: לְהַרְרִי
LXX: τῷ κάλλει μου
ε´: τῷ ὄρει μου
Aq: τῷ ὄρει μου
Sym: τῷ προπάτορί μου

זכר

(65) Psa 30:5
MT: לְזֵכֶר
LXX: τῇ μνήμῃ
ε´: ....
Aq: τῷ μνημοσύνῳ
Sym: ἀναμιμνήσκοντες

(66) Psa 89:48
MT: זְכָר-
LXX: μνήσθητι
ε´: ....
Aq: ....
Sym: μνημόνευσον

(67) Psa 89:51
MT: זְכֹר
LXX: μνήσθητι
ε´: ....
Aq: ....
Sym: μνημόνευσον

זמר

(68) Psa 29:1
MT: מִזְמוֹר
LXX: ψαλμὸς
ε´: ....
Aq: μελῴδημα
Sym: ᾠδὴ

(69) Psa 30:1
MT: מִזְמוֹר
LXX: ψαλμὸς
ε´: ....
Aq: μελῴδημα
Sym: ᾆσμα

TRANSLATION TECHNIQUE OF MINOR VERSIONS   525

(70) Psa 30:5
MT: זמרו
LXX: ψάλατε
ε´: ....
Aq: μελωδήσατε
Sym: ᾄδετε

(71) Psa 30:13
MT: יזמרך
LXX: ψάληι σοι
ε´: ....
Aq: μελωδήσηι σοι
Sym: ᾄδηι σε

(72) Psa 31:1
MT: מזמור
LXX: ψαλμός
ε´: ....
Aq: μελῴδημα
Sym: ᾆσμα

(73) Psa 49:1
MT: מזמור
LXX: ψαλμός
ε´: ....
Aq: μελῴδημα
Sym: ᾆσμα

חדל

(74) Psa 49:9
MT: וחדל
LXX: καὶ ἐκοπίασεν
ε´: ....
Aq: καὶ ἐπαύσατο
Sym: ἀλλὰ παυσάμενος

חול

(75) Psa 30:12
MT: למחול
LXX: εἰς χαρὰν
ε´: ....
Aq: εἰς χορὸν
Sym: εἰς χορὸν

חזה

(76) Psa 46:9
MT: חזו
LXX: ἴδετε
ε´: ....
Aq: ὁραματίσθητε
Sym: θεάσασθε

חזק

(77) Psa 31:25
MT: חזקו
LXX: ἀνδρίζεσθε
ε´: ....
Aq: ἐνισχύεσθε
Sym: κρατύνεσθε

(78) Psa 35:2
MT: החזק
LXX: ἐπιλαβοῦ
ε´: ....
Aq: ....
Sym: κράτησον

חירה

(79) Psa 49:5
MT: הירתי
LXX: τὸ πρόβλημά μου
ε´: ....
Aq: αἴνιγμά μου
Sym: ....

חיה

(80) Psa 30:4
MT: חייתני
LXX: ἔσωσάς με
ε´: ....
Aq: ἐζώωσάς με
Sym: ἀνεζώωσάς με

(81) Psa 49:10
MT: וִיחִי-
LXX: καὶ ζήσεται
 καὶ ζήσεται
ε': καὶ ζήσεται
--- --------
Aq: καὶ ζήσεται
--- --------
Sym: ζῶν διατελέσει
--- --------

(82) Psa 89:49
MT: יְחִיֶה
LXX: ὃς χρήσεται ---
ε': ὃς ζήσεται ---
Aq: -- ζήσεται ---
Sym: ὃς διατελέσει ζῶν

חיל

(83) Psa 18:33
MT: חיל
LXX: δύναμιν
ε': καὶ δύναμιν
Aq: εὐπορίαν
Sym: ....

(84) Psa 49:7
MT: עַל-חילם
LXX: ἐπὶ τῇ δυνάμει αὐτῶν
ε': ....
Aq: ἐπὶ -- εὐπορίᾳ αὐτῶν
Sym: --- τῇ δυνάμει ἑαυτῶν

(85) Psa 49:11
MT: חילם
LXX: τὸν πλοῦτον αὐτῶν
ε': τὴν δύναμιν αὐτῶν
Aq: --- εὐπορίαν αὐτῶν
Sym: τὴν ἰσχὺν αὐτῶν

חלד

(86) Psa 49:2
MT: חלד
LXX: τὴν οἰκουμένην
ε': τὴν κατάδυσιν
Aq: --- κατάδυσιν
Sym: τὴν ἔγκατα

(87) Psa 89:48
MT: מה-חלד
LXX: ἡ ὑπόστασις
ε': ἐκ καταδύτου
Aq: ἐκ καταδύσεως
Sym: ἡμερόβιος ὤν

חלה

(88) Psa 35:13
MT: בחלותם
LXX: τοὺς παρενοχλεῖν
 μοι
ε': ἐν τῷ παρενοχλεῖσθαι
 αὐτοὺς
Aq: ἐν ἀρρωστίαις
 αὐτῶν
Sym: ....
 ....

חלק

(89) Psa 36:3
MT: החליק
LXX: ἐδόλωσεν
ε': ....
Aq: ἐλείωσε
Sym: ἐξολισθάνειν

חמר

(90) Psa 46:4
MT: יחמרו
LXX: καὶ ἐταράχθησαν
ε': καὶ ταραχθήσονται
Aq: --- αὐστηρωθήσονται
Sym: καὶ θολουμένων

חנה

(91) Psa 46:10
MT: חנית
LXX: ὅπλον
ε': ....
Aq: δόρυ
Sym: λόγχας

TRANSLATION TECHNIQUE OF MINOR VERSIONS

חנן

(92) Psa 28:6
MT: תחנוני
LXX: τῆς δεήσεώς μου
ε': ....
Aq: --- δεήσεώς μου
Sym: τῆς ἱκεσίας μου

(93) Psa 30:9
MT: אתחנן
LXX: δεηθήσομαι
ε': ....
Aq: ....
Sym: ἱκετεύσω

(94) Psa 30:11
MT: וחנני
LXX: καὶ ἠλέησέν με
ε': καὶ δώρησαί μοι
Aq: καὶ δώρησαί μοι
Sym: --- ᾤκτειρέν με

(95) Psa 31:10
MT: חנני
LXX: ἐλέησόν με
ε': δώρησαί μοι
Aq: δώρησαί μοι
Sym: οἴκτειρόν με

(96) Psa 31:23
MT: תחנוני
LXX: τῆς δεήσεώς μου
ε': ....
Aq: --- δεήσεώς μου
Sym: τῆς ἱκεσίας μου

(97) Psa 35:19
MT: חנם
LXX: δωρεὰν
ε': μάτην
Aq: ....
Sym: ἀναιτίως

חנף

(98) Psa 35:16
MT: בחנפי
LXX: ἐπείρασάν με
ε': ἐν ὑποκρίσει
Aq: ἐν ὑποκρίσει
Sym: ἐν ὑποκρίσει

חסד

(99) Psa 31:8
MT: בחסדך
LXX: ἐπὶ τῷ ἐλέει σου
ε': ....
Aq: ἐν -- ἐλέωι σου
Sym: ἐν τῇ χάριτί σου

(100) Psa 31:22
MT: חסדו
LXX: τὸ ἔλεος αὐτοῦ
ε': ὅσιον αὐτοῦ
Aq: ἔλεον αὐτοῦ
Sym: ....

(101) Psa 31:24
MT: חסידיו
LXX: οἱ ὅσιοι αὐτοῦ
ε': ....
Aq: -- ὅσιοι αὐτοῦ
Sym: ....

(102) Psa 32:10
MT: חסד
LXX: ἔλεος
ε': ....
Aq: ....
Sym: ....

(103) Psa 89:29
MT: חסדי
LXX: τὸ ἔλεός μου
ε': ....
Aq: -- ἔλεός μου
Sym: ....

(104) Psa 89:34
MT: וחסדי
LXX: --- τὸ δὲ ἔλεός μου
ε´: ....
Aq: καὶ -- -- ἔλεόν μου
Sym: ....

(105) Psa 89:50
MT: חסדיך
LXX: τὰ ἐλέη σου
ε´: ....
Aq: -- ἐλέη σου
Sym: ....

חסה

(106) Psa 18:31
MT: החסים
LXX: τῶν ἐλπιζόντων
ε´: ....
Aq: ....
Sym: τῶν πεποιθότων

(107) Psa 31:2
MT: חסיתי
LXX: ἤλπισα
ε´: ......
Aq: ἐπεποίθησα
Sym: ἐπεποίθησα

(108) Psa 31:20
MT: לחוסים
LXX: τοῖς ἐλπίζουσιν
ε´: ....
Aq: ....
Sym: τοῖς προσδοκῶσίν

(109) Psa 46:2
MT: מחסה
LXX: καταφυγὴ
ε´: ....
Aq: ἐλπὶς
Sym: πεποίθησις

חפז

(110) Psa 31:23
MT: בחפזי
LXX: ἐν τῆι ἐκστάσει μου
ε´: ....
Aq: ἐν θαμβήσει μου
Sym: ἐν ἐκπλήξει μου

חפך

(111) Psa 30:12
MT: הפכת
LXX: ἔστρεψας
ε´: ....
Aq: ....
Sym: μετέβαλες

חפץ

(112) Psa 35:27
MT: חפצי
LXX: οἱ θέλοντες
ε´: ....
Aq: -- βουλόμενοι
Sym: ....

(113) Psa 35:27
MT: החפץ
LXX: οἱ θέλοντες
ε´: ....
Aq: ὁ βουλόμενος
Sym: ....

חפר

(114) Psa 35:26
MT: ויחפרו
LXX: καὶ ἐντραπείησαν
ε´: ....
Aq: καὶ καταισχυνθείησαν
Sym: καὶ κατορυγείησαν

חקק

(115) Psa 89:32
MT: חֻקָּי
LXX: τὰ δικαιώματά μου
ε': τὰ ἠκριβασμένα μου
Aq: -- ἀκριβείας μου
Sym: τὰ προστάγματά μου

חרג

(116) Psa 18:46
MT: ויחרגו
LXX: καὶ ἐχώλαναν
ε': ....
Aq: καὶ συσταλήσονται
Sym: καὶ ἐντραπήσονται

חרק

(117) Psa 35:16
MT: חרק
LXX: ἔβρυξαν
ε': ....
Aq: ....
Sym: ἔπριον

חרש

(118) Psa 35:22
MT: אל-תחרש
LXX: μὴ παρασιωπήσῃς
ε': ....
Aq: μὴ κωφεύσῃς
Sym: μὴ ἡσυχάσῃς

חתת

(119) Psa 89:41
MT: מחתה
LXX: --- δειλίαν
ε': εἰς ταπείνωσιν
Aq: --- πτῆξιν
Sym: --- ἥττησιν

טהר

(120) Psa 89:45
MT: מטהרו
LXX: ἀπὸ καθαρισμοῦ
ε': τοὺς κεκαθαρμένους ----
Aq: ---- κεκαθαρισμὸν αὐτοῦ
Sym: τὴν καθαρότητα αὐτοῦ

טוב

(121) Psa 31:20
MT: טובך
LXX: τῆς χρηστότητός σου
ε': τῆς ἀγαθωσύνης σου
Aq: --- ἀγαθόν σου
Sym: τὸ ἀγαθόν σου

ידה

(122) Psa 28:7
MT: אהודנו
LXX: ἐξομολογήσομαι αὐτῷ
ε': ....
Aq: ....
Sym: ὑμνήσω αὐτόν

(123) Psa 30:5
MT: והודו
LXX: καὶ ἐξομολογεῖσθε
ε': ....
Aq: --- ἐξομολογεῖσθε
Sym: καὶ ἐπαινεῖτε

(124) Psa 30:10
MT: היודך
LXX: μὴ ἐξομολογήσεταί σοι
ε': ....
Aq: ....
Sym: ....

(125) Psa 30:13
MT: אודך
LXX: ἐξομολογήσομαί σοι
ε': ....
Aq: ....
Sym: αἰνέσω σε

יחד

(126) Psa 35:17
MT: יְחִידָתִי
LXX: τὴν μονογενῆ μου
ε′: ....
Aq: --- μοναχήν μου
Sym: τὴν μονότητά μου

יחל

(127) Psa 31:25
MT: הַמְיַחֲלִים
LXX: οἱ ἐλπίζοντες
ε′: ....
Aq: οἱ περιμένοντες
Sym: ....

יחם

(128) Psa 89:47
MT: חֲמָתֶךָ
LXX: ἡ ὀργή σου
ε′: ....
Aq: -- χόλος σου
Sym: ὁ θυμός σου

יעץ

(129) Psa 32:8
MT: אִיעָצָה
LXX: ἐπιστηριῶ
ε′: ....
Aq: βουλεύσομαι
Sym: βουλεύσομαι

יצא

(130) Psa 89:35
MT: וּמוֹצָא
LXX: καὶ τὰ ἐκπορευόμενα
ε′: ....
Aq: καὶ --- ἔξοδον
Sym: οὐδὲ τὴν προφορὰν

ירד

(131) Psa 30:4
MT: מִיּוֹרְדִי-
LXX: ἀπὸ τῶν καταβαινόντων
ε′: ....
Aq: ἀπὸ τοῦ καταβῆναί με
Sym: τοῦ μὴ κατενεχθῆναί με

(132) Psa 30:10
MT: בְּרִדְתִּי
LXX: ἐν τῷ καταβῆναί με
ε′: ....
Aq: ....
Sym: κατενεχθέντος μου

ירה

(133) Psa 32:8
MT: וְאוֹרְךָ
LXX: καί συμβιβῶ σε
ε′: καί φωτιῶ σε
Aq: καί φωτίσω σε
Sym: καί ὑποδείξω σοι

ירח

(134) Psa 89:38
MT: כַּיָּרֵחַ
LXX: καὶ ὡς ἡ σελήνη
ε′: --- ὡς ἡ σελήνη
Aq: --- ὡς ἡ μήνη
Sym: --- ὡς ἡ μήνη

ירש

(135) Psa 31:5
MT: מֵרֶשֶׁת
LXX: ἐκ παγίδος
ε′: ....
Aq: ἀπὸ δικτύου
Sym: ἀπὸ δικτύου

ישב

(136) Psa 49:2
MT: ישבי
LXX: οἱ κατοικοῦντες
ε′: ....
Aq: -- καθήμενοι
Sym: ....

כאב

(137) Psa 32:10
MT: מכאובים
LXX: αἱ μάστιγες
ε′: ....
Aq: -- ἀλγήματα
Sym: -- καταπονήσεις

כון

(138) Psa 89:38
MT: יכון
LXX: κατηρτισμένη
ε′: ἑτοιμασθήσεται
Aq: ἑτοιμασθήσεται
Sym: ἑδραία

כזב

(139) Psa 89:36
MT: אכזב
LXX: ψεύσομαι
ε′: ....
Aq: διαψεύσομαι
Sym: ....

כלם

(140) Psa 35:26
MT: כלמה
LXX: καὶ ἐντροπὴν
ε′: ....
Aq: ....
Sym: καὶ ἀσχημοσύνην

כנור

(141) Psa 49:5
MT: בכנור
LXX: ἐν ψαλτηρίωι
ε′: ....
Aq: ἐν κιθάραι
Sym: διὰ ψαλτηρίου

כסל

(142) Psa 49:11
MT: יחד כסיל
LXX: ἐπὶ τὸ αὐτὸ ἄφρων
ε′: ....
Aq: ἅμα -- ---- ἀνόητος
Sym: ὁμοῦ -- ---- ἀνόητος

(143) Psa 49:14
MT: כסל
LXX: σκάνδαλον
ε′: ....
Aq: ἀνοησία
Sym: ἀνοίας

כעס

(144) Psa 31:10
MT: בכעס
LXX: ἐν θυμῷ
ε′: ....
Aq: ἐν παροργισμῶι
Sym: διὰ παροργισμὸν

כפר

(145) Psa 35:17
MT: מכפירים
LXX: ἀπὸ λεόντων

ε′: ....

Aq: ἀπὸ σκύμνων

Sym: ἀπὸ λεόντων ὀλοθρευόντων

לבש

(146) Psa 35:13
MT: לבושי
LXX: -- ἐνεδυόμην ---
ε´: ....
Aq: -- ἔνδυσίς μου
Sym: τὸ ἔνδυμα ---

(147) Psa 35:26
MT: ילבשו -
LXX: ἐνδυσάσθωσαν
ε´: ....
Aq: ....
Sym: ἀπφιεσθήτωσαν

לעג

(148) Psa 35:16
MT: לעגי
LXX: ἐξεμυκτήρισάν με
ε´: μυκτηρίζοντες --
Aq: λέξεων --
Sym: φθέγμασι --

מאס

(149) Psa 89:39
MT: ותמאס
LXX: καὶ ἐξουδένωσας
ε´: καὶ ἐγκατέλιπες
Aq: καὶ ἀπέρριψας
Sym: ....

מגן

(150) Psa 18:31
MT: מגן
LXX: ὑπερασπιστής
ε´: ....
Aq: θυρεός
Sym: ....

(151) Psa 18:36
MT: מגן
LXX: ὑπερασπισμὸν
ε´: ....
Aq: θυρεὸν
Sym: ....

(152) Psa 28:7
MT: ומגני
LXX: καὶ ὑπερασπιστής μου
ε´: ....
Aq: καὶ θυρεός μου
Sym: ....

(153) Psa 35:2
MT: מגן
LXX: ὅπλου
ε´: ....
Aq: θυρεοῦ
Sym: ἀσπίδος

מגר

(154) Psa 89:45
MT: מגרתה
LXX: κατέρραξας
ε´: ....
Aq: ἀποκατέσπασας
Sym: ἀνέστρεψας

מהר

(155) Psa 31:3
MT: מהרה
LXX: τάχυνον
ε´: ταχὺ
Aq: ταχέως
Sym: ταχὺ

מוג

(156) Psa 46:7
MT: חמוג
LXX: ἐσαλεύθη
ε´: τακήσεται
Aq: ἠδαφίσθη
Sym: διελύθη

מוט

(157) Psa 30:7
MT: אמוט
LXX: σαλευθῶ
ε´: ....
Aq: σφαλῶ
Sym: περιτραπήσομαι

TRANSLATION TECHNIQUE OF MINOR VERSIONS 533

(158) Psa 46:3
MT: ובמוט
LXX: καὶ -- -- μετατίθεσται
ε´: καὶ -- -- σαλεύεσθαι
Aq: καὶ ἐν τῷ σφάλλεσθαι
Sym: καὶ -- -- κλίνεσθαι

(159) Psa 46:6
MT: תמוט
LXX: σαλευθήσεται
ε´: σαλευθῇ
Aq: σφαλῇ
Sym: περιτραπήσεται

(160) Psa 46:7
MT: מטו
LXX: ἔκλιναν
ε´: ἐσαλεύθησαν
Aq: ἐσφάλησαν
Sym: περιετράπησαν

מור

(161) Psa 46:3
MT: בהמיר
LXX: ἐν τῶι ταράσσεσθαι
ε´: ....
Aq: ἐν τῶι ἀνταλλάσσεσθαι
Sym: ἐν τῶι συγχεῖσθαι

מלט

(162) Psa 89:49
MT: ימלט
LXX: ῥύσεται -------
ε´: ....
Aq: περισώσει -------
Sym: διαφυγεῖν ποιήσει

משח

(163) Psa 28:8
MT: משיחו
LXX: τοῦ χριστοῦ αὐτοῦ
ε´: ....
Aq: --- ἠλειμμένου αὐτοῦ
Sym: ....

(164) Psa 89:39
MT: אם-משיחך
LXX: τὸν χριστόν σου
ε´: τῶι χριστῶι σου
Aq: μετὰ ἠλειμμένου σου
Sym: πρὸς τὸν χριστόν σου

(165) Psa 89:52
MT: משיחך
LXX: τοῦ χριστοῦ σου
ε´: ....
Aq: --- ἠλιμμένου σου
Sym: ....

משל

(166) Psa 49:13
MT: נמשל
LXX: παρασυνεβλήθη
ε´: συνεβλήθη
Aq: παρεβλήθη
Sym: παρεικάσθη κτήνεσιν

נאר

(167) Psa 89:40
MT: נארחה
LXX: --- κατέστρεψας -----
ε´: ....
Aq: --- ἐσπάνισας -----
Sym: εἰς κατάραν ἔδωκας

נבל

(168) Psa 18:46
MT: יבלו
LXX: ἐπαλαιώθησαν
ε´: ....
Aq: ἀπορρυήσονται
Sym: ἀτιμωθήσονται

נגה

(169) Psa 18:29
MT: יגיה
LXX: φωτιεῖς
ε´: ....
Aq: φεγγώσεις
Sym: ....

נגע

(170) Psa 32:6
MT: יגיעו
LXX: ἐγγιοῦσιν
ε´: ....
Aq: καταντήσουσιν
Sym: ἐγγίσαι

נהל

(171) Psa 31:4
MT: ותנהלני
LXX: καὶ διαθρέψεις με
ε´: ....
Aq: καὶ διαβαστάσεις με
Sym: καὶ τημελήσεις μου

נזר

(172) Psa 89:40
MT: נזרו
LXX: τὸ ἁγίασμα αὐτοῦ
ε´: τὸ ἀφωρισμένον αὐτοῦ
Aq: -- ἀφόρισμα αὐτοῦ
Sym: -- στέφανον αὐτοῦ

נחה

(173) Psa 31:4
MT: תנחני
LXX: ὁδηγήσεις με
ε´: ....
Aq: καθοδηγήσεις με
Sym: ....

נחל

(174) Psa 28:9
MT: נחלתך
LXX: κληρονομίαν σου
ε´: ....
Aq: ....
Sym: κληρουχίαν σου

נחת

(175) Psa 18:35
MT: ונחתה
LXX: καὶ ἔθου
ε´: ....
Aq: καὶ κατεσκεύασε
Sym: καὶ ἑδράζων

נכה

(176) Psa 35:15
MT: נכים
LXX: μάστιγες
ε´: ....
Aq: πεπληγότες
Sym: πλῆκται

נכר

(177) Psa 18:45
MT: נכר
LXX: ἀλλότριοι
ε´: ....
Aq: ἀπεξενωμένου
Sym: ....

(178) Psa 18:46
MT: נכר
LXX: ἀλλότριοι
ε´: ....
Aq: ἀπεξενωμένου
Sym: ....

נצח

(179) Psa 31:1
MT: למנצח
LXX: εἰς τὸ τέλος
ε´: --- τῶι νικοποιῶι
Aq: --- τῶι νικοποιῶι
Sym: ἐπινίκιον

(180) Psa 36:1
MT: למנצח
LXX: εἰς τὸ τέλος
ε´: --- τῶι νικοποιῶι
Aq: --- τῶι νικοποιῶι
Sym: ἐπινίκιον

(181) Psa 46:1
MT: למנצח
LXX: εἰς τὸ τέλος
ε': --- τῶι νικοποιῶι
Aq: --- τῶι νικοποιῶι
Sym: ἐπίνικιος

(182) Psa 49:1
MT: למנצח
LXX: εἰς τὸ τέλος
ε': --- τῶι νικοποιῶ
Aq: --- τῶι νικοποιῶ
Sym: ἐπινίκιον

(183) Psa 49:10
MT: עוד לנצח
LXX: -- εἰς τέλος
ε': ἔτι εἰς νῖκος
Aq: ἔτι εἰς νῖκος
Sym: --- εἰς αἰῶνα

(184) Psa 89:47
MT: לנצח
LXX: εἰς τέλος
ε': ....
Aq: εἰς νῖκος
Sym: ....

נצל

(185) Psa 31:3
MT: הצילני
LXX: τοῦ ἐξελέσθαι με
ε': --- ἐξελοῦ με
Aq: --- ῥῦσαί με
Sym: --- ἐξελοῦ με

נצר

(186) Psa 31:24
MT: נצר
LXX: ἐκζητεῖ
ε': φυλάσσει
Aq: διατηρεῖ
Sym: φυλάσσει

(187) Psa 32:7
MT: תצרני
LXX: τῆς περιεχούσης με
ε': --- φυλάξεις με
Aq: --- διατηρήσεις με
Sym: τῆς περιεστώσης με

נקם

(188) Psa 18:48
MT: נקמות
LXX: ἐκδικήσεις
ε': ....
Aq: ....
Sym: τιμωρίας

נשא

(189) Psa 28:9
MT: ונשאם
LXX: καὶ ἔπαρον αὐτοὺς
ε': ....
Aq: ....
Sym: καὶ ὕψωσον αὐτοὺς

(190) Psa 89:51
MT: שאתי
LXX: οὗ ὑπέσχον
ε': ....
Aq: -- αἴροντός
Sym: ὃν ἐβάστασα

נתן

(191) Psa 18:33
MT: ויתן
LXX: καὶ ἔθετο
ε': ....
Aq: καὶ ἔδωκεν
Sym: καὶ παρέχων

(192) Psa 18:36
MT: ותתן
LXX: καὶ ἔδωκάς
ε': ....
Aq: ....
Sym: καὶ δώσεις

(193) Psa 18:41
MT: נתתה
LXX: ἔδωκάς
ε': ....
Aq: ....
Sym: παρέσχες

(194) Psa 18:48
MT: הַנּוֹתֵן
LXX: ὁ διδοὺς
ε': ....
Aq: ....
Sym: ὁ παρασχὼν

סבב

(195) Psa 32:7
MT: חֲסוֹבְבֵנִי
LXX: ἀπὸ τῶν κυκλωσάντων με
ε': --- -- περιεκύκλωσάν με
Aq: --- -- περικυκλώσεις με
Sym: --- -- κυκλώσεις με

(196) Psa 32:10
MT: יְסוֹבְבֶנּוּ
LXX: κυκλώσει
ε': ....
Aq: περικυκλώσει αὐτόν
Sym: κυκλώσει αὐτόν

(197) Psa 49:6
MT: יְסֻבֵּנִי
LXX: κυκλώσει με
ε': ....
Aq: ....
Sym: ....

סגר

(198) Psa 18:46
MT: מִמִּסְגְּרוֹתֵיהֶם
LXX: ἀπὸ τῶν τρίβων
αὐτῶν
ε': ....
Aq: ἀπὸ --- ἐπικλισμῶν
αὐτῶν
Sym: ἀπὸ --- περιφραγμάτων
αὐτῶν

(199) Psa 31:9
MT: הִסְגַּרְתַּנִי
LXX: συνέκλεισάς με
ε': ....
Aq: ἀπέκλεισάς με
Sym: ἐξέκλιωάς με

סכה

(200) Psa 31:21
MT: בְּסֻכָּה
LXX: ἐν σκηνῆι
ε': ἐν σκέπηι
Aq: ἐν συσκιασμῶι
Sym: ἐν σκέπηι

סלה

(201) Psa 32:7
MT: סלה
LXX: διάψαλμα
ε': ἀεί
Aq: ἀεί
Sym: ....

(202) Psa 46:4
MT: סלה
LXX: διάψαλμα
ε': ἀεί
Aq: ἀεί
Sym: ....

(203) Psa 46:12
MT: סלה
LXX: διάψαλμα
ε': ἀεί
Aq: ἀεί
Sym: ....

(204) Psa 49:14
MT: סלה
LXX: διάψαλμα
ε': ἀεί
Aq: ἀεί
Sym: ....

(205) Psa 89:38
MT: סלה
LXX: διάψαλμα
ε´: ἀεί σελ
Aq: ἀεί ---
Sym: ....

(206) Psa 89:46
MT: סלה
LXX: διάψαλμα
ε´: ἀεί σελ
Aq: ἀεί ---
Sym: ....

(207) Psa 89:49
MT: סלה
LXX: διάψαλμα
ε´: ἀεί σελ
Aq: ἀεί ---
Sym: ....

סלע

(208) Psa 31:4
MT: סלעי
LXX: κραταίωσίς μου
ε´: στερεός μου
Aq: πέτρα μου
Sym: πέτρα μου

סער

(209) Psa 18:36
MT: וסערני
LXX: ἀντελάβετό μου
ε´: ....
Aq: συνεπίσχυσέ μου
Sym: ὑποστηρίσει με

סתר

(210) Psa 30:8
MT: הסתרתה
LXX: ἀπέστρεψας δὲ
ε´: ἀπέκρυψας --
Aq: ἀπέκρυψας --
Sym: κρύψαντος δέ

(211) Psa 31:21
MT: תסתרם
LXX: κατακρύψεις αὐτοὺς
ε´: ....
Aq: ἀποκρυψεις ------
Sym: σκεπάσεις αὐτοὺς

(212) Psa 31:21
MT: בסתר
LXX: ἐν ἀποκρύφωι
ε´: ....
Aq: ἐν ἀποκρυφῆι
Sym: ἐν σκέπηι

(213) Psa 32:7
MT: סתר
LXX: καταφυγή
ε´: σκέπη
Aq: ἀποκρυφή
Sym: σκέπη

(214) Psa 89:47
MT: תסתר
LXX: ἀποστρέψῃ
ε´: ἀποκρύψεις
Aq: ἀποκρυβῇ
Sym: ἀποκρυβήσηι

עבר

(215) Psa 89:39
MT: התעברת
LXX: ἀνεβάλου
ε´: ὠργίσθης
Aq: ἀνυπερθέτησας
Sym: ἐχολώθης

(216) Psa 89:42
MT: עברי
LXX: οἱ παραπορευόμενοι
ε´: οἱ διαπορευόμενοι
Aq: -- παρερχόμενοι
Sym: οἱ παροδεύοντες

עגל

(217) Psa 46:10
MT: עגלות
LXX: καὶ θυρεοὺς
ε´: καὶ ἅρματα
Aq: --- ἁμάξας
Sym: --- ἁμάξας

עדה

(218) Psa 32:9
MT: עדיו
LXX: τὰς σιαγόνας αὐτῶν
ε´: ....
Aq: --- κατακόσμησιν αὐτοῦ
Sym: --- περιθέσεως -----

עוג

(219) Psa 35:16
MT: מעוג
LXX: μυκτηρισμῷ --
ε´: ἐξεχλεύασάν με
Aq: περιαθροισμοῦ --
Sym: πεπλασμένοις --

עון

(220) Psa 89:33
MT: עונם
LXX: τὰς ἀδικίας αὐτῶν
ε´: τὰς ἀνομίας αὐτῶν
Aq: --- ἀνομίαν αὐτῶν
Sym: ....

עור

(221) Psa 35:23
MT: העירה
LXX: ἐξεγέρθητι κε
ε´: ἐξεγέρθητι --
Aq: ἐξεγέρθητι --
Sym: γρηγόρησον --

עזז

(222) Psa 28:7
MT: עזי
LXX: βοηθός μου
ε´: ....
Aq: κράτος μου
Sym: ἰσχύς μου

(223) Psa 28:8
MT: עז-
LXX: κραταίωμα
ε´: ἰσχὺς
Aq: κράτος
Sym: ἰσχὺς

(224) Psa 28:8
MT: ומעוז
LXX: ὁ ὑπερασπιστὴς
ε´: καὶ ὑπερασπιστὴς
Aq: καὶ κραταίωμα
Sym: καὶ ἐνίσχυσις

(225) Psa 29:1
MT: ועז
LXX: καὶ τιμήν
ε´: καὶ ἰσχύν
Aq: καὶ κράτος
Sym: καὶ δύναμιν

(226) Psa 30:8
MT: עז
LXX: δύναμιν
ε´: ....
Aq: κράτος
Sym: κράτος

(227) Psa 31:3
MT: מעוז
LXX: ὑπερασπιστὴν
ε´: κατοικητήριον
Aq: κραταιώματος
Sym: ἰσχυρόν

(228) Psa 31:5
MT: מעוזי
LXX: ὁ ὑπερασπιστής μου κε
ε': ὁ ὑπερασπιστής μου --
Aq: -- κραταίωμα μου --
Sym: -- ἀηττησία μου --

(229) Psa 46:1
MT: עז
LXX: δύναμις
ε': ....
Aq: κράτος
Sym: ἰσχὺς

עזב

(230) Psa 89:31
MT: יעזבו
LXX: ἐγκαταλίπωσιν
ε': ....
Aq: καταλίπωσι
Sym: ....

עטה

(231) Psa 89:46
MT: העטית
LXX: κατέχεας
ε': περιέβαλες
Aq: ἀνεβόλησας
Sym: ἠμφίεσας

עלה

(232) Psa 30:4
MT: העלית
LXX: ἀνήγαγες
ε': ....
Aq: ἀνεβίβασας
Sym: ....

עלם

(233) Psa 46:1
MT: על-עלמות
LXX: ὑπὲρ τῶν κρυφίων
ε': ....
Aq: ἐπὶ --- νεανιοτήτων
Sym: ὑπὲρ τῶν αἰωνίων

(234) Psa 89:46
MT: עלומיו
LXX: τοῦ χρόνου αὐτοῦ
ε': τῆς νεότητος αὐτοῦ
Aq: --- νεανιοτήτων αὐτοῦ
Sym: τῆς νεότητος αὐτοῦ

עמר

(235) Psa 30:8
MT: העמדתה
LXX: παρέσχου
ε': ἔστησας
Aq: ἔστησας
Sym: ἔστησας

ענוה

(236) Psa 18:36
MT: וענותך
LXX: καὶ ἡ παιδεία σου
ε': καὶ ἡ πραΰτης σου
Aq: καὶ -- πραΰτης σου
Sym: καὶ τὸ ὑπακούειν σοι

ענה

(237) Psa 18:42
MT: ענם
LXX: εἰσήκουσεν αὐτῶν
ε': ....
Aq: ὑπήκουσεν αὐτῶν
Sym: ὑπήκουσεν αὐτῶν

(238) Psa 35:13
MT: עניתי
LXX: καὶ ἐταπείνουν ---
ε': --- ἐταπείνωσα οὖν
Aq: --- ἐκακούχουν ---
Sym: --- ἐκάκουν ---

עני

(239) Psa 18:28
MT: עני
LXX: ταπεινὸν
ε': πένητα
Aq: πένητα
Sym: πρᾶον

(240) Psa 31:8
MT: אֶת-עָנְיִי
LXX: τὴν ταπείνωσίν μου, **
ε´: τὴν πτωχείαν μου --
Aq: τὴν κακουχίαν μου --
Sym: τὴν κάκωσίν μου --

עָפָר

(241) Psa 18:43
MT: עָפָרö
LXX: ὡς χοῦν
ε´: ....
Aq: ....
Sym: ....

(242) Psa 30:10
MT: עָפָר
LXX: χοῦς
ε´: ....
Aq: ....
Sym: κόνις

עֶצֶם

(243) Psa 35:18
MT: עָצוּם
LXX: βαρεῖ
ε´: ....
Aq: ὀστεΐνῶι
Sym: παμπληθεῖ

עָקֵב

(244) Psa 89:52
MT: עִקְּבוֹת
LXX: τὸ ἀντάλλαγμα
ε´: τὰ ἴχνη
Aq: -- πτερνώσεις
Sym: τὰ ἴχνη

עִקֵּשׁ

(245) Psa 18:27
MT: עִקֵּשׁ
LXX: στρεβλοῦ
ε´: ....
Aq: ....
Sym: σκολιὸν

עֹרֶף

(246) Psa 18:41
MT: עֹרֶף
LXX: νῶτον
ε´: ....
Aq: τένοντα
Sym: αὐχένα

עָשָׂה

(247) Psa 31:24
MT: עֹשֵׂה
LXX: ποιοῦσιν
ε´: ....
Aq: ....
Sym: πράσσουσιν

עָשֵׁשׁ

(248) Psa 31:10
MT: עָשְׁשָׁה
LXX: ἐταράχθη
ε´: ....
Aq: αὐχμώθη
Sym: ἐθολώθη

פָּלָא

(249) Psa 31:22
MT: הִפְלִיא
LXX: ἐθαυμάστωσε
ε´: ....
Aq: ....
Sym: παραδοξάσας

פֶּלֶג

(250) Psa 46:5
MT: פְּלָגָיו
LXX: τὰ ὁρμήματα
ε´: αἱ διαιρέσεις
Aq: -- διαιρέσεις αὐτοῦ
Sym: -- διαιρέσεις -----

פלט

(251) Psa 31:2
MT: פלטני
LXX: ῥῦσαί με καὶ ἐξελοῦμαι
ε´: ῥῦσαί με ---

Aq: διάσωσόν με ---

Sym: διάσωσόν με ---

(252) Psa 32:7
MT: פלט
LXX: --- λύτρωσαί με
ε´: ....
Aq: --- διασώζων --
Sym: καὶ ἔκφευξις --

פעל

(253) Psa 31:20
MT: פעלת
LXX: ἐξειργάσω
ε´: ....
Aq: κατειγάσω
Sym: εἰργάσω

(254) Psa 46:9
MT: מפעלות
LXX: τὰ ἔργα
ε´: ....
Aq: -- κατέργασμα
Sym: ἃ διεπράξατο

פרץ

(255) Psa 89:41
MT: פרצת
LXX: καθεῖλες
ε´: ....
Aq: διέκοψας
Sym: διέκοψας

פרר

(256) Psa 89:34
MT: אפיר
LXX: διασκεδάσω
ε´: ....
Aq: ἀκυρώσω
Sym: διαλύσω

פשע

(257) Psa 36:2
MT: פשע
LXX: ὁ παράνομος
ε´: ---- ἀσέβεια
Aq: ---- ἀθεσία
Sym: περὶ ἀσυνθεσίας

(258) Psa 89:33
MT: פשעם
LXX: τὰς ἀνομίας αὐτῶν
ε´: τὰς ἀσεβείας αὐτῶν
Aq: --- ἀθεσίαν αὐτῶν
Sym: τὰς παραβάσεις αὐτῶν

פתח

(259) Psa 30:12
MT: פתחת
LXX: διέρρηξας
ε´: ....
Aq: περιέλυσας
Sym: ἀπέλυσας

פתל

(260) Psa 18:27
MT: תתפתל
LXX: διαστρέψεις
ε´: ....
Aq: ....
Sym: σκολιεύσῃ

צאן

(261) Psa 49:15
MT: כַּצֹּאן
LXX: ὡς πρόβατα
ε´: ....
Aq: ὡς ποίμνιον
Sym: ὡς βοσκήματα

צדק

(262) Psa 31:2
MT: בְּצִדְקָתְךָ
LXX: ἐν τῇ δικαιοσύνῃ σου
ε´: ....
Aq: ἐν -- δικαιοσύνῃ σου
Sym: ἐν τῇ ἐλεημοσύνῃ σου

(263) Psa 35:24
MT: כְצִדְקְךָ
LXX: κατὰ τὴν δικαιοσύνην μου --- ----- ---
ε´: κατὰ τὴν δικαιοσύνην
σου τὸ ἔλεός σου
Aq: κατὰ --- δίκαιόν σου
--- -- ----- ---
Sym: ....
.... -- ----- ---

(264) Psa 35:27
MT: צִדְקִי
LXX: τὴν δικαιοσύνην μου
ε´: ....
Aq: --- δίκαιόν μου
Sym: ....

(265) Psa 35:28
MT: צִדְקֶךָ
LXX: τὴν δικαιοσύνην σου
ε´: ....
Aq: --- δίκαιόν σου
Sym: ....

צור

(266) Psa 31:3
MT: מְצוּדוֹת
LXX: καταφυγῆς
ε´: ....
Aq: ὀχυρωμάτων
Sym: ....

(267) Psa 31:4
MT: וּמְצוּדָתִי
LXX: καὶ καταφυγή μου
ε´: ....
Aq: --- ὀχύρωμά μου
Sym: ....

צור

(268) Psa 18:32
MT: צוּר
LXX: θεὸς
ε´: στερεὸς
Aq: στερεὸς
Sym: κραταιὸς

(269) Psa 18:47
MT: צוּרִי
LXX: καὶ θεός μου
ε´: --- στερεός μου
Aq: --- στερεός μου
Sym: καὶ κραταιός μου

(270) Psa 31:3
MT: לְצוּר-
LXX: εἰς θν
ε´: --- στερεὸν
Aq: εἰς στερεὸν
Sym: εἰς ἀκρότομον

(271) Psa 31:22
MT: מָצוֹר
LXX: περιοχῆς
ε´: ....
Aq: ....
Sym: περιπεφραγμένῃ

(272) Psa 89:27
MT: וְצוּר
LXX: καὶ ἀντιλήπτωρ
ε': καὶ στερεὸς
Aq: καὶ στερεὸς
Sym: καὶ περιτείχισμα

(273) Psa 89:44
MT: צוּר
LXX: τὴν βοήθειαν
ε': τὴν στερρότητα
Aq: --- στερεὸν
Sym: τὴν στερρότητα

צוּר

(274) Psa 49:15
MT: וְצוּרָם
LXX: καὶ ἡ βοήθεια αὐτῶν
ε': καὶ ἡ ἰσχὺς αὐτῶν
Aq: καὶ -- χαρακτὴρ αὐτῶν
Sym: τὸ δὲ κρατερὸν αὐτῶν

צֶלַע

(275) Psa 35:15
MT: וּבְצַלְעִי
LXX: καὶ κατ' -- ------ ἐμοῦ
ε': καὶ ἐν τῇ ἀσθενείᾳ μου
Aq: καὶ ἐν -- σκασμῶι μου
Sym: --- -- σκάζοντος δὲ μου

צמת

(276) Psa 18:41
MT: אַצְמִיתֵם
LXX: ἐξωλόθρευσας
ε': ....
Aq: ἐξολοθρεύσω αὐτούς
Sym: ἀφώνους ἐποίησας

צִנָּה

(277) Psa 35:2
MT: וְצִנָּה
LXX: καὶ -- θυρεοῦ
ε': ....
Aq: καὶ -- ἀσπίδος
Sym: καὶ ἐν πανοπλίαι

צַעַד

(278) Psa 18:37
MT: צְעָדִי
LXX: τὰ διαβήματά μου
ε': ....
Aq: ....
Sym: τοῖς βαδίσμασί μου

צָפַן

(279) Psa 31:20
MT: צָפַנְתָּ
LXX: ἔκρυψας --------
ε': ....
Aq: συνέκρυψας --------
Sym: συνέκρυψας ἀπόθετον

(280) Psa 31:21
MT: תַּצְפְּנֵם
LXX: σκεπάσεις αὐτούς
ε': ....
Aq: συγκρύψεις αὐτούς
Sym: κρύψεις αὐτούς

צָרַף

(281) Psa 18:31
MT: צְרוּפָה
LXX: --- πεπυρωμένα
ε': καὶ πεπυρωμένον
Aq: --- πεπυρωμένον
Sym: --- δόκιμος

צָרַר

(282) Psa 31:8
MT: בְּצָרוֹת
LXX: ἐκ τῶν ἀναγκῶν
ε': ....
Aq: ἐν --- θλίψεσι
Sym: -- τὰς θλίψεις

(283) Psa 31:10
MT: צַר-
LXX: θλίβομαι
ε': ....
Aq: στενὸν
Sym: ....

(284) Psa 32:7
MT: מצר
LXX: ἀπὸ θλίψεως
ε´: ἀπὸ θλίβοντος
Aq: ἀπὸ θλίβοντος
Sym: ....

(285) Psa 89:43
MT: צריו
LXX: τῶν θλιβόντων αὐτὸν
ε´: ....
Aq: --- θλιβόντων αὐτὸν
Sym: ....

קדד

(286) Psa 35:14
MT: אם קדר
LXX: καὶ σκυθρωπάζων
ε´: ὡς ὁ σκυθρωπάζων
Aq: μητρὸς σκυθρωπάζων
Sym: ὁμομήτριον σκυθρωπὸς

קדש

(287) Psa 29:3
MT: קדש
LXX: ἅγίαι   αὐτοῦ
ε´: ἅγίαι   -----
Aq: ἡγιασμένῃ -----
Sym: ἅγίαι   -----

(288) Psa 30:5
MT: קדשו
LXX: τῆς ἁγιωσύνης αὐτοῦ
ε´: ....
Aq: --- ἡγιασμένωι αὐτοῦ
Sym: τὸν ἁγιασμὸν αὐτοῦ

קהל

(289) Psa 35:18
MT: בקהל
LXX: ἐν ἐκκλησίαι
ε´: ....
Aq: ....
Sym: ἐν πλήθει

קום

(290) Psa 18:40
MT: קמי
LXX: τοὺς ἐπανισταμένους --
ε´: .... --
Aq: ---- ἐπανεστηκότας μοι
Sym: τοὺς ἀνθισταμένους μοι

(291) Psa 35:2
MT: וקומה
LXX: καὶ ἀνάστηθι
ε´: ....
Aq: ....
Sym: --- στῆθι

(292) Psa 89:44
MT: הקימתו
LXX: ἀντελάβου αὐτὸν
ε´: ἔστησας αὐτὸν
Aq: ἀνέστησας αὐτὸν
Sym: ὑπέστησας αὐτὸν

קיץ

(293) Psa 35:23
MT: והקיצה
LXX: καὶ πρόσχες
ε´: καὶ ἐξυπνίσθητι
Aq: καὶ ἐξυπνίσθητι
Sym: καὶ διανάστα

קצה

(294) Psa 46:10
MT: עד-קצה
LXX: μέχρι τῶν περάτων
ε´: ἕως τῶν περάτων
Aq: ἕως --- τελευταίου
Sym: ἕως τῶν περάτων

קצץ

(295) Psa 46:10
MT: וקצץ
LXX: καὶ συγλάσει
ε´: ....
Aq: καὶ κατακόψει
Sym: καὶ κατέκοψε

קצר

(296) Psa 89:46
MT: הִקְצַרְתָּ
LXX: ἐσμίκρυνας
ε´: ....
Aq: ἐκολόβωσας
Sym: συνέτεμες

קרא

(297) Psa 30:9
MT: אֶקְרָא
LXX: κεκράξομαι
ε´: ....
Aq: καλέσω
Sym: βοήσω

(298) Psa 49:12
MT: קָרְאוּ
LXX: ἐπεκαλέσαντο
ε´: ....
Aq: ἐκάλεσαν
Sym: ὀνομάσαντες

(299) Psa 89:27
MT: יִקְרָאֵנִי
LXX: ἐπικαλέσεταί με
ε´: ....
Aq: καλέσει με
Sym: καλέσει με

קרץ

(300) Psa 35:19
MT: יִקְרְצוּ-
LXX: καὶ διανεύοντες
ε´: --- διανεύσουσιν
Aq: --- κνίζοντες
Sym: μὴ ἐπίδοιέν

רבב

(301) Psa 31:20
MT: רֹב-
LXX: πολὺ τὸ πλῆθος
ε´: ....
Aq: πολύ -- ------
Sym: πολύ -- ------

(302) Psa 32:6
MT: רַבִּים
LXX: πολλῶν
ε´: ....
Aq: πολλά
Sym: πολλά

(303) Psa 32:10
MT: רַבִּים
LXX: πολλαί
ε´: ....
Aq: πολλά
Sym: ....

(304) Psa 35:18
MT: רָב
LXX: μεγάληι
ε´: ....
Aq: πολλῆ
Sym: πολλῶι

(305) Psa 89:51
MT: כָּל-רַבִּים
LXX: πολλῶν --- --------
ε´: πάσας τὰς ἀδικίας
Aq: πάσας --- ἀδικίας
Sym: πάντων πολλῶν

רבה

(306) Psa 18:36
MT: תַּרְבֵּנִי
LXX: ἀνώρθωσέ με. εἰς τέλος
ε´: πληθυνεῖ με· --- -----
Aq: ἐπλήθυνέν με. --- -----
Sym: αὐξήσει με. --- -----

רגע

(307) Psa 30:6
MT: רֶגַע
LXX: ὀργή
ε´: συντέλεια
Aq: ἀθροισμὸς
Sym: πρὸς ὀλίγιστον

(308) Psa 35:20
MT: רִגְעֵי -
LXX: ὀργὴν
ε´: συντέλειαν
Aq: ἀθρόα
Sym: συναρπαγῆς

רדה

(309) Psa 49:15
MT: וַיִּרְדּוּ
LXX: καὶ κατακυριεύσωσιν
ε´: ....
Aq: καὶ ἐπικρατήσουσιν
Sym: καὶ ὑποτάξουσιν

רום

(310) Psa 18:28
MT: רָמוֹת
LXX: ὑπερηφάνων
ε´: ....
Aq: ὑψηλοὺς
Sym: ὑπερηφάνους

(311) Psa 18:47
MT: וְיָרוּם
LXX: καὶ ὑψωθήτω
ε´: ....
Aq: καὶ ὑψωθήσεται
Sym: καὶ ὑψηλὸς ἔστω

רוץ

(312) Psa 18:30
MT: אָרֻץ
LXX: ῥυσθήσομαι
ε´: δραμοῦμαι
Aq: δραμοῦμαι
Sym: καταδραμοῦμαι

רחב

(313) Psa 18:37
MT: תַּרְחִיב
LXX: ἐπλάτυνας
ε´: ....
Aq: πλατυνεῖς
Sym: εὐρυχώρησας

(314) Psa 31:9
MT: בַּמֶּרְחָב
LXX: ἐν εὐρυχώρωι
ε´: ....
Aq: ἐν πλατύτητι
Sym: ....

(315) Psa 35:21
MT: וַיַּרְחִיבוּ
LXX: καὶ ἐπλάτυναν
ε´: ....
Aq: ....
Sym: ....

רחק

(316) Psa 35:22
MT: תִּרְחַק
LXX: ἀποστῇς
ε´: μακρύνῃς
Aq: μακρύθῃς
Sym: μακρὰν γένῃι

ריב

(317) Psa 31:21
MT: מֵרִיב
LXX: ἀπὸ ἀντιλογίας
ε´: ....
Aq: ἀπὸ δικασίας
Sym: ἀπὸ ἀντιλογιῶν

(318) Psa 35:1
MT: יְרִיבַי
LXX: ---- ἀδικοῦντάς με
ε´: ---- δίκην μου
Aq: ---- δικαζομένοις με
Sym: τοὺς ἀντιδίκους μου

(319) Psa 35:23
MT: לְרִיבִי
LXX: εἰς τὴν δίκην μου
ε´: ....
Aq: εἰς --- δικαίωσίν μου
Sym: εἰς τὴν διαδικασίαν μου

רכס

(320) Psa 31:21
MT: מרכסי
LXX: ἀπὸ ταραχῆς
ε´: ....
Aq: ἀπὸ τραχυτήτων
Sym: ἀπὸ παραδειγματισμοῦ

רמה

(321) Psa 35:20
MT: מרמות
LXX: δόλους δὲ
ε´: δόλια
Aq: ἐπιθέσεων
Sym: δολίους

רנן

(322) Psa 32:7
MT: רני
LXX: τὸ ἀγαλλίαμά μου --
ε´: ....
Aq: αἴνε   μου --
Sym: εὐφημία   μου σὺ

(323) Psa 32:11
MT: והרנינו
LXX: καὶ καυχᾶσθε
ε´: καὶ ἀλαλάξατε
Aq: καὶ αἰνοποιεῖτε
Sym: καὶ εὐφημεῖτε

(324) Psa 35:27
MT: ירנו
LXX: ἀγαλλιάσαιντο
ε´: ἀγαλλιάσθωσαν
Aq: αἰνέσαιεν
Sym: εὐφημείτωσαν

רע

(325) Psa 35:14
MT: כרע-
LXX: ὡς ---- πλησίον
ε´: ....
Aq: ὡς ---- ἑταίρωι
Sym: ὡς πρὸς ἑταῖρον

רעה

(326) Psa 28:9
MT: ורעם
LXX: καὶ ποίμανον αὐτοὺς
ε´: ....
Aq: καὶ νέμησον αὐτοὺς
Sym: ....

(327) Psa 49:15
MT: ירעם
LXX: ποιμανεῖ αὐτοὺς
ε´: ....
Aq: νεμήσει αὐτοὺς
Sym: νεμήσεται αὐτοὺς

רעש

(328) Psa 46:4
MT: ירעשו -
LXX: --- ἐταράχθησαν
ε´: --- σεισθήσονται
Aq: --- σεισθήσεται
Sym: καὶ σειομένων

רפה

(329) Psa 46:11
MT: הרפו
LXX: σχολάσατε
ε´: ....
Aq: ἰάθητε
Sym: ἐάσατε

רצה

(330) Psa 30:6
MT: ברצונו
LXX: ἐν τῷ θελήματι αὐτοῦ
ε´: ....
Aq: ἐν --- εὐδοκίᾳ αὐτοῦ
Sym: ἐν τῆι διαλλαγῆι αὐτοῦ

(331) Psa 30:8
MT: ברצונך
LXX: ἐν τῷ θελήματί σου
ε´: ....
Aq: ἐν -- εὐδοκίᾳ σου
Sym: ἐν τῇ εὐδοκίᾳ σου

(332) Psa 49:14
MT: יִרְצוּ
LXX: εὐδοκήσουσιν
ε´: ....
Aq: δραμοῦνται
Sym: ....

רֶשַׁע

(333) Psa 32:10
MT: לָרָשָׁע
LXX: τοῦ ἁμαρτωλοῦ
ε´: ....
Aq: τοῦ ἀσεβοῦς
Sym: τοῦ παρανόμου

(334) Psa 36:2
MT: לָרָשָׁע
LXX: τοῦ ἁμαρτάνειν
ε´: τῷ ἁμαρτωλῶι
Aq: τῶι ἀσεβεῖ
Sym: τοῦ ἀσεβοῦς

שָׂגַב

(335) Psa 46:8
MT: מִשְׂגָּב
LXX: ἀντιλήπτωρ
ε´: ....
Aq: ὑπερέπαρσις
Sym: ὀχύρωμα

(336) Psa 46:12
MT: מִשְׂגָּב
LXX: ἀντιλήπτωρ ἡμῶν
ε´: ....
Aq: ὑπερεπαρτὴς ἡμῖν
Sym: ὀχύρωμα ἡμῶν

שִׂים

(337) Psa 46:9
MT: אֲשֶׁר־שָׂם
LXX: ἃ ἔθετο
ε´: ....
Aq: ὅσους ἔθηκεν
Sym: ἃς ἐποίησεν

(338) Psa 89:30
MT: וְשַׂמְתִּי
LXX: καὶ θήσομαι
ε´: ....
Aq: καὶ θήσω
Sym: καὶ ποιήσω

(339) Psa 89:41
MT: שַׂמְתָּ
LXX: ἔθου
ε´: ....
Aq: ἔθηκας
Sym: ἐποίησας

שָׂכַל

(340) Psa 32:8
MT: אַשְׂכִּילְךָ
LXX: συνετιῶ σε
ε´: ....
Aq: ἐπιστημώσω σε
Sym: ....

שָׂמַח

(341) Psa 35:19
MT: יִשְׂמְחוּ־
LXX: ἐπιχαρείησάν
ε´: ....
Aq: εὐφρανθείησάν
Sym: ....

(342) Psa 35:24
MT: יִשְׂמְחוּ־
LXX: ἐπιχαρείησάν
ε´: ....
Aq: εὐφρανθείησάν
Sym: ἐπιχαροῖεν

(343) Psa 35:26
MT: שְׂמֵחֵי
LXX: οἱ ἐπιχαίροντες
ε´: ....
Aq: οἱ εὐφραινόμενοι
Sym: οἱ ἐφηδόμενοι

(344) Psa 35:27
MT: וישמחו
LXX: καὶ εὐφρανθείησαν
ε′: ....
Aq: ....
Sym: καὶ εὐφραινέσθωσαν

(345) Psa 46:5
MT: ישמחו
LXX: εὐφραίνουσι
ε′: ....
Aq: ....
Sym: ....

(346) Psa 89:43
MT: השמחת
LXX: εὔφρανας
ε′: ἐπεύφρανας
Aq: ἐξεύφρανας
Sym: ἐπεύφρανας

שנא

(347) Psa 18:41
MT: ומשנאי
LXX: καὶ τοὺς μισοῦντάς με
ε′: ....
Aq: καὶ μισοποιοῦντάς με
Sym: ....

שרף

(348) Psa 46:10
MT: ישרף
LXX: κατακαύσει
ε′: ....
Aq: ἐμπρήσει
Sym: κατέκαυσεν

שבט

(349) Psa 89:33
MT: בשבט
LXX: ἐν ῥάβδῳ
ε′: ....
Aq: ἐν σκήπτρῳ
Sym: ....

שבר

(350) Psa 46:10
MT: ישבר
LXX: συντρίψει
ε′: ....
Aq: ....
Sym: ἐπέκλασεν

שבת

(351) Psa 46:10
MT: משבית
LXX: ἀνταναιρῶν
ε′: καταπαύων
Aq: διαλιμπάνων
Sym: ἔπαυσεν

(352) Psa 89:45
MT: השבת
LXX: κατέλυσας
ε′: ἀνέκοψας
Aq: διέλειψας
Sym: ἀπέπαυσας

שוא

(353) Psa 31:7
MT: שוא
LXX: διὰ κενῆς
ε′: ψευδεῖς
Aq: εἰκῆι
Sym: εἰκῆ

(354) Psa 35:17
MT: משאיהם
LXX: ἀπὸ τῆς κακουργίας
αὐτῶν ῥῦσαι
ε′: ἀπὸ τῆς κακουργίας
αὐτῶν -----
Aq: ἀπὸ --- συμφορῶν
αὐτῶν -----
Sym: ἀπὸ τῆς βίας
αὐτῶν -----

(355) Psa 89:48
MT: עַל-מֶה-שָּׁוְא
LXX: μὴ γὰρ ματαίως
ε': ἐπὶ τί ματαίως
Aq: ἐπὶ τί εἰκῆ
Sym: ἢ ἐπὶ τίνα ματαίωι

שוב

(356) Psa 35:13
MT: תָּשׁוּב
LXX: ἀποστραφήσεται
ε': ....
Aq: ἐπιστρέψει
Sym: ὑπέστρεψεν

(357) Psa 35:17
MT: הָשִׁיבָה
LXX: ἀποκατάστησον
ε': ἐπίστρεψον
Aq: ἐπίστρεψον
Sym: ....

(358) Psa 89:44
MT: אַף-תָּשִׁיב
LXX: ----- ἀπέστρεψας
ε': καίγε ἀπέστρεψας
Aq: καίπερ ἐπέστρεψας
Sym: ἀλλὰ καὶ ἀπέστρεψας

שוה

(359) Psa 18:34
MT: מְשַׁוֶּה
LXX: ἐξισῶν καταρτιζόμενος
ε': ------ καταρτιζόμενος
Aq: ἐξισῶν -------------
Sym: ἐξισῶν -------------

שוע

(360) Psa 18:42
MT: יְשַׁוְּעוּ
LXX: ἐκέκραξαν
ε': ....
Aq: ἀναβοήσουσιν
Sym: ἐπεκαλοῦντο

(361) Psa 31:23
MT: בְּשַׁוְּעִי
LXX: ἐν τῷ κεκραγέναι με
ε': ....
Aq: ἐν -- ἀναβοήσει μου
Sym: ἐπικαλουμένου ---

שור

(362) Psa 18:30
MT: שׁוּר
LXX: τεῖχος
ε': ....
Aq: τείχισμα
Sym: τείχους

שחק

(363) Psa 18:43
MT: וְאֶשְׁחָקֵם
LXX: καὶ λεπτυνῶ αὐτούς
ε': ....
Aq: καὶ λεανῶ αὐτούς
Sym: καὶ ἐλεπτοκόπησα αὐτούς

(364) Psa 89:38
MT: בַּשַּׁחַק
LXX: ἐν --- οὐρανῶι
ε': ἐν τῆι νεφέληι
Aq: ἐν --- ῥοπῇ
Sym: ἐν --- αἰθέρι

שחת

(365) Psa 49:10
MT: הַשָּׁחַת
LXX: --- καταφθοράν
ε': --- διαφθοράν
Aq: τὴν διαφθοράν
Sym: τὴν διαφθοράν

TRANSLATION TECHNIQUE OF MINOR VERSIONS

שטף

(366) Psa 32:6
MT: לשטף
LXX: ἐν κατακλυσμῷ
ε': ....
Aq: τοῦ κλύσαι
Sym: ἐπικλύζοντα

שיר

(367) Psa 28:7
MT: ומשירי
LXX: καὶ ἐκ -- θελήματός μου
ε': καὶ ἀπὸ τοῦ ᾄσματός μου
Aq: καὶ ἀπὸ -- ᾄσματός μου
Sym: καὶ ἐν -- ᾠδαῖς μου

(368) Psa 30:1
MT: שיר
LXX: ᾠδῆς
ε': ....
Aq: ᾄισματος
Sym: ....

(369) Psa 46:1
MT: שיר
LXX: ψαλμός
ε': ᾠδή
Aq: ᾆσμα
Sym: ᾠδή

שית

(370) Psa 49:15
MT: שתו
LXX: ἔθεντο
ε': καταχθήσονται
Aq: ....
Sym: ἔταξαν ἑαυτούς

שכן

(371) Psa 46:5
MT: משכני
LXX: τὸ σκήνωμα αὐτοῦ
ε': τὸ κατασκήνωμα αὐτοῦ
Aq: --- σκήνωμα -----
Sym: τῆς κατασκηνώσεως -----

(372) Psa 49:12
MT: משכנתם
LXX: --- σκηνώματα αὐτῶν
ε': ....
Aq: ....
Sym: τὰς κατασκηνώσεις αὐτῶν

(373) Psa 89:42
MT: לשכניו
LXX: τοῖς γείτοσιν αὐτοῦ
ε': ....
Aq: ....
Sym: ....

שלה

(374) Psa 30:7
MT: בשלוי
LXX: ἐν τῇ εὐθηνίᾳ μου
ε': ....
Aq: ἐν -- εὐθηνίᾳ μου
Sym: ἐν τῇ ἠρεμίᾳ μου

שלם

(375) Psa 31:24
MT: ומשלם
LXX: καὶ ἀνταποδίδωσι
ε': καὶ ἀποδιδοῖ
Aq: καὶ ἀποδίδωσι
Sym: ....

שמם

(376) Psa 46:9
MT: שמות
LXX: τέρατα
ε´: ἠφανισμένα
Aq: ἀφανισμους
Sym: καταργήσεις

שמע

(377) Psa 28:6
MT: שמע
LXX: εἰσήκουσε
ε´: ....
Aq: ἤκουσε
Sym: ἐπακούσας

(378) Psa 30:11
MT: שמע-
LXX: ἤκουσε
ε´: εἰσάκουσον
Aq: ἄκουσον
Sym: ἀκούσας

(379) Psa 31:23
MT: שמעת
LXX: εἰσήκουσας
ε´: ὑπήκουσας
Aq: ἤκουσας
Sym: ....

שנה

(380) Psa 89:35
MT: אשנה
LXX: ἀθετήσω
ε´: ἀλλοιώσω
Aq: ἀλλοιώσω
Sym: ἀλλάξω

שסס

(381) Psa 89:42
MT: שסהו
LXX: διήρπασαν αὐτὸν
ε´: ....
Aq: συνήρπασαν αὐτὸν
Sym: ....

שקר

(382) Psa 35:19
MT: שקר
LXX: -- ἀδίκως μάτην
ε´: -- ἀδίκως -----
Aq: -- φεύδους -----
Sym: οἱ ψευδεῖς -----

(383) Psa 89:34
MT: אשקר
LXX: ἀδικήσω
ε´: ....
Aq: ψεύσομαι
Sym: παραβήσομαι

תמד

(384) Psa 35:27
MT: תמיד
LXX: διαπαντὸς
ε´: ....
Aq: ἐνδελεχῶς
Sym: διηνεκῶς

תמם

(385) Psa 18:26
MT: תמים
LXX: ἀθώιου
ε´: ἀμώμου
Aq: τελείου
Sym: ἀκέραιον

(386) Psa 18:26
MT: תתמם
LXX: ἀθῷος ἔσηι
ε´: ἄμωμος ἔσηι
Aq: τελειωθήσηι
Sym: ἀκέραια πράξεις

(387) Psa 18:31
MT: תמים
LXX: ἄμωμος
ε´: ....
Aq: τελεία
Sym: ....

(388) Psa 18:33
MT: חמים
LXX: ἄμωμον
ε´: ....
Aq: τελείαν
Sym: ....

Part III

Psa 46:1-12

NB: Agreements with ε' against the LXX are underlined.

```
LXX: 1 εἰς τὸ τέλος      ὑπὲρ τῶν υἱῶν  κορε, ὑπὲρ τῶν
ε':  1 --  τῶι νικοποιῶι  -- τοῖς υἱοῖς ..............
Aq:  1 --  τῶι νικοποιῶι  -- ................ ἐπὶ --
Sym: 1 --  --  ἐπινίκιος·-- ........................

LXX: κρυφίων      ψαλμός. 2 ὁ θς   ἡμῶν καταφυγὴ καὶ δύναμις,
ε':  ........     ᾠδή      2 .................................
Aq:  νεανιοτήτων  ᾆσμα.   2 λανου²³ -- ἐλπὶς   " κράτος.
Sym: αἰωνίων      ᾠδή.    2 -- -- ἡμῖν πεποίθησις " ἰσχύς,

LXX: Βοηθὸς ἐν θλίψεσι ταῖς εὑρούσαις  ἡμᾶς σφόδρα. 3 διὰ
ε':  ................ -- εὑρέθη      -- ........ 3 ...
Aq:  Βοήθεια .......... -- εὑρέθης    -- ........ 3 ἐπὶ
Sym: "       .......... -- εὑρισκόμενος -- ....... 3 ...

LXX: τοῦτο  οὐ φοβηθησόμεθα ἐν τῶι ταράσσεσθαι   τὴν γῆν
ε':  .......................................................
Aq:  τούτωι ................ " " ἀνταλλάσσεσθαι -- ...
Sym: ..................... " " συγχεῖσθαι     -- ...

LXX: καὶ  -- -- μετατίθεσθαι ὄρη ἐν καρδίᾳ θαλασσῶν.
ε':  .... -- -- σαλεύεσθαι   ........................
Aq:  .... ἐν τῷ σφάλλεσθαι   ........................
Sym: .... -- -- κλίνεσθαι    ........................

LXX: 4 ἤχησαν   καὶ ἐταράχθησαν   τὰ ὕδατα αὐτῶν, --
ε':  4 ἠχήσουσι  "  ταραχθήσονται  ........ αὐτῆς, --
Aq:  4 ὀχλάσουσιν -- αὐστηρωθήσονται --   " αὐτοῦ, --
Sym: 4 ἠχούντων  "  θολουμένων     τῶν ὑδάτων  --   καὶ

LXX: ἐταράχθησαν τὰ ὄρη ἐν τῇ κραταιότητι αὐτοῦ. διάψαλμα.
ε':  σεισθήσονται -- .......... ὑπερηφανίᾳ   "  ἀεί.
Aq:  σεισθήσεται  -- .......... ὑπερηφανίᾳ   "  ἀεί.
Sym: σειομένων   -- ὀρέων " τῶι ἐνδοχασμῶι   "  ........

LXX: 5 τοῦ ποταμοῦ τὰ ὁρμήματα   --   εὐφραίνουσι τὴν πόλιν
ε':  5 ........... αἱ διαιρέσεις --   ............. .....
Aq:  5 -- ....... -- διαιρέσεις αὐτοῦ ............ -- ....
Sym: 5 ........... -- διαιρέσεις --   ............. .....
```

---

²³This looks as if a phrase from column 2 (the transliterated Hebrew) has accidentally replaced the reading for Aquila in column 3.

LXX: τοῦ θυ · -- ἡγίασεν τὸ σκήνωμα   αὐτοῦ ὁ   ὕψιστος.
ε': ...., -- ἅγιον " κατασκήνωμα ....
Aq: -- ... -- ἅγιον   -- ....   -- -- ὑψίστου.
Sym: ...., τὸ ἅγιον τῆς κατασκηνώσεως -- τοῦ   " .

LXX: 6 ὁ θς' ἐν μέσῳ αὐτῆς, -- οὐ σαλευθήσεται· βοηθήσει
ε': 6 ...., ἵνα μὴ σαλευθῇ   ....
Aq: 6 .... ἐγκάτῳ ....., οὐ " σφαλῇ: ....
Sym: 6 .... περιτραπήσεται· ....

LXX: αὐτῆι ὁ θεὸς τῶι πρὸς τρωὶ πρωί. 7 ἐταράχθησαν ἔθνη,
ε': .... τὸ .... -- .....   7 ἤχησαν   ,
Aq: .... νεῦσαι τὴν πρωίαν. 7 ὤχλασαν   ....,
Sym: .... -- περὶ τὸν ὄρθρον. 7 συνήχθησαν   ....,

LXX: ἔκλιναν   βασιλεῖαι· ἔδωκε   -- φωνὴν αὐτοῦ,
ε': ἐσαλεύθησαν ....,
Aq: ἐσφάλησαν βασιλεῖς· .....   ἐν φωνῇ ......,
Sym: περιετράπησαν ....· διδόντος ....,

LXX: ἐσαλεύθη ἡ γῆ. 8 יהוה τῶν δυνάμεων μεθ' ἡμῶν,
ε': τακήσετα ..... 8 ....
Aq: ἠδαφίσθη ..... 8 .... -- στρατιῶν ....,
Sym: διελύθη ..... 8 ....,

LXX: ἀντιλήπτωρ ἡμῶν ὁ θς Ἰακώβ. --   διάψαλμα. δεῦτε
ε': .... ἀεί. ....
Aq: ὑπερέπαρσις .... -- .... ἀεί.   --   .....
Sym: ὀχύρωμα   ....   --   .... ἔρχεσθε

LXX: καὶ ἴδετε   τὰ ἔργα   יהוה, ἃ   ἔθετο
ε': ....
Aq: -- ὁραματίσθητε -- κατέργασμα ....· ὅσους ἔθηκεν
Sym: -- θεάσασθε   ἃ διεπράξατο ...., ἃς ἐποίησεν

LXX: τέρατα   ἐπὶ τῆς γῆς. 10 ἀντανειρῶν πολέμους μέχρι
ε': ἠφανισμένα ἐν τῇ γῇ.   10 καταπαύσων .... ἕως
Aq: ἀφανισμοὺς ἐν τῇ γῇ.   10 διαλιμπάνων .... ἕως
Sym: καταρήσεις ἐν τῇ γῇ.   10 ἔπαυσεν   .... ἕως

LXX: τῶν περάτων   τῆς γῆς τόξον συντρίψει καὶ συγκλάσει
ε': ....
Aq: -- τελευταίου .... κατακόψει
Sym: ....ἐπέκλασεν " κατέκοψει

```
LXX: ὅπλον     καὶ θυρεοὺς κατακαύσει ἐν πυρί. 11 σχολάσατε
ε':  ............ ἅρματα ............. ........ 11 ..........
Aq:  δόρυ,   -- ἁμάξας ἐμπρήσει       ........ 11 ἰάθητε
Sym: λόγχας, --       "      κατέκαυσεν -- ..... 11 ἐάσατε

LXX: καὶ γνῶτε ὅτι ἐγώ εἰμι ὁ θς ὑψωθήσομαι ἐν τῆι γῆι.
ε':  ..........................................
Aq:  ..................................    "  --  "
Sym: ἵνα ........................ ὑψούμενος............

LXX: 12 יהוה τῶν δυνάμεων  μεθ' ἡμῶν, ἀντιλήπτωρ   ἡμῶν
ε':  12 .................................................
Aq:  12 .... -- στρατειῶν .........., ὑπερεπαρτὴς  ἡμῖν
Sym: 12 .........................., ὀχύρωμα ..........

LXX: ὁ θς 'Ιακώβ. --      διάψαλμα
ε':  ............ ἀεί        --
Aq:  ............ ἀεί        --
Sym: ............  --     ........
```

THE TREATMENT IN THE LXX OF THE THEME OF SEEING GOD

†ANTHONY HANSON

In this paper I propose to confine myself to six passages in the Pentateuch and one in Judges, as well as one in the Apocrypha. I pay no attention to the visions of God in the prophets, because these seem to have caused less difficulty to the translators and exegetes. In one of the most famous of prophetic visions, that described in Ezekiel 1, the prophet himself had gone to great pains in order to modify the anthropomorphic impression of his vision of God. I treat only those passages where the individuals are described as seeing God in the course of their active lives.

1. Genesis 32:31

Jacob, having wrestled with a mysterious being, calls the name of the place Penuel. This being is not called an angel in Genesis 32, but see Hos 12:5 (EVV 12:4), where the prophet says that Jacob strove with an angel (מלאך). The LXX renders this with ἄγγελος. The MT of 32:31 runs: כי ראיתי אלהים פנים אל פנים ותנצל נפשי, "For I have seen God face to face, and my life has been preserved." The LXX translates "Peniel" with εἶδος θεοῦ, but renders the next clause quite straightforwardly: εἶδον γὰρ θεὸν πρόσωπον πρὸς πρόσωπον καὶ ἐσώθη μου ἡ ψυχή. The only hint in the LXX here of an attempt to modify the claim to have seen God is that the LXX offers εἶδος θεοῦ instead of πρόσωπον θεοῦ.

Philo[1] refers to this passage twice. In *De Somniis* 1:79, commenting on "the sun rose upon him as he passed Penuel," he says that the sun is used here συμβολικῶς, to indicate the non-sensible means by which we apprehend him who is. And in *De Mutatione Nominum* 14-15 he remarks that even the powers (δυνάμεις) subordinate to God will not tell his name, thereby implying that he whom Jacob met was one of the powers, not God himself. This is exactly what we would expect of Philo's exegesis. The *Pal. Tg.* represents Jacob as saying: "I have seen face to face the angels from before God."[2] *Tg. Onq.* and *Tg. Ps.-J.* offer the same substitution of "the angel of the Lord" for God. *Tg. Ps.-J.* identifies the angel with Michael.[3]

It is possible, however, that the identification of the figure here with a named angel may be capable of being traced farther back than this. G. Brooke points out that *Tg. Neof.* here identifies the angel with Sariel (an anagram of Israel by *hilluf*). Sariel makes his first appearance in the Qumran documents. In 1QM 9:12-15 he appears in a list of four archangels. If we may conjecture that among the Qumran sectaries the angel of Jabbok was already identified with Sariel, we may have traced this identification to a period within perhaps a century of the LXX translation.[4] *Jubilees* ignores the incident altogether. Is this because the author found it embarrassing?

Exod 24:9-11

From the point of view of later tradition this is the most shocking of the passages in which people see God. Moses and Aaron, Nadab and Abihu, and seventy of the elders of Israel go up Mount Sinai "and they saw the God of Israel." The MT (24:10) is: ויראו את אלהי ישראל. The LXX renders this with: καὶ εἶδον τὸν τόπον οὗ εἰστήκει ἐκεῖ ὁ θεὸς τοῦ Ἰσραήλ. This is not only an attempt to avoid the directness of the MT, but must also witness to a Hebrew text which already contained this periphrasis. We could conjecturally restore it thus: ויראו המקום אשר עמד שם אלהי ישראל. Thus by the time that the MT was translated exegetical activity had already modified the directness of the original. The Vg has no such periphrasis but translates: "et viderunt Deum Israel." In 24:11 the MT uses another verb: ויחזו את האלהים. The verb חזה softens the crudeness somewhat, for it is often used of prophetic visions. In verse 11 the LXX has a double periphrasis: καὶ ὤφθησαν ἐν τῷ τόπῳ τοῦ θεοῦ "and they were seen in the place of God." This of course removes the offensive element altogether. The Vg goes serenely on with "videruntque."

Philo considers this passage more than once. In *De Somniis* 1:61-63 he discusses the various senses which the word τόπος can bear in scripture. In some of the senses it means the θεῖος λόγος, the divine Word, and he cites Exod 24:10 LXX as an example. Again in his *Questions and Answers on Exodus* he writes: "No one will boast of seeing the invisible God, (thus) yielding to arrogance...this 'place' is that of the logos."[5] Symmachus' version shows no sign of knowing the periphrasis which we find in the LXX. He translates καὶ εἶδον ὁράματι τὸν θεὸν 'Ισραήλ, "and they saw in a vision the God of Israel."[6] This confirms our impression that the Greek translators could accept the idea of seeing God in a vision rather than seeing him literally.

The targums, as we would expect, represent Moses and the others as having seen "the glory" of the God of Israel. But *Tg. Ps.-J.* and the ms. of the *Pal. Tg.* which Le Déaut calls Add. 27031 have an interesting piece of haggadah here. They say that only Nadab and Abihu lifted up their eyes boldly to behold the God of Israel. The others reverently kept their eyes on the ground. These two targums add that the punishment of the boldness of Nadab and Abihu was postponed until after their rebellion narrated in Num 16.

3. Exodus 33:11

Here we read that the Lord spoke to Moses "face to face, as a man speaks to his friend." The MT is: וידבר יהוה אל משה פנים אל פנים כאשר ידבר איש אל רעהו. The LXX translates: καὶ ἐλάλησεν κύριος πρὸς Μωυσῆν ἐνώπιος ἐνωπίῳ ὡς εἴ τις λαλήσει πρὸς τὸν ἑαυτοῦ φίλον. This sounds perfectly straightforward, but in 33:20 only nine verses later Moses is told that he cannot see God's face, פני in the MT. There פני is rendered with πρόσωπον. It is possible therefore that the LXX's use of ἐνώπιος ἐνωπίῳ may be a slight modification of the literal Hebrew meaning. According to Field, one ms. of the LXX has πρόσωπον πρὸς πρόσωπον.[7]

The targums of course modify the statement in verse 11. Le Déaut translates the Aramaic of *Tg. Neof.* with "de vive voix" and comments that it means literally "discours pour discours." He adds that the formula "face to face" is judged to be too anthropomorphic.[8] *Tg. Onq.* and *Tg. Ps.-J.* substitute "word for word" for "face to face" and *Ps.-J.* adds "the voice of the word was heard but the majesty of the presence was not seen."[9]

In the subsequent verses Moses asks to see God's glory (33:18). MT הראני נא את כבדך. The LXX has no difficulty here, since God refuses the request, saying: "you cannot see my face (פני), for man cannot see me and live." Philo with his usual ingenuity manages to interpret Moses' request so as to produce exactly the opposite sense to that of the Hebrew. Moses really means οὐκ ἂν ἴσχυσα δέξασθαι τὸ τῆς σῆς φαντασίας ἐναργὲς εἶδος, "I could not have borne the clear image of your appearance."[10]

Tg. Onq. removes the sentiment one stage further away from the original MT, rendering 33:20 with "Thou canst not see the face of my Shekinah."[11]

4. Numbers 12:8

Here God, in rebuking Aaron and Miriam, makes a clear distinction between how he speaks to the prophets and how he speaks to Moses. To prophets he speaks in a vision (MT מראה; LXX ὁράματι), or in a dream (MT חלום; LXX ἐν ὕπνῳ, 12:6). But to

Moses he speaks "mouth to mouth clearly, and not in dark speech; and he beholds the form of the Lord." The MT is: פה אל פה אדבר בו ומראה ולא בחידת ותמנת יהוה יביט. This is a very perplexing passage for later translators, both because מראה is here used of the mode in which God will communicate with Moses, though מראה has already been used of the way in which God communicates with prophets, and also because the idea that Moses could see the form of the Lord must seem dangerously anthropomorphic. The LXX renders it with: στόμα κατὰ στόμα λαλήσω αὐτῷ, ἐν εἴδει καὶ οὐ δι'αἰνιγμάτων, καὶ τὴν δόξαν κυρίου εἶδεν. The translator has rendered the same word מראה with ὅραμα in verse 6 and with εἶδος in verse 8. There is nothing surprising in this: the RSV does essentially the same thing, using "vision" in verse 6 and "clearly" in verse 8 for the same Hebrew word. W. Rudolph, who edited Numbers in *BHS*, suggested that for ומראה in verse 8 we should read ואמרה. But there is no textual support for this. The OL has "claritatem" for מראה here. The Vg manages to avoid the difficulty by translating "et palam et non per aenigmata et figuras Dominum videt," "and he sees the Lord openly and not by riddles and figures," though it must be admitted that this only alleviates the anthropomorphism slightly. The LXX has certainly modified the text by rendering תמנת יהוה with τὴν δόξαν κυρίου.

As we might well expect, the targums modify all this. *Tg. Neof.* offers: "with living voice have I talked with him; in vision and not in appearance, and it is the resemblance from before the Lord that he has contemplated."[12] The phrase "in

THE THEME OF SEEING GOD

vision" is בחזוין, the same root as is often used in scripture for prophetic visions. Both *Tg. Ps.-J.* and Add. 27031 insist that Moses only enjoyed this communion with God because he had abstained from sexual intercourse.

5. Deuteronomy 4:12

Moses reminds the people that on Sinai they only heard a voice; they did not see any form of God. This in itself may well be an example of scripture interpreting scripture. The author of Deuteronomy was just as much offended by the suggestion that anyone had actually seen God as was the LXX translator. The MT is: קול דברים אתם שמעים ותמונה אינכם ראים זולתי קול. The LXX renders this with: φωνὴν ῥημάτων ὑμεῖς ἠκούσατε καὶ ὁμοίωμα οὐκ εἴδετε, ἀλλ' ἢ φωνήν. We have noticed how in Num 12:8 התמונה is paraphrased by the LXX translator with τὴν δόξαν κυρίου. It is unnecessary for the translator to do that here, since it is explicitly denied that they saw any form. M, a tenth century ms. of the LXX now in Paris, reads μορφήν for ὁμοίωμα.[13] It is worth noting that in the *War Scroll* from Qumran one of the privileges of Israel is listed as "hearing the glorious voice, seeing the holy angels." By the period of the Qumran sect no doubt it had been agreed that Israel could have heard God's voice without impropriety, but what they saw was angels not God himself. This anticipates the targums. The Hebrew of 1QM 10:10-11 is: ושומעי קול נכבד ורואי מלאכי קודש.[14] The targums translate this passage quite straightforwardly, since it does not present them with any problems. The Vg offers:

"Vocem verborum eius audistis, et formam penitus non vidistis."

6. Judges 13:22

We now examine briefly a passage in Judges where someone is described as literally seeing God. Before Samson's birth Manoah and his wife are foretold of the event by an angel. When Manoah has seen the angel he exclaims: "We shall surely die, for we have seen God." The MT is: מות נמות כי אלהים ראינו. The LXX has apparently no difficulty with this, for it offers: θανάτῳ ἀποθανούμεθα, ὅτι θεὸν ἑωράκαμεν.[15] Perhaps the absence of any attempt to modify this arises from the fact that in the rest of the narrative the apparition is referred to as "the angel of the Lord."

It is remarkable that the *Bib. Ant.* of Pseudo-Philo in treating this incident entirely omits any mention of Manoah's fear at having seen God; so much so that Manoah says to the angel: "that thou mayest offer a sacrifice unto the Lord thy God."[16] Perhaps this goes some way towards confirming my suggestion that the author of *Jubilees* omitted the incident of Jacob's wrestling at Jabbok because he found it embarrassing. The targum, as we might expect, renders the MT with: "We shall surely die because we have seen the angel of Adonai."[17] The word for "seen" is חזינא.

7. Sirach 17:13

Finally we must consider an interesting passage from Sirach. It is 17:13, where the author is describing the momentous events on Mount Sinai:

"Their eyes saw his glorious majesty,
and their ears heard the glory of his voice."
The Greek is:

μεγαλεῖον δόξης εἶδον οἱ ὀφθαλμοὶ αὐτῶν,
καὶ δόξαν φωνῆς αὐτοῦ ἤκουσεν τὸ οὖς αὐτῶν.

The reference is to Israel as a whole, so this is a formal contradiction to Deut 4:12. The Hebrew has not survived, but it is not difficult to guess what must lie behind the phrase μεγαλεῖον δόξης εἶδον. The word μεγαλεῖον in the singular or the plural is quite a favourite with Ben Sira's grandson. There are two occurrences in which the Hebrew is extant. The first is 42:21, where μεγαλεῖα τῆς σοφίας αὐτοῦ translates the Hebrew גבורות חכמתו.[18] The second is 45:24d, where ἱερωσύνης μεγαλεῖον translates the Hebrew כהונה גדולה. Now twice in Deuteronomy the LXX translator has used μεγαλεῖον or a cognate word to render a cognate word of גדול. In Deut 11:2 τὰ μεγαλεῖα αὐτοῦ is the translation of the MT את גדלו, and in Deut 32:3 μεγαλωσύνη is the rendering of the Hebrew גדל. It is therefore not unreasonable to suggest that behind the Greek of μεγαλεῖον δόξης in Sirach 17:13 lies some such phrase as גודל כבודו. We may at least safely conclude that Ben Sira himself wished to avoid any suggestion that the Israelites on Mount Sinai saw God literally. He was probably writing within less than a hundred years of the period when the Pentateuch was translated into Greek.

Before concluding we ought to notice an apparent example of the opposite to the tendency we have encountered so far: a passage where the

LXX appears to be more direct and anthropomorphic than the MT. It is Exod 33:13: Moses simply asks to be instructed in God's design for Israel. But the LXX translation ἐμφάνισόν μοι σεαυτόν, "show me thyself," is far more direct than the MT הודיעני נא את דרכך "show me now thy way." From the point of view of later theology, this is a quite unexceptionable request. It seems most improbable that the LXX translator had our MT text before him: he would surely never have changed "Make me know thy way" to "show me thyself." The Vg also differs from the MT. It has "Ostende mihi faciem tuam." Quell suggests that the LXX translator had הראני נא ואראך "reveal thyself so that I may see thee." At any rate we may surely conjecture that the MT text is itself a modification of the original, an original which is reflected in both the LXX and the Vg. This is therefore not an example of the tendency reversed.

The passages we have examined of the treatment in the LXX of the theme of seeing God indicate, we may safely conclude, that within the LXX itself we can trace the beginning of the exegetical tradition, which, no doubt under the influence of Greek rationalism, softened down anthropomorphisms and modified cruder notions of how human beings may know God. The general impression which I carry away from this study is that, could we have all the evidence before us, much that dates in the form we know it from a comparatively late period was already in the tradition much earlier.

NOTES

1. *Philonis Alexandrini, Opera Quae Supersunt* (ed. L. Cohn and P. Wendland; Berlin: Reimer, 1888-1915).

2. *Targum du Pentateuque: I Genèse* (ed. and trans. R. Le Déaut; SC 245; Paris: Editions du Cerf, 1978) 308-309.

3. *The Targums of Onkelos and Jonathan ben Uzziel on the Pentateuch* (trans. J. W. Etheridge; London: Longman, 1862-65; reprinted New York: Ktav, 1968).

4. G. J. Brooke, *Exegesis at Qumran: 4QFlorigelium in its Jewish Context* (JSOTSup 29; Sheffield: JSOT Press, 1985) 32.

5. Philo, *Questions and Answers on Exodus* 2:37 (ed. and trans. R. Marcus; LCL; London: Heinemann; Cambridge, Mass: Harvard, 1953) 78-79.

6. See F. Field, *Origenis Hexaplorum Quae Supersunt* (Oxford: Clarendon Press, 1875; Reprinted Hildesheim: Olms, 1964) 1, in loc.

7. It is $F^b i$ in A. E. Brooke and N. McLean, *The Old Testament in Greek* (Cambridge: University Press, 1909) Vol. I, Part 2.

8. *Targum du Pentateuque: II Exode et Lévitique* (ed. and trans. R. Le Déaut; SC 256; Paris: Editions du Cerf, 1979) 262-63.

9. *The Targums of Onkelos and Jonathan be Uzziel on the Pentateuch* (trans. J. W. Etheridge) 433, 555. In all three targums the Aramaic is ממלל קבל ממלל.

10. *De Specialibus Legibus* 1:45.

11. *The Targums of Onkelos and Jonathan be Uzziel on the Pentateuch* (trans. J. W. Etheridge) 424.

12. *Targum du Pentateuque: III Nombres* (ed. and trans. R. Le Déaut; SC 261; Paris: Editions du Cerf, 1979) 116. The French is "de vive voix (je me suis entretenu) avec lui, en vision et non en apparence, et c'est la ressemblance de devant Yahve qu'il a contemplée."

13. *Exodus* (ed. J. W. Wevers; Septuaginta Vetus Testamentum Graecum 2.1; Göttingen: Vandenhoeck & Ruprecht, 1990).

14. See Y. Yadin, *The Scroll of the War of the Sons of Light against the Sons of Darkness* (Oxford: University Press, 1962) 306-307.

15. *Codex Alexandrinus* has εἴδομεν for ἑωράκαμεν.

16. M. R. James, *The Biblical Antiquities of Philo Now First Translated from the Old Latin Version* (Translations of Early Documents; New York: Macmillan, London: SPCK, 1917; reprinted with a Prologemonenon by L. H. Feldman; New York: Ktav, 1971) XLII, § 8, p. 197.

17. A. Sperber, *The Bible in Aramaic* (Leiden: Brill, 1959) II, 76.

18. See I Lévi, *The Hebrew Text of the Book of Ecclesiasticus* (SSS 3; Leiden: Brill, 1904; reprinted 1969).

ΕΔΡΑ AND THE PHILISTINE PLAGUE

JOHAN LUST

When preparing a dictionary of the Septuagint, the lexicographer is confronted with the undeniable fact that most biblical Greek is translation Greek. In addition to that, as a translation it is most often relatively literal. That means that it usually tries to render the Hebrew as faithfully as possible, word by word, even when the Greek language hardly allows this. When deviations from the original Hebrew or Aramaic seem to occur, this may be due to a number of reasons. The translator may have had in front of him a *Vorlage* differing from the MT, or he may have misread the parent text, or he may not have understood it, or he may have wished to reinterpret the original text, adapting it to a new situation. It is also possible that the problem lies on the side of the modern scholar. He may have a less developed knowledge of biblical Hebrew and of Alexandrian Greek than the translator. It is my conviction that, when possible, this fact and some of its related

problems should be reflected in a lexicon of the
Septuagint, even when it is to be a succinct one.
Therefore, in our attempt towards such a lexicon,
we have adopted it as our general policy to
indicate the differences between the MT and the
version read by the translator, if these
differences are easily explained on the level of
the graphemes, for instance when the MT has אמר
where the Greek obviously read אמן (Jer 15:11).
In doing so, it is not our intention to indicate
the causes accounting for the differences.

In the present contribution it is our intention
to study a more complex type of lexicographical
difference between the MT and the LXX, using the
case of ἕδρα as a model.[1]

1. The Problem

a. Hebrew Qere and Ketib

ἕδρα occurs 10 times in the LXX, spread over
two passages: Deut 28:27 (once) and 1 Kgdms 5-6 (9
times) in the story of the ark. In all these cases
it translates Hebrew עפלים (Ketib) or טחורים
(Qere). The meaning of the Hebrew terms in
question is not clear. Most often it is said that
the Ketib refers to the so called "bubonic
plague,"[2] an illness marked by swellings in groin
and armpits. The Qere seems to denote
"haemorrhoids." How did the translator understand
these terms? Did he intend to render the Qere or
the Ketib? Is his translation meant to be literal
or free and perhaps euphemistic? Or did he not
understand his *Vorlage*?

b. The Meanings of ἕδρα

The meanings of ἕδρα listed in the classical dictionaries do not seem to correspond directly to the Hebrew. According to Liddell and Scott[a] the first meaning is "sitting place: seat, chair, stool, bench," or "seat, abode, place, base," or the "back" of a horse "on which the rider sits," or "quarters" of the sky in which omens appear, or "seat" of a physiological process; the second meaning is "sitting" esp. of suppliants, or "sitting still," or "position," or "sitting, session" of a council; the third meaning is "seat, breech, fundament, rump;" and the fourth "face" of a regular solid (geom.).

No illnesses are mentioned. If the Hebrew was understood as referring to haemorrhoids, a Greek word meaning exactly that was available. Why did the translator not use it?

c. The Immediate Context in 1 Samuel

In 1 Sam 5:6 the term ἕδρα is used in different contexts. It functions as a direct object of the verb ποιέω and ἀποδίδωμι (6:4, 17) and in a more stereotyped manner as an indirect object of the verbs πατάσσω (εἰς) and πλήσσω (εἰς) (5:3, 9, 12). It is usually accepted that in these stereotyped expressions ἕδρα means "seat, breech, buttocks." The phrase is then translated as "He smote (them) in the seat, or buttocks, or anus." This may be understood as a euphemism for "He afflicted them with tumors or haemorrhoids." But how then is one to visualise the ἕδραι of the first case? These are to be made of gold and given as images of the ἕδραι with which those afflicted were smitten.

The context in 5:3 creates a further problem: there the expression ἐπάταξεν αὐτοὺς εἰς τὰς ἕδρας is followed immediately by τὴν Αζωτον καὶ τὰ ὅρια αὐτῆς. Grammatically these localities can hardly be an explicit identification of αὐτοῦς. They rather function as an apposition to ἕδρας. But then, how can these "buttocks" be connected with Azote (Ashdod) and its environs?[4]

d. MT, LXX and the Lucian version

Indirectly complicating our quest is the complexity of the Greek translation of 1 Sam 5:6.[5] At the end of v.3 of ch.5, the major mss of the Septuagint, but not the Lucian version, have a long "plus," equivalent to the reading of the MT in v.6. In addition to that, the LXX as well as the Lucian version have a "plus" in v.6 without equivalent in the MT. In that verse, at the beginning of the story, the Greek tradition brings the rats onto the scene which are presupposed by the Hebrew in 6:4, 5. It is usually accepted that the Greek felt the need to correct the Hebrew and to add supplementary information. However, the possibility may not be ruled out that the Greek preserved traces of a more original text.[6] Although the question of priority is not primarily important for our present study, the differences between the respective ancient Greek versions and the MT may reveal something about the meaning of the ἕδραι in the view of the translators.

e. The Context in Deut 28

A comparison with Deut 28:27 raises more questions. There the expression πατάσσω ἐν ταῖς ἕδραις[7] is taken up in a series of punishing

illnesses listed as curses for disobedience. In
the Hebrew text, each of them is preceded by the
ב -instrumentalis. All of them are rendered by
LXX, one by one, in the dative, sometimes
introduced by the preposition ἐν. However, there
is an exception. The וב before the second plague
is read as a local ב by the translator, the ו is
discarded, and the plague, which happens to be
called עפלים, is turned into an indication of
place connected with the first plague.

Why did the translator suddenly change his
translation policy? It is usually taken for
granted that the translation of the Torah served
as a model for the translators of the other
biblical books. Is this also true in this
particular case?

2. Qere and Ketib

The Ketib עפלים, which in 1 Sam 5:6, 9, 12;
6:4, 5 and in Deut 28:27 underlies Greek ἕδρα,
is in the Qere always replaced by טחורים. The
Ketib in question is said to be among the
expressions which depart from conventional
standards of "clean speech." According to the
Babylonian Talmud three more terms belong to the
same series of unacceptable expressions: שגל
(violate, ravish), חרא (faeces), שין (urine).[8]
They are to be replaced by euphemisms.

In all these instances, and especially in our
case, the difference of meaning between Qere and
Ketib seems to be rather slight.[9] This makes it
difficult to find out whether the Greek follows
the Qere or the Ketib. Nonetheless, several
authors pretend to know the precise difference

between the Qere and the Ketib as well as the choice of LXX. Thus McCarter states that עֹפֶל usually means "hill, mound," and also "swelling, tumor." He proceeds: "Evidently, however, עפלים could be understood to mean 'buttocks' at the time the first Greek translation was made. Hence the rendering of LXX ..."[10] Still according to McCarter, the Qere, on the other hand, introduced a term which was unambiguously connected with dysentery. Josephus supports the interpretation of the Qere.

J. Stoebe's views are different. In his opinion, עפלים means "tumors" in general, whereas טחורים definitely denotes "haemorrhoids," which explains the translation of LXX: εἰς τὰς ἕδρας...[11]

If we have to make a choice, we prefer the views of mcCarter. The LXX by no means always adopts the Qere. The clearest case is that of שין, "urine". The Qere for this term is the euphemistic periphrase מימי רגלים, "water of the feet". The difference from the Ketib is rather obvious. LXX unambiguously renders the Ketib: οὖρον (urine): 4 Kgdms 18:24; Isa 36:12.

In 1 Sam 5 and 6 the translator appears to have proceeded along similar lines, rendering the Ketib עפלים and not the Qere. Whereas it is not evident that this Hebrew word was ever understood as meaning "buttocks," as boldly stated by McCarter, it is generally accepted that the unvocalised term denoted both "boil" and "mound, hill, acropolis." In a following paragraph we will see that the Greek term ἕδρα had equivalent connotations.

Before we proceed with a study of the Greek

term in question, we may add one more remark concerning the Ketib עפל. One may suggest that later translators read אפל instead of עפל. This could explain why Symmachus and the Vulgate rendered this term by "secret parts." Indeed, אפל is often used in contexts where it refers to a deep threatening darkness full of secrets. How did the Greek render this term? Often the translator used σκότος, or one of its derivatives.[12] It may be significant that in 2 Kgs 5:24 the Hebrew עפל is rendered by σκοτεινός which suggests first that the translator read אפל and second that he understood this term not simply as darkness, but as a "dark or secret place."[13]

3. The Meaning of εἰς τὰς ἕδρας in Non-biblical Greek Literature

A comparison with its use in non-biblical Greek literature may give us a better grasp of the meaning of the Greek expression studied here. In most of its biblical attestations, the term ἕδρα is phrased in the accusative preceded by the preposition εἰς. A search on the TLG computer readable text of classical Greek literature[14] reveals two different uses of this phrase. It most often occurs in medical texts where it definitely means "anus." We may take an example from Hippocrates' ΠΕΡΙ ΑΙΜΟΡΡΟΙΔΩΝ: ἔπειτα τὸν αὐλίσκον ἐνθεὶς εἰς τὴν ἕδρην, "then insert the pipe in the anus."[15] It must be noted that in this context the singular prevails.

Less frequently, and not in medical literature, it indicates a "place" where something or somebody resides or belongs. With this meaning, the expression not only occurs in its singular form, but also in the plural. For an example we refer to Plato's ΤΙΜΑΙΟΣ: εἰς τὰς ἕδρας ὅθεν ἀνῇει ὁ νέος ἀήρ, "in the places out of which the new air came up."[16]

In the Bible, the substantive ἕδρα is repeatedly used with the verb πατάσσω or πλήσσω and the preposition εἰς. A combined search in the TLG data reveals that πατάσσω εἰς τὰς ἕδρας occurs exclusively in the biblical passages under discussion and in the Greek Church Fathers referring to 1 Sam 5 and 6. The story of the ark captured by the Philistines is not among the favourite texts of the Fathers. Nevertheless they repeatedly allude to our expression in their commentaries on Ps 78(77):66 where a similar phrase occurs: ἐπάταξε τοὺς ἐχθροὺς εἰς τὰ ὀπίσω. They use the Samuel text in order to explain the Psalm.

The earliest and most explicit example is to be found in Eusebius' works: "How He smote them in the rear (εἰς τὰ ὀπίσω) is explained by the story of the First Book of Kingdoms which runs as follows: ... ." Eusebius proceeds with an extensive quotation of 1 Sam 5:3(6),9-12 and concludes explaining why it is said in the Psalm that when God smote the enemy "in the rear, he brought on them a perpetual reproach:" "it was a reproach for them to be beaten ἐν ταῖς ἕδραις since those were the parts with which they were licentious."[17] There seems to be no doubt that in Eusebius' view, the ἕδραι in 1 Sam allude to the buttocks and the sexual organs. It is to be noted that Eusebius slightly changes the text of Samuel replacing εἰς by ἐν. In the following section we will comment upon this variant. It should also be observed that Eusebius and his successors do not refer to Deut 28:27 in order to explain the Psalm and the plague mentioned in 1 Sam 5 and 6.

Exceptionally, Theodoretus Cyrensis comments directly upon the story in 1 Sam 5 and 6.[18] He quotes 5:12 εἰς τὰς ἕδρας ἐπλήγησαν. He interprets it with the help of Aquila, whose translation he compares with Josephus' periphrastic rendition. Aquila refers to "cancerous ulcers" whereas Josephus labels the plague as dysentery. According to Theodoretus the one follows out of the other.

The results of the comparison with non-biblical literature are rather scanty but significant. The rare relevant texts, not influenced by the biblical passages in question, seem to indicate that εἰς τὰς ἕδρας can mean either "into the anus," especially in medical contexts, or "into a place" where somebody or something resides. In their reading of 1 Sam 5 and 6, Eusebius as well as Theodoretus and their successors appear to have inclined toward the first meaning.

4. Related Expressions in the Bible

Further light can perhaps be gained from related expressions within the Bible. In the Scriptures, πατάσσω εἰς occurs with other complements.[19] In some instances, the complement indicates the place (or the person) towards which somebody (or something) is thrown or smitten: thus πατάσσω εἰς τὴν γῆν,[20] to beat somebody to the ground. Εδρας in 1 Kgdms 5 and 6 cannot have this function. The context does not allow it: one cannot assume that the relevant lines intended to say that the Philistines were thrown towards, or beaten to, their ἕδρας. However, the complement of πατάσσω can also indicate the place whereupon somebody is struck: "He smote the Philistine on his forehead" (εἰς τὸ μέτωπον) 1 Kgdms 17:49;[21] "she smote him upon his neck" (εἰς τὸν τράχηλον) Jdt 13:8; or the place where somebody is stricken with a disease: "The Lord smote him in the bowels" (εἰς τὴν κοιλίαν) 2 Chron 21:18.[22] In the first two cases that of a physical blow, the context as a rule clearly indicates the instrument with which somebody is stricken: David smites Goliath with a stone, Judith beats Holofernes with his sword. In the last case, that of a disease, no instrument is mentioned. The expression in 1 Kgdms 5:6 seems to fall in the latter category: the Ashdodians were smitten in their seats.[23]

In this context, special mention should once more be made of the Greek version of Ps 78(77):66. We have already observed that the early Church Fathers explained this verse of the Psalm with a reference to 1 Sam 5. It is usually stated that they rightly did so, since the Psalm contains a historical survey which seems to allude to the story of the Ark. The expression used in the Greek version of v. 66 of the Psalm is very similar to that of 1 Samuel, but nevertheless it differs from it: ἐπάταξε τοὺς ἐχθροὺς εἰς τὰ ὀπίσω. In the Psalm, ὀπίσω replaces ἕδρας. The Hebrew shows more differences. The verb is the same in both instances, but, in the Psalm the indirect object has no prefixed ב although the

Greek translation seems to presuppose its presence. The translator of the Psalm probably found it in Samuel. For his rendition of the indirect object אחור, he chose the term ὀπίσω which is an equivalent to ἕδραι and equally ambiguous. It may indicate the buttocks as well as the rear guard of an army. These were probably the meanings he preferred for the context of the Psalm.

One wonders whether the translator was not first of all referring to a type of corporal punishment. He may have understood the Greek expression, both in the Psalm and in 1 Samuel, as meaning "spanking:" with his hand, mentioned explicitly in 1 Sam 5:3 and 6, God beats the Philistines on their "buttocks." This form of corporal punishment was well known in Greece and in its educational system. It is described by several classical authors as a degrading chastisement.[24] Theoretically, that could be the reason why in Ps 77:66 it is said to inflict "a perpetual reproach." However, the problem with this interpretation is that in classical Greek, this type of punishment is never described with the terminology used in our biblical passages.

A note should be added on the use of ἐν[25] with the verb πατάσσω. It is much more frequent than that of εἰς, and it is most often clearly distinguished from it. In many instances, the preposition ἐν introduces the locality in which somebody is defeated or killed: "He smote some of the Philistines in Machmas" (1 Kgdms 14:31). Elsewhere it frequently indicates the instrument or the illness with which somebody is beaten or stricken: "with (ἐν) the edge of the sword" (Judg 1:8 and passim), "with (ἐν) an evil sore" (Deut 28:35). In some instances, it refers to those who are struck: "The Lord had inflicted on (ἐν) the people a very great plague." It never seems to indicate a part of the body stricken with physical blows or with disease. This suggests that Eusebius' reading of 1 Kgdms 5:3(Hebrew 5), referred to in the above, can hardly be correct. The same applies to the reading of Deut 28:27 in the manuscripts preferred in the critical edition of Göttingen. In our discussion of this text we will return to this point.

Tentatively combining the evidence gained in this section with the previous, we suggest that the expression under discussion should be understood as referring to a plague with which the Philistines were smitten "in their seats." However, this conclusion does not yet allow us to define unambiguously what the translator had in mind when pointing at these "seats." The context may bring further clarification.

5. The Context in 1 Samuel

First of all we wish to draw attention to the end of 5:3 (5:6 in the Lucian version and in the MT): "Azotus and its environs." In our introduction we have already mentioned the critical observation of most commentators concerning this geographical indication; it seems to be appended rather clumsily to the foregoing expression "He beat them on their seats." If it had been intended as an apposition to "them," as proposed by McCarter,[26] then it should have mentioned the Azotians rather than the localities in which they live. It is our suggestion that "Azotus and its environs" was understood by the translator as an apposition to ἕδρα, here used with the meaning: "seat, place where somebody resides." This is exactly how the *Vetus Latina* interpreted the Greek, using "domus" (house, residence) as a Latin equivalent of Greek ἕδρα in this context: "et percussit illos in domibus eorum, in Azotum et regiones eius."[27] Note that in this version, Azotus and its environs are explicitly identified as the localities stricken with a plague. We may assume that the Latin translator got it right. In the above, we have demonstrated that his interpretation is perfectly suitable in the light of non-biblical Greek literature.

A suitable English translation of our passage then reads as follows: "He struck them (with illness) in their residences, that is in Ashdod and its environs."[28] This implies that the Greek text did not immediately specify the character of the illness. In the Lucianic version the specification is given in the next line: the Lord "brought rats over them and they propagated all over their ships and sprang up in the heart of their country. And there was a great terror of death in the city" (1 Sam 5:6).

The continuation causes more problems. In vv. 9-10 the Greek versions differ considerably from the MT. In the following section, we will have to return to these differences. Here we focus on the double mention of the ἕδραι in this passage.

The context of the first occurrence reads as

follows: "He smote the men of the city, small and great, εἰς τὰς ἕδρας." The Greek sentence is very similar to that in 5:3(6). Although here in v. 9, the apposition, identifying the "seats" with Ashdod and its environs, is missing, we are still inclined to translate ἕδρας by "residences." The *Vetus Latina*, preserved by Luciferus Calaritanus,[29] confirms this interpretation. It splits the phrase and expands it: "Et percussit vires civitatis, a minimo usque ad maximum, *et ebullivit illis mures* in sedibus." The insertion of a reference to the rats does not encourage us to understand the ἕδραι, translated by "sedes," as meaning "anuses" or "bottoms." The translator rather wants us to think of "areas" or "localities" in which rodents were propagating.

But how are we then to understand the continuation of the verse: "and they made themselves ἕδρας?"[30] Probably this notice originally belonged in ch. 6, after v. 5 where the Philistines are recommended to make five golden replicas of their "seats."[31] The question still remains: what was, in the eyes of the translator, the meaning of these "manufactured" seats? He may have hesitated. The term ἕδρα admitted several possibilities. He may have preferred this term for that reason. It allowed him to leave the choice to his readers. It is likely that he still identified the "seats" with the "residences" or cities or satrapies of the Philistines. The five golden replicas can be compared with Ezekiel's model of Jerusalem portrayed on a brick.[32] Their number is then easily explicable as the number of the five Philistine cities or countries.

An objection against our interpretation of the
ἕδραι may be found in 6:3. There the Philistines
are told to prepare offerings in order to get
"healed." Does this not imply that they were sick?
Where does the story mention any illness, if not
in the verses referring to the עפלים or ἕδραι? In
so far as the Hebrew is concerned, this reasoning
may be valid. It does not necessarily apply to
the Greek text. We have suggested that in the
eyes of the translator, the plague consisted of
swarms of rats causing illness and death.[33] In
his view, a deliverance from the rats also meant
healing.

Summarising this section we note that the Greek
versions in 5:3(6) strongly support an
interpretation of ἕδρα as a noun meaning
"locality, residence." The remaining occurrences
of the term in chs 5 and 6 can be understood along
the same line. The Old Latin confirms and even
reinforces this interpretation. An altogether
different picture is given in the Vulgar Latin.
There the relevant passages are understood as
referring to the "secret parts" of the human body
or the "anus."[34] Symmachus has a similar
interpretation of the Hebrew text. In the section
on the Qere and Ketib, we noted that this
interpretation may have been influenced by the
reading of עפל as אפל.

6. MT, LXX, and the Lucian Tradition

It is not our main intention here to offer an
in-depth study of the differences between the MT,
LXX, and Lucian version of our passage. Nevertheless, some comment is called for. There are two

major divergences between the MT and the LXX. First, the sequence is different: the second half of LXX 5:3 corresponds with MT 5:6. Second, LXX 5:3 has a plus which to a large extent corresponds with the longer reading of 5:6 in the Lucianic version. It introduces rats as a plague in the beginning of the story. There is no corresponding reference to rats in the MT, where they are not mentioned until 6:4 where the reader is not prepared for their appearance. McCarter is right when he observes that the statements concerning the rats in 6:4, 5, 11, and 18 seem to presuppose earlier mention of these rodents. The verses in question are concerned with golden rats used as offerings. The rationale for this must be the presence of rats in the plague. McCarter's solution is that the Lucianic version preserved their original mention in 5:6, whereas LXX restored it in the wrong place.[35] Although others are inclined to exclude the reading of LXX, and of L, as expansive, we tend to prefer McCarter's views.

Although this is not necessarily an argument in favour of its authenticity, one has to admit that the Lucian text has the more coherent version, especially in 5:6. It appears to acknowledge one plague only: that of the rats who cause a terror of death in the residences of the Philistines.[36] A similar picture is given in 6:1. Whereas the MT in that verse does not explicitly describe the plague, the Greek versions clearly refer to the propagating rats. This scenario corresponds with the Exodus narrative to which our story refers.

There also only one plague at a time is sent against the enemy.

In 5:9 and 12, the situation is more complicated. Especially in v 9 the textual problems are intricate. It is clear however that also in this verse, both the LXX and the Lucianic tradition refer to the rats whereas the MT does not. Moreover, the Greek versions anticipate 6:5 and its reference to the "making (καὶ ἐποίησαν = ויעשו) 'seats'." Instead of this the MT has: וישתרו עלהם עפלים. Usually the Hebrew is translated as follows: "and tumors broke out upon them." The Hebrew verb שתר is a hapax legomenon,[37] and its meaning is not well known. Nevertheless, it should be clear that its subject, the עפלים can hardly be understood as "localities." The reference is most probably to "swellings" or "tumors." It is remarkable that the Greek translators read either another verb in their *Vorlage*, or corrected it in order to avoid the notion of tumors.

In v 12 the Lucianic text appears to express an idea which the MT probably preserved in a mutilated state: "not only the living, but also the dying (οἱ ἀποθανόντες) were stricken by the plague in the ἕδρας or ἕδραις." Although here the rats are not mentioned, it is perfectly possible that the translator had them in mind. In his view, they threatened both the living and the dead in their mansions. Through the replacement of the article οἱ by the negation οὐκ before the "dying," the LXX was probably "corrected" towards the MT. It reads: "those who lived and did not die were stricken by the plague ..." The MT itself has a shorter version mentioning only those who did not die: "and the men who did not die were afflicted by the plague ..." This seems to imply a contradiction since it oddly enough suggests that those who did die, presumably by the plague, were not stricken by the plague.

We may conclude that the Lucianic tradition preserved the most coherent version of the story of the Philistines and the Ark. It knew of only one plague, that of rats propagating all over the Philistine towns.

7. The Relation With Deuteronomy

Up to now, we have basically dealt with 1 Sam 5 and 6, in its respective versions, referring only obliquely to Deut 28:27, the other passage in which our expression occurs. It is often said that the translation of the Torah functioned as a model for the translators of the other biblical books.[38] If that is indeed the case, then one may presume that the Greek version of Deut 28:27 inspired the translator of 1 Sam 5 and 6.

However, a further investigation reveals first that the general theory hardly applies to the translation of 1 Samuel, and second that the choice of the term ἕδρα in Deut 28:27 may have been influenced by its use in 1 Samuel, and not vice versa.

G. Gerleman[39] and L. C. Allen[40] have rightly noted a contrast between Paralipomena and Kingdoms. Whereas Paralipomena as a rule very closely follows the language of the Pentateuch, Kingdoms markedly diverges from it.

The lack of any affinity with the Pentateuch is

EΔPA AND THE PHILISTINE PLAGUE 587

especially remarkable in the translation of 1 Samuel. Already in 1906, in his study of *The Greek Translators of the Four Books of Kings*[41] H. St.J Thackeray had observed that the translator of 1 Sam had a want of familiarity with renderings employed in the Pentateuch. The first example brought to the fore by Thackeray is specific for the chapters we are dealing with: (τὸ) τῆς βασάνου renders אשם, "guilt-offering," in 1 Sam 6:3, 4, 8, 17. Nowhere in the Pentateuch, nor in any other biblical book, can the same translation be found. This is most striking in 1 Sam 6:3 where one reads the expression השיב אשם which seems to be coined after Num 5:8, the only other passage in which this phrase is used. Although the Hebrew in 1 Sam 6:3 is probably dependent on Numbers, the Greek is not. In passing we may note that the guilt-offering consists of images (צלם): 1 Sam 6:5, 11. The Greek here has ὁμοίωμα, whereas in the Pentateuch the translator prefers εἰκών (Gen 1:26, 27; 5:3; 9:6).

We may add a second example, also taken from the cultic realm. In 1 Sam 6:14 cows are offered as a burnt offering (עלה). The priestly regulations concerning such offerings are to be found in Lev 1:1-17 and 22:17-25. In these chapters the translator uses most often ὁλοκαύτωμα and never ὁλοκαύτωσις, the term preferred by the translator of 1 Sam 6.[42]

In most of the later biblical books, quotations and allusions to passages in the Hebrew Pentateuch were often phrased in the Greek in a manner identical with the LXX translation of their

Pentateuchal sources.[43] They are the clearest
indications of dependence. Again however, this
hardly applies to 1 Samuel. None of the examples
listed in Tov's article on the subject[44] are taken
from that book. Chapters 5 and 6 contain several
allusions to the Pentateuch. However, the
translation does not show signs of dependence.
The most explicit reference is to the plagues in
Egypt. In 1 Sam 6:4, 5 the Hebrew term for plague
is מגפה. The Greek renders it by πταῖσμα, a word
which occurs only here. In Exod 12:13 and
elsewhere in the Pentateuch, the same term is
translated as πληγή. A direct comparison with the
Egyptian plagues is to be found in 1 Sam 6:6, a
passage which clearly alludes to Exod 10:1-2 and
its Exodus account. Both texts mention a
hardening of the heart (לב כבד). In Exodus, the
LXX translates the Hebrew verb with σκληρύνω,
whereas in 1 Sam it uses βαρύνω. Note though that
in both contexts, the rare hifil of עלל is
rendered by ἐμπαίζω.

A more veiled allusion to the Pentateuch occurs
in 1 Sam 6:7. Here the reference seems to be to
Num 19:2 where a red "heifer that has not been
yoked" is slaughtered and burned. The expression
in between quotation marks returns literally in
1 Sam 6:7. However, the Greek translation is
completely different. 1 Sam 6:7 offers a
circumlocution, δύο βόας πρωτοτοκούσας, where Num
19:2 has a more literal rendition: δάμαλων ᾗ οὐκ
ἐπεβλήθη ἐπ' αὐτὴν ζυγός.

These data allow us to question the assumption
that the Greek of 1 Sam in general, and of chs 5
and 6 in particular, was inspired by the LXX

version of the Pentateuch. In as far as the use
of ἕδρα is concerned, the opposite may be true.
Indeed, in Deut 28:27 the choice of the term ἕδρα
is hard to explain without a comparison with 1 Sam
5 and 6. We have already noted that Deut 28:27
lists a series of illnesses. Εδρα does not fit in
that series. It is no disease. In order to make
it fit, the text had to be adapted. The
translator must have had a reason for this
intervention. It does not suffice to say that he
may not have understood the Hebrew terms שחור or
עפל. Even then, the context must have told him
that these words stood for sickening plagues. One
may suggest that he wished to avoid a literal
translation of both the Qere and the Ketib. Even
so, the normal translation technique of the
translator of Deuteronomy should have prompted him
to find an alternative closer to the original
text. The more plausible explanation is that he
had in mind the story of the ark and its plague.
This is easily conceivable when one admits that
the story of the ark was told independently from
its canonical context, and also translated
independently from it. An alternative scenario is
that an earlier translation of Deut 28:27 was
later rephrased under the influence of the Greek
version of Samuel.

If the translator of Deuteronomy was indeed
dependent on that of Kingdoms, then he probably
read εἰς (τὴν ἕδραν or τὰς ἕδρας) and not
ἐν (...). Indeed, in 1 Kingdoms he found εἰς and
not ἐν. Moreover, used with πατάσσω, ἐν, in
contrast with εἰς, usually does not refer to the
place on the body or the area stricken by a

disease. We have already noted that it rather indicates the locality in which an army is defeated, or in which people are physically stricken or killed, or the instrument with which somebody is beaten or killed. With Vaticanus and a series of minuscules we thus prefer to read εἰς, although J. Wever's critical edition, following other manuscripts, has ἐν. This reading may have been provoked by the context in Deuteronomy where this preposition ἐν recurs several times with the same verb. It may have been brought in by a copyist who overlooked the fact that ἐν in this context introduced diseases and not places such as ἕδρα.[45]

Conclusion

Many of the answers we have found to the questions phrased in the introduction remain tentative. Nevertheless they are worth summarising:
a. In their translation of the Hebrew, the ancient Greek versions seem to have intended to render the Ketib rather than the Qere.
b. The relevant data in the non-biblical Greek texts reveal that the expression εἰς τὰς ἕδρας should either refer to the "anus," or to "residences" or "localities." The combination of this expression with the verb πατάσσω cannot be found in non-biblical Greek. Related combinations suggest that the phrase πατάσσω εἰς τὰς ἕδρας describes a plague in the area of the anus, or in the area of the habitations of the victims.
c. The immediate context in 1 Samuel 5 and 6 directs us towards the acceptance of the second

possibility. It identifies the ἕδραι with the residences of the Philistines. The *Vetus Latina* supports this interpretation.

d. The most coherent narration of the plague, and perhaps also the more original one, is preserved in the Lucianic version. It does not hesitate between two plagues, that of the so-called haemorrhoids or bubos, and that of the rats. It definitely sees the rats as the plague which strikes the Philistines in their cities or residences.

e. The Greek translation of Deut 28:27, with its enumeration of several diseases, is probably dependent on 1 Sam 5 when it translates the עפלים.

NOTES

1. In another paper, forthcoming in the proceedings of the Congress on "Phoenicia and the Bible" held at Leuven in April 1989 and to be edited by E. Lipinski, we dealt with the translation of מלך by αρχων in Lev 18 and 20.

2. J. Campbell Gibson, "What is Bubonic Plague," *ExpT* 12 (1900-1901) 378-80; C. J. Dann, "'Mice' and 'Emerods,'" *ExpT* 15 (1903-1904) 476-78; J. Wilkinson, "The Philistine Epidemic of I Samuel 5 and 6," in *ExpT* 88 (1976-1977) 137-41. These three authors give a similar explanation of the plague, referring to the outbreak of the bubonic disease in Bombay in 1900-1901. It is somewhat amazing that the more recent articles do not have cross-references to the earlier ones in the same periodical. See also B. Brentjes, "Zur 'Beulen' - Epidemie bei den Philistern in 1. Samuel 5-6," *Altertum* 15 (1969) 67-74. F. S. Bodenheimer, *Animal and Man in Bible Lands* (Collection de

l'Acad. intern. d'histoire des sciences 10; 2 vol;
Brill 1960-1972) 1.201-202. For further bibliography, see the recent commentaries by J. Stoebe,
Das erste Buch Samuelis (KAT 8; Gütersloh: Mohn,
1973) 140; P. Kyle McCarter, *1 Samuel* (AB 8; New
York: Doubleday, 1980) 123; R. W. Klein *I Samuel*
(WBC 10; Waco, Texas: Word Books, 1983) 47.

3. *A Greek-English Lexicon. With a Supplement* (8th
ed; Oxford: Clarendon, 1968).

4. On the story of the Ark as a whole, see
recently A. F. Campbell, *The Ark Narrative (1 Sam
4-6; 2 Sam 6). A Form-Critical and Traditio-
Historical Study* (SBLDS 16; Missoula, Mont.
Scholars Press, 1975); F. Schiklberger, *Die Lade
Erzählung des ersten Samuel-Buches* (FzB 7;
Würzburg: Echter, 1973); P. D. Miller &
J. J. M. Roberts, *The Hand of the Lord. A
Reassessment of the "Ark Narrative"* (Baltimore:
John Hopkins University Press, 1977); K. A. D.
Smelik, "The Ark Narrative Reconsidered," *New
Avenues in the Study of the Old Testament* (ed. A.
S. Van der Woude; Leiden: Brill, 1989) 128-44.

5. For a good survey of the differences between
the LXX and the Lucianic texts, see J. Trebolle
Barrera, *Centena in libros Samuelis et Regum.
Variantes textuales y composicion Literaria en los
libros de Samuel y Reyes* (CSIC; Madrid: Consejo
Superior de Investigaciones Cientificas, 1989)
55-63. Most helpful in the same series is the
edition of the Lucianic text by N. Fernandez
Marcos & J. R. Busto Saiz, *El texto Antioqueno de
la Biblia Griega* (vol. I *1-2 Samuel*; Madrid:
Consejo Superior de Investigaciones Cientificas,
1989). Other important works on the Greek text of
Samuel are: J. Wellhausen, *Der Text der Bücher
Samuelis* (Göttingen: Vandenhoeck, 1871); S. R.
Driver, *Notes on the Hebrew Text of the Books of
Samuel* (2nd rev. ed; Oxford: Clarendon, 1913); N.
Peters, *Beiträge zur Text- und Literarkritik der
Bücher Samuel* (Freiburg im Br: Herder, 1899);
H. St. J. Thackeray, "The Greek Translators of the
Four Books of Kings" *JTS* 8 (1907) 262-78;
P. A. H. De Boer, *Research into the Text of
1 Samuel 1-16* (Amsterdam: H. J. Paris, 1938);
B. Johnson, *Die Hexaplarische Rezension des
1. Samuelbuches der Septuaginta* (Studia Theol.
Lund. 22; Lund: Gleerup, 1963); S. P. Brock, *The
Recensions of the LXX Version of 1 Samuel* (diss.
Oxford, 1966); E. Tov (ed.), *The Hebrew and Greek
Texts of Samuel* (1980 Proceedings IOSCS; Vienna;

Jersualem: Academon, 1980); S. Pisano, *Additions or Omissions in the Books of Samuel* (OBO 57; Freiburg: Universitätsverlag, 1984).

6. Thus McCarter, *1 Samuel*, 119 and Trebolle, *Centena in libros*, 56-57.

7. For variant readings see the edition of J. Wevers (Göttingen: Vandenhoeck & Ruprecht, 1977): ms B has the acc. sing. and several minuscules have the acc. plur.

8. B.Megillah, 25a. See R. Gordis, *The Biblical Text in the Making. A Study of the Kethib-Qere. Augmented Edition with a Prolegomenon* (New York: Ktav, 1971) esp. XVII-XVIII (correct b.Megillah 28a); see also the older but still useful works of Z. Frankel, *Vorstudien der Septuaginta* (Leipzig: Vogel, 1841) esp. 219-41 and A. Geiger, *Urschrift und Übersetzungen der Bibel* (Breslau: Hainauer, 1857) esp. 407-15.

9. Gordis, *Biblical Text in the Making*, 167, n. 1.

10. P. Kyle McCarter, *1 Samuel*, 123.

11. H. J. Stoebe, *Das erste Buch Samuelis*, 140.

12. Σκότος: Deut 28:29; Job 3:6; 10:22; 23:17; Ps 90(91):6; Isa 29:18; 58:10; Zeph 1:15; σκοτεινός: Prov 4:19; σκοτία: Job 28:3; σκοτομήνη: Ps 10(11):2. Elsewhere the translator preserved γνόφος: Exod 10:22; Josh 24:7; Jer 23:12; Joel 2:2; Amos 5:10, or γνοφώδης: Prov 7:9; and δορία: Isa 59:9.

13. More common words for "buttocks" or "secret parts" seem to have been the euphemistic רגלים (e.g., Nah 3:5), or ערות דבר (Deut 23:14); or שת (2 Sam 10:4; Isa 20:4); or אחור (Amos 4:2?; Ps 88:66?; Ezek 8:16). In none of these cases does the Greek render these terms with ἕδρα.

14. See L. Berkowitz & K. A. Squitier, *Theasaurus Linguae Graecae. Canon of Greek Authors and Works* (2nd ed; New York, Oxford: Oxford University Press, 1986).

15. VI,I; see R. Joly, *Hippocrate*, t.XIII (Collection des Universités de France; Paris: 1978) 149.

16. 60.c.3; see I. Burnet, *Platonis opera* (Scriptorum classicorum bibliotheca oxonensis; Oxford, 1902, reprint 1968). Only one plural form was

found in the TLG. A similar search in the Greek papyri had no positive result.

17. *Commentaria in Psalmos* (Migne 23) 937. Compare with Athanasius, *Expositio in Psalmum 78* (Migne 27) 356. Chrysostomos seems to be the first to comment directly upon the Samuel passage. He offers a synopsis, without further comment: *Synopsis Scripturae Sacrae* (Migne 56) 341.

18. Migne 81, 363, p. 542.

19. Leaving out the passages describing the punishment of the Philistines stealing the Ark and the list of plagues in Deut 28:27, the expression occurs about 15 times.

20. 1 Kgdms 26:8; 2 Kgdms 2:22; 18:11; 4 Kgdms 13:18; compare with 1 Kgdms 1:14; 19:10; Zech 9:4.

21. Reading of the Lucianic version.

22. Compare with 2 Kgdms 3:27; Ps 77(78):66; see also Gen 37:21 (smite somebody in his life, kill somebody).

23. Some special cases may be added here: in several instances εἰς introduces the number of those who are stricken: Judg 3:31; 2 Kgdms 8:13. In 4 Kgdms 10:27 the meaning is not clear: ἔταξαν αὐτὸν εἰς λυτρῶνας. According to the immediate context, the direct object seems to be Baal. In that case the expression seems to imply that the god went down the drain: he is thrown into the "toilet." However, the object can also be the house of Baal. That is certainly so in the MT. In that case the Greek should perhaps be read as follows: "He demolished the house of Baal and turned it into a 'privy'."

24. See e.g., Quintilianus, *Institutio oratoria*, 1,3,14-17.20.

25. For a more general and nuanced view on the use of ἐν or εἰς, see I. Soisalon-Soininen, "ἐν für εἰς in der Septuaginta" *VT* 32 (1982) 129-44.

26. *1 Samuel*, 122: "these words may have been added ... in the light of the following phrase, בעפלים, understood as 'on (their) mounds, (on) their acropoles'." In this sentence the "following phrase" should probably be changed into "preceding phrase."

27. See P. Sabatier, *Bibliorum Sacrorum Latinae Versiones antiquae seu Vetus Italica* (3 vol; Reims, 1743-9) II, 484. His witness is from the

4th century: Lucifer Calaritanus. A critical edition of Lucifer's work is available in G. F. Diercks, *Luciferi Calaritani Opera quae supersunt* (Corp. Christ. Series lat. 8; Turnhout: Brepols, 1978). The passage occurs in *De Athanasio*, I, XII, 15 (p. 22). A similar version is given in the marginal notes of the Leon codex published by C. Vercellone, *Variae lectiones vulgatae latinae bibliorum editionis* (2 vol; Rome: Spithöver, 1864) 203: "et percussit illos in domibus eorum; ipsum Azotum, et regiones eius." In v. 6, however, Sabatier has "et percussis in secretiore parte natium." This reading cannot be found in the critical edition of Diercks. It is identical with the version of the Vulgate and seems to be inspired by Symmachus. The Leon codex does not have an equivalent.

28. This may after all be original meaning of the Hebrew. Indeed, Hebrew עפל usually means "mound" where people reside. Compare with McCarter, *1 Samuel*, 122, 123.

29. Diercks, *Luciferi Calaritani*, 22.

30. In the edition of Diercks the *Vetus Latina* noted by Luciferus reads: "Et fecerunt sibi sedes pellicias." The marginal notes in mss L91, 92 (Leon codex) and L93-95 have: "et fercerunt ipsi sibi Gethaei cathedras aureas," see Fernandez Marcos, *El texto Antioqueno*, 16.

31. For ch. 6:4 the marginal notes of the *Vetus Latina* mss L91-95, published by Fernandez Marcos (*El texto Antioqueno*, 17) have: "Quinque sedes aureas facite similes sedibus vestris." In v. 11 the same marginal notes have: "et cathedras aureas posuerunt..."

32. Ezek 4:1. For a discussion of the function of these golden objects, see the commentaries and Brentjes, "Zur 'Beulen'," 67-74.

33. This does not necessarily imply that the translator was aware of the exact cause-effect relation between rats and illness. See Stoebe, *Das erste Buch Samuelis*, 151, with further bibliography on this topic. In this context, it may be interesting to note that ancient Jewish interpretations of the passage describe the relation between the rats and illness as follows: rats crawl forth out of the earth and jerk the entrails out of the bodies of the Philistines (Sifre Num 88; Sifre Z 96; compare Ps. Philo 55,

2-5. See L. Ginzberg, *The Legends of the Jews* (7 vol; Philadelphia: The Jewish Publication Society of America, 1968) 1.62-63 and 6.223-24; Bodenheimer, *Animal and Man*, 1.201. Without connecting them with the biblical scene of the Philistine plague, Bodenheimer also mentions sacred poisonous "shrews" or ratlike animals and their figurines in Egypt (1.41-42 and 2.24, fig. 11). The figurines can be compared with the golden replicas in the biblical story.

34. See the critical edition of *The Biblia Sacra iuxta Latinam Vulgatam Versionem, V, Samuel* (Rome: Typis Polyglottis Vaticanis, 1943). The respective renderings are as follows: 5:6, 12 "in secretiore parte natium;" 5:9 "prominentes extales;" 6:5 "quinque anos;" 6:11 "similitudinem anorum."

35. McCarter, *1 Samuel*, 119-20. Note that Josephus also introduces the rats at a position corresponding to 1 Sam 5:6 (*Ant.* 6:3).

36. For a similar interpretation in ancient Jewish exegesis, see note 33.

37. E. Nestle, "Miszellen," *ZAW* 29 (1909) 232 proposes reading a hitpael of שרה: "to let loose."

38. See E. Tov, "The Impact of the LXX Translation of the Pentateuch on the Translation of Other Books," *Mélanges Dominique Barthélemy* (eds. P. Casetti, O. Keel, A. Schenker, OBO, 38; Fribourg: Universitärsverlag, 1981) 577-92.

39. *Studies in the Septuagint* (Lunds Univ. Arsskr; Lund: Gleerup, 1946) 22-29.

40. *The Greek Chronicles* (2 vol; VTSup 25-26; Leiden: Brill, 1974) 1.23-26 and 57-59.

41. "The Greek Translators," 262-78, esp. 274. According to Thackeray, the translator had problems with the rendition of the Hebrew. This appears to have been true especially of the story of the Philistines and the Ark. Several words seem to have been unfamiliar to him. Thus in 6:8 he transliterates the Hebrew בארגז after his tentative translation ἐν θέματι. He adopted a similar procedure in 5:4 where he transliterated המפתן after his guesswork-translation τὰ ἐμπρόσθια. It is very possible that his translation of עפלים was also guesswork.

42. Leviticus has ολοκαυτομα about 56 times and ολοκαυτωσις 7 times, whereas 1 Sam has ολοκαυτωμα only once and ολοκαυτωσις 10 times.

43. Tov, "The Impact of the LXX Translation," 588.

44. Tov, "The Impact of the LXX Translation," 589-99.

45. Both the translator and the copyist must have understood ἕδρα as a noun indicating "the behind" or more precisely "the anus." This is also the translation of Symmachus who has εις τα κρυπτα.

IS THE ALTERNATE TRADITION OF THE DIVISION OF THE KINGDOM (3 KGDMS 12:24a-z) NON-DEUTERONOMISTIC?

ZIPORA TALSHIR

This paper deals with the tradition of the division of the kingdom preserved in the LXX of 3 Kgdms 12:24a-z. As a whole it has no counterpart in the Book of Kings. Nevertheless, it parallels parts of 1 Kgs 11, 12 and 14. Within the framework of the LXX it repeats the story of the same events described beforehand in the current translation of chapters 11-12. We therefore refer to it as the alternate tradition.

The alternate tradition starts with the introduction of Rehoboam's reign (§a). It then goes back to tell about Jeroboam's rise to power in the days of Solomon, his flight to Egypt, and his return, on Solomon's death, to his hometown Sareira (§§b-f). There the scene of the sick child takes place, including Ahijah's prophecy of doom (§§g-n). At the beginning of the following scene Jeroboam initiates the meeting in Shechem. At this point the prophecy by Shemaiah, promising

Jeroboam the ten tribes, is introduced. The negotiations fail (§§n-u). Shemaiah speaks again, this time to substantiate the division of the kingdom by God's will (§§x-z).

The comparison of the alternate tradition with the parallel material in the Book of Kings reveals that part of the components missing from the alternate tradition as against the MT are deuteronomistic by definition. Do the missing deuteronomistic elements suggest that the alternate tradition relies on pre-deuteronomistic sources and is itself non-deuteronomistic?[1] This would accord the alternate tradition immense value for the literary criticism of the Book of Kings, since it would be a sole representative of the supposed pre-deuteronomistic stage of the Book of Kings.[2]

We approach the subject from two aspects. On the one hand, we ask whether the alternate tradition in its present form is indeed non-deuteronomistic. On the other hand, we assess whether there is no explanation for the missing deuteronomistic sections, other than the non-deuteronomistic nature of the sources underlying the alternate tradition. We shall consider the relations between the alternate tradition and the parallel in the Book of Kings with reference to those points relevant to the deuteronomistic question.

a. Paragraph a, the introduction to Rehoboam's reign, is much shorter than its parallel in the MT of 1 Kgs 14:21-24. The definition of Jerusalem - העיר אשר בחר ה' לשום שמו שם מכל שבטי ישראל, "the

THE DIVISION OF THE KINGDOM   601

city the Lord had chosen out of all the tribes of Israel to establish his name there" - is lacking in the alternate tradition. Both the idea and the language are of deuteronomistic provenance. In keeping with criteria used in literary criticism of the Bible, the simple conclusion would be that these words were not part of the material at the disposal of the author of the alternate tradition. This is of course possible. However, the following argumentation shows that the history of the text should not be over- simplified.

The designation of Jerusalem as God's chosen city, not found in other introductory formulae, is in line with the irregular character of this particular introductory formula, which portrays the relationship between God and his people. The MT reads: ויעש יהודה הרע בעיני ה' ויקנאו אתו מכל אשר עשו אבתם בחטאתם אשר חטאו: ויבנו גם המה להם במות ומצבות ואשרים על כל גבעה גבהה ותחת כל עץ רענן: וגם קדש היה בארץ ככל התועבת הגוים אשר הוריש ה' מפני בני ישראל:, "Judah did what was displeasing to the Lord, and angered Him more than their fathers had done by the sins that they committed. They too built for themselves shrines, pillars, and sacred posts on every high hill and under every leafy tree; there were also male prostitutes in the land. [Judah] imitated all the abhorrent practices of the nations which the Lord had dispossessed before the Israelites" (14:22-24). In the alternate tradition all this is paralleled by no more than καὶ ἐποίησεν τὸ πονηρὸν ἐνώπιον Κυρίου καὶ οὐκ ἐπορεύθη ἐν ὁδῷ Δαυειδ τοῦ πατρὸς αὐτοῦ, presumably reflecting: ויעש הרע בעיני ה' ולא הלך בדרך דוד אביו, "and he did that which was evil in the sight of the Lord, and walked not in the way of David his father." The subject is obviously not Judah, but Rehoboam, as customary in the introductory formulae, and his sins are only very generally touched upon.

The outstanding characterization of Judah and Jerusalem at this particular stage in the Book of Kings is intended as the "identity card" of the newly formed state. As such it has a function in the large framework of the Book of Kings. It recalls the final address to the Northern Kingdom (2 Kgs 17:7ff), as well as the evaluation of Manasseh, who leads Judah to its destruction (2 Kgs 21 and 23:26-27). It is undoubtedly part of the late deuteronomistic composition.

Was there ever a previous edition of the Book of Kings which treated the reign of Rehoboam as it would any other reign, totally unaware of its crucial point in history? Is the alternate tradition a reliable witness to the existence of such an edition? Before answering this question one should consider the evidence of Chronicles and the LXX of 1 Kgs 14, both of which seemingly support the alternate tradition.

The subject of the passage in the LXX is explicitly Rehoboam, not Judah. Nevertheless, the long text of the MT is reflected almost literally. The result is a conflated text, undoubtedly secondary. It refers to Rehoboam but at the same time goes into a lengthy description of the sins of the people, complete with the reference to the sins of Rehoboam's (instead of the people's!) ancestors: καὶ ἐποίησεν Ροβοὰμ τὸ πονηρὸν ἐνώπιον

THE DIVISION OF THE KINGDOM

κυρίου καὶ παρεζήλωσεν αὐτὸν ἐν πᾶσιν οἷς ἐποίησαν οἱ πατέρες αὐτοῦ ... (3 Kgdms 14:22-24).[a]

From Chronicles two passages may be adduced:[3] First, 2 Chron 12:1: ויהי כהכין מלכות רחבעם וכחזקתו עזב את תורת ה' וכל ישראל עמו, "when the kingship of Rehoboam was firmly established, and he grew strong, he abandoned the Teaching of the Lord, he and all Israel with him." This is the Chronicler's own contribution to the history of Rehoboam, forming periods of good and evil in the king's reign, to accord with his system of retribution. It may, however, suggest that the Chronicler is aware of the version of Kings, which describes the sins of the people, since he specifies that all of Israel sinned, and not the king alone.[4]

The formal counterpart of the formula is 2 Chron 12:14: ויעש הרע כי לא הכין לבו לדרוש את ה', "he did what was wrong, for he had not set his heart to seek the Lord." Rehoboam is the subject, characterized by no more than a short sentence. Does the Chronicler witness a stage previous to the Book of Kings? Except for ויעש הרע, the passage is the unmistakable product of the Chronicler's language and thought. Therefore, we are inclined to think that he left out the passage of Kings in order to make room for his own formulation. Moreover, in Chronicles the introductory formula appears at the very end of Rehoboam's reign, as a kind of summary. This is a quite awkward point to go into a lengthy description of the people's sins. Consequently, his version cannot serve as proof for the secondary nature of 1 Kgs 14:22-24.

This should put us on guard as to the alternate tradition. Our author as well may have had his reasons to give up the detailed description of Judah's sins and phrase his estimation of Rehoboam in a commonplace description of the king's behaviour. Given the narrow scope of the alternate tradition, it would hardly be the right place for a broad characterization of Judah. The alternate tradition does not deal with the history of Judah, it is limited to the division of the kingdom. The author gives his attention to Rehoboam. Later on in his story he will make it quite clear that no one but Rehoboam is to blame for the loss of the Northern tribes.

Let us look now at the other side of the coin. The short text of the alternate tradition may well be judged as earlier than the elaborate passage in the MT, but had this text appeared in the Book of Kings, would it not be considered as part of its deuteronomistic framework? This means that if the alternate tradition is actually a witness of a previous stage of the Book of Kings, it is not the totally pre-deuteronomistic stage of popular tales, prophetic stories, etc., but rather an intermediary stage, in which the raw material was already embedded in a deuteronomistic framework.

Even as a survival of a first deuteronomistic edition, §a does not live up to the image of the alternate tradition as conceived by those scholars who highly favour its originality. In their opinion the introductory paragraph is clearly redactional; the real story, as all good stories, opened with καὶ ἦν ἄνθρωπος..., "and there was a man...," and concentrated exclusively on

Jeroboam.[5] §a was added as a link when the alternate tradition was introduced into its present context.[6] One cannot but wonder at the method behind this suggestion: the deuteronomistic elements in the MT absent from the alternate tradition prove that the latter is pre-deuteronomistic, while the deuteronomistic elements preserved in the alternate tradition are to be regarded as an addition to the original alternate tradition.

In my opinion §a is indispensable to the alternate tradition. It is the starting point of the story about to take place; otherwise, there is no indication as to the time of Jeroboam's activities. Besides, it is the sole preparation for Rehoboam's intervention in the story, at the meeting in Shechem. We note that this long scene (§§p-u), unlike the MT, makes no mention at all of Jeroboam. As in §a, here too Rehoboam is the leading character. The issue in the alternate tradition is not exclusively Jeroboam's rise to power, but also Rehoboam's fall and the division of the kingdom.

Finally, one cannot fail to notice that the alternate tradition constitutes a thorough revision of its source, be it close to the MT or belonging to a former deuteronomistic stage. It no longer uses the formulae to the end they were originally designated for: not for stating the end of one reign and the beginning of another, but as an introduction to the whole literary unit.

b. We now turn to the scene of the sick child and to the words of Ahijah to Jeroboam's wife. First and foremost we should note the different place of the whole scene in context. In the MT it stands at the close of the history of Jeroboam. In the alternate tradition it is located immediately on his return from Egypt.[7] This is the key to the understanding of the differences between the two versions of the prophecy.

The prophecy in the Book of Kings is extensive (14:7-16). It is composed of three levels: the fate of the child, the House of Jeroboam, and of all Israel. In the alternate tradition the prophecy contained in §§l-m is shorter, concentrating on the fate of the child and of the others related to Jeroboam.

The discrepancy is evident even where the child's fate is concerned, vv. 12-13 paralleled in §l and the second part of §m:

3 Kgdms 12:24
§l ἰδοὺ σὺ ἀπελεύσῃ ἀπ' ἐμοῦ καὶ ἔσται εἰσελθούσης σου τὴν πύλην εἰς Σαριρα καὶ τὰ κοράσιά σου ἐξελεύσονταί σοι εἰς συνάντησιν καὶ ἐροῦσί σοι τὸ παιδάριον τέθνηκεν
§m...
καὶ τὸ παιδάριον κόψεται οὐαι Κύριε ὅτι εὑρέθη ἐν αὐτῷ ῥῆμα καλὸν περὶ τοῦ Κυρίου

Reconstruction	1 Kgs 14:12-13
הנה את הלכה מאתי	ואת קומי לכי לביתך
והיה בבאך השערה צררתה	בבאה רגליך העירה
ונערתיך הצאנה לקראתך	---
ואמרו לך	---
הילד מת	ומת הילד
וליליד יספדו	וספדו לו כל ישראל
הוי אדון	---

THE DIVISION OF THE KINGDOM

```
                              ---                          וקברו אתו
                              ---              כי זה לבדו יבא לירבעם אל קבר
יען נמצא בו דבר טוב                                  יען נמצא בו דבר טוב
    ---    אל ה'      אלהי ישראל בבית ירבעם
```

In the alternate tradition the prophet's words are embellished with certain features, but missing others. There is no mention of כל ישראל, "all Israel," or אלהי ישראל, "the God of Israel," reducing the national tenor of the Book of Kings, nor is there any trace of בית ירבעם "the House of Jeroboam." The phrase בית ירבעם is typical of those passages - again deuteronomistic by definition - which express God's wrath against the dynasties of kings unworthy to rule over Israel. Why should such elements be missing from the alternate tradition? Again, one may argue that they were not yet part of its *Vorlage*. But they may as well have been deliberately left out by the author of the alternate tradition, since they obviously do not fit his setting of the story. In his story there is no place for either national mourning, or for royal terms, seeing that Jeroboam is not yet king.

The second level in the prophecy extends the child's fate to everyone related to Jeroboam. This has a partial parallel at the beginning of §m:
3 Kgdms 12:24

§m ὅτι τάδε λέγει Κύριος ἰδοὺ ἐγὼ ἐξολοθρεύσω τοῦ Ιεροβοὰμ οὐροῦτα πρὸς τοῖχον καὶ ἔσονται οἱ τεθνηκότες τοῦ Ιεροβοὰμ ἐν τῇ πόλει καταφάγονται οἱ κύνες καὶ τὸν τεθνηκότα ἐν τῷ ἀγρῷ καταφάγεται τὰ πετεινὰ τοῦ οὐρανοῦ

Reconstruction	1 Kgs 14:10-11
כי כה אמר ה'	---
הנני---	לכן הנני מביא רעה
---	אל בית ירבעם
והכרתי לירבעם	והכרתי לירבעם
משתין בקיר	משתין בקיר
---	עצור ועזוב בישראל
---	ובערתי אחרי בית ירבעם
---	כאשר יבער הגלל עד תמו
והיה המת	והיה המת
לירבעם בעיר	לירבעם בעיר
יאכלו הכלבים	יאכלו הכלבים
והמת בשדה	והמת בשדה
יאכלו עוף השמים	יאכלו עוף השמים
---	כי ה' דבר

Here too the national and dynastic features are missing, and again one has to bear in mind that they are unwarranted in the scene of the sick child where it stands in the alternate tradition: Jeroboam is not yet king, neither was he promised kingship. Naturally, his dynasty cannot be threatened.

Once more, as with §a, the question rises whether §m, though lacking certain deuteronomistic elements, is nonetheless deuteronomistic. Are not the phrases והכרתי לירבעם משתין בקיר והיה המת לירבעם בעיר יאכלו הכלבים והמת בשדה יאכלו עוף השמים characteristic of the same contexts as the missing elements? We find them in the threat to the House of Baasha (1 Kgs 16:3-4) and in its realization by Zimri (v. 11); in the threat to the House of Ahab (21:21-22, 24), and in the command to Jehu (2 Kgs 9:8-9). All these passages are obviously

THE DIVISION OF THE KINGDOM

interconnected and pertain to the same layer in the Book of Kings. Are they an elaboration of an earlier, personal version, of the kind preserved in the alternate tradition? This supposition may be supported by the fact that similar phrases occur outside the Book of Kings, not directly related to the fate of royal dynasties. Nabal the Carmelite is threatened: אם אשאיר מכל אשר לו עד הבקר משתין בקיר, "if by the light of morning I leave a single male of his" (1 Sam 25:22, also 34).[8] Still, the difference is outstanding. First in the story of Nabal the threat comes from David, while in the alternate tradition the menace is spoken by God, as customary in the Book of Kings. Secondly, attention is called to the phrasing of the threat: unlike in the story of Nabal, the verb reflected in the alternate tradition is כרת, another characteristic of the texts bearing on the extermination of rejected dynasties. Moreover, the alternate tradition says about Jeroboam more than is said about Nabal. The additional words והיה המת לירבעם בעיר יאכלו הכלבים והמת בשדה יאכלו עוף השמים are of significance to our question. These words are of a wider range than expected on a mere personal level; as such they betray their original context, and are best characterized as a remnant of a longer version, which the author could not keep as a whole but was reluctant to give up altogether.

No wonder that whoever insists on the old and original nature of the alternate tradition looks upon the first part of §m as an obstacle and dismisses it as a secondary addition.[9] This is totally unacceptable. Indeed the prophecy of doom

to some degree upsets the integrity of the
alternate tradition, but not because it is
deuteronomistic. One may wonder why at this early
stage in his history Jeroboam deserves the horrid
punishment envisaged in the prophecy. Also
noteworthy is the fact that the punishment will
not materialize within the compass of the
alternate tradition. Nevertheless, the message of
Jeroboam's destruction suits our author's attitude
towards Jeroboam. He would have liked to keep
every word to Jeroboam's discredit; however, the
way he constructed his story he could only refer
to Jeroboam the private man, not to Jeroboam the
king, founder of a possible dynasty.

The absence of vv. 7-9, 14-16 should be
explained on the same grounds. There is not
direct proof that they were indeed part of our
author's sources. But it is also clear that the
situation they describe does not accord with the
alternate tradition. The kingdom has not yet been
divided, nor has Jeroboam become ruler over
Israel; naturally he could not have accomplished
his reform of the cult, which was to leave its
mark on the northern kingdom and put it under the
spell of the sins of Jeroboam. This extensive
material relating to later stages in the history
of Jeroboam could not be used by the author in his
chronological setting of the events.

There is yet another angle to the issue. Other
elements which certainly do not bear a
deuteronomistic stamp, are also absent from the
alternate tradition. In the Book of Kings the
reader is supposed to know Ahijah from a previous
scene: הוא דבר עלי למלך על העם הזה, "the one who

predicted that I would be king over this people" (14:2). Our author could not keep this component. In his version Ahijah is first introduced in the scene of the sick child. The prophecy of Jeroboam's destiny as king of Israel is due at a later stage, and a different prophet will speak it. Similarly, the most distinguished literary feature of the story in the Book of Kings, the disguise of Jeroboam's wife, has no trace in the alternate tradition. Is it a late addition in the Book of Kings? Was it missing in our author's *Vorlage*? Hardly so. He simply had to give it up, since it did not fit in with the course of events of his composition. Here Jeroboam's wife has no reason to disguise herself to meet the prophet: Ahijah knows neither her nor her husband.

A seemingly logical question is raised to prove the priority of the alternate tradition: why would the author of the alternate tradition omit all the deuteronomistic parts if they were extant in his source? In my view there is a perfectly good reason. The perspective of the deuteronomistic material pertaining to the future is based on a much richer past of Jeroboam than he has at this point in the alternate tradition. Therefore, everything that explicitly relates to Jeroboam as king has no place in the story.

c. Similar considerations arise with respect to the other prophecy in the alternate tradition, concerning the destiny of Jeroboam as a ruler over the ten tribes of Israel. As against the lengthy words of Ahijah in 1 Kgs 11:29-39, the alternate tradition presents the terse prophecy of Shemaiah in §o. Actually, §o runs parallel to vv. 29-31, usually considered as the original, pre-deuteronomistic part of the prophecy, consisting mainly of a symbolic act, accompanied by few words to explain its meaning. The following verses, 32-39, abundant as they are in expressions typically deuteronomistic, have no trace in the alternate tradition.

Does the alternate tradition present the original, pre-deuteronomistic, short form of the prophecy? In my opinion, the clear-cut absence of the unit 32-39 raises doubts against the trustworthiness of the evidence presented by the alternate tradition. Verses 32-39 were not added *en bloc*.[10] Some elements, though deuteronomistic by definition, derive from the original composition; this is most obvious in v. 34, which defines the limited nature of Solomon's rule, and v. 37, which envisages a possibility of Jeroboam deserving a stable dynasty. I doubt whether in a consolidated literary work there has ever been a stage in which the prophecy regarding Jeroboam's destiny did not as much as mention the king who is about to lose the greater part of his kingdom. The core of vv. 32-39 is tightly connected with Solomon, his sins, his father's grace, and with his son, who will pay for his father's sins. In the alternate tradition there is no place for all this. Here the prophecy is totally cut off from the days of Solomon. There is no implication that it was pronounced in the time of Solomon or that the seed of the rupture had been sown in his days. Indeed, this fundamental difference stands out from the outset, since even in the passage which

still has a parallel in the alternate tradition a
connection with Solomon is deliberately avoided:
3 Kgdms 12:24
§o τάδε λέγει Κύριος ἐπὶ τὰς δέκα φυλὰς τοῦ
Ισραηλ

Reconstruction	1 Kgs 11:29-39
כה אמר ה'	...29-31
---	כי כה אמר ה' <u>אלהי ישראל</u>
על עשרה שבטי ישראל	הנני קרע את הממלכה מיד שלמה
---	ונתתי לך את עשרת השבטים
	32-39

Similarly, the author of Chronicles who blotted
out any possible connection between Jeroboam's
uprising and Solomon's misconduct, could not have
possibly told his reader that Rehoboam was
punished for his father's sins, or that he was
awarded Judah for the sake of his grandfather.
These ideas, which are the essence of vv. 32-39,
may not have been to the taste of our author
either. For him, as for the Chronicler, the
starting point of Jeroboam's story is the reign of
Rehoboam, not Solomon.[11] I would even suggest
that the promises made to Jeroboam in this
prophecy are out of the question for our author.
After all, the prophecy of doom was already
pronounced, rendering any hope for a stable and
enduring dynasty null and void.

d. Finally, we mention two passages echoing the
prophecies discussed above. In the Book of Kings
both prophecies are explicitly said to have been
fulfilled. The story of the sick child ends with:
ויקברו אתו ויספדו לו כל ישראל כדבר ה' אשר דבר ביד
עבדו אחיהו הנביא, "they buried him and all Israel

lamented over him, in accordance with the word that the Lord had spoken through his servant the prophet Ahijah" (14:18). The negotiations in Shechem come to an end with: ולא שמע המלך אל העם כי היתה סבה מעם ה' למען הקים את דברו אשר דבר ביד אחיה השילני אל ירבעם בן נבט, "the king did not listen to the people; for the Lord had brought it about in order to fulfill the promise which the Lord had made through Ahijah the Shilonite to Jeroboam the son of Nebat" (12:15). Both verses are missing in the alternate tradition. Does this prove the alternate tradition or its sources to be earlier than the prophetic-deuteronomistic layer in the Book of Kings?[12] In my opinion they were simply left out by the author to make room for his own carefully construed endings.

In the scene of the sick child the message is delivered to Jeroboam's wife gradually, by a threefold motif which has no parallel in the MT: the prophet's servant warns her of the grievous tidings she is about to hear from his master (§k); then the prophet himself tells her that on her return home her maid-servants will meet her with the message (§l); and finally, as she arrives at Sareira, she is met by the cry of mourning (§n). This is how he chooses to end his story, with an abrupt cry which suits the pain it expresses. Any additional word would be superfluous.

The differences in the conclusion of the negotiations in Shechem should be explained by the same token. The writer of 12:15 saw divine interference in Rehoboam's decision.[13] It seems that our author preferred a different explanation: according to him Rehoboam's stupidity is his fault

THE DIVISION OF THE KINGDOM 615

alone: ὅτι οὗτος ὁ ἄνθρωπος οὐκ εἰς ἄρχοντα οὐδὲ εἰς ἡγούμενον, "for this man is not for a prince or a ruler over us" (§t), again an independent contribution, unparalleled in the MT.

We have looked into the various cases relevant to the relationship between the alternate tradition and the MT as regards the stage of deuteronomistic redaction they represent. In certain instances - that of the missing fulfillment formulae - the only conceivable explanation lies in the different literary design of the story. In others - the outline of the prophecies - we argued that the parts missing in the alternate tradition did not fit its course of events. Finally, there are cases which prove that the author of the alternate tradition used a source of deuteronomistic provenance; as in §a, in which secondary use is made of the deuteronomistic formulae, and §m, which retains a deuteronomistic remnant of the prophecy against Jeroboam. If we are right in our evaluation of these two paragraphs, they bear evidence as to the rest of the material as well.

There is one last factor to be taken into consideration. If one assumes that certain deuteronomistic material was not yet in front of the author of the alternate tradition, it would mean that the rest of the material in the alternate tradition, which is paralleled in the Book of Kings, is of an earlier date than the deuteronomistic material missing in the alternate tradition. Would it stand to reason that the missing deuteronomistic passages are later than the episode of Shemaiah, the man of God, in 1 Kgs 12:21-24, found almost literally in §§x-z? It has been argued that this episode bears the stamp of the chronicler regarding the general situation, as well as in some particular expressions.[14] The most conspicuous of all is the national unit attributed to Rehoboam, namely, Judah and Benjamin. This well established notion of Chronicles-Ezra-Nehemiah is otherwise alien to the Book of Kings.[15] Moreover, it causes a major problem in the immediate context: in the centre of the words God addresses to Solomon (11:11-13), and of Ahijah's prophecy to Jeroboam (11:32-39), stands the concept of one tribe allotted to the House of David. 12:20, immediately preceding our passage, follows suit: לא היה אחרי בית דוד זולתי שבט יהודה לבדו, "there was none that followed the house of David, but the tribe of Judah only." This last verse certainly was part of our author's *Vorlage*; its parallel appears in §u, in a modified version, doing away with the incongruity: καὶ πορεύονται ὀπίσω αὐτοῦ πᾶν σκῆπτρον Ιουδα καὶ πᾶν σκῆπτρον Βενιαμιν, "and there followed him the whole tribe of Judah, and the whole tribe of Benjamin."

If indeed 12:21-24 is an addition later than the main deuteronomistic redaction of the Book of Kings, it would be difficult to claim that the alternate tradition, which comprises this passage, is based on a pre-deuteronomistic source. We could not claim with certainty that all the deuteronomistic material of the parallel in the Book of Kings was part of the source of the alternate tradition, but in view of the evidence

THE DIVISION OF THE KINGDOM 617

presented by 12:21-24 it seems that one has to look for an answer other than the early/late, pre-deuteronomistic/deuteronomistic relationship.

Those scholars who are keen on retaining the early image of the alternate tradition would not challenge the late character of the Shemaiah episode. They would rather label §§x-z as yet another late addition to the original alternate tradition, intended as a *Wiederaufnahme* of the running text which ends with the same episode (12:21-24). According to this method one could easily designate the previous scene, the meeting in Shechem, as a *Wiederaufnahme*, since it too is a repetition of the parallel scene in the standard LXX. It is an awkward solution when the material under discussion is by definition alternative. Moreover, §§x-z are part of the literary design of the alternate tradition: the second part of §n together with §o on the one hand, and §§x-z on the other, form a well construed framework to the in-between scene of the negotiations in Shechem.

We have followed two lines of argumentation, one regarding the deuteronomistic material missing from the alternate tradition, the other concerning those passages in the alternate tradition which nevertheless bear a deuteronomistic stamp.

We have argued that §§a,m,x-z, deuteronomistic and late as they are, should not be subjected to rules and methods standard in biblical literary criticism, and should not be removed from the alternate tradition in order to retain its claimed pre-deuteronomistic nature. They are not secondary additions to the original alternate tradition; they rather prove that the alternate tradition is based on a source basically similar to the Book of Kings

As for the missing deuteronomistic material, the alternate tradition is hardly a reliable witness to the existence of a pre-deuteronomistic stage of 1 Kgs 11-14. It is rather the other way round. The author of the alternate tradition remodels his sources, not fundamentally divergent from the Book of Kings, to create his own literary work.

We cannot be careful enough in using the evidence of sources such as the alternate tradition, found in the LXX, Chronicles or certain Qumranic compositions, as witnesses to the history of a text or tradition. Before adopting their evidence, we should ascertain that their unique features do not derive from the inner needs of their own composition.

NOTES

1. Debus, whose main interest in our story lies in its contribution to the understanding of the deuteronomistic pattern of redaction, gives an unequivocal answer to this question. In his opinion, the alternate tradition does not rely on a text of the type preserved in the Book of Kings. It was not subject to the massive deuteronomistic redaction characteristic of the Book of Kings: "Die nur in der griechischen Übersetzung erhaltene Sonderüberlieferung der Jerobeamgeschichte ist von der im hebräischen Kanon tradierten Textform unabhängig; sie beruht zwar auf denselben Quellen wie der masoretische Text, ist aber nicht durch

die deuteronomistische Redaktion gegangen,"
J. Debus, *Die Sünde Jerobeams* (FRLANT 95;
Göttingen: Vandenhoeck & Ruprecht, 1967) 85.

2. Debus, *Die Sünde Jerobeams*, 90: "Unsere
Untersuchung von LXX-B brachte als Ergebnis ...
dass die von grossen literarischen Wert ist, weil
sie eine vordeuteronomistische Stufe der
Textüberlieferung darstellt."

3. A. Bendavid was right in placing 1 Kgs 14:22a
parallel to both 2 Chron 12:1 and 14; see his
Parallels in the Bible (Jerusalem: Carta, 1972) ad
locum.

4. Admittedly, the separate evaluation of the king
and the people could be the Chronicler's own
formulation, not necessarily influenced by the
Book of Kings. It continues in v. 12: ובהכנעו שב
ממנו אף ה' ... וגם ביהודה היו דברים טובים, "after
he had humbled himself, the anger of the Lord was
averted ... In Judah, too, good things were
found."

5. A. T. Olmstead, "Source Study and the Biblical
Text," *AJSL* 30 (1913) 20-21.

6. Since Debus (*Die Sünde Jerobeams*, 85-86) admits
that the formulaic material which constitutes §a
indicates that a deuteronomistic writer is at
work, he finds it absolutely necessary to rid the
alternate tradition of it.

7. For the special role of the story of the sick
child in the composition of the alternate tradition see my book, *The Alternate Tradition of the
Division of the Kingdom (3R XII 24a-z)* (Jerusalem:
Simor, 1989) 177-81 (Hebrew).

8. Note, however, that inspite of the different
context, this chapter yields the same contrast as
the Book of Kings between he whose remembrance is
blotted out, that is Nabal, and he who is destined
to have a faithful House, that is David; see
v. 28.

9. Thus Winckler, who presents the alternate
tradition as void of any tendencies; see H.
Winckler, "Das elfte Kapitel des ersten
Königsbuches, seine geschichtliche Nachrichten
und seine Bedeutung für die Quellenscheidung,"
Alttestamentliche Untersuchungen (Leipzig:
Pfeiffer, 1892) 13; or, Trebolle-Barrera, who
claims that this paragraph is the first addition
to the original story of the sick child, an

addition which later attracted further stereotypes of the nature of 1 Kgs 14; see J. C. Trebolle-Barrera, *Salomón y Jeroboan* (Salamanca: Universidad Pontificia, 1980) 166.

10. If vv. 32-39 are a uniform work, vv. 29-31 should be included. Thus, Noth, consistent in his method, views the prophecy, vv. 29-39, as a whole deuteronomistic composition; see M. Noth, *Könige* (BKAT IX/1; Neukirchen-Vluyn: Neukirchener Verlag, 1968) 245-46.

11. They both mention Jeroboam's uprising against Solomon in flash-back only (§§b-c; 2 Chron 13:6-7).

12. See the study by von Rad, who described the prophecies and their fulfilment as a main principle in the deuteronomistic concept of the Book of Kings: G. von Rad, "Die deuteronomistische Geschichtstheologie in den Königsbüchern," *Deuteronomium-Studien* (FRLANT 58; 2nd ed; Göttingen: Vandenhoeck & Ruprecht, 1948) 52-64 = "The Deuteronomistic Theology of History in the Books of Kings," *Studies in Deuteronomy* (Trans. D. Stalker; London: SCM, 1953) 74-91. See also Dietrich's study, advocating the threefold deuteronomistic redaction in the Book of Kings, one of which is prophetic: W. Dietrich, *Prophetie und Geschichte* (FRLANT 108; Göttingen: Vandenhoeck & Ruprecht, 1972). And see further the distinctions introduced by I. L. Seeligmann, "Die Auffassung von der Prophetie," *Congress Volume, Göttingen 1977* (VTSup 29; Leiden: Brill, 1978) 258-70.

13. A parallel, outside the scheme of prophecies and their fulfilment in the Book of Kings, is 2 Sam 17:14: ויאמר אבשלום וכל איש ישראל טובה עצת חושי הארכי מעצת אחיתפל וה' צוה להפר את עצת אחיתפל הטובה לבעבור הביא ה' אל אבשלום את הרעה "and Absalom and all the men of Israel said, 'The counsel of Hushai the Archite is better than the counsel of Ahithophel.' For the Lord had ordained to defeat the good counsel of Ahithophel, so that the Lord might bring evil upon Absalom."

14. See R. Kittel, *Die Bücher der Könige* (HKAT 5; Göttingen: Vandenhoeck & Ruprecht, 1900): "Sie sind ein Stuck Midrasch in der Weise der Chronik." Montgomery expressly argues that they are the Chronicler's explanation for the division of the kingdom: J. A. Montgomery, *The Books of*

Kings (ICC; Edinburgh: T. & T. Clark, 1951). Also Noth, *Könige* 279; E. Würthwein, *Das Erste Buch der Könige* (ATD 11:1; Göttingen: Vandenhoeck & Ruprecht, 1977) 161; E. Nielsen, *Shechem. A Traditio-Historical Investigation* (2nd ed; Copenhagen: Gad, 1959) 204-206.

15. In my opinion, this passage is not exclusively characteristic of Chronicles. It is closer to the Book of Jeremiah. Again the exact definition of Rehoboam's share is of special interest. In Kings, as in Jeremiah, Judah and Benjamin are separate units: ויקהל את כל בית יהודה ואת שבט בנימן, "he assembled all the house of Judah, and the tribe of Benjamin" (12:21; 2 Chron 11:1 ויקהל את בית יהודה ובנימן, "he assembled the house of Judah and Benjamin"), and presumably also v. 23 (compare 2 Chron 11:3). And in Jeremiah: ... ובאו מערי יהודה ומסביבות ירושלם ומארץ בנימן ומן השפלה ומן ההר ומן הנגב ... "... from the cities of Judah ... from the land of Benjamin ..." (Jer 17:26; also 32:44; 33:13). In contrast, in the post-exilic literature it is one unit designated as יהודה ובנימן. It seems that the different terms express a different political reality. I cannot accept Kallai's attitude, who argues that 12:20 and 12:21-24 reflect two historical stages close to each other and to the division of the kingdom: Z. Kallai, "Judah and Israel - A Study in Israelite Historiography," *IEJ* 28 (1978) 251-61. Or others, who see in 12:21-24 an exact image of the period it describes, e.g., K. D. Schunk, *Benjamin. Untersuchungen zur Entstehung und Geschichte eines israelitischen Stammes* (BZAW 83; Berlin: de Gruyter, 1963) 142, 146-47.

INDEX OF ANCIENT AND CLASSICAL SOURCES

BIBLICAL REFERENCES

References in the first list refer primarily to the Hebrew Bible but frequently also cover discussion of Greek and other versional evidence. Items are included in the LXX index which are discussed solely or largely in their own right or have a versification different from that in the Hebrew Bible.

Genesis	374	46:3	61
1:26	587	Exodus	6
1:27	587	1:5	68
2:2	222	1:22	14
2:4a	351	2:21	14
2:19	337	3:16	256
4:25	233	7:4	256
5:3	587	7:10	256
6:2	318-20	8:14	256
9:6	587	10:1-2	588
11:1	337	10:11	256
18:18	61	10:21	257
18:24-25	284	10:22	496
22:1	337	12:13	588
30:11	347	17:16	256
31:39	265	18:6	265
32:31	557	20:11	18
		21:5	272
		21:29	256
		22:3	256, 272
		22:4	266, 267
		22:6	256
		22:11	272
		22:12	272
		22:16	272
		22:22	272
		22:25	272
		23:22	272
		23:31	256
		24:9-11	559

24:10	559	35	85, 397
24:11	559	35:1	83
25-31	82, 382, 402	35:3	392, 400
25-28	396	35:4	85
25	85, 92, 94, 382	35:5-16	85, 86
25:15	400	35:5	390
25:17-22	89	35:10	389
25:21	392	35:11-19	396
25:23-40	89	35:12	89
25:23-24	91	35:14	87, 392
25:23	392	35:15	84, 90
25:31-40	93	35:22	83, 390
25:31	92	35:24	390
25:32-33	92	35:31	390
25:33	400	36-40	402
25:39	93	36-39	100
26	382	36	383
26:1	99	36:1-8a	99
26:29	84	36:2	390
26:36-37	94, 98	36:8b-9	99
27	382	36:10-34	383
27:16-17	94, 98, 99	36:21-24	83, 103
28	382	36:23	103
28:4	256	36:28	85
28:6	97	36:35-38	99
28:12	96, 98	36:35-36	99
28:29	97, 98	36:37-38	94, 96, 98, 99
29	382	37-38	383
30-31	396, 397	37:2	103
30:16	96, 97	37:5	392, 393
31:7-11	396	37:6-16	86, 87
31:13	392	37:6	86, 103, 392
32:11	256	37:9-16	83, 103
33:11	560, 561	37:10	86, 392
33:13	566	37:11	103
33:18	561	37:12	86
33:20	560	37:13	103
34:10	351, 376	37:14	86, 392
34:13	375	37:16	86, 103
34:18-35:3	85	37:17	103, 392
35-40	81-106, 382	37:18	92

INDEX OF ANCIENT AND CLASSICAL SOURCES 625

37:22	103	40:32	389
37:23	103	40:33	105
37:24	94, 103	40:36	390
37:25-28	86, 383		
37:25	86	Leviticus	
37:26	103	1:1-17	587
37:27	84, 91, 92, 101	2:1	246, 272
37:29	88	2:4	246, 272
38	87, 383	2:12	68
38:1-12	104	2:14	68
38:1	88	3:1	68
38:8	88, 101, 384	4:25	261
38:9-23	99	4:26	261
38:9	392	7:12	246, 272
38:10-12	89, 106	10:6	259
38:17	89, 393	10:7	260
38:18-19	94, 95, 96, 98, 99	11:27	258, 260
38:18	95, 105	13:3	260, 264
38:19	89, 95, 105	13:7	272
38:23	391	13:22	272
38:25-28	95, 97	13:27	272
38:25	392	13:35	272
38:27	97	13:42	259, 264
39	383, 397	14-17	36
39:1-31	393	14:16	261, 264
39:1b-31	99	14:17	258, 260
39:3	390	14:18	260
39:6	90	14:42	259
39:7	97, 98, 99	14:48	272
39:21	390	15:2	258
39:23	390	15:3	260, 261, 264, 265, 266-67
39:33-43	396		
39:33-41		15:24	272
39:36	392	16:12	259
39:42-43	396	16:19	258
40	383	17:2	260
40:1-16	396	17:3	258, 259
40:8-27	83	17:4	36, 258, 260, 261, 265, 267
40:17	83, 392		
40:18-33	396	17:5	259
40:20	389, 392	18	591

18:26	62	26:4	53-54
18:27	258, 261	26:5	54-57, 360
18:28	258	26:6	56-57
18:30	259, 260	26:8	58
19:2	260	26:9	58
19:3	261	26:10	59
19:7	272	26:11	55, 59-60
19:16	60, 61	26:12	60
19:37	62	26:13	61
20	591	26:19	260
20:2	258, 265	26:20	258, 265
20:3	258	26:22	259
20:4	272	26:24	259, 260, 261
21:6	259	26:43	62
21:7	259, 261	26:46	62
21:8	258, 260, 261, 264	26:14	62
		26:15	62-63
21:15	258	27:12	258, 259
21:22	258	27:13	259
22:17-25	587	27:14	259
22:18	258	27:15	259
22:21	260	27:17	260, 265
22:22	258	27:19	259, 260
22:24	260, 265		
22:25	258, 260, 264	Numbers	
23:21	261	1:2b	71
23:24	261	3:10	375
23:27	260, 261	3:12	14
23:28	261	3:40	70-71
23:32	261	4:6	72
23:36	261	4:7	73, 392
24:9	259	4:8	72
24:10	260	4:9	392
24:12	259	4:11	72
24:14	258	4:12	72
25:29	259	4:14	74
25:30	260	5:8	587
25:31	258, 259, 260	6:14	272
25:32	259, 260	6:15	272
25:34	259	6:22-27	289
25:35	259, 261, 265	11:8	273

12:6	20, 561, 562	6:6	18
12:8	561, 562, 563	7-8	36-37
14:12	14	7:1	17
14:18	14	7:5	375
16	560	7:11	18
16:5	20	7:15	37
16:36-40	384	7:23	67
18:6	274	8:1	18
19:2	588	8:12-14	275
19:3	21	8:12	37
20:13	36	8:19	37, 272
21:11	36	9:2	37
21:12	36	10:8	288
21:20	36	10:13	18
22:9	21	11:2	565
22:10	21	11:8	17, 18
22:23	252	11:10	17
22:31	252	11:11	17
23:1	375	11:13	272
23:2	375	11:22	272
23:4	375	11:29	17
23:14	375	12:11	18
23:29	375	12:13	375
23:30	375	12:14	18
24:24	361	12:15	281
27:23	36	12:22	280, 285
30:13	272	12:22-23	280
30:16	272	13:7-12	281
35:26	272	13:7	281-82
		13:13-19	283
Deuteronomy		13:13-14	295
1:27	271	13:14, 16	283-84
2:36	68	13:19	18
4:5	17	15:5	272
4:12	563-64, 565	15:19-23	285
4:14	17	15:22	285, 295
4:26	17	17:2-7	285
4:40	18	17:3	285
5:15	18	17:9	287-88, 296
6:1	17	17:14-15	343
6:2	18	18:5	288-89

INDEX OF ANCIENT AND CLASSICAL SOURCES

18:10	233, 246	5:13-14	252
18:14	233, 246	6-9	164
19:17	296	6	164, 167
21:1-9	289	6:5-10	183-84
21:5	289	6:5	167, 168
21:6	289	6:6	167
21:12	290-91	6:7	167, 168
23:14	593	6:8	167
23:21	17	6:9	167
28:1	272	6:10	167
28:21	17	7:12-15	184
28:27	572-73, 577, 586-91	7:12	168
		7:13	161, 168
28:36	343	7:14	169
28:63	17	7:15	169, 170
30:16	17	7:16-18	144
30:18	17	8	164
32:3	565	8:3-19	169
32:8	20, 29	8:3-5	169, 184-85
31:5	66-67	8:4	170
31:13	17	8:7-9	170, 185
31:21	337	8:7	170
32	29	8:8	170
32:10	56	8:10-14	170
32:15	275	8:10	171
32:43	29	8:11	171
33:8-11	34-35	8:14	171
33:10	336	8:18	171, 172
32:47	17	8:31	172
		8:34-35	173
Joshua		8:34	172
2-4	164	8:35	172, 173
2:11-12	165	10:1	173
2:11	165	10:3-11	173
2:12	165	10:3-5	173, 185
3-5	173	10:4	174
3:15-17	166	10:5	174
3:15-16	183	10:8-10	174
3:15	167, 172	10:10	174
4	167	10:11	174, 185
4:3	167	17	164, 174

22:19	346	2:14	234, 239
22:29	375	2:15	233, 234
22:34	375	2:16	223, 233, 234, 237, 239, 244, 248
23:10	56		
23:12	272	2:17	236, 239
		2:18	229
Judges	5	2:20	227, 228, 229, 236
6:19	273		
6:25	347	2:21	226, 227, 233, 234
6:28	347		
6:30-32	347	2:22	32, 228, 233, 239
8:7	54	2:23-24	32
8:16	54, 55	2:23	229, 237
13:22	564	2:24	239, 246
14:12	272	2:25	233, 234
		2:27	236
1-2 Samuel	15	2:28	236
1 Sam 1- 2 Sam 10	225	2:29	228, 229, 245, 273
		2:30	233
1 Samuel		2:31-32	149, 239, 246, 271, 273
1:22-2:5	30-31		
1:11	229, 248, 272	2:32	227, 236
1:12	234	2:36	228
1:13	233	3:4	228, 233
1:22-2:6	271	3:15	137, 153, 154
1:22	230, 239, 240, 247	3:20-4:1	142
		3:21	142-43
1:23	19, 218, 228	4:1a	143
1:24	19, 32, 133, 142, 153, 154, 226, 233, 234, 236, 238, 239, 246, 248, 269	5:3	571, 572, 576, 579-83
		5:4	596
		5:5	580
		5:6	571, 572, 573, 576, 579, 580, 581, 584
1:25	217, 227		
2:2	233, 237, 242		
2:4	227	5:8-10	271
2:8-10	271	5:8	229, 234, 236
2:9	229, 239, 246	5:9-12	576
2:10	227, 239, 245	5:9	227, 228, 571, 573, 581, 585
2:12-25	271		

5:10	227, 229, 233, 234, 236, 581	12:25	272
		13:5	138-39
5:11	229	13:15	147
5:12	571, 573, 577, 585-86	14:32	229
		14:41-42	152
6:1	233, 246, 584	14:41	147, 148, 151
6:2	246	14:42	145, 146, 148
6:3	228, 233, 587	14:47	228
6:4	149, 233, 571, 572, 573, 584, 587, 588	15:12-13	144-45, 151
		15:27	218, 236, 246
		15:29	228, 239
6:5	572, 573, 584, 587, 588	15:30	242
		15:31	236
6:7	588	16:14-23	254
6:8	587, 596	17-18	253
6:9	239	17:4	228
6:11	584, 587	20:6	272
6:14	587	20:7	272
6:17	571, 587	20:9	272
6:18	149, 584	20:21	272
8:6	234	20:30	19
8:18	228, 239	22:20-23	139
9:7	237	23:6	139-40
9:18	228	24	25
9:19	228	24:15	236
9:24	230	24:18	237
10:1	133, 143-44	24:19	236
10:4	233	25:3	229
10:12	228	25:22	609
10:14	234	25:34	609
10:21	144	25:36	140, 141
10:25-26	271	26:11	229
10:25	228, 236, 244	26:12	234
10:26	228, 233, 242, 270	27-30	155
		27:10	229, 230
10:27-11:1	228, 271	28:1	237
11:1	239, 252	29:4	155
11:8	228	29:10	141, 153, 154, 155
11:9-10	240		
11:9	237	30:24	145, 151
12:8	138	30:29	229

INDEX OF ANCIENT AND CLASSICAL SOURCES 631

31:3	228	6:3-4	148, 226
31:6	16	6:3	228, 245
		6:5	227, 228, 249
2 Samuel		6:6	227, 229, 236
2:5	228	6:7	235, 240, 249
2:7	241	6:9	228, 249
2:15	233	6:13-17	271
2:22	135, 136	6:13	229, 234, 245, 248, 251
3:1	228, 233		
3:3	229, 236, 246	6:20	235
3:7	236, 245	7:5-7	368
3:21	272	7:11-14	150
3:23-5:14	31, 271	7:23	69, 223, 229, 236, 245, 250
3:23	228		
3:27	234	8:4	233
3:28-29	229, 233	8:7-8	271
3:28	234	8:7	239, 246, 249
3:29	227, 229	10:4	593
3:33	228	10:5	236, 249
3:34	228, 229, 234, 242	10:6-7	271
		10:6	68, 237, 241
3:25	234	11-24	225
3:32	236	11:3	238
3:34	234, 245	11:4	230, 231, 238, 245
3:36	236		
4:1	32, 236, 245	11:5	242
4:2	32, 236, 245	12:14	231, 233
4:4	230	12:15	238
4:10	234	12:16	237, 238
4:12	32, 228, 233, 237, 245	12:17	230
		13:3	230
5:1	237	13:21-22	140
5:6	233	13:21	140, 240
5:8	230, 242	13:24	230
5:9	16, 228, 249	13:27	136, 140, 141, 240
5:11	234		
5:13	241	13:28	143
5:21	16	13:32	235
6:2-9	271	13:34	136, 146
6:2	229, 237, 249, 274	13:37	237
		13:39	227

INDEX OF ANCIENT AND CLASSICAL SOURCES

14-15	37	1:6	140
14:30	79, 146	7:40	272
15:2	235, 242	7:45	272
15:3	79	8:27	368, 371
15:19-20	153	9:6	272
15:20b	137, 140	11-14	618
15:31	235	11	599
17:14	620	11:11-13	616
17:28	272	11:29-39	611-13
18:3	230, 238, 272	11:29-31	612
18:6	231	11:32-39	612, 613, 616
18:9	227, 230	11:34	612
18:10	235	11:37	272, 612
18:11	230	12	599
18:18	135, 136	12:15	614
19:8	235	12:16	271
19:10	235	12:20	616, 621
19:12	243	12:21-24	616-17
20:10	230	12:21	621
20:22	136	14	599, 602
21:6	230	14:2	610-11
22:33	230	14:7-16	606
22:36	231	14:10-11	608
22:37	235, 240	14:12-13	606-607
22:39	235	14:18	614
22:43	235	14:21-24	600
22:46	230	14:22-24	601-605
22:48	231	14:22a	619
22:49	231	14:25-26	250
22:51	230	16:3-4	608
23:1	230, 245	16:11	608
23:3	230	20:39	272
24:15	230	21:21-22	608
24:16	230, 240, 251, 271	21:24	608
24:17	227	22:28	272
24:18	238		
		2 Kings	
1-2 Kings	15, 152	4:38-41	272
		5:24	575
1 Kings		9:8-9	608
		10:7	273

INDEX OF ANCIENT AND CLASSICAL SOURCES

14:7	394	Ezekiel	
14:22	394	1	557
14:25	394	4:1	595
15:35	394	8:16	593
17:7	602	18:1-20	284
18:4	394	34:26	53
18:8	394	34:27	61
21	602	37:26	58
23:26-27	602		
		Hosea	
Isaiah	358, 363	12:5	557
8:11-18	205	13:6	275
8:11	205, 206, 207, 208		
		Joel	
8:12-13	206	2:6	273
8:15	206		
9:1	211	Amos	
10:14	363-64	4:2	593
14:19	344	6:8	55, 59, 79
17:8		9:13	55, 360-61, 378
20:4	593		
23:1-2	69	Micah	
25:8	328	3:3	273
27:9	375	6:8	351
30:17	56		
46:7a	368	Nahum	
48:7	351, 376	2:6	314
53:11	199	2:10	273
53:12	199	3:5	593
		3:18	315
Jeremiah			
11:13	375		
15:11	570	Psalms	
17:24	272	18	235
17:26	621	18:26-48	507
22:4	272	18:26	522, 552 (2x)
32:14	621	18:27	521 (2x), 540, 541
33:13	621	18:28	539, 546
38:17	272	18:29	519, 533
42:10	272	18:30	522, 523, 546, 550
46:27	57		

18:31	519, 528, 532, 543, 552	30:10	521, 529, 530, 540
18:32	542	30:11	527, 552
18:33	519, 526, 535, 553	30:12	524, 525, 528, 541
		30:13	523, 525, 529
18:34	550	31:1-10	507
18:35	534	31:1	525, 534
18:36	532, 535, 537, 539, 545	31:2	520, 528, 541, 542
		31:3	532, 535, 538, 542
		31:4	534, 537, 542
18:37	543, 546	31:5	530, 539
18:40	544	31:7	520, 549
18:41	536, 540, 543, 549	31:8	522, 527, 540, 543
		31:9	536, 546
18:42	539, 550	31:10	527, 531, 540, 543
18:43	540, 550	31:20-25	507
18:45	534	31:20	528, 529, 541, 543, 545
18:46	529, 533, 534, 536		
		31:21	536, 537 (2x), 543, 546, 547
18:47	542, 546		
18:48	522, 535, 536	31:22	527, 540, 542
28:6-9	507	31:23	522, 527, 528, 550, 552
28:6	527, 552		
28:7	520, 529, 532, 538, 551	31:24	519, 527, 535, 540, 551
28:8	533, 538 (2x)	31:25	519, 525, 530
28:9	534, 535, 547	32:6-11	507
29:1-3	507	32:6	534, 545, 551
29:1	524, 538	32:7	535, 536, 537, 541, 544, 547
29:2	523		
29:3	544	32:8	523, 530, 530, 548
30:1-13	507	32:9	520, 538
30:1	524, 551	32:10	520, 527, 531, 536, 545, 548
30:2	523		
30:4	525, 530, 539	32:11	522, 547
30:5	524, 525, 529, 544	33:9	376
		35:1-2	507
30:6	520, 545, 547	35:1	546
30:7	532, 551	35:2	525, 532, 543, 544
30:8	524, 537, 538, 539, 547	35:13-28	507
		35:13	526, 532, 539, 550
30:9	527, 545		

INDEX OF ANCIENT AND CLASSICAL SOURCES 635

35:14	523, 544, 547	46:11	547
35:15	520, 523, 534, 543	46:12	536, 548
		49:1-15	507
35:16	527, 529, 532, 538	49:1	525, 535
		49:2	526, 531
35:17	530, 531, 549, 550	49:3	519
		49:4	520, 523
35:18	524, 540, 544, 545	49:5	525, 531
		49:6	536
35:19	527, 545, 548, 552	49:7	520, 524, 526
		49:9	525
35:20	523 (2x), 546, 547	49:10	526, 535, 550
35:21	546	49:11	521, 526, 531
35:22	529, 546	49:12	519, 545, 551
35:23	538, 544, 546	49:13	523, 533
35:24	542, 548	49:14	531, 536, 548
35:25	520	49:15	520, 521, 542, 543, 546, 547, 551
35:26	520, 522, 528, 531, 532, 548		
		50:12-13	368
35:27	522, 528 (2x), 542, 547, 549, 552	68:31	78
		78:9	78
		78:66	576, 578
35:28	524, 542	89:26-53	507
36:1-6	507	89:27	543, 545
36:1	534	89:29	519, 521, 527
36:2	541, 548	89:30	548
36:3	526	89:31	523, 539
46:1-12	507, 554-56	89:32	529
46:1	535, 539, 551	89:33	538, 541, 549
46:2	528	89:34	519, 528, 541, 552
46:3	533 (2x), 533	89:35	521, 530, 552
46:4	522, 524, 526, 536, 547	89:36	531
		89:38	519, 530, 531, 537, 550
46:5	540, 549, 551		
46:6	521, 533	89:39	532, 533, 537
46:7	524, 532, 533	89:40	521, 533, 534
46:8	548	89:41	521, 522, 529, 541, 548
46:9	525, 541, 548, 552		
		89:42	537, 551, 552
46:10	526, 538, 544 (2x), 549 (2x)	89:43	544, 549
		89:44	543, 544, 550

89:45	529, 532, 549	119:105	120, 123
89:46	537, 539 (2x), 545	119:106	127
89:47	521, 530, 535, 537	119:107	122, 125, 126
		119:108	120, 122, 125
89:48	524, 526, 550	119:109	120, 127
89:49	522, 526, 533, 537	119:110	120, 127
		119:111	127
89:50	519, 528	119:113	120
89:51	524, 535, 545	119:114	123
89:52	533, 540	119:116	125
89:66	593	119:117	127
101:1	119	119:119	120-21
102:1	119	119:128	122
102:18	126	119:129	127
102:24	122	119:130	121, 122
102:26	122	119:131	122
102:27	123	119:140	113
102:29	122	119:142	123
107:18	59	119:152	123
109:31	122	119:153	127
119:16	123	119:154	113
119:17	123, 124	119:155	113
119:18	123	119:156	125
119:20	124	121:2	113
119:37	124, 126	122:3	113
119:41	126	123:1	113
119:42	113	124:7	113
119:43	126	130:2	113
119:44	126	137:1	113
119:45	126	139:17	113
119:49	120	141:10	113
119:59	125	143:3	113
119:61	125	143:5	113
119:68	122	143:6	113
119:70	124	144:1	113
119:71	120	145:2	113
119:82	123	145:3	113
119:83	126	145:6	113
119:85	125	145:15	113
119:87	126	148:5	122
119:92	125	148:5b	376

Proverbs
6:23	317
8	373
11:2	353
22:17-23:12	350
24:27	256

Job
26:7	367
38:23	78
41:22	273

Lamentations
5:22	272

Qohelet
2:14	347
2:15	376
3:19	376
9:2-3	376
9:18	78

Daniel
	353, 358
3:19	256
4	377
5	377
7:11	355
7:21	78
8:3	69
8:4	69
8:25	363
11	207
11:29	343, 356
11:30	356, 361-63

Nehemiah
9:25-26	275

1 Chronicles
3:1	229
6:12-13	248
6:18-19	248
8:33	251
8:34	251
9:39	251
9:40	251
10:6	16
11:1	237
11:7-8	16
11:8	228, 249
13:5	249
13:6	229, 237, 249
13:7	226
13:8	227, 249
13:9	227, 236, 249
13:10	235, 240, 249
13:12	228, 249
14:1	234
14:3	241
14:12	16
15:26	229, 234, 245, 248
17:21	69, 229, 236, 245, 250
18:8	250
19:5	249
19:6-7	241
19:6	237
21:16	252
21:17	227

2 Chronicles
11:1	621
12:1	603, 619
12:9	250
12:14	603, 619
13:6-7	620
21:18	578
31:1	375
35:13	273

LXX

Genesis
1:1	335
18:18	61
22:1	328
37:21	594
46:3	61

Exodus
10:22	593
25:39	93
25:33	385
35-40	81-106
35-39	86, 92
35	396
35:12	89-91
35:27	90
36-40	402
36-38	98
36-37	91, 100
36:1-8a	99
36:8b-38	99
36:9	99
36:10	99, 390
36:12	99
36:13	90
36:15	99
36:28	390
36:29	99
36:30	99, 390
36:32	99
36:37	99
37:1-2	99
37:3-6	99
37:3	99
37:5	99
37:7-21	99
37:8-10	89
37:15	89, 393
37:16	99
37:17	89
37:21	391
38	88, 387
38:4	392, 400
38:5-12	86, 87
38:5	392, 400
38:6-12	92
38:9	392, 400
38:13-17	93
38:13	392
38:14	92, 101
38:18-26	383, 393
38:22-26	92
38:22-24	88
38:25	88
38:26	88
38:27	389
39	396, 397
39:13-23	396
39:17	392
40	396

Leviticus
1:15	66
5:16	259
18:26	62
19:16	60, 61
19:37	62
22:14	259
22:20	258
24:8	66
26:4	53, 75
26:4	53-54
26:5	54-57
26:6	56-57, 76
26:8	58
26:9	59
26:10	59
26:11	59, 76
26:12	60, 75, 78
26:13	61

INDEX OF ANCIENT AND CLASSICAL SOURCES 639

26:14	62	16:13	16
26:15	62-63		
26:43	62	1 Kingdoms	316
26:46	62	1:14	594
27:27	259	5-6	570, 577
27:31	259	5:3	580-83, 584
		5:6	578-83, 584
Numbers		6:5	582, 585
1:2b	71	6:9	347
3:9	247, 248	14:31	579
3:40	70-72	17:49	578
4:6	72	19:10	594
4:7	73	26:8	594
4:8	72		
4:11	72	2 Kingdoms	
4:12	72	2:22	594
4:14	74	3:27	594
8:16	248	8:13	594
18:6	248	18:11	594
		24:1-9	71
Deuteronomy			
2:36	68	3 Kingdoms	
4:14	17	8:26	370
6:1	17	8:27	370-72
11:11	17	12:24a-z	599-621
11:29	17	12:24a	599, 600-605, 615, 617
28:12	53		
28:27	570	12:24b-f	599
28:29	593	12:24b-c	620
28:35	580	12:24g-n	599
31:5	66-67	12:24k	614
		12:24l-m	605-611
Joshua	316	12:24l	614
9:1-2	173	12:24m	615, 617
9:2	172	12:24n-u	600
24:7	593	12:24n	614
		12:24o	611-13, 617
Judges		12:24p-u	605
1:8	580	12:24x-z	600, 616-17
3:31	594	12:32-33	347
13:8	336	13	347

14:22-24	603	3 Maccabees	
16:32	347	2:7	371
		2:9	369, 371, 372
4 Kingdoms		3:27	377
10:27	594		
12:3	336	Psalms	317
13:8	594	10:2	593
16:10	376	32:9	376
17:27	336	67:30	78
17:28	336	77:9	78
18	347	77:66	576, 578, 594
18:22	376	90:6	593
18:24	574	106:18	59
21:1-3	376		
23	347	Proverbs	
		4:19	593
Paralipomena	586	7:9	593
1 Esdras	316, 348	Job	
2:3	349	3:6	593
		10:22	593
2 Esdras		23:17	593
1:2	349	28:3	593
Judith		Wisdom	
13:8	578	9:1-2	373
		9:15	372-73
1 Maccabees		9:17	373
1:59	346		
		Ben Sira	13, 223, 305, 316
2 Maccabees		Prologue	338, 365, 471
2:19	375	17:13	564-65
6:2	348	42:21	565
6:19	377	45:24d	565
6:28	377	50:12	375
7:28	366-68	50:14	375
7:37	376	50:14b	375
9:28	344		
14:34	370	XII Prophets	316
14:35	369, 371, 372		
		Hosea	

INDEX OF ANCIENT AND CLASSICAL SOURCES

4:19	376	65:11	347
8:11	376		
10:1	376	Jeremiah	316
10:2	376	23:12	593
10:8	376	26:27	57
		43:4	28
Amos		43:5	28
2:8	376	43:6	28
3:14	376		
5:10	593	Ezekiel	
6:8	59	6:4-13	376
9:13	55	8:5	376
		30:9	378
Micah		34:27	61
4:2	336		
Joel		Daniel	
2:2	593	3	133
Nahum			
2:6	314	New Testament	
3:10	315		
		Luke	
Habakkuk		3:23	493
2:18	337		
2:19	336	Acts	
		6:9	4
Zephaniah		17:24-25	379
1:15	593		
		1 Corinthians	
Zechariah		15:54	328
9:4	594		
		2 Corinthians	
Isaiah	195-209, 316, 363	6:16	
8:11-16	205		
10:14	363		
29:18	593	PSEUDEPIGRAPHA	
33:21	378		
36:12	574	Adam and Eve	
58:10	593	38:3	336
59:9	593		

INDEX OF ANCIENT AND CLASSICAL SOURCES

2 Apoc. Bar.		307	463-67
13:2	337	308-11	495
		310-11	307
Ap.Const.		312-21	496
2.5.7	336	312	499
		317	499
1 Enoch			
6:2	319	Jubilees	223, 321, 559, 564
Ep. Aristeas	305-308, 317, 320,	4:15	319
		12:26	337
	326, 359, 387, 404, 432, 434, 441, 442, 443, 450, 453, 457, 462, 463, 475, 476, 479, 485, 486	Pseud-Philo Bib.Ant. 3:8 55:2-5	318, 319, 564 337 595
4	486	Test. Levi	
9	487	14:4	336
11	487		
12	486	Sybilline Or.	
13	486	III	207
22	486		
28	487		
30	306, 486	**DEAD SEA SCROLLS**	
32	307	1QDeut^a	295
35	486	1QIsa^a	22, 26, 37-38, 39, 42, 113, 114-16, 130, 195-202, 204-208, 209, 211
39	494, 500		
41	485, 486		
46-47	307		
121	307	1QIsa^b	114-16, 195-97, 199-201, 209, 211
128-72	502		
128-71	487	1QH	223
172	500	1QM 9:12-15	558
175	501	10:10-11	563
176	307		
180	485	2QDeut^c	38, 40, 42
187-294	500, 502		
301	485, 500	4QExod^b	102
302	501	4QExod^f	83, 102

INDEX OF ANCIENT AND CLASSICAL SOURCES

4QpalExod^m	83, 215, 25-57, 266	4QPhyl J	18
4QLev^{d*}	35-36, 42	4QPhyl M	18
4QNum^b	20-21, 27, 36, 42	4QPhyl N	275
4QDeut^c	33, 42, 45, 282, 295	4Q158	216, 256, 266
4QDeut^f	297	4QVisionSamuel (160)	154
4QDeut^h	33-35, 42, 46	4QpIsa^c	115-16
4QDeut^j	20, 35, 42, 46	4QFlor (174)	46
4QDeut^q	20, 29-30, 42	4QTest (175)	34-35, 46, 336
4QpaleoDeut^r	67	4QOrNab	377
4QJosh^a	161, 164, 167-74, 183-85, 188, 189	4QPssJosh (379)	166
4QJosh^b	161, 164, 165-67, 174, 183, 188	4QMMT	278
4QSam^a	19, 21, 25, 26, 30-33, 42, 114-16, 134, 142, 149, 154, 215-55	5QDeut	36-37, 39, 42
		5QKings	40
		5QIsa (5Q3)	195, 210
4QSam^b	20, 114-16	pap7QExod	49
4QSam^c	37, 42, 79, 114-16, 147	pap7QEpJer	49
4QIsa^{a-r}	195-97	8QGefl	117
4QIsa	24	8QPhyl	18
4QJer^a	21	8HevXIIgr	2, 4, 49, 301-306, 314-18, 326, 328, 336, 510
4QJer^b	21, 26, 28-29, 42		
4QJer^d	26, 28-29, 42	11QpaleoLev	114-16, 216, 255, 257-68
4QDan^a	114-16	11QPs^a	112-30
4QDan^b	114-16	11QT^a	
4QDan^c	114-16	3-13:7	82
4QLXXLev^a	49, 50, 51, 52-63, 65, 74-76	3-10	84
		3	101
4QLev^b	49	3:8-16	92
4QLXXNum	49, 50, 51, 70-74, 400	3:8-12	85-87, 88
		3:8	86
4QLXXDeut	49, 50	3:10	84, 86, 88
4QUnid gr	49	3:13	87
pap4Qpara Exod gr	49, 50	3:14-16	87-88
		3:14-15	87
4QPhyl B	18	3:16	88
		3:16b-17	87

3:17	88-89	54:19-21	281-82
7	90, 91	55:2-14	283-84
7:12-13	89-91	55:2-7	283
7:13	89, 91	55:3	283
7:14	90	55:6	283
8:5-6	91	55:15-56:04	285-87
8:7	91-92	55:17-18	285
9	99	56:05-11	287-88
9:3-4	92	56:07-1	287
9:3	92	60:1-15	288-89
9:4	92-93	60:10-11	288
9:11-12	93-94	61:7-9	287
9:11	93	61:8-9	297
10	91, 94-100, 101	61:8	296
10:1-17	95	61:9	296
10:2	94	63:05-8	289-90
10:4	95, 105	63:4-5	289
10:5	95, 96, 97, 106	63:10-64:03	290-91
10:6	94	63:12-13	290
10:7	94		
10:8-17	95		
10:8	95	PHILO	
10:9	95		
10:10	95, 105	Philo	54, 80, 308, 310,
10:11	95, 105		317, 320, 326-27,
10:12	95		332, 364, 374,
10:14	95		405, 442, 450,
10:15	94		461, 477, 486,
10:16	94		499
10:17	95	De Somniis	
10:18	94	1:61-63	559
15:3-17:5	98	1:79	558
33:13	84	De Mutatione	
36:3	84	Nominum 14-15	558
39:8-10	98, 106	De Spec.	
39:11-13	98, 106	Legibus 1:45	561, 567
52:7-12	285	Life of Moses	
52:10-11	285	2:25-44	304, 480
53:07-53:8	280-81	2:42	497
53:3	289	2:44	498
54:19-55:1	281-83	Quest. & Answ.	

INDEX OF ANCIENT AND CLASSICAL SOURCES 645

on Exodus			561
2:37	560, 567	Palestinian Tg.	558, 560
		Add. 27031	560, 563
		Ps.-Jonathan	53, 227, 558, 560, 561, 563
JOSEPHUS		Samaritan Tg.	276
Josephus	217, 364, 374, 404, 450, 462, 497, 574, 577	MISHNAIC AND RELATED LITERATURE	
Antiquities			
1:10	480	m.Sanh. 4:1	284
1:22	328	m.Shab. 7:2	500
1:27	335	m.Sota 7:6	297
6:3	596	m.Sota 9:6	290
7:121	68	m.Tamid 5:1	297
8:111	379	m.Tamid 7:2	297
12:11-18	480		
12:11	480, 492	t.Sanh. 14:3	284
12:12-18	486	t.Sanh. 14:5	296
12:12	487		
12:51	485	b.Meg. 16b	317
12:55	485	b.Meg. 25a	573, 593
12:99	500	b.Menah. 88b	105
12:108-109	308-309	b.Shabb. 12b	337
12:110	499	b.Shabb. 19a	501
War		b.Shebu. 47b	271
5:212-14	105	b.Yebam. 48a	297
Against Apion			
1:43	210	Sifre Deuteronomy	
1:148	355	94	296
2:44-45	480	153	297
2:44	487	209	290
		212	297
		Sifre Numbers	
TARGUMS		88	595
		96	595
Targums	23, 105, 124, 126, 319, 320, 321, 331, 563, 564	Meg. Taanit	440-44, 476, 495, 503
Neofiti	337, 558, 562		
Onqelos	265, 276, 558,		

INDEX OF ANCIENT AND CLASSICAL SOURCES

PAPYRI

P.Fouad 266 64
P.Oxyrh. 11.1381 324, 338

CLASSSICAL AND PATRISTIC LITERATURE
(including versional writers)

Aelian
VH 3.7   499
Annanius   439-40
Apollodorus   493
Aquila   3, 71, 73, 193,
                   303, 316, 317,
                   318, 319, 326,
                   329, 330, 367,
                   505, 506, 508,
                   510-14, 515, 516,
                   517, 519-56
Aristobulus   405, 448, 449,
                   450, 461, 462,
                   468, 469, 470,
                   476, 480, 482,
                   483, 486, 487,
                   488, 502
Aristotle   376
Arrian
Anab. 3.1.1   500
Athanasius
Exposito in
  Ps. 78 356   594
Augustine
De Civ. Dei
  18.42   481
De Mir. Sacrae
  Script. 1.9   481

Bar Hebraeus   422, 482, 492, 493

Chronography 407, 412, 435, 443
Basil of
  Seleucia   497
  PG 85:421-22 481, 492
Berossus
  Babyloniaca 355, 377

Caecius
  Plaut. Schol. 488
Cedrenus   482, 487, 492, 499
Celsus   374
Chron. Pas. I 482
Chrysostom   407, 470-71, 489, 490
Against Judaiz.
  Christians   481, 502
Homilies on
  Genesis 4.4 481
Homilies on
  Matthew 5.2 407, 481, 489
Synop. Script.
  Sacrae 341   594
Cicero   202, 310, 311, 312
Claudius
  Ptolemaeus   498
Clement of
  Alexandria   405, 450, 461, 482
Strom.
  1.22.148   480, 483, 487, 489
Cosmas
  Indicopleustes
  Topog. Christ. 481, 487
Cyril
  Lexicon   358
Cyril of
  Alexandria   495
  Contra
  Iulian. 1.16 406, 435-37
Cyril of
  Jerusalem   451, 499

INDEX OF ANCIENT AND CLASSICAL SOURCES 647

Cat. Lectures
4.34   481, 487

Democritus   367
Demosthenes   376
Diodorus
  Siculus   354, 357
Bibl. Historica
31.2.1   377
Diogenes
  Laertius   405, 455, 456,
                459, 488
Dionysius the
  Areopagite   312
Dionysius
  Tell-Mahre
Syriac Chron. 481
(see also Eusebius)

Epiphanius   471, 472, 474-75,
                476, 477, 491,
                498
Panarion Haer.
3.3   494
4.1   494
29.4.1   494
29.5.1-4   494
51.16.2   493
Wts & Meas.   406, 412, 421-24,
                424-35, 443, 481,
                487, 492, 493
Eratosthenes   429-30, 444, 445,
                452, 454, 468,
                470, 494
Euripides
Heracles
1341-46   369
Eusebius   405, 422, 423,
                444, 447, 451,
                452, 453, 454,
                459, 460, 470,
                471, 472, 474-75,
                476, 477, 491,
                492, 498
Armen. Chron. 407, 437-40, 481,
                490, 492
Comm. in Ps. 576-77, 594
Hist. Eccl.
5.8.11   483
7.32.16   480, 483, 488, 501
8.1.8   499
13.12.2   480
Lat. Chron.   406, 417, 418,
                420, 424-35, 436,
                445-46, 448, 449,
                461, 468, 472,
                480, 486, 492, 501
Praep. Evan.
8.1   487
8.1.5   480, 485
8.1.8   499
8.2-5   486
8.5   499
13.12.2   487
Syr. Chron.   407
Euthymius
  Zigabenus
In Psalmos   482
Eutychius
PG 11   484
Excerpta Latina
  Barberi   484

Filaster   451, 482
Div. Haer. 142483

Hermippus   455, 459
Hippocrates
Peri Haim.   6.1575, 593
Horace   310, 311, 312

Iamblichus of Chalkis	322-34, 338	Livy	354, 357
		Lysias	376
De Mysteriis	322-33	Lucian(ic)	37, 46, 225-57, 287, 581, 583-86, 591
Ioannes Lydus			
De Magistrat.	481		
De Mensibus	481	Lucifer Calaritanus	595
Ioan. Malalas	481		
Ion. Zonaras	482		
Iosephi Hypomnesticum	482	Maimonides	105
		Manetho	449
Irenaeus	451, 482, 483	Melito of Sardis	338
Ag. Heresies 2.22.5	493	Michael the Syrian	482, 489, 492
Isidore			
Etymol. 6.3.5	481	Chronice	407, 440
Jerome	202, 311, 417, 437, 438, 439, 440, 499	Nachmanides	105, 132
		Nicephorus	492
		PG 100:1009	482
Chronicle (see also Eusebius)	480-81	Nicetas of Heraclea	407, 471, 483, 498
Comm. in Ezek. 5.12	481	Catena in Pss	482, 488, 490
Comm. in Mich. 2.9	481	Origen	64, 120, 328, 357
Praef. in Pent. 28.181	481	Panodorus	439-440
		Parmenides	367
Justin	328, 336, 405, 421, 450, 477, 485, 498, 499	Peri Hypsous	374
		Plato	368
		Laws 716a	352
Apology 1.31	480	716b	352
Dial. with Trypho 71	480	Phaedo 81c	373
88	493	Sophist 246a-c	367
Exhort. to the Greeks 13	480, 486-87, 498	Theaet. 155e	367
		Timaeus 27c1-47e2	351
		60c3	576, 593
Ktesias	354	Plutarch	
		Aristides-Cato maior	
Leo Gramm.	482, 488, 492, 499	Cato 31	368

INDEX OF ANCIENT AND CLASSICAL SOURCES

Moralia 189d	488, 499	Tertullian	450
Pollux	450, 480, 492	*Apology* 18	480, 487
Polybius	353, 357	Theodoretus	483, 577
Historiae		Theodotion	37, 69, 71, 104, 106, 120, 162, 178, 179, 193, 287, 303, 317, 318, 319, 367, 505, 506, 508, 510, 517
29.27.4	377		
29.27.8	377		
45.12	377		
Polycarp	329		
Porphyry	374, 418, 468, 469, 470, 491, 492, 493		
		Thomas of Harkel	329
Pseudo-Athanasius	407, 451, 471, 489		
		Xenophanes	368
Synopsis	481		
Pseudo-Theodoretus	407, 471, 483, 488, 498	Zacharias of Mitylene	481
		Syr. Chron.	406, 435-37
Tractatus Ineditus	482, 490	Zosimus Panopolitanus	483
		De Zythorum	483
Qoran	330		
Quintilianus			
Institutio Or.			
1, 3, 14	594		
Rashi	105, 132		
Solomon			
Book of the Bee	482, 492		
Symmachus	3, 4, 73, 124, 193, 317, 319, 320, 337, 505, 506, 508, 514-15, 516, 517, 519-56, 560, 575, 583, 595		
Syncellus	407, 440, 471-72, 482, 487, 492, 499		

INDEX OF MODERN AUTHORS

Ackroyd, P.R.	376	Benoit, P.	186, 334
Adler, A.	377	Berardino, A. di	498
Aejmelaeus, A.	63, 78, 106, 212, 381-402	Berkowitz, L.	593
		Berlin, A.	156
Akavia, A.A.	496	Bickerman, E.J.	478, 490, 493, 499
Aland, B.	376		
Aland, K.	376	Biel, J.C.	377
Alexander, P.S.	318, 337	Birdsall, J.N.	503
Allen, L.C.	586	Bogaert, P.M.	45
Aly, Z.	64, 79	Bodenheimer, F.S.	591, 596
Anbar, M.	131, 155	Bodine, W.R.	336
Artom, E.A.	45	Boer, P.A.H.	592
Auld, A.G.	175, 176, 191, 192	Boling, R.	160, 186, 188, 190, 191
		Boulluec, A. le	399
Baentsch, B.	46, 399, 400	Brentjes, B.	591, 595
		Brinkmann, A.	157
Baillet, M.	38, 40, 50, 77	Brock, S.P.	1, 213, 301-38, 502, 506, 592
Barr, J.	211, 212, 334, 335, 341, 345	Brooke, A.E.	294, 567
		Brooke, G.J.	77, 81-106, 129, 150, 157, 213, 294, 297, 503, 558, 567
Bartelink, G.J.M.	211		
Barthélemy, D.	3, 44, 78, 143, 144, 147, 156, 210, 211, 246, 273, 274, 295, 301, 302, 303, 332, 334, 336, 338, 505, 506, 508, 509, 510, 514, 515, 516	Brooks, C.E.P.	497
		Brooks, E.W.	489
		Brownlee, W.H.	209
		Budde, K.	273
		Burguire, P.	489
Bauer, W.	376	Burnet, I.	593
Becker, I.	487, 488, 492	Burrows, M.	209
		Burton, S.	503
Bendavid, A.	619	Busto Saiz, J.R.	592
Ben Hayyim, Z.	276		

INDEX OF MODERN AUTHORS

Campbell, A.F.	592	Diercks, G.F.	595
Carson, D.A.	213, 337	Dietrich, W.	620
Casetti, P.	375, 596	Dieu, L. de	43
Casson, L.	501	Dillmann, A.	131
Castellus	14	Dimant, D.	297
Chabot, J.B.	478, 489, 492	Dinkler, E.	379
Charlesworth, J.H.	129, 486	Dorival, G.	478, 484, 485, 503
Chouraqui	331	Driver, S.R.	19, 31, 43, 156, 271, 592
Claassen, W.	129		
Cohen, N.G.	502	Dubberstein, W.H.	497
Cohn, L.	567	Duncan, J.	33-35, 45, 46
Collins, A. Yarbro	486		
Collins, N.	403-503		
Colson, F.H.	334	Eissfeldt, O.	376
Colwell, E.C.	269, 271	Elat, M.	274
Conzelmann, H.	370, 378	Elliger, K.	46
Cook, C.	494	Elliott, J.K.	188
Cook, J.	107-30	Emerton, J.A.	375
Coste, J.M.	212	Engels, D.W.	500, 501
Cox, C.	44, 77, 158, 212	Epp, E.	162, 188
		Etheridge, J.W.	567
Cross, F.M.	30, 44, 83, 159, 160, 161, 163, 164, 170, 177, 181, 186, 188, 216, 217, 237, 246, 269, 270, 271, 273, 342		
		Feldman, L.H.	568
		Fernandez Marcos, F.	156, 157, 176, 192, 592, 595
		Fernandez Vallina, J.	156
		Field, F.	561, 567
Daniel, S.	375	Finegan, J.	479, 490, 491, 493
Dann, C.J.	591		
Davies, W.D.	478	Finkelstein, L.	295, 296, 297, 478
Davila, J.R.	45		
Dawe, R.D.	271		
Dean, J.E.	478, 481, 487, 489, 492, 493, 494	Fishbane, M.	44, 132, 156
		Fitzmyer, J.A.	109, 210
Dearing, V.A.	189, 270	Flowers, B.	270
Déaut, R. Le	560, 567	Foresti, F.	272, 273
Debus, J.	618-19	Fotheringham, J.K.	496
Deist, F.E.	130	Fowler, H.N.	379
Delcor, M.	102	Fraenkel, D.	77, 211
Dibelius, M.	370, 378	Frankel, Z.	294, 593

INDEX OF MODERN AUTHORS

Fraser, P.M. 479, 488, 491, 494, 501
Freedman, D.N. 102
Fuller, R.E. 45

Garbini, G. 210
Gardiner, A.H. 500
Garcia Martinez, F. 45, 102
Geiger, A. 271, 593
Gercke, A. 44
Gerleman, G. 586
Gesenius, F.H.W. 43
Gibson, J.C. 591
Gingerich, O. 496
Ginzberg, L. 596
Gooding, D.W. 90, 103, 104, 270, 274, 386-87, 399
Goodman, M. 478
Gordis, R. 593
Gordon, R.P. 131-58
Goshen-Gottstein, M. 270
Gottlieb, H. 158
Gottschalk, H. 503
Gould, S.J. 182-83, 194
Grabbe, L.L. 505-56
Graham, W.C. 493
Greenspahn, F. 497
Greenspoon, L. 159-94
Gronewald, M. 157

Hadas, M. 479, 485, 486, 488, 500
Hamilton, F.J. 489
Hammershaimb, E. 158
Hanhart, R. 1, 50, 64, 339-799
Hanson, A.T. 557-67
Harl, M. 337, 478
Hart, J.H.A. 491
Hassencampius 43
Hastings, A. 503

Hastings, J. 483, 485
Hays, W.L. 270
Helm, R. 478, 489, 497
Hempel, J. 151
Herter, H. 157
Hicks, R.D. 488
Hilgert, E. 497
Hirsch, E. 151
Holl, K. 493
Holmes, S. 176, 190, 192
Hopfe, L.M. 295
Hottingerus 43
Hyvarinen, K. 512

Isserlin, B.S.J. 486

Jacoby, F. 491
Jakeways, R. 496, 503
James, M.R. 568
Janzen, J.G. 44
Jastram, N. 36, 45
Jeansonne, S.Pace 64, 79
Jellicoe, S. 193, 479, 484, 486, 502
Johnson, B. 592
Joly, R. 593
Jonas, H. 370

Kahle, P. 74
Kallai, Z. 621
Karpp, H. 334
Karst, J. 479, 481, 489
Katz, P. 302, 319, 337
Keel, O. 375, 596
Keil 147
Kelly, L.G. 335
King-Re, K. 14, 26

Kittel, R.	620	Marquis, G.	212
Klein, F.N.	336	Mathews, K.A.	186, 257, 271, 275
Klein, R.W.	12, 44, 592	McCarter, P.K.	30, 45, 143, 157, 230, 574, 580, 584, 592, 593, 595, 596
Klijn, A.F.J.	334		
Koch, D.A.	338		
Koenen, L.	64, 79, 491		
Koenig, J.	211, 213	McLean, N.	294, 567
Kooij, A. van der	38, 195-213, 399	Meecham, H.G.	491, 498
		Megalli, M.D.	497
Kraft, R.A.	77, 514	Mercati, J.	507
Kuenen,	401	Metal, Z.	43
Kuhl, C.	131-33, 151	Metzger, B.M.	269
Kuschke, A.	45	Meyer, R.	45
Kutscher, E.Y.	109, 209	Milgrom, J.	95, 97, 105
		Milik, J.T.	36, 39, 40, 77, 295
Lagarde, P. de	70, 342		
Lang, B.	151	Millar, F.	478
Langlois, V.	489	Miller, P.D.	592
Lee, J.A.	484	Min, Y.J.	44
Lehmann, M.R.	297	Montevecchi, O.	335
Levi, I.	568	Montgomery, J.A.	348, 376, 620
Lewontin, R.C.	182, 194		
Lindars, B.	1-7, 77, 78, 105, 503	Morrow, F.J.	196, 197, 210, 211
Lifshitz, B.	302, 334	Mosshammer, A.A.	478, 490, 492, 493, 495, 498, 499
Lipinski, E.	591		
Loewenstamm, S.E.	276	Moxon, I.	503
Lohfink, N.	45	Mulder, M.J.	294
Long, B.O.	156	Munnich, O.O.	336, 478
Lust, J.	274, 569-97	Mutzenbecher, E.H.	377
Luther, M.	324, 353		
		Nestle, E.	483, 484, 485, 596
Maas, P.	25, 32, 44, 222, 270, 271		
		Neves, J.C.M. das	213
Mack, B.L.	497, 499	Newsom, C.A.	160, 186, 189, 191
Maier, J.	102, 297		
Marcus, R.	334, 335, 567	Nielsen, E.	621
		Nieuwoudt, B.A.	130
Margolis, M.L.	162, 173, 176, 180-81, 189, 190, 191, 193	Norden, E.	44, 370, 378
		Noth, M.	396, 399,

INDEX OF MODERN AUTHORS

400, 401, 620

Oates, J.	494
O'Connell, K.G.	104, 106, 334, 506, 513
Oesch, J.M.	212
O'Flaherty, W.D.	188, 189
Oikonomos, C.	484, 485
Olmstead, A.T.	619
Oppolzer, T.R. von	496
Orlinsky, H.M.	12, 44, 47, 176, 192, 334, 478, 485, 486
Ottley, R.R.	79, 505
Pace, S.	79
Parker, R.	497
Paul, A.	335, 337
Pelletier, A.	334, 478, 480, 483, 489
Pestman, P.W.	479, 490
Petavius	410
Peters, N.	592
Pfeiffer, R.	479, 488
Pietersma, A.	44, 77
Pisano, S.	134-51, 153-55, 157, 274, 593
Polak, F.H.	3, 31, 215-76
Popper, J.	399
Preaux, C.	338
Puech, E.	258, 259, 260, 261, 275
Purvis, J.D.	276
Qimron, E.	95, 105, 109
Quast, U.	77, 211
Quell,	566
Rad, G. von	620
Rappaport, U.	297
Reider, J.	511
Reynolds, L.D.	270
Roberts, J.J.M.	592
Robinson, J.M.	379
Rofe, A.	175, 191, 272, 274, 295, 375
Rosenzweig	331
Rudolph, W.	378, 562
Sabatier, P.	594
Sadaqa, A.	46
Salvesen, A.	337
Samuel, A.E.	478, 490, 491, 492, 494, 498
Sanday, W.	156
Sanders, J.A.	129
Sanderson, J.E.	83, 187, 255, 275, 400
Sandevoir, P.	399
Scaliger, J.J.	377, 378
Schenker, A.	375, 596
Schiffman, L.H.	106, 277-97, 503
Schiklberger, F.	592
Schleusner, J.F.	377
Schunk, K.D.	621
Schurer, E.	478
Schwarz, W.	335, 338
Seeligmann, I.L.	132, 207, 213, 343, 358, 363, 375, 378, 620
Seldenus	43
Sibinga, J.S.	333
Siegel, S.	272
Skehan, P.W.	45, 49, 50, 77, 196, 201, 202, 209, 210, 211
Smelik, K.A.D.	592
Smend, R.	399
Smith, C.G.	503
Smith, M.	336

Soggin, J.A.	159, 186	Trebolle Barrera, J.	64, 78, 133, 153, 154, 155, 156, 592, 593, 619, 620
Soisalon-Soininen, I.	211, 212, 400, 594		
Sollamo, R.	212, 400	Trever, J.C.	209
Speiser, E.A.	274	Tucker, G.M.	12
Sperber, A.	568	Turner, E.G.	498
Sprengling, M.	493	Turner, N.	511
Squitier, K.A.	593	Tweddle, L.	503
Stalker, D.	620		
Stec, D.	503	Ulrich, E.C.	1, 27, 30, 44, 46, 49-80, 102, 187, 188, 209, 217, 225, 230, 246, 269, 271, 273, 274, 335, 400, 503
Stegemann, H.	102, 103		
Steuernagel, C.	131		
Stoebe, J.	147, 574, 592, 593, 595		
		Usserius	43
Sukenik, E.L.	209		
Swanson, D.D.	105	Vaux, R. de	77
Swete, H.B.	79, 488, 505	Vercellone, C.	595
		Vermes, G.	336, 478
		Vermeylen, J.	212
Tadmor, H.	271		
Talmon, S.	132, 156, 160, 188, 269, 270, 271	Wacholder, B.Z.	497, 498
		Wallis Budge, E.A.	482, 489, 493
Talshir, Z.	599-621		
Taylor, T.	322, 338	Walters, P.	302, 337
Terian, A.	499	Walters, S.D.	272
Thackeray, H.St.J.	479, 487, 489, 493, 587, 592, 596	Way, A.S.	378
		Weinfeld, M.	271
Thenius, O	19, 31, 43, 143, 342	Welles, C.	494
		Wellhausen, J.	19, 31, 43, 131, 272, 273, 274, 342, 592
Tigay, J.	44		
Toeg, A.	148	Wendland, P.	479, 480-83, 487, 488, 489, 490, 492, 502, 567
Tov, E.	1, 11-47, 50, 63, 77, 78, 81, 102, 129, 130, 160, 161, 164, 166, 174, 175, 176, 181, 186, 187, 188, 189, 190, 191, 192, 193, 194, 210, 211, 212, 217, 247, 257, 269, 271, 272, 273, 274, 275, 294, 295, 296, 297, 303, 334, 335, 375, 487, 510, 588, 592, 596, 597		
		Wernberg-Moller, P.C.H.	210
		West, M.L.	270
		Westwood, J.O.	494
		Wevers, J.	50, 51, 65-67, 72-73, 75, 77, 78, 79, 80, 211, 259, 294, 319, 400, 485, 567, 590, 593
		White, S.A.	33, 45, 295,

297
Wicksteed, P.H. 399
Wiener, H.M. 131, 275
Wigtil, D.N. 338
Wilamowitz-
 Moellendorff,
 U. von 378
Wilkinson, J. 591
Williams, F. 494
Williamson, H.G. 213, 337
Willis, J. 271
Wills, L. 102, 103, 294
Wilson, A.M. 102, 103, 294
Wilson, N.G. 270
Winckler, H. 619
Woods, F.H. 135, 156
Wordsworth, J. 157
Woude,
 A.S. van der 295, 592
Woudstra, M. 159, 186
Wright, B.G. 212
Wurthwein, E. 621

Yadin, Y. 82, 85, 87, 88, 89, 91-98, 101, 102, 103, 104, 105, 106, 294, 295, 296, 297, 568
Ysebaert, Y. 336

Zakai, D. 496
Zakovitch, Y. 191, 375
Ziegler, J. 26, 37-38, 44, 200, 201, 211, 212
Zuntz, G. 338, 486, 503

JOHN COLLINS, GEORGE NICKELSBURG
Ideal Figures in Ancient Judaism: Profiles and Paradigms (1980)
Code: 06 04 12

ROBERT HANN
The Manuscript History of the Psalms of Solomon (1982)
Code: 06 04 13

J.A.L. LEE
A Lexical Study of the Septuagint Version of the Pentateuch (1983)
Code: 06 04 14

MELVIN K. H. PETERS
A Critical Edition of the Coptic (Bohairic) Pentateuch
Vol. 5: Deuteronomy (1983)
Code: 06 04 15

T. MURAOKA
A Greek-Hebrew/Aramaic Index to I Esdras (1984)
Code: 06 04 16

JOHN RUSSIANO MILES
Retroversion and Text Criticism:
The Predictability of Syntax in An Ancient Translation
from Greek to Ethiopic (1985)
Code: 06 04 17

LESLIE J. MCGREGOR
The Greek Text of Ezekiel (1985)
Code: 06 04 18

MELVIN K.H. PETERS
A Critical Edition of the Coptic (Bohairic) Pentateuch,
Vol. 1: Genesis (1985)
Code: 06 04 19

ROBERT A. KRAFT AND EMANUEL TOV (project directors)
Computer Assisted Tools for Septuagint Studies
Vol 1: Ruth (1986)
Code: 06 04 20

CLAUDE E. COX
Hexaplaric Materials Preserved in the Armenian Version (1986)
Code: 06 04 21

MELVIN K.H. PETERS
A Critical Edition of the Coptic (Bohairic) Pentateuch
Vol. 2: Exodus (1986)
Code: 06 04 22

CLAUDE E. COX (editor)
VI Congress of the International Organization for Septuagint
and Cognate Studies: Jerusalem 1986
Code: 06 04 23

JOHN KAMPEN
The Hasideans and the Origin of Pharisaism:
A Study of 1 and 2 Maccabees
Code: 06 04 24

THEODORE BERGREN
Fifth Ezra:
The Text, Origin, and Early History
Code: 06 04 25

BENJAMIN WRIGHT
No Small Difference:
Sirach's Relationship to Its Hebrew Parent Text
Code: 06 04 26

TAKAMITSU MURAOKA (editor)
Melbourne Symposium on Septuagint Lexicography
Code: 06 04 28

JOHN JARICK
Gregory Thaumaturgos' Paraphrase of Ecclesiastes
Code: 06 04 29

JOHN WILLIAM WEVERS
Notes on the Greek Text of Exodus
Code: 06 04 30

CLAUDE E. COX
VII Congress of the International Organization for Septuagint and Cognate Studies
Code: 06 04 31

J.J.S. WEITENBERG and A. DE LEEUW VAN WEENEN
Lemmatized Index of the Armenian Version of Deuteronomy
Code: 06 04 32

GEORGE J. BROOKE AND BARNABAS LINDARS, S.S.F. (editors)
Septuagint, Scrolls and Cognate Writings: Papers Presented to the International Symposium on the Septuagint and Its Relations to the Dead Sea Scrolls and Other Writings

MICHAEL E. STONE
A Textual Commentary on the Armenian Version of IV Ezra
Code: 06 04 34

Order from:
Scholars Press Customer Services
P.O. Box 6996
Alpharetta, GA 30239-6996
1-800-437-6692

Other Titles in the Septuagint and Cognate Studies Series

ROBERT A. KRAFT (editor)
Septuagintal Lexicography (1975)
Code: 06 04 01
Not Available

ROBERT A KRAFT (editor)
1972 Proceedings: Septuagint and Pseudepigrapha Seminars (1973)
Code: 06 04 02
Not Available

RAYMOND A. MARTIN
Syntactical Evidence of Semitic Studies in Greek Documents (1974)
Code: 06 04 03
Not Available

GEORGE W. E. NICKELSBURG, JR. (editor)
Studies on the *Testament of Moses* (1973)
Code: 06 04 04
Not Available

GEORGE W.E. NICKELSBURG, JR. (editor)
Studies on the *Testament of Joseph* (1975)
Code: 06 04 05
Not Available

GEORGE W.E. NICKELSBURG, JR. (editor)
Studies on the *Testament of Abraham* (1976)
Code: 06 04 06

JAMES H. CHARLESWORTH
Pseudepigrapha and Modern Research (1976)
Code: 06 04 07
Not Available

JAMES H. CHARLESWORTH
Pseudepigrapha and Modern Research with a Supplement (1981)
Code: 06 04 07 S

JOHN W. OLLEY
"Righteousness" in the Septuagint of Isaiah: A Contextual Study (1979)
Code: 06 04 08

MELVIN K. H. PETERS
An Analysis of the Textual Character of the Bohairic of Deuteronomy (1980)
Code: 06 04 09
Not Available

DAVID G. BURKE
The Poetry of Baruch (1982)
Code: 06 04 10

JOSEPH L. TRAFTON
Syriac Version of the Psalms of Solomon (1985)
Code: 06 04 11

www.ingramcontent.com/pod-product-compliance
Lightning Source LLC
Chambersburg PA
CBHW021348290426
44108CB00010B/154